Still ... of war ... to ... great sluggers ...

# SULTANS

### OF

# SWAT

# SULTANS

## OF

# SWAT

The Four Great Sluggers
of the New York Yankees

AS ORIGINALLY REPORTED BY

𝕿𝕳𝖊 𝕹𝖊𝖜 𝖄𝖔𝖗𝖐 𝕿𝖎𝖒𝖊𝖘

with an Introduction by Yogi Berra

St. Martin's Press ❧ New York

www.stmartins.com

Design by Phil Mazzone

Library of Congress Cataloging-in-Publication Data

Sultans of swat : the four great sluggers of the New York Yankees / the New York Times with an introduction by Yogi Berra.
   p.  cm.
  ISBN 0-312-34014-1
  EAN 978-0-312-34014-8
  1. New York Yankees (Baseball team)—History.  2. Ruth, Babe, 1895–1948.  3. Mantle, Mickey, 1931–1995.
  4. Gehrig, Lou, 1903–1941.  5. DiMaggio, Joe, 1914–1999.  6. Batting (Baseball).  I. New York Times Company.

  GV875.N4S85 2006
  796.357'092'2–dc22
  [B]                                             2005052039

First Edition: April 2006

10  9  8  7  6  5  4  3  2  1

# CONTENTS

# INTRODUCTION

## by Yogi Berra

Bronx Bombers: Lou Gehrig and Babe Ruth, picking their bats in 1930, combined for 1,207 home runs during their legendary careers. (INTERNATIONAL PHOTOS)

DON'T COMPARE THEM because you can't. It's impossible to compare eras and say today's players are better or worse. How would our Yankee teams compare to other great Yankee teams—how would I know? What's true is each had something in common: good players. Ruth and Gehrig and DiMaggio and Mantle were great, that's for sure. But what people forget is how much each guy loved the game. Each gave everything he had to baseball. Each helped make Yankee history and tradition. It's a tradition I'm lucky and proud to be part of.

Funny, where I grew up, nobody cared or knew about the Yankees. Growing up in St. Louis in the 1930's, all we knew were the Cardinals and Browns, and maybe we liked the Cardinals a little better because they were. In the later years of the Depression, the W.P.A. ran an instructional clinic at Sherman Park and some of the Cardinals players would come and talk to a bunch of us kids. And Joe Medwick—my favorite player— happened to be a regular customer when I was a 12-year-old newspaper hawker on the street corner.

All summer all we did was play baseball. Those were the days. Occasionally a lady on our street, Mrs. Domenica, would take us to Sportsman's Park to see those Cardinals—the Gashouse Gang. We'd sit in the left-field grandstand and see Medwick, Dizzy Dean and Frankie Frisch, but to be honest, I always preferred playing than watching.

The Yankees? Babe Ruth might as well as been a cartoon character because he didn't seem real. There was no TV then and all you heard and read about Ruth is being this great popular character who hit monster home runs. Never saw him play nor did I ever see Lou Gehrig. Gehrig emerged as a star in 1925, same year I was born.

When I started following baseball in the 1930's, Italian-American players were a rarity. I did notice the Yankees had Tony Lazerri, Frank Crosetti, Joe DiMaggio, but it was the Cardinals who fired my imaginations and big-league dreams, especially me and Joe Garagiola, who grew up right across the street from me. When the Cardinals held tryouts in Sportsman's Park in the summer of 1942, it was a great thrill. Me and Joe dreamed of making the Cardinals—and Joe's came true. After the tryout Branch Rickey, the Cardinals general manager, gave Joe a $500 signing bonus. Me? I got discouraged. Rickey told me I'd never become a major-leaguer.

What I didn't know was that Leo Browne, who ran our American Legion program, told George Weiss, the Yankees farm director, about me. After the Cardinals beat the Yankees in the World Series that October, Weiss told the Yankees bullpen coach John Schulte, who lived in St. Louis, to check around on me. So one day Schulte came to our house, said he'd never seen me play, but had talked to some people. He was willing to offer me the same $500 to sign with the Yankees organization, and $90 a month to play for Norfolk in the Piedmont League. My father didn't want me to play ball. My brothers finally convinced him to give me the chance. So he signed it. I was 17 and joining the New York Yankees organization. I hadn't a clue what lay ahead.

After playing in Norfolk in 1943, I served in the Navy, then joined Newark, the Yankees' top farm team, in

1946. Being short and blocky, I wasn't your classic-looking ballplayer. But I could always hit pretty good, and liked to hit bad pitches. There were a lot of stories written and said about me, not all of them true. One true one is when I first walked into Yankee Stadium in my Navy uniform on a weekend liberty, someone said I didn't look like a ballplayer. Peter Sheehy, the clubhouse manager, said I didn't even look like a sailor.

And in spring training 1947, one of the writers told Bucky Harris, our manager, "You're not really thinking of keeping him, are you? He doesn't even look like a Yankee." All the teasing and razzes never bothered me. If you have pride, that's all that matters. I had a real pride in being a Yankee, being part of something that was awfully good. Like I said, maybe it's something about the uniform.

What I know is all my years on the Yankees we were a tight-knit team, everybody pulling for each other, never any jealousies. We wanted to win, bad. Sure we had some pretty good ballplayers. When I came up we had DiMaggio, Henrich, Rizzuto, Keller, not too shabby. Those guys made a lasting impression on the young guys. Nobody played harder, nobody did that little extra better than them. They took the game serious and instilled that pride. When Casey Stengel became our manager in 1949, he did the same. "Don't ever forget," he told us, "once you put on that shirt with the Yankee emblem on it, you become a Yankee and you stay a Yankee. Great things are expected of you just because you're wearing that uniform. Don't ever let it down."

There's no other place like Yankee Stadium, either. I learned that real quick. Two weeks into my rookie year was Babe Ruth Day. He had throat cancer and was pretty weak. His voice was like a whisper and he wasn't up to putting on his old uniform. But just seeing him was enough. This was the greatest player ever, the reason they built Yankee Stadium, and I just got chills watching him. Then he said farewell. Never thought I'd see him again.

A couple of months later, we were playing the Browns in St. Louis and Ruth came to Sportsman's Park—another stop on his farewell tour. Before the game, a photographer grabbed my arm and told me to take a picture next to Babe. I didn't know what to say I was so nervous. Then Babe put his hand out to me. He said real softly, "Hiya kid." A year later he was gone.

I played a number of games in right field in my rookie year. A few times I thought about Babe, since I was standing where he stood. In 1949, the Yankees brought in Bill Dickey as a coach and to help my catching. He was a great player and a teammate of Babe's and Lou Gehrig's—and probably Gehrig's closet friend. Once I asked Dickey about Gehrig since I'd never seen him play. He told me he was the most serious-minded and best competitor he ever saw. Could outmuscle any pitch and was strong as an ox. He played all those games because it was his job and the team needed him. How can you not respect that? I was surprised when Dickey told me Gehrig got jittery before World Series games. But like Dickey said, he wouldn't be human if he didn't.

DiMaggio once told me when he first came up, Gehrig always made him feel welcome. He was just a kid, a long way from home, and I think he had a good influence on him. Nobody I knew played the game with the heart DiMag showed.

People laugh when I said Dickey learned me his experience, but Gehrig helped Dickey as a young player, too, and that's part of that tradition—someone's always giving help and advice. When Phil Rizzuto first came up in 1941 he was trying to take the shortstop job away from Frank Crosetti. And the guy who gave him the most help and advice was Crosetti.

I played with DiMaggio for five years and there wasn't anything he didn't do perfect. Sure he was quiet, but not silent. He wasn't one to get up on a soapbox or preach a sermon. We all kind of left him alone; I could still see him drinking his coffee and smoking his cigarettes by his locker, by himself. But he'd join in card games on the train and some of us would go out to eat with him, if he asked you. He just didn't like to be bothered a lot. Kept a lot of feelings to himself. One time I couldn't resist playing a gag on him. He was at his locker opening his mail and out popped a long, squirmy worm. For some reason, DiMag knew it was me and started chasing me around the locker room—we had a good laugh over it.

The main thing is DiMag cared so much about winning. Did everything right. Played hurt. Expected everyone to bust their butt, too. And if you didn't he'd let you know.

He was always great with me. Him and Tommy Henrich were still connected to the great teams of the 1930s, and they made sure the younger guys did things the Yankee way, the little things. Hit to the opposite filed. No mental mistakes. Always hustle. Never get down on yourself.

DiMag was real class. Always came to the ballpark in those tailored suits, very businesslike. I think his desire rubbed off on everybody. I'll always remember 1949 when he missed the first 65 games we played. He had that bone spur in his heel—it was almost impossible to walk without pain. Then he joined us in Boston, our biggest rival, and helped us sweep the series. It was almost unbelievable. He hadn't played all year and then played like he hadn't been away. Even the Red Sox fans cheered him.

Nineteen fifty-one was DiMag's last year and Mickey Mantle's first. I don't know what you can say about Mickey except he was as good a teammate you could have, one heck of a guy. Boy we had fun. I still miss him, too. For raw talent, I don't think Mickey ever knew how good he was. Nobody had his mix of power, speed and good baseball sense. He was lightning-fast when he first came up—fastest guy I'd ever seen. Then he has those knee injuries; there no telling how much more he could've done if he had two good legs. Darn he was strong. He swung so hard and he'd hit those huge home runs. He'd hit them 600 feet and I'd hit them half that and remind him they still count the same. Well, he liked to put on a show. Guys in the other dugout would stop everything to watch him in batting practice.

Mickey was a tremendous competitor. Tremendous desire. Always wanted to play no matter how bad he hurt. For years he batted third, me fourth, and I'd see him almost with tears in his eyes he was hurting so bad. But he played—played more games as a Yankee than anyone.

Sure he liked to go out in those days—we all did—he and Whitey asked me to stay out late with them. But I'd always leave around 11—told them they didn't have to catch the next day, but I did. Once Mickey got on me that calling a game wasn't too tough, so one day I arranged for him to call the signs from centerfield. Then I'd relay his signals—if he stood up it was a fastball, if he bent down it was a curve—to Whitey. By the seventh inning, I think we were ahead 2–0, and Mickey came over to me in the dugout and said, "I got you this far, now you finish." Told me he didn't want the pressure of calling a wrong pitch that would cost us.

People always think Mickey and Roger Maris were rivals—that's wrong. It was a great thing when they hit all those homers in 1961. Sure they wanted to break Babe Ruth's record—what athlete wouldn't? We really didn't care who hit more, as long as we won. There's nothing Mickey wouldn't do for you—he cared about the game so much, cared about his teammates better than anyone I ever knew. Even when I became manager in 1964, Mickey busted his tail. Had a great comeback season, playing hurt the whole time. Remember the World Series and that homer off Barney Schultz in Game 3? Well, right before he got up, he told me if he was going to hit it out. Then he hit the first pitch into the upper deck.

Like I always say, I was born at the right time. I was lucky to play with the Yankees. If I had to do it over again, I'd do it again. There's such a tradition of success, so much history. Every person who walks in Yankee Stadium knows it and sees it. Ruth, Gehrig, DiMaggio and Mantle, what can you say? They were the best. They said they felt lucky to be Yankees, too.

---

*Former Yankee great Yogi Berra is the author of* Ten Rings: My Championship Seasons *(HarperCollins).*

# BABE RUTH

No  player had more impact on baseball than George Herman Ruth. He won 94 games as a pitcher, but his uncanny knack for hitting home runs far and frequently separated him from all others in the 1920's and 1930's. By the time he had hit his 700th home run in 1934, only two other players had even hit more than 300 homers. (THE NEW YORK TIMES PHOTO ARCHIVES)

May 7, 1915

## NEW YORK CLUBS DEFEAT BOSTON'S TWO TEAMS—PHILLIES DEFEAT DODGERS

─────────

### HIGH AND COOK SPILL RED SOX IN 13TH

─────────

### Yankees Win Close and Hard-Fought Battle at the Polo Grounds, 4 to 3.

─────────

Those Yanks won another game up at the Polo Grounds yesterday, after fighting the Boston Red Sox tooth and nail for thirteen innings. Doc Cook, with a healthy smash to the right, sent Hugh High over the plate with the winning run when one man was out in the thirteenth. The score was 4 to 3. It was the first extra-inning game of the season, and about 5,000 fans were worked up to mid-August enthusiasms over the tussle.

The Bostons looked like sure enough winners up to the ninth inning. At that time Boston was leading 3 to 2. In the last of the ninth, with two out, Daniel Boone set off some fireworks with a two-base slam to centre which scored Dock Cook with the tying run. About this time Cy Pieh went in to pitch for the Yankees, and too much cannot be said about Pieh's efforts in the pitching line. He held the threatening Red Sox in check and mowed them down in order when they had desperate designs on the game. He did a smart piece of work in the eleventh inning, when the Sox got two men on bases. Pieh tightened up and retired the side on strike-outs.

For Boston, the big left-handed pitcher, Babe Ruth, was all that a pitcher is supposed to be, and some more. He put his team into the running in the third inning by smashing a mighty rap into the upper tier of the right-field grand stand. Ruth also had two other hits to his credit. His pitching throughout was of high order, and it was only after the hardest kind of effort that the Yanks were able to break through his service.

Boston introduced an accomplished new infielder in McNally, who cavorted playfully around third base. Charley Wagner has returned to the game and is now playing second base and the Red Sox line-up looks like a formidable combination. The team is handicapped, however, because of the absence of Joe Wood, Vean Gregg and Leonard from active service.

Jack Warhop's pitching was not badly abused by the Bostons. They did not hit him very often, but when they did connect, the ball seemed to have every intention of going out of the lot. Ruth was the first batsman to face Warhop in the third inning and with no apparent effort he slammed a home run into the grand stand.

The Yankees tied the score in the fourth inning. Cook was safe on Wagner's error and he stole second. Peck popped to Wagner and Boone was safe on McNally's weird toss to first. As Nunamaker forced Boone at second, Cook scored. The Red Sox went to the front in the seventh. With one out, Bill Carrigan doubled to left. After Ruth struck out, and Hooper walked, Wagner jammed a hit to left, scoring Carrigan.

In the eighth, Boston got another. Duffy Lewis hit a double to left and Hoblitzel sacrificed. Scott's double to left centre sent Lewis home. The Yankees began to get busy in the eighth inning. With one gone, Maisel singled and stole second, going around to third on Carrigan's wild toss to second. As McNally was throwing out Roy Hartzell at first, Maisel scored.

Then followed the giddy ninth when Dan Boone wrought havoc with Ruth's pitching. In that round, Pipp was an easy out at first and Cook was hit by a pitched ball. Cole stole second. Peck sent a high fly to Hoblitzel, and then Boone crashed his double to right centre, scoring Cook and tying the score.

The Yankees had a splendid opportunity to win in the eleventh inning. Pipp opened the session with a single, and after two men had been retired, Ruth was afraid to take a chance with Boone, so he gave him an intentional pass, and, Nunamaker, following Daniel, hoisted a high fly to Hooper in right.

Pieh's great pitching saved the Yanks the game in the eleventh. Henriksen, pinch-hitting for Bill Carrigan, doubled and sent Scott around to third. Pieh then struck out the next two batters.

High opened the thirteenth inning with a single and stole second. After Pipp had struck out, Cook produced his timely single to right and High romped home with the game.

On Monday, a crowd of more than 8,000 sailors from the fleet will be the guests of the Yankee owners at the Polo Grounds. The score:

| BOSTON. | | | | | | NEW YORK. | | | | | |
|---|---|---|---|---|---|---|---|---|---|---|---|
| | AB | R | H | PO | A | | AB | R | H | PO | A |
| H'per, rf. | 5 | 0 | 0 | 1 | 1 | Maisel, 3b. | 5 | 1 | 2 | 3 | 1 |
| Wag'r, 2b. | 5 | 0 | 3 | 4 | 2 | Hart'l, lf. | 4 | 0 | 0 | 0 | 0 |
| Sp'k'r, cf. | 4 | 0 | 0 | 2 | 0 | High, cf. | 6 | 1 | 3 | 4 | 2 |
| Lewis, lf. | 6 | 1 | 3 | 2 | 0 | Pipp, 1b. | 6 | 0 | 1 | 14 | 0 |
| Hob'l, 1b. | 5 | 0 | 0 | 20 | 0 | Cook, rf. | 5 | 2 | 2 | 2 | 0 |
| Scott, ss. | 5 | 0 | 1 | 0 | 6 | P'k'gh, ss. | 5 | 0 | 0 | 2 | 6 |
| McN'y, 3b. | 6 | 0 | 0 | 2 | 5 | Boone, 2b. | 4 | 0 | 2 | 4 | 3 |
| Car'gan, c. | 4 | 1 | 1 | 3 | 1 | Nua'er, c. | 5 | 0 | 0 | 10 | 2 |
| *Henr'n | 1 | 0 | 1 | 0 | 0 | Warh'p, p., | 2 | 0 | 0 | 0 | 1 |
| Tho's, c. | 0 | 0 | 0 | 2 | 0 | ‡Mul'en | 1 | 0 | 0 | 0 | 0 |
| Ruth, p | 5 | 1 | 3 | 1 | 5 | | | | | | |
| Total | 46 | 3 | 12 | 37 | 20 | Total | 45 | 4 | 10 | 39 | 17 |

*Batted for Carrigan in eleventh inning.

†One out when winning run was scored.

‡Batted for Warhop in eighth inning.

Errors—Wagner, McNally, Carrigan, Ruth, Maisel, Pieh.

| Boston | 0 | 0 | 1 | 0 | 0 | 0 | 1 | 1 | 0 | 0 | 0 | 0—3 |
|---|---|---|---|---|---|---|---|---|---|---|---|---|
| New York | 0 | 0 | 0 | 0 | 1 | 0 | 0 | 1 | 1 | 0 | 0 | 1—4 |

Two-base hits—Carrigan, Lewis, Scott, Boone. Home run—Ruth. Stolen bases—Cook, 2; Maisel, Hooper, Hartzell, High. Earned runs—New York, 2; Boston, 3. Sacrifice hits—Speaker, Hartzell, Hoblitzel. Double play—Peckinpaugh and Pipp. Left on bases—New York, 9; Boston, 10. First base on errors—New York, 2; Boston, 2. Bases on balls—Off Warhop, 4; off Ruth, 3.

Hits—Off Warhop, 10 in 8 innings; off Pieh, 2 in 5 innings. Hit by pitcher—By Ruth (Cook). Struck out—By Warhop, 1; by Pick, 6; by Ruth, 3. Wild pitch—Ruth. Umpires—Messrs. Evans and Mullaney. Time of game, two hours and thirty-five minutes.

---

September 6, 1918

## RED SOX BEAT CUBS IN INITIAL BATTLE OF WORLD'S SERIES

### RUTH STAR IN TALE OF BOSTON VICTORY

#### Detailed Play, Inning by Inning, Shows Mastery of Big Red Sox Twirler.

CHICAGO, Sept. 5.—While the managers and umpires were conferring an immense horseshoe of roses was brought to the home plate and presented to Fred Mitchell, manager of the Chicago team. Charles Deal, third baseman of the locals, was given a big bouquet of roses.

The umpires were assigned as follows: balls and strikes, O'Day; first base, Hildebrand, second base, Klem; third base, Owens.

The game in detail was as follows:

FIRST INNING.—Red Sox—Hooper was cheered as he walked to the plate. Vaughn's first pitch was a strike. Hooper bumped the second offering down the first base line and was out, Merkle to Vaughn. Shean took two strikes and then dropped a Texas leaguer in right. Strunk forced Shean, Deal to Pick, the Chicago second baseman losing a chance for a double play by a momentary fumble. Strunk tried to advance to second on a short passed ball and was thrown out, Killifer to Hollocher. NO RUNS. ONE HIT. NO ERRORS.

FIRST INNING.—Cubs—Flack fanned, the third strike being called when it shot over the outside corner, shoulder high. Hollocher grounded out, Shean to McInnis. Mann sent a duplicate grounder at Shean, but the ball hopped over the second baseman's head for a single. Paskert singled sharply to left and Mann went to third, Paskert taking second on the throw to the far corner. Merkle ran his string to three and two and then walked, filling the bases. This brought up Pick, who made his world series debut in a world series pinch. Pick, on the fourth pitch, flied to Whiteman. NO RUNS. TWO HITS. NO ERRORS.

SECOND INNING.—Red Sox—Whiteman opened with a single to centre. It was a fast grounder between Hollocher and Pick. McInnis sacrificed, Vaughn to Merkle, placing a nice bunt close to the line, Whiteman going to second. Scott took a ball and a strike, fouled into the stands for the second strike, and then flied to Flack. Thomas's grounder bounced high in the air, but a fast play retired him, Merkle to Vaughn. NO RUNS. ONE HIT. NO ERRORS.

SECOND INNING.—Cubs—Ruth's control seemed not of the best. His first two pitches to Deal were high and wide. The next two were called strikes and Deal then grounded out, Ruth to McInnins. Killifer was applauded when he came to bat. He grounded out, Shean to McInnis. Vaughn also drew a patter of applause from the fans. He fouled out to Agnew. NO RUNS. NO HITS. NO ERRORS.

THIRD INNING.—Red Sox—Agnew waited till the call was three balls and two strikes and then fouled out to Killifer. Ruth was cheered when he came up. He drove a hard liner to centre. Paskert stumbled, but recovered quickly and captured the ball. Hooper caught a curve on the end of his bat and drove it safely to left. Hooper went out stealing, Killifer to Hollocher. NO RUNS. ONE HIT. NO ERRORS.

THIRD INNING.—Cubs—Flack singled to short centre, the hit dropping between Shean and Strunk. Hollocher sacrificed, Thomas to McInnis, the veteran first baseman making a good catch of a wide throw. Flack went to second on the play. Mann grounded out, Shean to McInnis, Flack taking third. Paskert grounded out, Scott to McInnis. NO RUNS. ONE HIT. NO ERRORS.

FOURTH INNING.—Red Sox—Vaughn lost control and passed Shean. Strunk bunted a pop fly to Vaughn. Whiteman made his second hit, a looping drive which just cleared Hollocher's mitt. Shean went to second. Shean scored on McInnis's hard single to left, Whiteman moving to second. Scott bunted a pop fly, which Deal caught on the run, Whiteman barely scrambled back to second in safety. Thomas fanned, swinging heavily at the third strike. ONE RUN. TWO HITS. NO ERRORS.

FOURTH INNING.—Cubs—Merkle drove a high fly to Hooper. Pick fanned, offering weakly at the third strike, which was low and wide. Deal put up a high fly which Hooper had no trouble in capturing. NO RUNS. NO HITS. NO ERRORS.

FIFTH INNING.—Red Sox—Agnew out, Deal to Merkle. Ruth was again cheered when he came up to bat. Vaughn worked carefully and fanned the big Boston pitcher. The feat drew the first pot cheering from the shivering crowd. Hooper grounded out, Vaughn to Merkle. NO RUNS. NO HITS. NO ERRORS.

FIFTH INNING.—Cubs—Killifer's high fly dropped into Whiteman's hands. Vaughn fouled twice, then swung at a curve and missed for the third strike. Flack was hit on the head, but showed no ill effects as he went to first. Hollocher flied to Strunk. NO RUNS. NO HITS. NO ERRORS.

SIXTH INNING.—Red Sox—Shean ran his string up to the three-and-two count and then let the third strike go by. Strunk drove a sharp grounder at Vaughn, who threw him out to Merkle. Flack captured Whiteman's foul fly after a short run. NO RUNS. NO HITS. NO ERRORS.

SIXTH INNING.—Cubs—The crowd began to root for a Chicago run as Mann came to the plate. The left fielder responded with an easy fly to Hooper. Paskert hit safely to centre, and the rooting started again. Merkle drove a hit through the box and over second base, Paskert advancing to the middle station. Pick, with orders to sacrifice, popped a foul fly on his first attempt. He then grounded out to McInnis unassisted, both runners moving up. With an opportunity to sew up the game, Deal flied to Whiteman. NO RUNS. NO HITS. NO ERRORS.

SEVENTH INNING.—Red Sox—McInnis flied to Paskert in short centre. Hollocher made a fine stop of Scott's sharp grounder and threw him out at first. Thomas fanned on three pitched balls. NO RUNS. NO HITS. NO ERRORS.

SEVENTH INNING.—Cubs—The band halted the proceedings by playing "The Star-Spangled Banner." The players, with the exception of Thomas, stood at civilian salute, the Great Lakes sailor coming to the military pose. Killifer flied to Strunk, Vaughn hit far to Scott's right, but the Boston shortstop skidded over and made a one-handed pickup, throwing his man out at first. Flack grounded out, Scott to McInnis. There were less than half a dozen balls pitched in this inning. NO RUNS. NO HITS. NO ERRORS.

EIGHTH INNING.—Red Sox—Agnew went out, Deal to Merkle. For the third time the crowd rooted for a hit from Ruth. He fanned out three pitched balls, fouling the first and swinging heavily at two sharp-breaking curves that followed. Hooper out, Pick to Merkle. NO. RUNS. NO HITS. NO ERRORS.

EIGHTH INNING.—Cubs—Hollocher grounded down the first-base line, and was out to McInnis, unassisted. Mann flied to Whiteman. The crowd turned its attention to the formation of six warplanes which flew over the field. Paskert let the third strike go by and was called out. NO RUNS. NO HITS. NO ERRORS.

NINTH INNING.—Red Sox—Shean walked. Strung sacrificed, Vaughn to Merkle, Shean moving to second. Whiteman fanned, the third strike being a foul tip. McInnis was purposely passed. Scott grounded out, Vaughn to Merkle. NO RUNS. NO HITS. NO ERRORS.

NINTH INNING.—Cubs—Merkle flied to Whiteman. O'Farrell batted for Pick. He waited carefully until the count was three and two and then popped to Thomas. Deal beat out a hit down the third-base line. McCabe ran for Deal. On the hit and run Killifer flied to Hooper. NO RUNS. NO HITS. NO ERRORS.

# RED SOX BEAT CUBS IN INITIAL BATTLE OF WORLD'S SERIES

## ONE RUN GIVES RED SOX FIRST GAME OF SERIES

### Babe Ruth's Mighty Arm Holds Cubs Scoreless Through Nine Torrid Innings.

### McINNIS'S BAT SETTLES IT

### Boston First Baseman Drives Ball to Left Field for Hit Which Scores Shean.

*Special to The New York Times.*

CHICAGO, Sept. 5.—Far different from any incident that has ever occurred in the history of baseball was the great moment in the first world's series game between the Chicago Cubs and the Boston Red Sox, which came at Comisky Park this afternoon during the seventh inning stretch. As the crowd of 19,274 spectators—the smallest that has witnessed the diamond classic in many years—stood up to take their afternoon yawn, that has been the privilege and custom of baseball fans for many generations, the band broke forth to the strains of "The Star-Spangled Banner."

The yawn was checked and heads were bared as the ball players turned quickly about and faced the music. Jackie Fred Thomas of the U.S. Navy was at attention, as he stood erect, with his eyes set on the flag fluttering at the top of the lofty pole in right field. First the song was taken up by a few, then others joined, and when the final notes came, a great volume of melody rolled across the field. It was at the very end that the onlookers exploded into thunderous applause and rent the air with a cheer that marked the highest point of the day's enthusiasm.

The mind of the baseball fan was on the war. The patriotic outburst following the singing of the national anthem was far greater than the upheaval of emotion which greeted Babe Ruth, the Boston southpaw, when he conquered Hippo Jim Vaughn and the Cubs in a seething flinging duel by a score of 1 to 0. The cheers for America's stirring song were greater even than the demonstration offered Vaughn when he twice made the mighty Ruth whiff the air.

### Game Brilliantly Played.

This was an unusually brilliant exhibition of baseball for world's series play. There were no misplays, no errors of judgment, no let-up in the tense, earnest work of the rival players. Stripped of much of the pomp and glamour usually attending world's series games, the players this afternoon were not so high-strung. They were at their very best and played the kind of baseball expected in critical games during the season.

The Cubs successfully stilled the perilous home-run bat of Ruth, but they overlooked the menace of his pitching arm. Manager Barrow operated a little surprise when he sent Ruth to the mound. Joe Bush had warmed up and was ready to take the pitching responsibility, but the Baltimore mauler was named for the task.

Hippo Vaughn pitched a great game. At only one moment was there a blemish on his performance. That one weak spot, which caused him to bow before the superior flinging of Ruth, was a base on balls to Dave Shean in the fourth inning.

Shean was the first batsman to face Vaughn in that round. There was a bit of white tape on Shean's injured left finger. Maybe it was the knowledge of this bruised finger that caused Vaughn to be a bit careless in pitching to the Boston second sacker. Anyway, Hippo gave Shean a pass. Amos Strunk attempted to sacrifice, but instead he lifted up a pop fly which Vaughn nipped after a high jump.

George Whiteman, who has not had serious consideration in the series, slammed a steaming one-base drive to centre field, and Shean stood safely at second.

## McInnis Decides Game.

Next came to the bat Stuffy McInnis, the modest little graduate of the baseball university of Connie Mack. Jack McInnis is a cool, cautious citizen in a pinch of this kind. If Manager Barrow had his choice, he could not have chosen a better man than this same sawed-off lad from Gloucester.

Jim Vaughn's repertoire of curves responded beautifully to the twist of his fingers, and there was no fear in his heart as he speeded the ball over to little Jack. McInnis set himself, took a tremendous swing, and the ball hummed its way out to left field, while Shean started on a wild dash from second base.

Leslie Mann, Chicago's left fielder, raced over and checked the truant ball. Shean did not even stop to look, but tore around third base toward home as Mann picked up the ball and hurled it to Killifer. Shean may have had a badly injured finger, but there was nothing the matter with his feet, for he galloped home, taking the last few yards with a long, desperate slide, and beat the ball in by inches.

There was the ball game right there.

Whatever danger there was of Ruth's weakening was gone, for after that he was exhilarated with the thrill of triumph. That one lone run grew larger as the pitchers battled along, both displaying an impenetrable mysticism of curves. That lonesome unit grew taller and taller in the mind of Babe Ruth, until, when the ninth inning came, it was as high as the aviation altitude record.

This is the first world's series 1 to 0 game since the great Mathewson, in the heyday of his glory, pitched the Philadelphia Athletics to defeat by that score in 1905. If the greatest reason for playing this world's series this year was to give the boys overseas something to talk about besides war, this game today surely will serve the purpose. The cables and the wireless tonight had many things to flash across which will be topics of conversation for the courageous crusaders.

There was no getting away from the fact that there was a touch of sadness in the world's series clash today. Empty seats, rows and rows of them, brought home to every man and woman in the crowd that the lads who have sat in those seats in the past were far, far from home on the world's grimmest mission.

It is not surprising that only a few over 19,000 went through the gates. The far-reaching hand of war has thinned the ranks of the fans; it has thinned the ranks of the players, and even the most enthusiastic of today's onlookers would not help but realize that this will probably be the last world's series for a long, long time.

These were the thoughts uppermost in every one's mind in that seventh inning stretch, when the baseball park suddenly blazed forth in an outburst of patriotism which caused every mother's son in the stands to forget all about baseball.

Around the camp fires in France and on the decks of Uncle Sam's battleships in foreign waters they will be talking, telling each other tomorrow about that miraculous play by Everett Scott in the seventh inning, when Scotty fairly wished himself over into left field to spear Jim Vaughn's savage smash on his bare, stinging hand and throw the pitcher out at first while he was still tangled up like a pretzel in midair.

## Flack's Head Solid.

Yes, and the boys overseas will be telling each other what a hard, solid head Max Flack has. They will surely smile and wish their heads were as hard as Flack's, who took the full force of one of Babe Ruth's shoots right on the top of his cap in the fifth inning and sunk to the ground.

It was a fearful bang which resounded through the stands as the ball and Flack's head met. Three doctors and half a dozen undertakers forgot about the game and were on their toes in a second, thinking that an important case was at hand. Naturally, you imagine that Flack was badly hurt. You have another imagine, because Max jumped up and walked down to first base without even rubbing his head. A toppiece like that would hardly need a steel helmet on the other side.

There was another great fielding play when Charley Hollocher, the sensational Cub shortstop, nipped Scott's hit in the bud in the seventh inning and transformed it into a plain every day out with a marvelous stop and just as marvelous a toss to first base.

The Cubs went down to defeat fighting bitterly. Right up to the last putout Mitchell's men were still confident that they would break through Ruth's tricky curves. They twice had Ruth and Boston on the run, but it is much to the credit of the Boston men's gameness that they were able to stem the tide and turn the Cubs back when they were threatening dangerously.

## Cubs Have Early Chance.

The first inning saw the Cubs with victory within their grasp. After Flack had been called out on strikes in the opening inning and Hollocher had been neatly tossed out at first by Scott, Mann poked a fickle grounder down toward Shean at second base. The bouncing ball just touched a loose pebble enough to cause it to hop outrageously over Shean's head for a single. Dode Paskert jammed a single through the big hole between Scott and Thomas, and Mann raced to third.

The ball had taken a bad bounce off Whiteman's shins in left field, and as Whiteman recovered the ball and hurled it to third in a vain effort to cut off Mann, Paskert raced to second.

Here was the table all set for a nice run luncheon. Fred Merkle was the bat and unanimously elected to serve it. Ruth didn't pitch any good ones to Merkle because he knows the former Giant first baseman of old. Merkle was patient and got a pass filling the bases.

If any one but Charley Pick was at the bat with this great chance staring him in the face, the result might have been different, but Pick is a youngster and was plainly nervous with so much responsibility packed on to his young shoulders. The best he could do was to lift a fly to Whiteman in left and end the Cubs' greatest opportunity of the day.

Indeed, the Cubs again had a good chance in the sixth. In this inning Mann rocked the ball out to Harry Hooper in right field. Paskert stung a hit to centre and Merkle slapped one to the same bailiwick, and Ruth was becoming plainly worried. So was Manager Ed Barrow, and he gave Joe Bush the high sign, and Joe, far out in right field, again resumed the task of warming up which he had been diligently pursuing from the moment the game started. Pick, still nervous, was placed in this all important predicament again and this time he rolled a sacrifice down to Jack McInnis and two runners advanced a station nearer home and glory.

## Deal Has Fine Chance.

With men on third and second and two out, Charley Deal, who proved his worth in a situation of this kind back in the great series of 1914, came to the bat and had good wishes of every one in Chicago with him. Deal fell far short of his 1914 reputation, and instead of sending the crowd into hysteria of joy he poked a fly to Whiteman and again the Cubs' chances were flickering away.

There was still one saucy kick left in the Cubs when they came to the bat in the last of the ninth. Most of the crowd had taken it for granted that not a Chicago bat could prod the kind of pitching that Ruth was showing, and they had started for the exits. Merkle shot a rocket to Whiteman, and O'Farrell, batting for Pick, popped to Thomas.

Deal brought the spectators hustling back to their seats when he rolled the ball down the infield toward third and beat Thomas's toss to first base. McCabe was injected into the pastime to serve as Deal's propelling power.

Bill Killifer set his teeth tightly and took one last grand slam at the ball and shot a high ballooner between right and centre fields.

As the ball rose higher and higher Hooper and Strunk both set out after it. They both yelled that they had it exclusively, and, amid the cheering, their words fell on deaf ears.

On and on they came toward each other, and it looked as if a head-on collision was in the making. Hooper yelled again as he approached Strunk, and as the players were about to collide, Strunk stepped back and Hooper made the catch.

### THE SCORE OF YESTERDAY'S GAME.

| BOSTON (A.) | AB. | R. | BH. | PO. | A. | E. | CHICAGO (N.) | AB. | R. | BH. | PO. | A. | E. |
|---|---|---|---|---|---|---|---|---|---|---|---|---|---|
| Hooper, rf | 4 | 0 | 1 | 4 | 0 | 0 | Flack, rf | 3 | 0 | 1 | 2 | 0 | 0 |
| Shean, 2b | 2 | 1 | 1 | 0 | 3 | 0 | Hollocher, ss | 3 | 0 | 0 | 2 | 1 | 0 |
| Strunk, cf | 3 | 0 | 0 | 2 | 0 | 0 | Mann, lf | 4 | 0 | 1 | 0 | 0 | 0 |
| Whiteman, lf | 4 | 0 | 2 | 5 | 0 | 0 | Paskert, cf | 4 | 0 | 2 | 2 | 0 | 0 |
| McInnis, 1b | 2 | 0 | 1 | 10 | 0 | 0 | Merkle, 1b | 3 | 0 | 1 | 9 | 2 | 0 |
| Scott, ss | 4 | 0 | 0 | 0 | 3 | 0 | Pick, 2b | 3 | 0 | 0 | 1 | 1 | 0 |
| Thomas, 3b | 3 | 0 | 0 | 1 | 1 | 0 | Deal, 3b | 4 | 0 | 1 | 1 | 3 | 0 |
| Agnew, c | 3 | 0 | 0 | 5 | 0 | 0 | Killifer, c | 4 | 0 | 0 | 7 | 2 | 0 |
| Ruth, p | 3 | 0 | 0 | 0 | 1 | 0 | Vaughn, p | 3 | 0 | 0 | 3 | 5 | 0 |
| | | | | | | | ᵃO'Farrell | 1 | 0 | 0 | 0 | 0 | 0 |
| | | | | | | | ᵇMcCabe | 0 | 0 | 0 | 0 | 0 | 0 |
| Total | 28 | 1 | 5 | 27 | 8 | 0 | Total | 32 | 0 | 6 | 27 | 14 | 0 |

ᵃBatted for Pick in ninth.
ᵇRan for Deal in ninth.

| | | | | | | | | | | |
|---|---|---|---|---|---|---|---|---|---|---|
| Boston | 0 | 0 | 0 | 1 | 0 | 0 | 0 | 0 | 0—1 |
| Chicago | 0 | 0 | 0 | 0 | 0 | 0 | 0 | 0 | 0—0 |

Sacrifice hits—McInnis, Hollocher, Strunk. Left on bases—Americans, 5; Nationals, 8. Bases on balls—Off Ruth, 1; off Vaughn, 3. Hit by pitcher—By Ruth, (Flack.) Struck out—By Ruth, 4; by Vaughn, 6. Time of game—1 hour and 50 minutes. Umpires—O'Day at plate; Hildebrand at first; Klem at second; Owens at third.

# MATHEWSON DEDUCES FROM WORLD'S SERIES THAT NATIONAL LEAGUE OUTCLASSES RIVAL

## RUTH STANDS ALONE AS A HEAVY HITTER

### His Remarkable Batting Feats Provide Greatest Feature of 1919 Baseball Season

The history of the 1919 baseball season is now ready for the chronicler, and the first chapter of any history that may be written belongs, on results accomplished, to big Babe Ruth, the mastodonic mauler of the Boston Red Sox, whose feats with the willow have discounted everything that went before in batting annals since the game was introduced. A world's series has come and gone, the supposedly stronger contender for first honors has been toppled and the championship rests with the National League for the second time in ten years. For the American League rests the honor of having produced the greatest batsman the game ever has known.

Ruth has won his laurels in a manner that leaves no doubt as to being the hardest hitter in the history of the game. He did not pile up his huge total of twenty-nine home runs through the aid of some neighborly fence on his home park, as so frequently happens, when a player is able to hit more than seven or eight home runs in one season. Ruth in the past year hit a ball beyond a barrier of every park in the American League and in several cities he made drives which old timers readily class as record drives. If any player of the past hit home runs on every park in the circuit the performance has escaped notice, which hardly would be probable.

The Boston slugger hit what New York critics agree was the longest drive ever made at the Polo Grounds, the ball going above the roof of the right field stand and continuing on its way to a neighboring field. Joe Jackson once put a ball over the stand but it was not traveling as fast as the Ruth slam when it disappeared from view. At Navin Field, Detroit, Ruth hit a ball beyond the street wall in a game during the past summer. This wall stands beyond a runway through which the bleacherites make their way to the uncovered stands. At Sportsman's Park in St. Louis, Ruth hit the longest drive ever recorded there, and at his home field, Fenway Park, in Boston, the big slugger has made several drives beyond the best mark reached by any other player.

**Great Driving Power.**

An idea of the remarkable driving power shown by Ruth in his record-making campaign this season is provided in the hitting he has done at Comiskey Park in Chicago and Navin Field in Detroit. Ruth has driven three homers into the right-field bleachers at Chicago, as many as the entire collection of American League sluggers has averaged in a season since the park was built. He has hit five home runs to the right-field section of Navin Field, and here he goes beyond the average season crop for home runs to this distant section. Cleveland's right field has a fence forty-five feet high, and Ruth hit two beyond this barrier this year.

Since the tendency of later days is to built larger parks than those used in the old days, there seems to be little likelihood of any slugger displacing the record set by Ruth this season. It must be remembered, too, that he missed several games played by the Red Sox early in the year, also that the major league schedule called for only 140 games. Ruth took part in only 130 games during the 1919 season, or twenty-four less than the schedule called for normally. With those twenty-four extra games added, there is no telling how high Ruth would run that home run total.

It is not with the idea of disparaging the high totals reached by Ed Williamson in 1884, or Buck Freeman in 1899, to say that both had easier fences to shoot at in the old days than Ruth, or any other player, has at the present time. Williamson met conditions as he found them and it is to his credit that he was able to set up a figure which no player of his day, or of the next thirty-four years, could duplicate. Freeman, with two home runs less than Williamson made, undoubtedly was one of the star sluggers of a later era. However, since so many comparisons have been made between the figures of Ruth and those of Williamson and Freeman, it is only fair to the great Red Sox slugger to say that he hardly had to equal those old-time marks to prove his superiority over both as a long-distance hitter.

Clark Griffith has been quoted as saying that Freeman had a neighborly fence at the home park of the Washington Club when he compiled his record in the late '90s, while the capital was represented in the old twelve-club National League. According to figures recently unearthed, Freeman made fifteen of his home runs at Washington, and got no more than two on any other park that year. He got two at Chicago, St. Louis, and Louisville, and one at Cleveland, Brooklyn, Boston, and New York. Williamson hit 25 of his 27 home runs on the old Congress Street grounds in Chicago and the remaining two at Buffalo. Gavvy Cravath, when he set the later-day record, 24 home runs in 1915, did most of his home-run hitting at the Phillies' Park, where the right-field fence is short and the outfield bleacher offers a convenient spot for a ball to bound into.

### Babe Hits 'Em Everywhere.

How different has been the work of Ruth during the season just closed. His home field, Fenway Park, is one of the most difficult in baseball from a home-run standpoint, and some of the best hitters of the game have never hit a ball into the right or centre field bleachers at Boston. Ruth hit nine home runs in Boston during the recent season and he made at least two on all other parks except that at Washington, where he hit for the circuit only once. The tabulation of Ruth's home-run drives by cities is as follows: Boston, 9; Detroit, 5; New York, 4; Chicago, 3; St. Louis, 3; Cleveland, 2; Philadelphia, 2; Washington, 1. No park has been too difficult for Ruth.

With all the facts at hand, there can be no denying that Ruth's performance as a home-run hitter outshines the marks of the sluggers of other years in a wider degree than in the difference in the figures. His wonderful batting ability has needed no particular field to prey on. He has demonstrated throughout the league that he stands alone in long-distance hitting of recent years, and there is a marked tendency among old-timers to give him credit as being the greatest slugger in the history of the game.

Ruth is a comparative youngster in baseball, and he should shine for many years to come as a home-run hitter. He started slowly, with only nine home runs in his first three seasons in the big league—four in 1915, three in 1916, and two in 1917. He played comparatively few games in those campaigns, being used mainly as a pitcher, but even under these conditions he showed no such slugging ability as in the curtailed seasons of 1918 and 1919. He made eleven home runs last season, which ended Labor Day, and added twenty-nine this year. His home run total since coming into the majors has reached forty-nine, and he undoubtedly will pass all the previous marks of the heavy hitters. The fences are not too far away for this particular slugger.

# RUTH BOUGHT BY NEW YORK AMERICANS FOR $125,000, HIGHEST PRICE IN BASEBALL ANNALS

## YANKS BUY BABE RUTH FOR $125,000

### Highest Purchase Price in Baseball History Paid for Game's Greatest Slugger.

### WILL GET NEW CONTRACT

### Miller Huggins Is Now in California to Sign Home-run King at Large Salary.

### SLATED FOR RIGHT FIELD

### Acquisition of Noted Batsman Gives New York Club the Hard-Hitting Outfielder Long Desired.

Babe Ruth of the Boston Red Sox, baseball's super-slugger, was purchased by the Yankees yesterday for the largest cash sum ever paid for a player. The New York Club paid Harry Frazee of Boston $125,000 for the sensational batsman who last season caused such a furor in the national game by batting out twenty-nine home runs, a new record in long-distance clouting.

Colonel Ruppert, President of the Yanks, said that he had taken over Ruth's Boston contract, which has two years more to run. This contract calls for a salary of $10,000 a year. Ruth recently announced that he would refuse to play for $10,000 a year next season, although the Boston Club has received no request for a raise in salary.

Manager Miller Huggins is now in Los Angeles negotiating with Ruth. It is believed that the Yanks manager will offer him a new contract which will be satisfactory to the Colossus of the bat.

President Ruppert said yesterday that Ruth would probably play right field for the Yankees. He played in left field for the Red Sox last season, and had the highest fielding average among the outfielders, making only two errors during the season. While he is on the Pacific Coast Manager Huggins will also endeavor to sign Duffy Lewis, who will be one of Ruth's companions in the outfield at the Polo Grounds next season.

**Home Run Record in Danger.**

The acquisition of Ruth strengthens the Yankees club in its weakest department. With the added hitting power of Ruth, Bob Shawkey, one of the Yankee pitchers, said yesterday the New York club should be a pennant winner next season. For several seasons the Yankees have been experimenting with outfielders, but never have been able to land a consistent hitter. The short right field wall of the Polo Grounds should prove an easy target for Ruth next season and, playing seventy-seven games at home, it would not be surprising if Ruth surpassed his home-run record of twenty-nine circuit clouts next Summer.

Ruth was such a sensation last season that he supplanted the great Ty Cobb as baseball's greatest attraction, and in obtaining the services of Ruth for next season the New York club made a ten-strike which will be received with the greatest enthusiasm by Manhattan baseball fans.

Ruth's crowning batting accomplishment came at the Polo Grounds last Fall when he hammered one of the longest hits ever seen in Harlem over the right field grandstand for his twenty-eighth home run, smashing the home record of twenty-seven, made by Ed Williamson way back in 1884. The more modern home-run record, up to last season, had been held by Buck Freeman, who made twenty-five home runs when a member of the Washington club in 1899. The next best home-run hitter of modern times is Gavvy Cravath, now manager of the Phillies, who made twenty-four home runs a few seasons ago.

Ruth's home-run drives were distributed all over the circuit, and he is the one player known to the game who hit a home run on every park on the circuit in the same season.

## Specializes in Long Hits.

Ruth's batting feats last season will stand for many years to come, unless he betters the record himself with the aid of the short right field under Coogan's Bluff. The record he made last season was a masterpiece of slugging. He went up to the bat 432 times in 130 games and produced 139 hits. Of these hits 75 were for extra bases. Not only did he make 29 home runs, but he also made 34 two-baggers and 12 three-baggers. Ruth's batting average for extra base hits was .657, a mark which probably will not be approached for many years to come.

Ruth scored the greatest number of runs in the American League last season, crossing the plate 103 times. Cobb scored only 93 runs last year. Ruth was so dangerous that the American League pitchers were generous with their passes and the superlative hitter walked 101 times, many of these passes being intentional. Ruth also struck out more than any other batsman in the league, fanning 58 times. He also made three sacrifice hits and he stole seven bases.

Ruth is a native of Baltimore and is 26 years old, just in his prime as a baseball player. He was discovered by Jack Dunn, owner of the Baltimore Club, while playing with the baseball team of Mount St. Joseph's, a school which Ruth attended in that city, in 1913. In 1914 Ruth played with the Baltimore team and up to that time little attention had been paid to his batting. It was as a pitcher he attracted attention in Baltimore. Boston bought Ruth along with Ernie Shore and some other players in 1914. The price paid for Ruth is said to have been $2,700.

## Holds World's Series Record.

Ruth was a big success in the major league from the start. In 1916, when the Red Sox won the pennant, he led the American League pitchers in effectiveness and in the world's series of 1916 and 1918, Ruth hung up a new world's series pitching record for shut-out innings. He pitched twenty-eight scoreless consecutive innings, which beat the record of twenty-seven scoreless innings made in the world's series games by Christy Mathewson of the Giants.

For the past few seasons Ruth's ambition has been to play regularly. While he was doing only pitching duty with Boston he was a sensational pinch hitter and when he played regularly in the outfield last season he blossomed forth as the most sensational batsman the game has ever known. He was also a great success as a fielder and last season he made only two errors and had 230 putouts. He also had twenty-six assists, more than any outfielder in the American League. This was because of his phenomenal throwing arm. His fielding average last season was .992. Ruth didn't do much pitching last season. He pitched thirteen games and won eight and lost five.

Manager Huggins is expected back in New York at the end of next week with Ruth's contract in his inside pocket. It is believed that the New York Club will not try to hold Ruth to the Boston contract which he has decided is unsatisfactory.

The new contract which the Yankees have offered Ruth is said to be almost double the Boston figure of $10,000 a year. While he is out on the coast interviewing Ruth, Huggins is also getting into line not only Duffy Lewis, but also Bob Meusel, the sensational young slugger of the Pacific Coast League, who is regarded by baseball scouts as the minor league find of the year.

## The Perfect Hitter.

Ruth's principle of batting is much the same as the principle of the golfer. He comes back slowly, keeps his eyes on the ball and follows through. His very position at the bat is intimidating to the pitcher. He places his feet in perfect position. He simply cannot step away from the pitch if he wants to. He can step only one way—in. The weight of Ruth's body when he bats is on his left leg. The forward leg is bent slightly at the knee. As he stands facing the pitcher more of his hips and back are seen by the pitcher than his chest or side. When he starts to swing his back is half turned toward the pitcher. He goes as far back as he can reach, never for an instant taking his eye off the ball as it leaves the pitcher's hand.

The greatest power in his terrific swing comes when the bat is directly in front of his body, just half way in the swing. He hits the ball with terrific impact and there is no player in the game whose swing is such a masterpiece of batting technique.

## FRAZEE DISCUSSES SALE.

### "Red Sox Were Fast Becoming a One-Man Team," Says Owner.

BOSTON, Jan. 5.—Harry H. Frazee of the Boston Americans said tonight that he has sold "Babe" Ruth to the New York Americans because he thought it was an "injustice" to keep him with the Red Sox, who "were fast becoming a one-man team." He did not make public the purchase price.

Ruth, who is the world champion home run hitter, recently returned his three-year contract, which called for a payment of $10,000 a year, without his signature, demanding a much larger salary. Mr. Frazee said he would use the money obtained from the New York Club for the purchase of other players and would try to develop the Red Sox into a winning team.

## RUTH NOT SURPRISED.

### Home-Run King Says He Expected Red Sox Would Sell Him.

LOS ANGELES, Cal., Jan. 5.—Babe Ruth, champion home-run hitter, tonight said he had no information regarding his reported sale by the Boston Americans to the New York American club until told by The Associated Press that Colonel Ruppert, President of the Yankees, had announced the deal.

"I am not surprised, however," he added. "When I made my demand on the Red Sox for $20,000 a year, I had an idea they would choose to sell me rather than pay the increase, and I knew the Yankees were the most probable purchasers in that event."

Ruth said he had not yet seen Miller Huggins, manager of the Yankees, who was reported to be in Southern California to negotiate with the ball player.

May 2, 1920

## RUTH DRIVES BALL OVER GRAND STAND

### Colossal Clout of Home-Run King Helps Yankees in Their 6 to 0 Victory Over Red Sox.

### BOB SHAWKEY IN FINE FORM

### Only One Visitor Passes First Base—Three New York Players Are Chased to the Clubhouse.

May Day disturbances of one sort and another stirred up a lot of commotion at the Polo Grounds yesterday. Soviet uprisings among the Yankee players put the Boston Red Sox to rout, 6 to 0. Revolutionary measures, aimed at the umpires, Dineen and Nallin, wrought havoc with baseball law and order and steamed up a funny little riot. Attorney-General Palmer wasn't there to handle it, so the umpires took the matters in their own hands and three Yankee players—Mays, Shore and O'Doul—were deported. Although disgraced, they left laughingly.

Babe Ruth sneaked a bomb into the park without anybody knowing it and hid it in his bat. He exploded the weapon in the sixth, when he lambasted a home run high over the right field grand stand into Manhattan Field. This was Babe's first home run of the championship season, and it was a sock-dolager. The ball flitted out of sight between the third and fourth flagstaffs on the top of the stand. Ruth smashed it over the same place when he broke the world's home run record last season. The only other citizen who has even slapped the ball over the stand was Joe Jackson, a few seasons back.

Another dangerous explosive was pushed into the game by Duffy Lewis. He followed Ruth's example and soaked a home run into the left field bleachers. From the Red Sox point of view, it was a tough day for good baseball government.

### Three Yankees Chased.

Rumblings of unrest came from the Yankee bench in the fifth inning. The soapbox orator proved to be Carl Mays. He was preaching free speech and anarchy in large chunks, hurling them all at Will Dineen, the umpire. Will stands for the kind of Americanism which suspends all the house rules in relation to umperical authority. His fellow ump, Dick Nallin, thinks the same. In fact, all umpires think alike.

Ernie Shore and Frank O'Doul joined in the outrageous and alarming wave of free speech, directing their treacherous vaporings against Dick Nallin.

The umpires brought their heads together. Not in collision, you understand. Nallin stuck his ear in close proximity to Will Dineen's chiseled lips. What right has these proletariat ball players to raise a voice against the concrete wall of authority? Who were these unruly scamps to shout against the infallible word of the umpire?

Will and Dick placed the iron heel on the necks of the common ball players, displaying no softness of feeling or kindness of heart. Mays, Shore and O'Doul were sent from the bench to the Siberia of the club house, without even a hearing as provided under the constitution.

Some 12,000 onlookers witnessed the insurrection. Were they with the forces of umperical law and order? They were not. They were for the underdog. They whooped it up for the poor downtrodden common victims. They yelled in soprano, alto, bass and baritone against the high-handed demonstration of the law of the diamond.

### Pennock Is Hit Hard.

It was a satisfying ball game for the Yanks. They started hitting at last and poked the ball hard as it came from the hands of the southpaw, Herb Pennock. Herb survived for six innings. Harry Harper took up the burden and he was so wild that he gave way to a pitcher named Fortune. He was anything but that. After the seventh inning Manager Ed Barrow thought his name ought to be changed to bankruptcy.

Bob Shawkey pitched for the Yanks, and at last hit his stride. He held the Sox to four hits, none of them dangerous. Sixteen of the Red Sox went out on fly balls. Hooper, who reached second base in the ninth inning, was the only visiting player to pass first base. He died at second. Bob had the leather sphere spinning prettily and the Boston batsmen strained their backs lofting high flies.

The Yanks got a run in the first. Ward walked and went along on Peckinpaugh's sacrifice. Pipp cracked a single to right and sent Ward home. Ruth rolled to Pennock and forced Pipp at second. Foster chucked Lewis out at first and ended the inning. Ruth did better in the fourth. He doubled against the right field wall and went to third on Lewis's out at first.

Ruth then promulgated a fine piece of base running. Pratt hit a grounder to Scott, who tossed the runner out at first. Babe started down the third base line with the swing of Scott's arm and crossed the plate before McInnis could get the ball to Walters at the plate.

The score:

| NEW YORK (A.) | Ab | R | H | Po | A | BOSTON (A.) | Ab | R | H | Po | A |
|---|---|---|---|---|---|---|---|---|---|---|---|
| Ward, 3b | 3 | 1 | 1 | 0 | 2 | Hooper, rf | 4 | 0 | 1 | 1 | 0 |
| Peck'p'gh, ss | 2 | 0 | 1 | 3 | 1 | McNally, 2b | 3 | 0 | 1 | 2 | 2 |
| Pipp, 1b | 3 | 0 | 1 | 6 | 0 | Menosky, 1f | 4 | 0 | 0 | 2 | 1 |
| Ruth, rf | 4 | 2 | 2 | 2 | 0 | Hendryx cf | 3 | 0 | 1 | 1 | 0 |
| Lewis, 1f | 4 | 1 | 1 | 6 | 0 | McInnis, 1b | 3 | 0 | 0 | 12 | 0 |
| Pratt, 2b | 4 | 0 | 0 | 2 | 1 | Foster, 3b | 3 | 0 | 0 | 0 | 5 |
| Bodie, cf | 3 | 0 | 2 | 3 | 0 | Scott, ss | 3 | 0 | 1 | 3 | 2 |
| Ruel, c | 3 | 1 | 2 | 5 | 2 | Walters, c | 2 | 0 | 0 | 2 | 2 |
| Shawkey, p | 3 | 1 | 0 | 0 | 1 | Devine, c | 1 | 0 | 0 | 1 | 1 |
|  |  |  |  |  |  | Pennock, p | 2 | 0 | 0 | 0 | 0 |
|  |  |  |  |  |  | Harper, p | 0 | 0 | 0 | 0 | 0 |
|  |  |  |  |  |  | Fortune, p | 0 | 0 | 0 | 0 | 0 |
|  |  |  |  |  |  | ªEibel | 1 | 0 | 0 | 0 | 0 |
| Total | 29 | 6 | 10 | 27 | 7 | Total | 29 | 0 | 4 | 24 | 13 |

ªBatted for Fortune in ninth.
Error—Menosky.

| | | | | | | | | | | |
|---|---|---|---|---|---|---|---|---|---|---|
| New York | 1 | 0 | 0 | 1 | 0 | 2 | 2 | 0 | ..—6 |
| Boston | 0 | 0 | 0 | 0 | 0 | 0 | 0 | 0 | 0—0 |

Two-base hits—Ruth, Bodie. Home runs—Ruth, Lewis. Sacrifice hit—Peckinpaugh. Double play—Ruel and Pipp. Left on bases—New York 6. Boston 3. Bases on balls—Off Pennock 2, Harper 2, Fortune 2, Shawkey 1. Hits—Off Pennock 8 in 6 innings; Harper none in 1–3, Fortune 2 in 1 2–3. Struck out—By Shawkey 3, Pennock 1. Losing pitcher—Pennock. Umpires—Dineen and Nallin. Time—2 hours, 8 minutes.

### Babe Ruth's Latest Homer Raises His Total to Fifty.

Babe Ruth's colossal smash over the grand stand at the Polo Grounds yesterday was the fiftieth home run the super-slugger has made in his major league career of six years. He joined the Red Sox in 1915 and in that year played only 42 games, making 4 home runs. In 1916 Ruth made only 3 home runs in 67 games, but in those days he was used only occasionally as a pinch hitter and gave most of his time to pitching. In 1917 Ruth, serving as a pitcher, had a chance to make only 2 home runs, but in 1918, when he was used more frequently in the field, he hammered out 11 circuit drives. Last year he made 20 homers, a new world's record, and the slam yesterday completed a striking list of 50.

Ruth has played in 396 games, has been at bat 1,134 times, had made 203 runs, 349 hits and 50 homers. His batting average during his major league career is .309.

July 20, 1920

## BABE SETS RECORD, THEN ADDS ANOTHER

Super-Slugger Hits Twice for Circuit While Yanks Split with White Sox.

### HUGMEN WIN OPENER, 8–2

But Drop Second Contest, 8–5, When Gleason Clan Raps Thormahlen Hard.

### SHAWKEY BACK ON MOUND

Veteran Baffles Chicago in First Game—Rain Holds Up Play for Forty-five Minutes.

The big slam has arrived and a record which made baseball followers gasp in amazement less than a year ago has passed into the discard.

Babe Ruth, crowned last September the greatest home run hitter in major league history, yesterday turned loose the powerful swing that the baseball world has been anxiously awaiting since last Thursday, when he equaled the mark of twenty-nine home runs set up in 1919. Amid a deafening din such as only 28,000 delirious fans can make, Babe jogged around the bases while a crowd in the right field bleachers fought for possession of the ball with which the home run record was shattered.

The big event of the double-header between the Yankees and White Sox developed with Pipp on first base in the fourth inning of the second game, at a time when the Hugmen were trailing on the empty end of a 1 to 0 score. Four times in the first game the crowd had entreated the Sultan of Swat to come through with his epoch-making home run, but the big fellow had not delivered. Twice he walked, once he turned an ordinary single into a two-bagger by a burst of speed that surprised the White Sox, and on his last trip to the plate he forced a runner at second base. The Yankees won that game 8 to 2.

Ruth had drawn his usual pass when he faced Dickie Kerr, the bantam-weight of major league boxmen, for the first time in the second battle, which eventually went against the Yankees, 8 to 5. In the fourth inning, with one out and Pipp on first base, the White Sox bantam ran the string to two strikes and two balls against Babe and then tried to sneak a curve past the end of Babe's bat. There was a resounding smack as bat met ball and the noise from the stand swelled in volume before the ball had started its descent. Every last fan knew that this was the much awaited punch. Nemo Leibold, playing a deep right field for the Wizard of Wallop, backed until his shoulders rubbed against the fence of the right field bleachers and then he gazed upward as the ball sailed over his head. It wasn't the longest hit Ruth has made into this section, but it was longer than any other ball player ever has a hit at the Polo Grounds.

### Babe Wears a Broad Smile.

Ruth was just as happy over his success as was the crowd. While the fans howled in glee, tossed hats around the stand in reckless abandon and made the big stand a mass of waving arms, Ruth completed his journey to the plate and then beamed back with a smile that spurred the crowd on to great exertion, if that were possible. Doffing his cap, the conventional response which usually stills a cheering crowd of fans, had no effect here. Several times on his way to the bench Ruth bowed his acknowledgments, but the din continued after he disappeared in the dugout. His march to left field at the close of the inning was the signal for another outburst, and the applause was renewed when he came in after the White Sox had retired in the fourth inning.

The record-breaking hit was one of a pair which Ruth unlimbered in the second game, but there was no joy for Babe as the jogged around the bases and back to the bench on the second homer, which ran the season's string to thirty-one. It arrived when the Yanks were defeated, and that always serves to take interest out of circuit hits for Ruth, much as the fans revel in such performances, whether the Yanks are winning or losing. Babe was the first citizen to toe the plate in New York's half of the ninth inning, and the score was 8 to 4 against them. He lined hard into the lower section of the right field stand and carried over New York's last run of the afternoon. Peckinpaugh and Joe Jackson also hit home runs in this game and Ping Bodie had favored with one of his long clouts in the opener.

A small-sized cloudburst, which deluged the Polo Grounds about 12:30 o'clock but missed the greater part of Manhattan, threatened at one time to wash both games off the slate. Then Miller Huggins decided that he would play one game. The early appearance of Old Sol caused a change in plans, and it was decided to start at 2 o'clock, a half hour late, and play the two games. After two innings had been played dark clouds appeared again over the field and a few raindrops gave the hint of another downpour. Then came a race against the rain with the Yankees trying to get in the four and one-half innings which would protect the six runs which they scored in the first two frames.

## Rain Breaks Too Late.

The crowd took keen interest in the race, cheered every putout on either side which hurried the game along, and howled with joy when Eddie Collins fouled to Ward for the third out in Chicago's fifth inning. That assured a Yankee victory if there was no more baseball, and the fans evidently wanted the victory more than they wanted two games. After a delay of forty-five minutes the teams were able to resume play and the Yankees breezed along to an 8-to-2 victory.

Shawkey's brilliant pitching tamed the Sox completely in the opener. It was Bob's first start since he tore a muscle in his side in a game at St. Louis on June 23 and his work yesterday indicated that he is back to normal form. The Sox scored one run through an error by Peckinpaugh and another which was complimentary. It came in the ninth inning on two singles, the first batter being allowed to run at will on the bases. The Yanks hit Wilkinson hard and bunched the hits to good effect.

Peck's single, Pipp's triple and a single by Bodie gave the Yanks two runs in the first inning, two outs and a pass to Ruth coming between the triple and Ping's safe clout. Four more runs were added in the second inning on Ruth's double, a single by Shawkey, another single by Peck, Pratt's double, a pass to Ruth and an error at the plate by Schalk on an attempted double steal. In the fifth the Hugmen added two more runs on Ruth's double and Bodie's drive into the left field bleachers for a home run.

The White Sox got their first run in the sixth on Jackson's single, a fumble by Peck, a fielder's choice and Risberg's sacrifice fly. In the ninth Schalk singled, was allowed to reach second and third unmolested, and he scored on Leibold's single to centre. Chicago got to Shawkey for nine hits, but they were well scattered.

## Thormahlen Yanked in Eighth.

Kerr and Thormahlen, two southpaws, went to the rubber for the second game. The Yankee sidewheeler was derricked in the eight, when one clean hit and two trick singles filled the bases with none out. An error at the plate by Hannah helped the Sox to take the lead in the seventh, after the Yankees had picked up a two-run advantage. Shore finished the eighth, departed for a pinch hitter and McGraw finished the game.

Jackson's home run into the right field stand put the White Sox in front in the second inning, but the Hugmen went ahead in the fourth when Pipp singled to left and Ruth hit into the right field bleachers for his thirtieth home run of the year. Peck's double, Pipp's sacrifice and Pratt's triple in the sixth added another run.

Chicago went to the front in the seventh with three runs on Felsch's walk, singles by Collins and Risberg, Hannah's error at the plate, Leibold's scratch hit and a line single by E. Collins. In the eighth, Jackson, Felsch and J. Collins got singles which filled the bases and Thormahlen was replaced by Shore. Ernie made a wild pitch which sent one run over, Schalk's squeeze play sent in another, a throw to centre field by Hannah accounted for a third, and Leibold's single for the fourth.

Peck hit into the left field bleachers in New York's eighth inning and Ruth hit into the right field stand in the ninth.

The scores:

# FIRST GAME

| NEW YORK (A.) | Ab | R | H | Po | A | CHICAGO (A.) | Ab | R | H | Po | A |
|---|---|---|---|---|---|---|---|---|---|---|---|
| P'paugh, ss | 5 | 2 | 2 | 3 | 4 | Leibold, rf | 5 | 0 | 1 | 1 | 0 |
| Pipp, 1b | 5 | 1 | 3 | 6 | 2 | E. Collins | 5 | 0 | 0 | 7 | 2 |
| Pratt, 2b | 4 | 1 | 1 | 1 | 3 | Weaver, 3b | 4 | 0 | 2 | 1 | 3 |
| Ruth, 1f | 2 | 1 | 1 | 2 | 0 | Jackson, 1f | 3 | 1 | 2 | 2 | 1 |
| Meusel, rf | 4 | 0 | 1 | 1 | 0 | Felsch, cf | 4 | 0 | 1 | 3 | 0 |
| Bodie, cf | 4 | 1 | 2 | 5 | 0 | J. Collins, 1b | 4 | 0 | 1 | 6 | 0 |
| Ward, 3b | 3 | 0 | 1 | 1 | 0 | Risberg, ss | 2 | 0 | 1 | 2 | 5 |
| Ruel, c | 4 | 1 | 1 | 6 | 0 | Schalk, c | 4 | 1 | 1 | 2 | 2 |
| Shawkey, p | 3 | 1 | 1 | 2 | 1 | Wilkinson, p | 3 | 0 | 0 | 0 | 1 |
| | | | | | | ªJourdan | 1 | 0 | 0 | 0 | 0 |
| Total | 34 | 8 | 13 | 27 | 10 | Total | 35 | 2 | 9 | 24 | 14 |

ªBatted for Wilkinson in ninth.

Errors—Peckinpaugh, Jackson, Schalk.

| | | | | | | | | | | |
|---|---|---|---|---|---|---|---|---|---|---|
| New York | 2 | 4 | 0 | 0 | 2 | 0 | 0 | 0 | ..—8 |
| Chicago | 0 | 0 | 0 | 0 | 0 | 1 | 0 | 0 | 1—2 |

Two-base hits—Ruel, Pratt, Felsch, Ruth. Three-base hit—Pipp. Home run—Bodie. Stolen bases—Bodie, Schalk, Leibold (2). Sacrifice hit—J. Collins. Double plays—Pratt, Peckinpaugh and Pipp (2); Risberg, E. Collins and J. Collins. Left on bases—Chicago 9, New York 7. Bases on balls—Off Wilkinson 5, Shawkey 2. Struck out—By Wilkinson 2, Shawkey 4. Umpires—Messrs. Chill and Moriarity. Time of game—One hour and fifty-five minutes.

# SECOND GAME

| NEW YORK (A.) | Ab | R | H | Po | A | CHICAGO (A.) | Ab | R | H | Po | A |
|---|---|---|---|---|---|---|---|---|---|---|---|
| P'paugh, ss | 4 | 2 | 2 | 0 | 2 | Leibold, rf | 5 | 0 | 2 | 2 | 0 |
| Pipp, 1b | 3 | 1 | 1 | 12 | 1 | E. Collins, 2b | 5 | 0 | 1 | 1 | 4 |
| Pratt, 2b | 4 | 0 | 1 | 1 | 3 | Weaver, 3b | 5 | 0 | 0 | 1 | 5 |
| Ruth, 1f | 3 | 2 | 2 | 3 | 0 | Jackson, 1f | 5 | 2 | 2 | 2 | 0 |
| Meusel, rf | 4 | 0 | 1 | 2 | 0 | Felsch, cf | 4 | 2 | 2 | 1 | 1 |
| Bodie, cf | 4 | 0 | 2 | 2 | 0 | J. Collins, 1b | 4 | 2 | 2 | 14 | 0 |
| Ward, 3b | 4 | 0 | 1 | 2 | 5 | Risberg, ss | 5 | 0 | 1 | 1 | 3 |
| Hannah, c | 3 | 0 | 0 | 4 | 1 | Schalk, c | 4 | 1 | 2 | 4 | 0 |
| Th'mahlen, p | 2 | 0 | 0 | 0 | 1 | Kerr, p | 3 | 1 | 0 | 1 | 4 |
| Shore, p | 0 | 0 | 0 | 0 | 1 | | | | | | |
| ªLewis | 1 | 0 | 0 | 0 | 0 | | | | | | |
| McGraw, p | 0 | 0 | 0 | 1 | 0 | | | | | | |
| Total | 32 | 5 | 10 | 27 | 14 | Total | 40 | 8 | 12 | 27 | 17 |

Errors—Peckinpaugh, Pratt, Hannah (2).

| Chicago | 0 | 1 | 0 | 0 | 0 | 0 | 3 | 4 | 0—8 |
|---------|---|---|---|---|---|---|---|---|-----|
| New York | 0 | 0 | 0 | 2 | 0 | 1 | 0 | 1 | 1—5 |

Two-base hits—Peckinpaugh. Three-base hits—Pratt, Ward. Home run—Ruth (2), Jackson, Peckinpaugh. Stolen bases—Risberg, Schalk. Sacrifice hits—Pipp, Kerr. Double plays—Risberg, E. Collins and J. Collins; Weaver and J. Collins. Left on bases—Chicago 8, New York 2. Bases on balls—Off Thormahlen 2, Kerr 1. Hits—Off Thormahlen 9 in 7 innings (none out in 8th), Shore 2 in 1, McGraw 1 in 1. Struck out—By Thormahlen 1, Kerr 2. Wild pitch—Shore. Losing pitcher—Thormahlen. Umpires—Moriarity and Chill. Time of game—One hour and forty-five minutes.

### *List of Babe Ruth's Homers In His Climb to New Record*

Babe Ruth started his 1920 home-run campaign against a southpaw, and it was against a southpaw that he broke his former record. He has made 17 circuit drives against right handers and 14 against left handers. Ruth's 1920 record is as follows:

#### MAY.

| Date. Pitcher and Club. | | Men on Base. | Place. |
|---|---|---|---|
| 1—Pennock, Bos | (L) | 0 | N. Y. |
| 2—Jones, Bos | (R) | 1 | N. Y. |
| 11—Wilkinson, Chi | (R) | 1 | N. Y. |
| 11—Kerr, Chi | (L) | 0 | N. Y. |
| 12—Williams, Chi | (L) | 0 | N. Y. |
| 23—Wellman, St. L | (L) | 1 | N. Y. |
| 25—Leonard, Det | (L) | 1 | N. Y. |
| 26—Dause, Det | (R) | 0 | N. Y. |
| 27—Harper, Boston | (L) | 0 | Boston |
| 27—Karr, Boston | (R) | 0 | Boston |
| 29—Bush, Boston | (R) | 1 | Boston |
| 31—Johnson, Wash | (R) | 1 | N. Y. |

## JUNE.

| | | | |
|---|---|---|---|
| 2—Zachary, Wash | (L) | | N. Y. |
| 2—Carlson, Wash | (R) | 0 | N. Y. |
| 2—Snyder, Wash | (R) | 0 | N. Y. |
| 10—Okrie, Det | (L) | 1 | Det. |
| 13—Myers, Cleve | (R) | 0 | Cleve. |
| 16—Faber, Chi | (R) | 1 | Chi. |
| 17—Williams, Chi | (L) | 2 | Chi. |
| 23—Shocker, St. L | (R) | 0 | St. L. |
| 25—Pennock, Bos | (L) | 0 | N. Y. |
| 25—Pennock, Bos | (L) | 0 | N. Y. |
| 30—Bigbee, Ath | (R) | 0 | Phila. |
| 30—Perry, Ath | (R) | 1 | Phila. |

## JULY.

| | | | |
|---|---|---|---|
| 9—Oldham, Det | (L) | 0 | N. Y. |
| 10—Dauss, Det | (R) | 0 | N. Y. |
| 11—Ehmke, Det | (R) | 0 | N. Y. |
| 14—Davis, St. L | (R) | 0 | N. Y. |
| 15—Burwell, St. L | (R) | 2 | N. Y. |
| 19—Kerr, Chi | (L) | 1 | N. Y. |
| 19—Kerr, Chi | (L) | 1 | N. Y. |

# RUTH'S RECORD HIT HELPS YANKS WIN

## Babe Makes History With Drive Into Centre Field Bleachers at the Polo Grounds.

### FIRST TO PERFORM FEAT

## Slugger Also Gets Another Homer, Pitches Five Innings and Fans Ty Cobb.

### TIGERS DEFEATED, 13 TO 8

## Baker and Hawks get Circuit Clouts—Schang Painfully Injured When Struck by Pitched Ball.

The Yankees tried out a young pitcher called Babe Ruth yesterday afternoon, and he impressed the on-lookers as a most promising performer. The heavy-clouting Tigers got only one safe hit off his slants in the first four innings, but tapped him a bit in the fifth, when they made three earnest blows. He was tested in the field and at the bat also, and performed like a corner, although all he was able to do with the cudgel was a couple of home runs. It is believed he will be valuable to the team with a trifle more seasoning.

The score of the game was 13 to 8 with the local troupe on the proper side of the tally. It was a free-hitting affray, as may be surmised from the figures. The Babe departed from the mound, with his side arms and all the honors of war, in the sixth period after allowing a single and passing a man. Mays and Ferguson attended to the rest of the twirling for the Manhattanites. For the visitors, Ehmke went the route and lives to tell the tale, but he will never be the same man again after the terrible banging he sustained.

Ruth's first four-bagger was made in the third chapter with nobody aboard the bases. His second circuit punch of the afternoon, and his twenty-first of the season, came in the seventh and Peck was on second at the time, having just doubled to centre. This latter slam of Ruth's deserves a complete column of resounding praise, for it was a thunderous blow into the centre field bleachers, just to the right of the screen, a territory never before invaded by a batted ball. The Babe has had it upon his mind to perpetrate this Big Bertha shot for some time, but never seemed to get around to it. No other player ever threatened the mark which Ruth reached yesterday.

There were other home run artists present aside from the concoctor of this double header. Nelson Hawks drove the ball to the right centre field fence in the second and made it a four-base hit by a great burst of speed. Frank Baker got the other one in the third. His was a drive into the stand.

### Schang Is Injured.

One unfortunate happening disturbed the serenity of the fans. Wallie Schang was hit on the right forearm by a twister from Ehmke's hand in the third inning, sustaining a painful injury. He will probably be out of the game for two or three weeks. The pain caused by the blow made him loose consciousness for a minute, but he recovered and was able to walk back to the bench.

After Young had been disposed of by Peck's throw to Pipp in the opening inning, the Babe took a few minutes off while he repaid some of Sunday's courtesies by passing Bush and Cobb. Heilmann fouled to Baker and Ward scooped up Vaughn's tap and nailed him at first.

The Yankees got no hits in their half of the opening session, but they got something far more satisfactory. This treasure was a perfectly valid run built out of various scrappy elements. Bobby Roth took his time about offering at Ehmke's slants and strolled on four wide ones in consequence. He stole second and dashed to third while Peck was being thrown out by Bush. Ruth got four heaves far from the plate and meandered complainingly to first. Pipp drove a sacrifice fly to Veach and Roth galloped home. Meusel forced Ruth at second, Jones to Young.

That was a good enough run as runs go, but either of the brace of Yankee tallies that showed up in the second was its superior in merit. After Baker's long hoist had been plucked by Hellman, Ward singled to left off the tips of Jones's outstretched fingers. Schang flied to Young. Nelson Hawks, the Calgary Whiz, fired with indignation over finding himself at the bottom of the batting order, vented his venom by crashing the ball to the most distant point in the right field for the entire circuit, flowing Ward across the plate. Roth followed with a one-base slap to Jones, who threw badly to first after recovering the sphere, and Bobby got to second. Peck fanned for the last out.

One run in the first and two in the second started a sequence which the Huggins athletes felt moved to continue—for a while at least. Their three tallies in the third were procured by about as solid a bit of slugging as has often been effected in a couple of minutes. The healthy Babe to whom the Yankees are acting as a lot of fathers was the first man up. Now Ruth didn't owe anybody any home runs, but sheer exuberance of spirits led him to pepper that faithful old right field stand in its lower stratum with much vigor. It was a very fancy four-bagger and it met with the exuberant approval of the throng.

Pipp passed away on a tap to Blue. Bob Meusel landed on the rotund missile and conveyed it to the left field fence for two bases. Frank Baker gave it a ride, too, but much further and in the opposite direction. The one-time home run king projected the ball into the stand close to the point where Ruth's slam had landed. This ticket was good for two, so Meusel rode home on it as well as Baker.

## Tigers Launch Attack.

With the tally placed at 6 to 0 by this outburst, the Tigers felt it incumbent upon them to be up and stirring. So they stirred quite a bit in the fifth and cooked up four runs. Young started things with a double to the left hand regions. He went the remainder of the distance home when Peck foozled Bush's grounder. Hoffman, who had taken the place of Schang after the latter's injury, dropped the third strike on Cobb just as Bush was stealing, and the latter reached second while Ty was being thrown out. Hellman's triple to the right centre field outskirts scored Bush and Hellman wound up his trip when Veach likewise whaled a three-baser to the same region. When Blue got a pass a double steal was launched and Hoffman's throw to Peck was wide, although the shortstop caged it in his trained left. Veach tallied on this episode.

The score was now 6 to 4, and the Yankees didn't care to be so near to the Tigers in the reckoning. Therefore they indulged in a mauling bee in the latter portion of the fifth and took those four runs right back again.

Bob Meusel got a pass at the outset of this jamboree and galloped to third on Baker's sharp single to centre. Both of them reported at the plate on Ward's three-base crash to left centre. After Hoffman had faded away through the efforts of Bush and Blue, Hawks whipped out a single to centre and Ward tallied. Hawks scampered clear around to the far turn on Roth's one-base rap to the central garden and scored while Peck was forcing Roth.

The Huggins brigade took unto themselves another run in the sixth on a single by Baker and a double by Ward. In the seventh, after Peck had laid the ball in centre for two bases, Babe Ruth perpetrated his enormous slam into the centre field bleachers referred to above rather casually.

Three singles and an infield out produced a marker for the Tigers in the seventh, and they got a pair of them in the eighth by virtue of a trio of singles and a couple of sacrifice flies. Their ninth-inning score came on singles by Young and Bush, abetted by a bit of sluggish fielding.

The score:

| NEW YORK (A.) | Ab | R | H | Po | A | DETROIT (A.) | Ab | R | H | Po | A |
|---|---|---|---|---|---|---|---|---|---|---|---|
| Roth, rf | 4 | 1 | 2 | 3 | 0 | Young, 2b | 4 | 2 | 2 | 4 | 1 |
| Peck'p'gh, ss | 5 | 1 | 1 | 3 | 4 | Bush, ss | 5 | 2 | 2 | 1 | 6 |
| Ruth, p, cf | 3 | 2 | 2 | 2 | 0 | Cobb, cf | 5 | 1 | 1 | 0 | 0 |
| Pipp, lb | 4 | 0 | 0 | 7 | 1 | Hellmann, rf | 5 | 1 | 3 | 1 | 0 |
| Meusel, lf | 4 | 2 | 2 | 2 | 0 | Veach, cf | 4 | 2 | 2 | 3 | 0 |
| Baker, 3b | 5 | 3 | 3 | 1 | 0 | Blue, 1b | 2 | 0 | 1 | 9 | 2 |
| Ward, 2b | 5 | 2 | 3 | 4 | 3 | Jones, 3b | 5 | 0 | 0 | 1 | 1 |
| Schang, c | 1 | 0 | 0 | 0 | 0 | Bassler, c | 4 | 0 | 1 | 4 | 0 |
| Hoffman, c | 3 | 0 | 1 | 2 | 0 | Ehmke, p | 4 | 0 | 1 | 1 | 1 |
| Hawks, cf | 3 | 2 | 2 | 3 | 0 | ªShorten | 1 | 0 | 0 | 0 | 0 |
| Mays, | 1 | 0 | 0 | 0 | 0 | | | | | | |
| Ferguson, p | 1 | 0 | 0 | 0 | 0 | | | | | | |
| Total | 39 | 13 | 16 | 27 | 8 | Total | 39 | 8 | 13 | 24 | 11 |

ªBatted for Ehmke in ninth.
Errors—Peckingpaugh, Pratt, Bush.

| New York | 1 | 2 | 3 | 0 | 4 | 1 | 2 | 0 | ..—13 |
|---|---|---|---|---|---|---|---|---|---|
| Detroit | 0 | 0 | 0 | 0 | 4 | 0 | 1 | 2 | 1—8 |

Two-base hits—Meusel, Young, Ward, Peckinpaugh. Three-base hits—Hellmann, Veach, Ward. Home run—Ruth (2), Hawks, Baker. Stolen bases—Roth, Bush, Veach, Blue (2). Sacrifices—Pipp, Veach, Blue. Left on Bases—New York 8, Detroit 13. Bases on balls—Off Ruth 7, Ehmke 4. Hits—Off Ruth 5 in 5 innings (none out in sixth), Mays 5 in 2 (none out in eighth), Ferguson 3 in 2. Hit by pitcher—By Ehmke (Schang). Struck out—By Ruth 1, by Ehmke 3. Passed balls—Bassler, Hoffman. Winning pitcher—Ruth. Umpires—Dineen and Connolly. Time of game—2:28.

# RUTH IN ROW WITH UMPIRE AND FAN AT POLO GROUNDS

### Following Dispute Over Decision Babe Throws Dirt in the Official's Face.

## CHASES ROOTERS IN STAND

### Attempts to Attack Spectator—Banished From Game, May Be Fined or Suspended.

## HOME-RUN KING NOT SORRY

### Says He Merely Resented Insulting Remarks—Ban Johnson Must Decide Case of Yanks' Star.

Babe Ruth today faces another indefinite suspension from baseball. At the Polo Grounds yesterday, only six days after he had been restored to good standing by Judge K. M. Landis, Baseball Commissioner, following more than five weeks' suspension, the home-run slugger threw a handful of dust into the face of Umpire Hildebrand and was put out of the game. Incensed by the jeers of the crowd, Ruth then climbed into the stand and tried to punish a fan he said made insulting remarks.

It was in the third inning of the game with the Washington Senators, which the Yankees won by a score of 6 to 4. With one man out, Ruth singled to centre. When Sam Rice of the Senators fumbled the ball slightly Ruth tried to stretch his hit into a two-bagger. He slid into second base in a cloud of dust and umpire Hildebrand called him out.

This decision sent the home-run slugger into a rage. He leaped to his feet with the quickness of a cat and he brought up with him a handful of dirt, which he threw in the direction of the umpire. From the grandstand it seemed that the dust spattered over Hildebrand's face and neck. Some of it seeped down inside his collar and the rest fell on his arm and on the front of his blue uniform.

Hildebrand at once waved Ruth out of the game, and the Babe walked back to the Yankee bench. Every step of the journey was a signal to the crowd to jeer and hoot. To this demonstration Ruth made the retort courteous. He lifted his cap in courtly manner, a satirical gesture that had only the effect of increasing the volume of jeers and hisses.

### Climbs Into Grandstand.

A minute later Ruth was not so gracious and smiling. Back at the Yankee bench sat two Pullman conductors. One of them shouted something at Ruth which the Babe didn't like. In a flash he vaulted to the roof of the dugout, clambered through a box filled with people and started up the aisle in the direction of his tormentor.

As Ruth approached the fan receded. He climbed back over the tops of the seats, put several rows between him and the Babe and from this point of safety listened to a series of scathing remarks from the irate player. Several neutral bystanders pushed Ruth away gently, and some of the crowd—those further away—yelled, "Hit the big stiff!" When nobody followed the advice Ruth climbed back on the field, disappeared inside the bench for an instant and then walked across the field to the clubhouse.

On this second march he was again booed, but some of the crowd cheered and applauded. To these friends Ruth lifted his cap.

At the Hotel Ansonia, where Ruth has an apartment, the homerun hitter gave his version of the affair last night. He said he wasn't a bit sorry for his action in invading the grandstand.

"They can boo and hoot me all they want," said Ruth. "That doesn't matter to me. But when a fan calls insulting names from the grandstand and become abusive I don't intend to stand for it. This fellow today, whoever he was, called me a 'low-down bum' and other names that got me mad, and when I went after him he ran.

"Furthermore, I didn't throw any dirt in Hildebrand's face. It didn't go into his face, only on his sleeve. I don't know what they will do to me for this. Maybe I'll be fined or suspended for kicking on the decision, but I don't see why I should get any punishment at all. I would go into the stand again if I had to."

## May Get Off With Fine.

The Pullman conductor whose remarks started the trouble refused to give his name. Shortly after the incident was over he was requested by the Yankee authorities to leave the park, and he did so.

Baseball men last night were agreed that Ruth would be punished in some way, but there were many who believed that a heavy fine would be the extent of the action by Ban Johnson, President of the American League. One high official, who refused to permit his name to be used, said that probably Ruth would only be fined, and this because of his attack on the umpire.

If baseball precedent, however, is followed, Ruth will draw an indefinite suspension. The nearest parallel to his case is that of Ty Cobb, now manager of the Detroit Tigers, who climbed into the stand after a fan during a game at the Yankees' old Hilltop grounds in 1911. Cobb, then at the peak of his career, was set down indefinitely by President Johnson, and the Detroit team promptly sent on its celebrated "sympathy strike," refusing to play until its star player was reinstated. The strike was overcome and Cobb stayed out for ten days before Johnson lifted the ban.

Ruth's case is complicated by the fact that he also threw dust in the umpire's face and had been put out of the game before he made his sortie into the grandstand. In any event, however, it is not considered likely that he will be out for more than ten days, if that long. It was pointed out by baseball men last night that under the terms of an American League agreement made in Chicago in February, 1920, any indefinite suspension must be lifted at the end of ten days or else be subject to action by a board of review.

This rule was passed as a result of the Carl Mays case, when the pitcher was indefinitely barred by Ban Johnson. If Ruth is not reinstated before ten days his case will go before the Board of Review, the members of which are Colonel Jacob Ruppert, one of the two owners of the Yankees, and Clark Griffith, President of the Washington Club. If this board cannot agree, the case goes to a Federal Judge in Chicago for settlement.

## Landis Has No Jurisdiction.

Judge Landis, Commissioner of Baseball, has no jurisdiction in the case. The decision is up to President Johnson, who will receive confidential reports from Umpire Hildebrand, the recipient of the handful of dust, and from Umpire Dick Nallin, who was in charge of yesterday's game. The umpires' testimony was wired to American League headquarters last night, and a decision may be expected today.

Colonel Jacob Ruppert, President of the club, was out of town yesterday and did not know of the latest outbreak of Ruth's until he was told by a New York Times reporter last night.

"Probably Ruth acted in the heat of the moment," the Colonel said, "but even so he deserves to be punished for what he did. It's very unfortunate, coming so soon after Ruth's reinstatement. As I said, I was not at the game, and therefore can't speak as an eyewitness."

## Huston and Huggins Silent.

The same reticence was shown by Colonel T. L. Huston, Ruppert's partner, and by Manager Miller Huggins. "I have nothing to say," Huston told reporters. Huggins referred questioners to the owners of the club.

Another Yankee official declared that he does not look for a suspension. "Cobb was set down because he trashed the fan severely," this official said. "Ty didn't stop at merely 'bawling' the other fellow out, as Ruth did. There has been several cases in both the American and National Leagues where players have gone up to a fan and castigated him verbally, and the custom has been to reprimand the offender or, at most, to fine him."

Other baseball observers, however, recalled that Ban Johnson has been unusually strict in upholding his umpires this year. Shortly after the beginning of the season he barred Miller Huggins indefinitely for merely talking roughly to an umpire, and the suspension lasted several days. Ruth's prominence and the fact that last Fall he defied Judge Landis and baseball law by going on a barnstorming trip are regarded as factors that may influence Johnson to make the punishment as stiff as possible.

Only once before in his major league career did Ruth have serious trouble with an umpire. Back in 1919 he struck Brick Owens when the umpire called a strike on him during a game at Fenway Park, Boston. The Babe then was a member of the Boston Red Sox. He was suspended indefinitely by Ban Johnson and not reinstated until five days had passed.

Already thirty-eight days behind his home run record, Ruth would be hit hard by any additional layoff. Ten days more out of the game would mean that he would have missed more than a quarter of the season, and in that case to tie his last year's record of fifty-nine home runs would be nearly impossible. Kenneth Williams of the Browns has twelve homers to the Babe's one, and if again suspended Ruth might lose his home run crown.

## Two Homers for Meusel.

In fact, right now Ruth is two homers behind Bob Meusel, who was one of his partners on the ill-fated barnstorming trip last Fall which resulted in Judge Landis's five-week sentence. Meusel was very much in the limelight yesterday. He started the game even with the Bambino in the matter of four-baggers and he ended two ahead, both drives coming after Ruth had been banished from the field.

The Yankees won by only two runs, 6 to 4, and as late as the first half of the sixth inning they were tied with the hustling Senators, who hit Waite Hoyt with a certain amount of éclat and tied the score after the Yanks had taken a 4–1 lead.

In the same inning the Hugmen score another run, and that won the game. But for safety's sake, Bob Meusel came to the plate in the eighth and, espying a spot in the corner of the left field bleachers, pumped a low line drive against the bull's eye. Bob's previous homer was made in the fourth inning. He started the inning by taking hold of one of Tom Phillips's curves and depositing it clear on the other side of the high fence at the rear of the left field bleachers. It was considerable of a blow, and it was extremely timely, coming on the heels, so to speak, of Ruth's incursion into the stand and excursion from the park.

Two home runs helped the Senators to keep in the running. With one out in the first frame Sam Rice, who delivered a circuit drive on Wednesday, sent a hard drive spinning between Witt and Ruth. The ball rolled to the fence while Rice was skimming around the bases.

In the same inning the home lads scored twice on Witt's walk, Ward's bunt, which he beat out; Ruth's sacrifice and Baker's neat single to center. They picked up a couple of more in the fourth on Meusel's homer, a walk to Scott and Hoyt's surprising double against the right field grandstand.

## Judge Hits for Circuit.

This made the game appear safe, but the Senators had one punch left, which they delivered in the sixth. As a starter Harris was hit by a pitched ball, and Ward fumbled Rice's splash to second base. Then came the second Washington home run, Judge driving the ball into a box in the upper right field tier.

The score was tied, but Pipp and Scott untied it in the same inning. After Meusel had flied out, Pipp drove to right for one base, and Scott immediately followed with a whistling double down the third-base line. Pipp came all the way from first with a run. In the eighth Meusel's second home run made it 6 to 4, where it stood to the end. Brillheart, a new left-hander, pitched for the Senators after the seventh, when Milan batted for Phillips.

Chick Fewster almost got himself put out of the game in the seventh. He was called out at the plate by Nallin, and Chick was so enraged that he kicked dust all over the umpire's nice new shine. After kicking with both feet and mouth, Chick was led out to center field, and the game went on.

The score:

| NEW YORK (A.) | Ab | Rr | H | Po | A | WASHINGTON (A.) | Ab | Rr | H | Po | A |
|---|---|---|---|---|---|---|---|---|---|---|---|
| Witt, cf | 2 | 1 | 0 | 2 | 0 | Harris, 2b | 4 | 1 | 1 | 2 | 5 |
| Fewster, lf | 1 | 0 | 1 | 1 | 0 | Rice, rf | 4 | 2 | 1 | 5 | 1 |
| Ward, 2b | 3 | 1 | 1 | 2 | 1 | Judge, 1b | 4 | 1 | 2 | 3 | 0 |
| Ruth, lf | 1 | 0 | 1 | 0 | 0 | Brower, rf | 4 | 0 | 0 | 0 | 0 |
| Miller, lf, cf | 2 | 0 | 0 | 2 | 0 | Goslin, lf | 4 | 0 | 1 | 2 | 0 |
| Baker, 3b | 4 | 0 | 2 | 2 | 3 | Shanks, 3b | 3 | 0 | 0 | 2 | 0 |
| Meusel, rf | 4 | 1 | 1 | 0 | 0 | Gharrity, c | 4 | 0 | 1 | 3 | 0 |
| Pipp, 1b | 4 | 1 | 1 | 15 | 0 | P'paugh, ss | 4 | 0 | 0 | 2 | 3 |
| Scott, ss | 3 | 1 | 1 | 1 | 6 | Phillips, p | 2 | 0 | 0 | 0 | 1 |
| Schang, c | 4 | 0 | 1 | 2 | 0 | aMilan | 1 | 0 | 0 | 0 | 0 |
| Hoyt, p | 3 | 0 | 1 | 0 | 4 | Brillheart, p | 0 | 0 | 0 | 0 | 0 |
| | | | | | | bSmith | 1 | 0 | 0 | 0 | 0 |
| Total | 30 | 6 | 11 | 27 | 14 | Total | 35 | 4 | 6 | 24 | 10 |

aBatted for Phillips in seventh.
bBatted for Brillheart in ninth.
Errors—Ward, Baker.

| New York | 2 | 0 | 0 | 2 | 0 | 1 | 0 | 1 | ..—6 |
|---|---|---|---|---|---|---|---|---|---|
| Washington | 1 | 0 | 0 | 0 | 0 | 3 | 0 | 0 | 0—4 |

Two-base hits—Hoyt, Scott. Home runs—Rice, Meusel (2), Judge. Stolen base—Fewster. Sacrifice—Ruth.

Double plays—Phillips, Harris and Judge; Harris, Peck and Judge. Left on bases—New York 5, Washington 7. Bases on balls—Off Hoyt 1, Phillips 3. Struck out—by Hoyt 2, Phillips 1, Brillheart 1. Hits—Off Phillips, 8 in 6 innings, Brillheart, 3 in 2. Hit by pitcher—By Phillips (Scott), Hoyt (Harris and Shanks). Losing pitcher—Phillips. Umpires—Nallin, Hildebrand and Evens. Time of game—1:43.

# 74,200 SEE YANKEES OPEN NEW STADIUM; RUTH HITS HOME RUN

## Record Baseball Crowd Cheers as Slugger's Drive Beats Red Sox, 4 to 1.

## 25,000 ARE TURNED AWAY

## Gates to $2,500,000 Arena Are Closed Half an Hour Before Start of Game.

## MANY NOTABLES ATTEND

## Governor Smith Throws Out First Ball—Shawkey, in Great Form, Allows Only Three Hits.

Governors, generals, colonels, politicians and baseball officials gathered together solemnly yesterday to dedicate the biggest stadium in baseball, but it was a ball player who did the real dedicating. In the third inning, with two team mates on the base lines, Babe Ruth smashed a savage home run into the right field bleachers, and that was the real baptism of the new Yankee Stadium. That also won the game for the Yankees, and all the ceremony which had gone before was only a trifling preliminary.

The greatest crowd that ever saw a baseball game sat and stood in this biggest of all baseball stadia. Inside the grounds, by official count, were 74,200 people. Outside the park, flattened against doors that had long since closed, were 25,000 more fans, who finally turned around and went home, convinced that baseball parks are not nearly as large as they should be.

The dream of a 100,000 crowd at a baseball game could easily have been realized yesterday if the Yankee Colonels had only piled more concrete on concrete, more steel on steel, and thus provided the necessary space for the overflow. In the face of this tremendous outpouring all baseball attendance records went down with a dull thud. Back in 1916, at a world's series game in Boston, some 42,000 were present, and wise men marveled. But there were that many people at the Yankee Stadium by 2 o'clock yesterday, and when the gates were finally closed to all but ticket holders at 3 o'clock the Boston record had been exceeded by more than 30,000.

### Shawkey Pitches Fine Game.

It was an opening game without a flaw. The Yankees easily defeated the Boston Red Sox, 4 to 1. Bob Shawkey, war veteran and the oldest Yankee player in point of service, pitched the finest game in his career, letting the Boston batters down with three scattered hits. The Yankee raised their American League championship emblem to the top of the flagpole—the chief feature of an opening-day program that went off perfectly. Governor "Al" Smith, throwing out the first ball of the season, tossed it straight into Wally Schang's glove, thus setting another record. The weather was favorable and the big crowd was handled flawlessly.

Only one more thing was in demand, and Babe Ruth supplied that. The big slugger is a keen student of the dramatic, in addition to being the greatest home run hitter. He was playing a new role yesterday—not the accustomed one of a renowned slugger, but that of a penitent, trying to "come back" after a poor season and a poorer world's series. Before the game he said he would give a year of his life if he could hit a home run in his first game in the new stadium. The Babe was on trial, and he knew it better than anybody else.

He could hardly have picked a better time and place for the drive that he hammered into the bleachers in the third inning. The Yankees had just broken a scoreless tie by pushing Shawkey over the plate with one run. Witt was on third base, Dugan on first, when Ruth appeared at the plate to face Howard Ehmke, the Boston pitcher. Ruth worked the count to two and two, and then Ehmke tried to fool him with one of those slow balls that the Giants used successfully in the last world's series.

The ball came in slowly, but it went out quite rapidly, rising on a line and then dipping suddenly from the force behind it. It struck well inside the foul line, eight or ten rows above the low railing in front of the bleachers, and as Ruth circled the bases he received probably the greatest ovation of his career. The biggest crowd in baseball history rose to its feet and let loose the biggest shout in baseball history. Ruth, jogging over the home plate, grinned broadly, lifted his cap at arm's length and waved it at the multitude.

## Home Run Settles Outcome.

That home run was useful as well as dramatic and decorative. It drove three runs across the plate, and those runs, as later events proved, were the margin by which the Yankees won. All the New York scoring was in that one inning, and the Red Sox, although they touched Shawkey for one run in the seventh, could not close the gap.

But the game, after all, was only an incident of a busy afternoon. The stadium was the thing. For the Yankee owners it was the realization of a dream long cherished. For the fans it was something they had never seen before in baseball. It cost about $2,500,000 to build, and eleven months were spent in the construction work. It is the most costly stadium in baseball, as well as the biggest.

First impressions—and also last impressions—are of the vastness of the arena. The stadium is big. It towers high in the air, three tiers piled one on the other. It is a skyscraper among baseball parks. Seen from the vantage point of the nearby subway structure, the mere height of the grandstand is tremendous. Baseball fans who sat in the last low of the steeply sloping third tier may well boast that they broke all altitude records short of those attained in an airplane.

Once inside the grounds, the sweep of the big stand strikes the eye most forcibly. It throws its arms far out to each side, the grandstand ending away over where the bleachers begin. In the centre of the vast pile of steel and concrete was the green spread of grass and diamond, and fewer ball fields are greener than that on which the teams played yesterday.

The Yankees' new home, besides being beautiful and majestic, is practical. It was emptied yesterday of its 74,000 in quicker time than the Polo Grounds ever was. Double ramps from top to bottom carried the stream of people steadily and rapidly to the lower exits, which are many and well situated. Fans from the bleachers and far ends of the grandstand poured out onto the field and were swept through gates in left field. The grandstand crowd passed through exists opening on both Doughty Avenue and 157th Street, which lies along the south side of the stadium.

## Throng Handled Without Confusion.

The record-breaking throng was handled with almost no confusion at all. Transportation facilities were strained before the game because of the big flow of people from downtown points, but the subway's elevated and surface lines handled the heavy traffic without a break after the game. There was little congestion in the 161st Street station of the Lexington Avenue subway, much of the crowd walking to nearby elevated and surface lines.

The fans were slow in coming to the stadium. When the gates were thrown open at noon only about 500 persons were in line before the ticket windows. But by 1 o'clock the guardians of law and order in front of the main entrance began finding their hands full. The supply of 50,000 unreserved grandstand and bleacher seats began dwindling rapidly, and by 2 o'clock the huge grandstand was beginning to bulge at the sides. Ten minutes later the gates to the main stand were ordered closed, and patrons who arrived more than an hour before game time were greeted with the "Standing Room Only!" sign and the gentle announcement that bleacher seats *only* were available. When 3 o'clock came around even the bleachers were packed solidly with humanity, and after that there was nothing to do but close the gates and padlock them.

Inspector Thomas Riley, in charge of police arrangements outside the grounds estimated that 25,000 fans were turned away, and officials of the club agreed with this estimate.

Kenesaw M. Landis, High Commissioner of Baseball, travelled to the scene in democratic style. He disembarked from an Interborough train shortly before 2 and was caught up in the swirl before the main entrance, being rescued finally by the police and escorted inside the stadium.

Preceding him by an hour was the Seventh Regiment Bans, which arrived at 1 o'clock and immediately launched on a musical program. Just about the same time the Yankees and Red Sox deployed on the scene, the champions looking neat and natty in new home uniforms of white. The Bostonians were a symphony in red— red sweaters, red-peaked caps, red-striped stockings. At their head was Frank Chance, Peerless Leader of the old-time Cubs, returned now to lead the Red Sox out of the baseball wilderness.

### Governor Greeted Warmly.

Then at 3 o'clock the spotlight shifted from the players to the celebrities of opening day. Governor Smith moved down to his box, accompanied by Mrs. Smith, and got a rousing greeting. Judge Landis, in gray overcoat, doffing his wide brimmed hat in greeting, came on to the field and immediately strode out to centre field, where the American League flag was waiting. The Seventh Regiment Band assembled near the Yankee bench on the third base side, and John Philip Sousa, in bandmaster's uniform, took his baton in hand and moved to the head of the musicians. The two teams clustered into platoon formation and the parade began.

Once out at the flagpole, the old traditional ritual of opening day began. While the band played "The Star-Spangled Banner," the Stars and Stripes were pulled slowly to the peak of the flagpole. After it fluttered the red, white and blue American League pennant, and as the last note of the national anthem died away and the halyards were made fast, the big crowd let loose a roar that floated across Harlem and far beyond.

That wasn't the end of it, by any means. Back to the home plate came the band and the players and the notables. In the front line of march were the Yankee colonels: Ruppert and Huston, side by side and beaming broadly; Judge Landis, Mrs. Smith, the Governor and Harry Frazee, the Boston club owner. It was noticed for the first time that Mayor Hylan was absent, and club officials explained that the city's chief executive was unable to attend because of illness. Byron Bancroft Johnson, President of the American League, was also missing because of a sudden attack of influenza.

Major Gen. Robert Lee Bullard, commander of the Department of the East, and his staff took part in the exercises, and other prominent military men present were Major Gen. Frank T. Hines, Director of the Veterans' Bureau; Major Gen. F. W. Sladen, Superintendent of West Point; Major Gen. Wigie of Governors Island and Major Charles D. Daley and Captain M. B. Ridgeway of West Point. State commander Callan represented the American Legion and Captain Robert Woodside the Veterans of Foreign Wars.

Governor Smith and Judge Landis were escorted to their boxes along the third base side, and the photographers then got in their deadly work. Mr. Smith was snapped throwing an imaginary first ball. Judge Landis had to take off his hat and have his white locks photographed. Somebody stepped up and presented a big floral horseshoe to the Yankee club, and Colonel Ruppert and Managers Huggins and Chance were lined up for a picture in front of this. Charles A. Stoneham, President of the Giants, was taken in friendly converse with the Yankee owners.

## Babe Ruth Receives Gift.

Then the teams converged around the plate, and Babe Ruth was presented with a case containing a big bat—a delicate hint to the slugger, possibly. After Babe had blushingly mumbled his thanks, Governor Smith stood up in his box, took a shiny white ball between his thumb and first finger and threw it carefully at Wally Schang.

Now here was the first deviation from a decent and proper opening day program. Tradition demands that the thrower miss the objective by several feet. But the Governor, unwinding the official arm, hit Schang's glove as well as Bob Shawkey ever did. Old-time baseball men considered it a distinct social error.

After that there was nothing to do but to play the game. Frank Chance walked out on the coaching line. The Yankees scattered briskly to their positions, Everett Scott going to shortstop as a signal to the world that the record of 986 consecutive games would not be broken yet. Umpire Tommy Connolly, dean of the American League staff, who unexpectedly appeared to take charge of the game, mumbled something to the effect that the contest might begin, and Shawkey, twirling his red sleeved arms, pitched, "Ball One" to the first batter, Chick Fewster, who used to play with the Yankees. The season was started.

## Burns Gets First Hit.

The first hit off him—in fact, the first hit in the new stadium—came from the bat of first baseman George Burns in the second inning, but Burns was cut down trying to steal and the rally died down. In the sixth Ehmke singled to centre with none out and that was the second hit. In the seventh, after Burns walked, Norman McMillan, traded by the Yanks last Winter, prodded a triple to right centre, and that was the third hit. It was the only one which did any damage, for Burns scampered home from first with the solo Boston run of the game.

The Yanks' big third inning started with Ward's single to left, the first Yankee hit. Scott bunted him to second, but Ward was nipped at third on Shawkey's grounder straight at Ehmke. Shawkey moved up to second while Ward was being run down. Witt coaxed a pass out of Ehmke, and Shawkey came in from second when Dugan dropped a single in short centre. Witt trotted to third, and the stage was set for Ruth's blast into the right-field bleachers.

In the fourth the Yanks got after Ehmke again, but lost a run because of bad work on the bases. To start the inning Bob Meusel got a two-bagger out of a Texas League fly to short left, Fewster barely getting his glove under the ball. But Schang bunted to Ehmke and Meusel was nailed by a shade at third base. Ward then fanned, but Scott rammed a hard hit double between Collins and Skinner. Schang tried to come all the way from first on the drive and was out for his pains, a fast relay from Collins to Burns to Devormer slaying the catcher at the plate.

Ruth got his first walk in the fifth, and the crowd joined in a chorus of boos and jeers that smacked of the good old days of 1921. The Yanks went out in order in the sixth, and Shawkey's single was the only incident in the seventh, which was Ehmke's last inning. Menosky batted for him, and Fullerton finished up for Chance's team. He walked Ruth again in the eighth and was heartily hooted by the assembled citizenry.

Shawkey's only sign of weakening came in the seventh, when he passed Burns and McMillan tripled. There was still only one out, but Sailor-Bob fanned the veteran Shanks and Dugan made a clever play on Devormer's hard grounder for the third out. Fine support helped Shawkey again in the eighth. Fewster was hit with none out but Scott got in front of Collins's ground ball and started a fast double play through Ward and Pipp. This was the last time the Red Sox showed signs of life.

# Ruth Makes Error.

Everything wasn't milk and honey for Ruth. To start the fifth he muffed Harris's high fly to short right, juggling the ball twice then letting it hit the turf. This faux pas placed Harris on second, and Shawkey passed McMillan after fanning Burns. With runners on second and first and only one out the Yankee veteran settled down, outwitted Shanks on a third strike and made Devormer roll gently to Pipp.

The Yanks looked like a new team on their own ball field. They hustled every minute, kept their heads up and struck hard when the time came to strike. Aaron Ward played one of the best games of his life at second base, and his stop of Ehmke's fast grounder behind second in the third inning was by all odds the finest fielding play of the game.

Everett Scott, who sprained his ankle last week, was not the fastest athlete on the field, but he showed little effect from the injury. He handled five chances deftly at shortstop and wasted no time in getting around the bases when he doubled to right centre in the fourth. It was Scott's 987th consecutive game; only thirteen more and he will be up to the 1,000 mark.

The score:

| NEW YORK (A.) | | | | | | BOSTON (A.) | | | | | |
|---|---|---|---|---|---|---|---|---|---|---|---|
| | Ab | R | H | Po | A | | Ab | R | H | Po | A |
| Witt, cf | 3 | 1 | 1 | 3 | 0 | Fewster, ss | 3 | 0 | 0 | 2 | 6 |
| Dugan, 3b | 4 | 1 | 1 | 1 | 1 | Collins, rf | 4 | 0 | 0 | 2 | 1 |
| Ruth, rf | 2 | 1 | 1 | 3 | 0 | Skinner cf | 4 | 0 | 0 | 0 | 0 |
| Pipp, 1b | 3 | 0 | 0 | 12 | 0 | Haris, lf | 4 | 0 | 0 | 0 | 0 |
| Meusel, lf | 4 | 0 | 1 | 0 | 0 | Burns, 1b | 3 | 1 | 1 | 9 | 2 |
| Schang, c | 4 | 0 | 0 | 4 | 2 | McMillan, 2b | 2 | 0 | 1 | 2 | 0 |
| Ward, 2b | 3 | 0 | 1 | 3 | 5 | Shanks, 3b | 3 | 0 | 0 | 3 | 0 |
| Scott, ss | 2 | 0 | 1 | 1 | 4 | Devormer, c | 3 | 0 | 0 | 6 | 2 |
| Shawkey, p | 3 | 1 | 1 | 0 | 0 | Ehmke, p | 2 | 0 | 1 | 0 | 4 |
| | | | | | | ªMenosky | 1 | 0 | 0 | 0 | 0 |
| | | | | | | Fullerton, p | 0 | 0 | 0 | 0 | 0 |
| Total | 28 | 4 | 7 | 27 | 12 | Total | 20 | 1 | 3 | 24 | 15 |

ªBattled for Ehmke in eighth.

| | | | | | | | | | | |
|---|---|---|---|---|---|---|---|---|---|---|
| New York | 0 | 0 | 4 | 0 | 0 | 0 | 0 | 0 | ..—4 |
| Boston | 0 | 0 | 0 | 0 | 0 | 0 | 1 | 0 | 0—1 |

Two-base hits—Meusel, Scott. Three-base hit—McMillan. Home run—Ruth. Sacrifice—Scott. Double play—Scott, Ward and Pipp. Left on bases—New York, 5, Boston, 4. Bases on balls—Off Shawkey, 2, Ehmke, 3, Fullerton, 1. Struck out—By Shawkey, 5, Ehmke, 4, Fullerton, 1. Hits—Off Ehmke 7 in 7 innings, Fullerton none in 1. Hit by pitcher—By Shawkey (Fewster). Losing pitcher—Ehmke. Umpires—Connolly, Evans and Holmes. Time of game—2:05.

---

# RUTH OUT OF DANGER AFTER CONVULSIONS ON ARRIVAL HERE

## Hurts Head in Fall on Train, but Escapes Concussion of the Brain.

## HAS AN ATTACK OF "FLU"

## Was Unconscious 90 Minutes and Was Carried Through Car Window on Stretcher.

## MUST STAY IN HOSPITAL

## Relapse Followed Fried Potatoes for Breakfast—Doubtful About Playing in Opening Game.

Babe Ruth, the mighty batsman of the New York Yankees and idol of the baseball world, arrived unconscious at the Pennsylvania Station here yesterday afternoon from his Spring training trip. Shortly after the train left Manhattan Transfer the mighty Babe collapsed in the dressing room of the car and struck his head on the wash basin. For a time it was feared that he had suffered a concussion of the brain and possibly had fractured his skull.

Ruth lay unconscious in the car, which was held on the main track, for an hour and five minutes before he could be removed. For another half hour he was unconscious in the station before the ambulance arrived to take him to St. Vincent's Hospital at Seventh Avenue and Eleventh Street, but soon after reaching the hospital he regained consciousness and recognized those about him. It was not until then that Dr. Edward King, who had attended the great hitter in his many illnesses and ailments during the past nine years pronounced his patient out of danger.

Dr. King's statement follows:

"Ruth's condition is not serious. He is run down and has low blood pressure and there is an indication of a slight attack of the flu. What he needs is rest. He should have been in bed a week ago. He has a slight temperature of 101, two degrees above normal. He is resting easily and his condition is satisfactory. It is possible he may be out in two or three days and that he may play in the opening game of the season. Ruth is such a powerful fellow that he is liable to recover over night if he wants to, as he has in the past."

Although the official diagnosis of Ruth's condition was a slight attack of influenza, it also was said that his training diet had much to do with his collapse. Ruth's appetite has long been a subject of discussion, and on several occasions, especially recently, it has been said that the great batsman was "eating himself out of baseball." Physicians familiar with Ruth's habits and diet said that his condition probably was due as much to overeating as to anything else. Fried potatoes for breakfast yesterday morning are said to have contributed to his sudden relapse.

### Resting Quietly This Morning.

Ruth was resting quietly early this morning, with ice packs on his head. Dr. King, before he left at midnight, said he felt optimistic.

Ruth was sent on ahead of his team after he collapsed at Asheville, N.C., last Tuesday. He first was taken ill last Sunday, but despite his condition, he insisted on playing in the exhibition games of last Sunday and Monday, getting two home runs in the Sunday contest and another, which won the game for the Yankees, the following day. On Tuesday, however, his condition became more critical, and when he collapsed at Asheville he was ordered to bed, and it was decided to send him on to New York as soon as he was able to travel.

Earlier in the day reports had circulated throughout the United States and even in England that Ruth was dead. These rumors were played up on the first pages of London newspapers. They were not definitely denied until the train on which the player was traveling reached Washington early yesterday morning. When the train arrived at the capital newspaper men rushed aboard. Paul Kritchell, scout for the Yankees, who was accompanying Ruth on the trip from the South, put an end to the rumors at once.

At that time he was resting in his berth, and it was reported that he had spent a very comfortable night, and was apparently in better physical condition than he had been since he was first stricken. However, just after the train left Manhattan Transfer, Ruth collapsed again.

The Babe was cleaning up for his arrival in New York, happy at the prospect of seeing his wife, who had preceded him, arriving here on Monday, and who was at the station to meet him. He sent Kritchell to get a comb, and when the Yankee scout returned he found the great hulk of the mighty hitter crumpled in a heap on the floor. Kritchell tried in many ways to revive the fallen star, but without success. He summoned aid, and Ruth was carried to his berth, where his huge form was stretched out unconscious.

As soon as the train arrived at the Pennsylvania Station, messengers were sent scurrying for the staff surgeon of the railroad. Dr. J. M. Murphy was one of the first to reach the side of the unconscious athlete.

### Mrs. Ruth at Station.

Mrs. Ruth, accompanied by Mrs. C. C. White, a close friend of the Ruths and who had accompanied Mrs. Ruth from St. Petersburg, Fla., were at the station to meet the Babe. Mrs. Ruth, arrayed in bright Spring attire, appeared calm at her husband's condition, but when she heard of the new complications that had set in, a little cry escaped from her lips, her eyes filled with tears, and she rushed to the side of her husband.

Edward Barrow, business manager of the Yankees; Charles McManus, his assistant, and Ed Holley, major league scout, also were allowed to enter the ward where the home-run king lay in a state of coma. All others, and there were many who had gathered at the station to welcome Ruth and to wish him well and a quick recovery from what was believed to be only a slight illness, were driven back by the station guards. Stretcher-bearers were sent for and soon returned with a rolling stretcher to carry the Babe to the ambulance which had been ordered from St. Vincent's Hospital as soon as it was learned that Ruth was in a more critical condition than had been anticipated.

The crowd waited anxiously for the Babe to appear, but minutes passed and there was no word from the little group which had gathered around the unconscious form. Drawn curtains prevented any view of what was going on in the car and no reports were forthcoming. The minutes ticked off into an hour and there was a tense strain on the part of those who waited for a word of Ruth's condition.

While the crowd waited another train carrying the Boston Braves en route to Boston drew up on a the adjoining track and the members of the National League club, which had trained at St. Petersburg, where Ruth and the Yankees also prepared for the pennant race, came out to learn the latest reports. The Braves had heard earlier reports on Ruth's death and were relieved to discover that these reports were untrue, but their concern was renewed when they learned that he had suffered a relapse.

Rube Marquard, former Giant and Robin pitcher, and Dave Bancroft, manager of the Braves, went to the car wherein Ruth was confined with a message of sympathy from their club, but Ruth's condition was so grave at that time that they were not allowed to enter and their train sped on its way again with the Babe still in a coma.

## Ambulance Breaks Down.

Finally, at 2:15, Ruth's unconscious form was moved through a window and on to a stretcher. Accompanied by Mrs. Ruth, who had not left his side since she learned of his collapse; Barrow, Holley and Kritchell, Ruth was carried to the baggage room on a freight elevator. There it was learned that the steering gear of the ambulance from St. Vincent's Hospital had broken and it was necessary to summon another from the New York Hospital.

Three times before the ambulance finally arrived Ruth went into convulsions, lashing out with arms and legs and muttering incoherently. The first attack seized him about 2:20 P.M. Shortly before he had regained consciousness momentarily. His eyelids fluttered and he looked at his wife, who was bent over him.

"I feel rotten, Helen," he whispered. Mrs. Ruth smiled through her tear-dimmed eyes, but before she could answer her husband had lapsed into unconsciousness again. Those were the first intelligible words he had spoken since his collapse on the train, and the last until he revived at the hospital.

Soon after he was seized with his first delirious attack and it took six men to hold him on the stretcher. His arms suddenly flew wide and his legs kicked out. He almost rose to a sitting position before those standing beside the stretcher were able to subdue him. Mrs. Ruth's eyes filled with tears again, but she bravely brushed them away and continued to stand stoically beside his prostrate form.

About ten minutes later Ruth suffered another attack of convulsions, and again he was forced back and quieted. Christopher di Crocco, the ambulance surgeon, who had arrived, then administered a hypodermic injection. But this failed to quiet the Babe, and just before he was put in the ambulance he was seized with a third attack and almost leaped off the stretcher before he could be quieted. Another hypodermic was administered before he was finally put into the ambulance and taken to the hospital.

Two more convulsions occurred during the trip from the station to the hospital and another just as he was being carried from the ambulance into the hospital. The last was the most serious and it took the combined strength of seven attendants to keep him on the stretcher as it was carried through the crowd of silent onlookers who had gathered at the building.

## Is Rushed to Hospital.

The trip from the Pennsylvania Station to the hospital was an eventful one. The streets were cleared for the ambulance, which sped silently along, as the horn had been broken. Mrs. Ruth, who had held up bravely under the ordeal while at the station, broke down and wept after the ambulance got under way. She made the trip on the front seat with the driver.

Arriving at the hospital Ruth was carried up to Room 19, and after Dr. King had made a thorough examination of the patient and pronounced him in no danger, either from the attack of influenza or from the bump on his head, the Babe suddenly regained consciousness, recognizing his wife first, then Barrow and Dr. King. By 4 o'clock Ruth was laughing and talking and twenty minutes later he said he was going to take a nap. His head, which ached from the blow received while falling on the train, was packed with ice.

It was a strange entrance into the city of his greatest triumphs for the mighty Ruth. A few short weeks ago he left amid the plaudits of the crowd, smiling and robust. Through his training period in the sunny South, first at Hot Springs, Ark., and then at St. Petersburg, every move of the great slugger had been followed by the fans. Reports of his rounding into form were received here with enthusiasm, and his hitting record during the Spring exhibition games was a source of encouragement to the Yankee officials and the baseball public.

Then came the collapse of Ruth at Asheville, N.C., which shocked the baseball world. Ruth made encouraging progress, however, on the trip north until he fainted yesterday morning. Kritchell said that he and the Babe had played pinochle on the train Wednesday night and that the slugger appeared to be well on the road to recovery.

Mrs. Ruth, waiting for her husband at the station, did not seem especially perturbed over Ruth's condition, evidently believing it only a recurrence of the influenza that has attacked him several times before. She chatted with newspaper men before the train arrived, seemingly at ease. But when the Babe failed to appear ten minutes after the train had reached the station she became anxious and on hearing of his relapse rushed to his side. Dorothy Ruth, the young daughter of the star, was on her way to New York from the Babe's farm at Sudbury, Mass., when Ruth collapsed. She arrived later in the afternoon, after her father had been taken to the hospital.

### Goes Into Convulsions.

There was grave concerns over Ruth's condition when he was carried from the train, but the anxiety reached its height when he went into convulsions while waiting for the ambulance to arrive.

Mrs. Ruth stood at his head, with tear-dimmed eyes, bravely struggling to keep her composure. Barrow, Kritchell, Dr. Murphy and attendants were lined along the side of the stretcher, when suddenly the Babe lashed out right and left with arms and legs. Immediately those within distance jumped to the side of the stretcher and held the big man down. Barrow, a sad and serious expression on his face, stroked the Babe's cheek as if he were a child, but soon after the Babe lashed out again.

The crowd which had gathered plainly showed its concern, and when the hypodermic injections failed to quiet the Babe it appeared serious. Dr. Murphy flashed an electric torch in Ruth's unseeing eyes, not more than three inches away, but the Babe never blinked. Only once, when he spoke to his wife, did he appear at all conscious.

This break in Ruth's health is not the first that has occurred since he became a nationally famous figure because of his sensational home-run hitting. The husky looking star is in reality one of the most brittle and susceptible characters in baseball. Last Spring he collapsed at Hot Springs from influenza, and on several other occasions he has been out of the game from one injury or another. His ankles, which are extremely small for the great size of his body, together with his wrists, have been constant sources of worry to the slugger. Several times he has fallen unconscious on the field after coming into collision with the wall or a teammate in racing after a fly ball. However, despite these many ailments and illnesses, Ruth's physical strength always has pulled him through with exceptional rapidity. He suffers injuries as easily if not more so than most athletes, but at the same time he recovers from them quickly.

### Say Ruth Is "Very Careless."

The reason for Ruth's many attacks of illness was disclosed last night by a physician who has attended him for several years.

"The big fellow doesn't take care of himself," the physician said. "He leads an active life and he eats heartily. He becomes overheated while playing, then he jumps into an automobile and drives rapidly. He's subject to colds and when he gets one he pays no attention to it. The result is that it settles and then he's really sick."

Questions as to whether the Babe kept late hours and dissipated in the Winter brought a laugh.

"He's very careless," the physician added.

## LONDON PRESS INTERESTED.

### Report of Ruth's Death Receives Front Page Display.

LONDON, April 9.—The London press, which serves a public knowing nothing about baseball except that it is some sort of game like "rounders," gave the report of Babe Ruth's death today a prominence which the passing of a mere financier or politician would not have achieved.

The first evening paper on the streets with the story gave it a top head on the front page, alongside the dispatch telling of the stoning of the hotel in Damascus, Syria, where Lord Balfour was stopping. Other papers followed with pictures and stories from one to two columns in length, dealing with the "Babe's fame as "King of Baseball," and his great salary—a sum which has always caused amazement in conservative England.

So great was the interest that the papers immediately began calling on the American correspondents in London for special articles.

In England baseball itself means nothing, but there was none who could not get a thrill from the human interest aspects of this baseball prodigy's career.

## WASHINGTON IS STIRRED.

### Early Morning Reports of Ruth's Death Arouse Capital.

WASHINGTON, April 9.—Report that Babe Ruth, the home-run king, had died en route to Washington started in the early morning hours when his train was speeding through Southwestern Virginia. Originating apparently in Canada, the report spread with almost incredible rapidity.

Even before the train reached Washington newspaper offices here were kept busy answering inquiries, and train dispatchers along the route of the train were set to work checking up on the report.

When the train pulled into the Union Station a group of station officials and others immediately boarded it. They were told Ruth apparently was in better physical condition than he was when he left the North Carolina town where he was stricken after a fight against influenza.

Among these were officials of the Southern Railroad, who had been routed out of their beds and who previously had set in motion the intelligence machinery of the road in an effort to ascertain the facts.

As an instance of the rapidity with which the rumor spread, Government clerks en route to their work, heard whisperings of it and it was a topic of conversation and speculation among groups gathered here and there on the street corners and elsewhere.

## RUMORS BESIEGE YANKEES.

### Huggins and Players Kept Busy Denying Ruth's Death.

CHARLOTTE, N.C., April 9.—The usual crop of rumors came down upon the Yanks here today in the wake of Ruth's illness. Huggins got scores of telegrams requesting details of the Bambino's death and the false report was rife in Charlotte. It got to be so persistent that even those who should have known better began to believe there might be some truth in it.

Just before the game started Dazzy Vance came over to the press box and asked if Ruth were still alive. He will probably think he is very much alive if he has to pitch against him in either one of the games in Brooklyn.

It is understood here that the way the report of Ruth's death got started was that he missed connections at Sallsbury, N.C., and had to take a later train, thus delaying his arrival in Washington.

August 30, 1925

# RUTH FINED $5,000; COSTLY STAR BANNED FOR ACTS OFF FIELD

## Manager Huggins of Yankees Imposes Penalty at St. Louis for "Misconduct."

## OFFENDER ORDERED HOME

## Leaves Hotel With Suitcase, but Later Cancels Reservation on Train.

## WAS BOUGHT FOR $135,000

## Home Run King Also Loses part of $52,000 Salary During His Indefinite Suspension.

ST. LOUIS, Aug. 29 (AP).—George Herman (Babe) Ruth, baseball's premier slugger, today was fined $5,000 and suspended indefinitely by Manager Miller Huggins of the Yankees for "general misconduct." Ruth made no comment when Huggins told him to pack up and leave St. Louis for New York. The home-run king checked out of his hotel immediately, ostensibly to follow Huggins's orders.

Later Huggins said Ruth had been penalized for "misconduct off the field."

"I absolutely refuse to discuss the circumstances which led to the fine and suspension except to say that Ruth was guilty of misconduct off the field," Huggins stated, and refused to add to this.

"Does this mean that Ruth is out of the game for the remainder of the season?" Huggins was asked.

"That's entirely up to me, and I will decide that when the time comes," he replied.

"Was Ruth's misconduct what is generally known as breaking the training rules?"

"I have refused to answer that question. The misconduct was off the field of play."

"Does 'misconduct off the field' mean drinking?" Huggins was asked.

"Of course it means drinking," said Huggins, "and it means a lot of other things besides. There are various kinds of misconduct. Patience has ceased to be a virtue. I have tried to overlook Ruth's behavior for a while, but I have decided to take summary action to bring the big fellow to his senses.

"I am disciplining him for general misconduct off the ball field, detrimental the best interests of the club during the present road trip. I am not saying anything about his actions on the ball field.

"Every one knows he has been having an off year and his weak batting has been excused on account of his illness this Spring.

"When he started playing the first of June he was on probation more or less, bound to take care of himself physically and live up to the rules of club discipline.

"He has forgotten all about these restrictions on this trip, hence the fine and suspension."

Late tonight it was learned that Ruth had exchanged his railroad ticket for one on the Pennsylvania Railroad leaving here about noon tomorrow.

## Did Not Consult Ruppert.

Manager Huggins said tonight he had penalized Babe Ruth without consulting Colonel Ruppert, the owner of the Yankees, or Secretary Edward F. Barrow of the club. He acted on his own responsibility entirely, he said.

First news that there had been trouble came this afternoon when the Yankees took the field for the game against the Browns, and Ruth was absent from that line-up. Inquirers were informed that Ruth had deserted the club and gone to New York, but when Huggins was confronted with the report he admitted the fine and suspension, and that he had ordered the slugger to New York.

Employes at the Buckingham Hotel declared that Ruth was smiling and seemingly not worried by the turn of events. They said he left with his suitcases without giving any forwarding address. It was learned at Union Station here that Ruth had canceled reservations, previously arranged, on the 6 P.M. New York train.

At an early hour tonight Ruth could not be reached for a statement. He was said to have appeared at a residence in the West End, but left a few minutes before newspaper men arrived, saying that he intended catching a 6 o'clock train for New York. Ruth was not on the train, however, and had not appeared at the station when it departed.

This is only one of the numerous escapades of the New York star, who in addition to being proclaimed baseball's most valuable player in 1922 is the highest salaried player in the history and probably was the greatest drawing card of all time.

During the Fall of 1921 Ruth violated the rules of organized baseball prohibiting "barnstorming" tours by members of the pennant-winning teams. For that incident Ruth was suspended without pay for the first thirty days of the 1922 season. On other occasions Ruth's temperament similarly exhibited itself, resulting in disputes with umpires.

## No Comment by Officials Here.

No official comment could be obtained last night from Yankee executives. Efforts to reach Colonel Jacob Ruppert, the club President, and Ed Barrow, the Yankee business manager, were unsuccessful. At Colonel Ruppert's home it was said he was spending the day in the country and was not expected back until late at night. Barrow was out of town for the week-end.

This is a record fine in baseball for a minor or major league player. No other such penalty has been levied. Considering that Ruth is paid a salary that is believed to be $52,000 a year, and under the rules of baseball his salary will cease during the term of his suspension, it is likely that the present difficulty will cost Ruth a greater sum than many star players receive for an entire year's services. It has been calculated that Ruth receives $296 a day during the playing season.

# Ruth's Home Run Total 299.

No athlete probably ever has had the brilliant, sensational career that has George Herman Ruth. An orphan in a Baltimore home, Ruth sprang into prominence as a member of the Baltimore Orioles and was sold to the Boston Red Sox in 1914 for a price said to be $2,900. In 1919 he set the sport world agog when he crashed out twenty-nine home runs, a feat that every slugger in the major leagues had striven to attain.

The remarkable popularity of Ruth and the attention his wonderful feats attracted have stimulated interest in baseball to a degree that probably did more than any other single thing to bolster the sport in the year after the infamous White Sox scandal. From the day Ruth began making homers and gaining his fame, baseball parks began filling, and the drab days that were feared passed, and the greatest years, financially, at least, in the history of organized baseball followed and continued as long as Ruth, with his gigantic bat and his colorful personality, dominated the national pastime.

In this respect Ruth is beyond doubt the most expensive investment in baseball's history. As an attraction at the gate he is invaluable, and the price that would be asked for his services, if he were for sale, can only be guessed at, but it certainly would be a king's ransom.

He became a mild sensation and his fame spread to the Yankees, who paid the then record price of $135,000 for his services. This transaction took place in the Winter of 1919. It caused great grief in Boston, but great joy in New York. With the world at his feet, with his picture on the front page of many newspapers and his name on the tip of every baseball fan's tongue, the colorful Babe set out to create a new mark, and he did. Playing his first season, that of 1920 with the Yankees, Ruth made fifty-four home runs, a mark that was simply amazing. His name became a household word and his fame spread around the globe.

But the prince of sluggers was not satisfied. In 1921 he sought new worlds to conquer, and he found them. He added the sum of five home runs to his 1920 total, bringing his record up to fifty-nine. He has never done better than that. Baseball men say he never will and that it will be a long, long time before another exceeds that mark.

Counting the fifteen homers he has made this season, the mighty hitsmith had compiled a grand total of 299 since becoming a major leaguer. The third year he was with the Yanks, 1922, he made thirty-five homers, and in 1923 he made forty-one circuit drives. Last season he made forty-six and led the American League in batting, a goal he long cherished. His batting mark was .378.

His decided slump in 1922 was due to a suspension at the hands of Baseball Commissioner Landis. At the conclusion of the 1921 season Ruth, despite the orders of Landis, went on a barnstorming tour, and for this he was set down until May 20, 1922. Thus he lost six weeks of the playing season, and it spoiled his chances of breaking his record of the year before.

How strong a hold Ruth has on the public is shown by the manner in which the world sought news of his illness this past Spring. Ruth, following a training period at St. Petersburg, Fla., where he injured his hand and was out of the game for a time, started home with the Yankees, but at Asheville, N.C., on April 7, while alighting from the train Ruth collapsed. He was carried to a hotel and the news of his sickness was flashed around the world. He was brought home on April 9 and was taken to St. Vincent's Hospital, where he was critically ill for many weeks. He underwent several operations, the original illness of grippe having developed complications. He finally rejoined his team and played in his first game of the season on June 1.

Ruth was born in Baltimore on Feb. 7, 1894. He went to school at Mount St. Mary's Industrial School, Baltimore, and played ball there until he was picked up by Jack Dunn of the Baltimore Orioles. He was tried out as a southpaw pitcher and was then sold to Boston.

# RUTH HITS 3 HOMERS AND YANKS WIN, 10–5; SERIES EVEN AGAIN

---

### Babe Breaks Six Records Hitting Two Balls Out of Park, One Into Distant Bleachers.

---

## EVEN ST. LOUIS CHEERS HIM

---

### 40,000 See Yankees Get 14 Hits Off Five Pitchers—Hoyt Gives 14, Too, but Survives.

---

## VICTORY CLINCHED IN FIFTH

---

### Five Bases on Balls and a Double Net 4 Runs—Pennock vs. Sherdel Today—Sixth Game Here.

---

### By JAMES R. HARRISON.

*Special to The New York Times.*

ST. LOUIS, Oct. 6.—Contrary to reports, the king is not dead. Long live the king, for today he hit three home runs and smashed six world's series records as completely as his fellow-Yankees smashed the Cardinals, to tie the world's series at two victories apiece.

After all, there is only one Ruth. He is alone and unique. Tonight he is securely perched on the throne again, and the crown does not rest uneasy on his royal head. For to his record of fifty-nine homers in one season he added today the achievement of three home runs in one world's series game.

Behind his bulky, swaggering figure, the Yankees marched to an overwhelming victory, 10 to 5. When they were going down for the third and almost the last time, Ruth tossed them the rope of three homers. He took personal charge of the world's series and made the game his greatest single triumph. He led the charge of a faltering battalion and turned the tide of battle so much that tonight most of the neutral critics were conceding the championship to the Yankees.

**Yanks Find Batting Eye.**

Hearing the old familiar ring of Ruth's big bat, the Yankees came out of their coma, made ten runs and fourteen hits and bore the Cardinals to earth with a rugged, slashing attack.

Besides setting world's series records that may stand for all time, George Herman Ruth hit a baseball where only two other men had hit it—into the centrefield bleachers of Sportsmans Park. It is 430 feet to the bleacher fence. The wall is about twenty feet high. Back of it stretches a deep bank of seats, and almost squarely in the middle of this bank Ruth crashed the third homer that made all the history.

It was not one of his longest drives but it was by all odds his best, for it automatically wiped four marks off the record book. It was, as noted above, the first time anybody had hit that many homers in a series game. It made Ruth's number of homers for all series games seven, beating by one the former record of "Goose"

Goslin. It made his total bases in one game twelve, three more than Harry Hopper in 1915. His extra bases on long hits amounted to nine. Again three better than any other man had ever done.

Beside those four marks, which were shattered by the one heroic blow, Ruth broke two more. He scored four runs, the most which any player had scored in a world's series game, beating a record of three set by Mike Donlin in 1905, which has been equaled often. Ruth also raised his own record of eighteen extra bases achieved in world series games to a grand total of twenty-seven.

Ruth's first contribution to the gayety of more than 40,000 fans today came in the first inning, when Flint Rhem, the first of five Cardinal pitchers, decided that a fast ball, adroitly served, would fool the king. Ruth swung under the ball and raised it high in the air. The pellet flouted out to right field, hugging the foul line and blown by the wind toward foul territory.

## Over the Fence It Goes.

At the last moment, with the ball veering closer and closer to the chalk line of extinction, it disappeared over the stand and fell to the broad avenue below—not two feet from the foul line.

In the third, when Ruth came up next, young Mr. Rhem had changed his mind and decided that a fellow who could hit speed that far might be slightly deceived by a pitch of slower pace. So he tossed up a dew-drop slow ball between the waist and shoulder and on the inside corner.

Ruth must have been expecting it, for he leaned back, swung from the floor and, with perfect timing, drove a long, high and hard poke over the bleacher roof in deep right-centre.

In both cases he swung at the first ball. Two pitches and two home runs. Two pitches and the game was practically over, with the Yanks inspired and rejuvenated and crowding to the plate to hit with old-time vim.

Two pitches and, who knows, the series was practically over. With his star left-hander, Pennock, thoroughly rested and ready to pitch tomorrow, Miller Huggins has the upper hand once more, with the Yanks finally awake and out of their batting slump.

After the third inning, the Cardinal pitchers treated Mr. Ruth with great aloofness and attempted no familiarities but one. That one was disastrous. In the sixth inning, Herman Bell, a young right-hander, was pitching. Combs opened with a single too deep for Thevenow to handle. Koenig fanned and Bell was so pleased with this conquest that he attempted conclusions with Ruth, which was equivalent to tampering with a stick of dynamite.

When the count was finally three and two Mr. Bell did a foolish thing. He drew back his arm and cut loose with a fast ball straight through the middle. When Ruth is hitting as he was today, there is not a pitcher in the world who can afford this gamble. Even a school-boy pitcher knows better than that.

Ruth waded into the fast ball and put all his shoulders and back behind the 52-ounce bat that has brought more ruin than any other in baseball. He caught the ball as flush as an expert marksman. It was a terrific blow and there was no doubt where it was going.

Douthit ran back as far as he could, and having no scaling irons or ladder, stood helplessly while the ball shot over the wall and landed in the laps of the St. Louis rooters. It was still going with unabated speed when it arrived. It struck with force and bounced up, and then there came the finest ovation that St. Louis has ever given a visiting athlete.

## Babe Gets Ovation.

Three home runs in one world's series game! Only seven men in modern baseball have hit three in any ordinary game. Even the hardened partisans of St. Louis had to admit the grandeur of the feat. In Boston or New

York or several other cities they would have torn the grandstand down and given Babe the pieces, but for St. Louis it was a gigantic tribute that poured out from more than 40,000 throats.

The folks in the grandstand were inclined to be a bit conservative. A few bitter-enders committed the lèse-majesté of booing the king, but out in the bleachers it was all tumult and uproar. The boys in the sun seats in left, where Ruth was stationed, got to their feet as if one man. They waved papers and programs and Cardinal banners and tossed a few ancient straw hats out on the field.

There have been few more gallant figures than Ruth leading the charge of the Yanks today. It had been a dark hour for the New York gladiators. Before the game, it was reported, Ban Johnson, President of the American League, went to the Yankee dressing room to give the players the sort of talk that a football coach delivers to his men before the big game. There was a general conviction that the Cards were the better team and would win, an opinion that was not changed until the slumbering menace in Babe Ruth's bat awoke and made a new team of the Yanks.

There have been few figures as gallant as Ruth as he strode from the bench to receive the trice-repeated homage of an enemy crowd—his portly frame swaggering ever so slightly, his face alight with the fire of determination.

If the Babe was going down, he would go down fighting. There was only one man who could jar the Yanks out of their depressing slump. It is still a one-man team and the happy fortune today was that that one man found his batting eye and blazed the trail for his dejected colleagues.

## A Lively Ball Game.

With the greatest home-run hitter of them all hitting three homers, it was, naturally enough, a lively occasion. The game was long and one-sided, but it was a good one—a great game, indeed, with attacks and counterattacks, a seesawing score. Twenty-eight hits on both sides and sensation following sensation, even to the almost disastrous collision of two Cardinal outfielders.

The paid attendance was 38,825, more than 1,000 above yesterday's first St. Louis game. This number of people paid $166,190 at the gate, bringing the total receipts of the series up to $730,001, a new record.

The previous record for receipts in four games was $723,104 made in 1923. The record for players' share, also made in that year, was $368,783.

With the playing of the fourth game, the players ceased to share in the receipts. However, the players' pool totaled $372,300, a world's series record, surpassing by more than $4,000 the record set in 1923. Of this total the world's series player will share in only 70 per cent., as the remaining 30 per cent goes to the second, third and fourth place teams in the pennant races of the two leagues.

On this basis the world's series players will divide $260,610. Each club has twenty-five eligible players, which means that each player for the winning teams will receive about $6,254 and each player for the losing team will get $4,168. Both these sums are records in world's series.

The series is sure to go back to New York, and that means a Saturday game at the Stadium, with the two club owners cutting heavily into the net proceed. With Pennock at hand, refreshed by a four-day rest, and the New York war clubs again playing the music of the solid wallop, the Yanks are favorites here to win, when last night they were poor second-money choices.

It was, until today, a lifeless world's series. Three games had been played and in none of them was there a great play or a thrilling rally, or hardly an event that the baseball field had not seen dozens of times before.

## The Series Awake.

But today the series awoke and put on its best show. And there was sparkling fielding and the heavy ring of busy bats and enough mistakes to keep the fans on edge from the start to finish.

The Cardinals opened brusquely on Waite Hoyt, but fell behind until the fourth. Then four hits and three runs put them one to the good, and raise the grave suspicion that Mr. Hoyt would take an early trip to the clubhouse. But to gain those three runs in the fourth Hornsby had to take out Rhem. Arthur Reinhart, his left-handed successor, threw the game away in the fifth by setting another world's series record, and giving five bases on balls. Four, as a matter of fact, were charged to Reinhart and the fifth to Herman Bell. With only one hit the Yanks scored four runs, and in the sixth Ruth struck another home run blow and the game was over.

With all this friendly assistance, Hoyt was able to stagger through, although he did not pitch a good game. He struck out eight, but was so much in trouble that Urban Shocker pitched almost a complete game in the bullpen, where he was joined later by Shawkey and Pennock, as the Cardinals made their constant threats.

Once Rhem had passed out, Hornsby was at sea and called on four more pitchers in vain. Reinhart, Bell, a young southpaw named William Hallahan and the right-hander Vic Keen, strayed forth from the bench at odd moments, with Keen showing in the ninth the only flash of ability.

There was one other record tied during the sunny afternoon. Between and among them the Cardinal pitchers issued ten bases on balls.

In the fourth the exultant fans were frightened speechless as Chick Hafey and Taylor Douthit, two of the outfield guard, crashed together in pursuit of a fly and were knocked groggy. Lazzeri was on first base with one out when Joe Dugan looped a fly to left centre. Douthit rushed over from centre and Hafey dashed in from left. Eyes glued on the ball, they saw nothing else in the world. Players of more experience would have avoided the crash. Either of them could have caught the ball, but as Douthit touched it he bumped into Hafey, and the ball flew to the ground. Both players were stretched out apparently unconscious.

They were so badly dazed that neither could get up and chase the ball. Bell rushed out from third and retrieved it, but by that time Lazzeri was almost at the plate.

## Doctor Rushes Out.

Douthit, as he rushed in, rammed his elbow against Hafey's chest and stomach; and the left fielder was the worse hurt of the two. He went down on his side and lay still. Players of both teams ran out. On their heels came the St. Louis trainer and the club doctor. For a moment it looked like a stretcher case, with the Cardinals out two good ball players, but smelling salts, a dash of cold water and frenzied towel-swinging did the trick and brought them both back to normal.

Douthit did one of the gamest things of the series only a minute later. With Dugan on second, Severeid sliced a pretty single to dead centre. Although only six seconds before he had been reclining on his back, Douthit sprinted in and tore loose a wonderful throw which nailed Joe fast at the plate.

It was one of four great throws today. In the second Lazerri hit against the left field bleachers, but was out at third on Thevenow's fine relay of the ball from Douthit. In the fourth Douthit tried to score from second on a single, but was cut down by Ruth's marvelous line fling straight into Severeid's glove.

Again in the sixth, Meusel singled to right and tried a smart maneuver by rounding first base slowly and then suddenly putting on a burst of speed, hoping that Southworth would be taken in by the trick. Billy, however, was wide awake. He erased the big city slicker at second with a throw true and straight.

There was still another interval when the medical talents of the club trainer were needed to resuscitate an athlete. In the fourth, Bob Meusel suddenly stopped the game and walked into the diamond to complain of a dizzy spell and failing eyesight. The fans were not surprised to hear it, for they believed that by that time the

Cardinals had knocked all the Yanks dizzy. Expert first-aid ministrations by Trainer Woods restored Robert, and there were no more complaints during the afternoon.

Rhem, in the first inning, struck out Combs and Koenig, but after this gay beginning, he tossed the celebrated fast ball to Mr. Ruth who stowed it away on the outside of the park. Meusel walked and Gehrig singled to right. The Cards had trouble getting hold of the ball and Meusel, smartly, kept on running from first to the plate. That he didn't make it was no fault of the strategy, for a better slide would have landed him safe and sound.

For the Cardinals, Douthit outran a tap to deep short, and Southworth sent him to third with a single through second. Hornsby emulated Ruth to some degree by dashing a rugged hit to right, scoring Douthit and moving Southworth to second.

## Cardinals Hitting Fiercely.

The Cardinal hitting was fierce, and Hornsby wisely ordered Bottomley to keep the attack going instead of bunting. Bottomley, however, flied to Ruth and Lester Bell did likewise to Combs. Hoyt got out of a very bad hole by fanning Hafey.

Lazzeri's two bagger to left opened the second. Tony thought the ball was going into the stand, and loafed down to first. So was a second late in arriving at third, where Bell did a nice job of touching. Followed Severeid's single, on which Lazzeri could have scored. It was one of three or more runs tossed away by the opulent Yanks.

The second Ruthian product enlivened the third inning. The score was now: Ruth 2, St. Louis 1. The Yanks showed more signs of life in the fourth, when Lazerri walked and scored during the Hafey-Douthit head-on collision, which also allowed Dugan to reach second. On Severeid's single Joe was tagged out at home, Joe's speed being less than his earnest intentions.

The fourth was almost the end for Waite Hoyt. Up to this time he had done excellent work. Although his curve was nothing to boast about, he had nice control and an effective change of pace, working the corners with low fast balls that were called strikes but were hard to hit.

Koenig charged out to left to make a rattling good catch of L. Bell's fly. Hafey singled and then the Yankee shortstop made up for his good work by fumbling O'Farrell's grounder, and error which nearly cost the game, giving the Cards three unearned runs.

It was a bad break of luck for Hoyt. Thevenow whipped a two-bagger an inch inside first base and Hafey scored while O'Farrell paused at second. Hornsby had no confidence in Rhem and yanked him for Pinch Hitter Toporcer. It was a move that Roger lived to regret, for Rhem certainly would have done better than the miscellaneous collection of talent which followed him.

Toporcer didn't deliver much at that, though his sacrifice fly to Combs scored O'Farrell with the tying run. Combs's throw was fast, but badly aimed.

## Douthit's Two-Bagger.

Here, Douthit sent a rollicking two-bagger out to the bleacher wall in right centre and put his team a run ahead, while the local enthusiasts went crazy with joy. Sportsman's Park was a madhouse for two or three minutes, and the purple-faced rooters went into another spasm when Southworth singled to left. Douthit went for home and Ruth stopped him dead. The vocal storm subsided somewhat.

Back came the Yanks in the fifth to have the game presented to them on a silver platter. Reinhart, a stalwart left-hander with a tricky service like Sherdel's, was nervous and wild. Altogether he gave the most pathetic spectacle of many a world's series. He walked Combs without getting over even one strike, and the Yanks got a break when Koenig popped a fluky double down the right-field line, the ball landing in the one exact spot where no fielder could reach it.

Hornsby slipped when he picked up the ball, and Combs was fast enough to score. With Ruth at bat, Reinhart went on an ascension and neglected to take his parachute with him.

True, he favored Ruth with a strike, but the other four were balls. Another walk to Meusel filled up the bases and Reinhart went from bad to worse by chucking two bad ones to Gehrig.

Here was the point where Hornsby should have acted. He had Herman Bell warmed up, and it was no secret that Reinhart was now in the clouds. The left-hander steadied a little, but when the count was two and two he walked Gehrig, forcing Koenig in and sending New York ahead.

Bell took up the assignment with the bases still full and no one out, and no one thinking of getting out. Lazzeri's fly to Southworth scored Ruth while Meusel occupied third after the catch. Dugan's grounder spouted up in the air and during his subsequent demise at the hands of O'Farrell, Meusel raced home with the fourth run.

In the sixth came Combs's single and the third of the Ruth home-run series. The score was now 9 to 4. The Cards in their half of the inning made attempts at reprisals. O'Farrell and Thevenow singled, but Flowers, a hitter for Bell, fanned. Douthit and Southworth were powerless.

A single by Severeid, Hoyt's sacrifice, and Combs's two-bagger inside third put the Yanks into double figures in the seventh. Protected by his big lead, Hoyt went along in able style now. When O'Farrell led off with a single in the eighth, there was a flutter in the New York bull pen, but it was all a mistake. Hoyt struck out Thevenow and also Holm, who batted for Hallahan. Douthit flied to centre.

Wee Willie Sherdel will come back for the Cards tomorrow and the Cards need that victory very much, for it will be their last home game. Tomorrow night the procession wends back to New York.

### OFFICIAL SCORE OF FOURTH GAME OF WORLD'S SERIES

NEW YORK YANKEES.

| | AB. | R. | H. | TB. | 2B. | 3B. | HR. | BB. | SO. | SH. | SB. | PO. | A. | E |
|---|---|---|---|---|---|---|---|---|---|---|---|---|---|---|
| Combs, cf | 5 | 2 | 2 | 3 | 1 | 0 | 0 | 1 | 1 | 0 | 0 | 4 | 0 | 0 |
| Koenig, ss | 6 | 1 | 1 | 2 | 1 | 0 | 0 | 0 | 3 | 0 | 0 | 1 | 3 | 1 |
| Ruth, lf | 3 | 4 | 3 | 12 | 0 | 0 | 3 | 2 | 0 | 0 | 0 | 1 | 1 | 0 |
| Meusel, rf | 2 | 1 | 1 | 1 | 0 | 0 | 0 | 3 | 0 | 0 | 0 | 1 | 0 | 0 |
| Gehrig, 1b | 3 | 0 | 2 | 3 | 1 | 0 | 0 | 1 | 1 | 1 | 0 | 8 | 0 | 0 |
| Lazzeri, 2b | 3 | 1 | 1 | 2 | 1 | 0 | 0 | 1 | 0 | 1 | 0 | 1 | 3 | 0 |
| Dugan, 3b | 4 | 0 | 1 | 2 | 1 | 0 | 0 | 1 | 0 | 0 | 0 | 1 | 2 | 0 |
| Severeid, c | 4 | 1 | 3 | 3 | 0 | 0 | 0 | 1 | 0 | 0 | 0 | 10 | 0 | 0 |
| Hoyt, p | 4 | 0 | 0 | 0 | 0 | 0 | 0 | 0 | 1 | 1 | 0 | 0 | 0 | 0 |
| Total | 34 | 10 | 14 | 28 | 5 | 0 | 3 | 10 | 6 | 3 | 0 | 27 | 9 | 1 |

## ST. LOUIS CARDINALS.

| | AB. | R. | H. | TB. | 2B. | 3B. | HR. | BB. | SO. | SH. | SB. | PO. | A. | E |
|---|---|---|---|---|---|---|---|---|---|---|---|---|---|---|
| Douthit, cf | 5 | 1 | 2 | 3 | 1 | 0 | 0 | 0 | 0 | 0 | 0 | 2 | 2 | 0 |
| Southworth, rf | 5 | 0 | 3 | 3 | 0 | 0 | 0 | 0 | 0 | 0 | 0 | 1 | 2 | 0 |
| Hornsby, 2b | 5 | 1 | 2 | 2 | 0 | 0 | 0 | 0 | 2 | 0 | 1 | 3 | 4 | 0 |
| Bottomley, 1b | 4 | 0 | 1 | 1 | 0 | 0 | 0 | 1 | 0 | 0 | 0 | 6 | 1 | 0 |
| L. Bell, 3b | 4 | 0 | 1 | 1 | 0 | 0 | 0 | 0 | 0 | 1 | 0 | 3 | 0 | 0 |
| Hafey, lf | 5 | 1 | 1 | 1 | 0 | 0 | 0 | 0 | 2 | 0 | 0 | 0 | 0 | 0 |
| O'Farrell, c | 4 | 1 | 2 | 2 | 0 | 0 | 0 | 0 | 0 | 0 | 0 | 8 | 1 | 0 |
| Thevenow, ss | 4 | 1 | 2 | 3 | 1 | 0 | 0 | 0 | 1 | 0 | 0 | 3 | 2 | 0 |
| Rhem, p | 1 | 0 | 0 | 0 | 0 | 0 | 0 | 0 | 1 | 0 | 0 | 0 | 1 | 0 |
| aToporcer | 0 | 0 | 0 | 0 | 0 | 0 | 0 | 0 | 0 | 1 | 0 | 0 | 0 | 0 |
| Reinhart, p | 0 | 0 | 0 | 0 | 0 | 0 | 0 | 0 | 0 | 0 | 0 | 0 | 0 | 0 |
| H. Bell, p | 0 | 0 | 0 | 0 | 0 | 0 | 0 | 0 | 0 | 0 | 0 | 0 | 0 | 0 |
| bFlowers | 1 | 0 | 0 | 0 | 0 | 0 | 0 | 0 | 1 | 0 | 0 | 0 | 0 | 0 |
| Hallahan, p | 0 | 0 | 0 | 0 | 0 | 0 | 0 | 0 | 0 | 0 | 0 | 1 | 0 | 0 |
| cHolm | 1 | 0 | 0 | 0 | 0 | 0 | 0 | 0 | 1 | 0 | 0 | 0 | 0 | 0 |
| Keen, p | 0 | 0 | 0 | 0 | 0 | 0 | 0 | 0 | 0 | 0 | 0 | 0 | 1 | 0 |
| Total | 39 | 5 | 14 | 16 | 2 | 0 | 0 | 1 | 8 | 2 | 1 | 27 | 14 | 0 |

aBatted for Rhem in the fourth.
bBatted for H. Bell in the sixth.
cBatted for Hallahan in the eighth.

### SCORE BY INNINGS

| | | | | | | | | | | |
|---|---|---|---|---|---|---|---|---|---|---|
| New York | 1 | 0 | 1 | 1 | 4 | 2 | 1 | 0 | 0—10 |
| St. Louis | 1 | 0 | 0 | 3 | 0 | 0 | 0 | 0 | 1—5 |

Left on bases—New York, 10, St. Louis 10. Bases on Balls—Off Rhem 2, Reinhart 4, H. Bell 1, Hallahan 3, Hoyt 1. Struck out—By Rhem 4, H. Bell 1, Hallahan 1, Hoyt 8. Hits—Off Rhem 7 in 4 innings, Reinhart 1 in none (pitched to five men in fifth inning), H. Bell 4 in 2, Hallahan 2 in 2, Keen none in 1. Balk—H. Bell. Losing pitcher—Reinhart. Umpires—Klem (N. L.) at plate, Dinneen (A. L.) at first base, O'Day (N. L.) at second base, Hildebrand (A. L.) at third base. Time of game—2:39.

Babe Ruth watches the ball after hitting his 60th home run of the season on Sept. 30, 1927, at Yankee Stadium during a game against the Washington Senators. (ASSOCIATED PRESS)

October 1, 1927

**Home Run Record Falls as Ruth Hits 60th; Pirates Lose; Giants Out of Race**

RUTH CRASHES 60TH TO SET NEW RECORD

**Babe Makes It a Real Field Day by Accounting for All Runs in 4–2 Victory.**

1921 MARK OF 59 BEATEN

**Fans Go Wild as Ruth Pounds Ball Into Stands With One On, Breaking 2–2 Tie.**

CONNECTS LAST TIME UP

**Zachary's Offering Converted Into Epochal Smash, Which Old Fan Catches— Senators Then Subside.**

Babe Ruth scaled the hitherto unattained heights yesterday. Home run 60, a terrific smash off the southpaw pitching of Zachary, nestled in the Babe's favorite spot in the right field bleachers, and before the roar had ceased it was found that this drive not only had made home run record history but also was the winning margin in a 4 to 2 victory over the Senators. This also was the Yanks' 109th triumph of the season. Their last league game of the year will be played today.

When the Babe stepped to the plate in that momentous eighth inning the score was deadlocked. Koenig was on third base, the result of a triple, one man was out and all was tense. It was the Babe's fourth trip to the plate during the afternoon, a base on balls and two singles resulting on his other visits plateward.

The first Zachary offering was a fast one, which sailed over for a called strike. The next was high. The Babe took a vicious swing at the third pitched ball and the bat connected with a crash that was audible in all parts of the stand. It was not necessary to follow the course of the ball. The boys in the bleachers indicated the route of the record homer. It dropped about half way to the top. Boys, No. 60 was some homer, a fitting wallop to top the Babe's record of 59 in 1921.

While the crowd cheered and the Yankee players roared their greetings the Babe made his triumphant, almost regal tour of the paths. He jogged around slowly, touched each bag firmly and carefully and when he embedded his spikes in the rubber disk to record officially Homer 60 hats were tossed into the air, papers were torn up and tossed liberally and the spirit of celebration permeated the place.

The Babe's stroll out to his position was the signal for a handkerchief salute in which all the bleacherites, to the last man, participated. Jovial Babe entered into the carnival spirit and punctuated his Ringly strides with a succession of snappy military salutes.

## Ruth 4, Senators 2.

Ruth's homer was a fitting climax to a game which will go down as the Babe's personal triumph. The Yanks scored four runs, the Babe personally crossed the plate three times and bringing in Koenig for the fourth. So this is one time where it would be fair, although not original, to record Yankee victory 109 as Ruth 4, Senators 2.

There was not much else to the game. The 10,000 persons who came to the stadium were there for no other purpose than to see the Babe make home run history. After each of Babe's visits to the plate the expectant crowd would relax and wait for his next effort. They saw him open with a base on balls, follow with two singles and then clout the epoch-making circuit smash.

The only unhappy individual within the Stadium was Zachary. He realized he was going down in the records as the historical home run victim, in other words the great Zachary was one of the most interested spectators of the home run fight. He tossed his glove to the ground, muttered to himself, turned to his mates for consolation and got everything but that. There is no denying that Zachary was putting everything he had on the ball. No pitcher like to have recorded after his name the fact that he was Ruth's victim on his sixtieth homer.

The ball that the Babe drove, according to the word from official sources, was a pitch that was fast, low and on the inside. The Babe pulled away from the plate, then stepped into the ball, and wham! According to Umpire Bill Dinneen at the plate and Catcher Muddy Ruel the ball traveled on a line and landed a foot inside fair territory about half way to the top of the bleachers. But when the ball reached the bleacher barrier it was about ten feet fair and curving rapidly to the right.

## Fan Rushes to Babe With Ball.

The ball which became Homer 60 was caught by Joe Forner of 1937 First Avenue, Manhattan. He is about 40 years old and has been following baseball for thirty-five, according to his own admission. He was far from modest and as soon as the game was over rushed to the dressing room to let the Babe know who had the ball.

For three innings both sides were blanked. The Senators broke through in the fourth for two runs.

The Yanks came back with one run in their half of the fourth. Ruth opened with a long single to right and moved to third on Gehrig's single to centre. Gehrig took second on the throw to third. Meusel drove deep to Goslin, Ruth scoring and Gehrig taking third after the catch.

With two out in the sixth Ruth singled to right. Gehrig's hit was so fast that it went right through Gillis for a single, Ruth holding second. The Babe tied the score on Meusel's single to centre. Lazzeri was an easy third out.

The box score:

| WASHINGTON (A.) | | | | | | | NEW YORK (A.) | | | | | | |
|---|---|---|---|---|---|---|---|---|---|---|---|---|---|
| | ab. | r. | h. | po. | a. | e. | | ab. | r. | h. | po. | a. | e. |
| Rice, rf | 3 | 0 | 1 | 2 | 0 | 0 | Combs, cf | 4 | 0 | 0 | 3 | 0 | 0 |
| Harris, 2b | 3 | 0 | 0 | 3 | 4 | 0 | Koenig, ss | 4 | 1 | 1 | 3 | 5 | 0 |
| Canzel, cf | 4 | 0 | 1 | 1 | 0 | 0 | Ruth, rf | 3 | 3 | 3 | 4 | 0 | 0 |
| Gotlin, lf | 4 | 1 | 1 | 5 | 0 | 0 | Gehrig, 1B | 4 | 0 | 2 | 10 | 0 | 1 |
| Judge, 1b | 4 | 0 | 0 | 8 | 0 | 0 | Meusel, lf | 3 | 0 | 1 | 3 | 0 | 0 |
| Ruel, c | 2 | 1 | 1 | 2 | 0 | 0 | Lazerri, 2b | 3 | 0 | 0 | 2 | 2 | 0 |
| Bluege, 3b | 3 | 0 | 1 | 1 | 4 | 0 | Dugan, 3b | 3 | 0 | 1 | 1 | 1 | 0 |
| Gillis, ss | 4 | 0 | 0 | 2 | 1 | 0 | Bengough, c | 3 | 0 | 1 | 1 | 3 | 0 |
| Zachary, p | 2 | 0 | 0 | 0 | 1 | 0 | Pipgras, p | 2 | 0 | 0 | 0 | 2 | 0 |
| ªJohnson | 1 | 0 | 0 | 0 | 0 | 0 | Pennock, p | 1 | 0 | 0 | 0 | 1 | 0 |
| Total | 30 | 2 | 5 | 24 | 10 | 0 | Total | 30 | 4 | 9 | 27 | 13 | 1 |

ªBatted for Zachary in ninth.

| | | | | | | | | | | |
|---|---|---|---|---|---|---|---|---|---|---|
| Washington | 0 | 0 | 0 | 2 | 0 | 0 | 0 | 0 | 0—2 |
| New York | 0 | 0 | 0 | 1 | 0 | 1 | 0 | 2 | ..—4 |

Two-base hits—Rice. Three-base hit—Koenig. Home run—Ruth. Stolen Bases—Ruel, Bluege, Rice. Sacrifice—Meusel. Double play—Harris and Bluege, Gillis, Harris and Judge. Left on bases—New York, 4, Washington, 7. Bases on balls—Off Pipgras, 4, Pennock, 1, Zachary, 1. Struck out—By Zachary 1. Hits—Off Pipgras 4 in 6 innings, Pennock 1 in 3. Hit by pitcher—By Pigras (Rice). Winning pitcher—Pennock. Umpires—Dinneen, Connolly and Owens. Time of game—1:35.

**Yankees Win Series, Taking Final, 7 to 3; Ruth Hits 3 Homers**

---

**New York Team Sets Record of Eighth Straight by Beating the Cards Fourth Time in Row.**

---

## BOTTLES THROWN AT RUTH

---

**St. Louis Fans Angry After His Second Homer—Makes Great Catch to End Game.**

---

## SECOND VICTORY FOR HOYT

---

**Gehrig and Durst Also Make Home Runs—Total Receipts for Series $777,290.**

---

By JAMES R. HARRISON.

*Special to The New York Times.*

ST. LOUIS, Oct. 9.—Establishing records that will live as long as the game itself, scaling a baseball Matterhorn where no other foot had ever trod before, the Yankees made it four in a row over the Cardinals today, 7 to 3, as Babe Ruth, for the second time in his incredible career, hit three homers in one world's series game.

For the second successive year this super team of supermen defeated its National League rivals in four straight games to build for itself a monument that still will be standing when the names of Ruth and Gehrig and Huggins are mellow memories out of the distant past.

And to climax his marvelous career, to reach the greatest heights ever attainted by any ball player, George Herman Ruth did again today what no other man had done even once. Three times he drove the ball over the right field bleachers. He finished with the highest world's series batting average on record .625 while his co-partner and protégé, Lou Gehrig, hit one homer to set a new series record for runs driven in—nine.

### Game Is Unparalleled.

This was a game unparalleled in baseball history, not merely because, for the first time in that history, a team had won its second world's series in four straight games. Not merely because Ruth hit three homers for the second time in his career or because Gehrig drove in his ninth run. Not merely because the Yankees hammered out five homers in one game and set a new mark.

No, it was unparalleled mainly because it saw the Yankees rising triumphantly to overcome the greatest obstacles that might face a world's series team. Because it saw George H. Ruth and the badly crippled New Yorkers reach the very climax of their greatness to do deed that will be remembered as long as the game lives. If there was any lingering doubt, if anywhere in this broad land there were misguided souls who believed that Babe Ruth was not the greatest living ball player, they should have seen him today.

They should have seen him hooted and hissed, come to the plate three times, twice against Wee Willie Sherdel and once against the great Pete Alexander, and send three mighty drives whistling over that right-field pavilion.

They should have seen him swaggering and waving a friendly fist at the world as he romped out to left field—the play boy of baseball—to be greeted by a barrage of pop bottles thrown by a few sportsmen who thought that the Babe had been struck out in the seventh, a moment before he clouted his second homer to tie the score. Misguided sportsmen who could not appreciate the incredible feats of this incredible man.

### Try to Spoil Catch.

They should have seen him at the very end of the game as he drove an injured knee forward at top speed, dashing down the foul line and past the field boxes to make a one-hand catch while St. Louis partisans threw paper and programs at him to blind his vision.

They should have seen him, that great catch completed, continue to run in, holding the ball aloft in his gloved right hand—the picture of triumph and glee and kindly defiance of the whole world.

It was thus that the world's series of 1928 passed into history—with Ruth triumphant, with Ruth rampant on a field of green, with Ruth again stranger than fiction and mightier than even his most fervent admirers had dreamed he would be.

"The king is not dead, long live the king!" they might have shouted as this amazing play boy, this boisterous soul, in the great hour of his career, added new records to a list already stretching ten years back into baseball history.

### Path Strewn With Flowers.

They threw bottles and programs and newspapers at him today, did a few small-souled St. Louis fans, but as he ran from the field his path was strewn with the invisible flowers of invisible persons who know real baseball greatness when they see it.

Overshadowed by Ruth were even other heroes of this Yankee ball team which started the series as the under dog and ended it as the greatest world's series team of all time.

Overshadowed was Henry Louis Gehrig—Gehrig who today tied Ruth's record of four homers in one series and set a new mark for runs driven in. Overshadowed was little Miller Huggins, who now is tied with John Mc-Graw and Connie Mack in number of world's championship—three. Overshadowed was Waite Hoyt, who won his second game from the Cardinals, and Tony Lazzeri and all the other soldiers of this immortal battalion.

No, this game was the Ruth and nothing but the Ruth. So was the series, in which, besides his home-run feats, he established a new record for runs scored in one series with nine and for homers in his nine series with thirteen and tied Joe Harris's mark of twenty-two total bases in one series. Except that Ruth hit his in four games and Harris in seven.

### Drama in the Seventh.

The seventh inning was one of the greatest in world's series annals. Hoyt, thanks to two errors in the fourth, was on the short end of a 2–1 score, when that inning dawned. Wee Willie Sherdel, though roughly handled by the Yanks, had escaped extinction so far.

The only run off him had been Ruth's first homer in the fourth round. The game little southpaw threw a curve a half foot inside the plate. It was not a ball to swing at, but Ruth isn't human. He smacked it clear over the right-field bleachers without even touching that structure.

At the outset of the seventh Koenig popped to Maranville. Then Sherdel planted two strikes across the plate and had G. H. Ruth in a bad way. Immediately after the second strike Sherdel tried a quick return, tried to sneak the ball over while Ruth, his head turned, was exchanging quips and bright repartee with Catcher Earl Smith.

The sneak delivery was right across there, but Umpire Charley Pfirman refused to call it. He ruled that such a delivery was illegal in a world's series and was upheld by the three other umpires, who pointed out to the Cards that such a ruling had been agreed upon before the series and that both teams had been notified.

None the less, the Cardinals squawked bitterly. McKechnie and his lieutenants, sergeants and buck privates streamed out from the bench, exuding perspiration and indignation. They were joined at the plate by nine other Cardinals, led by Fordham Frank Frisch. The squawking was loud and enthusiastic. The general verdict was that Mr. Pfirman, if he ever took the blindfolded cigarette test, wouldn't need a bandage.

But though the Cardinals howled and the crowd joined in, the umpire's verdict stood. It was still two and nothing on the Babe. The next was a ball outside. Ball two was also off the plate. Then Sherdel wound up again and threw a slow curve outside.

With no perceptible effort, with an easy swing, the Bambino met the ball and knocked it toward the right-field bleachers. The crowd gasped and then groaned as the ball, flying high and never losing momentum, cleared the roof of the pavilion. Through a narrow aperture at the back you could see a white speck fall and then disappear into the great open spaces of Grand Boulevard.

As he went around the bases Ruth was triumph itself. Mockingly he waved his hands at the crowd. As he passed second base he sent a salute to his friendly enemies in the left-field bleachers. He turned toward home still waving a mocking and derisive hand at a crowd too stunned to give this feat the ovation it deserved.

### Tried to Catch King Asleep.

So they had tried to sneak a third strike over on Ruth, eh! They tried to catch the king asleep, did they! Must have been afraid to throw it when he was looking, for see what happened when he was.

And then, in the wake of Babe Ruth, came the Yankee attack, the New York shock troops, fierce and dauntless, fast moving and hard hitting. Look out, the Yanks are coming!

One the second ball pitched by Willie Sherdel, Gehrig came back with that big bat of his and hammered a homer to the roof of the right-field stand, close to the foul line. Ruth had tied the score, Gehrig had put his team ahead. What a pair! What men! Between them they had made this world's series a shamble, a source of humiliation and sorrow for the National League, which in eight straight games against this unbelievable Yankee team had met nothing but one-sided defeat.

And again the terrible Yankees swung into double trot and leaped into action. Meusel jabbed a single to left and Wee Willie Sherdel, protesting in vain, was taken out of the box—Willie Sherdel, who in four games against the Yanks had pitched well but had never won.

From the bullpen came Grover Cleveland Alexander, not so awe-inspiring as he had been two years ago when he shuffled in from another bullpen to stave off a Yankee attack.

Old Alex had some tough breaks today. Lazzeri raised a fly to left field which Hafey lost in a blinding October sun. Chick ran away from the ball instead of toward it, and Orsatti, though making a game try, got only his finger-tips on the leather.

This synthetic two-bagger advanced Meusel to third, and then Robertson, batting for Dugan, grounded to Frisch, who tried to nab Meusel at the plate, but was too late.

With Lazzeri on third, one out and the Yanks two runs ahead, Huggins pulled out Bengough. There was a commotion on the Yankee bench and then out strode a straight, graceful figure of a man, a trimly built fellow who admits no rivals in the centre-field business. In other words, Earl Combs, the Kentucky Rosebud.

## Graceful Act by Huggins.

This was the Combs who hurt his wrist and was put out of the series before it started, whose loss, it was feared, might wreck the Yankees' chances. Here he was now—coming in at the last moment—a graceful act on the part of Miller Huggins.

There didn't seem to be anything wrong with Earl's batting eye. He steamed a line drive to right with old-time vigor. Harper made a nice catch, but Lazzeri scored from third with the fourth run of as exciting an inning as was ever played.

Now the Yanks were three runs ahead, and after Hoyt had cut down the Cards in their half the Hugmen added two more in the eighth. Durst began it with a drive into the right field bleachers—the fourth Yankee homer. Alexander wasn't getting much on the ball.

When Ruth came up Alex threw a called strike and then essayed a curve on the inside corner. What a foolish mistake! What bad control by a man who was one of the masters of control! For the Babe met this ball squarely and drove it again to right, and, to show you how badly the Babe was slipping, this ball only hit on the roof of the pavilion. The big boy was certainly starting to slump.

Incidentally, all three homers were hit off curve balls on the inside of the plate. If an American League pitcher ever did such a thing three times in one afternoon, he would be given away to the South Norwalk club.

"I got two more 'cousins' to add to my list—Sherdel and Alexander," said the Babe after the game. "Cousin" is a baseball slang for a pitcher easy to hit. All the St. Louis pitchers are cousins of G. Herman, for it was at Sportsman's Park, two years ago, that he hit three homers in one game.

Though rapped for eleven hits, Hoyt pitched a careful and capable game and justified the claim that he is in the front rank of right-handed pitchers. His support was not good; in fact, for six innings the Yanks were far from impressive. Their fielding was mediocre and they had plenty of chances to score, but were feeble in the pinches. However, they are an old and steady team; they have been through the mill and enjoy unbounded confidence in themselves, and they never looked like a beaten team.

This team has something that every great person has—whether a great athlete or a great actor, or a great lawyer, or a great businessman. It has a certain intangible something, a confidence, almost cockiness, that it is the best team on earth. It has poise, aplomb, insouciance—a calm, sure faith in itself that shines forth and is radiated to the other team and the enemy crowd.

## Cards Awed and Beaten.

In this series the Cardinals were awed and beaten before they had swung a bat.

What a series it was, too; a gay, joyous romp for the American League, which is brimming with pride over the Yankees—and with some amazement, too, it must be admitted. Surely the junior circuit, founded twenty-eight years ago by Ban Johnson, had its biggest day this afternoon as its Yankee envoys scored their eighth successive victory over the older organization, to beat the former record by two.

And equally so, it was a day of bitterness and regrets for the National League, which could not even give the Yanks a run for their money in two successive Octobers.

In their hour of defeat the Cardinals need sympathy more than censure and so we shall not dwell on their shortcomings and failures. Naturally, they gave their best. Today, in a desperate effort to inject new life and blood into his team, Bill McKechnie benched Taylor Douthit and Jimmy Wilson, sending Ernie Orsatti to centre and Earl Smith behind the plate.

It was rather tough on Wilson to be taken out at this late date after he has been worn down to a shadow by the nerve-wracking task of catching almost every game the Cards have played since June.

*37,331 Paid $161,902 to See*
*Fourth Game of World's Series*

### STANDING.

|  | Won. | Lost. | Pct. |
|---|---|---|---|
| Yankees | 4 | 0 | 1.000 |
| Cardinals | 0 | 4 | .000 |

### SCORES.

First game—New York 4, St. Louis 1.
Second game—New York 9, St. Louis 3.
Third game—New York 7, St. Louis 3.
Fourth game—New York 7, St. Louis 3.

### FOURTH GAME.
*Paid attendance, 37,331.*

| | |
|---|---|
| Total receipts | $161,902.00 |
| Advisr'y Council's share | 16,190.20 |
| Players' share | 87,427.08 |
| Each club's share | 14,571.18 |
| Each league's share | 14,571.18 |

### TOTALS FOR SERIES.
*Paid attendance, 199,075.*

| | |
|---|---|
| Total receipts | $777,290.00 |
| Advisr'y Council's share | 77,729.00 |
| Players' share | 419,736.60 |
| Each club's share | 69,956.10 |
| Each league's share | 69,956.10 |

### Company for the Cards.

The Cardinals' great trouble was that they could not stop Ruth and Gehrig. In this great sorrow they have plenty of company, the company of seven American League clubs, including the Athletics.

The Cardinals played even worse ball than the Pirates last October and it is the only barb we care to shoot at them. Not another team in baseball could have beaten the Yanks in this series, so why pick on the poor old Cardinals, who are now down and out and have received all the kicks that the human system can assimilate in any given space of time?

Anyway, what the Yanks have done in their last two world's series has been incredible and super-human. They can't be weighed and measured by ordinary standards as long as they have two fiends in human form like G. Herman Ruth and H. Louis Gehrig, by far the two greatest ball players ever on one team.

Babe Ruth

Always we will remember Babe Ruth today—as he ran around the bases after those three homers, as he picked up pop bottles in left field and kidded with the crowd before turning his back on that menacing throng. But particularly we shall remember him as he looked when he charged along the foul line and in front of the field boxes—230 pounds of the best ball player that ever lived—swerving in toward the wooden railing, his gloved right hand outstretched and his legs pounding while fans stood up and pelted paper missives at him.

## Holds the Ball Aloft.

Then we shall remember how he caught that baseball incredibly and held it up for the world to see in his right hand. Of all our baseball memories that shall be the clearest-etched and most unforgettable. Ruth, indomitable, unconquerable, triumphant. An amazing man, this George Herman Ruth.

The Cardinals had a grand opening in the first inning, but what is a little thing like an opening to the Cards? With one out, Ruth, blinded by the sun, let High's easy fly fall safely for a two-bagger, but Hoyt fanned Frisch at three and two, walked Bottomley, and then stopped Hafey on a feeble grounder to the box.

More St. Louis ineptness in the second. Smith singled with one gone. McKechnie flashed the hit-and-run sign, but Hoyt threw that particular pitch at Maranville's head and Smitty was out standing up at second, whereupon the Rabbit socked a double to right, Meusel playing in none too well, but Sherdel bounded to Gehrig.

Finally the Cards scored a run. To open the third Orsatti planted a fly in short centre and by daring base running made two bases. Pascal should have had him at second. High caught the Yanks off guard and beat out a bunt, and Frisch contributed a sacrifice fly which scored Orsatti. Bottomley and Harper, the latter striking out, chloroformed a promising rally.

The Cards worked hard for that tally and the Yanks made theirs with a minimum of labor. The Babe led off the fourth in an admirable fashion, sending a liner whistling over the right field stand. The count was two balls and one strike and Sherdel would have been satisfied to make it four and nothing. He slipped a curve six inches inside the plate—a bad ball obviously—but Ruth stepped away from it and nailed the ball half way down his bat and gave it a long ride.

Sherdel followed by walking Gehrig, Meusel flied deep to Orsatti, Lazzeri singled to left—his first hit of the series—but Dugan and Bengoug were unable to come through with assistance.

Koenig was a Santa Claus in the fourth and made the Cards a present of a run. After Smith had singled he was forced by Maranville. Koenig had a sure double play in sight but made the wildest wild throw on record, heaving the ball into the lap of a spectator fifteen rows back in the grandstand. Maranville, of course, went to second.

Sherdel flied to centre, and with Orsatti at bat the Yankees baited a trap for Maranville. The idea was for Bengoug to return the ball to Hoyt who would wheel quickly and throw to Koenig, who meanwhile would have sneaked up behind Maranville.

## Koenig Misses Signal.

The thing worked perfectly except that Koenig missed the signal and failed to do any sneaking. And so when Hoyt turned and threw, there was no Yankee at second and the pill, naturally enough, went on to centre field while Maranville churned for the plate and scored.

Hoyt and Pascal singled with none out in the fifth, but the Yanks couldn't move a wheel. Koenig popped to Frisch, Ruth grounded to Bottomley, Gehrig walked and Meusel forced out Columbia Lou.

Again in the sixth the first two Yankees, Lazzeri and Dugan, hit singles, but the next three worthies were a total loss.

You know all about the riotous doings of the seventh frame. In the eighth Cedric Durst whaled a homer into the right field stand and Ruth did likewise.

The Cardinals scored once in the ninth with the consent of Mr. Hoyt, who let Martin, who ran for Smith, run wild on the bases and score on a single by High.

The paid attendance for today was 37,331, bringing the total paid attendance for the four games to 199,075, which is short of the total for four games last year. The total receipts were $777,290. The receipts for today were $166,902.

## OFFICIAL BOX SCORE OF FOURTH WORLD'S SERIES GAME

### NEW YORK YANKEES.

| | AB. | R. | H. | TB. | 2B. | 3B. | HR. | BB. | SO. | SH. | SB. | PO. | A. | E. |
|---|---|---|---|---|---|---|---|---|---|---|---|---|---|---|
| Pascal, cf | 4 | 0 | 1 | 1 | 0 | 0 | 0 | 0 | 0 | 0 | 0 | 3 | 0 | 0 |
| Durst, cf | 1 | 1 | 1 | 4 | 0 | 0 | 1 | 0 | 0 | 0 | 0 | 0 | 0 | 0 |
| Koenig, ss | 5 | 0 | 1 | 1 | 0 | 0 | 0 | 0 | 0 | 0 | 0 | 4 | 2 | 1 |
| Ruth, lf | 5 | 3 | 3 | 12 | 0 | 0 | 3 | 0 | 0 | 0 | 0 | 2 | 0 | 0 |
| Gehrig, 1b. | 2 | 1 | 1 | 4 | 0 | 0 | 1 | 3 | 0 | 0 | 0 | 7 | 0 | 0 |
| Meusel, rf | 5 | 1 | 1 | 1 | 0 | 0 | 0 | 0 | 2 | 0 | 0 | 0 | 0 | 0 |
| Lazzeri, 2b | 4 | 1 | 3 | 4 | 1 | 0 | 0 | 0 | 0 | 0 | 1 | 1 | 2 | 0 |
| Durocher, 2b | 1 | 0 | 0 | 0 | 0 | 0 | 0 | 0 | 0 | 0 | 0 | 0 | 0 | 0 |
| Dugan, 3b | 3 | 0 | 1 | 1 | 0 | 0 | 0 | 0 | 0 | 0 | 0 | 0 | 0 | 0 |
| Robertson, 3b | 2 | 0 | 0 | 0 | 0 | 0 | 0 | 0 | 0 | 0 | 0 | 0 | 0 | 0 |
| Bengough, c | 3 | 0 | 1 | 1 | 0 | 0 | 0 | 0 | 0 | 0 | 0 | 8 | 1 | 0 |
| [a]Combs | 0 | 0 | 0 | 0 | 0 | 0 | 0 | 0 | 0 | 1 | 0 | 0 | 0 | 0 |
| Collins, c | 1 | 0 | 1 | 2 | 1 | 0 | 0 | 0 | 0 | 0 | 0 | 2 | 0 | 0 |
| Hoyt, p | 4 | 0 | 1 | 1 | 0 | 0 | 0 | 0 | 0 | 1 | 0 | 0 | 2 | 1 |
| Total | 40 | 7 | 15 | 32 | 2 | 0 | 5 | 3 | 2 | 2 | 1 | 27 | 7 | 2 |

[a]Batted for Bengough in the seventh.

### ST. LOUIS CARDINALS

| | AB. | R. | H. | TB. | 2B. | 3B. | HR. | BB. | SO. | SH. | SB. | PO. | A. | E. |
|---|---|---|---|---|---|---|---|---|---|---|---|---|---|---|
| Orsatti, cf | 5 | 1 | 2 | 3 | 1 | 0 | 0 | 0 | 2 | 0 | 0 | 4 | 0 | 0 |
| High, 3b | 5 | 0 | 3 | 4 | 1 | 0 | 0 | 0 | 0 | 0 | 0 | 0 | 1 | 0 |
| Frisch, 2b | 4 | 0 | 0 | 0 | 0 | 0 | 0 | 0 | 1 | 1 | 0 | 3 | 1 | 0 |
| Bottomley,1b | 3 | 0 | 0 | 0 | 0 | 0 | 0 | 1 | 2 | 0 | 0 | 10 | 1 | 0 |
| Hafey, lf | 3 | 0 | 1 | 1 | 0 | 0 | 0 | 1 | 1 | 0 | 0 | 1 | 0 | 0 |
| Harper, rf | 3 | 0 | 0 | 0 | 0 | 0 | 0 | 1 | 1 | 0 | 0 | 2 | 0 | 0 |
| Smith, c | 4 | 0 | 3 | 3 | 0 | 0 | 0 | 0 | 0 | 0 | 0 | 4 | 1 | 0 |
| [a]Martin | 0 | 1 | 0 | 0 | 0 | 0 | 0 | 0 | 0 | 0 | 0 | 0 | 0 | 0 |
| Maranville, ss | 4 | 1 | 2 | 3 | 1 | 0 | 0 | 0 | 0 | 0 | 1 | 3 | 1 | 0 |
| Sherdel, p | 3 | 0 | 0 | 0 | 0 | 0 | 0 | 0 | 1 | 0 | 0 | 0 | 0 | 0 |
| Alexander, p | 0 | 0 | 0 | 0 | 0 | 0 | 0 | 0 | 0 | 0 | 0 | 0 | 3 | 0 |
| [b]Holm | 1 | 0 | 0 | 0 | 0 | 0 | 0 | 0 | 0 | 0 | 0 | 0 | 0 | 0 |
| Total | 35 | 3 | 11 | 14 | 3 | 0 | 0 | 3 | 8 | 1 | 1 | 27 | 8 | 0 |

[a]Ran for Smith in the ninth.
[b]Batted for Alexander in the ninth.

| | | | | | | | | | | |
|---|---|---|---|---|---|---|---|---|---|---|
| New York | 0 | 0 | 0 | 1 | 0 | 0 | 4 | 2 | 0—7 |
| St. Louis | 0 | 0 | 1 | 1 | 0 | 0 | 0 | 0 | 1—3 |

Runs batted in—New York: Ruth 3, Durst 1, Gehrig 1, Robertson 1, Combs 1. St. Louis: Frisch 1, Holm 1. Double plays—Koenig and Gehrig, Bottomley and Maranville. Left on bases—New York 11, St. Louis 9. Bases on Balls—Off Hoyt 3, Sherdel 3. Struck out—By Hoyt 8, Sherdel 1, Alexander 1. Hits—Off Sherdel, 11 in 6 1–3 innings; Alexander 4 in 2 2–3. Losing pitcher—Sherdel. Umpires—Pfirman (N.L.) at plate, Owens (A.L.) at first base, Rigler (N.L.) at second base, McGowan (A.L.) at third base. Time of game—2:25.

---

October 10, 1928

## Cardinals' Fate Is Settled by Powerful Attack of Yankees, Including 5 Homers

### YANKEE HOMERS PUT CARDINALS TO ROUT

### Siege Guns Get Into Action in Seventh After Sherdal Stems Them for Six Innings.

### CARDS WITHER UNDER FIRE

### Hoyt Eases Up With Lead Secure and Permits One Extra Run—Touched for 11 Hits.

### RUTH'S START IS WEAK

### Hits Into Double Play in the First Inning, but Makes It Up With Three Circuit Wallops.

### By RICHARDS VIDMER.

*Special to The New York Times.*

ST. LOUIS, Oct. 9.—The Yankees said it with homers! The conventional way is to say it with flowers, but the flowers today were for the Cards. They were funeral wreaths.

Under the greatest display of power outside Niagara Falls the Yanks buried the champions of the National League in the fourth and final game of the world's series. The Cards struggled and strained with might and main to keep their heads above sea level. Through six sensational innings they toiled and moiled, fretted and fumed and fought, and at the end of that strenuous, sweating siege they had made just two runs.

It was one more run than the Yankees had made, but the game was not yet over. The caissons hadn't rolled

Babe Ruth and his wife after a fishing trip in 1929. (Times Wide World Photos, Washington Bureau)

## Homers Kill Cards' Chances.

What a little rabbit had run his legs off to accomplish, what a little left-hander had pitched his heart out to hold, the mastodon maulers with their murderous maces wiped out in a flash. And they laughed in derision. They said it with homers.

The Cards had made two runs by the effort and energy born of desperation and a dying desire, but the Yankees said it with homers. Gehrig hit one, Durst hit one and Babe Ruth hit three. Those five furious flashes ended the last ray of hope for Cardinals cohorts. They ended the world's series of 1928. They broke the Cardinals' back and a little pitcher's heart. The Yankees are the Yankees still and the Yankees are champions of the world.

There were other tallies later on, scores that meant nothing and might never have happened if the heavy artillery had fired only blanks. The final score was 7 to 5, but the homers sent the Yankees home victorious in four successive games for the second series in a row.

Wee Willie Sherdel, the Lilliputian left-hander, stood on the mound and held off the annihilating attack of the mastodons for six struggling sessions. Rabbit Maranville ran his legs off, even against his manager's orders, to gain a lead for the Lilliputian. But Sherdel pitched in vain. The Rabbit's running got him nowhere. The Yankees thundered to triumph.

Even a couple of their colossal clouts would have been sufficient behind the praiseworthy pitching of

Waite Hoyt, who could have held the Cards to two runs instead of three and would have if it had been necessary, but once a gigantic body starts rolling it doesn't stop suddenly.

## Hoyt Yields Eleven Hits.

Hoyt gave the Cardinals eleven hits today where he gave them only three in the first game of the series. He gave them three runs where they made only one in the opener. Yet he pitched just as well if not better because when the crisis came he was stronger, steadier and more certain.

Koenig singled in the Yankees' half of the first but Ruth hit into a double play to end the inning. In the Cardinals' half of the same session High flied to left for what should have been the second out, but Ruth was playing the sun field and it fell for a double. As a rule left field is the shade section in the St. Louis park but with the games starting earlier than usual the glare was in that direction today.

After High's dubious double, Hoyt struck out Frisch, more in anger than in sorrow, but he walked Bottomley. That gave the Cards a chance to score, but they didn't. Hoyt was himself again and Hafey bounced to the box.

In the second there was another moment of anxiety. With one out Smith walked and Maranville doubled, but before the Rabbit's punch Hoyt had broken up a hit and run play. Somehow he sensed the situation and when Smith went lumbering into second, Hoyt shot the ball straight at Maranville's midsection. Instead of hitting, the Rabbit had to keep from being hit and Smith was thrown out. So the Rabbit's double that followed drove nobody home. There was nobody to be driven home.

Bengough made the longest single on record to start the third for the Yanks, the ball hitting the left field fence on the first bounce, but Hafey was waiting for it on the rebound and his throw to second would have headed off any one less fleet than mercury. Bengough is less fleet than the winged-footed god and wisely held first.

But nothing came of that drive. Hoyt neatly sacrificed Bengough to second but High stopped Paschal's drive with one hand and the Yankees with the same gesture. So it was not until the last half of the third that the scoreless tie was broken.

Orsatti doubled to center to start with, but only because he was more desperate than smart. The hit was a mere Texas leaguer back of second base which Paschal couldn't catch no matter how fast he ran in. Orsatti, however, not being satisfied, even thankful, at getting such a lucky single, kept right on going to second. It looked like public suicide, but Paschal's throw was low and wide and the understudy comedian—Orsatti used to double for Buster Keaton in the movies—reached his destination in safety.

High then dragged a bunt down the first base line which was perfection. Gehrig had to take the ball and no one could get to first in time to cover, so Orsatti reached third. Then Frisch hit a long fly to Paschal and Orsatti scored the first run of the game after the catch.

The Cardinals had struggled desperately for that tally and they were joyous at being one run ahead, but their joy turned to dejection a moment later. All that they had accomplished by squeezing and squirming Babe Ruth did with one mighty wave of his bludgeon. He bounced the ball off the right-field roof for a home run. It was only his first, but it tied the score.

A tie wasn't enough, though. It wasn't nearly enough. In the Cardinals' half of the same inning they forged to the front again, because the Rabbit was smarter than his manager. Smith singled to start the inning, but Maranville forced him at second and when Koenig, trying to complete a double play, threw the ball into the first base boxes the Rabbit scampered on to the half-way mark.

Sherdel flied to Paschal for the second out and Orsatti fanned for the third out, but before he did the Rabbit scampered home. He lingered off second and drew a quick throw from Hoyt in an attempt to catch him.

Hoyt's throw was perfect except for one thing. There was no one there to catch it. Though Hoyt didn't notice this until after the ball left his hands, the Rabbit did and he streaked toward third like a flash.

### Ignores McKechnie's Signals.

As Maranville rounded third he saw the waving hands of Bill McKechnie, his boss, frantically signaling him to stop. But the Rabbit paid no heed. Over the bag he sped and started for home without hesitating, while McKechnie had apoplexy. But the Rabbit kept on and scored. Once more the Cardinals were ahead, but that was the last time they ever were to be.

Through the fifth and sixth innings Sherdel fought the Yankees off. They filled the bases with two out in the fifth, but a brilliant play by Maranville on a hit by Meusel that would have driven in at least two runs had it escaped the Rabbit's clutches stopped them. Lazzeri and Dugan both hit safely before any one was out to start the sixth, and later Lazzeri stole third. But no one would drive either them home. Then in the seventh the caissons came dolling along.

The Babe was the first man up. Sherdel slipped two strikes over the plate without pitching a ball. Then the Babe wasn't looking. Straight through the center of the plate the white streak sped before the Babe could get himself set, but it didn't count.

There's a rule in the American League that nullifies quick pitches. There's no such rule in the National and Sherdel thought it was worth trying. But there was an agreement before the series started that the American League rule would prevail in such a case, and Ruth only laughed while the Cardinals cried.

Then, still laughing, the Behemothian Babe hit the ball over the roof of the right field stands, tying the score once more. After that, death and destruction followed. Gehrig hit his fourth home run of the series over the roof of the same section of seats immediately and Sherdel's heart was broken. When Meusel followed with a single to left he gave up and Grover Cleveland Alexander came in to take his place and do what he could to quell the riot which so suddenly had broken out.

### Yanks Keep Up the Pace.

But Alex could do nothing about it. The Yanks had started and they wouldn't be stopped. Lazzeri doubled, Robertson grounded to Frisch, who tried to head off Meusel at the plate and got no one. Combs, batting for Bengough, hit a sacrifice fly that scored Lazzeri and four runs were in. The Yanks were three runs ahead.

They showered pop bottles at Ruth when he took his place in left field, the bleacher boys laboring under the belief that he really was struck out by Sherdel's quick pitch. But they were standing up and cheering for him when he came out again in the eighth, for in the first half of that inning Durst hit a home run and the Babe followed with his third of the day, one of the longest he ever hit anywhere and repeating the performance he put on here in the series of 1926, when the Cards beat the Yankees for the diadem of the diamond. They got their revenge for that today.

### COMPOSITE SCORE OF WORLD'S SERIES GAMES

G., games; A.B., at bat; R., runs; H., hits; T.B., total bases; 2B., two-base hits; 3B., three-base hits; H.R., home runs; B.B., bases on balls; S.O., struck out; S.B., stolen bases; Bat. Ave., batting averages; P.O., put outs; A., assists; E., errors; T.C., total chances; Flfg. Ave., fielding average.

*(continued)*

## NEW YORK YANKEES

| | G | AB | R | H | TB | 2B | 3B | HR | BB | SO | SB | Bat Ave | PO | A | E | TC | Fldg Ave |
|---|---|---|---|---|---|---|---|---|---|---|---|---|---|---|---|---|---|
| Paschal, cf | 3 | 10 | 0 | 2 | 2 | 0 | 0 | 0 | 1 | 0 | 0 | .200 | 8 | 0 | 0 | 8 | 1.000 |
| Durst, cf | 4 | 8 | 3 | 3 | 6 | 0 | 0 | 1 | 0 | 1 | 0 | .375 | 3 | 0 | 0 | 3 | 1.000 |
| Koenig, ss | 4 | 19 | 1 | 3 | 3 | 0 | 0 | 0 | 0 | 1 | 0 | .158 | 8 | 11 | 2 | 21 | .905 |
| Ruth, rf., lf | 4 | 16 | 9 | 10 | 22 | 3 | 0 | 3 | 1 | 2 | 0 | .625 | 8 | 1 | 0 | 9 | 1.000 |
| Gehrig, 1b | 4 | 11 | 5 | 6 | 19 | 1 | 0 | 4 | 6 | 0 | 0 | .545 | 33 | 0 | 0 | 33 | 1.000 |
| Meusel, lf., rf | 4 | 15 | 5 | 3 | 7 | 1 | 0 | 1 | 2 | 5 | 2 | .200 | 5 | 0 | 0 | 5 | 1.000 |
| Lazzeri, 2b | 4 | 12 | 2 | 3 | 4 | 1 | 0 | 0 | 1 | 0 | 2 | .250 | 2 | 7 | 2 | 11 | .818 |
| Durocher, 2b | 4 | 2 | 0 | 0 | 0 | 0 | 0 | 0 | 0 | 1 | 0 | .000 | 1 | 1 | 0 | 2 | 1.000 |
| Dugan, 3b | 3 | 6 | 0 | 1 | 1 | 0 | 0 | 0 | 0 | 0 | 0 | .167 | 3 | 0 | 0 | 3 | 1.000 |
| Robertson, 3b | 3 | 8 | 1 | 1 | 1 | 0 | 0 | 0 | 1 | 0 | 0 | .125 | 2 | 1 | 1 | 4 | .750 |
| Bengough, c | 4 | 13 | 1 | 3 | 3 | 0 | 0 | 0 | 1 | 1 | 0 | .231 | 33 | 2 | 0 | 35 | 1.000 |
| Collins, c | 1 | 1 | 0 | 1 | 2 | 1 | 0 | 0 | 0 | 0 | 0 | 1.000 | 0 | 0 | 0 | 2 | 1.000 |
| Hoyt, p | 2 | 7 | 0 | 1 | 1 | 0 | 0 | 0 | 0 | 0 | 0 | .143 | 0 | 3 | 1 | 4 | .750 |
| Pipgras, p | 1 | 2 | 0 | 0 | 0 | 0 | 0 | 0 | 0 | 0 | 0 | .000 | 0 | 1 | 0 | 1 | 1.000 |
| Zachary, p | 1 | 4 | 0 | 0 | 0 | 0 | 0 | 0 | 0 | 1 | 0 | .000 | 0 | 1 | 0 | 1 | 1.000 |
| *Combs | 1 | 0 | 0 | 0 | 0 | 0 | 0 | 0 | 0 | 0 | 0 | .000 | 0 | 0 | 0 | 0 | .000 |
| Total | | 134 | 27 | 37 | 71 | 7 | 0 | 9 | 13 | 12 | 4 | .276 | 103 | 28 | 6 | 142 | .958 |

*Pinch hitter

## ST. LOUIS CARDINALS

| | G | AB | R | H | TB | 2B | 3B | HR | BB | SO | SB | Bat Ave | PO | A | E | TC | Fldg Ave |
|---|---|---|---|---|---|---|---|---|---|---|---|---|---|---|---|---|---|
| Douthit, cf | 3 | 11 | 1 | 1 | 1 | 0 | 0 | 0 | 1 | 1 | 0 | .091 | 6 | 1 | 0 | 7 | 1.000 |
| Orsatti, cf | 4 | 7 | 1 | 2 | 3 | 1 | 0 | 0 | 1 | 3 | 0 | .286 | 4 | 0 | 0 | 4 | 1.000 |
| High, 3b | 4 | 17 | 1 | 5 | 7 | 2 | 0 | 0 | 1 | 3 | 0 | .294 | 2 | 5 | 0 | 7 | 1.000 |
| Frisch, 2b | 4 | 13 | 1 | 3 | 3 | 0 | 0 | 0 | 2 | 2 | 2 | .231 | 8 | 14 | 0 | 22 | 1.000 |
| Bottomley, 1b | 4 | 14 | 1 | 3 | 8 | 0 | 1 | 1 | 2 | 6 | 0 | .214 | 35 | 2 | 0 | 37 | 1.000 |
| Hafey, lf | 4 | 15 | 0 | 3 | 3 | 0 | 0 | 0 | 1 | 4 | 0 | .200 | 8 | 0 | 1 | 9 | .889 |
| Harper, rf | 3 | 9 | 1 | 1 | 1 | 0 | 0 | 0 | 2 | 2 | 0 | .111 | 5 | 0 | 0 | 5 | 1.000 |
| Holm, rf | 3 | 6 | 0 | 1 | 1 | 0 | 0 | 0 | 0 | 1 | 0 | .167 | 4 | 0 | 0 | 4 | 1.000 |
| Wilson, c | 3 | 11 | 1 | 1 | 2 | 1 | 0 | 0 | 0 | 3 | 0 | .091 | 14 | 2 | 2 | 18 | .889 |
| Smith, c | 1 | 4 | 0 | 3 | 3 | 0 | 0 | 0 | 0 | 0 | 0 | .750 | 4 | 1 | 0 | 5 | 1.000 |
| Maranville, ss | 4 | 13 | 2 | 4 | 5 | 1 | 0 | 0 | 1 | 1 | 1 | .308 | 11 | 3 | 1 | 15 | .933 |
| Thevenow, ss | 1 | 0 | 0 | 0 | 0 | 0 | 0 | 0 | 0 | 0 | 0 | .000 | 1 | 0 | 0 | 1 | 1.000 |
| Sherdel, p | 2 | 5 | 0 | 0 | 0 | 0 | 0 | 0 | 0 | 2 | 0 | .000 | 0 | 3 | 0 | 3 | 1.000 |
| S. Johnson, p | 2 | 0 | 0 | 0 | 0 | 0 | 0 | 0 | 0 | 0 | 0 | .000 | 0 | 0 | 0 | 0 | .000 |
| Alexander, p | 2 | 1 | 0 | 0 | 0 | 0 | 0 | 0 | 0 | 0 | 0 | .000 | 0 | 4 | 0 | 4 | 1.000 |
| Mitchell, p | 1 | 2 | 0 | 0 | 0 | 0 | 0 | 0 | 0 | 0 | 0 | .000 | 0 | 1 | 1 | 2 | .500 |
| Haines, p | 1 | 2 | 0 | 0 | 0 | 0 | 0 | 0 | 0 | 0 | 0 | .000 | 0 | 1 | 0 | 1 | 1.000 |
| Rhem, p | 1 | 0 | 0 | 0 | 0 | 0 | 0 | 0 | 0 | 0 | 0 | .000 | 0 | 0 | 0 | 0 | .000 |
| *Blades | 1 | 1 | 0 | 0 | 0 | 0 | 0 | 0 | 0 | 1 | 0 | .000 | 0 | 0 | 0 | 0 | .000 |
| †Martin | 1 | 0 | 1 | 0 | 0 | 0 | 0 | 0 | 0 | 0 | 0 | .000 | 0 | 0 | 0 | 0 | .000 |
| Total | | 131 | 10 | 27 | 37 | 5 | 1 | 1 | 11 | 29 | 3 | .206 | 102 | 37 | 5 | 144 | .965 |

(*continued*)

COMPOSITE SCORE BY INNINGS

| | | | | | | | | | |
|---|---|---|---|---|---|---|---|---|---|
| New York | 4 | 2 | 4 | 5 | 0 | 3 | 6 | 3 | 0—27 |
| St. Louis | 2 | 3 | 1 | 1 | 1 | 0 | 1 | 0 | 1—10 |

Runs batted in—New York: Gehrig 9, Ruth 4, Meusel 3, Durst 3, Robertson 2, Paschal 1, Dugan 1, Bengough 1, Pipgras 1. St. Louis: Bottomley 3, Douthit 1, High 1, Frisch 1, Holm 1, Wilson 1, Alexander 1.

Games won—New York 4, St. Louis 0. Pitchers' records—Games won, Hoyt 2, Pipgras 1, Zachary 1; games lost, Sherdel 2, Alexander 1, Haines 1. Hits—Off Hoyt 14 in 18 innings, Pipgras 4 in 9, Zachary 9 in 9, Sherdel 15 in 13 1–3, S. Johnson 4 in 2, Alexander 10 in 5, Mitchell 2 in 5 2–3, Haines 6 in 6, Rhem 0 in 2. Bases on balls—Off Hoyt 6, Pipgras 4, Zachary 1, Sherdel 3, Alexander 4, Mitchell 2, Haines 3, S. Johnson 1. Struck out—By Hoyt 14, Pipgras 8, Zachary 7, Sherdel 3, Alexander 2, Mitchell 2, Haines 3, S. Johnson 1, Rhem 1. Hit by pitcher—By Mitchell (Pipgras), by Zachary (Douthit). Sacrifices—Lazzeri, Dugan, Pipgras, Combs, Hoyt, Frisch 2. Double plays—Koenig, Lazzeri and Gehrig; Koenig, Durocher and Gehrig; Koenig and Gehrig; Frisch, Maranville and Bottomley; High, Frisch and Bottomley; Bottomley and Maranville. Left on bases—New York 24, St. Louis 27.

---

October 2, 1932

# YANKEES BEAT CUBS FOR 3D IN ROW, 7–5, AS 51,000 LOOK ON

---

## Ruth and Gehrig, Each With 2 Homers, Set Pace as New York Nears Series Title.

---

### BABE'S FIRST TALLIES 3

---

#### His Second Brings Wild Acclaim—Hartnett and Cuyler Also Deliver Circuit Drives.

---

### PENNOCK STARTS ON MOUND

---

#### Veteran Relieves Pipgras in Ninth and Halts Chicago Rally—Governor Roosevelt in Crowd.

---

### By JOHN DREBINGER.

CHICAGO, Oct. 1.—Four home runs, two by the master hitter of them all, Babe Ruth, and the other pair by his almost equally proficient colleague, Columbia Lou Gehrig, advanced the New York Yankees to within one game of their third world's series sweep today.

The American League champions once again overpowered the Cubs to win their third straight game of the current classic which, for the first time, went on display in this city.

A Big Gun Fires a Shot on the Links at Mamaroneck: Babe Ruth plays a round of golf as part of his preseason training. (Times Wide World Photos)

Those four blows made the final score 7 to 5. They crushed not only the National League standard-bearers, but a gathering of 51,000 which jammed Wrigley Field to the limits of its capacity and packed two wooden temporary bleachers outside the park. Included in the gathering was Governor Roosevelt of New York, the Democratic Presidential candidate.

It was by far the most turbulent and bitterly fought engagement of the series thus far. The Cubs, inspired by a show of civic enthusiasm, battled fiercely and courageously.

They even struck back with a couple of lusty homers on their own account, one by Kiki Cuyler, the other by Gabby Hartnett.

### Wallop Retires Pipgras.

Hartnett's wallop came in the ninth and brought about the retirement of George Pipgras, the first Yankee pitcher to appear in the series who had also taken part in the clean-sweep triumphs of 1927 and 1928.

But this move merely provided a setting that added still further to the glamour of the Yankee triumph. For it brought on the scene one of the greatest world's series pitchers of all time, the talented Herbie Pennock, who started pitching in these classics back in 1914. In that long interval he had recorded five personal triumphs without a single defeat. Consequently he did not mean to let this game slip from his fingers even though credit for the victory still would remain with Pipgras.

In short, the famous Squire of Kennett Square sharply halted the belated Cub rally, fairly smothering the desperate bid of the Chicagoans with consummate ease and skill.

With a Cub lurking on the base paths poised to dart for the plate, Pennock fanned a pinch-hitter and retired the next two on soft infield taps, one of which he fielded himself. The other was snared by Gehrig for the final put-out.

## Chance to Add to Record.

Thus, with three victories tucked away against no defeats, the Yankees, now skillfully piloted by Joe McCarthy, who bossed these same Cubs only two years ago, have advanced to a point where they need only one more game to clinch the world's championship. In addition they have a chance to add still further to their remarkable world's series record. They have now completed eleven straight series encounters without suffering a single reversal.

Both the game and all its trimmings provided a much livelier spectacle than either of the two previous encounters. In sharp contrast to the rather matter-of-fact manner in which New York had accepted the first two battles, the crowd today was as keyed up as the players, if not more so.

It was a warm day, clear and sunny, though rather windy. There was a gay, holiday spirit in the air that never forsook the gathering, for Chicago puts a great deal more fervor in its baseball than does New York. It seemed as though the fans of this mid-Western metropolis simply would not believe how severely and decisively their champions had been manhandled by the mighty Yankees in the first two games in the East.

## Ruth's Drive Awes Throng.

They roared their approval of every good play made by the Cubs. They playfully tossed bright yellow lemons at Babe Ruth and booed him thoroughly as the great man carried on a pantomime act while standing at the plate.

Then they sat back, awed and spellbound, as the Babe, casting aside his buffoonery, smashed one of the longest home runs ever seen at Wrigley Field.

It was an amazing demonstration by baseball's outstanding figure, who a few weeks ago was ill and confined to his bed. It confounded the crowd, which in paid attendance numbered 49,986 and which had contributed $211,912 in receipts.

The Cubs took the field with their hopes resting upon the stout right arm of Charlie Root, but Charlie was unequal to the task. He failed to survive five rounds, retiring immediately after Ruth and Gehrig had blasted their second two homers. These came in succession in the fifth like a flash of lightning and a clap of thunder.

Both were held fairly well in restraint in the latter rounds by Pat Malone and the left-handed Jackie May. But aside from providing the crowd with a chance to give vent to boos, the earlier damage these two had inflicted proved far sufficient to carry the day.

Ruth and Gehrig simply dominated the scene from start to finish, and they began their performance early. When the two marched to the plate during the batting rehearsal they at once thrilled the crowd by uncorking a series of tremendous drives into the temporary wooden bleachers.

## Almost Clears Bleachers.

The Babe's very first practice shot almost cleared the top of the wooden structure, and he followed it with several more prodigious drives. Gehrig produced some more, and each time the ball soared into those densely packed stands the crowd gasped. The spectacle certainly could not have been very heartening to the Cubs.

And when the battle proper began, both kept right on firing. The Babe's two homers were his first in the current series, but they sent his all-time world's series record for home runs to fifteen. For Gehrig, his two gave him a total of three for the series and an all-time record of seven.

Fittingly enough, the Babe was the first to touch off the explosion and his opening smash sent the Yanks away to a three-run lead in the very first inning. In fact, the crowd had scarcely recovered its composure after it had accorded a tumultuous reception when it was forced to suffer its first annoyance.

There was a sharp wind blowing across the playing field toward the right-field bleachers that threatened to raise havoc with the players, and it did very shortly.

### Jurges Makes Wild Throw.

Eager and tense, the crowd watched Root pitch to Earle Combs, the first Yankee batter. It at once roared approbation as Combs sent a drive squarely into the hands of young Billy Jurges who was again playing short-stop for the Cubs in place of the injured Mark Koenig.

But the next moment the throng voiced its dismay as Jurges unfurled a throw that sailed high over Manager Charlie Grimm's head at first and into the Yankee dugout.

Root was plainly flustered as Combs, under the prevailing ground rule, was allowed to advance to second base. Root strove to steady himself, but he passed Joey Sewell and faced Ruth. Cheers and jeers mingled as the great Yankee batter made his first official appearance at the plate in Chicago's portion of the setting.

Root pitched cautiously, fearful of what would happen if he allowed the Babe to shoot one high in the air with the brisk breeze behind it. His first two offerings went wide of the plate. Then he put one over, and away the ball went. It was a lofty shot that soared on and on until it dropped deep in the temporary stands. Thus, the Cubs, who had planned to fight so desperately for this game, already were three runs to the bad.

### Cubs Fight Courageously.

But desperately they fought, nevertheless, and in the lower half of the same inning they gave their cohorts the chance to do some whole-hearted cheering by getting one of these tallies back.

The wind, which had annoyed Root so much, also seemed to trouble Pipgras. He passed Herman, where-upon the crowd set up a roar as though the series already had been won. Woody English was retired on a fly to Ruth, who was performing in left field today in order to avoid the glare of the sun.

But Kiki Cuyler, who might have been the hero of this struggle had Ruth and Gehrig been playing else-where, lifted a two-bagger over Ben Chapman's head in right against the wire screening in front of the bleach-ers, and Herman scored amid tumultuous cheering.

But two innings later Gehrig, after an uneventful first inning, stepped into the picture. Leaning heavily into Root's pitch, he sent another mighty shot soaring into the right-field bleachers. That made the score 4 to 1.

At this point, however, the Cubs staged their most gallant fight of the day. With one out in the lower half of the third, Cuyler again produced a jubilant uproar by shooting a homer into the right-field stands, and this at once inspired his comrades to redouble their efforts against Pipgras. Stephenson slashed a single to right, and though he was forced by Johnny Moore Manager Grimm lined a drive to right that Chapman did not play any too well. The ball shot past the Alabama arrow for a two-bagger and Moore scored all the way from first.

That left the Cubs only one run in arrears, and in the fourth they drew even amid the most violent vocal demonstration of the afternoon. Jurges, eager to make amends for his earlier miscue, slapped a low liner to left, and the crowd howled with glee as Ruth failed in a heroic attempt to make a shoe-string catch of the ball. Jurges gained two bases on the hit.

## Ruth Doffs His Cap.

Good naturedly, the Babe doffed his cap in acknowledgment to the adverse plaudits of the fans and the play went on. Tony Lazzeri made a spectacular catch of Herman's high, twisting pop-fly back of second base. But the next moment Tony booted English's grounder and Jurges raced over the plate with the tally that tied the score at 4-all.

But it seems decidedly unhealthy for any one to taunt the great man Ruth too much and very soon the crowd was to learn its lesson. A single lemon rolled out to the plate as Ruth came up in the fifth and in no mistaken motion the Babe notified the crowd that the nature of his retaliation would be a wallop right out the confines of the park.

Root pitched two balls and two strikes, while Ruth signaled with his fingers after each pitch to let the spectators know exactly how the situation stood. Then the mightiest blow of all fell.

It was a tremendous smash that bore straight down the centre of the field in an enormous arc, came down alongside the flagpole and disappeared behind the corner formed by the scoreboard and the end of the right-field bleachers.

---

### *49,986 Fans Paid $211,912*
### *At Third World's Series Game*

#### STANDING OF THE CLUBS.

|                | Won. | Lost. | P.C. |
|----------------|------|-------|------|
| Yankees        | 3    | 0     | 1.000 |
| Cubs           | 0    | 3     | .000 |

#### THIRD GAME STATISTICS.

| | |
|---|---|
| Attendance (paid) | 49,986 |
| Receipts | $211,912.00 |
| Commissioner's share | 31,786.80 |
| Players' share | 108,075.12 |
| Each club's share | 18,012.52 |
| Each league's share | 18,012.52 |

---

It was Ruth's fifteenth home run in world's series competition and easily one of his most gorgeous. The crowd, suddenly unmindful of everything save that it had just witnessed an epic feat, hailed the Babe with a salvo of applause.

Root, badly shaken, now faced Gehrig and his feelings well can be imagined. The crowd was still too much excited over the Ruth incident to realize what was happening when Columbia Lou lifted an enormous fly high in the air. As it sailed on the wings of the lake breeze the ball just cleared the flagpole and dropped in the temporary stand.

Grimm, the player-manager of the Cubs, called time. Consolingly he invited Root to retire to the less turbulent confines of the clubhouse and ordered Pat Malone to the mound.

Pat filled the bases with three passes but he escaped the inning without further trouble. From then on the game, like its two predecessors, passed on to its very obvious conclusion with the exception of a final flurry in the ninth.

### May Takes Up Mound Duties.

Two very fine plays by Grimm and Moore rescued Malone from possible trouble in the sixth. He also went well through the seventh despite a second misplay by Jurges and a single by Crosetti, then he faded out for a pinch-hitter. Jackie May, lone lefthander of the Chicago pitching staff, came to the mound to pitch in the eighth.

Jackie got by that inning exceedingly well, closing out by inducing Ruth to slap into a double play. But in the ninth Jackie found that trouble can be found at either end of the Yankee batting order.

The lake breeze had now developed into a young gale and it seemd as though the Yanks strategically had decided upon capitalizing on it to the full. Gehrig, Lazzeri and Chapman successively touched off three sky-rocket infield flies that in their decent veered in all directions.

Woody English caught the first one right in the centre of the diamond after bumping into three of his comrades. But Gabby Hartnett, the ambitious Cub catcher, insisted on going after the second one and dropped it.

Then Herman muffed Dickey's hit and the Yankees had two aboard, one of which scored immediately on Chapman's double to left, a low drive for which the Cubs seemingly were totally unprepared. That blow removed May, and Bud Tinning, and apprentice right-hander, collected the last two outs that finally checked the Yanks.

### Hartnett's Drive Stirs Crowd.

The score was now 7 to 4, and, as Pipgras had done some really fine pitching from the fifth through the eighth, the crowd appeared definitely wilted. But it seems to be a simple matter to revive a Chicago crowd, and when Hartnett, first Cub up in the ninth, walloped a homer over the left-field wall into the temporary bleachers there was again a mighty roar.

The applause doubled in volume when Jurges whistled a single into left, and Manager McCarthy decided to withdraw Pipgras, for he had still another trump card up his sleeve. It was Herbie Pennock, and the veteran southpaw's finishing strokes to the combat produced another masterpiece.

Hemsley, batting for Tinning, struck out on three tantalizing slow balls. Herman topped one into the dirt in front of the plate which Pennock himself fielded, and Gehrig smothered English's grounder. That also smothered the Cubs.

Johnny Allen is scheduled to pitch tomorrow for the Yankees. His opponent will be Guy Bush. The weather forecast is fair and warmer.

## BOX SCORE OF THIRD GAME OF WORLD'S SERIES

### CHICAGO CUBS.

| | ab. | r. | h. | tb. | 2b. | 3b. | hr. | bb. | so. | sh. | sb. | po. | a. | e. |
|---|---|---|---|---|---|---|---|---|---|---|---|---|---|---|
| Herman, 2b | 4 | 1 | 0 | 0 | 0 | 0 | 0 | 1 | 0 | 0 | 0 | 1 | 2 | 1 |
| English, 3b | 4 | 0 | 0 | 0 | 0 | 0 | 0 | 1 | 0 | 0 | 0 | 0 | 3 | 0 |
| Cuyler, rf | 4 | 1 | 3 | 7 | 1 | 0 | 1 | 0 | 0 | 0 | 0 | 1 | 0 | 0 |
| Stephenson, lf | 4 | 0 | 1 | 1 | 0 | 0 | 0 | 0 | 0 | 0 | 0 | 1 | 0 | 0 |
| J. Moore, cf | 3 | 1 | 0 | 0 | 0 | 0 | 0 | 1 | 0 | 0 | 0 | 3 | 0 | 0 |
| Grimm, 1b | 4 | 0 | 1 | 2 | 1 | 0 | 0 | 0 | 0 | 0 | 0 | 8 | 0 | 0 |
| Hartnett, c | 4 | 1 | 1 | 4 | 0 | 0 | 1 | 0 | 0 | 0 | 0 | 10 | 1 | 1 |
| Jurges, ss | 4 | 1 | 3 | 4 | 1 | 0 | 0 | 0 | 0 | 0 | 1 | 3 | 3 | 2 |
| Root, p | 2 | 0 | 0 | 0 | 0 | 0 | 0 | 0 | 1 | 0 | 0 | 0 | 0 | 0 |
| Malone, p | 0 | 0 | 0 | 0 | 0 | 0 | 0 | 0 | 0 | 0 | 0 | 0 | 0 | 0 |
| May, p | 0 | 0 | 0 | 0 | 0 | 0 | 0 | 0 | 0 | 0 | 0 | 0 | 0 | 0 |
| Tinning, p | 0 | 0 | 0 | 0 | 0 | 0 | 0 | 0 | 0 | 0 | 0 | 0 | 0 | 0 |
| aGudat | 1 | 0 | 0 | 0 | 0 | 0 | 0 | 0 | 0 | 0 | 0 | 0 | 0 | 0 |
| bKoenig | 0 | 0 | 0 | 0 | 0 | 0 | 0 | 0 | 0 | 0 | 0 | 0 | 0 | 0 |
| cHemsley | 1 | 0 | 0 | 0 | 0 | 0 | 0 | 0 | 1 | 0 | 0 | 0 | 0 | 0 |
| Total | 35 | 5 | 9 | 18 | 3 | 0 | 2 | 3 | 2 | 0 | 1 | 27 | 9 | 4 |

### NEW YORK YANKEES.

| | ab. | r. | h. | tb. | 2b. | 3b. | hr. | bb. | so. | sh. | sb. | po. | a. | e. |
|---|---|---|---|---|---|---|---|---|---|---|---|---|---|---|
| Combs, cf | 5 | 1 | 0 | 0 | 0 | 0 | 0 | 0 | 2 | 0 | 0 | 1 | 0 | 0 |
| Sewell, 3b | 2 | 1 | 0 | 0 | 0 | 0 | 0 | 2 | 0 | 0 | 0 | 2 | 2 | 0 |
| Ruth, lf | 4 | 2 | 2 | 8 | 0 | 0 | 2 | 1 | 1 | 0 | 0 | 2 | 0 | 0 |
| Gehrig, 1b | 5 | 2 | 2 | 8 | 0 | 0 | 2 | 0 | 0 | 0 | 0 | 13 | 1 | 0 |
| Lazzeri, 2b | 4 | 1 | 0 | 0 | 0 | 0 | 0 | 1 | 1 | 0 | 0 | 3 | 4 | 1 |
| Dickey, c | 4 | 0 | 1 | 1 | 0 | 0 | 0 | 1 | 0 | 0 | 0 | 2 | 1 | 0 |
| Chapman, rf | 4 | 0 | 2 | 3 | 1 | 0 | 0 | 1 | 1 | 0 | 0 | 0 | 0 | 0 |
| Crosetti, ss | 4 | 0 | 1 | 1 | 0 | 0 | 0 | 1 | 0 | 0 | 0 | 4 | 4 | 0 |
| Pipgras, p | 5 | 0 | 0 | 0 | 0 | 0 | 0 | 0 | 5 | 0 | 0 | 0 | 0 | 0 |
| Pennock, p | 0 | 0 | 0 | 0 | 0 | 0 | 0 | 0 | 0 | 0 | 0 | 0 | 1 | 0 |
| Total | 37 | 7 | 8 | 21 | 1 | 0 | 4 | 7 | 10 | 0 | 0 | 27 | 13 | 1 |

aBatted for Malone in seventh.

bBatted for Tinning in ninth.

cBatted for Koenig in ninth.

### SCORE BY INNINGS.

| | | | | | | | | | | |
|---|---|---|---|---|---|---|---|---|---|---|
| New York . . . | 3 | 0 | 1 | 0 | 2 | 0 | 0 | 0 | 1—7 |
| Chicago . . . | 1 | 0 | 2 | 1 | 0 | 0 | 0 | 0 | 1—5 |

Runs batted in—New York: Ruth 4, Gehrig 2, Chapman 1.

Chicago: Cuyler 2, Grimm 1, Hartnett 1.

Left on bases—New York 11, Chicago 6. Double plays—Sewell, Lazzeri and Gehrig; Herman, Jurges and Grimm. Hits—Off Root 6 in 4 1–3 innings, Malone 1 in 2 2–3, May 1 in 1 1–3, Tinning 0 in 2–3, Pipgras 9 in 8 (none out in ninth), Pennock 0 in 1. Struck out—By Root 4, Malone 4, May 1, Tinning 1, Pipgras 1, Pennock 1. Bases on balls—Off Root 3, Malone 4, Pipgras 3. Hit by pitcher—By May (Sewell). Winning pitcher—Pipgras. Losing pitcher—Root. Umpires—Van Graflan (A.L.) at the plate; Magerkurth (N.L.) at first base; Dinneen (A.L.) at second base; Klem (N.L.) at third base. Time of game—2:11.

---

July 7, 1933

# Ruth's Home Run Gives American League Team Margin of Victory at Chicago

## AMERICAN LEAGUE BEATS RIVALS, 4–2

### 49,000 See Ruth's Homer Yield Two Runs as Nationals Are Toppled.

## LONG HIT COMES IN THIRD

### Frisch Also Gets Circuit Smash—Gomez, Crowder, Grove Baffle Losers.

### By JOHN DREBINGER.

*Special to THE NEW YORK TIMES.*

CHICAGO, July 6.—The National League is still trying to catch up with Babe Ruth, but apparently with no more success than in recent world's series conflicts.

Today, in the presence of a capacity throng of 49,000 in Comiskey Park, the great man of baseball fittingly whaled a home run into the right-field pavilion that gave the American League's all-star cast the necessary margin to bring down the pick of the National League in the "game of the century."

That smash, propelled off Willie Hallahan, star left-handed pitcher of the Cardinals, and with a runner on base, gave the team piloted by the venerable Connie Mack the victory by a score of 4 to 2. There was nothing the equally sagacious John J. McGraw could do about it.

McGraw, coming out of retirement for this singular event, the first of its kind in the history of the two major leagues, threw practically all his available manpower into the fray.

### Stage Mild Uprising.

But there seemed to be no way whatever of effacing the effect of that Ruthian wallop, even though the National League later staged a mild uprising of their own with Frankie Frisch, the erstwhile Fordham flash, banging a homer into the stands.

Mack and McGraw, matching wits for the first time since their last world's series clash in 1913, each sent three hurlers to the mound, but to Mack went the honors because the greater power was to be found in the mighty bludgeons of the American Leaguers.

Mack's selections were Vernon Gomez, ace left-hander of the Yankees; Alvin Crowder, star right-hander of the Senators, and finally, his own master southpaw, Lefty Bob Grove. Each went three innings, and only off Crowder were the National League forces able to make any headway. They scored both their tallies off the Washington flinger.

Hallahan, Lon Warneke, brilliant right-hander of the Cubs, and Carl Hubbell, foremost left-hander of the National League, did the pitching for McGraw. Though the battle plan had been that this trio, too, should work three rounds apiece, the plan bogged down when Hallahan sagged in the third.

It was in this round that Ruth belted his homer. Before the round had ended the tall Warneke had to be rushed to Hallahan's assistance. It seems that when the Babe smacks one, the whole park rocks and few survive.

### Hallahan Not Effective.

Hallahan, who unfortunately had pitched a full nine-inning game for the Cardinals only the day before yesterday, was obviously not quite himself as he squared off with Gomez. The latter, incidentally, also had had only a single day's rest after pitching a trying game against the Senators on the Fourth, but the willowy Yankee left-hander apparently is made of a little sterner stuff.

Hallahan's troubles began in the second when, with one out, he passed Dykes and Cronin. He seemed out of his difficulties when he retired Rick Ferrell and had only Gomez to face, but the gallant Castillian, known for his eccentricities, here did a very odd thing.

Admittedly one of the weakest hitters in all baseball in this "game of the century" with the greatest clouter assembled, he struck the first damaging blow. He rifled a single to center and Dykes tallied.

In the third, Hallahan's misfortunes engulfed him in less than a jiffy. He passed Gehringer and tried to whip one past Ruth. But the Babe drove it on a low line, just inside the right filed foul pole and into the lower pavilion. The crowd, sweltering in the heat of a broiling sun, roared in acclamation.

### Warneke Goes to Rescue.

Hallahan then pitched four more wide ones to Lou Gehrig, who also was waving his bat menacingly, and the tall, angular Warneke came rushing on the scene. He checked the American Leaguers for a time, but in the sixth dropped a run himself when Cronin singled, Ferrell sacrificed and Earl Averill, batting for Crowder, also singled.

Only for a brief moment did Gomez appear in trouble. That was at the start of the second when Chick Hafey and Bill Terry opened fire with a pair of one-base wallops. But Berger slapped into a double play and Bartell struck out. Gomez then swept through the third without allowing a man to reach first.

Crowder did equally well through the fourth and fifth, but in the sixth Warneke did a surprising thing. He banged a long hit down the right field foul line which the aging Ruth did not play any too well. Before the ball had been retrieved, Warneke had converted the smash into a triple.

Pepper Martin's out sent the Chicago pitcher hustling over the plate with the Heydler circuit's first run and a moment later Frisch slashed a drive into the lower right pavilion for the circuit.

## Crowder Halts Attack.

Through Chuck Klein followed with a single, Crowder clamped down the lid and the high spot of the National League's attack has passed.

With the seventh, baseball's two greatest southpaws, Grove and Hubbell, took the mound. Both blanked the opposition, though the McGraw legions did threaten Grove twice.

Terry opened the seventh with his second single of the day and Pie Traynor, pinch-hitting for Bartell, doubled to right center, between Simmons and Ruth. But Grove fanned Gabby Hartnett, retired Woody English on a fly and the back of that rally was broken.

In the eighth Frisch, flashing as of yore, drove a single to right. There was a cry of keen expectancy from the National League supporters in the crowd as Hafey sent a soaring fly heading in the direction of the right-field pavilion. But the Babe caught this one just as he was about to back into the wall, and the last National League threat faded.


## Three Mack Stars Idle.

With the exception of Hal Schumacher, who was held in reserve in case Hubbell ran into difficulties, McGraw used all his available players. But the finish saw Mack with still lot of punch up his sleeve which he never had to use. Jimmy Foxx, Tony Lazzeri and Bill Dickey did not get into the fray at all.

The official attendance was 49,200, which was not a record for Comiskey Park, but on this occasion no standing room was permitted by order of Commissioner Landis. The receipts totaled $51,000, which will be turned over to the National Association of Professional Baseball Players, which takes care of retired ball players in need.

During the early preliminaries the great crowd could not have found itself more occupied had a nine-ringed circus been in progress. Never before had baseball put on a show with all its great luminaries on stage at the same time.

Ruth, of course, was the chief magnet of the autograph seekers. But there was plenty of attention bestowed upon the other great performers such as Terry, Klein, Foxx, Simmons and Cronin.

One of the warmest receptions of the day was tendered to Lefty Grove when the crowd's attention was called to the fact that the famous Mack southpaw was warming up in the bull pen.

But the greatest ovation of all seemed to go to Hubbell as the Giant left-hander started tuning up his mighty arm that pitched eighteen scoreless innings last Sunday.

There was some disappointment when these two aces did not start the game, especially as the two starting hurlers, Hallahan and Gomez, both had pitched in regular league assignments on Tuesday.

## BOX SCORE OF CHICAGO GAME

### NATIONAL LEAGUE

| | AB | R | H | TB | 2b | 3b | hr | bb | so | sh | sb | po | a | e |
|---|---|---|---|---|---|---|---|---|---|---|---|---|---|---|
| Martin, St. L., 3b | 4 | 0 | 0 | 0 | 0 | 0 | 0 | 0 | 1 | 0 | 0 | 0 | 3 | 0 |
| Frisch, St. L., 2b | 4 | 1 | 2 | 5 | 0 | 0 | 1 | 0 | 0 | 0 | 0 | 5 | 3 | 0 |
| Klein, Phila., rf | 4 | 0 | 1 | 1 | 0 | 0 | 0 | 0 | 0 | 0 | 0 | 3 | 0 | 0 |
| P. Waner, Pitt., rf | 0 | 0 | 0 | 0 | 0 | 0 | 0 | 0 | 0 | 0 | 0 | 0 | 0 | 0 |
| Hafey, Cincin., lf | 4 | 0 | 1 | 1 | 0 | 0 | 0 | 0 | 0 | 0 | 0 | 0 | 0 | 0 |
| Terry, N.Y., 1b | 4 | 0 | 2 | 2 | 0 | 0 | 0 | 0 | 0 | 0 | 0 | 7 | 2 | 0 |
| Berger, Boston, cf | 4 | 0 | 0 | 0 | 0 | 0 | 0 | 0 | 0 | 0 | 0 | 4 | 0 | 0 |
| Bartell, Phila., ss | 2 | 0 | 0 | 0 | 0 | 0 | 0 | 0 | 1 | 0 | 0 | 0 | 3 | 0 |
| aTraynor, Pitt. | 1 | 0 | 1 | 2 | 1 | 0 | 0 | 0 | 0 | 0 | 0 | 0 | 0 | 0 |
| Hubbell, N.Y., p | 0 | 0 | 0 | 0 | 0 | 0 | 0 | 0 | 0 | 0 | 0 | 0 | 0 | 0 |
| bCuccinello, Bklyn | 1 | 0 | 0 | 0 | 0 | 0 | 0 | 0 | 1 | 0 | 0 | 0 | 0 | 0 |
| J. Wilson, St. L., c | 1 | 0 | 0 | 0 | 0 | 0 | 0 | 0 | 0 | 0 | 0 | 2 | 0 | 0 |
| cO'Doul, N.Y. | 1 | 0 | 0 | 0 | 0 | 0 | 0 | 0 | 0 | 0 | 0 | 0 | 0 | 0 |
| Hartnett, Chi., c | 1 | 0 | 0 | 0 | 0 | 0 | 0 | 0 | 1 | 0 | 0 | 2 | 0 | 0 |
| Hallahan, St. L., p | 1 | 0 | 0 | 0 | 0 | 0 | 0 | 0 | 0 | 0 | 0 | 1 | 0 | 0 |
| Warneke, Chi., p | 1 | 1 | 1 | 3 | 0 | 1 | 0 | 0 | 0 | 0 | 0 | 0 | 0 | 0 |
| English, Chi., ss | 1 | 0 | 0 | 0 | 0 | 0 | 0 | 0 | 0 | 0 | 0 | 0 | 0 | 0 |
| Total | 34 | 2 | 8 | 14 | 1 | 1 | 1 | 0 | 4 | 0 | 0 | 24 | 11 | 0 |

### AMERICAN LEAGUE

| | AB | R | H | TB | 2b | 3b | hr | bb | so | sh | sb | po | a | e |
|---|---|---|---|---|---|---|---|---|---|---|---|---|---|---|
| Chapman, N.Y., lf., rf. | 5 | 0 | 1 | 1 | 0 | 0 | 0 | 0 | 1 | 0 | 0 | 1 | 0 | 0 |
| Gehringer, Detr., 2b | 3 | 1 | 0 | 0 | 0 | 0 | 0 | 2 | 0 | 0 | 1 | 1 | 3 | 0 |
| Ruth, N.Y., rf | 4 | 1 | 2 | 5 | 0 | 0 | 1 | 0 | 2 | 0 | 0 | 1 | 0 | 0 |
| West, St. L., cf | 0 | 0 | 0 | 0 | 0 | 0 | 0 | 0 | 0 | 0 | 0 | 0 | 0 | 0 |
| Gehrig, N.Y. 1b | 2 | 0 | 0 | 0 | 0 | 0 | 0 | 2 | 1 | 0 | 0 | 12 | 0 | 1 |
| Simmons, Chi., cf., lf | 4 | 0 | 1 | 1 | 0 | 0 | 0 | 0 | 0 | 0 | 0 | 4 | 0 | 0 |
| Dykes, Chi., 3b | 3 | 1 | 2 | 2 | 0 | 0 | 0 | 1 | 0 | 0 | 0 | 2 | 4 | 0 |
| Cronin, Wash., ss | 3 | 1 | 1 | 1 | 0 | 0 | 0 | 1 | 0 | 0 | 0 | 2 | 4 | 0 |
| R. Ferrell, Boston, c | 3 | 0 | 0 | 0 | 0 | 0 | 0 | 0 | 0 | 1 | 0 | 4 | 0 | 0 |
| Gomez, N.Y., p | 1 | 0 | 1 | 1 | 0 | 0 | 0 | 0 | 0 | 0 | 0 | 0 | 0 | 0 |
| Crowder, Wash., p | 1 | 0 | 0 | 0 | 0 | 0 | 0 | 0 | 0 | 0 | 0 | 0 | 0 | 0 |
| dAverill, Cleve. | 1 | 0 | 1 | 1 | 0 | 0 | 0 | 0 | 0 | 0 | 0 | 0 | 0 | 0 |
| Grove, Phila., p | 1 | 0 | 0 | 0 | 0 | 0 | 0 | 0 | 0 | 0 | 0 | 0 | 0 | 0 |
| Total | 31 | 4 | 9 | 12 | 0 | 0 | 1 | 6 | 4 | 1 | 1 | 27 | 11 | 1 |

aBatted for Bartell in seventh. bBatted for Hubbell in ninth.
cBatted for Wilson in sixth.    dBatted for Crowder in sixth.

National League    0    0    0    0    0    2    0    0    0—2

American League   0    1    2    0    0    1    0    0    ..—4

Runs batted in—American League: Ruth 2, Gomez, Averill.

National League: Martin, Frisch.

Left on bases—American League 10, National League 5. Double plays—Bartell, Frisch and Terry; Dykes and Gehrig. Hits—Off Hallahan 2 in 2 (none out in third), Warneke 6 in 4, Hubbell 1 in 2, Gomez 2 in 3, Crowder 3 in 3, Grove 3 in 3. Struck out—By Hallahan 1, Warneke 2, Hubbell 1, Gomez 1, Grove 3. Bases on balls—Off Hallahan 5, Hubbell 1. Winning pitcher, Gomez; losing pitcher, Hallahan. Umpires—Dinneen (A.L.) at the plate; Klem (N.L.) at first, McGowan (A.L.) at second, Rigler (N.L.) at third, for the first four and one-half innings; Klem (N.L.) at the plate, McGowan (A.L.) at first Rigler (N.L.) at second, Dinneen (A.L.) at third, for the remainder of game. Time of game—2:05.

———

July 14, 1934

## Ruth's Record of 700 Home Runs Likely To Stand for All Time in Major Leagues.

*Special to* THE NEW YORK TIMES.

DETROIT, July 13.—A record that promises to endure for all time was attained on Navin Field today when Babe Ruth smashed his seven-hundredth home run in a lifetime career. It promises to live, first, because few players of history have enjoyed the longevity on the diamond of the immortal Bambino, and, second, because only two other players in the history of baseball have hit more than 300 home runs.

In his twenty-first year of play, and what is expected to be his farewell season, Ruth rounded out the record he had set for himself before retiring.

He has another mark he is shooting at and which he should attain before the end of the current campaign. He wants to go out with 2,000 bases on balls to his credit, a reflection of the respect rival pitchers have for him. He is only a few short of the mark.

Lou Gehrig and Rogers Hornsby are the only players who have exceeded 300 home runs in their careers. Gehrig boasts 314 and Hornsby 301. The improbability of a parallel to the Ruth mark is appreciated with the knowledge that Gehrig will have to survive ten more years of play, and then average about 40 home runs a year, to equal it.

Today a youth was happy and richer by $20. Even before he circled the bases, Ruth was shouting to mates on the field: "I want that ball! I want that ball!" Emissaries were sent scurrying after the youth who recovered the ball after it cleared the fence, and it was restored to Ruth in the Yankee dugout, in exchange for $20.

Ruth paid $20 for his five-hundredth home-run ball, hit in Cleveland, and a similar amount for the home-run ball that touched the 600 mark three years ago. This one was hit in St. Louis.

Ruth had his greatest home-run year in 1927, when he created the modern season's record of 60. He hit 59 in 1921, and 54 in both 1920 and 1928. In 1930 he smashed 49.

Following is a table of the home runs hit by Ruth in championship games and world's series contests:

## CHAMPIONSHIP GAMES.

| Year | Team | Homers | Year | Team | Homers |
|------|------|--------|------|------|--------|
| 1914 | Red Sox | 0 | 1926 | Yankees | 47 |
| 1915 | Red Sox | 4 | 1927 | Yankees | 60 |
| 1916 | Red Sox | 3 | 1928 | Yankees | 54 |
| 1917 | Red Sox | 2 | 1929 | Yankees | 46 |
| 1918 | Red Sox | 11 | 1930 | Yankees | 49 |
| 1919 | Red Sox | 29 | 1931 | Yankees | 46 |
| 1920 | Yankees | 54 | 1932 | Yankees | 41 |
| 1921 | Yankees | 59 | 1933 | Yankees | 34 |
| *1922 | Yankees | 35 | 1934 | Yankees | 14 |
| 1923 | Yankees | 41 | Total | | 700 |
| 1924 | Yankees | 46 | | | |
| †1925 | Yankees | 25 | | | |

*Out until May 20, suspended for barnstorming after 1921 world's series.
†Out until June with illness after collapsing during training trip.

## WORLD'S SERIES GAMES.

| Year | Team Against | Homers | Year | Team Against | Homers |
|------|--------------|--------|------|--------------|--------|
| 1915 | Phillies | 0 | 1926 | Cardinals | 4 |
| 1916 | Dodgers | 0 | 1927 | Pirates | 2 |
| 1918 | Cubs | 0 | 1928 | Cardinals | 3 |
| 1921 | Giants | 1 | 1932 | Cubs | 2 |
| 1922 | Giants | 0 | Total | | 15 |
| 1923 | Giants | 3 | | | |

# RUTH HITS 700TH AS YANKS SCORE 4–2

## Reaches Goal of His Career With Mighty Homer in the Third Against Tigers.

### GEHRIG, ILL, FORCED OUT

## Consecutive-Game Streak May End—Dickey's Two-Bagger Decides the Contest.

### By JAMES P. DAWSON.

*Special to THE NEW YORK TIMES.*

DETROIT, July 13.—The incomparable Babe Ruth reached his goal today with his 700th home run, a wallop that helped in sending the Yankees back into the lead in the American League pennant race.

It came in the third inning, a drive of about 480 feet high over the right-field wall. Earle Combs was on first when Ruth drove the ball out of the lot, fashioning two runs off Tom Bridges, the Detroit pitcher.

It seemed the blow would carry victory for Charley (Red) Ruffing, who was locked in an intense pitching duel with Bridges as 21,000 looked on.

In the end, however, it was a two-base drive off the bat of reliable Bill Dickey in the eighth inning which brought the triumph by a count of 4 to 2 and restored to the Yankees their slender lead over the Tigers in first place.

### Wallop Sends Two Home.

Dickey's hit, one of two for the backstop, chased Ruth and Ben Chapman home with the runs that put the game on the Yankees' side of the ledger.

Tonight the Yanks are happy, and Ruth is the happiest of all. They humbled the ace right-hander of the Tigers' hurling staff with a nine-hit attack and can look forward less apprehensively now to the remaining two games in this crucial series.

Ruffing, hammered to shelter in his last two championship starts and in his all-star game effort as well, selected the right time to return to his winning ways. He gave the Tigers six scant hits.

A pass and a double, with a high fly, brought the first Tiger run in the third, and the only other score came in the eighth, when Ruffing let the Tigers cluster a single and a triple.

### Gehrig's Status in Doubt.

Lou Gehrig, playing in his 1,426th consecutive championship game, was involuntarily withdrawn in the second inning, suffering from an attack of lumbago which may very well bring an end to his unique record. Whether he will play tomorrow was undetermined tonight.

With one out in the third, Combs singled. Then, after Saltzgaver had fanned, Ruth, with the count three and two, blasted his fourteenth homer of the season.

That was all the Yankee scoring until the eighth, when, with one out, Ruth drew a pass and took second on Rolfe's single. Rolfe was caught off first, then Chapman walked. Dickey here slashed a double to centre.

Manager McCarthy sent Red Rolfe to short and shifted Saltzgaver to first and Crosetti to third.

The box score:

| NEW YORK (A.) | | | | | | | DETROIT (A.) | | | | | | |
|---|---|---|---|---|---|---|---|---|---|---|---|---|---|
| | ab. | r. | h. | po. | a. | e. | | ab. | r. | h. | po. | a. | e. |
| Combs, cf | 5 | 1 | 1 | 4 | 0 | 0 | Fox, rf | 5 | 0 | 0 | 4 | 1 | 0 |
| Saltz'r, 3b, 1b | 4 | 0 | 0 | 7 | 1 | 0 | White, cf | 2 | 1 | 0 | 2 | 0 | 0 |
| Ruth, lf | 3 | 2 | 1 | 1 | 0 | 0 | Goslin, lf | 4 | 0 | 1 | 1 | 0 | 0 |
| Byrd, lf | 0 | 0 | 0 | 0 | 0 | 0 | Ge'inger, 2b | 4 | 0 | 1 | 1 | 1 | 0 |
| Gehrig, 1b | 1 | 0 | 1 | 1 | 0 | 0 | Rogell, ss | 4 | 1 | 1 | 2 | 4 | 0 |
| Rolfe, ss | 2 | 0 | 1 | 1 | 2 | 0 | Gr'nberg, 1b | 4 | 0 | 2 | 8 | 0 | 0 |
| Chapman, rf | 3 | 1 | 1 | 0 | 0 | 0 | Cochrane, c | 3 | 0 | 1 | 8 | 2 | 0 |
| Dickey, c | 4 | 0 | 2 | 5 | 0 | 0 | Owen, 3b | 3 | 0 | 0 | 1 | 0 | 0 |
| Cros'ti, ss, 3b | 3 | 0 | 1 | 2 | 3 | 0 | Bridges, p | 3 | 0 | 0 | 0 | 2 | 0 |
| Heffner, 2b | 4 | 0 | 1 | 6 | 0 | 0 | ªWalker | 1 | 0 | 0 | 0 | 0 | 0 |
| Ruffing, p | 4 | 0 | 0 | 0 | 0 | 0 | | | | | | | |
| Total | 33 | 4 | 9 | 27 | 6 | 0 | Total | 33 | 2 | 6 | 27 | 10 | 0 |

ªBatted for Bridges in ninth.

| New York | 0 | 0 | 2 | 0 | 0 | 0 | 0 | 2 | 0—4 |
|---|---|---|---|---|---|---|---|---|---|
| Detroit | 0 | 0 | 1 | 0 | 0 | 0 | 0 | 1 | 0—2 |

Runs batted in—Ruth 2, Gehringer, Dickey 2, Greenberg.

Two-base hits—Greenberg. Home runs—Ruth. Stolen bases—White, Chapman, Cochrane. Double play—Fox and Gehringer. Left on bases—Detroit 8, New York 8. Bases on balls—Off Bridges 4, Ruffing 4. Struck out—By Bridges 8. Ruffing 8. Wild pitches—Bridges 2. Umpires—Donnelly, McGowan and Owens. Time of game—2:12.

September 25, 1934

## American League Pennant Is Clinched by Idle Tigers as Yankees Are Beaten.

### TIGERS, ILDE, WIN FLAG AS YANKS BOW

## McCarthymen, Blanked by Red Sox, 5–0, Eliminated From League Pennant Race.

### RUTH IN FAREWELL STAND

## Merena, Rookie, Holds New York to 4 Hits—First Title for Detroit Since 1909.

### By JOHN DREBINGER

At 5 o'clock yesterday afternoon the Yankees, officially as well as very dolefully, passed out of the American League pennant race as they sustained a shutout defeat at the hands of a southpaw recruit, John Merena.

To the Red Sox went the ball game, 5 to 0, and as the Yankee position, given up as untenable weeks ago, was of a sort that could stand for no more defeats, the championship of the American circuit went to Detroit.

The Tigers, with an open day in the schedule, virtually had the flag thrust upon them while doing nothing more energetic than rocking in their hotel-lobby chairs. This is the first pennant for Detroit since 1909.

To the Yanks and some 2,000 diehards who remained faithful to the last, all this, while decidedly not unexpected, was very sad, especially as the occasion also marked the farewell appearance of the McCarthy forces at the Stadium this year.

### Five More Games for Yanks.

They still have five more games to play, but these will be struggled through in Philadelphia and Washington, and nothing very important will depend on any of them. They can win them all, but this will not win back the pennant that was tossed away in July and August. They can also lose them all with impunity, for they cannot be dislodged from second place.

Even the final passing of the great man Ruth, who has announced this as his last season as a regular, was shorn of all the dramatics that usually associated themselves with this illustrious character of the game.

Still limping painfully, the Babe started in right field, caught one fly for which he scarcely had to move, drew a base on balls as he came to bat in the first inning, hobbled to first and called for a runner.

### Fans Cheer Babe Lustily.

As he trudged up from the base and headed into the Yankee dugout, the 2,000 cheered as lustily as the circumstances would permit. To a man, the crowd would liked to have cheered a more boisterous exit.

As for the rest of the Yanks, though no limping was perceptible, they seemed to be hobbled to something, too, for they gathered only four hits off young Merena, whom Manager Bucky Harris acquired only a few days ago; hit two flies to the outfield, advanced three men as far as second and only one to third.

Fordham Johnny Murphy was the victim of all this Yankee ineptness, which was rather unfortunate, as Johnny did some pretty good pitching of his own, allowing only seven blows.

But after dropping a run in the first when Almada singled, stole second and counted on Cooke's single, the scholarly Johnny received a body blow in the second when Red Rolfe tossed two Boston runs over the plate, all on a wild throw after fumbling a sacrifice bunt.

## Yankees Chiefs Confer.

Just what the Yankees plan to do about giving themselves some additional lift to carry them over the top next year is still probably in an embryonic state, but it seemed to be getting a fair start in what is known as the "royal box" on the mezzanine tier, where sat the entire general staff, including Colonel Ruppert himself.

Needless to say, the interest of the Yankee war lords in the game was more or less a casual one. But from a distance the conversation looked to be of a very serious nature, indeed.

Despite defeat, the Yanks nevertheless finished with an edge over the Red Sox on the season's play, winning twelve of the twenty-two games between the two.

The box score:

| BOSTON (A.) | ab. | r. | h. | po. | a. | e. | NEW YORK (A.) | ab. | r. | h. | po. | a. | e. |
|---|---|---|---|---|---|---|---|---|---|---|---|---|---|
| Niemie, 2b | 4 | 0 | 0 | 4 | 5 | 0 | Crosetti, ss | 1 | 0 | 1 | 2 | 3 | 0 |
| Werber, 3b | 4 | 0 | 1 | 0 | 5 | 0 | Rolfe, 2b | 4 | 0 | 0 | 1 | 2 | 2 |
| Almada, cf | 5 | 2 | 3 | 1 | 0 | 0 | Ruth, rf | 0 | 0 | 0 | 1 | 0 | 0 |
| Cooke, lf | 4 | 0 | 2 | 1 | 1 | 0 | Hoag, rf | 3 | 0 | 0 | 1 | 0 | 0 |
| Graham, rf | 4 | 0 | 1 | 0 | 0 | 0 | Gehrig, 1b | 2 | 0 | 2 | 15 | 0 | 0 |
| R. Ferrell, c | 4 | 0 | 0 | 2 | 1 | 0 | Selkirk, lf | 4 | 0 | 0 | 2 | 0 | 1 |
| Morgan, 1b | 3 | 1 | 0 | 16 | 0 | 1 | Lazzeri, 2b | 4 | 0 | 0 | 1 | 4 | 0 |
| Lary, ss | 2 | 1 | 0 | 3 | 5 | 0 | Chapman, cf | 3 | 0 | 1 | 1 | 0 | 0 |
| Merena, p | 2 | 1 | 0 | 0 | 1 | 0 | Jorgens, c | 2 | 0 | 0 | 3 | 0 | 0 |
| | | | | | | | Murphy, p | 3 | 0 | 0 | 0 | 4 | 0 |
| Total | 32 | 5 | 7 | 27 | 18 | 1 | Total | 26 | 0 | 4 | 27 | 13 | 3 |

| | | | | | | | | | | |
|---|---|---|---|---|---|---|---|---|---|---|
| Boston | 1 | 2 | 1 | 0 | 0 | 0 | 0 | 0 | 1—5 |
| New York | 0 | 0 | 0 | 0 | 0 | 0 | 0 | 0 | 0—0 |

Runs batted in—Cooke, Ferrell, Werber.

Two-base hit—Chapman. Stolen bases—Almada, Cooke. Sacrifices—Merena, Niemie. Double plays—Lary, Niemi and Morgan; Crosetti and Gehrig; Werber, Niemie and Morgan. Left on bases—New York 6, Boston 8. Bases on balls—Off Merena 4, Murphy 6. Struck out—By Murphy 3, Merena 2. Passed ball—R. Ferrell. Umpires—McGowan and Dinneen. Time of game—1:14.

## 58,339 Acclaim Babe Ruth In Rare Tribute at Stadium

### Baseball's Most Famous Figure Is Honored By Season's Biggest Crowd— Exercises Broadcast to Fans Throughout World

#### By LOUIS EFFRAT

Wherever organized baseball was played yesterday Babe Ruth was honored. Ceremonies at the Yankee Stadium, where the Babe was given the greatest ovation in the history of the national pastime, were broadcast throughout the world, and what Ruth and others had to say was piped to other ball parks.

However, for the real impact, for the fullest effect and for the solemnity of the occasion, one had to be among the 58,339 followers of the game at the Stadium, often referred to as the "House That Ruth Built." This was "Babe Ruth Day."

Older, grayer, no longer the robust Babe who wrote diamond history, George Herman Ruth stood before a microphone at home plate. He talked to the crowd, the biggest baseball turnout of the year. And what he had to say was extemporaneous. Babe said he did not need to write down things that came from the heart. Francis Cardinal Spellman delivered the invocation, Commissioner A.B. Chandler, American League President Will Harridge, National League President Ford Frick and Larry Cutler, a 13-year-old lad who represented the American Legion players, were the other speakers.

A bit unsteady at the outset, the Babe, in a raspy voice that obviously had been weakened by recent serious operations, dwelt principally on the youth of the land. Ruth's main interest now is the American Legion baseball program, for which he has been signed a consultant, and it was to the boys that he directed his talk.

"Thank you very much, ladies and gentleman," he began. "You know how bad my voice sounds. Well, it feels just as bad. You know this baseball game of ours comes up from the youth. That means the boys. And after you've been a boy, and grow up to know how to play ball, then you come to the boys you see representing themselves today in our national pastime."

Now the Babe's big smile was visible to everyone. Still a very sick man, he emphasized his remarks with a clenched fist and a wave of the hand.

"The only real game in the world, I think, is baseball," he continued. "As a rule, some people think if you give them a football or a baseball or something like that, naturally, they're athletes right away. But you can't do that in baseball. You've gotta start from way down at the bottom, when you're 6 or 7 years old. You can't wait until you're 15 or 16. You've gotta let it grow up with you, and if you're successful and you try hard enough, you're bound to come out on top, just like these boys have come to the top now.

"There's been so many lovely things said about me, I'm glad I had the opportunity to thank everybody. Thank you."

#### Strides to Yanks' Dugout.

Then with a wave to the fans, the Babe walked down into the New York dugout. He had had his "Day."

Several weeks of vacationing under a Florida sun brought the Babe to the Stadium a tanned, but still sick man. Just before he spoke, Ruth started to cough and it appeared that he might break down because of the thunderous cheers that came his way. But once he started to talk, he was all right, still the champion. It was the many men who surrounded him on the field, players, newspaper and radio persons, who choked up.

Underneath the stands, Ruth again started to cough and he had a few trying minutes before he was able to move to a box adjoining the Yankee dugout. There he joined Mrs. Ruth, his daughter, Mrs. Julian Flanders, and a friend, Emory C. Perry. Ruth remained until the start of the eighth inning of the Yankees-Senators game. He left with the score, 0–0, and did not see the Washington club score a run in the eighth and win, 1–0.

Cardinal Spellman was unable to remain for the ball game. Before he departed, though, there was a behind-the-scene-get-together. "You've been a great inspiration to the boys and I want to tell you, you've been a great inspiration to me," said Cardinal Spellman, who then left with Msgr Walter Kellenberg.

The crowd which had booed Commissioner Chandler cheered him when he paid tribute to Ruth. Presidents Harridge and Frick also paid their respects. The former gave Ruth a plaque, inscribed by American League club owners, while Frick handed the Babe a book containing autographs of every player, club owner and official in the National League. Thirteen-year-old Cutler welcomed the Babe back to baseball.

### Gifts From Team, League.

The Yankees, for whom Ruth used to play, and the American League, handed envelopes to the Babe. It was believed that these contained checks for sizable sums. However, the donors were reluctant to discuss this. President Larry MacPhail of the Yankees said: "Anything about what we gave Ruth will have to come from him."

The Babe's comment was: "I have not opened or looked at a single thing I received."

Now 53 years old, the one-time Sultan of Swat, who hit sixty homers in 1927, and a total of 714 since he broke into the majors with the Boston Red Sox as a left-handed pitcher in 1915, has been out of baseball as an active player since 1935. He retired that season after moving from the Yankees to the Boston Braves of the National League. He returned in 1938 for a brief term as a Dodger coach.

No one in baseball has matched the Babe's ability to swat home runs. With his big bat he set a record that may never be equaled. His fortune rose with his fame and in one season he was paid $80,000. Other players benefited by Ruth's great deeds—attendance, salaries and playing conditions becoming better all around.

The Babe Ruth of yesterday was not the Babe Ruth of yesteryear; this was not the Babe Ruth who "called his shot" in the 1932 World Series, when he pointed to a spot in the centre-field bleachers and promptly belted a homer there; this was not the Ruth who made enemy pitchers' knees shake.

### Autographs for Players.

But everyone showed admiration for the man who revolutionized the game. Joe DiMaggio, George McQuinn, Frankie Crosetti, Bucky Harris and others crowded around the Babe, asked and got his autograph. Were it not for special protection the Babe would have had his hands full with thousands of fans, who also wanted his autograph. If permitted, the Babe would gladly have complied with every wish.

Among those who paid their respects to the Babe was 79-year-old Edward Grant Barrow, former president of the Yankees. It was Barrow, back in 1920, who brought Ruth from Boston to New York, and converted him into an outfielder, so that the Yankees could make the most of Ruth's slugging prowess. Barrow was inconspicuous in a mezzanine box. What thoughts were running through Cousin Ed's head while he gazed at the Babe were not revealed.

Ruth probably was a tired but happy man when he went home last night. "Babe Ruth Day" was a long time in coming, but when it arrived, it was a tremendous day. Even the sun, which had been playing hide-and-seek, cooperated, the rain holding off until just after the game had been finished.

Now the Babe plans to devote his time to helping promote kids' baseball. As soon as he feels strong enough, he will dig into the American Legion program. There is even talk about a "Babe Ruth Foundation." The Babe will have something to say about it soon.

August 17, 1948

## Ruth Set Fifty-four Major League Records and Ten Additional Marks in American Circuit

### SLUGGER STARRED IN 10 WORLD SERIES

### Ruth Set Major League Homer Mark on Total of 714—Hit Over 40 Eleven Seasons

### HAD MOST WALKS IN 1923

### All-Time Batting Great Also Struck Out Most Times in Career Lasting 22 Years

Babe Ruth held fifty-four major league records and was tied for four others. In addition, he had ten strictly American League records to his credit and was tied for five more. His outstanding performances follow:

### Regular Season

Highest slugging percentage (extra base hits) season, 100 or more games—.847, New York, 142 games, 1920 (major league record).

Highest slugging percentage American League—.692, Boston and New York, 21 years 1914–1934 inclusive (major league record).

Most years leading American League in slugging percentage, 100 or more games—13, Boston and New York, 1918–1931, except 1925 (major league record).

Most runs, season (American League)—177, New York, 152 games, 1921.

Most years leading American League in runs—8, Boston and New York, 1919, 1920, 1921, 1923, 1924, 1926, 1927, 1928 (major league record).

Most home runs—714, Boston (A.), New York (A.) and Boston (N.), 22 years, 1914 to 1935 inclusive. 708 in A.L. and 6 in N.L. (major league record).

Most home runs, league—708, Boston and New York, 21 years, 1914–1934 inclusive (American League).

Most home runs, season—60, New York, 151 games, 1927 (major league record).

Most home runs, two consecutive seasons—114, New York, 60 in 1927, 54 in 1928 (major league record).

Most years leading American League in home runs—12, Boston and New York, 1918 (tied), 1919, 1920, 1921, 1923, 1924, 1926, 1927, 1928, 1929, 1930, 1931 (tied)—(major league record).

Speaking to the crowd at the park and the nation over radio on Babe Ruth Day at Yankee Stadium, 1947. (THE NEW YORK TIMES)

Most consecutive years leading American League in home runs—6, New York, 1926 to 1931 (tied in 1931).

Most home runs, season, on road—32, New York, 1927 (major league record).

Most years, 50 or more home runs American League—4, New York, 1920, 1921, 1927, 1928 (major league record).

Most consecutive years, 50 or more home runs season, American League—2, New York, 1920–1921; 1927–1928 (major league record).

Most years, 40 or more home runs, American League—11, New York, 1920, 1921, 1923, 1924, 1926, 1927, 1928, 1929, 1930, 1931, 1932 (major league record).

Most consecutive years, 40 or more home runs, American League—7, New York, 1926–1932 inclusive, (major league record).

Most years, 30 or more home runs, American League—13, New York, 1920 to 1933, excepting 1925 (major league record).

Most times, two or more home runs in one game—72, Boston (A.), New York (A.) and Boston (N.), 22 years, 1914–1935; 71 in American League, 1 in National League (major league record).

Most times, three home runs in a double-header—7, New York 1920 to 1933 (major league record).

Most home runs with bases filled in one season—4, Boston, 130 games, 1919 (tied American and major league records).

Most home runs with bases filled in two consecutive games—2, New York, Sept. 27; 29, 1927, also Aug. 6, second game, Aug. 7 first game 1919 (tied American League record).

Most home runs, 5 consecutive games—7, New York, June 10, 11, 12, 13, 14, 1921 (American League record and tied major league record).

Most home runs, two consecutive days—6, New York, May 21, 21, 22, 22, 1930, 4 games (American League record).

Most home runs, one week—9, New York, May 18 to 24, second game, 1930, 8 games (tied American League record).

Most total bases, season—457, New York, 152 games, 1921 (major league record).

Most years leading American League in total bases—6, Boston and New York, 1919, 1921, 1923, 1924, 1926, 1928 (tied American League record).

Most extra-base hits—1,356, Boston (A.), New York (A.) and Boston (N.); 22 years, 1914 to 1935 inclusive (major league record); 506 doubles, 136 triples, 714 home runs.

Most long hits, American League—1,350, Boston and New York, 21 years, 1914–1934 inclusive (major league record for one league); 506 doubles; 136 triples, 708 home runs.

Most extra-base hits in one season—119, New York, 152 games, 1921 (major league record); 44 doubles, 16 triples, 59 home runs.

Most years leading American League in extra-base hits—7, Boston and New York, 1918, 1919, 1920, 1921, 1923, 1924, 1928.

Most consecutive years leading American League in extra-base hits—4, Boston and New York, 1918, 1919, 1920, 1921 (major league record).

Most extra bases on long hits—2,920 Boston (A.), New York (A.) and Boston (N.), 22 years, 1914–1935 inclusive (major league record).

Most extra bases on long hits, American League— 2,902, Boston and New York, 21 years, 1914–1934 inclusive (major league record).

Most extra bases on long hits in one season—235, New York, 152 games, 1921 (major league record).

Most years leading American League in extra bases on long hits—9, Boston and New York, 1918, 1919, 1920, 1921, 1923, 1924, 1926, 1928 (major league record).

Most consecutive years leading American League in extra bases on long hits—4, Boston and New York, 1918, 1919, 1920, 1921 (major league record).

Most years 200 or more extra bases on long hits—4, New York, 1920, 1921, 1927, 1928 (major league record).

Most years, 100 or more extra bases on long hits—14, Boston and New York, 1919–1933 inclusive, except 1925 (tied American League record).

Most runs batted in—2,209, Boston (A.) and New York (A.) and Boston (N.), 22 years, 1914–1935 inclusive (major league record).

Most runs batted in, American League—2,197, Boston and New York, 21 years, 1914–1934 inclusive.

Most years leading American League, runs batted in—6, Boston and New York, 1919, 1920, 1921, 1923 (tied), 1926, 1928 (tied).

Most consecutive years leading American League, runs batted in—3, Boston and New York, 1919, 1920, 1921.

Most years, 100 or more runs batted in—13, Boston and New York, 1919–1933 except 1922 and 1925 (tied American and major league records).

Most consecutive years, 150 or more runs batted in, league—3, New York, 1929, 1930, 1931 (tied American and major league records).

Most bases on balls—2,055, Boston (A.), New York (A.) and Boston (N.), 22 years, 1914–1935 inclusive (major league record).

Most bases on balls, American League—2,036, Boston and New York, 21 years, 1914–1934 inclusive.

Most bases on balls in one season—170, New York, 152 games, 123 (major league record).

Most years leading American League in bases on balls—11, New York, 1920; 1921, 1923, 1924, 1926, 1927, 1928, 1930, 1931, 1932, 1933 (major league record).

Most consecutive years leading American League in bases on balls—4, New York, 1930, 1931, 1932, 1933 (major league record).

Most years 100 or more bases on balls, American League—13, Boston and New York, 1919, 1920, 1921, 1923, 1924, 1926, 1927, 1928, 1930, 1931, 1932, 1933, 1934 (major league record).

Most consecutive years, 100 or more bases on balls, league—5, New York, 1930–1935 inclusive (tied American League record).

Most strikeouts, 1,330, Boston (A.), New York (A.) and Boston (N.), 22 years, 1914–1935 inclusive (major league record).

Most strikeouts, American League, 1,306, Boston and New York, 21 years, 1914–1934 inclusive.

## World Series

Most series played, 10, Boston (1915, 1916, 1918); New York (1921, 1922, 1923, 1926, 1927, 1928, 1932).

Most series batting .300 or better—6, New York (1921, 1923, 1926, 1927, 1928, 1932).

Highest batting percentage, four or more games, one series—.625, New York, 1928.

Most runs, total series—37, New York (A.).

Most runs, one series—Nine (four-game series)—New York, 1928; eight (six-game series), New York, 1923; eight (six-game series), New York (1923).

Most runs, one game—4, New York, 1926 (tie).

Most consecutive games, one or more runs, one or more series—9, New York.

Most hits, one series—10, (four-game series), New York (1928).

Most two-base hits, one series—3 (four-game series), New York 1928.

Most home runs, total series—15, New York, 1921, 1923, 1926, 1927, 1932.

Most home runs, one series—3 (six-game series), New York, 1923; 4 (seven-game series), New York, 1926.

Most home runs, one game—3, New York, 1928.

Three home runs, one game—New York, 1932.

Most total bases, one series—22 (four-game series), New York, 1928; 19 (six-game series), New York, 1923.

Most total bases, one game—12, New York 1926, 1928.

Most extra-base hits, one series—6 (four-game series), New York, 1928; five (six-game series), New York, 1923 (tied).

Most extra-base hits, total series—22, Boston and New York.

Most extra bases on long hits, total series—54, Boston and New York.

Most extra bases on long hits, one game—9, New York, 1926, 1928.

Most times player batting in three runs on long hit—2, New York, 1927, 1932 (tied).

Most bases on balls, total series—33, Boston and New York.

Most bases on balls, one series—8 (six-game series), New York, 1923; 11 (7-game series), New York, 1926.

Most bases on balls, one game—4, New York, 1926 (tied).

Most strike-outs, total series—30, Boston and New York.

August 17, 1948

## Babe Ruth, Baseball Idol, Dies At 53 After Lingering Illness

### Famous Diamond Star Fought Losing Battle Against Cancer for 2 Years—End Comes Suddenly After Encouraging Rally

### By MURRAY SCHUMACH

Babe Ruth died last night. The 53-year old baseball idol succumbed to cancer of the throat at Memorial Hospital at 8 o'clock, less than two hours after a special bulletin had announced he was "sinking rapidly."

The home-run king's death came five days after he had been placed on the critical list. It ended nearly two years of fighting against a disease that had sent him repeatedly to hospitals.

About a half hour before his death the famous Yankee slugger said a prayer. Last rites of the Roman Catholic Church had been administered on July 21.

After his death, the Rev. Thomas H. Kaufman of Providence College, Providence, R.I., who had blessed him shortly before death, said: "The Babe died a beautiful death. He said his prayers and lapsed into a sleep. He died in his sleep."

At the deathbed, besides the priest, were the Babe's wife, Claire, his two adopted daughters, Mrs. Daniel Sullivan and Mrs. Richard Flanders; his sister, Mrs. Wilbur Moberly; his doctor, his lawyer, and a few of his closest friends.

There was a hush around the hospital when the end came. The group of youngsters who had gathered about the red-brick hospital since Wednesday when the name of George Herman Ruth first appeared on the critical list, were home having dinner.

In the marble lobby, where late last week groups of boys had occasionally tarried, sometimes leaving flowers for the great right fielder, there were juts a handful of adults, all of them waiting to see other patients.

On the ninth floor, where the Babe had spent his final illness, nurses and doctors talked in whispers. Those who had seen him had been shocked at the change since the days of his baseball prime.

The powerful six-footer who had once electrified Americans with sixty homers in a season, had wasted away. The famous round face had become so hollowed that his snub nose looked long. The once black hair so often seen when the Babe doffed his cap rounding the bases, was almost white.

Deeply moved, Father Kaufman said little as he left after having been with the Babe most of the day. Others in the party were just as uncommunicative and hastened past the dozens of youngsters who quickly gathered in East Sixty-eighth Street outside the hospital.

The Babe's death brought tributes from men equally famous in other fields. Among those who sent messages were President Truman and former President Herbert Hoover. Included in the many tributes from baseball figures were those from Will Harridge, president of the American League, and Ford Frick, head of the National League.

Members of the Ruth family said that although funeral plans had not yet been completed, it had been arranged tentatively that a mass would be sung in St. Patrick's Cathedral at 11 A.M. Thursday. Meanwhile the body was to be taken to the Universal Funeral Chapel, 595 Lexington Avenue.

### Relapse Comes Suddenly.

Though the public had been aware for several days of the baseball idol's grave condition, his relapse yesterday was surprising because he had shown steady improvement over the week-end. On Sunday he had left his bed for twenty minutes.

Even yesterday morning, the first bulletin issued at 10:20 o'clock, showed a continuation of this trend. It said the former Yankee slugger had spent a comfortable night and was "holding his own." "There has been no significant change," the announcement said.

In the next few hours, however, the patient's temperature began to rise. Early in the afternoon his condition was obviously worse. At 2:20 P.M. the second bulletin noted that pulmonary complications that had not been present the previous day had returned in "moderate" degree. At the same time the Babe showed difficulty in taking nourishment.

But the full extent of his relapse did not become evident until nearly three hours later. In a special bulletin at 5:10 P.M.—ordinarily hospital authorities would have waited until 9 P.M. for the next report—it was announced:

"Pulmonary complications have become worse since this morning. Condition considered more critical."

Even then, however, visitors to the hospital were unaware that anything unusual was taking place. The groups of youngsters that on previous days had gathered outside the twelve-story building were missing. There was no excitement in the lobby, and most of the green chairs were unoccupied.

At 6:25 o'clock the second special bulletin was issued. As the word passed down from the patient's room on the ninth floor to the lobby, photographers began testing their equipment.

Within five minutes, a flurry of telephone calls that set switch-board lights flashing made it apparent that news of the Babe's extremely critical condition had spread beyond the hospital.

From the moment it became known last Wednesday that Babe Ruth was critically ill, his condition became a matter of nation-wide concern exceeding that usually accorded to the country's most important public officials, industrialists and princes of the church.

## RUTH'S PAY BY SEASONS

### DURING BASEBALL CAREER

Babe Ruth's salary by seasons for his professional baseball career follows:

| Year | Team | Salary | Year | Team | Salary |
|------|------|--------|------|------|--------|
| 1914 | Baltimore (I.L.) | $600 | 1926 | New York (A.L.) | 52,000 |
| *1914 | Boston (A.L.) | 1,300 | 1927 | New York (A.L.) | 70,000 |
| 1915 | Boston (A.L.) | 3,500 | 1928 | New York (A.L.) | 70,000 |
| 1916 | Boston (A.L.) | 3,500 | 1929 | New York (A.L.) | 70,000 |
| 1917 | Boston (A.L.) | 5,000 | 1930 | New York (A.L.) | 80,000 |
| 1918 | Boston (A.L.) | 7,000 | 1931 | New York (A.L.) | 80,000 |
| 1919 | Boston (A.L.) | 10,000 | 1932 | New York (A.L.) | 75,000 |
| 1920 | New York (A.L.) | 20,000 | 1933 | New York (A.L.) | 50,000 |
| 1921 | New York (A.L.) | 30,000 | 1934 | New York (A.L.) | 35,000 |
| 1922 | New York (A.L.) | 52,000 | 1935 | Boston (N.L.) | 40,000 |
| 1923 | New York (A.L.) | 52,000 | 1938 | Brooklyn (N.L.) | 15,000 |
| 1924 | New York (A.L.) | 52,000 | Total | | $925,900 |
| 1925 | New York (A.L.) | 52,000 | | | |

*Bought by Red Sox from Baltimore and farmed to Providence (I.L.).

Headed by President Truman and Cardinal Spellman, American leaders in many fields inquired about his health and wished him recovery. By last night more than 15,000 messages had been received at the hospital from all over the United States and Canada.

The range of greetings to the ailing man, who was more famous in his heyday than Presidents, showed how strong a hold he still had on the people.

On the one hand, Mayor James M. Curley of Boston set aside Friday in his city as "Babe Ruth Day," thus following the precedent established in New York on July 26. At the other extreme, hundreds of youngsters huddled outside the hospital or drifted into the lobby for a few moments.

Though many persons had long been aware that the famous slugger was very ill, the first announcement of his critical condition on Wednesday came as a shock. He had entered Memorial Hospital on June 24, presumably for observation and rest.

Last Monday, when it became known that he had a cold, the situation was not considered alarming by the public, particularly when, the next day, his condition was reported improved. The Babe had been in and out of hospitals since Nov. 26, 1946, when he was admitted to French Hospital.

On Wednesday, however, it was obvious that this illness might be Ruth's last. Only his wife, immediate relatives and close friends were allowed to see him. He was running a high temperature, hospital officials said then, and there were pulmonary complications. Police Headquarters added telephone operators because of the surge of public interest.

The next day, though the Babe improved slightly, his condition was still critical. That evening his personal physician conferred with Dr. George Baehr, president of the New York Academy of Medicine.

By Friday, the hospital was issuing its reports only three times a day and the patient was reported to be continuing his recovery. His temperature went down and he began taking nourishment. However, he was still on the critical list.

That night, at the Yankee Stadium, more than 60,000 fans stood for a minute in silent prayer for the man whose bat had furnished so much baseball drama.

Over the week-end the patient's improvement continued. His temperature went down and he took more nourishment. On Sunday he even left his bed for twenty minutes after spending what the hospital bulletin called "the most restful night of the past ten days."

August 17, 1948

## Throng at Yankees-Giants Game Stands At Polo Grounds for a Moment of Silence

News of Babe Ruth's death came last night to the Polo Grounds a few minutes before the New York Yankees—the team on which he starred for so many years—was about to take the field against the New York Giants in their annual game for possession of the Mayor O'Dwyer Trophy.

Over the public address system, announcer Jim Gorey told the huge gathering of Ruth's passing and asked the crowd to stand for a moment of silent prayer. Men, women and children rose, the men with heads bared, while the members of the two teams doffed their caps and stood in front of the dugouts.

The moment of silence over, the Giants trotted out on the field to defend their territory against the "alien" Yankees—and the crowd roared. It was just as the Babe would have it, a game he would have been watching.

Mayor O'Dwyer, scheduled to hurl the first ball, arrived too late for the ceremony but not too late to express his regrets.

"All I have to say," he declared, "is what the whole town and the whole nation has to say—God bless him and may he have a happy landing."

Before Col. Jake Ruppert and Col. Til Huston erected the Yankee stadium—the house that Ruth built—the Babe was hitting home runs in the Polo Grounds. His passing was in the tradition, for the Yankees were playing the Giants before a gathering of about 18,000 to raise funds for the city's agencies devoted to the sandlot baseball.

The players in the opposing dugouts, the Giants in the "home" team cubicle to the first base side of the plate, and the Yanks in the "visitors" quarters to the third base side of home, were sobered and saddened by the news. They shuffled about on the benches silently.

# NATION'S LEADERS MOURN BABE RUTH

## Truman Joins With Others in Expressing Sorrow Over Death of Baseball Star

President Truman joined with leaders in the sports world and in other fields throughout the nation last night in expressing sorrow at the passing of Babe Ruth. Charles G. Ross, White House press secretary, said the President was informed of the baseball star's death soon after it was announced and arranged to send a message of condolence to Mrs. Ruth.

The White House had called the Memorial Hospital here last week at Mr. Truman's request to inquire about the Babe's condition.

Former President Herbert Hoover said in a statement here: "He was a great sportsman in the very best sense of the term."

Mr. Hoover recalled that when a small boy asked him for his autograph during a public gathering in Los Angeles, the lad requested and received three copies "because it takes two of yours to trade for one of Babe Ruth's."

Word of Babe Ruth's death reached Governor Dewey and Gov. Earl Warren of California while the Republican standard bearers were conferring at Albany on campaign plans, according to the Associated Press. They issued the following statement:

Governor Dewey: "George Herman Ruth was the idol of millions of sports-loving Americans. A spectacular baseball player whose equal may never be reached, Babe Ruth was above all a great American. An inspiration to generations of youth all over the country, he typified the fair play, honesty and clean sportsmanship that exemplified American sport. An ambassador of good-will, he took these American sports ideals to the four corners of the earth. In his passing, I have lost a good friend. He will be greatly missed by the many, millions of his fans who knew and loved him."

Governor Warren: "A great American has passed on. Few men in American history have been a greater inspiration to the youth of our land. Throughout his life he played the game fair and hard and never gave up to the very end. Those of us who not only admired him, but knew him feel a deep sense of personal loss in his passing."

### Chandler Pays Tribute

Baseball Commissioner A. B. (Happy) Chandler said:

"His was the American story, the boy who came up from obscurity to learn the people's game and go on to be a great national hero. His deeds will be an inspiration for the children of the world who will try to emulate him."

### League President's Tribute

Will Harridge, president of the American League, said: "Babe Ruth was the greatest single figure and personality in the history of baseball. The indomitable sportsmanship and courage he displayed so many years on the playing field, which he showed through his long illness, stands as a part of a glorious Ruth legend that will live on always in the annals of our national sport and be an inspiration to youth forever."

Ford Frick, president of the National League:

"Babe Ruth needed every inch of that big chest of his to protect the world's largest heart. I knew the Babe well when I traveled with the Yankees as a baseball writer, and I never saw a man with more heart—and you can interpret that as meaning both courage on the field and consideration for others."

Edward G. Barrow, former president of the New York Yankees, who converted Babe Ruth from a southpaw pitcher into an outfielder who became the all-time homerun king, almost collapsed when he received the news at his home in Larchmont.

"Oh, my God," he said. "I just can't believe it. I am terribly shocked and terribly sorry. He was certainly the greatest player of them all. This is a tremendous personal loss to me and even greater loss for all America."

## Last Reunion On June 28

Barrow's last reunion with Ruth was on June 18 at Yankee Stadium when the players of the 1923 world championship Yankees gathered for their silver anniversary. Both broke into tears when they embraced on the diamond. Mr. Barrow, who now is more than 80 years old, had many differences with Ruth, mostly in regards to the star's fabulous salary and his indifference to training rules, but beneath it all there existed a warm friendship.

Other tributes were:

BURT SHOTTON, Manager Brooklyn Dodgers—All of us in baseball mourn the passing of a great and courageous fellow. But today's players in particular owe a debt of gratitude to Babe Ruth. His spectacular fests on the diamond widened interest in the game, drew record crowds and enabled club owners to double and even triple the capacity of big-league parks.

GEORGE WEISS, general manager of the Yankees—The Yankee organization deeply mourns the passing of Babe Ruth. He will always be the outstanding symbol of Yankee baseball.

EMIL FUCHS, once president and for a brief period manager of the Boston Braves, who hired Ruth as a player and "assistant manager" after the Babe drew his release from the Yankees—Ruth was a great figure in the game and but for certain circumstances would probably still be alive and here at Braves Field today. He was a colorful figure—how colorful we will realize when today's big attendances return to normal.

BILLY SOUTHWORTH, manager of Boston Braves—In all the years I have been associated with baseball I cannot recall any one event which has saddened so many ball players as the news that Babe Ruth had passed away.

LEO DUROCHER, Giants manager, who played on one of the Ruth clubs—I am shocked at the news. Somehow I thought he would pull through. Babe was a great competitor. His passing is a loss not only to baseball but to sports generally.

FRANKIE FRISCH, who played on the Cardinals against the Yanks in World Series competition—I played against the Babe many, many times, and I never have seen a greater player. He will never be forgotten.

FRANKIE CROSETTI, only remaining Yankee player who was a contemporary of Ruth—I will always consider it one of the greatest thrills to have played with the Babe.

BUCKY HARRIS, leader of the Yankee squad, who played against Ruth in his heyday—There will never be another like him. He was a great competitor and a great guy.

BILL MEYER, Pirate manager and one of the few men now in baseball who batted against Ruth when he pitched for the Red Sox—That he was also a great pitcher as well as a hitter is almost forgotten.

GEORGE KELLY, coach of the Cincinnati Reds, who opposed Ruth in World Series games while with the Giants—All ball players owe Babe a debt of gratitude for the high salaries that have come to baseball.

TRIS SPEAKER, who played with Ruth in Boston when the Babe entered the American League—A great loss to the baseball world, and, especially, to the kids, for he was their champion.

MUDDY RUEL, Cleveland coach who was a teammate of Ruth's shortly after World War I—No baseball player ever meant so much to so many. Millions of youngsters looked to him as an idol and an incentive.

August 17, 1948

## Ruth's Highlights

### HIS FIRST GAME
### Cleveland at Boston, July 21, 1914

| CLEVELAND (A.) | ab. | r. | h. | po. | a. | e. | BOSTON (A.) | ab. | r. | h. | po. | a. | e. |
|---|---|---|---|---|---|---|---|---|---|---|---|---|---|
| Jack Graney, lf | 4 | 1 | 2 | 4 | 0 | 1 | Olaf Henriksen, lf | 4 | 0 | 0 | 0 | 0 | 0 |
| Terry Turner, 3b | 3 | 0 | 0 | 0 | 4 | 0 | Duffy Lewis, lf | 1 | 0 | 1 | 0 | 0 | 0 |
| Joe Jackson, rf | 4 | 0 | 2 | 2 | 0 | 0 | Everett Scott, ss | 4 | 1 | 1 | 2 | 3 | 0 |
| Larry Lajole, 2b | 4 | 0 | 0 | 0 | 0 | 0 | Tris Speaker, cf | 4 | 1 | 1 | 3 | 1 | 1 |
| Jay Kirke, 1b | 4 | 1 | 2 | 6 | 2 | 1 | Larry Gardner, 3b | 4 | 1 | 3 | 1 | 4 | 0 |
| Ray Chapman, ss | 4 | 1 | 1 | 3 | 1 | 0 | Hal Javrin, 1b | 3 | 0 | 1 | 15 | 2 | 0 |
| Nemo Leibold, cf | 2 | 0 | 0 | 2 | 0 | 0 | Walter Rehg, rf | 4 | 0 | 0 | 0 | 0 | 0 |
| Steve O'Neill, c | 3 | 0 | 1 | 6 | 2 | 2 | Steve Yerkes, 2b | 2 | 1 | 0 | 0 | 6 | 0 |
| Bill Mitchell, p | 0 | 0 | 0 | 0 | 1 | 0 | Bill Carrigan, c | 2 | 0 | 1 | 6 | 0 | 0 |
| | | | | | | | Babe Ruth, p | 2 | 0 | 0 | 0 | 4 | 0 |
| | | | | | | | Hub Leonard, p | 0 | 0 | 0 | 0 | 1 | 0 |
| Total | 31 | 3 | 8 | 24 | 10 | 4 | Total | 30 | 4 | 8 | 27 | 21 | 1 |

| | | | | | | | | | |
|---|---|---|---|---|---|---|---|---|---|
| Cleveland | 0 | 0 | 0 | 1 | 0 | 0 | 2 | 0 | 0—3 |
| Boston | 1 | 0 | 0 | 2 | 0 | 0 | 1 | 0 | x—4 |

Three-base hits—Gardner. Sacrifices—Turner, Leibold, Janvrin. Stolen bases—Speaker, Yerkes. Left on bases—Boston 5, Cleveland 2, Struck out—By Mitchell 5, Ruth 1, Leonard 4. Hits—Off Ruth 8 in 7 innings, Leonard 0 in 2. Winning pitcher—Ruth. Umpires—Connolly and O'Loughlin. Time of game—1:53.

## HIS 60TH HOME RUN
### Washington at New York, Sept. 30, 1927

| WASHINGTON (A.) | ab. | r. | h. | po. | a. | e. | NEW YORK (A.) | ab. | r. | h. | po. | a. | e. |
|---|---|---|---|---|---|---|---|---|---|---|---|---|---|
| Sam Rice, rf | 3 | 0 | 1 | 2 | 0 | 0 | Earle Combs, rf | 4 | 0 | 0 | 3 | 0 | 0 |
| Bucky Harris, 2b | 3 | 0 | 0 | 3 | 4 | 0 | Mark Koenig, ss | 4 | 1 | 1 | 3 | 5 | 0 |
| Chick Ganzel, cf | 4 | 0 | 1 | 1 | 0 | 0 | Babe Ruth, rf | 3 | 3 | 3 | 4 | 0 | 0 |
| Goose Goslin, lf | 4 | 1 | 1 | 5 | 0 | 0 | Lou Gehrig, 1b | 4 | 0 | 2 | 10 | 0 | 1 |
| Joe Judge, 1b | 4 | 0 | 0 | 8 | 0 | 0 | Bob Meusel, lf | 3 | 0 | 1 | 3 | 0 | 0 |
| Muddy Ruel, c | 2 | 1 | 1 | 2 | 0 | 0 | Tony Lazzeri, 2b | 3 | 0 | 0 | 2 | 2 | 0 |
| Ossie Bluege, 3b | 3 | 0 | 1 | 1 | 4 | 0 | Joe Dugan, 2b | 3 | 0 | 1 | 1 | 1 | 0 |
| Jack Gillis, ss | 4 | 0 | 0 | 2 | 1 | 0 | Ben Bengough, c | 3 | 0 | 1 | 1 | 2 | 0 |
| Tom Zachary, p | 2 | 0 | 0 | 0 | 1 | 0 | Geo. Pipgras, p | 2 | 0 | 0 | 0 | 2 | 0 |
| [a]Walter Johnson | 1 | 0 | 0 | 0 | 0 | 0 | Herb Pennock, p | 1 | 0 | 0 | 0 | 1 | 0 |
| Total | 30 | 2 | 5 | 24 | 10 | 0 | Total | 30 | 4 | 9 | 27 | 13 | 1 |

[a]Batted for Zachary in ninth.

| Washington | 0 | 0 | 0 | 2 | 0 | 0 | 0 | 0 | 0—2 |
|---|---|---|---|---|---|---|---|---|---|
| New York | 0 | 0 | 0 | 1 | 0 | 1 | 0 | 2 | x—4 |

Runs batted in—Ruth 2, Gehrig, Meusel, Ruel, Bluege.

Two-base hits—Rice. Three-base hit—Koenig. Home run—Ruth. Stolen bases—Ruel, Bluege, Rice. Double plays—Harris and Bluege; Gillies, Harris and Judge. Bases on balls—Off Pipgras 4, Pennock 1, Zachary 1. Struck out—By Zachary 1. Hit by pitcher—By Pipgras 1. Winning pitcher—Pennock. Umpires—Dinneen, Collony and Owens.

# HIS BIGGEST DAY
## New York at Chicago (N.L.), World Series game
### Oct. 1, 1932, where he called his home run shot against Charlie Root.

| NEW YORK (A.) | ab. | r. | h. | po. | a. | e. | CHICAGO (N.) | ab. | r. | h. | po. | a. | e. |
|---|---|---|---|---|---|---|---|---|---|---|---|---|---|
| Earle Combs, rf | 5 | 1 | 0 | 1 | 0 | 0 | Bill Herman, 2b | 4 | 1 | 0 | 1 | 2 | 1 |
| Joe Sewell, 3b | 2 | 1 | 0 | 2 | 2 | 0 | Woody English, 3b | 4 | 0 | 0 | 0 | 3 | 0 |
| Babe Ruth, rf | 4 | 2 | 2 | 2 | 0 | 0 | Kiki Cuyler, rf | 4 | 1 | 3 | 1 | 0 | 0 |
| Lou Gehrig, 1b | 5 | 2 | 2 | 13 | 1 | 0 | R. Stephenson, lf | 4 | 0 | 1 | 1 | 0 | 0 |
| Tony Lazzeri, 2b | 4 | 1 | 0 | 3 | 4 | 1 | John Moore, cf | 3 | 1 | 0 | 3 | 0 | 0 |
| Bill Dickey, c | 4 | 0 | 1 | 2 | 1 | 0 | Chas. Grimm, 1b | 4 | 0 | 1 | 8 | 0 | 0 |
| Ben Chapman, rf | 4 | 0 | 2 | 0 | 0 | 0 | Leo Hartnett, c | 4 | 1 | 1 | 10 | 1 | 1 |
| Frank Crosetti, ss | 4 | 0 | 1 | 4 | 4 | 0 | Billy Jurges, ss | 4 | 1 | 3 | 3 | 3 | 2 |
| Geo. Pipgras, p | 5 | 0 | 0 | 0 | 0 | 0 | Charles Root, p | 2 | 0 | 0 | 0 | 0 | 0 |
| Herb Pennock, p | 0 | 0 | 0 | 0 | 1 | 0 | Pat Malone, p | 0 | 0 | 0 | 0 | 0 | 0 |
| | | | | | | | Jake May, p | 0 | 0 | 0 | 0 | 0 | 0 |
| | | | | | | | Bud Tinning, p | 0 | 0 | 0 | 0 | 0 | 0 |
| | | | | | | | aMarv Gudat | 1 | 0 | 0 | 0 | 0 | 0 |
| | | | | | | | bMark Koenig | 0 | 0 | 0 | 0 | 0 | 0 |
| | | | | | | | cRollie Hemsley | 1 | 0 | 0 | 0 | 0 | 0 |
| Total | 37 | 7 | 8 | 27 | 13 | 1 | Total | 35 | 5 | 9 | 27 | 9 | 4 |

aBatted for Malone in seventh.
bBatted for Tinning in ninth.
cBatted for Koenig in ninth.

| New York | 3 | 0 | 1 | 0 | 2 | 0 | 0 | 0 | 1—7 |
|---|---|---|---|---|---|---|---|---|---|
| Chicago | 1 | 0 | 2 | 1 | 0 | 0 | 0 | 0 | 1—5 |

Runs batted in—Ruth 4, Gehrig 2, Cuyler 2, Grimm, Chapman, Hartnett.

Two-base hits—Chapman, Cuyler, Jurges, Grimm. Home run—Ruth 2, Gehrig 2, Cuyler, Hartnett. Stolen base—Jurges. Double plays—Sewell, Lazzeri and Gehrig; Herman, Jurges and Grimm. Struck out—By Root 4, Malone 4, May 1, Tinning 1, Pipgras 1, Pennock 1. Bases on balls—Off Root 3, Malone 4, Pipgras 3. Hits—Off Root 6 in 4 1–3 innings, Malone 1 in 2 2–3, May 1 in 1 2–3, Tinning 0 in 2–3, Pipgras 9 in 8, Pennock 0 in 1. Hit by pitcher—By May 1. Winning pitcher—Pipgras. Losing pitcher—Root. Umpires—Van Graflan, Magerkurth, Dinneen and Klem. Time of game—2:11. Attendance—49,986.

# LOU GEHRIG

Postage stamp of Lou Gehrig, 1989.

## Yanks Win at Last—Robins Beat Giants in 12th

---

### BABE'S TYING BLOW HELPS YANKEES WIN

---

### Convalescent Slugger's Two-Bagger in Eighth Starts Senators' Downfall by 8 to 5.

---

### BOB MEUSEL GETS 2 HOMERS

---

### Second Drive Brings Combs and Witt in Right After the Bambino's Big Bang.

---

### RADICAL SHIFT BY HUGGINS

---

### Gehrig Supplants Pipp, Shanks Has Ward's Place and Bengough Does the Catching.

---

### By JAMES R. HARRISON.

He may be a trifle peaked and pallid, but the Babe still packs a terrific wallop. He may still be a pale and interesting invalid, but the Washington Senators found him a healthy and able-bodied citizen in the eighth inning yesterday, when his ringing two-bagger to right centre drove in the tying run at the Stadium.

The ball soared over Joe Harris's head and rolled to the right field bleachers on the short bound. With a little sharper trajectory toward the bleachers the pill would have drifted into the sun seats for a home run. As it was, Bob Meusel followed with a four-base gem to left centre—his second homer of the game—and the three resulting tallies gave the Yanks an 8–5 victory over the Senators.

Day by day the Babe is getting better and better. In four official times at bat he gathered two hits. He was hit by a pitched ball the first time, fanned the second, singled the third, grounded out the fourth and doubled in the fifth.

After slapping the two-bagger in the eighth George retired to let Whitey Witt scamper for him. Whitey was one of the advance guard which preceded Meusel to the plate.

Miller Huggins took his favorite line-up and shook it to pieces. Wally Pipp, after more than ten years as regular first baseman, was benched in favor of Lou Gehrig, the former Columbia University fence-wrecker. Aaron Ward, another old standby, surrendered second base to Howard Shanks. Steve O'Neill and Wally Schang perched themselves comfortably on the bench while Benny Bengough donned the mask and protector.

### Only Three Regulars at Hand.

The most radical shakeup of the Yankee line-up in many years left only three regulars of last season in the batting order—Dugan, Ruth and Meusel. Gehrig made two singles and a double in his first three trips to the front. Shanks's single played a prominent role in the first run, and Bengough covered himself with glory and perspiration by socking three clean singles in four times at bat. And still they say that little Bennah can't hit.

The Yanks were a run in arrears when Veach, hitting for Wanninger, pried loose the eighth with a single to right, Ernie Johnson ran for him. Dugan sacrificed and Combs got a walk.

Along came Ruth. The outfielders went back to the edge of the greensward. Babe looked over Allen Russell's assortment carefully and finally picked out one he liked. He took an old-time lunge at it and whipped a fly to right centre. Despite the fleetest footwork of Messrs. Rice and Joe Harris, the ball landed in the great open spaces and reached the bleachers in a couple of bounces. Johnson scored. Combs legged it to third and the Bambino trudged along to second.

Meusel followed with a thunderous clout to left centre. Combs and Wit were over in a jiffy. The ball landed on the running track and bounced to the fence. Meusel coming over the plate without the formality of a slide. It was California Bob's fourteenth homer of the season.

### Shocker Retires in Fifth.

Urban Shocker lasted only five innings under the Senatorial gunfire. In the second frame Bluege singled and Peck doubled to right for one run. The Yanks feasted on George Mogridge in the same inning. Gehrig, Shanks, Bengough and Shocker singled in succession for two runs, and after Wanninger's out Dugan drove in Bengough with a hit to left.

Three to one, but the Senators tied it in the third when Stan Harris singled and Joseph Ignatius Judge tickled a homer into the right field bleachers.

Meusel's first homer, a smack into the bleachers in right centre, sent the Yanks out in front again in the same inning, by which time Russell had taken the burden off Mogridge's shoulders. But in the fifth the Senators came even again on Ruel's single, Russell's sacrifice and Rice's base hit. When Bucky Harris singled, Shocker receded in favor of Ferguson, who showed unexpected prowess by fanning Judge and Goslin.

Off Ferguson the Nationals counted what looked like the triumphant tally in the sixth. Joe Harris pried it open with a single and Bluege did the sacrificial stuff successfully. On Peckinpaugh's single to left centre Harris trekked homeward.

Ferguson tolerated no runs and only two hits thereafter and kept away from trouble while his playmates assassinated Mr. Russell in the eighth. This was only as it should be.

The score:

| NEW YORK (A.) | Ab | R | H | Po | A | WASHINGTON (A.) | Ab | R | H | Po | A |
|---|---|---|---|---|---|---|---|---|---|---|---|
| Wan'ger, ss | 4 | 0 | 1 | 2 | 5 | Rice, cf | 5 | 0 | 2 | 0 | 0 |
| aVeach | 1 | 0 | 1 | 0 | 0 | S. Harris, 2b | 5 | 1 | 2 | 6 | 1 |
| E. John'n, ss | 0 | 1 | 0 | 0 | 0 | Judge, 1b | 4 | 1 | 1 | 7 | 2 |
| Dugan, 3b | 2 | 0 | 2 | 1 | 1 | Goslin, lf | 4 | 0 | 0 | 2 | 0 |
| Combs, cf | 4 | 1 | 0 | 3 | 1 | J. Harris, rf | 4 | 1 | 1 | 2 | 0 |
| Ruth, rf | 4 | 0 | 2 | 2 | 0 | Bluege, 3b | 3 | 1 | 1 | 1 | 1 |
| bWitt | 0 | 1 | 0 | 0 | 0 | Peck'p'gh, ss | 4 | 0 | 3 | 1 | 1 |
| Paschel, rf | 0 | 0 | 0 | 1 | 0 | Ruel, c | 4 | 1 | 2 | 5 | 1 |
| Meusel, lf | 5 | 2 | 2 | 2 | 0 | Mogridge, p | 0 | 0 | 0 | 0 | 1 |
| Gehrig, 1b | 5 | 1 | 3 | 8 | 1 | cLiebold | 1 | 0 | 0 | 0 | 0 |
| Shanks, 2b | 4 | 1 | 1 | 2 | 2 | Russell, p | 1 | 0 | 0 | 0 | 4 |
| Bengough, c | 4 | 1 | 3 | 5 | 0 | dRuether | 1 | 0 | 0 | 0 | 0 |
| Shocker, p | 2 | 0 | 1 | 0 | 0 | | | | | | |
| Ferguson, p | 2 | 0 | 0 | 1 | 2 | | | | | | |
| Total | 37 | 8 | 16 | 27 | 12 | Total | 36 | 5 | 12 | 24 | 11 |

Errors—None

aBatted for Wanninger in eighth.

bRan for Ruth in eighth.

cBatted for Mogridge in third.

dBatted for Russell in ninth.

| | | | | | | | | | | |
|---|---|---|---|---|---|---|---|---|---|---|
| New York | 0 | 3 | 1 | 0 | 0 | 0 | 0 | 4 | ..—8 | |
| Washington | 0 | 1 | 2 | 0 | 1 | 1 | 0 | 0 | 0—5 | |

Two-base hits—Peckinpaugh, Gehrig, Ruth. Three-base hits—Peckinpaugh. Home runs—Judge, Meusel (2). Sacrifices—Russell, Bluege, Dugan (2). Left on bases—New York 11, Washington 6. Bases on balls—Off Russell 3. Struck-out—By Mogridge 1, by Russell 4, by Shocker 1, by Ferguson 3. Hits—Off Mogridge 6 in 2 innings, Russell 10 in 6, Shocker 8 in 4 1–3, Ferguson 4 in 4 2–3. Hit by pitcher—By Mogridge (Ruth). Winning pitcher—Ferguson. Losing pitcher—Russell. Umpires—Hildebrand, Connolly and Evans. Time of game—2:00.

Lou Gehrig gets the 1927 American League Most Valuable Player Award. (TIMES WIDE WORLD PHOTOS)

October 12, 1927

## Gehrig Gets American League Most Valuable Player Award

### BEST-PLAYER AWARD GOES TO LOU GEHRIG

### Yankee First Baseman is Voted Most Valuable Performer in American League.

### GETS 56 POINTS OUT OF 64

### Lazzeri Receives Single Vote as Yanks Best Man—Heilmann Next, With 35; Lyons Follows, With 34.

### By The Associated Press.

CHICAGO, Oct. 11.—Lou Gehrig, star first baseman with the world champion Yankees, tonight was proclaimed the most valuable player in the American League for the 1927 season.

Selection of Gehrig, who gave Babe Ruth a sizzling battle for home run honors and finished with a total of forty-seven, more than any other player has made in baseball history except Ruth himself, was made by a committee of baseball writers representing the cities of the league. All but one of the first choice votes were given to Gehrig, who won the coveted honors with 58 points out of a possible 64.

Gehrig's nearest competitors for the honors were Harry Heilmann, Detroit outfielder and 1927 batting champion of the American League, and Ted Lyons, star pitcher with the Chicago White Sox. Heilmann had 35 points, while 34 went to Lyons.

### One Vote Cast for Lazzeri.

The only dissenting vote was cast for Tony Lazzeri, as the most valuable player for the Yankees, while all the others chose Columbia Lou, not only as the most valuable player of the Yankees but the greatest in the league. Twenty-five players were named in this year's competition.

President Ban Johnson of the American League, in announcing the results of the balloting, praised Gehrig as a great example for the youth today. Gehrig causes umpires no trouble, President Johnson said, attends strictly to business and has always given the club his best efforts.

Gehrig, finished third in the batting list in the American League, closed the season with the honor of driving in more runs than any other player in the league.

In 154 games Gehrig was at bat 584 times. He made 218 hits for a total of 427 bases. These included 53 doubles, 18 triples and his 47 homers. He drove in 175 runs, averaging better than a run a game. Gehrig is regarded as a natural ball player. He is a steady fielder, but his terrific hitting was the important thing in his favor.

### Gehrig Native of New York.

Gehrig, born in New York on June 19, 1903, began his baseball career with the High School of Commerce of New York. He later played at Columbia. He joined the Yankees in 1923 and was later sent to Hartford. He returned to the New York club in time to play in the last ten games of the 1924 season, when the veteran Wally Pipp went to the Reds. Gehrig, who had been Pipp's understudy, became the guardian of first base.

Stockily built and somewhat shorter than Ruth, Gehrig follows through in batting with the same powerful swing that enabled the Babe to set a baseball record of all times with his sixty home runs.

The result of the balloting for this season's award follows:

| | Points | | Points |
|---|---|---|---|
| Henry Lou Gehrig, first base, New York | 56 | Horace Lizenbee, pitcher, Washington | 5 |
| Harry Heilmann, outfield, Detroit | 35 | Edmund Miller, outfield, St. Louis | 5 |
| Ted Lyons, pitcher, Chicago | 34 | Alex Meizler, outfield, Chicago | 4 |
| Gordon Cochrane, catcher, Philadelphia | 18 | Ira Flagstead, outfield, Boston | 3 |
| Al Simmons, outfield, Philadelphia | 18 | Charles Jamieson, outfield, Cleveland | 3 |
| Leon Goslin, outfield, Washington | 15 | Walter Shang, catcher, St. Louis | 3 |
| Harold Ruel, catcher, Washington | 15 | Fred Schultz, outfield, St. Louis | 3 |
| James Dykes, infield, Philadelphia | 14 | Willis Hudlin, pitcher, Cleveland | 2 |
| Luke Sewall, catcher, Cleveland | 13 | William Regan, second base, Boston | 2 |
| Tony Lazzeri, second base, New York | 8 | Jack Rothrock, infield, Boston | 2 |
| R.E. Reeves, shortstop, Washington | 7 | Bryan Harris, pitcher, Boston | 1 |
| Frank O'Rourke, third base, St. Louis | 6 | Phillip Tedt, first base, Boston | 1 |
| Jack Tavener, shortstop, Detroit | 6 | | |

### Sisler First to Gain Honor.

The most valuable player award was inaugurated in the American League in 1922 when George Sisler of the St. Louis Browns was the winner. Babe Ruth took the honor in 1923 and the following year Walter Johnson of the Senators was voted the most valuable player. Roger Peckinpaugh of the Senators won the vote in 1925 and last year George Burns of the Indians was named.

The award in the American League is made each year under a rule that no player may be named more than once. In the national League the rule is that a player may be chosen any number of times.

May 5, 1929

# 3 HOMERS BY GEHRIG HELP YANKS WIN, 11–9

## Gets Trio of Circuit Drives for 2nd Time in Career in Victory Over White Sox.

## RUTH CONNETCS WITH NO. 3

## Meusel Also Contributes 4-Bagger in 16-Hit Barrage Against 3 Chicago Pitchers.

## 25,000 WITNESS STRUGGLE

## Hoyt Knocked Out in 6th, but Hard Clubbing by Mates Brings New York Triumph.

### By JOHN DREBINGER.

*Special to The New York Times.*

CHICAGO, May 4.—Opening their first swing of the year around the Western loop of the American League, the Yankees clubbed the White Sox into submission here this afternoon by a score of 11 to 9, and in the midst of all this turmoil, which brought a deal of woe to a gathering of 25,000, Miller Huggins made a startling discovery. It is to the effect that the Yankees really need no pitcher.

Waite Hoyt, holding three successive victories to his credit and the distinction of being the only Huggins hurler to date to start and finish a game, blew up with a loud detonation in the sixth and at that moment life was all misery for Miller Huggins.

But along about this time Huggins's clouters, of which he has many, stepped in and in scarcely no time at all turned the little Miller's grief to smiles.

## Five Homers by Yankees.

This grand array of clouters pummeled three White Sox pitchers, Red Faber, Hal McKain and Danny Dugan to a pulp with sixteen hits. Five of these blows were homers. Three of the homers were made by Lou Gehrig, to bring his season's total to six. Babe Ruth got one, to give him his No. 3 of the year, and Bob Meusel got the other one.

In addition to this, Ruth also cracked a valuable double, drove in two other runs with a single, and Gehrig also drove in one other tally with a one-base thump. Comiskey's Park tonight was fairly riddled full of holes.

Incidentally, this was the second time in his young career as pretender to the home run crown still worn by Ruth that Gehrig hit three in a day. The first time he did this was on June 23, 1927, against the Red Sox. The all-time record for homers in one game is held by Bobby Howe and Ed Delehanty at four each. Their performance came before 1900.

## White Sox Score in First.

Hoyt was anything but secure in getting away, but had the good fortune to escape with only one run being scored against him in the first. He walked Metzler and Kerr singled. Kamm was retired, but Clancy lifted a sacrifice fly to Ruth and Metzler counted. Two more passes followed and Hoyt was in more trouble, but squirmed out of it, holding Cissell to a fly.

In the second inning Gehrig squared matters for the Yankees by clouting his fourth home run of the season, a tremendous smash that sailed high over the double-decked stand in right field, but in the third the White Sox stepped in front again when Cissell slapped a homer into the left-field stands. This blow accounted for two runs, as Hoffman had singled a moment before.

In the meantime, Faber was moving along at a terrific clip. The Gehrig homer in the second was the only interruption to a string of nine outs in the first three frames. But in the fourth, Red began to slip, a double by Ruth and a single by Gehrig giving the Yankees a run, and in the fifth the old man of forty Summers and Winters went down completely.

## Hoyt Opens With Single.

A single by Hoyt started it. Then came a single by Combs, another single by Ruth, a pass to Gehrig, a single by Meusel and a double by Lazzeri. In between all this clubbing came to White Sox errors, and when the inning was over the Yanks had four runs and McKain had supplanted Faber in the box.

But the Yanks enjoyed their 6-to-3 lead only until the next inning, when Hoyt was leveled to the floor for the first time this year. Between a pair of outs, Watwood doubled and Grouse singled. Metzler also singled, scoring Watwood, and when Kerr drew a pass the bases were filled. Then Kamm singled to left, scoring two runners, and when Dickey took Ruth's throw in and fired the ball wildly past third everybody came in, with Kamm bringing up the rear. This gave the Sox all told five runs for the inning and Wiley Moore came in to relieve Hoyt.

But all this only served to enrage the Yanks greatly, and in the seventh they opened on the luckless Mr. McKain their fiercest outburst of hitting of the year.

Combs doubled, and after Koenig had sacrificed him to third, Ruth crashed his third homer of the year into the upper tier of the right-field stand. No sooner had the furor of this hit subsided than Gehrig slammed one almost into the same spot for his second of the day and fifth of the season.

That wrote finis for McKain, and Danny Dugan, unsuspecting, young and left-handed, came on. To break the monotony Meusel greeted him with a homer inside the park. The hit bounced off the centre-field wall and Bob beat a string of relays to the plate with a burst of speed such as he probably has not shown in a great many years.

In the ninth, with Dugan still pitching, Gehrig, now thoroughly wound up, belted his third home run of the day and sixth of the season into the upper right-field tier for the Yanks' eleventh and final tally of the long afternoon.

Mr. Faber fairly overwhelmed the three Yanks to face him after Gehrig opened the second with a homer. The elderly gentleman fanned Meusel, Lazzeri and Durocher without so much as letting them see what he was throwing.

After Cassell cracked his homer in the third, Crouse almost added another one to the Sox total when his high wallop just missed clearing the right-field wall and dropping into the lower tier. However, it wasn't even a hit, for languid Bob Meusel got out to the wall about the same time, and with a great leap caught the ball in his gloved hand.

Ruth, even when he is bringing misery in the home team, seldom fails to amuse the fans. After scoring two with his single in the fifth he got himself trapped between first and second when Faber cut off Metzler's throw from left. The Babe, stood perfectly still until Faber was almost on top of him, then he lit out for first and made the bag with a long slide when Clancy dropped Red's toss.

George Pipgras, who has made three starts to date without getting by with any of them, is slated to try it again in the second game of the series here tomorrow.

The box score:

| NEW YORK (A.) | ab. | r. | h. | po. | a. | e. | CHICAGO (A.) | ab. | r. | h. | po. | a. | e. |
|---|---|---|---|---|---|---|---|---|---|---|---|---|---|
| Combs, cf | 5 | 2 | 3 | 3 | 0 | 0 | Metzler, lf | 4 | 2 | 2 | 1 | 1 | 1 |
| Koenig, 3b | 4 | 0 | 0 | 1 | 0 | 0 | Kerr, 2b | 4 | 1 | 1 | 1 | 6 | 0 |
| Ruth, lf | 3 | 2 | 3 | 3 | 0 | 0 | Kamm, 3b | 5 | 1 | 1 | 1 | 3 | 1 |
| Gehrig, 1 b | 4 | 4 | 4 | 11 | 1 | 1 | Clancy, 1b | 4 | 0 | 0 | 10 | 0 | 1 |
| Meusel, rf | 3 | 1 | 3 | 3 | 0 | 0 | Hofman, cf | 4 | 2 | 3 | 3 | 0 | 1 |
| Lazzeri, 2b | 8 | 1 | 1 | 0 | 6 | 0 | Watwood, rf | 4 | 1 | 1 | 2 | 0 | 0 |
| Durocher, ss | 5 | 1 | 1 | 0 | 2 | 0 | Cassell, ss | 5 | 1 | 2 | 1 | 0 | 0 |
| Dickey, c | 5 | 0 | 0 | 1 | 0 | 1 | Crouse, c | 4 | 1 | 1 | 8 | 0 | 0 |
| Hoyt, p | 3 | 1 | 1 | 0 | 1 | 1 | Faber, p | 1 | 0 | 0 | 0 | 1 | 0 |
| Moore, p | 1 | 0 | 0 | 0 | 1 | 0 | McKain, p | 1 | 0 | 0 | 0 | 0 | 0 |
| | | | | | | | Dugan, p | | | | | | |
| Total | 42 | 11 | 16 | [27?] | [10?] | | Total | 37 | 9 | 1 | 27 | 11 | 4 |

```
New York    0   1   0   1   4   0   4   0   1—11
Chicago     1   0   2   0   0   5   0   0   1—9
```

Runs batted in—Ruth 4, Gehrig 4, Meusel 2, Lazzeri, Cassell 2, Clancy, Metzler, Kamm 2, Watwood.

Two base hits—Ruth, Lazzeri, Watwood, Combs 2. Home runs—Gehrig 3, Cassell, Ruth, Meusel. Sacrifices—Clancy, Faber, Koenig. Left on bases—New York 8, Chicago 9. Bases on balls—Off Hoyt 4; Faber 1, Moore 1. Struck out—By Faber 3, McKain 1, Hoyt 1, Dugan 1. Hits—Off Faber [?] in 4 2–3 innings, McKain 4 in 1 2–3; Hoyt 3 in [3?] 1–3. Wild pitch—Faber. Winning pitcher—Moore. Losing pitcher—McKain. Umpires—Guthrie, McCarthy and Hildebrand. Time of game—2:20.

## Three Homers Each for Ruth and Gehrig as Yanks Win Twice; Giants, Robins Lose

### RUTH HITS THREE MORE AS YANKS WIN TWO

#### Drives 2 Homers in First Game, 1 in Second, Against Athletics—Ties 2 Marks.

### NOW HAS TWELVE HOME RUNS

#### Gehrig Connects Three Times, Once With the Bases Filled, in Nightcap.

### LEAGUE RECORD IS BROKEN

#### Ten Circuit Smashes by Both Clubs in Second Contest Erase Mark of Eight for Single Game.

#### By WILLIAM E. BRANDT.

*Special to The New York Times.*

PHILADELPHIA, May 22.—Babe Ruth's big bat shot three more homers over Shibe Park's right field wall today, but the rest of the Yankees chimed in, as well as divers and sundry Athletics, so that the cannonading resounded far and wide for nearly five hours and a half and near the finish the combined home-run hitting of the two teams tied a major league record and set a new American League record.

While the slogging records tottered and toppled the Yanks finished on the long end of the score in both games, 10 to 1 in the first and 20 to 13 in the second, thus gaining their first victories of the year over the champions and heading home tonight with an even break for the four-game series here.

Twenty-three thousand fans saw Ruth hit his tenth homer off Ehmke and his eleventh off Rommel in the third and fourth innings of the first game, then his twelfth off Quinn in the second game's second inning. He thus tied existing records for total homer production by an individual in three successive games and four successive games.

#### Three Times for Ruth.

Seven times previously in baseball annals a slugger has made five homers in three successive games. Twice it was Ruth, so that today he became the first player ever to bunch five homers in three successive games three times.

Only three times previously has a player ever bunched six homers in four games, and Ruth, in 1921, was the first. Since then Ken Williams and Chuck Klein have tied the feat, but today Ruth became to first man to do it twice.

Upon the bat of Henry Lou Gehrig, Ruth's apt pupil, fell the day's chief laurel for intensive homer production. In the second game Columbia's heaviest hitting alumnus poled the ball beyond the playing field's limits three times. In the first he did it against Bill Shores with the bases filled. In the fourth, with Lazzeri on base, he reached Rommel for his ninth of the season. He hit his season's tenth off Glenn Liebhardt in the ninth, with one on base.

Lou's feat today made him the first player ever to hit three homers in one league game on three different occasions.

Ruth, who has hit three homers in a game three times, did it twice in world's series games and here yesterday for the first time in a league game.

### Foxx Connects for Two.

That second game held six homer which neither Ruth nor Gehrig had a hand in. Beside Lou's three and Babe's one, Lazzeri poled one into the left field stands and for the Athletics Foxx hit two, while Dykes, Simmons and Bishop crashed one each.

These ten homers tied the major league record for total homers in one game, set by the Phillies and the Cardinals on May 11, 1923. It set a new league record, the former mark of eight having been hung up by the Athletics and Detroit on June 3, 1921.

The box scores:

### FIRST GAME.

| NEW YORK (A.) | ab. | r. | h. | po. | a. | e. | PHILADELPHIA (A.) | ab. | r. | h. | po. | a. | e. |
|---|---|---|---|---|---|---|---|---|---|---|---|---|---|
| Combs, cf | 4 | 2 | 1 | 2 | 0 | 0 | Bishop, 2b | 4 | 0 | 0 | 0 | 0 | 0 |
| Byrd, rf | 1 | 0 | 0 | 1 | 0 | 0 | Williams, 2b | 2 | 0 | 0 | 0 | 1 | 1 |
| Lary, ss | 5 | 2 | 3 | 1 | 3 | 0 | Haas, cf | 1 | 0 | 2 | 3 | 0 | 1 |
| Ruth, lf | 5 | 2 | 3 | 4 | 0 | 0 | Dykes, 3b | 2 | 0 | 1 | 1 | 6 | 0 |
| Lazzeri, 2b | 5 | 1 | 2 | 3 | 0 | 0 | Simmons, lf | 3 | 0 | 0 | 1 | 0 | 0 |
| Reese, 2b | 0 | 0 | 0 | 1 | 1 | 0 | Cramer, lf | 1 | 0 | 1 | 1 | 0 | 0 |
| Gehrig, 1b | 5 | 1 | 4 | 8 | 1 | 0 | Foxx, 1b | 4 | 0 | 0 | 11 | 1 | 0 |
| Hargrave, c | 4 | 0 | 0 | 4 | 0 | 0 | Miller, rf | 3 | 0 | 1 | 1 | 0 | 1 |
| Cooke, rf | 4 | 0 | 0 | 1 | 0 | 0 | Harris, rf | 1 | 0 | 0 | 2 | 0 | 0 |
| Chapman, 2b | 5 | 1 | 1 | 1 | 1 | 0 | Perkins, c | 4 | 0 | 0 | 5 | 1 | 1 |
| Pipgras, p | 5 | 1 | 2 | 1 | 1 | 0 | Roley, ss | 1 | 0 | 0 | 0 | 0 | 0 |
| | | | | | | | Mahaffey | 1 | 0 | 0 | 0 | 1 | 0 |
| | | | | | | | ªKeesey | 1 | 0 | 0 | 0 | 0 | 0 |
| | | | | | | | Ehmke, p | 0 | 0 | 0 | 0 | 0 | 0 |
| | | | | | | | Rommell, p | 0 | 0 | 0 | 0 | 0 | 0 |
| | | | | | | | McNair, ss | 3 | 1 | 1 | 2 | 0 | 0 |
| Total | 43 | 10 | 16 | 27 | 7 | 0 | Total | 31 | 1 | 6 | 27 | 10 | 4 |

ªbatted for Mahaffey in ninth.

| | | | | | | | | | | |
|---|---|---|---|---|---|---|---|---|---|---|
| New York | 2 | 1 | 2 | 3 | 0 | 0 | 0 | 0 | 2—10 |
| Philadelphia | 0 | 0 | 0 | 0 | 0 | 0 | 1 | 0 | 0—1 |

Runs batted in—Lazzeri 2, Pipgras, Ruth 3, Gehrig, Chapman 2, Haas.

Two-base hits—Lazzeri, Gehrig. Three-base hit—Haas. Home Runs—Pipgras, Ruth 2, Chapman. Stolen base—Lary. Sacrifices—Roley, Hargrave. Double play—Lary, Reese and Gehrig. Left on bases—New York 8, Philadelphia 8. Bases on balls—Off Pipgras 4, Mahaffey 1. Struck out—By Pipgras 3, Ehmke 1, Rommel 2, Mahaffey 3. Hits—Off Ehmke 8 in 2 innings (none out in 3d), Rommel 4 in 2, Mahaffey 4 in 5. Losing pitcher—Ehmke. Umpires—Dinneen, Nallin and Geisel. Time of game—1:50.

## SECOND GAME.

| NEW YORK (A.) | ab. | r. | h. | po. | a. | e. | PHILADELPHIA (A.) | ab. | r. | h. | po. | a. | e. |
|---|---|---|---|---|---|---|---|---|---|---|---|---|---|
| Combs, cf | 5 | 1 | 2 | 4 | 0 | 0 | Bishop, 2b | 3 | 3 | 1 | 2 | 3 | 0 |
| Lary, ss | 6 | 2 | 2 | 1 | 0 | 0 | Haas, cf | 6 | 1 | 2 | 0 | 1 | 0 |
| Ruth, lf | 4 | 2 | 1 | 3 | 0 | 0 | Dykes, 3b | 5 | 1 | 1 | 7 | 0 | 0 |
| Lazzeri, 2b | 4 | 5 | 4 | 1 | 7 | 0 | Simmons, lf | 1 | 3 | 3 | 4 | 0 | 0 |
| Reese, 2b | 1 | 0 | 0 | 0 | 0 | 0 | Foxx, 1b | 5 | 2 | 2 | 6 | 0 | 0 |
| Gehrig, 1b | 5 | 3 | 3 | 8 | 0 | 0 | Miller, rf | 4 | 1 | 2 | 1 | 0 | 0 |
| Dickey, c | 6 | 2 | 3 | 7 | 0 | 0 | Schang, c | 5 | 0 | 2 | 6 | 0 | 1 |
| Cooke, rf | 1 | 1 | 3 | 0 | 0 | 0 | ªMcNair, ss | 0 | 0 | 0 | 0 | 0 | 0 |
| Byrd, rf | 2 | 1 | 2 | 1 | 0 | 0 | Perkins, c | 3 | 0 | 0 | 0 | 0 | 0 |
| Chapman, 3b | 6 | 2 | 3 | 1 | 0 | 0 | Boley, ss | 5 | 1 | 2 | 0 | 4 | 0 |
| Hoyt, p | 1 | 0 | 0 | 1 | 0 | 0 | Shores, p | 0 | 0 | 0 | 0 | 0 | 0 |
| McEvoy, p | 1 | 0 | 0 | 0 | 0 | 0 | Quinn, p | 0 | 0 | 0 | 1 | 0 | 0 |
| Johnson, p | 0 | 0 | 0 | 0 | 1 | 0 | Rommel, p | 1 | 1 | 0 | 0 | 0 | 0 |
| Sherid, p | 1 | 1 | 0 | 0 | 0 | 0 | Earnshaw, p | 2 | 0 | 0 | 0 | 0 | 1 |
| | | | | | | | Grove, p. | 0 | 0 | 0 | 0 | 0 | 0 |
| | | | | | | | ᵇHarris | 1 | 0 | 0 | 0 | 0 | 0 |
| | | | | | | | Liebhardt, p | 0 | 0 | 0 | 0 | 0 | 0 |
| Total | 43 | 20 | 23 | 27 | 8 | 0 | Total | 41 | 13 | 15 | 27 | 8 | 2 |

ªRan for Schang in eighth.
ᵇBatted for Grove in eighth.

| | | | | | | | | | | |
|---|---|---|---|---|---|---|---|---|---|---|
| New York | 7 | 2 | 0 | 2 | 0 | 1 | 2 | 1 | 5—20 | |
| Philadelphia | 0 | 1 | 4 | 2 | 0 | 5 | 0 | 0 | 1—13 | |

Runs batted in—Lazzeri 4, Gehrig 8, Chapman 3, Ruth 2, Dickey, Lary, Combs, Simmons 2, Dykes 2, Foxx 6, Bishop, Boley.

Two-base hits—Cooke 2, Lazzeri 2, Miller, Haas, Schang, Chapman. Home-runs—Ruth, Gehrig 3, Simmons, Dykes, Foxx 2, Lazzeri, Bishop. Stolen bases—Chapman 2. Sacrifices—Hoyt, Gehrig, Simmons. Double-play—Bishop and Foxx. Left on bases—New York 12, Philadelphia 10. Bases on balls—Off Hoyt 1, McEvoy 2, Johnson 1, Sherid 3, Shores 2, Earnshaw 4, Grove 2, Liebhardt 4. Struck out—By Hoyt 1, McEvoy 1, Johnson 2, Sherid 1, Earnshaw 4, Grove 1. Hits—Off Hoyt 6 in 2 2–3 innings, McEvoy 1 in 1–3 (none out in 4th), Johnson 4 in 2 1–3, Sherid 4 in 3 2–3, Shores 3 in 0 (none out in 1st), Quinn 7 in 2, Rommel 3 in 2, Earnshaw 4 in 2 2–3, Grove 2 in 1 1–3, Liebhardt 4 in 1. Passed balls—Schang, Dickey. Hit by pitcher—By Shore (Lazzeri). Winning pitcher—Sherid. Losing pitcher—Earnshaw. Umpires—Nallin, Geisel and Dinneen. Time of game 3 hours.

Yankee Star with Catch He Made Off Florida: Lou Gehrig with the six-foot, nine-inch sailfish he landed recently on a fishing expedition off Long Key. (TIMES WIDE WORLD PHOTOS)

June 4, 1932

## Gehrig Ties All-Time Record With Four Straight Home Runs as Yankees Win

### EQUALS TWO MARKS IN 20 TO 13 VICTORY

### Lou Ties Record of Four Circuit Drives in One Game as the Athletics Are Beaten.

### DUPLICATES LOWE'S FEAT

### He Connects in First Four Times at Bat and Nearly Makes Fifth in Ninth.

### RUTH PRODUCES HIS 15TH

### Total Base Marks Fall, With 50 for Yanks, 77 for Both Clubs—Victors Tie Team Homer Record.

### By WILLIAM E. BRANDT.

*Special to THE NEW YORK TIMES.*

PHILADELPHIA, June 3—Henry Louis Gehrig's name today took rank in baseball's archives along with Bobby Lowe and Ed Delehanty, the only other sluggers who, in more than half a century of recorded diamond battles, ever hit four home runs in one major league game.

Largely because of Gehrig's quartet of tremendous smashes the Yankees outstripped the Athletics in a run-making marathon, winning 20 to 13, and twice losing the lead because of determined rallies by the American League champions.

Homers by Combs, Lazzeri and Ruth, the latter the Babe's fifteenth of the season, enabled the Yankees to tie the all-time record of seven homers by one club in one game, performed three times before 1900 by Detroit, New York and Pittsburgh, of the old National League and once in modern times, by the Athletics on June 3, 1921.

### Yankees Set Team Mark.

The Yanks, with their twenty-three hits, also set a new modern club-batting record for total bases, with fifty, which eclipsed the previous modern major league mark of forty-six and the American League's best total of forty-four. This achievement fell short by only five bases of the all-time record, set by Cincinnati in 1923. Both club's total of seventy-seven bases also set an American League mark.

Gehrig in his first four times at bat hammered the ball outside the playing area. In the first and fifth innings he sailed balls into the stands in left centre. In the fourth and seventh he fired over the right-field wall.

Saltzgaver was on base when Lou connected in the first inning, but the other three came with the bases empty. His fifth-inning home run, which made him the first man in baseball history ever to hit three homers in one game for the fourth time, came after Combs and Ruth had reached Earnshaw for drives over the right-field wall.

### Lazzeri Clears Bases.

Lazzeri's drive into the left-field stands in the ninth, the last Yankee homer, came with the bases filled. In Philadelphia's half of the ninth, Jimmy Foxx, the major league leader, sent his nineteenth homer of the year shooting into the left-field stands.

Cochrane had driven the ball over the right-field wall in the first inning, but the collective homer total, nine, fell one short of the major league record for both teams in a game.

The outcome of the game evened the series, two to two, but the crowd of 5,000 seemed to concentrate on encouraging Gehrig to hit a fifth homer and thus surpass a brilliant record in baseball's books.

Lou had two chances. He grounded out in the eighth, but in the ninth he pointed a terrific drive which Simmons captured only a few steps from the furthest corner of the park. A little variance to either side of its actual line of flight would have sent the ball over the fence or into the stands.

### One Base Under Record.

As it was, Lou's four homers tied the all-time record of Lowe in hitting for the circuit in four successive times at bat in 1894. Only three of Delehanty's were in successive times at bat. Both Lowe and Delehanty had a single in the same game with their four homers, so that Gehrig fell one short of tying their record for total bases.

Gehrig's four made his season's total eleven, six of which have been hit against Philadelphia, four off Earnshaw and two off Mahaffey.

The defeat of the Mackmen, coupled with the Indianan's double victory, dropped the Athletics to fifth place, Cleveland supplanting them in fourth.

Lazzeri's homer with the bases filled was his fifth hit of the game. He and Gehrig each drove in six runs. The box score:

| NEW YORK (A.) | ab. | r. | h. | po. | a. | e. | PHILADELPHIA (A.) | ab. | r. | h. | po. | a. | e. |
|---|---|---|---|---|---|---|---|---|---|---|---|---|---|
| Combs, cf | 5 | 2 | 3 | 3 | 0 | 0 | Bishop, 2b | 4 | 2 | 2 | 3 | 2 | 0 |
| Saltzg'er, 2b | 4 | 1 | 1 | 3 | 2 | 0 | Cramer, cf | 5 | 1 | 1 | 1 | 0 | 0 |
| Ruth, lf | 5 | 2 | 2 | 3 | 0 | 1 | aRoettiger | 1 | 0 | 0 | 0 | 0 | 0 |
| Hoag, lf | 0 | 1 | 0 | 1 | 0 | 0 | Miller, lf | 0 | 0 | 0 | 0 | 0 | 0 |
| Gehrig, 1b | 6 | 4 | 4 | 7 | 0 | 1 | Cochrane, c | 5 | 1 | 1 | 10 | 2 | 0 |
| Chapman, rf | 3 | 3 | 2 | 4 | 0 | 0 | bWilliams | 1 | 0 | 0 | 0 | 0 | 0 |
| Dickey, c | 4 | 2 | 2 | 5 | 0 | 0 | Sim'ns, lf, cf | 4 | 2 | 0 | 2 | 0 | 0 |
| Lazzeri, 3b | 6 | 3 | 5 | 0 | 1 | 0 | Foxx, 1b | 3 | 3 | 2 | 8 | 0 | 0 |
| Crosetti, ss | 6 | 1 | 2 | 0 | 5 | 2 | Coleman, rf | 6 | 2 | 2 | 2 | 1 | 0 |
| Allen, p | 2 | 0 | 0 | 1 | 0 | 1 | McNair, ss | 5 | 1 | 3 | 1 | 2 | 0 |
| Rhodes, p | 1 | 0 | 1 | 0 | 0 | 0 | Dykes, 3b | 4 | 1 | 1 | 0 | 1 | 0 |
| Brown, p | 1 | 0 | 0 | 0 | 1 | 0 | Earnshaw, p | 2 | 0 | 0 | 0 | 2 | 1 |
| Gomez, p | 1 | 1 | 1 | 0 | 0 | 0 | cPass | 1 | 0 | 1 | 0 | 0 | 0 |
| | | | | | | | Mahaffey, p | 0 | 0 | 0 | 0 | 0 | 0 |
| | | | | | | | Walberg, p | 0 | 0 | 0 | 0 | 0 | 0 |
| | | | | | | | Krausse, p | 0 | 0 | 0 | 0 | 0 | 0 |
| | | | | | | | dMadjeski | 1 | 0 | 0 | 0 | 0 | 0 |
| | | | | | | | Rommel, p | 0 | 0 | 0 | 0 | 1 | 0 |
| Total | 46 | 20 | 23 | 27 | 9 | 5 | Total | 42 | 13 | 13 | 27 | 11 | 1 |

aBatted for Cramer in eighth.
bBatted for Cochrane in ninth.
cBatted for Earnshaw in fifth.
dBatted for Krausse in eighth.

| | | | | | | | | | | |
|---|---|---|---|---|---|---|---|---|---|---|
| New York | 2 | 0 | 0 | 2 | 3 | 2 | 3 | 2 | 6—20 | |
| Philadelphia | 2 | 0 | 0 | 6 | 0 | 2 | 0 | 2 | 1—13 | |

Runs batted in—Gehrig 6, Combs, Ruth, Crosetti 2, Saltzgaver, Lazzeri 4, Chapman, Dickey, Cochrane 2, Cramer 3, Coleman 3, Foxx, McNair 2.

Two-base hits—Lazzeri, McNair, Ruth, Coleman. Three-base hits—Bishop, Cramer, Chapman, Lazzeri, Foxx. Home runs—Gehrig 4, Cochrane, Combs, Ruth, Lazzeri, Foxx. Stolen bases—Lazzeri. Sacrifices—Bishop, Saltzgaver. Double plays—Cochrane and McNair; Bishop and Foxx; Coleman and Cochrane. Left on bases—New York 6, Philadelphia 11. Bases on balls—Off Allen 5, Rhodes 2, Brown 1, Earnshaw 2, Walberg 1, Rommel 3. Struck out—By Allen 2, Gomez 1, Earnshaw 3, Walberg 1. Hits—Off Allen 7 in 3 2–3 innings, Rhodes 1 in 1 1–3, Brown 3 in 2, Gomez 2 in 2, Earnshaw 3 in 5, Mahaffey 6 in 1 (none out in the seventh), Walberg 2 in 1, Krausse 4 in 1, Rommel 3 in 1. Wild pitch—Rhodes. Winning pitcher—Brown. Losing pitcher—Mahaffey. Umpires—Geisel, McGowan and Van Grafian. Time of game—2:55

Lou Gehrig. (TIMES WIDE WORLD PHOTOS)

October 17, 1936

## Second 'Most Valuable' Player Award Bolsters Gehrig's All-Time Star Rating

### GEHRIG TIES MARK FOR PLAYER PRIZE

#### Writers Name Yankees' Power Hitter 'Most Valuable' in League a Second Time.

### THREE OTHERS WON TWICE

#### Cochrane, Johnson and Foxx Achieved Honor—Appling Next in Voting.

By The Associated Press.

For the second time in his remarkable career, Lou Gehrig, burly first baseman of the Yankees, yesterday was named the American League's "most valuable player" by the Baseball Writers Association.

Leader of one of the most devastating team batting attacks in the history of the game, Gehrig topped the league with forty-nine homers, batted .354, drove in 152 runs, ran his stretch of consecutive games to 1,808, and led the Yankees to American League and world series championships.

Luke Appling, brilliant White Sox shortstop and new American League batting champion, was second in the voting. Earl Averill of the Indians was third, and Charley Gehringer, Tigers, fourth.

Only three other players have received the award twice—Mickey Cochrane of the Tigers in 1928–1934, Walter Johnson, Senators, in 1913–1924, and Jimmie Foxx, Red Sox, 1932–1933. Gehrig won the award for the first time in 1927.

## Basis of Award.

The selection was made by a committee of eight writers, one from each city in the American League. Each member of the committee picked his ten best players, the first on each list getting 10 points, the second 9, the third 8, and so on.

Under this system, Gehrig was first on four of the eight lists and totaled 73 points. Appling received three first place votes and a total of 65 points, Averill was given 48 points, and Gehringer, who received the other first place vote, 39.

Following Gehringer on the list were Bill Dickey, Yankee catcher, 29 points; Joe Kuhel, Senators, and Vernon Kennedy, White Sox, 27, and Joe DiMaggio, Yankees, 26.

Others who received five or more votes were Tommy Bridges, Tigers, 25; Hal Trosky, Indians, 19; Jimmy Foxx, Red Sox, 16; Gerald Walker, Tigers, 14; Beau Bell, Browns, 10; Wally Moses, Athletics, 7, and Bob Grove, Red Sox, who won the award in 1931, 5.

## Greenberg Not Included.

Hank Greenberg, Detroit first baseman, who won the award last year, was not considered in the voting because he was out of the line-up most of the year with a fractured wrist.

Never under .300 batting mark after his first full season in the majors in 1925, Gehrig has beaten his .354 mark of this year four times. He hit .379 in 1930; .374 in 1928, .373 in 1927 and .363 in 1934, when he won the league batting championship. Gehrig also led the league in runs scored in 1933 and 1935.

Others who received votes from the committee were Manager Jimmy Dykes, White Sox, and his out-fielder, Rip Radcliff, 3 each; Sammy West, Browns, 2, and Eric McNair, Red Sox, and Zeke Bonura, White Sox, 1 each.

Players receiving honorable mention:

Monte Pearson, Tony Lazzeri, Pat Malone, Charley Ruffing, Frank Crosetti and Bump Hadley, Yankees; Goose Goslin, Marvin Owen and Schoolboy Rowe, Tigers; Johnny Allen, Roy Weatherly, Sammy Hale and Billy Sullivan, Indians; Julius Solters, Jim Bottomley and Lyn Lary, Browns.

Also Harry Kelley and Bob Johnson, Athletics; Jimmy DeShong, Johnny Stone, Buddy Lewis, Pete Appleton, Buck Newsom, Ben Chapman and Ralph Kress, Senators; Luke Sewell, White Sox, and Wes Ferrell, Red Sox.

## Personnel of Committee.

Members of the committee who made the selections were John Malaney, Boston Post; Irving Vaughan, Chicago Tribune; Gordon Cobbledick, Cleveland Plain Dealer; Charles Ward, Detroit Free Press; Rud Rennie, New York Herald Tribune; James C. Isaminger, Philadelphia Inquirer; James Gould, St. Louis Post Dispatch; Shirley Povich, Washington Post.

Stuart Bell of the Cleveland Press, associate president, was ex officio, committee chairman.

The complete list of the American League's most valuable players:

1911—Ty Cobb, Tigers
1912—Tris Speaker, Red Sox
1913—Walter Johnson, Senators
1914—Eddie Colins, Athletics
1922—George Sisler, Browns
1923—Babe Ruth, Yankees
1924—Walter Johnson, Senators
1925—Roger Peckinpaugh, Senators
1926—George Burns, Indians
1927—Lou Gehrig, Yankees

1928—Mickey Cochrane, Athletics
1929—Lew Fonseca, Indians
1930—Joe Cronin, Senators
1931—Bob Grove, Athletics
1932—Jimmie Fox, Athletics
1933—Jimmie Fox, Athletics
1934—Mickey Cochrane, Tigers
1935—Hank Greenberg, Tigers
1936—Lou Gehrig, Yankees

The Chalmers Award covered the period from 1911–14, then was discontinued. The awards were made by the league from 1922–28. The Associated Press polled baseball writers for the awards in 1929 and 1930. The Baseball Writers Association has made the awards since 1931.

July 8, 1937

## Yankees Drive in Seven Runs as American League Easily Wins All-Star Game

### GEHRIG AND GOMEZ STAR IN 8–3 VICTORY

### Lou Bats in 4 on Homer and Double to Help American League Beat National

### LEFTY EXCELS ON MOUND

### But Hubbell is Routed Quickly—32,000 at Capital See President Start Game

#### By JOHN DREBINGER

*Special to THE NEW YORK TIMES*

WASHINGTON, July 7.—Amid a blazing hot setting which included in its cast President Roosevelt and a sweltering, shirt-sleeve crowd of 32,000 that jammed every available inch of Griffith Stadium, the might of the American League returned to power today as the carefully-chosen forces of Joseph V. McCarthy crushed Bill Terry's handpicked National League array in major league baseball's fifth annual all-star game.

Lou Gehrig                123

Lou Gehrig and Joe DiMaggio. (THE NEW YORK TIMES ARCHIVES)

The final score was 8 to 3, to give the American Leaguers their fourth victory of the five games played to date and the most decisive triumph ever recorded since this mid-Summer classic was inaugurated in 1933.

Financially, the game was a grand success, the gross gate receipts totaling $28,475, the greater part of which will go to a benevolent fund for indigent ball players. The paid attendance numbered 31,391.

President Roosevelt threw out the first ball. But before long, not that ball, but many others, received a terrific cuffing while events in this inter-league struggle reverted sharply to the older order of things.

For where a year ago the flower of the National League's pitching spun back the American circuit's power for its lone victory in the series, the cream of the senior loop's hurling craft was churned to a rich froth today.

## Star Pitchers Fall

The invincible Dizzy Dean, the matchless Carl Hubbell and the fireball Van Lingle Mungo all went down in a grand crash as the American Leaguers, paced by four members of the world champion Yankees, literally swept them off their feet.

In fact, more than an American League victory the day proved a smashing individual triumph for Marse Joe's marauding Yanks, leading more than one to remark that there really are in existence now three major leagues, The Yankees, The American and the National.

Of the eight American League runs that came hustling over the plate seven were driven in by Yankee bludgeons. Columbia Lou Gehrig alone accounted for four.

He drove in two with a towering home run drive over the right field wall off Dean in the third inning and three rounds later hammered one of Mungo's blazing shoots into deep center for a double to drive in two more.

Red Rolfe banged in two others with a sweeping triple off Hubbell in the fourth and Bill Dickey banged home the seventh Yankee tally with a two-bagger off Lee Grissom in the fifth.

Charlie Gehringer of the Tigers sent in the only other American League run with a single behind the Rolfe three-bagger that sent the famous screwball maestro of the Giants, Hubbell, out of the arena before he had completed a single inning.

## More Help From Yanks

And when to this you add the fact that Vernon (Lefty) Gomez started the American League horde off on the right foot by blasting away from the mound with three scoreless innings, in which he allowed only a single blow, it takes no deep amount of delving into the vital statistics to discover how much part the Yanks played in this one-sided conflict.

Even defensively they flashed with Joe DiMaggio unfurling a bullet throw from deep right field in the sixth that nipped the one serious threat the National League made all day.

Against all this Terry fought back stubbornly with all the resources he had at his command. But he had only one man to match the power of those American sluggers.

Jersey Joe Medwick, perhaps the greatest right-handed hitter since the palmy days of Rogers Hornsby, blazed a brilliant trail as he strove almost single handed to keep his colleagues in the fight. In five times up, he uncorked four line-drive hits, two of them doubles.

It was, indeed, pretty much a struggle between the Yanks and Medwick and the celebrated member of St. Louis' famed Gas House Gang simply found himself outnumbered.

## Harder Also Hurls Well

In addition to Gomez, Tommy Bridges, the trim, right-hander of the Detroit Tigers, and Mel Harder of the Cleveland Indians pitched three innings apiece for the triumphant American Leaguers and it was only off bridges that the Terry cast was able to make any impression at all.

It was the sort of attack which with gilt-edged pitching might have won, but the McCarthy forces knocked all the gilt off before the conflict had gone more than half way.

In vain Terry flung all six of his hurlers into the fray. With the exception of Cy Blanton, none escaped getting hit in the grand total of thirteen blows, through Bucky Walters, working the eighth, managed to keep from getting scored on.

Thirteen hits also fell to the lot of the National Leaguers, but with the exception of the two Medwick doubles and another two-bagger inserted by Melvin Ott in the role of pinch hitter, all were singles. In sharp contrast to this five of the American Leaguers' blows were for extra bases, which rather graphically tells the whole story.

The crowd, which arrived early, jammed traffic in all directions and then amused itself milling around in the general quest for the right seats, got its first thrill at 1:15 o'clock when the portals behind the right wing of the grand stand swung open and the long, sleek open town car of the President rolled out on the playing field.

There were rousing cheers as the Rooseveltian smile beamed on one and all. A military band in square formation at home plate struck up "Hail to the Chief," while the players of both teams lined at attention along the first base foul line.

## Griffith Escorts President

Then followed no end of to do as the President was escorted to his box alongside the Washington dugout by Clark Griffith, owner of the Senators, while news photographers jostled each other and clicked their cameras in feverish haste.

Now the scene shifted to the tall flagpole in centerfield, where to the strains of "The Star-Spangled Banner" a detachment of Boy Scouts hoisted Old Glory. More cheers for everybody and again all eyes reverted back to the Presidential box, where the President prepared to toss out the first ball after having it formally presented to him by the rival pilots, McCarthy and Terry.

The Rooseveltian arm swept back, the players surged forward and as the white pellet arched through the air a football scramble ensued that for a few moments resembled that memorable battle of Sportsman's Park.

In this initial skirmish the National League drew its first and what eventually proved its only victory of the day for when the heap of the nation's greatest players untangled themselves Jo-Jo Moore of the Giants had the ball tightly clasped in his fingers.

From then on thrills came fast and furious as the long and lean Dean and the equally slender Gomez started firing away.

## Typical Reception for Dean

For most of the capital fans it was their first view of the Gas House Gang's celebrated hurler and they greeted his first appearance with cheers and jeers, indicating they already had acquainted themselves with the manner in which only a Dean is received on an alien ball field.

For two innings, Dean's smooth and effortless delivery kept him abreast of Gomez. He issued a pass to DiMaggio in the first and a pair of singles by Earl Averill and Dickey jolted him in the second.

But the fates had something more disturbing in store for Dizzy. He had retired Rolfe and Gehringer as the first two outs in the third and was within one out of stalking out of there with his customary jauntiness when the blow fell.

DiMaggio singled sharply to center, almost decapitating the great Dean. Then Diz squared off against Gehrig. He had fanned Lou in the first inning and seemed quite sure of himself.

Nor did a resounding foul smack that Gehrig sent flying over the grandstand roof seem to disturb his equanimity. But with the count 3 and 2 there was a terrific jolt and the crowd rose as one to see the ball sail high over the right-field barrier.

Gomez gave the National Leaguers no chance at all. Anky Vaughan singled in the first and was the only one to get on base through all of Lefty's three innings.

With the arrival of Bridges in the fourth, however, the Nationals swung into action, or rather Medwick did. Herman singled, took second on an out and counted on Medwick's first double.

But in the same round with Hubbell sedately stepping on the scene the American Leaguers burst out with even greater fury.

Hubbell's tenure of office was even stormier and far more brief than Dean's. For the American Leaguers, still rankled by the manner in which Hub once had fanned five of their greatest hitters in a row back in 1934, fell on him with a vengeance.

With one out, Dickey walked, and Sammy West of the Browns rammed a hit through Johnny Mize, the Cardinal first sacker. Bridges fanned for the second out and it looked as though the Hub would survive, but Rolfe unveiled his triple to right center and two scored. Came Gehringer's single to right scoring the Yankee third sacker and a third tally flitted home.

Hubbell was withdrawn by Terry and replaced by Blanton of the Pirates. Cy fanned DiMaggio for the third out and then immediately retired himself for a pinch hitter in the fifth.

## Ott Connects in Pinch

That pinch-hitter, Ott, helped the Nationals to their second run off Bridges with a two-bagger to right after Gabby Hartnett had singled. But it took a fly to the outfield by Paul Waner to drive in that run, and the Nationals were still three shy.

Grissom, pitching the fifth for the Nationals, made an imposing entry as he fanned Gehrig and Averill. But then trouble nailed him, too, as Joe Cronin and Dickey cracked him for a pair of doubles, and the Americans had another run, to which they added two more off Mungo in the sixth when Gehrig hit his mighty two-bagger which just missed being a triple.

This inning, too, saw the National Leaguers make their last desperate stand. In fact, for a few exciting moments it looked as though they would rout Bridges and put themselves back in the fight.

The redoubtable Medwick and Frank Demaree of the Cubs singled. A fly by Mize drove in Jersey Joe. Then, after Hartnett had forced Demaree for the second out, Rolfe fumbled Dick Bartell's grounder and the National Leaguers had two on.

Terry here made another strategic move. He ordered Burgess Whitehead to run for the lumbering Gabby, and Rip Collins, Cubs' slugging first sacker, came to bat for Grissom. Collins singled sharply to right and the Nationals looked to have another run as the fleet Whitehead rounded third.

But the ball thrown by DiMaggio's powerful arm proved even swifter and Whitey was nailed at the plate for the third out.

Perhaps some day they'll inaugurated a three-cornered all-star struggle, with the Yankees battling as a unit.

### BOX SCORE OF THE GAME

NATIONAL LEAGUE

| | ab. | r. | h. | tb. | 2b. | 3b. | hr. | bb. | so. | sh. | sb. | po. | a. | e. |
|---|---|---|---|---|---|---|---|---|---|---|---|---|---|---|
| Waner, Pitts., rf | 5 | 0 | 0 | 0 | 0 | 0 | 0 | 0 | 0 | 0 | 0 | 1 | 0 | 0 |
| Herman, Chic., 2b | 5 | 1 | 2 | 2 | 0 | 0 | 0 | 0 | 0 | 0 | 0 | 1 | 4 | 0 |
| Vaughan, Pitts., 3b | 5 | 0 | 2 | 2 | 0 | 0 | 0 | 0 | 0 | 0 | 0 | 3 | 0 | 0 |
| Medwick, St. L., lf | 5 | 1 | 4 | 6 | 2 | 0 | 0 | 0 | 0 | 0 | 0 | 1 | 0 | 0 |
| Demaree, Chic., cf | 5 | 0 | 1 | 1 | 0 | 0 | 0 | 0 | 0 | 0 | 0 | 2 | 1 | 0 |
| Mize, St. L., 1b | 4 | 0 | 0 | 0 | 0 | 0 | 0 | 0 | 0 | 0 | 0 | 7 | 0 | 0 |
| Hartnett, Chic., c | 3 | 1 | 1 | 1 | 0 | 0 | 0 | 0 | 0 | 0 | 0 | 6 | 0 | 0 |
| [b]Whitehead, N.Y. | 0 | 0 | 0 | 0 | 0 | 0 | 0 | 0 | 0 | 0 | 0 | 0 | 0 | 0 |
| Mancuso, N.Y., c | 1 | 0 | 0 | 0 | 0 | 0 | 0 | 0 | 0 | 0 | 0 | 1 | 0 | 0 |
| Bartell, N.Y., ss | 4 | 0 | 1 | 1 | 0 | 0 | 0 | 0 | 0 | 0 | 0 | 2 | 3 | 0 |
| Dean, St. L., p | 1 | 0 | 0 | 0 | 0 | 0 | 0 | 0 | 0 | 0 | 0 | 0 | 1 | 0 |
| Hubbell, N.Y., p | 0 | 0 | 0 | 0 | 0 | 0 | 0 | 0 | 0 | 0 | 0 | 0 | 0 | 0 |
| Blanton, Pitts., p | 0 | 0 | 0 | 0 | 0 | 0 | 0 | 0 | 0 | 0 | 0 | 0 | 0 | 0 |
| [a]Ott, N.Y. | 1 | 0 | 1 | 2 | 1 | 0 | 0 | 0 | 0 | 0 | 0 | 0 | 0 | 0 |
| Grissom, Cincin., p | 0 | 0 | 0 | 0 | 0 | 0 | 0 | 0 | 0 | 0 | 0 | 0 | 0 | 0 |
| [c]Collins, Chic. | 1 | 0 | 1 | 1 | 0 | 0 | 0 | 0 | 0 | 0 | 0 | 0 | 0 | 0 |
| Mungo, Bklyn, p | 0 | 0 | 0 | 0 | 0 | 0 | 0 | 0 | 0 | 0 | 0 | 0 | 1 | 0 |
| [e]Moore, N.Y. | 1 | 0 | 0 | 0 | 0 | 0 | 0 | 0 | 0 | 0 | 0 | 0 | 0 | 0 |
| Walters, Phila., p | 0 | 0 | 0 | 0 | 0 | 0 | 0 | 0 | 0 | 0 | 0 | 0 | 0 | 0 |
| Total | 41 | 3 | 13 | 16 | 3 | 0 | 0 | 0 | 0 | 0 | 0 | 24 | 10 | 0 |

| | ab. | r. | h. | tb. | 2b. | 3b. | hr. | bb. | so. | sh. | sb. | po. | a. | e. |
|---|---|---|---|---|---|---|---|---|---|---|---|---|---|---|
| Rolfe, N.Y., 3b | 4 | 2 | 2 | 4 | 0 | 1 | 0 | 1 | 0 | 0 | 0 | 0 | 2 | 2 |
| Gehringer, Det., 2b | 5 | 1 | 3 | 3 | 0 | 0 | 0 | 0 | 0 | 0 | 0 | 2 | 5 | 0 |
| DiMaggio, N.Y., rf | 4 | 1 | 1 | 1 | 0 | 0 | 0 | 1 | 2 | 0 | 0 | 1 | 1 | 0 |
| Gehrig, N.Y., 1b | 4 | 1 | 2 | 6 | 1 | 0 | 1 | 0 | 2 | 0 | 0 | 1 | 1 | 0 |
| Averill, Cleve., cf | 3 | 0 | 1 | 1 | 0 | 0 | 0 | 1 | 1 | 0 | 0 | 2 | 0 | 0 |
| Cronin, Boston, ss | 4 | 1 | 1 | 2 | 1 | 0 | 0 | 0 | 0 | 0 | 0 | 3 | 4 | 0 |
| Dickey, N.Y., c | 3 | 1 | 2 | 3 | 1 | 0 | 0 | 1 | 0 | 0 | 0 | 2 | 0 | 0 |
| West, St. L., lf | 4 | 1 | 1 | 1 | 0 | 0 | 0 | 0 | 0 | 0 | 0 | 5 | 0 | 0 |
| Gomez, N.Y. p | 1 | 0 | 0 | 0 | 0 | 0 | 0 | 0 | 1 | 0 | 0 | 0 | 0 | 0 |
| Bridges, Det., p | 1 | 0 | 0 | 0 | 0 | 0 | 0 | 0 | 1 | 0 | 0 | 0 | 1 | 0 |
| dFoxx, Boston | 1 | 0 | 0 | 0 | 0 | 0 | 0 | 0 | 0 | 0 | 0 | 0 | 0 | 0 |
| Harder, Cleve., p | 1 | 0 | 0 | 0 | 0 | 0 | 0 | 0 | 0 | 0 | 0 | 1 | 1 | 0 |
| Total | 35 | 8 | 13 | 21 | 3 | 1 | 1 | 4 | 7 | 0 | 0 | 27 | 15 | 2 |

aBatted for Blanton in fifth.
bRan for Hartnett in sixth.
cBatted for Grissom in sixth.
dBatted for Bridges in sixth.
eBatted for Mungo in eighth.

### SCORE BY INNING

| | | | | | | | | | | |
|---|---|---|---|---|---|---|---|---|---|---|
| National League | 0 | 0 | 0 | 1 | 1 | 1 | 0 | 0 | 0—3 |
| American League | 0 | 0 | 2 | 3 | 1 | 2 | 0 | 0 | ..—8 |

Runs batted in—Gehrig 4, Medwick, Rolfe 2, Gehringer, Waner, Dickey, Mize.

Left on bases—National League 11, American League 7. Double play—Bartell and Mize. Struck out—By Dean 2, Hubbell 1, Blanton 1, Grissom 2, Mungo 1. Bases on balls—Off Dean 1, Hubbell 1, Mungo 2. Hits—Off Dean 4 in 3 innings, Hubbell 3 in 2–3, Blanton 0 in 1–3, Grissom 2 in 1, Mungo 2 in 2, Walters 2 in 1, Gomez 1 in 3, Bridges 7 in 3, Harder 5 in 3. Winning pitcher—Gomez. Losing pitcher—Dean. Umpires—McGowan (A.L.) behind the plate; Pinelli (N.L.) at first base; Quinn (A.L.) at second base; Barr (N.L.) at third base for first four and one-half innings; Barr behind the plate, Quinn at first, Pinelli at second, McGowan at third for remainder of game. Time of game—2:30.

Veteran First Baseman and His Successor. Lou Gehrig and Babe Dahlgren in Detroit on May 2, 1939. (WIRED PHOTO—TIMES WIDE WORLD)

May 3, 1939

## Gehrig Voluntarily Ends Streak at 2,130 Straight Games

### LOU, NOT HITTING, ASKS REST ON BENCH

### Gehrig's String, Started June 1, 1925, Snapped as Yanks Start Series in Detroit

### RETURN OF ACE INDEFINITE

### But Iron Man Who Holds Many Records Hopes to Regain Form in Hot Weather

#### By JAMES P. DAWSON

*Special to* THE NEW YORK TIMES.

DETROIT, May 2.—Lou Gehrig's matchless record of uninterrupted play in American League championship games, stretched over fifteen years and through 2,130 straight contests, came to an end today.

The mighty iron man, who at his peak had hit forty-nine home runs in a single season five years ago, took himself out of action before the Yanks marched on Briggs Stadium for their third game against the Tigers this year.

With the consent of Manager Joe McCarthy, Gehrig removed himself because he, better than anybody else, perhaps, recognized his competitive decline and was frankly aware of the fact he was doing the Yankees no good defensively or on the attack. He played last Sunday in New York against the Senators.

When Gehrig will start another game is undetermined. He will not be used as a pinch-hitter.

The present plan is to keep him on the bench. Relaxing and shaking off the mental hazards he admittedly has encountered this season, he may swing into action in the hot weather, which should have a beneficial effect upon his tired muscles.

## Dahlgren Gets Chance

Meanwhile Ellsworth (Babe) Dahlgren, until today baseball's greatest figure of frustration, will continue at first base. Manager McCarthy said he had no present intention of transferring Tommy Henrich, the youthful outfielder whom he tried at first base at the Florida training camp. Dahlgren had been awaited the summons for three years.

It was coincidental that Gehrig's string was broken almost in the presence of the man he succeeded as Yankee first baseman. At that time Wally Pipp, now a business man of Grand Rapids, Mich., was benched by the late Miller Huggins to make room for the strapping youth fresh from the Heartford Eastern League club to which the Yankees had farmed him for two seasons, following his departure from Columbia University. Pipp was in the lobby of the Book Cadillac Hotel at noon when the withdrawal of Gehrig was effected.

"I don't feel equal to getting back in there," Pipp said on June 2, 1925, the day Lou replaced him at first. Lou had started his phenomenal streak the day before as a pinch-hitter Peewee Wanninger, then the Yankee shortstop.

This latest momentous development in baseball was not unexpected. There had been signs for the past two years that Gehrig was slowing up. Even when a sick man, however, he gamely stuck to his chores, not particularly in pursuit of his all-time record of consecutive play, although that was a big consideration, but out of a driving desire to help the Yankees, always his first consideration.

## Treated for Ailment

What Lou had thought was lumbago last year when he suffered pains in the back that more than once forced his early withdrawal from games he had started was diagnosed later as a gall bladder condition for which Gehrig underwent treatment all last Winter, after rejecting a recommendation that he submit to an operation.

The signs of his approaching fade-out were unmistakable this Spring at St. Petersburg, Fla., yet the announcement from Manager McCarthy was something of a shock. It came at the end of a conference Gehrig arranged immediately after McCarthy's arrival by plane from his native Buffalo.

"Lou just told me he felt it would be best for the club if he took himself out of the line-up," McCarthy said following their private talk. "I asked him if her really felt that way. He told me he was serious. He feels blue. He is dejected.

"I told him it would be as he wished. Like everybody else I'm sorry to see it happen. I told him not to worry. Maybe the warm weather will bring him around.

"He's been a great ball player. Fellows like him come along once in a hundred years. I told him that. More than that, he's been a vital part of the Yankee club since he started with it. He's always been a perfect gentleman, a credit to baseball.

"We'll miss him. You can't escape that fact. But I think he's doing the proper thing."

## Lou Explains Decision

Gehrig, visibly affected, explained his decision quite frankly.

"I decided last Sunday night on this move," said Lou. "I haven't been a bit of good to the team since the season started. It would not be fair to the boys, to Joe or to the baseball public for me to try going on. In fact, it would not be fair to myself, and I'm the last consideration.

"It's tough to see your mates on base, have a chance to win a ball game, and not be able to do anything about it. McCarthy has been swell about it all the time. He'd let me go until the cows came home, he is that considerate of my feelings, but I knew in Sunday's game that I should get out of there.

"I went up there four times with men on base. Once there were two there. A hit would have won the ball game for the Yankees, but I missed, leaving five stranded as the Yankees lost. Maybe a rest will do me some good. Maybe it won't. Who knows? Who can tell? I'm just hoping."

Gehrig's withdrawal from today's game does not necessarily mean the end of his playing career, although that seems not far distant. When that day comes Gehrig can sit back and enjoy the fortune he has accumulated as a ball player. He is estimated to have saved $200,000 from his earnings, which touched a high in 1938, when he collected $39,000 as Yankee salary.

When Gehrig performed his duties as Yankee captain today, appearing at the plate to give the batting order, announcement was made through the amplifiers of his voluntary withdrawal and it was suggested he get "a big hand." A deafening cheer resounded as Lou walked to the dugout, doffed his cap and disappeared in a corner of the bench.

Open expressions of regret came from the Yankees and the Tigers. Lefty Vernon Gomez expressed the Yankees' feelings when he said:

"It's tough to see this thing happen, even though you know it must come to all of us. Lou's a great guy and he's always been a great baseball figure. I hope he'll be back in there."

Hank Greenberg, who might have been playing first for the Yanks instead of the Tigers but for Gehrig, said: "Lou's doing the right thing. He's got to use his head now instead of his legs. Maybe that Yankee dynasty is beginning to crumble."

## Scott Former Record Holder

Everett Scott, the shortstop who held the record of 1,307 consecutive games until Gehrig broke it, ended his streak on May 6, 1925, while he was a member of the Yankees. However, Scott began his string, once considered unapproachable, with the Red Sox.

By a strange coincidence, Scott gave way to Wanninger, the player for whom Gehrig batted to start his great record.

With only one run batted in this year and a batting average of .143 representing four singles in twenty-eight times at bat, Lou had fallen far below his record achievements of previous seasons, during five of which he led the league in runs driven home.

| | G. | AB. | R. | H. | RBI. | HR. | PC. |
|---|---|---|---|---|---|---|---|
| 1925 | *126 | 437 | 73 | 129 | 68 | 21 | .295 |
| 1926 | 155 | 572 | 135 | 179 | 107 | 16 | .313 |
| 1927 | 155 | 584 | 149 | 218 | 175 | 47 | .373 |
| 1928 | 154 | 562 | 139 | 210 | 142 | 27 | .374 |
| 1929 | 154 | 553 | 127 | 166 | 126 | 35 | .300 |
| 1930 | 154 | 581 | 143 | 220 | 174 | 41 | .379 |
| 1931 | 155 | 619 | 163 | 211 | 184 | 46 | .341 |
| 1932 | 156 | 596 | 138 | 208 | 151 | 34 | .349 |
| 1933 | 152 | 583 | 138 | 198 | 139 | 32 | .334 |
| 1934 | 154 | 579 | 128 | 210 | 165 | 49 | .363 |
| 1935 | 149 | 535 | 125 | 175 | 119 | 30 | .329 |
| 1936 | 155 | 579 | 167 | 205 | 152 | 49 | .354 |
| 1937 | 157 | 569 | 138 | 200 | 159 | 37 | .351 |
| 1938 | 157 | 576 | 115 | 170 | 114 | 29 | .295 |
| 1939 | 8 | 28 | 2 | 4 | 1 | 0 | .143 |
| Total | 2,141 | 7,953 | 1,880 | 2,704 | 1,976 | 493 | .340 |

*Includes eleven games before consecutive streak started.

Some of his more important records follow:

Most consecutive games—2,130.
Most consecutive years, 100 games or more—14.
Most years, 150 games or more—12.
Most years, 100 runs or more—13.
Most consecutive years, 100 runs or more—13.
Most home runs with bases full—23.
Most years, 300 or more total bases—13.
Most years, 100 runs or more driven in—13.
Most games by first baseman in one season—157.
Most home runs in one game—4
Most runs batted in, one season—184 (American League).

The Yankees' captain and Joe McCarthy. (TIMES WIDE WORLD PHOTOS)

June 22, 1939

## Infantile Paralysis Terminates Gehrig's Playing Career

### GEHRIG IS FORCED TO QUIT BASEBALL

#### Mayo Clinic Report Bars Lou From Playing—He Takes Verdict Philosophically

### STAYS AS YANKEE CAPTAIN

#### Will Receive Full Salary for Year—Ended Record Streak of 2,130 Games May 2

#### By ARTHUR J. DALEY

Lou Gehrig, the robust Iron Horse whose baseball endurance record of 2,130 consecutive games may never be broken, is suffering from a mild attack of infantile paralysis, it was disclosed yesterday upon the return of the Yankee captain from a week-long examination at the Mayo Clinic.

This shocking news was revealed by President Edward Grant Barrow of the Yankees just before yesterday's game at the Stadium. As a result, the spectacular career of the big first baseman is at an end.

It was on May 2 of this year that Gehrig, aware that his continued presence in the line-up was a detriment to the team, voluntarily withdrew to complete his unbroken string at 2,130 games. Last year he had started to slip and this season his downhill descent was alarming. When he quit he was batting only .143.

## Text of the Report

With his health worrying him he visited the Mayo Clinic at Rochester, Minn., for a thorough examination. Tuesday night he returned to New York by airplane and on his arrival at the Stadium yesterday presented Mr. Barrow with the following report from the Mayo Clinic:

To whom it may concern:

This is to certify that Mr. Lou Gehrig has been under examination at the Mayo Clinic from June 13 to June 19, 1939, inclusive.

After a careful and complete examination, it was found that he is suffering from amyotrophic lateral sclerosis. This type illness involves the motor pathways and cells of the central nervous system and in lay terms is knows as a form of chronic poliomyelitis (infantile paralysis).

The nature of this trouble makes it such that Mr. Gehrig will be unable to continue his active participation as a baseball player inasmuch as it is advisable that he conserve his muscular energy. He could, however, continue in some executive capacity.

(Signed) H. C. HABEIN, M.D.

## Barrow Receives Data

Along with this formal statement Gehrig had with him a complete set of charts, X-rays and all manner of detailed reports. He presented them to President Barrow and the two, along with Manager Joe McCarthy, were closeted for about ten minutes.

Then Barrow summoned the baseball writers. Holding the statement in his hand he said:

"Gentlemen, we have bad news. Gehrig has infantile paralysis."

The writers stared at him in disbelief. It seemed inconceivable that the broad-shouldered iron man could be laid low in such fashion.

As for Gehrig, he merely grinned. "I guess I have to accept the bitter with the sweet," he said. "If this is my finish I'll take it."

Neither he nor Barrow could venture to guess what Gehrig's future would be. "We'll keep him on the active player list at full salary for this year at least," declared Barrow. That full salary, by the way, is said to be $35,000.

Columbia Lou said that he had been given a list of doctors in every city in the American League circuit where he could go for treatments. But he had not the faintest idea of what those treatments would be.

## Fails to Solve Mystery

Nor could he supply any solution to the mystery of when or where he had contracted the disease. Whether or not he ever would recover was beyond his ken as well. Perhaps in a few years, he seemed to think, he might shake loose from the grip of the infantile paralysis, but since he became 36 years old on Monday that would definitely place him beyond the pale of active playing days.

When Gehrig walked into the Yankee dressing room he found his team-mates waiting for him uneasily. As the door opened some one started to cheer and then the rafters rocked with the acclaim he received from his fellows. They wanted to show him that they still were with him to the man.

The big captain dressed and sat on the bench with his fellow Yankees clustered around him as he described all the tests he had had out at the Mayo Clinic, telling his story with a ready laugh and ever-present grin. They tried to look unconcerned and as if nothing had happened. It was a brave attempt, but it failed. Bill Dickey, Gehrig's roommate, sat on the steps, his chin on a bat, staring morosely at Lou and never saying a word.

When he stepped up to the plate before the game to hand the batting order to the umpires in his role as captain, the crowd gave Lou a rousing cheer, most of the fans in total ignorance of what had happened.

But Lou Gehrig, the player, has come to the end of the trail, thus ending one of the most amazing careers in baseball.

## Played at Commerce High

That career began more than a score of years ago with the High School of Commerce in New York City. Then he pitched, played the outfield and first base for Columbia. The Yankees signed him in 1923 but he saw service in only thirteen games before being shipped to Hartford in the Eastern League, where he batted .304. A year later it was the same process—ten games with the Yankees and the rest of the season with Hartford. That time, however, he hit .369.

In 1925 the Yanks held onto their prize. Wally Pipp was the regular first baseman, but on June 1 Gehrig entered the line-up as a pinch hitter. He singled, and Miller Huggins decided to gamble on the strapping youngster the next day. He gave him a try at first base, and Gehrig stayed there without interruption until May 2 last.

### RECORD WITH YANKEES

#### REGULAR SEASON

|  | G. | R. | H. | RBI. | HR. | TB | PC. |
|---|---|---|---|---|---|---|---|
| 1923 | 13 | 6 | 11 | 9 | 1 | 20 | .423 |
| 1924 | 10 | 2 | 6 | 6 | 0 | 7 | .500 |
| 1925 | 126 | 73 | 129 | 68 | 21 | 233 | .295 |
| 1926 | 155 | 135 | 179 | 107 | 16 | 314 | .313 |
| 1927 | 155 | 149 | 218 | 175 | 47 | 447 | .373 |
| 1928 | 154 | 139 | 210 | 142 | 27 | 364 | .374 |
| 1929 | 154 | 127 | 166 | 126 | 35 | 322 | .300 |
| 1930 | 154 | 143 | 220 | 174 | 41 | 419 | .379 |
| 1931 | 155 | 163 | 211 | 184 | 46 | 410 | .341 |
| 1932 | 156 | 138 | 208 | 151 | 34 | 370 | .349 |
| 1933 | 152 | 138 | 198 | 139 | 32 | 359 | .334 |
| 1934 | 154 | 128 | 210 | 165 | 49 | 409 | .363 |
| 1935 | 149 | 125 | 176 | 119 | 30 | 312 | .329 |
| 1936 | 155 | 167 | 205 | 152 | 49 | 403 | .354 |
| 1937 | 157 | 138 | 200 | 159 | 37 | 366 | .351 |
| 1938 | 157 | 115 | 170 | 114 | 29 | 301 | .295 |
| 1939 | 8 | 2 | 4 | 1 | 0 | 4 | .143 |
| Total | 2,164 | 1,888 | 2,721 | 1,991 | 494 | 5,060 | .340 |

| | G. | R. | H. | RBI. | HR. | TB. | AV. |
|---|---|---|---|---|---|---|---|
| 1926 | 7 | 1 | 8 | 3 | 0 | 10 | .348 |
| 1927 | 4 | 2 | 4 | 5 | 0 | 10 | .308 |
| 1928 | 4 | 5 | 6 | 9 | 4 | 19 | .545 |
| 1932 | 4 | 9 | 9 | 8 | 3 | 19 | .529 |
| 1936 | 6 | 5 | 7 | 7 | 2 | 14 | .292 |
| 1937 | 5 | 4 | 5 | 3 | 1 | 11 | .294 |
| 1938 | 4 | 4 | 4 | 0 | 0 | 4 | .286 |
| Total | 34 | 30 | 43 | 35 | 10 | 87 | .361 |

During that time he compiled all sorts of records. In 1925 he hit under .300, and also in 1938, his last full season, he was under that mark. But in between his averages read .313, .373, .374, .300, .379, .341, .349, .334, .363, .329, and .351. His lifetime average is .340. He was in seven world series for a lifetime series average of .361, twice batting over .500.

No accurate picture can be given of his earnings in his fifteen seasons with the Yankees, but the general impression is that he has received $361,500. Together with his cuts of the world series his total income has been around $400,000.

Last season the iron man began to fade. His reflexes were not as sharp as they had been and his hitting fell off. That was strange, because ball players rarely lose their batting eyes with advancing years. It is generally their legs that go first.

In training camp at St. Petersburg last Spring Gehrig seemed to be over the hill. His drives lacked power and he slumped so seriously in fielding that he was covering no territory at all. When he made only four hits in the first eight games this year Columbia Lou seemed to feel that he should quit.

He played against the Washington Senators on April 30, but when the Yankees resumed their schedule at Briggs Stadium in Detroit on May 2 Captain Gehrig handed to the umpire a line-up that did not have Player Gehrig on it for the first time in fifteen years. The clever-fielding Babe Dahlgren took his place and has been at it ever since.

A week ago Monday the Bronx Bombers engaged in an exhibition game with their farm team at Kansas City. Gehrig played three innings, but did nothing to convince himself that he was ready to return.

### LOU'S BRAVERY DISCLOSED
#### Mayo Clinic Reveals How Gehrig Received News of Ailment

ROCHESTER, Minn., June 21 (AP). Lou Gehrig, baseballs' Iron Man, showed he had iron in his make-up when Mayo Clinic physicians told him he had chronic poliomyelitis and could never again play baseball, it was disclosed today.

Discovery that he could not return to the Yankee line-up was made several days ago. Neither physicians not Gehrig would announce the findings here, the Yankee slugger preferring to tell club officials first.

During a series of tests and examinations physicians ascertained more and more of Gehrig's condition. Announcement of the findings was not made to Gehrig abruptly. His knowledge of his complaint came about gradually.

Gehrig bravely received the news, merely saying:

"I suspected something was wrong." He realized, he said, that he was slowing up and seemed not greatly shocked.

The former Yankee slugger was cheerful throughout further examinations.

Monday he was a guest at an informal birthday party, and at no time did he show any evidence that he had heard the verdict. One of his last acts at the airport yesterday before leaving was to autograph a 10-cent baseball for a small boy.

Gehrig told clinic representatives he is prepared to adjust himself to his new condition in life.

## DR. FISHBEIN COMMENTS
### Finding on Gehrig Discussed by Medical Journal Editor

CHICAGO, June 21 (AP).—Dr. Morris Fishbein, editor of The Journal of the American Medical Association, made the following comment today on the diagnosis of Lou Gehrig's illness:

"The diagnosis of chronic infantile paralysis used to describe a wasting of the muscles of the neck and upper parts of the body.

"It passed from general use when infantile paralysis was better known and segregated as a separate disease.

"The diagnosis of amyotrophic lateral sclerosis is a well established scientific diagnosis of a condition in which there is a hardening of the tissues in the spinal column and a wasting of the muscles dependent upon it."

## SALARY TOTAL $361,500
### Gehrig's Earnings for Regular Season Play With Yanks

When Lou Gehrig receives his full salary for this season he will have been paid $361,500 by the Yankees for his services as a regular on the club if the first baseman has drawn the salaries generally reported to have been paid him.

In 1925, when he became a Yankee regular, he received only $3,750, but last year he was reported to have been paid $39,000, or more than ten times the amount which he drew in his initial full season with the club.

A compilation of his salary year by year does not include his share in seven world series, so his total baseball earnings have been approximately $400,000.

The salary tabulation follows:

| | | | |
|---|---|---|---|
| 1925 | $ 3,750 | 1933 | $ 23,000 |
| 1926 | 6,500 | 1934 | 23,000 |
| 1927 | 7,500 | 1935 | 31,000 |
| 1928 | 25,000 | 1936 | 31,000 |
| 1929 | 25,000 | 1937 | 36,750 |
| 1930 | 25,000 | 1938 | 39,000 |
| 1931 | 25,000 | 1939 | 35,000 |
| 1932 | 25,000 | Total | $361,500 |

# Marks Credited to Gehrig

## REGULAR SEASON

Most consecutive games—2,130.

Most consecutive years, 100 games or more—14.

Most years, 150 games or more—12.

Most years, 100 runs or more—13.

Most consecutive years, 100 runs or more—13.

Most years, 100 or more runs batted in—13 (tied with Ruth).

Most years, 150 or more runs batted in—7.

Most consecutive years, 100 or more runs batted in—13.

Most runs batted in, one season—184 (American League).

Most times, four long hits in one game—5.

Most years, 400 or more total bases—5.

Most years, 300 or more total bases—13.

Most home runs with bases filled—23.

Most consecutive home runs in one game—4 (modern record).

Most total bases, game (modern record)—16 (Tied with Ruth and Klein).

Most years, leading league, runs batted in—5 (tied with Ruth).

Most years, leading league games played, season—8.

First baseman, participating in most double plays, season—157.

## WORLD SERIES

Highest batting percentage, total series—.361 (7 series).

Most runs, one series—9 (tied with Ruth).

Most runs batted in, total series—35.

Most runs batted in, one series—9.

Most home runs, one four-game series—4.

Most home runs, 3 consecutive games—4.

Most extra bases on long hits, one series—13.

# 61,808 FANS ROAR TRIBUTE TO GEHRIG

## Captain of Yankees Honored at Stadium—Calls Himself 'Luckiest Man Alive'

### By JOHN DREBINGER

In perhaps as colorful and dramatic a pageant as ever was enacted on a baseball field, 61,808 fans thundered a hail and farewell to Henry Lou Gehrig at the Yankee Stadium yesterday.

To be sure, it was a holiday and there would have been a big crowd and plenty of roaring in any event. For the Yankees, after getting nosed out, 3 to 2, in the opening game of the double-header, despite a ninth-inning home run by George Selkirk, came right back in typical fashion to crush the Senators, 11 to 1, in the nightcap. Twinkletoes Selkirk embellished this contest with another home run.

But it was the spectacle staged between the games which doubtless never will be forgotten by those who saw it. For more than forty minutes there paraded in review two mighty championship hosts—The Yankees of 1927 and the current edition of Yanks who definitely are winning their way to a fourth straight pennant and a chance for another world title.

### Old Mates Reassemble

From far and wide the 1927 stalwarts came to reassemble for Lou Gehrig Appreciation Day and to pay their own tribute to their former comrade-in-arms who had carried on beyond all of them only to have his own brilliant career come to a tragic close when it was revealed that he had fallen victim of a form of infantile paralysis.

In conclusion, the vast gathering, sitting in absolute silence for a longer period than perhaps any baseball crowd in history, heard Gehrig himself deliver as amazing a valedictory as ever came from a ball player.

So shaken with emotion that at first it appeared he would not be able to talk at all, the mighty Iron Horse, with a rare display of that indomitable will power that had carried him through 2,130 consecutive games, moved to the microphone at home plate to express his own appreciation.

And for the final fadeout, there stood the still burly and hearty Babe Ruth alongside of Gehrig, their arms about each other's shoulders, facing a battery of camera men.

All through the long exercise Gehrig had tried in vain to smile, but with the irrepressible Bambino beside him he finally made it. The Babe whispered something to him and Lou chuckled. Then they both chuckled and the crowd roared and roared.

### Late Rally Fails

The ceremonies began directly after the debris of the first game had been cleared away. There had been some vociferous cheering as the Yanks, fired to action by Selkirk's homer, tried to snatch that opener away from the Senators in the last few seconds of the ninth. But they couldn't quite make it and the players hustled off the field.

Then, from out of a box alongside the Yankee dugout there spryly hopped more than a dozen elderly gentlemen, some gray, some shockingly baldish, but all happy to be on hand. The crowd recognized them at once, for they were the Yanks of 1927, not the first Yankee world championship team, but the first, with Gehrig an important cog in the machine, to win a world series in four straight games.

Down the field, behind Captain Sutherland's Seventh Regiment Band, they marched—Ruth; Bob Meusel, who had come all the way from California; Waite Hoyt, alone still maintaining his boyish countenance; Wally Schang, Benny Bengough, Tony Lazzeri, Mark Koenig, Jumping Joe Dugan, Bob Shawkey, Herb Pennock, Deacon Everett Scott, whose endurance record Gehrig eventually surpassed; Wally Pipp, who faded out as the Yankee first sacker the day Columbia Lou took over the job way back in 1925, and George Pipgras, now an umpire and, in fact, actually officiating in the day's games.

At the flagpole, these old Yanks raised the world series pennant they had won so magnificently from the Pirates in 1927 and, as they paraded back, another familiar figure streaked out of the dugout, the only one still wearing a Yankee uniform. It was the silver-haired Earle Combs, now a coach.

## Old-Timers Face Plate

Arriving in the infield, the old-timers strung out, facing the plate. The players of both Yankee and Senator squads also emerged from their dugouts to form a rectangle, and the first real ovation followed as Gehrig moved out to the plate to greet his colleagues, past and present.

One by one the old-timers were introduced with Sid Mercer acting as toastmaster. Clark Griffith, venerable white-haired owner of the Senators and a Yankee himself in the days when they were known as Highlanders, also joined the procession.

Gifts of all sorts followed. The Yankees presented their stricken comrade with a silver trophy measuring more than a foot and a half in height, their thoughts expressed in verse inscribed upon the base.

Manager Joe McCarthy, almost as visible affected as Gehrig himself, made this presentation and hurried back to fall in line with his players. But every few minutes, when he saw that the once stalwart figure they called the Iron Horse was swaying on shaky legs, Marse Joe would come forward to give Lou an assuring word of cheer.

Mayor La Guardia officially extended the city's appreciation of the services Columbia Lou had given his home town.

"You are the greatest prototype of good sportsmanship and citizenship," said the Mayor, concluding with "Lou, we're proud of you."

Postmaster General Farley also was on hand, closing his remarks with "for generations to come, boys who play baseball will point with pride to your record."

When time came for Gehrig to address the gathering it looked as if he simply would never make it. He gulped and fought to keep back the tears as he kept his eyes fastened on the ground.

But Marse Joe came forward again, said something that might have been "come on, Lou, just rap out another," and somehow those magical words had the same effect as in all the past fifteen years when the gallant Iron Horse would step up to the plate to "rap out another."

## Gehrig Speaks Slowly

He spoke slowly and evenly, and stressed the appreciation that he felt for all that was being done for him. He spoke of the men with whom he had been associated in his long career with the Yankees—the late Colonel Jacob Ruppert, the late Miller Huggins, his first manager, who gave him his start in New York; Edward G. Barrow, the present head of baseball's most powerful organization; the Yanks of old who now stood silently in front of him, as well as the players of today.

"What young man wouldn't give anything to mingle with such men for a single day as I have for all these years?" he asked.

"You've been reading about my bad break for week now," he said. "But today I think I'm the luckiest man alive. I now feel more than ever that I have much to live for."

The gifts included a silver service set from the New York club, a fruit bowl and two candlesticks from the Giants, a silver pitcher from the Stevens Associates, two silver platters from the Stevens employees, a fishing rod and tackle from the Stadium employees and ushers, a silver cup from the Yankee office staff, a scroll from the Old Timers Association of Denver that was presented by John Kieran, a scroll from Washington fans, a to-bacco stand from the New York Chapter of the Baseball Writers Association of America, and the silver trophy from his team-mates.

The last-named present, about eighteen inches tall with a wooden base, supported by six silver bats with an eagle atop a silver ball, made Gehrig weep. President Barrow walked out to put his arms about Lou in an effort to steady him when this presentation was made. It appeared for an instant that Gehrig was near collapse.

On one side of the trophy were the names of all his present fellow-players. On the other was the following touching inscription:

**TO LOU GEHRIG**

*We've been to the wars together,*
*    We took our foes as they came,*
*And always you were the leader*
*    And ever you played the game.*

*Idol of cheering millions,*
*    Records are yours by the sheaves,*
*Iron of fame they hailed you*
*    Decked you with laurel leaves.*

*But higher than that we hold you,*
*    We who have known you best,*
*Knowing the way you came through*
*    Every human test.*

*Let this be a silent token*
*    Of lasting friendship's gleam,*
*And all that we've left unspoken,*
*    Your pals of the Yankee team.*

As Gehrig finished his talk, Ruth, robust, round and sun-tanned, was nudged toward the microphone and, in his own inimitable, blustering style, snapped the tears away. He gave it as his unqualified opinion that the Yanks of 1927 were greater than the Yanks of today, and seemed even anxious to prove it right there.

"Anyway," he added, "that's my opinion and while Lazzeri here pointed out to me that there are only about thirteen or fourteen of us here, my answer is, shucks, we only need nine to beat 'em."

Then, as the famous home-run slugger, who also has faded into retirement, stood with his arms entwined around Gehrig's shoulders, the band played "I Love You Truly," while the crowd took up the chant: "We love you, Lou."

All given spontaneously, it was without doubt one of the most touching scenes ever witnessed on a ball field and one that made even case-hardened ball players and chroniclers of the game swallow hard.

When Gehrig arrived in the Yankee dressing rooms he was so close to a complete collapse it was feared that the strain upon him had been too great and Dr. Robert E. Walsh, the Yankees' attending physician, hurried to his assistance. But after some refreshment, he recovered quickly and faithful to his one remaining task, that of being the inactive captain of his team, he stuck to his post in the dugout throughout the second game.

Long after the tumult and shouting had died and the last of the crowd had filed out, Lou trudged across the field for his familiar hike to his favorite exit gate. With him walked his bosom pal and team-mate, Bill Dickey, with whom he always rooms when the Yanks are on the road.

Lou walks with a slight hitch in his gait now, but there was supreme confidence in his voice as he said to his friend:

"Bill, I'm going to remember this day for a long time."

So, doubtless, will all the others who helped make this an unforgettable day in baseball.

June 3, 1941

# GEHRIG, "IRON MAN" OF BASEBALL, DIES AT THE AGE OF 37

### Rare Disease Forced Famous Batter to Retire in 1939—Played 2,130 Games in Row

### SET MANY HITTING MARKS

### Native of New York, He Became Star of Yankees—Idol of Fans Throughout Nation

Lou Gehrig, former first baseman of the New York Yankees and one of the outstanding batsmen baseball has known, died at his home, 5204 Delafield Avenue, in the Fieldston section of the Bronx, last night. Death came to the erstwhile "Iron Man" at 10:10 o'clock. He would have been 38 years old on June 19.

Regarded by some observers as the greatest player ever to grace the diamond, Gehrig, after playing in 2,130 consecutive championship contests, was forced to end his career in 1939 when an ailment that had been hindering his efforts was diagnosed as a form of paralysis.

The disease was chronic, and for the last month Gehrig had been confined to his home. He lost weight steadily during the final weeks and was reported twenty-five pounds under weight shortly before he died.

## Member of Parole Board

Until his illness became more serious Gehrig went to his office regularly to perform his duties as a member of the New York City Parole Commission, a post he had held for a year and a half following his retirement from baseball. Ever hopeful that he would be able to conquer the rare disease—amyotrophic lateral sclerosis, a hardening of the spinal cord—although the ailment was considered incurable by many, Gehrig stopped going to his desk about a month ago to conserve his strength.

Two weeks ago he was confined to his bed, and from that time until his death his condition grew steadily worse. He was conscious until just before the end. At the bedside when he died were his wife, the former Eleanor Twitchell of Chicago; his parents, Mr. And Mrs. Henry Gehrig; his wife's mother, Mrs. Nellie Twitchell, and Dr. Caldwell B. Esselstyn.

It was said last night that funeral services would be private and would be held tomorrow morning at 10 o'clock in the Christ Episcopal Church in Riverdale. The Rev. Gerald V. Barry will officiate.

The body was taken this morning to the E. Willis Scott Funeral Parlor at 4 West Seventy-sixth Street.


## Record Spanning Fifteen Years

When Gehrig stepped into the batter's box as a pinch hitter for the Yankees on June 1, 1925, he started a record that many believe will never be equaled in baseball. From that day on he never missed a championship game until April 30, 1939—fifteen seasons of Yankee box scores with the name Gehrig always in the line-up. He announced on May 2, 1939, that he would not play that day, and thus his streak came to an end.

But as brilliant as was his career, Lou will be remembered for more than his endurance record. He was a superb batter in his heyday and a prodigious clouter of home runs. The record book is liberally strewn with his feats at the plate.

Only in his first season, 1925, and in his last full campaign, 1938, did he fail to go over the .300 mark. Once he led the American League in hitting with .363, but on three occasions he went over that without winning the batting crown—.373, .374 and .379.

But baseball has had other great hitters before and other great all-around players. It was the durability of Gehrig combined with his other qualities that lifted him above the ordinary players and in a class all his own.

An odd little incident gave Gehrig his start and an even stranger disease, one almost totally unknown for a robust athlete, brought it to an end. Columbia Lou's string of consecutive games began, innocently enough, when the late Miller Huggins sent him up to bat for Peewee Wanninger on June 1, 1925. The husky 22-year-old promptly singled.

Huggins was impressed by the way Gehrig had delivered, but according to the tale that is told he had no notion of using him as a first baseman. The Yankees had a star at the initial sack in those days, Wally Pipp. But Pipp was troubled with frequent headaches.

On June 2 he was bothered by pains in his head.

"Has anyone an aspirin tablet?" asked Pipp.

Huggins overheard him and, on a sheer hunch, decided to use the "kid"—Gehrig—at first base. He never left the line-up again until his voluntary resignation fourteen years later. Perhaps that story is not cut from the whole cloth. Gehrig has denied it, but Pipp insists just as vehemently that is it true. At any rate, it is an interesting sidelight on how a spectacular career was begun.

## Slipped in 1938

The beginning of the Gehrig playing days was abrupt but the ending was a much slower process. In 1937 the Iron Horse batted .351, his twelfth successive season over the .300 mark. But in 1938 the Yankee captain slipped to .295, the same figure he had established in his 1925 campaign.

Not only his hitting but his fielding had lost much of its crispness. Batted balls that the Gehrig of old had gobbled up easily skidded past him for base hits. In fact, the situation had developed to such an extent that there was continual talk in Spring training in 1939 that the endurance record was approaching its completion.

This became even more obvious in the early games of the campaign. Yankee followers were amazed to see how badly Gehrig had fallen from the peak. He was anchored firmly near first base and only the fielding wizardry of Joe Gordon to his right saved Gehrig from looking very bad. The second sacker over-shifted to cover the hole between him and his captain. Lou couldn't go to his right any more.

At bat Gehrig was not even a pale shadow of his former self. Once he had the outfielders backing up to the fences when he stepped to the plate. But this time he could hardly raise the ball out of the infield. On one occasion when he caromed a looping single to left—a certain double for even a slow runner—Gehrig was thrown out at second, standing up.

## Last Game Against Senators

That day he saw the handwriting on the wall. And on April 30, 1939, he played his last big league game against the Washington Senators. The Bombers lost and Gehrig realized that he was a detriment to his team. When the Yanks took to the field again in Detroit on May 2, Gehrig—his batting average down to .143—withdrew from the lineup, his first missed game after 2,130 straight.

He acted as nonplaying captain from that point on. On June 12, when the Yankees engaged in an exhibition game in Kansas City, Lou played the last three innings, did nothing and promptly left for the Mayo Clinic. He was there a week, determined to discover just what was the matter with him. That something was wrong he was certain.

On June 21 the diagnosis was made. It was that he had a mild attack of paralysis. His career thus was brought to an abrupt conclusion. And an amazing career it had been.

## Tribute by 61,808 at Retirement

The public's reaction to Gehrig's swift retirement gave rise to one of the most inspiring and dramatic episodes in sport when on July 4, in ceremonies preceding the afternoon's holiday double-header, a crowd of 61,808 joined in the Lou Gehrig Appreciation Day exercises at the Yankee Stadium and thundered a "hail and farewell" to baseball's stricken Iron Horse.

Players, officials, writers and employees at the park showered Lou with gifts, the climax of the spectacle coming when the Yankees themselves paraded on the field their world championship team of 1927. From far and wide these diamond stalwarts had returned to join in the tribute to their former team-mate, who had managed to carry on long after their own retirement from the game.

The group included such Yankee immortals as Babe Ruth, Waite Hoyt, Bob Meusel, Herb Pennock, Joe Dugan, Tony Lazzeri, Mark Koenig, Benny Bengough, Wally Schang, Everett Scott, Wally Pipp, George Pipgras and Bob Shawkey.

Overcome by this spontaneous reception, Gehrig finally mastered his emotions, and, in perhaps the most remarkable valedictory ever delivered in a sport arena, literally poured his heart out to his great throng of listeners, thanking them for their appreciation and assuring them, with characteristic pluck, thatbhe still considered himself "the luckiest fellow on earth, with much to live for."

From then until the end of the season Gehrig stuck by his guns as retired field captain, and spent every day on the bench. He accompanied the club on all its road trips, and at the finish sat through all four of the 1939 world series games in which his colleagues crushed another National League rival.

With the close of the campaign, Lou retired himself within a small circle of friends, spent much time in fishing, a sport second only to baseball in its fascination for him, and on Oct. 11 figured in another surprise move when Mayor La Guardia announced his appointment to a ten-year term as a member of the three-man Municipal Parole Commission at a salary of $5,700 a year. He tackled with considerable enthusiasm this newest job that was to launch him upon a new chapter in his astounding career.

## In Spotlight Again

Although anxious to go quietly about his new task and remain as much as possible in complete retirement, Gehrig was catapulted prominently into the spotlight in mid-August of the 1940 pennant campaign when a New York newspaper, in a featured article, intimated that the extraordinary collapse of the four-time world champion Yankees might be attributable to the possibility that some of the players may have become infected with Gehrig's disease.

The story brought vehement protests from the Yankee players, who insisted they were suffering from no physical ailments and then, as if in final rebuttal to the charge, the Yanks, within a few days after publication of the article, launched their spectacular drive which was to lift them from fifth place into the thick of the flag race throughout the month of September.

In the meantime, Gehrig had papers served for a $1,000,000 libel action, while the publication printed an

Lou Gehrig slugging ball on Columbia University's South Field in the early 1920's. Hamilton Hall is in the background. (UNITED PRESS INTERNATIONAL/BETTMANN NEWSPHOTOS)

apology to Gehrig, stating that thorough investigation revealed that Lou's ailment was not communicable. No legal action was taken after this.

Gehrig was born in New York on June 19, 1903.

His career began unobtrusively enough when, as a husky youngster, he reported for the High School of Commerce nine in New York. He was tried in the outfield, where he was no Joe DiMaggio at catching fly balls.

Lou Gehrig at Columbia University. (UNITED PRESS INTERNATIONAL/BETTMANN NEWSPHOTOS)

He was tried as a pitcher but was wild. He was tried as a first baseman and clicked. In later years Lou explained that, with his ever ready grin, by saying "We were mighty short on infielders in those days."

In his first season on the Commerce team he batted .170. Then he started hitting until he cracked the headlines with a crash in 1920. Commerce, the New York schoolboy champions, played Lane Tech of Chicago in a scholastic "world series." The single game was played at Wrigley Field and Gehrig was awed by his surroundings. But he was not too awed. In the ninth inning with Commerce one run behind and the bases full he drove a home run over the right field fence.

## Columbia All-Around Player

Buster Gehrig was beginning to take shape. He matriculated at Columbia, pitching, outfielding and playing at first. He was a good enough college pitcher but did have the knack of hitting home runs. For one year there he also tried football, but that sport did not have the same appeal that baseball bore.

The diamond game carried such a zest for him that he quit before he had been long at Morningside Heights, joining the Yankees in 1923. He played thirteen games before Huggins decided that he was not yet ready for major league ball. Farmed out to Hartford in the Eastern League, he batted .304 for the rest of the season. Back with the Yanks the next campaign he followed the identical procedure. He took part in ten games and then it was a return trip to Hartford, where he began to belabor the fences in the circuit, hitting .369. That figure was an eye-opener to Huggins, who recalled him the following season.

That was in 1925. Gehrig batted .295 in 126 games and then he began to rocket through baseball firmament. His first full season showed him with .313, but after that his successive batting averages were .373, .374, .300, .379, .341, .349, .334, .363, .329, .354, .351, and finally he was back to .295 in his last full campaign. The .363 average gave him the batting championship in 1934, but signal honors had come to him before that. In 1927, his second full season with the Yankees, he was voted the most valuable player in the American League.

Seven times he participated in world series and, oddly enough, was a star on the Yankees of 1926–27–28 and with the all-star contingent of 1936–37–38. Each of these groups has its supporters as the greatest baseball team of all time. Ruth-Gehrig-Meusel, the famed "Murderers' Row," or DiMaggio-Gehrig-Dickey? Those were the batting fulcrums around which the teams revolved. Columbia Lou was the lone tie between the two.

His series deeds have been awe-inspiring. His lifetime average in world series games was .361—his full regular average .340—and twice he hit over the fantastic mark of .500 with .545 in 1928 and .529 in 1932. Babe Ruth, however, holds the series record of .625 in 1928.

That is an oddity in itself, Gehrig with two terrific averages but still behind the Babe. Yet for the better part of his career the Iron Horse was to be in the shadow of Ruth. Lou entered baseball when the Babe was riding high, straddling the sport such as no man has straddled it before or since.

Gehrig never left that shadow. His all-time home run production was 494, a figure topped by only two men, Ruth and Jimmy Foxx, who at the end of 1940 had reached a 500 total. For many years Lou gave the Babe his closets pursuit in the home-run derby, but he never caught him until the Babe's last year as a Yankee. Only when the King was on the decline did the Crown Prince win the home-run championship of the league, 49 in 1934.

For one thing, Gehrig did not have the flamboyant Ruth personality. They were team-mates but far apart, one quiet, reserved and efficient and the other boisterous, friendly and efficient. Let it not be deduced that the Iron Horse was not of the friendly type. He was pleasant at all times, but unlike Ruth he never considered the world at large as his particular friend. Whereas the Babe would greet all and sundry with a booming "Hiya, kid?" Lou's was a more personalized welcome.

They were sharp contrast, those two, both hulking men but as far apart as the two poles. Ruth was Gehrig's boyhood idol, and with the passing years Lou never lost that respect for the Home Run King. And in spite of his own tremendous record, Gehrig was always subordinated to Ruth.

What a pair they made at the plate, coming up to bat in order! Each was likely to drive the ball out of the park. Frequently either or both did just that. In fact, one of the many records that Lou set was that of hitting the most home runs with the bases filled, a startling twenty-three. Another was of four homers in one game.

The Ruthian association affected Gehrig's salary in two respects. In one way the heavy blow that Ruth struck at the payroll kept Lou from getting a compensation as close to the Babe's as their relative batting averages would indicate. Yet, on the other hand, the Bambino lifted the scale so high that Gehrig probably received more than he would have had there been no Ruth to blaze the trail.

## Made Fortune in Game

Like most payrolls, the Yankee one is not open to public gaze, but is more public property than an ordinary business. So the amount of money Gehrig received each season is part guess and part accurate knowledge, especially in the most recent years when the Federal income tax rolls ceased being secret.

The general estimate is that the Iron Horse received a total of $361,500 in salary from the Yankees. Since he participated in seven world series where the share always was heavy his total income from baseball is estimated at $400,000.

Gehrig received $3,750 in his first season, $6,500 in his second year. This advanced $1,000 in 1927 and then the Iron Horse moved in to big-money class. He never dropped out of five figures for the rest of his career.

For the next five years he received $25,000 and then he dropped to $23,000 for 1933 and 1934, after which he received $31,000 in 1935 and 1936, $36,750 in 1937, $39,000 in 1938 and $35,000 for 1939, a campaign in which he played only eight games.

Baseball contracts are peculiar things, strictly one way. The club has the upper hand at all times and can sever any contract at will. Had they so desired the Yanks could have dropped Gehrig the day the report from the Mayo Clinic arrived. But he was kept on full salary for the remainder of the year.

So firm was his place in the Yankee scheme of things that Manager Joe McCarthy refused to break the Gehrig string even when there was clamor to the effect that the Iron Horse himself would benefit from it. Marse Joe shook his head to that. "Gehrig plays as long as he wants to play," he said. No many ball players would be granted such a privilege.

But in this respect McCarthy knew his man and knew him well. He realized that once Lou discovered his form had departed and that he was hindering the progress of the team he would call it quits. And that is what happened.

Had it not been for the attack of paralysis Gehrig might have continued as a part-time performer. Ball players do not go as fast as he went. The disintegration always is gradual enough for managers and club owners to make preparations. But the Yankees were caught without an adequate substitute for him, only the light-hitting but sure-fielding Babe Dahlgren.

Previously, being Gehrig's replacement had been the height of frustration. There was just no hope that he ever would give way to any one else. In their thorough fashion the Yankees had had several first basemen on their farm teams. All of them pleaded to be sold or traded elsewhere so that they would be able to play regularly.

One was Buddy Hassett, now at first base for the Boston Braves. Another was George McQuinn, hard-hitting initial sacker for the St. Louis Browns. Many others have paraded into the Yankee orbit and out again, balked of their desire by the stalwart figure of Lou Gehrig.

The day before he entered the Mayo Clinic for the examination baseball celebrated its centennial at Cooperstown and the Hall of Fame was dedicated. Ruth already had been elected to it and within a short time another bronze plaque joined the Babe's as Henry Lou Gehrig took his proper place among the all-time greats that this sport had produced.

For though Baseball's Hall of Fame committee decided to hold no elections for new candidates in 1939, it chose, upon recommendation of the Baseball Writers Association of America, to make an exception and name Gehrig as the lone Hall of Fame award for the year.

## Gehrig's Impressive Records

The major records that Gehrig made:

### REGULAR SEASON

Most consecutive games—2,130.
Most consecutive years, 100 games or more—14.
Most years, 150 games or more—12.
Most years, 100 runs or more—13.
Most consecutive years, 100 runs or more—13.
Most years, 100 or more runs batted in—13 (tied with Ruth).
Most years, 150 or more runs batted in—7.
Most consecutive years, 100 or more runs batted in—13.
Most runs batted in, one season—184 (American League).
Most times, four long hits in one game—5.
Most years, 400 or more total bases—5.
Most years, 300 or more total bases—13.

Most home runs with bases filled—23.
Most consecutive home runs in one game—4 (modern record).
Most total bases, game (modern record)—16 (tied with Ruth and Klein).
Most years, leading league, runs batted in—5 (tied with Ruth).
Most years, leading league games played, season—8.
First baseman participating in most double plays, season—157.

## WORLD SERIES

Highest batting percentage, total series—.361 (7 series).
Most runs, one series—9 (tied with Ruth).
Most runs batted in, total series—35.
Most runs batted in, one series—9.
Most home runs, one four-game series—4.
Most home runs, 3 consecutive games—4.
Most extra bases on long hits, one series—13.

June 1, 1986

*Views of Sport*

### Some Days in June With the Yankees' Quiet Hero

By RAY ROBINSON

For Lou Gehrig, the ill-fated Iron Horse of baseball, June was always a watershed month.

He was born on East 94th Street in Manhattan on June 19, 1903.

His 2,130-consecutive game streak with the New York Yankees began when he pinch-hit on June 1, 1925.

He hit four consecutive home runs against the Philadelphia Athletics on June 3, 1932 (and he was, incidentally, deprived of primary headline attention when John McGraw, after 30 years as manager of the New York Giants, resigned that day).

He died, just short of his 38th birthday, on June 2, 1941, exactly 45 years ago tomorrow.

• • •

In the enduring years of Yankee dominance Lou Gehrig always lived and played in the bulging shadow Babe Ruth. In popular parlance, Gehrig was the designated Crown Prince to Ruth's Kingship. But that didn't stop me from preferring the dimpled, modest Lou to baseball's Zeus, the larger-than-life Bambino. I chose Gehrig over Ruth because the Babe could win applause just by crossing the street, or even by strikeout.

Somehow, I wanted my heroes to be less outrageous, less flamboyant. That image seemed to fit Gehrig, stubbornly dedicated in his day-to-day role as captain of the Yankees. A handsome, sturdy man who became a living legend of dependability, Lou lashed screaming line drives compared to the Babe's higher-than-heaven home runs.

So, of all the world champion Yankees it was Lou Gehrig I loved the most. There was something else. He had enrolled at Columbia in 1922, the college that had also produced Eddie Collins, Connie Mack's Hall of Fame second baseman, some 15 years before. My father was graduated from Columbia and was privileged to see Collins play in college. Though he wasn't much of a baseball fan, my father appreciated the greatness of Collins. His pride in Columbia caused him to nurse special feelings for Gehrig, too.

"I remember Lou hitting fly balls off the steps of Low Library or off the brick walls of the Journalism Building," my father told me. He judged that such blows were easily 500 feet from home plate on Columbia's South Field. Such stories only reinforced my admiration. As I grew into my 11th year I was determined to meet The Quiet Hero, an altogether fitting appellation bestowed on Gehrig by Frank Graham, a newspaperman who had covered the Yankees for many years.

• • •

My early journalistic efforts were in behalf of P.S. 165's newspaper and it was my ambition to interview Lou for that paper. So one day I sat down with a friend and composed a letter, which was mailed to the Gehrig home in New Rochelle, N.Y.

In truth, we held out scant hope that he would ever respond. But these doubts were shredded magnificently when a hand-written letter arrived several days later. I can still remember the careful penmanship. Yes, he would be happy to see us. "Just use this letter to come to the clubhouse," he wrote.

Within 24 hours, my friend and I made the trip by uptown subway to Yankee Stadium, where the Washington Senators were to play the Yankees. I assume we played hooky that day. What a small price to pay for an audience with Larrupin' Lou!

That May day was cloudless, the skies Columbia blue, of course. In those days games began at 3:30 in the afternoon, but we arrived at the cavernous ball park by 1 o'clock. Foolishly, we assumed the prized letter would be an instant ticket of admission. But the gendarme guarding the Yankee clubhouse door informed us otherwise.

"You can wait here," he said, waving his pudgy arms in the general direction of the entire borough of the Bronx.

As the game began, we listened intently for crowd noises that might hint at Yankee rallies. Gehrig doubles, or perish forbid, Babe blasts. Once there was an enormous, growling roar that my friend wanted to bet was a homer with the bases loaded by Lou (a feat that Gehrig performed 23 times, a major league career mark).

Now the sun started to go down and we hoped the game was coming to an end. But the Yankees of those days were known as the team of "Five O'clock Lightning," a handy summation of their penchant for late-inning uprisings. My friend and I were tired and thirsty and had little more in our pockets than the return fare for the subway. Then, suddenly all was quiet within the stadium. We knew the game had ended and soon we would see Gehrig.

Being earnest reporters, we learned the Yanks had won again and that George Pipgras was the winning pitcher. Somebody said Tony Lazzeri had got the decisive hit. We tried to figure how long it would take Lou to shower and dress. Other youngsters also lingered around the clubhouse exit, but, with our precious letter, we felt smugly superior to all of them.

When Lou finally appeared, he was hatless, coatless, tieless; his thick brown hair—no blow-dry in those years—was still damp from his shower. He had the kind of deep tan that most of today's players have forfeited to night games. As he started to walk down the street to his car, we set out in breathless pursuit.

• • •

"Mr. Gehrig! Mr. Gehrig!" we called. He stopped and turned. The man looked enormous to two 11-year-olds. "We have a letter from you."

By now he was curious and advanced toward us. My friend handed him the letter. He gazed at it, recognized his own handwriting.

"Did you boys enjoy the game?" he asked.

"We couldn't get in," my friend informed him.

"Oh, I'm sorry," he said. "You should have told me you were coming, I would have left tickets for you." The voice, true to the accents of New York, was pleasant.

"Could we interview you now, Mr. Gehrig?" I asked, unwilling to acknowledge the failure of a mission.

"I'm afraid not," he answered. "I'm in a hurry to get home."

"But we waited all afternoon," my friend insisted, as bold as an apprentice reporter could be.

Lou smiled.

"I wish I'd known you were here," he offered. Then he reached into his pants pocket and withdrew two crumbled tickets. "Let's make it another day," he said, handing us the tickets. "I'll be happy to see you then."

"Thanks," my friend and I said, in unison, as we admired the tickets.

"Did you boys really wait all afternoon?" Lou continued.

"Yes we did, Mr. Gehrig," I said.

"I'm really very sorry," he repeated. Then, with a wave of his large hand, he entered his car. We watched as he drove away, into the traffic leading away from the stadium.

"He's some great guy," my friend said to me. I nodded in awe and silent agreement.

• • •

The last time I saw Gehrig was on July 4, 1939, at Lou Gehrig Appreciation Day at Yankee Stadium. Many of his old teammates, including Ruth, from whom he had been estranged due to some private hurt, were there, along with nearly 62,000 fans.

John Kieran, *The New York Times* columnist, wrote a splendid inscription on a trophy presented to Lou by his teammates. It began:

> *We've been to the wars together,*
> *We took our foes as they came*
> *And always you were the leader,*
> *And ever you played the game.*

Gehrig was already dying of amyotrophic lateral sclerosis (a disease that now bears his name). While the hushed thousands listened in teary silence, Lou hoarsely insisted over the public-address system that carried his valedictory that he was "the luckiest man on the face of the earth."

June 3, 1941, was my graduation day from Columbia. Lou had died the day before. As I walked across the campus, I recalled my father's stories about how Lou used to hit baseballs on South Field, at 116th Street and Broadway. I remembered, too, that my friend and I had never returned for an interview.

At a moment that I should have been joyous, I felt a strange melancholy.

*Views of Sport*

## When the Iron Horse Came to a Stop

### By RAY ROBINSON

For the first time in his long playing life with the New York Yankees—through Prohibition, the Flapper Age, the Roaring Twenties, the Great Depression and the New Deal—Lou Gehrig, baseball's Iron Horse, accepted a salary cut in the winter of 1939.

Gehrig's off year in 1938—he batted .295, close to 50 points off his lifetime pace—gave General Manger Ed Barrow the opening to decrease Gehrig's pay to $36,000, some $3,000 less than he had received the previous year. True to his style, Gehrig didn't battle or threaten; he would just strive, he promised, to regain his form. If others, including his wife, Eleanor, privately thought he was slipping, he continued to reject such a notion.

In the first days at spring training camp in St. Petersburg, Fla., Gehrig worked hard on his body, convinced that his zealous conditioning program would heal whatever was ailing him.

But by mid-March, after 10 exhibition games, Gehrig was hitting barely over .100, with no extra-base hits. His reflexes seemed even slower than they had been in 1938 and his familiar scythe-like swing was missing. Fans in Tampa, Bradenton and St. Petersburg now yelled "One out" or "Two out" when Gehrig walked to the plate.

Suspicions were rampant that Gehrig's abilities had retreated so far over the winter that Manager Joe Mc-Carthy might have to think seriously about replacing him, despite Gehrig's long streak of consecutive games.

"I began to fear that Lou might get hurt if I didn't get him out of there," said McCarthy.

• • •

In one batting practice session, Joe DiMaggio, Gehrig's teammate, watched with disbelief as Gehrig missed 19 straight pitches. "They were all fastballs, too, the kind of pitches that Lou would normally hit into the next county," said DiMaggio.

On another afternoon, as Gehrig was trying to put on his pants after a game, he fell down. When Pete Sheehy, the clubhouse attendant, and DiMaggio ran over to pick Gehrig up, Gehrig waived them away. He said he could get up by himself.

Previously, Gehrig's sporadic slumps had always engendered good-natured needling. Now, such joking ceased, for it was insensitive to shout "Hey, old man," at someone who was obviously suffering.

As the Yankees broke camp and headed north, Gehrig had played in 27 games without hitting a home run or a triple. The club had four exhibition games left with the Brooklyn Dodgers, who were touring with them. In the first of those games in Norfolk, Va., Gehrig cracked out four hits, his highest output of the spring. Among those hits were two homers.

When the team arrived in New York, the news of Gehrig's "revival," reported dutifully in the papers, raised hopes that Gehrig's silent spring had been a bad dream.

With the powerful team under his command—DiMaggio, Tommy Henrich, Bill Dickey, Charlie (King Kong) Keller, Joe Gordon, Red Rolfe, Frank Crosetti and pitchers like Red Ruffing, Lefty Gomez, Monte Pearson and Johnny Murphy—McCarthy felt he could afford to be patient with his captain.

When the season began at Yankee Stadium on April 20, Gehrig was at first base against the Red Sox. But what the fans saw, in Gehrig's 2,123d straight game, was a scarcely recognizable athlete. The first time he batted Gehrig received a rousing burst of applause, almost as if the fans were trying to tell Gehrig how much they wanted to see him recapture his old glory. But when Lefty Grove of the Red Sox walked DiMaggio intentionally to face Gehrig, reality struck home.

A few days later, with the Yankees playing the Athletics, George Caster, a Philadelphia right-hander, declined to pitch close to Gehrig. "I was afraid," said Caster, "that if I pitched him tight he wouldn't have the reflexes to get out of the way. His body seemed to have slowed up."

On April 29 the Senators beat the Yanks, 3–1. Gehrig singled in three at-bats against left-hander Ken Chase. It was the 2,721st—and final—hit of his career.

On Sunday, April 30, President Franklin D. Roosevelt visited New York to open the New York World's Fair at Flushing Meadows. At Yankee Stadium 24,000 chose to watch a ball game instead of journeying to the fair.

Gehrig arrived early on that glorious spring day to work on his hitting. In batting practice he managed to hit a few balls that barely reached the right-field bleachers. In infield practice Timmy Sullivan, the Yanks' mascot, worked faithfully with Gehrig, as his idol desperately tried to field ground balls.

For the fifth time in eight games, Gehrig went hitless, as the Senators beat the Yanks 3–2. After the game a buzz of disgruntlement pervaded the Yankee clubhouse. Some players openly expressed doubt then team could win with Gehrig in the lineup. Overhearing the remarks, Gehrig was deeply shaken. That night he discussed his situation with Eleanor. She asked only if he still got satisfaction out of playing.

"How can I, when I'm hurting the team?" he responded.

The Yankees had a day off before opening a series in Detroit on May 2, 1939, 50 years ago this week. When Gehrig arrived in his hotel room, he decided, at last, to step down after 2,130 consecutive games, a mark that will probably remain invulnerable as long as baseball is played.

Gehrig asked McCarthy to join him in his room. Anticipating what Gehrig was about to tell him, McCarthy hated to hear it.

"I'm benching myself, Joe," Gehrig announced.

After a moment's silence, McCarthy asked: "Why?"

"For the good of the team, Joe," Gehrig said. "I just can't seem to get going. Nobody has to tell me how bad I've been and how much of a drawback to the club. The time has come for me to quit."

"You don't have to quit," said McCarthy. "Take some time off to rest. Maybe you'll fell all right again."

Gehrig then went on to explain that an incident in the last game at the Stadium had convinced him it was time to put up his spikes.

In the ninth inning a ball had been hit between the pitcher's mound and first base. Murphy, the pitcher, had fielded it cleanly but had to wait for Gehrig to struggle to first base to take his throw. It should have been an easy play for Gehrig. It wasn't.

"When Murphy came over to tell me what a nice play I'd made," said Gehrig, "I knew it was time for me to get out."

McCarthy understood. "All right, Lou," he said. "I'll put Dahlgren in today, but any time you want to get back in there, it's your position."

•   •   •

On that May 2d afternoon the Yankee clubhouse under the stands in Briggs Stadium, was like a morgue. Even before Coach Art Fletcher tapped Babe Dahlgren on the shoulder to inform him he was starting at first base, the grapevine had reached the players. Most of them spoke in whispers, as they started to dress for a game they wished would never take place.

"Good luck, Babe," said Fletcher. In a state of near-shock, Dahlgren suited up and trotted out on the field to warm up. He noticed Gehrig, dedicated to the end, in the outfield chasing fungoes with the pitchers. For an hour Gehrig worked with his reluctant body, as if he was trying to shake the demons loose. Then he walked dejectedly towards the dugout.

With photographers clamoring for pictures, Gehrig returned to the field to pose with Dahlgren. Even if Dahlgren felt it was time to make his own reputation, he regarded himself as a culprit; he looked into Gehrig's eyes and saw tears there.

"Come on, Lou," said Dahlgren. "You better get out of there. You've put me in a terrible spot."

Gehrig tried to smile reassuringly at his successor. But the famous dimpled smile never came. Instead, he slapped Dahlgren on the back. "Go out there and knock in some runs," he said.

When the game was set to begin, Gehrig shuffled out with a Yankee lineup in his hand that excluded his own name. Umpire Stephen Basil accepted it. Then the announcement to the 11,379 people in the ball park, echoed over the public address system. "Dahlgren, first base," the voice pronounced.

These were Detroit fans, but they were also baseball fans. Most of them stood up and applauded. It went on for two minutes. His head down, Gehrig tipped his cap and disappeared into the Yankee dugout.

That Sunday's *New York Times* ran a memorable photo of Gehrig sitting on the dugout steps, gazing wistfully out at the field. The headline over the picture said:

"PITCHERS ONCE FEARED HIS BAT."

Two years later, on the evening of June 2, 1941, Gehrig was dead, at 38, of amyotrophic lateral sclerosis, a neuromuscular ailment in which the muscles atrophy and the patient becomes paralyzed. To this day, A.L.S., now known as Lou Gehrig's disease, remains incurable.

# JOE DIMAGGIO

Joe DiMaggio, a gallant and graceful center fielder, wore No. 5 and became a successor to Babe Ruth (3) and Lou Gehrig (4) in the Yankee Pantheon. When he hit in 56 consecutive games in 1941, a record that still stands today, the Yankee Clipper became an instant and indelible folk hero. (ASSOCIATED PRESS)

### *Yankees Obtain Di Maggio, Coast League Batting Star, in Player Transaction*

---

## CARLETON OF CARDS IS TRADED TO CUBS

---

### Tinning, Ward and Cash Go to St. Louis for Hurler—Yanks to Get Di Maggio in Fall.

---

## INDIANS, BROWNS IN DEAL

---

### Campbell Sent to Cleveland for Weiland, Burnett and Unannounced Sum.

---

#### By The Associated Press.

LOUISVILLE, Ky., Nov. 21.—The Chicago Cubs tonight sent Pitchers Bud Tinning and Dick Ward and cash to St. Louis Cardinals for Tex Carleton, right-handed pitcher.

Carleton won sixteen games and lost eleven for the world champions during the past season. Tinning won four and lost six for the third-place Cubs. Ward, who was with the Cubs for a while last season as a relief pitcher, was sent to Los Angeles, where he won thirteen and lost four.

News of this trade, made public during the minor league meetings here, followed an announcement that the Yankees had acquired Joe Di Maggio, San Francisco outfielder, who established a Pacific Coast record in 1933 by hitting safely in sixty-one consecutive games. Under present arrangements, Di Maggio will report to the Yanks next Fall.

#### Star Injured Last Season.

There was a hitch in this transaction, however, as the Yanks wanted to make certain that Joe was not slowed down permanently by a knee injury last season. Under the terms the New York club is to send five players to San Francisco next fall, two on option and three outright.

Lou Gehrig and Joe DiMaggio. (ASSOCIATED PRESS)

The Yankees were advised that Di Maggio not only was physically fit but that he was even a better prospect than Paul Waner was when he came from the Pacific Coast League to the Pirates. While names of the players who are to be sent to the Seals were not disclosed, unofficial reports indicated that Pitcher Floyd Newkirk and Pitcher Nosbert would be among them.

The Cleveland Indians announced they had sent Pitcher Bob Weiland, Infielder Johnny Burnett and cash to the Browns in return for Outfielder Bruce Campbell.

It was the overwhelming consensus among the baseball men here that Rogers Hornsby, St. Louis manager, had driven home another of his clever deals. Although Weiland, a southpaw, had a good season with the Boston Red Sox in 1933, he was ineffective last season and was sent to Cleveland. He compiled a record of two victories and ten defeats.

Campbell batted .281 in 138 games last season, but his infielding did not suit Hornsby. Burnett played in seventy-one games and batted .299.

Pittsburgh and the Cubs were attempting to make a deal whereby Outfielder Lindstrom and Pitcher Larry French would go to the Cubs for Pitcher Guy Bush and Babe Herman, an outfielder, who may play first base next season. The reported difficulties were that the Pirates wanted Shortstop Woody English instead of Herman.

### Washington to White Sox.

George Washington, Indianapolis outfielder, who lost the American Association batting championship by one point last season, was sold to the White Sox for $20,000, Pitcher Phil Gallivan and Infielder Billy Sullivan.

Twenty minutes after the Washington deal Indianapolis traded Sullivan to St. Paul for Third Baseman Otto Bluege.

Cleveland signed Steve O'Neill as coach, getting him from Toledo of the American Association for two players, Pitcher Forrest Twogood and another, to be named later.

Meanwhile the National Association of Professional Baseball Leagues opened its annual convention with an attendance of 900, approved committee reports and reelected J. Alvin Gardner, Texas League president, to the executive committee for a three-year term.

The International League tonight adopted a 154-game schedule for 1935, opening April 17 and closing September 8.

If there is still a little world series, and this was still in doubt as representatives of the International and the American Association met to settle their differences, the International will continue its present system of play-offs. If no little world series is scheduled, a meeting will be held to determine a new system.

Ike Boone has signed a two-year contract to manage the Toronto club in the International League, and Albany has sold Outfielder Joe Dugas to Montreal, it was announced.

Asheville of the Piedmont League sold Pitcher MacComisky and Infielder Hal Bennett to Albany. Baltimore sold First Baseman Sol Mishkin to Galveston of the Texas League and sent Pitcher Max Butcher to the same club on option.

### Di Maggio Young Star.

SAN FRANCISCO, Nov. 21 (AP).—Joe Di Maggio, whose transfer to the Yankees was disclosed today, will be 20 years old on Sunday. The baseball career of the six-foot one-inch 190-pounder began when his brother, Vince, was playing the outfield for the Seals in 1932. The Seals were looking for a shortstop. Vince convinced the owner his younger brother was a prospect for the position.

Joe played the last three games of the 1932 season. The next Spring Joe went to the outfield and made such an impression that the Seals kept him and released his brother.

He played in 187 games in 1933, hit for an average of .340 and batted home 169 runs. His twenty-eight home runs gave him fourth place in this department. A wrenched knee handicapped him last season, but in 101 games he hit .341 and drove home sixty-nine runs.

May 4, 1936

### *Yankees' Strong Attack Routs Browns at Stadium; Giants Win; Dodgers Lose*

## DIMAGGIO'S 3 HITS HELP YANKS SCORE

### Joe Plays Brilliantly in His Big League Debut as Browns Are Beaten by 14–5.

## NEW YORK GETS 17 BLOWS

## Four Runs in First and Three in Second Clinch Verdict Before 25,000.

### By KINGLSEY CHILDS

The "Three Spaghetti Boys" of the Yankees: Frank Crosetti, Toni Lazzeri and Joe DiMaggio. The latter has been the rookie sensation of the year, as all know, with a batting average of better than .325 and an imposing flock of home runs to his credit. (TIMES WIDE WORLD PHOTOS)

Considerably more proficient in frequently smacking timely hits of various dimensions to virtually every corner of the ball park, the Yankees climbed back into the winning column yesterday as the Browns invaded the Stadium for the opener of a three-game series.

Although the rival batters furnished the opposing pitchers with anything but sweet music, they provided plenty of harmony for the 25,000 customers, the vast majority of whom were delighted in the 14-to-5 victory recorded by the McCarthymen.

Joe DiMaggio, making his American League debut, fared well and got a big hand from the fans. He clouted a triple and two singles six turns at bat and was the only Yankee to get a hit from Russ Van Atta, who pitched the eighth.

Like the Yankees, who collected seventeen safeties from four moundsmen, the Browns, in dropping their eighth straight contest, also maced the ball hard. The visitors made thirteen good drives, but they were more scattered and did not do as much damage as the Yankee wallops.

### New York Pitching Better

The home forces also had the better of the bargain in so far as concerns pitching. Neither Vernon (Lefty) Gomez, who was shelled from the slab in the fifth, nor Johnny Murphy, who finished capably, was quite as generous as the St. Louis twirlers, particularly Elon Hogsett.

It was during the latter's stay in the box that the Yankees obtained their final run in the seventh with a minimum of effort—more specifically, a single by Lou Gehrig after DiMaggio had been retired.

Hogsett, recently obtained by Rogers Hornsby's crew from the Tigers via the trade route, thereupon proceeded to walk Bill Dickey and hit Myril Hoag with a pitched ball. Then the rangy southpaw uncorked a wild pitch that permitted Gehrig to tally.

Prior to that frame, with Ben Chapman and Gehrig leading the attack, the Yankees had counted in all except one inning, generally clustering the markers to demonstrate more impressively their superiority.

### Knott Routed in First

They began by routing Jack Knott, starting hurler, with one out in the first session, combining Frank Crosetti's triple and a double by Chapman with three walks and an error by Knott. Earl Caldwell, another right-hander, came to the rescue and tamed the New Yorkers temporarily.

But in the second, the McCarthymen added three counters to the four they obtained in the opening frame, successive singles by Red Rolfe, DiMaggio and Gehrig and a triple by Chapman being the salient factors. Caldwell, however, remained until a pinch hitter batted for him in the sixth, although he yielded another pair of runs in the fourth.

The sixth, with Hogsett twirling, was the big inning for the McCarthymen, for they massed six hits for four counters. Singles by Gehrig, Chapman, George Selkirk and Murphy followed Rolfe's double and DiMaggio's triple.

The Browns feasted principally upon Gomez's slants, belting his deliveries for nine safeties and gaining all their runs during his tenure in the box. They registered three in the first inning and added one each in the third and fifth stanzas.

After successive doubles by Lyn Larry and Ray Pepper in the latter frame, Murphy relieved the southpaw and kept the Browns at bay thereafter.

### Rain Causes Temporary Halt

Darkness, followed by a heavy downpour of rain, forced Umpire Bill Summers to halt the encounter in the last half of the sixth. After a fifteen-minute respite play was resumed.

Chapman had a perfect day at the plate, getting two triples, a double and a single in four times up. But he pulled up lame after clouting his one-base blow to right field in the seventh and retired in favor of Hoag.

Ralston Hemsley, Browns' catcher, was felled when a pitched ball bounded up from the ground and landed close to his left ear while Gehrig was at bat in the first frame. Hemsley finished the inning, but then left the contest. Angelo Guiliani replaced him.

The box score:

| ST. LOUIS (A.) | ab | r. | h. | po | .a. | e. |
|---|---|---|---|---|---|---|
| Lary, ss | 5 | 1 | 1 | 1 | 2 | 0 |
| Pepper, cf | 5 | 1 | 3 | 5 | 1 | 0 |
| Solters, lf | 5 | 1 | 2 | 3 | 0 | 0 |
| B'tomley, 1b | 3 | 1 | 1 | 4 | 0 | 0 |
| Bell, rf | 4 | 1 | 1 | 2 | 0 | 0 |
| Clift, 3b | 3 | 0 | 2 | 0 | 2 | 0 |
| Hemsley, c | 1 | 0 | 0 | 1 | 1 | 0 |
| Guiliani, c | 3 | 0 | 0 | 6 | 1 | 0 |
| Carey, 2b | 4 | 0 | 3 | 2 | 1 | 0 |
| Knott, p | 0 | 0 | 0 | 0 | 0 | 1 |
| Caldwell, p | 2 | 0 | 0 | 0 | 1 | 0 |
| aColeman | 1 | 0 | 0 | 0 | 0 | 0 |
| Hogsett, p | 0 | 0 | 0 | 0 | 0 | 0 |
| bWest | 1 | 0 | 0 | 0 | 0 | 0 |
| Van Atta, p | 0 | 0 | 0 | 0 | 0 | 0 |
| Total | 37 | 5 | 13 | 24 | 9 | 1 |

| NEW YORK (A.) | ab | r. | h. | po. | a. | e. |
|---|---|---|---|---|---|---|
| Crosetti, ss | 5 | 1 | 1 | 2 | 4 | 0 |
| Rolfe, 3b | 5 | 3 | 2 | 0 | 0 | 1 |
| DiMaggio, lf | 6 | 3 | 3 | 1 | 0 | 0 |
| Gehrig, 1b | 5 | 5 | 4 | 7 | 0 | 0 |
| Dickey, c | 3 | 1 | 0 | 8 | 1 | 0 |
| Chapman, cf | 4 | 0 | 4 | 1 | 0 | 0 |
| Hoag, cf | 0 | 1 | 0 | 2 | 0 | 0 |
| Selkirk, rf | 3 | 0 | 1 | 4 | 1 | 0 |
| Lazzeri, rf | 5 | 0 | 1 | 2 | 2 | 0 |
| Gomez, p | 2 | 0 | 0 | 0 | 0 | 0 |
| Murphy, p | 3 | 0 | 1 | 0 | 1 | 0 |
| Total | 41 | 14 | 17 | 27 | 9 | 1 |

aBatted for Caldwell in sixth.
bBatted for Hogsett in eighth.

| St. Louis | 301 | 010 | 000—5 |
|---|---|---|---|
| New York | 430 | 204 | 10..—14 |

Runs batted in—Bell, Clift, 2, Chapman 5, Lazzeri 2, Gehrig 2, Dickey, Pepper 2, Lary, DiMaggio, Selkirk.

Two-base hits—Clift, Chapman, Pepper, Rolfe. Three-base hits—Crosetti, Chapman 2, DiMaggio. Home run—Pepper. Double play—Selkirk and Gehrig; Crosetti and Gehrig; Lazzeri, Murphy and Gehrig. Left on bases—New York 11, St. Louis 7. Bases on balls—Knott 3, Caldwell 1, Hogsett 3, Gomez 1, Murphy 1. Struck out—By Gomez 3. Murphy 4, Caldwell 4, Van Atta 1. Hits—Off Knott 2 in 1–3 inning, Caldwell 7 in 4, Hogsett 7 in 2 2–3, Van Atta 1 in 1, Gomez 9 in 4, Murphy 4 in 5. Hit by pitcher—By Hogsett (Hoag). Wild pitch—Hogsett. Winning pitcher—Murphy. Losing pitcher—Knott. Umpires—Summers, Johnston and Owens. Time of game—2:47.

### *Pirates and Giants Divide Twin Bill; Yankees Triumph*

---

### *Yanks Win, DiMaggio Tying Mark With Two Homers in One Inning*

---

## Drives Feature McCarthymen's Ten-Run Attack in Fifth as White Sox Lose, 18–11—Gehrig's Four Hits Give Him 101 for Season—Powell Connects With Bases Full.

---

### By JOHN DREBINGER

*Special to THE NEW YORK TIMES.*

CHICAGO, June 24.—With Colonel Ruppert viewing the spectacle and wearing at the same time his best smile, the only one, indeed, that could be seen in the gathering of 7,000, the Yankees today put on a gorgeous show for the edification of their employer.

Joe DiMaggio hit two home runs, and Frank Crosetti, Jake Powell and Bill Dickey each exploded one. Even if our own pitching was not of the best, the twenty-four blows that sailed off the Yankee bats sufficed to bring down the White Sox with a grand crash and a final score of 18 to 11.

### Yankees Extend Lead

That gave the McCarthymen the lead in the current series, two to one, restored their hold on first place over the Red Sox to five and a half games and gave our Colonel, here essentially to attend a brewers' convention, a marvelous appetite for an excellent repast.

DiMaggio's two homers, his seventh and eighth of the season, came in one inning to tie a major league record and supply the highlight of a 10-run rally which the Yanks touched off in the fifth to wreck the encounter for the Sox beyond repair.

The first DiMaggio clout, made off Babe Phelps, came with one on, and the second one, off Russell Evans, found two on the bases, to give Joe credit for driving in five tallies in a single round, only one behind the all-time record. DiMaggio also hit two doubles.

In the same inning, Powell unfurled his homer and bagged four on the shot, the clout coming with the bases full.

### Lou Still Has Home Range

Dickey, prior to unloading his homer in the ninth, had warmed up on three singles, while Crosetti, who opened the first with his four-master, subsequently contributed two more singles.

Lou Gehrig's home run bludgeon was a little out of working order, but nothing serious. All Lou did was to pound out four hits, two of them doubles.

On taking an inventory this morning McCarthy found he had lost something more than the ball game in yesterday's bruising encounter. Tony Lazzeri reported on deck with a badly damaged finger that may keep the veteran second sacker on the sidelines for several days.

When Gehrig fetched up with his third blow it gave Lou the distinction of being the first player in the majors this year to gain his one hundredth hit. His seasonal total at the close of the day was 101.

By hitting two homers in one round DiMaggio tied a major league record held jointly by four others, Ken Williams, Hack Wilson, Bill Regan and Hank Leiber.

The box score:

| NEW YORK (A.) | ab | r. | h. | po. | a. | e. | CHICAGO (A.) | ab | r. | h. | po. | a. | e. |
|---|---|---|---|---|---|---|---|---|---|---|---|---|---|
| Crosetti, ss | 6 | 3 | 3 | 4 | 1 | 0 | Radcliff, lf | 5 | 3 | 3 | 4 | 0 | 0 |
| Rolfe, 3b | 6 | 3 | 3 | 0 | 2 | 0 | Rosenthal, cf | 4 | 2 | 2 | 1 | 0 | 0 |
| DiMaggio, rf | 6 | 3 | 4 | 1 | 1 | 0 | Hass, rf | 4 | 2 | 0 | 0 | 0 | 0 |
| Gehrig, 1b | 5 | 4 | 4 | 9 | 0 | 1 | Bonura, 1b | 2 | 1 | 1 | 9 | 1 | 0 |
| Dickey, c | 5 | 2 | 4 | 6 | 1 | 0 | Appling, ss | 4 | 0 | 2 | 2 | 2 | 0 |
| Selkirk, lf | 4 | 1 | 1 | 3 | 0 | 0 | Hayes, 2b | 5 | 0 | 1 | 3 | 5 | 0 |
| Powell, cf | 6 | 1 | 1 | 3 | 0 | 0 | Dykes, 3b | 5 | 0 | 0 | 0 | 7 | 0 |
| Heffner, 2b | 5 | 0 | 2 | 1 | 7 | 0 | Sewell, c | 2 | 1 | 1 | 4 | 1 | 0 |
| Gomez, p | 2 | 0 | 1 | 0 | 1 | 0 | Shea, c | 1 | 1 | 0 | 2 | 0 | 0 |
| Malone, p | 3 | 1 | 1 | 0 | 1 | 0 | Cain, p | 1 | 0 | 0 | 0 | 1 | 0 |
| | | | | | | | Phelps, p | 1 | 0 | 0 | 0 | 0 | 0 |
| | | | | | | | Evans, p | 1 | 0 | 0 | 1 | 1 | 0 |
| | | | | | | | ᵃKreevich | 1 | 0 | 1 | 0 | 0 | 0 |
| | | | | | | | Chelini, p | 1 | 1 | 1 | 1 | 0 | 0 |
| Total | 48 | 18 | 24 | 27 | 14 | 1 | Total | 37 | 11 | 12 | 27 | 18 | 0 |

ᵃBatted for Evans in eighth.

| New York | 230 | 0100 | 201—18 |
|---|---|---|---|
| Chicago | 301 | 300 | 022—11 |

Runs batted in—Crosetti, Dickey 4, Appling 2, Gehrig, Selkirk 3, Hayes 2, Sewell, Bonura 3, DiMaggio 5, Powell 4, Rosenthal 2.

Two-base hits—Rolfe, Bonura, Gehrig 2, Heffner, DiMaggio 2. Three-base hits—Radcliff. Home runs—Crosetti, Sewell, DiMaggio 2, Powell, Dickey. Double play—Gomez, Crosetti and Gehrig; Appling, Hayes and Bonura; Hayes, Appling and Bonura; Dykes, Hayes and Bonura. Left on bases—New York 7, Chicago 10. Bases on balls—Off Gomez 6, Cain 2, Phelps 1, Malone 5, Evans 1. Struck out—By Gomez 3. Cain 2, Phelps 1, Malone 3, Evans 1, Chelini 1. Hits—Off Gomez 6 in 3 2–3 innings, Cain 7 in 2 2–3, Phelps 7 in 1 1–3, Evans 9 in 4, Malone 6 in 5 1–3, Chelini 1 in 1. Winning pitcher—Malone. Losing pitcher—Phelps. Umpires—Dineen, Geizel and Hubbard. Time of game—2:29.

### *Even Break Keeps Giants in Lead; Dodgers Take Two; Yanks Win and Play Tie*

---

### Yankees Rout Browns by 16 to 9, Then Draw, 8–8, in Eleven Innings

---

### DiMaggio Smashes 3 Homers in Nightcap, Which Is Called to Make Train—Clift, St. Louis, Also Gets 3 for Day—Seven Runs in 9th Win Opener—New York Lead Now Half Game

---

### By James P. Dawson

*Special to THE NEW YORK TIMES.*

ST. LOUIS, June 13.—More than five hours of baseball ended at Sportsman's Park today with the Yankees gaining a decision over the Browns in one end of a double-header and getting a tie in the other.

The Yanks romped off with the first game by 16 to 9 in their biggest hitting and scoring splurge of the season. They were battling the Browns tooth and nail in the nightcap when the skirmish was called with the score 8-all after eleven innings because dusk was fast enveloping the field and the necessity for making even belated train connections was imperative.

The season's biggest American League crowd here, 12,249, left without grumbling as both clubs rushed for their trains.

### Drop Part of Lead

The day's doings cost the McCarthymen part of their lead. They now show the way to the second-place White Sox by a half game.

Joe DiMaggio stood out preeminently in this day of weird play which saw the Yankees smite six of Rogers Hornsby's pitches for thirty-one hits that held five homers, three of them in a row by DiMaggio, and were good for fifty-eight bases.

DiMaggio struck his three round-trippers in the nightcap and drove in five runs. The blow boosted his total of homers to fourteen, gave him the honor of striking nine over a stretch of as many games, five of them in four skirmishes, and extended the string of contests in which he has hit consecutively to fifteen.

Bill Dickey also hit a homer for the Yankees in the nightcap, a blow that was good for two runs in a six-run fifth inning which jarred Julio Bonetti, young Brown hurler.

### More Destructive Blows

DiMaggio's blows were the more destructive. His first fashioned three of the first four Yankee runs in the fifth. His second brought the Yanks within striking distance of the Browns in the seventh after they had hammered Bump Hadley to shelter and feasted generously on the offerings of Pat Malone. His third, struck in the ninth, brought the Yanks even with the enemy.

Not all the home-run hitting was done by the Yankees. Harland Clift hit one clean out of the park on Hadley in the fourth. He also smashed two in the opener.

Twenty hits in the opener established a season's high for the New Yorkers. The Browns added thirteen to the general bombardment. Fourteen runs in the last four innings, seven of them in the ninth, pulled the Yanks through. Joe Vosmik and Tony Lazzeri also connected for the circuit.

Johnny Broaca, it was revealed today by Dr. Robert F. Hyland, is handicapped by a torn ligament in the socket of his right arm, and the condition has ossified. It is a complaint somewhat similar to that which overtook Paul Dean, and there is little that can be done about it.

Monte Pearson, an X-ray examination showed, has a spur, a callous growth, on his right elbow, which must be subjected to intensive diathermic treatment. During the treatments Person must not undertake to do much throwing.

George Selkirk was back in action for the first time since he pulled up lame in Cleveland more than a week ago. He made four hits in the opener.

## The Box Scores

### FIRST GAME

| NEW YORK (A.) | ab | r. | h. | po. | a. | e. | | ST. LOUIS (A.) | ab | r. | h. | po. | a. | e. |
|---|---|---|---|---|---|---|---|---|---|---|---|---|---|---|
| Crosetti, ss | 5 | 1 | 2 | 1 | 4 | 0 | | Davis, 1b | 4 | 1 | 2 | 7 | 0 | 0 |
| Rolfe, 3b | 5 | 1 | 3 | 3 | 2 | 0 | | West, cf | 5 | 0 | 1 | 2 | 0 | 0 |
| DiM'gio, cf | 5 | 1 | 1 | 2 | 0 | 0 | | Vosmik, lf | 5 | 1 | 3 | 2 | 0 | 0 |
| Gehrig, 1b | 6 | 3 | 3 | 9 | 0 | 1 | | Bell, rf | 5 | 1 | 1 | 1 | 0 | 0 |
| Dickey, c | 4 | 3 | 2 | 6 | 0 | 0 | | Clift, 3b | 5 | 2 | 2 | 1 | 2 | 0 |
| Selkirk, rf | 6 | 3 | 4 | 1 | 0 | 0 | | Knickb'r, ss | 4 | 1 | 0 | 4 | 4 | 0 |
| Henrich, lf | 5 | 1 | 0 | 3 | 0 | 1 | | Huffman, c | 4 | 1 | 2 | 8 | 0 | 0 |
| Lazzeri, 2b | 6 | 2 | 2 | 2 | 3 | 0 | | Carey, 2b | 4 | 1 | 1 | 2 | 1 | 0 |
| Murphy, p | 1 | 0 | 1 | 0 | 2 | 1 | | Hildeb'd, p | 2 | 1 | 1 | 0 | 0 | 0 |
| Makosky, p | 4 | 1 | 2 | 0 | 0 | 0 | | Blake, p | 0 | 0 | 0 | 0 | 0 | 0 |
| | | | | | | | | Knott, p | 0 | 0 | 0 | 0 | 0 | 0 |
| | | | | | | | | Walkup, p | 0 | 0 | 0 | 0 | 1 | 0 |
| | | | | | | | | Koupal, p | 0 | 0 | 0 | 0 | 0 | 0 |
| | | | | | | | | ᵃAllen | 1 | 0 | 0 | 0 | 0 | 0 |
| Total | 47 | 16 | 20 | 27 | 11 | 3 | | Total | 39 | 9 | 13 | 27 | 8 | 0 |

ᵃBatted for Knott in eighth.

New York      020 003 227—16
St. Louis      201 310 200—9

Runs batted in—Vosmik 4, Murphy 2, Carey, Clift 3, Selkirk, Dickey 2, Henrich, Crosetti, Rolfe 2, Lazzeri 4, Makosky, DiMaggio, Davis.

Two-base hits—Murphy, Hildebrand, Gehrig, Selkirk. Three-base hits—Selkirk, Dickey, Rolfe. Home runs—Clift 2, Vosmik, Lazzeri. Stolen base—Crosetti. Sacrifice—Hildebrand. Double plays Knickerbocker and Davis; Rolfe, Lazzeri and Gehrig. Left on bases—New York 11, St. Louis 6. Bases on balls—Off Murphy 2, Hildebrand 5, Blake 1, Knott 1. Struck out—By Murphy 1, Hildebrand 2, Knott 3, Makosky 4, Koupal 2. Hits—Off Murphy 7 in 3 2–3 innings, Makosky 6 in 5 1–3, Hildebrand 8 in 6, Blake 1 in 0 (pitched to two batters in seventh, Knott 4 in 2, Walkup 5 in 1–3, Koupal 2 in 2–3. Winning pitcher—Makosky. Losing pitcher—Walkup. Umpires—Kolls, Basil and Summers. Time of game—2:26.

## SECOND GAME

| NEW YORK (A.) | ab | r. | h. | po. | a. | e. | ST. LOUIS (A.) | ab | r. | h. | po. | a. | e. |
|---|---|---|---|---|---|---|---|---|---|---|---|---|---|
| Crosetti, ss | 5 | 1 | 0 | 2 | 3 | 0 | Davis, 1b | 5 | 2 | 2 | 14 | 0 | 0 |
| Rolfe, 3b | 6 | 1 | 3 | 1 | 2 | 0 | West, cf | 5 | 1 | 2 | 3 | 0 | 0 |
| DiMaggio, cf | 6 | 3 | 3 | 5 | 0 | 0 | Vosmik, lf | 5 | 0 | 0 | 4 | 0 | 0 |
| Gehrig, 1b | 3 | 1 | 2 | 10 | 0 | 0 | Bell, rf | 4 | 2 | 2 | 3 | 0 | 0 |
| Dickey, c | 4 | 1 | 2 | 10 | 0 | 0 | Clift, 3b | 6 | 1 | 2 | 0 | 4 | 0 |
| Selkirk, rf | 4 | 0 | 0 | 1 | 0 | 0 | K'kbocker, ss | 6 | 0 | 2 | 2 | 2 | 0 |
| Henrich, lf | 4 | 1 | 1 | 3 | 0 | 0 | Hemsley, c | 5 | 0 | 1 | 5 | 2 | 0 |
| Lazzeri, 2b | 5 | 0 | 0 | 1 | 4 | 0 | Carey, 2b | 5 | 1 | 2 | 2 | 2 | 0 |
| Hadley, p | 1 | 0 | 0 | 0 | 0 | 0 | Bonetti, p | 3 | 1 | 0 | 0 | 1 | 1 |
| Malone, p | 1 | 0 | 0 | 0 | 1 | 0 | | | | | | | |
| Makosky, p | 1 | 0 | 0 | 0 | 2 | 0 | | | | | | | |
| aRuffing | 1 | 0 | 0 | 0 | 0 | 0 | | | | | | | |
| Total | 41 | 8 | 11 | 33 | 12 | 0 | Total | 44 | 8 | 13 | 33 | 11 | 1 |

aBatted for Malone in eighth.

| | | |
|---|---|---|
| New York | 000 060 101 00—8 |
| St. Louis | 000 350 000 00—8 |

Runs batted in—Clift 3, DiMaggio 5, Dickey 2, West 2, Vosmik, Bell, Knickerbocker, Lazzeri.

Two-base hits—Gehrig 2, Davis 2, West 2, Knickerbocker. Home runs—Clift, DiMaggio 3, Dickey. Stolen base—Henrich. Sacrifices—Vosmik, Bonetti. Double plays—Helmsley and Knickerbocker; Clift, Carey and David; Lazzeri, Crosetti and Gehrig. Left on bases—New York 7, St. Louis 10. Bases on balls—Off Hadley 3, Bonetti 5, Makosky 3. Struck out—By Hadley 3, Bonetti 5; Malone 2, Makosky 3. Hits—Off Hadley 4 in 4 innings (none out in fifth), Malone 5 in 3, Makosky 4 in 4. Umpires—Basil, Summers and Kolls. Time of game—2:41.

## *Chandler Triumphs for Yanks; Giants Lose Again; Dodgers Split Double Bill*

### YANKEES' 17 BLOWS ROUT BROWNS, 14–5

### McCarthymen Pound Trio of St. Louis Pitchers—Drive 8 Extra-Base Hits

### DiMAGGIO SMASHES NO. 31

### Threatens Babe Ruth's Home-Run mark of 1927—Gehrig, Rolfe Also Connect

### By JAMES P. DAWSON

A milestone in baseball was passed or closely approached, according to the point of view, at the Stadium yesterday, when the Yankees took their farewell of the hapless St. Louis Browns.

In one of the heaviest hitting days of the year the McCarthymen pounded Brownie hurling for seventeen hits as they buried Jim Bottomley's crew, 14 to 5, before 18,924 fans.

In this terrific cannonading Joe DiMaggio hammered his thirty-first home run of the season into the distant upper left field stand. Lou Gehrig clouted No. 21 into the lower right field stand to start the carnage in the first inning, and in the sixth Red Robert Rolfe hit his fourth of the year into the same section.

There were two triples, three doubles and nine singles in this devastating fire, Gehrig showing the way by hitting the cycle, a single, double, triple and homer in five trips to the plate. On his fifth trip Lou narrowly missed a second homer in his favorite parking grounds.

### Gets Drive in Seventh

But it was DiMaggio's circuit blow, which arrived in the seventh inning, that precipitated the record controversy. With this blow the sensational Italian either passed the intermediate mark Babe Ruth made in 1927, the year in which he hit sixty homers, or approached within striking distance of the Ruth level.

DiMaggio's thirty-first round-tripper, a blast that traveled more than 400 feet, arrived in the Yankees' eighty-ninth game, according to the baseball standings. Ruth's was struck in the ninetieth game the Yanks played in 1927. This year's totals, however, do not include two tied games which would boost the Yankee total of actual games played this year to ninety-one, since the two tied skirmishes go into the records.

This highly technical point, together with the minor consideration that DiMaggio in reality has played but eighty-four games—he missed five at the beginning of the season—sent the statisticians scurrying to the archives and produced an argument that is likely to endure.

No amount of argument, however, could minimize the satisfaction at DiMaggio's steady hammering for the circuit or cloud the possibility of his surpassing the Ruth mark if he maintains his present pace. The Babe had sixty-four games to go when he hit No. 31. He struck seventeen in September of that year. DiMaggio has sixty-five games to go and can get ahead of the Ruth schedule if he hits more than five homers in the next eleven games.

## Tune Up for White Sox

Leading up to this discussion was a demonstration of Yankee artillery fire that left three Brown pitchers prostrate as the McCarthymen tuned up for the important White Sox series which opens with a double-header tomorrow. Lou Koupal was the first victim of this attack. He fell by the wayside before the second inning was completed under a six-hit hammering that was touched off by Gehrig's first-inning homer and produced six runs.

The unsuspecting Julio Bonetti then came on the scene to take a ten-hit, six-run lambasting featured by Rolfe's sixth-inning homer and DiMaggio's circuit drive in the seventh, each with one man aboard. Bonetti was recalled after he had completed the seventh. Then Bill Trotter came on the scene and the Yanks made it unanimous by pounding him for a couple of runs in the eighth, Myril Hoag's third blow of the day, a triple, being the medium for both runs.

Under protection of this clouting Spurgeon Chandler celebrated his return to the Yankee firing line by spinning through a twelve-hit performance. It was his first start since returning from Newark. He gave Harland Clift a home-run ball in the fifth with one aboard, and served another to Ben Huffman, pinch-hitting in the eighth with one on.

But the enemy fire that might ordinarily have sounded a recall was lost in the shuffle of Yankee hits and the clatter of Yankee runs.

## Got Three in Tied Game

In considering the relation of the tied games in DiMaggio's record the fact that DiMaggio hit three homers off the same Julio Bonetti in one of them must not be overlooked.

The Yankees lost half a game of the league leading margin as the second-place White Sox took two contests from the Athletics.

The box score:

| ST. LOUIS (A.) | ab | r. | h. | po. | a. | e. | NEW YORK (A.) | ab | r. | h. | po. | a. | e. |
|---|---|---|---|---|---|---|---|---|---|---|---|---|---|
| Davis, 1b | 5 | 0 | 1 | 9 | 1 | 0 | Crosetti, ss | 1 | 0 | 0 | 0 | 0 | 0 |
| West, cf | 5 | 0 | 1 | 0 | 0 | 0 | Heffner, ss | 4 | 2 | 3 | 2 | 4 | 0 |
| Vosmik, lf | 5 | 1 | 2 | 2 | 1 | 0 | Rolfe, 3b | 5 | 2 | 1 | 0 | 3 | 0 |
| Clift, 3b | 3 | 1 | 1 | 2 | 4 | 0 | DiMaggio, cf | 3 | 3 | 3 | 3 | 0 | 1 |
| Bell, 3b | 5 | 0 | 0 | 2 | 0 | 0 | Gehrig, 1b | 5 | 1 | 4 | 13 | 1 | 0 |
| Knickb'r, ss | 2 | 0 | 0 | 3 | 2 | 0 | Dickey, c | 2 | 0 | 1 | 1 | 0 | 0 |
| Carey, ss | 3 | 0 | 1 | 1 | 1 | 0 | Powell, lf | 5 | 0 | 0 | 3 | 0 | 0 |
| Lipscomb, 2b | 4 | 2 | 3 | 3 | 3 | 0 | Lazzeri, 2b | 4 | 3 | 2 | 1 | 5 | 0 |
| Heath, c | 1 | 0 | 0 | 1 | 1 | 0 | Hoag, rf | 4 | 3 | 3 | 2 | 0 | 0 |
| Hemsley, c | 2 | 0 | 0 | 1 | 0 | 0 | Chandler, p | 3 | 0 | 0 | 2 | 1 | 0 |
| Trotter, p | 0 | 0 | 0 | 0 | 0 | 0 | | | | | | | |
| Koupal, p | 1 | 0 | 1 | 0 | 1 | 0 | | | | | | | |
| Bonetti, p | 2 | 0 | 1 | 0 | 1 | 0 | | | | | | | |
| Huffman, c | 1 | 1 | 1 | 0 | 0 | 0 | | | | | | | |
| Total | 39 | 5 | 12 | 24 | 15 | 0 | Total | 36 | 14 | 17 | 27 | 14 | 1 |

| St. Louis | 010 020 020—5 |
| New York | 240 002 42..—14 |

Runs batted in—Gehrig 3, Koupal, Heffner 3, DiMaggio 3, Clift 2, Rolfe 2, Huffman 2, Hoag, Chandler.

Two-base hits—Lipscomb 2, Gehrig, Carey, DiMaggio, Heffner. Three-base hits—Gehrig, Hoag. Home runs—Gehrig, Clift, Rolfe, DiMaggio, Huffman. Sacrifices—Chandler 2. Double plays—Lipscomb, Knickerbocker and Davis; Davis and Carey. Left on bases—New York 9, St. Louis 10. Bases on balls—Off Chandler 3, Koupal 3, Bonetti 4, Trotter 1. Struck out—By Bonetti 2, Chandler 1. Hits—Off Koupal 6 in 1 2–3 innings, Bonetti 10 in 5 1–3, Trotter 1 in 1. Hit by pitcher—By Bonetti (DiMaggio). Passed ball—Heath. Losing pitcher—Koupal. Umpires—Ormsby, Quinn and McGowan. Time of game—2:13.

---

October 25, 1939

### *DiMaggio Voted Most Valuable Player in American League*

## YANKS' STAR WINS WITH 280 POINTS

### DiMaggio Heads 15 Ballots in Annual Poll of 24 American League Baseball Writers

## FOXX NEXT, FELLER THIRD

### Williams, Ruffing and Dickey, Who Tops Three Lists, Also Draw Over 100 Tallies

#### By The Associated Press.

CHICAGO, Oct. 24—Joe DiMaggio, whose big bat earned him the batting championship and helped propel the Yankees to a fourth straight world title, today was named the most valuable player in the American League for the 1939 season.

The 24-year-old center fielder, who thus won a trophy from The Sporting News, received a total of 280 of a possible 336 points in balloting by a committee of the Baseball Writers Association of America.

DiMaggio, who hit .381, got fifteen first place votes of 14 points each. Three writers of the committee of twenty-four placed him second, three third, one fourth and two fifth. Votes for second place through tenth were rated from 9 points down to 1.

Thus DiMaggio capped his finest season since he came up to the Yanks in 1936. In that year he hit .323 and he followed with averages of .346 and .325, respectively, in 1937 and 1938. This past season he hammered 30 homers and drove in 126 runs.

## Foxx Three-Time Winner

Jimmy Foxx, Red Sox first baseman, who won the valuable player award for the third time last year, captured second place. He received 170 points, a testimonial to a fine season in which illness kept him out of action for a long period. Although he drew only one first-place ballot, two scribes placed him second and eleven made him their third choice. Only one writer failed to place the Boston star.

Bob Feller, the Indians' young pitching star, who won twenty-four games, was third with 155. Fourth place went to Ted Williams, the Red Sox freshman outfielder, who led the league with 142 runs batted in. Williams received 126 points, although he did not get any first-place vote, as Feller drew three.

Charlie Ruffing, New York pitcher, who won twenty-one games, also failed to get a first-place mention, but piled up 116 points for fifth place, 6 ahead of Bill Dickey. The Yankees' star catcher was the first choice of three writers, but was unplaced by eleven.

The other two to receive first-place consideration were Pitcher Emil Leonard of Washington, who won twenty games for a sixth-place team, and Mike Kreevich, White Sox outfielder. Leonard compiled 71 points and Kreevich 38. Ranking ahead of Kreevich, however, were Bob Johnson, Athletics' outfielder, with 52, and Joe Gordon, New York second baseman, with 43.

## Honor Roll Selected

The honor roll, a tabulation of ten extra votes not counting for points, was topped by first baseman George McQuinn of the Browns and pitcher Tommy Bridges of the Tigers, each being named eleven times. Manager Joe Cronin and Lefty Grove of Boston, third baseman Ken Keltner of Cleveland and Gordon, each with nine votes.

The writers on the selection committee were John Malaney, Gerry Moore and Victor Stout, Boston; James Gallagher, Ed Burns and Howard Roberts, Chicago; Gordon Cobbledick, Ed McAuley and Frank Gibbons, Cleveland; H. G. Salsinger, Charles P. Ward and Leo MacDonell, Detroit; Dan Daniel, Rud Rennie and Ed Murphy, New York; James Isaminger, Al Horwits and Frank Yeutter, Philadelphia; Glen Waller, James Gould and Ray Gillespie, St. Louis; Shirley Povich, Burton Hawkins and Frank O'Neill, Washington.

The distribution of points follows:

| | | | |
|---|---|---|---|
| Joe DiMaggio, New York | 280 | Charlie Gehringer, Detroit | 21 |
| Jimmy Foxx, Boston | 170 | Lefty Grove, Boston | 17 |
| Bob Feller, Cleveland | 155 | Joe Cronin, Boston | 15 |
| Ted Williams, Boston | 126 | Ted Lyons, Chicago | 13 |
| Charlie Ruffing, New York | 116 | Hank Greenberg, Detroit | 12 |
| Bill Dickey, New York | 110 | Buck Newsom, Detroit | 11 |
| Emil Leonard, Washington | 71 | Johnny Rigney, Chicago | 9 |
| Bob Johnson, Philadelphia | 52 | Joe Kuhel, Chicago | 8 |
| Joe Gordon, New York | 43 | Charlie Keller, New York | 7 |
| Mike Kreevich, Chicago | 38 | Jeff Heath, Cleveland | 7 |
| Clint Brown, Chicago | 34 | Gerald Walker, Chicago | 7 |
| Ken Keltner, Cleveland | 26 | Frankie Hayes, Philadelphia | 7 |
| George McQuinn, St. Louis | 24 | Tommy Bridges, Detroit | 7 |

Red Rolfe, New York . . . . . . . . . . . . . . 6
Barney McCosky, Detroit. . . . . . . . . . . 6
Eric McNair, Chicago . . . . . . . . . . . . . 5
Hal Trosky, Cleveland . . . . . . . . . . . . . 4

George Case, Washington . . . . . . . . . . 3
Myril Hoag, St. Louis. . . . . . . . . . . . . . 3
Rudy York, Detroit . . . . . . . . . . . . . . . 1
Luke Appling, Chicago . . . . . . . . . . . . 1

## List of Award Winners

Winners of the award since its inception follow:

| | | | | |
|---|---|---|---|---|
| 1922—George Sisler | St. Louis | | 1933—Jimmy Foxx | Philadelphia |
| 1923—Babe Ruth | New York | | 1934—Mickey Cochrane | Detroit |
| 1924—Walter Johnson | Washington | | 1935—Hank Greenberg | Detroit |
| 1925—Roger Peckinpaugh | Washington | | 1936—Lou Gehrig | New York |
| 1926—George Burns | Cleveland | | 1937—Charlie Gehringer | Detroit |
| 1927—Lou Gehrig | New York | | 1938—Jimmy Foxx | Boston |
| 1928—Mickey Cochrane | Philadelphia | | 1939—Joe DiMaggio | New York |
| 1929–30—No award | | | 1922–28, league award voted by baseball | |
| 1931—Lefty Grove | Philadelphia | | writers; 1931–39, Baseball Writers | |
| 1932—Jimmy Foxx | Philadelphia | | Association award. | |

July 12, 1939

## *62,892 See American League Beat National for 5–2 Lead in All-Star Games*

### HOMER BY DIMAGGIO MARKS 3–1 VICTORY

## American League Pounds Lee in 4th and 5th to Defeat Nationals at Stadium

### FELLER BRILLIANT IN BOX

## Halts Rally in 6th and Blanks Losers Thereafter—Goodman Hurt Trying for Catch

### By JOHN DREBINGER

Riding high on the wings of a Joe DiMaggio home run and finishing with a blinding burst of speed on the part of its foremost pitching wizard, Bobby Feller, the American League reasserted its superiority over the National League at the Yankee Stadium yesterday by winning the seventh annual All-Star game, 3 to 1.

The victory, cheered impartially by a vast gathering of 62,892 onlookers, who paid $75,701 to see the show, completely reversed the order of a year ago in Cincinnati, when the National forces had finished on top, and marked the fifth triumph for the American League in the seven games played starting in 1933.

It was not, perhaps, the most dramatic game ever played between the keen and sometimes bitter rivals of baseball's two major leagues. But it had its moments when the crowd, basking in the sunlight of a perfect Summer afternoon, reared up and roared its approval.

And at the finish there was occasion again to acclaim Marse Joe McCarthy, head man of the world champion Yankees, who skillfully piloted the American League troops to victory over gay Gabby Hartnett, the florid boss of the Cubs, who directed the battle lines of the vanquished.

## Underdogs Draw Cheers

There was the tug for the underdog, so inherent a characteristic of New York crowds, when the National Leaguers, 2-to-1 long shots in the betting, made off with a 1–0 lead in the first three innings.

Paul Derringer, ace right-hander of the National League's front running Reds, slightly outpitched burly Charlie (Red) Ruffing of the Yanks in that opening brush to gain the one-run margin, and the crowd magnanimously conceded the point. It even applauded vociferously when Linus Frey, one of five of Bill McKechnie's Cincinnatians in the starting line-up, rammed that tally home with a rousing two-base smash.

But in the fourth the American Leaguers, doubtless fired to action by the presence of no fewer than six world champion Yankees in their battlefront, surged irresistibly to the fore with a pair of runs wrenched from big Bill Lee, strapping right-hander of the Cubs.

George Selkirk of the Yanks banged in one of these with a single. A momentary crack-up in the Nationals' usually airtight defense, a fumble by Arky Vaughan, Pirate shortstop, let in the other.

An inning later the matchless DiMaggio, hailed as the wonder player of his time, stepped majestically into the picture all by himself. With nobody on the base-paths and practically nothing at all going on at the time, Jolting Joe leaned into one of Lee's most ardent deliveries and sent the ball sailing high through the clear blue sky into the left wing of the lower grandstand.

## Some Runs for Bridges

That gave Tommy Bridges, trim right-hander of the Tigers, a two-run margin to work on in his three-inning duel with the towering Lee, who at the moment was also glowering.

Then came the game's most dramatic moment in the sixth when the National Leaguers, striving desperately to retrieve their lost ground, filled the bases with only one out.

But at this moment McCarthy, the strangely silent Buffalo Irishman they all concede is a master builder of marvelous ball clubs but who, never having been a great ball player himself, they all say knows nothing of finesse and the finer points of diamond technique, pulled a managerial ten strike.

Out came the suddenly faltering Bridges and out of the bullpen came Feller who, at the moment, was merely warming up for his final stretch of three innings.

There was a breathless suspense as the youthful prodigy and Iowa farm boy, who still walks as if stalking through a potato field, trudged to the mound, took a few more warm-up pitches and then squared away.

His opponent at the plate was Vaughan, now desperately bent to make amends for his grievous misplay that had shunted the American Leaguers ahead in the fourth.

## Vaughan Hits First Pitch

Feller delivered just one pitch, Vaughan swung and connected, but it was nothing more than a harmless grounder to Gordon, called the modern Flash, and in a fraction of a jiffy there was a double play with the National Leaguers' last chance to win the game definitely snuffed out.

For the remaining three innings there remained nothing more for the crowd to do save marvel at the marvelous things this young 20-year-old fellow named Feller can do with a baseball. The National Leaguers in the same interval definitely proved they could do nothing at all.

Bobby allowed just one hit. Melvin Ott, the lone Giant in the National League's battle lines, although his boss, Colonel Bill Terry, was coaching on third base, singled in the ninth for his second hit of the game.

But that was all. For Feller, whose promised greatness had hung in the balance for several years until he definitely established himself as one of the pitching wonders of his age this season, swept down to the wire with the bit between his teeth.

He struck out Johnny Mize, getting the Cardinals' renowned slugger who came up as a pinch hitter on three pitched balls. Then, with the count three and two on Stanley Hack, Bobby fearlessly slammed over a third strike on the Cubs third sacker.

Hack, who had kept his bat on his shoulder while this unforeseen development came to pass, now fired his bat vehemently into the ground and started following Umpire George Magerkurth off the field, calling the while upon the heavens to bear witness to the fact that here, indeed, was an umpire stone blind.

But when they call that third one on you for the final out of the game, you may as well carry your plea to a man stone deaf as try to argue with an umpire. Magerkurth marched resolutely off the field and Hack merely followed him. Perhaps it was an act that all umpires and ball players know by heart.

Incidentally, the American Leaguers, by calling upon Feller to pitch those final three innings after he had checked the Nationals in the sixth, committed a technical infraction of the rule that specifies no pitcher in the All-Star game may hurl more than three innings unless the last one becomes embroiled in an overtime contest.

## No Quibbling Over Point

But the National Leaguers apparently were above quibbling over technicalities. From Terry, whom all respect as one of the game's most profound students, down the line, the National Leaguers always had insisted they could pin Feller's ears back any time they met.

They were till valiantly but unsuccessfully trying to prove their case as Mize and Hack took those final third strikes.

The day was one of ill fortune for the Ford Frick circuit on other counts as well. Ival Goodman, the Reds' star outfielder, damaged his left shoulder trying to make a spectacular catch of Selkirk's hit that drove in the American's first tally.

Goodman finished the inning, but when his shoulder began to pain him he was taken under the stand for examination by Dr. Robert Emmet Walsh, the Yanks' attending physician. The player was rushed to St. Elizabeth Hospital for X-ray examination and at first it was feared he was suffering from a broken collarbone.

But Dr. Walsh's final report was that Goodman's injured shoulder, which fortunately is not on his throwing side, was merely dislocated and that the Red outfielder would be out of action for no more than ten days to two weeks. However, with some crucial pennant clashed coming on, even this was bad enough and Manager McKechnie, present as a spectator, passed some anxious moments until he got his final report.

It seems there is always somebody getting hurt in these All-Star games, staged for the benefit of aging indigent ball players. It was in Washington, in 1936, that Dizzy Dean, just as he was completing his three-inning stint on the mound, was struck on the foot by a line drive off Earl Averill's bat and suffered a broken toe. All of the great Dizzy's subsequent misfortunes dated from that ill-fated afternoon.

The crowd, second largest in the history of the series—topped only by the 68,000 turnout in Cleveland in 1935—was a trifle late in arriving, which seemed to induce some early apprehension that the thing perhaps might develop into a flop. But the virtually perfect weather soon had the fans pouring through the turnstiles in droves and by game time most of the vacant spaces in the triple deck stands and sweeping bleachers were blotted out.

Derringer did a masterful job on the mound for the National League in the first three innings. Roger Cramer of the Red Sox singled to left field on the first pitch, but he was the only American Leaguer to reach first on the Red right-hander except Cramer's manager, the doughty Joe Cronin, just a shortstop in the ranks for this day, who bashed a single to right in the second.

## Ruffing in Trouble

Ruffing kept pace with this for two innings, giving only a single by Ernie Lombardi, ponderous backstop of the Reds. But in the third Big Red plunged deep into trouble.

Vaughan outgalloped an infield hit to Cronin and, though Derringer struck out, Hack dropped a pop fly single in short left just inside the foul line. Frey then hammered a two-bagger down the right field foul line just outside Hank Greenberg's big reach and Vaughan scored, with Hack pulling up at third.

The National Leaguers were really getting rough with Ruffing and their constituents in the stands were beginning to make themselves heard. For New York crowds, of course, are not entirely non-partisan. They have their Giant and Yankee rooters, and the latter already had identified themselves by roundly booing Terry, Hartnett's first lieutenant, during the pre-game exercise.

As for the Dodger fans, they seemed for the most part to sit in sullen silence, inasmuch as only two of their favorites, Dolph Camilli and Babe Phelps, appeared, and only to the extent of pinch-hitting. Whitlow Wyatt, who was to have pitched the final three innings, found an ailing left leg too painful for him to play, while an injury had forced Cooke Lavagetto off the National League squad several days ago.

Be that as it may, there was some whole-hearted jeering when Ruffing intentionally passed Goodman to fill the bases in this third inning push of the National Leaguers with one run already in and only one out.

But Ruffing quickly regained his customary poise. He slipped a third strike over on Frank McCormick of the Reds, who played first base throughout the game, and then induced Lombardi to end the inning with a harmless infield fly. Ruffing adroitly had squirmed out of a ticklish spot with the loss of only a single run and he now drew a rousing cheer from the Yankee fans in the stands as he withdrew from the battle.

In the next inning, with Lee just taking over Derringer's pitching chores, the Americans launched their victory drive. DiMaggio, up for his second turn at bat, grounded out, but his Yankee colleague, Bill Dickey, walked. Greenberg then singled to left. Although a standout in his circuit for a number of years, Hank was making his first All-Star appearance at first base, now that Lou Gehrig's star had finally sunk, while Jimmy Foxx was invited to sit on the bench.

Lee bore down with all he had against Cronin and fanned the Red Sox chieftain, but Selkirk slashed a low line drive to right. Goodman dived headlong into the ball and for a moment appeared to have made a sensational catch, but the ball got away from him and the single drove Dickey home with the tying run. A moment later came a second tally to put the American Leaguers in front when Vaughan booted Gordon's sharp grounder, Greenberg counting on the misplay.

Two were out and nobody on base when DiMaggio sent his high fly soaring just inside the foul line and into the lower left stand. Ironically, the ball sailed right over the head of the National League's lone DiMaggio rival, Joe Medwick, the Cardinal's slugging outfielder, who had retreated as far as the stands would permit him to.

Bridges, in the meantime, had given only a single pass in the fourth and fifth, but the Nationals suddenly rushed the Detroiter in the sixth. McCormick grounded out, but Lombardi singled solidly to left for his second hit.

Cronin then booted Medwick's sharp grounder for the American's only misplay and Ott followed with a bounding smash toward right. Gordon made a phenomenal stop of the ball and though this failed to check the hit it nevertheless prevented Lombardi from scoring.

The National Leaguers, however, had the bases filled, only one out and the crowd roared expectantly for something to explode. But down in the American League dugout a momentous decision was reached that perhaps saved the game.

Bridges was invited to retire and Feller, preparing to start his work on the mound with the beginning of the seventh, came in to try his hand at once. Vaughan swung on his first pitch and Gordon, Cronin and Greenberg did the rest as they throttled the National Leaguers with a lightning double play.

It was the Frick circuit's last serious threat, for Feller was virtually invincible in the next three innings. With one down he issued his only pass to Hack in the seventh, but then retired Frey and Terry Moore, the Card outfielder who had replaced the injured Goodman.

In the eighth, with two down, Medwick streaked a line drive toward right. But Gordon staged his second sensational fielding play as he leaped high in the air to collect the ball.

Lou Fette of the Bees did an equally fine pitching job in opposing the American Leaguers in the seventh and eighth, but it was all in vain. The combined gifted talents of Hartnett and Terry simply could do nothing about helping their charges solve the mystifying slants of Feller's pitches.

Ott singled in the ninth, but Vaughan flied out. Then came the two called third strikes on Mize and Hack and another All-Star conflict passed into history.

Oddly, the Nationals outhit their rivals, seven blows to six. But they failed twice to capitalize on their chances when they had the bases filled and that killed their day.

## Box Score of the Game

### NATIONAL LEAGUE

| | ab. | r. | h. | tb. | 2b. | 3b. | hr. | sh. | sb. | bb. | so. | po. | a. | e. |
|---|---|---|---|---|---|---|---|---|---|---|---|---|---|---|
| Hack, Chicago, 3b. | 4 | 0 | 1 | 1 | 0 | 0 | 0 | 0 | 0 | 1 | 3 | 1 | 1 | 0 |
| Frey, Cincinnati, 2b. | 4 | 0 | 1 | 2 | 1 | 0 | 0 | 0 | 0 | 0 | 0 | 0 | 4 | 0 |
| Goodman, Cincinnati, 3b. | 1 | 0 | 0 | 0 | 0 | 0 | 0 | 0 | 0 | 1 | 0 | 0 | 0 | 0 |
| cHerman, Chicago | 1 | 0 | 0 | 0 | 0 | 0 | 0 | 0 | 0 | 0 | 1 | 0 | 0 | 0 |
| T. Moore, St. Louis, c.f. | 1 | 0 | 0 | 0 | 0 | 0 | 0 | 0 | 0 | 0 | 0 | 0 | 0 | 0 |
| McCormick, Cincinnati, 1b. | 4 | 0 | 0 | 0 | 0 | 0 | 0 | 0 | 0 | 0 | 1 | 7 | 1 | 0 |
| Lombardi, Cincinnati, c. | 4 | 0 | 2 | 2 | 0 | 0 | 0 | 0 | 0 | 0 | 0 | 6 | 0 | 0 |
| Medwick, St. Louis, 1.f. | 4 | 0 | 0 | 0 | 0 | 0 | 0 | 0 | 0 | 0 | 1 | 1 | 0 | 0 |
| Ott, New York, c.f., r.f. | 4 | 0 | 2 | 2 | 0 | 0 | 0 | 0 | 0 | 0 | 0 | 4 | 0 | 0 |
| Vaughan, Pittsburgh, s.s. | 3 | 1 | 1 | 1 | 0 | 0 | 0 | 0 | 0 | 1 | 0 | 4 | 1 | 1 |
| Derringer, Cincinnati, p. | 1 | 0 | 0 | 0 | 0 | 0 | 0 | 0 | 0 | 0 | 1 | 0 | 0 | 0 |
| bCamilli, Brooklyn | 1 | 0 | 0 | 0 | 0 | 0 | 0 | 0 | 0 | 0 | 1 | 0 | 0 | 0 |
| Lee, Chicago, p. | 0 | 0 | 0 | 0 | 0 | 0 | 0 | 0 | 0 | 0 | 0 | 0 | 0 | 0 |
| dPhelps, Brooklyn | 1 | 0 | 0 | 0 | 0 | 0 | 0 | 0 | 0 | 0 | 0 | 0 | 0 | 0 |
| Fette, Boston, p. | 0 | 0 | 0 | 0 | 0 | 0 | 0 | 0 | 0 | 0 | 0 | 1 | 0 | 0 |
| eMize, St. Louis | 1 | 0 | 0 | 0 | 0 | 0 | 0 | 0 | 0 | 0 | 1 | 0 | 0 | 0 |
| Total | 34 | 1 | 7 | 8 | 1 | 0 | 0 | 0 | 0 | 3 | 9 | 24 | 7 | 1 |

| | ab. | r. | h. | tb. | 2b. | 3b. | hr. | sh. | sb. | bb. | so. | po. | a. | e. |
|---|---|---|---|---|---|---|---|---|---|---|---|---|---|---|
| Cramer, Boston, r.f. | 4 | 0 | 1 | 1 | 0 | 0 | 0 | 0 | 0 | 0 | 1 | 3 | 0 | 0 |
| Rofle, New York, 3b. | 4 | 0 | 1 | 1 | 0 | 0 | 0 | 0 | 0 | 0 | 0 | 1 | 0 | 0 |
| DiMaggio, New York, c.f. | 4 | 1 | 1 | 4 | 0 | 0 | 1 | 0 | 0 | 0 | 0 | 1 | 0 | 0 |
| Dickey, New York, c. | 3 | 1 | 0 | 0 | 0 | 0 | 0 | 0 | 0 | 1 | 0 | 10 | 0 | 0 |
| Greenberg, Detroit, 1b. | 3 | 1 | 1 | 1 | 0 | 0 | 0 | 0 | 0 | 1 | 0 | 7 | 1 | 0 |
| Cronin, Boston, s.s. | 4 | 0 | 1 | 1 | 0 | 0 | 0 | 0 | 0 | 0 | 1 | 2 | 3 | 1 |
| Selkirk, New York, l.f. | 2 | 0 | 1 | 1 | 0 | 0 | 0 | 0 | 0 | 2 | 0 | 0 | 0 | 0 |
| Gordon, New York, 2b. | 4 | 0 | 0 | 0 | 0 | 0 | 0 | 0 | 0 | 0 | 1 | 2 | 5 | 0 |
| Ruffing, New York, p. | 0 | 0 | 0 | 0 | 0 | 0 | 0 | 0 | 0 | 0 | 0 | 0 | 0 | 0 |
| aHoag, St. Louis | 1 | 0 | 0 | 0 | 0 | 0 | 0 | 0 | 0 | 0 | 1 | 0 | 0 | 0 |
| Bridges, Detroit, p. | 1 | 0 | 0 | 0 | 0 | 0 | 0 | 0 | 0 | 0 | 1 | 1 | 0 | 0 |
| Feller, Cleveland, p. | 1 | 0 | 0 | 0 | 0 | 0 | 0 | 0 | 0 | 0 | 1 | 0 | 0 | 0 |
| Total | 31 | 3 | 6 | 9 | 0 | 0 | 1 | 0 | 0 | 4 | 6 | 27 | 9 | 1 |

aBatted for Ruffing in third.
bBatted for Derringer in fourth.
cBatted for Goodman in fifth.
dBatted for Lee in seventh.
eBatted for Fette in ninth.

### SCORE BY INNINGS

National League    0 0 1   0 0 0   0 0 0—1
American League    0 0 0   2 1 0   0 0 ..—3

Runs batted in—Frey, Selkirk, DiMaggio.

Earned runs—National League 1, American League 2. Left on bases—National League 9, American League 8. Double play—Gordon, Cronin and Greenberg. Struck out—By Ruffing 4 (Hack, Medwick, Derringer, McCormick); by Bridges 3 (Camilli, Hack and Herman); by Feller 2 (Mize and Hack); by Derringer 1 (Hoag); by Lee 4 (Cronin, Bridges, Cramer and Feller); by Fette 1 (Gordon). Bases on balls—Off Ruffing 1 (Goodman); off Bridges 1 (Vaughan); off Feller 1 (Hack); off Lee 3 (Dickey, Greenberg, Selkirk); off Fette 1 (Selkirk). Hits—Off Ruffing, 4 in 3 innings; Bridges, 2 in 2 1–3 innings; Feller, 1 in 3 2–3 innings; Derringer, 2 in 3 innings; Lee, 3 in 3 innings; Fette, 1 in 2 innings. Winning pitcher—Bridges. Losing pitcher—Lee. Umpires—Hubbard (A. L.) at plate, Goetz (N. L.) at first base, Rommel (A. L.) at second base, Magerkurth (N. L.) at third base, for the first four and one-half innings, Magerkurth at the plate, Rommel at first, Goetz at second, Hubbard at third thereafter. Time of game—1:55. Attendance—62,892.

### *DiMaggio Bats Way to Record, 42 Games in Row; Giants Win: Dodgers Divide*

## YANKEES CONQUER SENATORS, 9–4, 7–5

### DiMaggio, Getting Hit in Each Contest, Beats Modern Mark—Keeler Record 44 Games

## 31,000 HAIL BATTING ACE

### Henrich, Gordon, Keller Keep Homer Streak Intact—Lead Over Indians 1½ Lengths

### By JAMES P. DAWSON

*Special to* THE NEW YORK TIMES.

WASHINGTON, June 29—Joe DiMaggio scaled new heights today.

In a Yankee sweep of a double-header with the Senators that attracted 31,000 fans to the seething caldron that was Griffith Stadium, the New Yorkers' batting marvel set a modern record for hitting in consecutive games.

With his only hit of the first encounter, a rousing double that rolled to the 422-foot sign on the bleacher wall, in the sixth inning, DiMaggio tied the modern record, hitting safely in forty-one successive contests, set by George Sisler.

This mark had withstood the assault of major league players since 1922.

In the nightcap DiMaggio was turned back three times before he connected. Finally, in the seventh inning Joe sent a screaming single to left that boosted his string to forty-two consecutive games and sent him in quest of the all-time major league record, forty-four games, made in 1897 by Willie Keeler, who "hit them where they ain't."

### The Crowd Forgets Heat

The fact that the thermometer hovered around 98 was forgotten in the excitement of this epochal clubbing by one of the greatest players baseball ever has known. The fans roared thunderous acclaim to the record-maker, first as he tore madly for second on his double in the opener, then as he loped to first on his single in the nightcap.

DiMaggio's teammates, to a man, were as excited as schoolboys over his feat. That the Yankees stretched their home-run record to forty in their last twenty-five games by hitting for the circuit in each struggle was an anti-climax. That they swept two games by scoring 9 to 4 and 7 to 5 was incidental, even though the McCarthyman thus took the lead of a game and a half over the second place Indians in the American League.

DiMaggio was jubilant, albeit slightly embarrassed over the fuss.

"Sure, I'm tickled, who wouldn't be?" he said, in the clubhouse between games as he donned a fresh suit, after a shower. "It's a great thing. I've realized an ambition. But I don't deserve the credit all alone.

"You have to give Mr. McCarthy some of it. I got many a break by being allowed to hit that '3 and 0' pitch. It brought me many a good ball to swing at. You know, he's got to give you the signal on '3 and 0' pitches and he was right with me all the time.

## Glad the Strain Is Over

"I'm glad the strain is over. Now I'm going after that forty-four-game mark and I'll keep right on swinging and hitting as long as I can."

DiMaggio explained he hit a low, fast ball to tie the record. "I never really was concerned about the mark until around the thirty-third game," he said. "Yesterday, in Philadelphia, I think, was the first time I was really nervous. I was tense out there today, too."

DiMaggio made his record-equaling hit off Dutch Leonard, adding a new pitching victim to his list. He swung at the first pitch, looked at a ball, then banged his double.

In the nightcap Arnold Anderson almost knocked DiMaggio down with a pitch in the seventh inning, but Joe swung at the next one and hammered a clean single to left. The cheers grew in volume when DiMaggio tore over the plate on Charley Keller's triple with the seventh Yankee run.

Tommy Henrich's fourteenth homer, with one aboard, in the ninth frame of the opener kept the Yankee circuit-hitting mark going. In the nightcap Joe Gordon hammered his No. 12 in the second and Keller his No. 16 in the fourth to raise the Yankee record to at least one four-bagger in each of their last twenty-five games. Sid Hudson was the victim of both blows.

## Ruffing Weakens Suddenly

In the first game the Yanks insured victory with a twelve-hit clouting of Leonard and Alejandro Carrasquel. Charley Ruffing pitched a one-hitter for five innings, but in the sixth the Senators and the heat weakened him. He was replaced after a four-run shellacking. Johnny Murphy came out of the bull-pen to turn back ten batters in a perfect job.

The Yanks made three runs in the fifth when Gordon singled and Phil Rizzuto and Ruffing doubled. Three more came in the sixth. DiMaggio struck his record-tying double, then came a pass to Keller, a sacrifice, a passed ball, an error by Jake Early and the retirement of Rizzuto, who tried to stretch a single into a double as Gordon sneaked home.

Two singles and a pass netted a run off Carrasquel in the eighth and in the ninth Henrich stroked his homer after Johnny Sturm had singled.

Four Yankee errors in the first three innings, three by Gordon, complicated matters in the nightcap. Manager Joe McCarthy called on three hurlers, while Bucky Harris used four. In the end, however, Yankee clubbing overwhelmed the Senators, a pinch double by George Selkirk with the bases full in the sixth inning chasing in two runs that pulled the Yanks out of a 4-all tie. To this were added the single by DiMaggio and Keller's triple in the seventh.

## Fans Bar Batting Practice

DiMaggio was mobbed even before the games. Fans interfered with his batting practice to get his autograph. He took it all good naturedly.

DiMaggio's favorite bat disappeared between games. A fan, discovered with the bat in the stand, refused to return it.

It became known today that DiMaggio, after the game yesterday in Philadelphia, had visited a sick boy, 10-year-old Tony Morell, at Jefferson Hospital. Lefty Gomez, DiMaggio's roomie, accompanied him.

When the visit came to light today DiMaggio pleaded that it be given no publicity.

The box score:

## FIRST GAME

| NEW YORK (A.) | ab | r. | h. | po. | a. | e. | WASHINGTON (A.) | ab | r. | h. | po. | a. | e. |
|---|---|---|---|---|---|---|---|---|---|---|---|---|---|
| Sturm, 1b | 5 | 1 | 1 | 9 | 1 | 0 | Archie, 3b | 4 | 1 | 1 | 2 | 1 | 0 |
| Rolfe, 3b | 5 | 0 | 0 | 1 | 4 | 0 | Cramer, cf | 3 | 0 | 0 | 4 | 0 | 0 |
| Henrich, re | 5 | 1 | 2 | 1 | 0 | 0 | Lewis, rf | 4 | 1 | 1 | 0 | 0 | 0 |
| DiMaggio, cf | 4 | 1 | 1 | 1 | 0 | 0 | Travis, ss | 4 | 1 | 2 | 1 | 2 | 0 |
| Keller, lf | 3 | 2 | 2 | 6 | 0 | 0 | Vernon, 1b | 4 | 1 | 1 | 12 | 1 | 0 |
| Dickey, c | 2 | 0 | 1 | 4 | 0 | 0 | Early, c | 4 | 0 | 1 | 3 | 1 | 1 |
| Gordon, 2b | 4 | 2 | 1 | 1 | 3 | 0 | Case, lf | 3 | 0 | 0 | 1 | 1 | 0 |
| Rizutto, ss | 4 | 1 | 3 | 3 | 1 | 0 | Blood'th, 2b | 3 | 0 | 0 | 3 | 6 | 0 |
| Ruffing, p | 3 | 1 | 1 | 0 | 1 | 0 | Leonard, p | 1 | 0 | 0 | 1 | 2 | 0 |
| Murphy, p | 1 | 0 | 0 | 1 | 0 | 0 | aBolton | 1 | 0 | 0 | 0 | 0 | 0 |
| | | | | | | | Carrasquel, p | 1 | 0 | 0 | 0 | 1 | 0 |
| Total | 36 | 9 | 12 | 27 | 10 | 0 | Total | 32 | 4 | 6 | 27 | 15 | 1 |

aBatted for Leonard in fifth.

New York       000  033  012—9
Washington     000  004  000—4

Runs batted in—Ruffing 2, Rolfe, Travis, Vernon, Early 2, Rizutto, Henrich 2.

Two-base hits—Rizutto, Ruffing, DiMaggio, Vernon. Three base hit—Early. Home run—Henrich. Sacrifice—Dickey. Double plays—Leonard, Bloodworth and Vernon; Rolfe, Gordon and Sturm; Early and Travis. Left on bases—New York 5, Washington 3. Bases on balls—Off Leonard 2, Ruffing 2, Carrasquel 1. Struck out—By Leonard 2, Ruffing 1, Carrasquel 2, Murphy 2. Hits—Off Ruffing 6 in 5 2–3 innings; Murphy 0 in 3 1–3, Leonard 8 in 6, Carrasquel 4 in 2. Hit by pitcher—By Carrasquel (DiMaggio). Passed ball—Early. Winning pitcher—Ruffing. Losing pitcher—Leonard. Umpires—Quinn, Grieve and McGowan. Time of game—2:03.

## SECOND GAME

| NEW YORK (A.) | ab | r. | h. | po. | a. | e. | WASHINGTON (A.) | ab | r. | h. | po. | .a. | e. |
|---|---|---|---|---|---|---|---|---|---|---|---|---|---|
| Sturm, 1b | 5 | 1 | 3 | 11 | 1 | 0 | Archie, 3b | 5 | 1 | 2 | 1 | 2 | 0 |
| Rolfe, 3b | 4 | 1 | 1 | 0 | 2 | 0 | Cramer, cf | 4 | 2 | 2 | 3 | 0 | 0 |
| Henrich, rf | 4 | 0 | 0 | 1 | 0 | 0 | Lewis, rf | 5 | 1 | 3 | 3 | 1 | 0 |
| DiMaggio, cf | 5 | 1 | 1 | 2 | 0 | 0 | Travis, ss | 5 | 0 | 2 | 3 | 2 | 1 |
| Keller, lf | 5 | 1 | 2 | 1 | 0 | 0 | Vernon, 1b | 5 | 0 | 1 | 9 | 2 | 0 |
| Gordon, 2b | 3 | 2 | 2 | 5 | 5 | 3 | Early, c | 3 | 0 | 0 | 3 | 0 | 0 |
| Rizutto, ss | 3 | 1 | 1 | 3 | 4 | 1 | Case, lf | 4 | 0 | 1 | 2 | 0 | 0 |

| | | | | | | | | | | | | | |
|---|---|---|---|---|---|---|---|---|---|---|---|---|---|
| Silvestri, c | 3 | 0 | 0 | 3 | 1 | 0 | Bl'dw'th, 2b | 3 | 0 | 0 | 3 | 1 | 0 |
| Stanceu, p | 2 | 0 | 0 | 0 | 1 | 0 | Hudson, p | 1 | 0 | 0 | 0 | 0 | 0 |
| [a]Selkirk | 1 | 0 | 1 | 0 | 0 | 0 | [b]Myer | 1 | 1 | 1 | 0 | 0 | 0 |
| Peek, p | 1 | 0 | 0 | 1 | 0 | 0 | Anderson, p | 1 | 0 | 0 | 0 | 0 | 0 |
| Bonham, p | 0 | 0 | 0 | 0 | 0 | 0 | Masterson, p | 0 | 0 | 0 | 2 | 0 | 0 |
| | | | | | | | [c]Welaj | 1 | 0 | 0 | 0 | 0 | 0 |
| | | | | | | | Kennedy, p | 0 | 0 | 0 | 0 | 0 | 0 |
| Total | 36 | 7 | 11 | 27 | 14 | 4 | Total | 38 | 5 | 12 | 27 | 11 | 1 |

[a]Batted for Leonard in fifth.

| | | | |
|---|---|---|---|
| New York | 210 | 102 | 100—7 |
| Washington | 102 | 100 | 001—5 |

[a]Batted for Stanceu in sixth.
[b]Batted for Hudson in fourth.
[c]Batted for Masterson in eighth.

Runs batted in—DiMaggio, Lewis 2, Gordon, Travis 2, Keller 2, Selkirk 3.

Two-base hits—Sturm, Lewis, Selkirk. Three base hits—Sturm, Keller. Home runs—Gordon, Keller. Sacrifice—Early. Double plays—Bloodworth, Travis and Vernon; Gordon, Rizzuto and Sturm 3. Left on bases—New York 8, Washington 9. Bases on balls—Off Stanceu 1, Anderson 3, Peek 1, Kennedy 3. Struck out—By Stanceu 3, Hudson 2, Kennedy 1, Peek 1. Hits—Off Stanceu 7 in 5 innings, Peek 5 in 3 2–3, Bonham 0 in 1–3, Hudson 6 in 4, Anderson 5 in 2 2–3, Masterson 0 in 1 1–3, Kennedy 0 in 1. Passed ball—Early. Winning pitcher—Stanceu. Losing pitcher—Anderson. Umpires—Grieve, McGowan and Quinn. Time of game—2:13. Attendance—31,000.

---

July 3, 1941

### *DiMaggio Sets All-Time Hitting Record as Yankees Win: Dodgers Triumph*

## HOME RUN IN FIFTH TOPS KEELER MARK

### DiMaggio's Wallop Stretches His Hitting Streak to 45 Games—Old Record 44

## YANKS HALT RED SOX, 8–4

### Win Sixth Straight to Extend First-Place Margin Over Indians to 3 Contests

### By JOHN DREBINGER

Joe DiMaggio hitting a home run against the Philadelphia Athletics, during his 56-game streak in 1941. (ASSOCIATED PRESS)

Sweeping majestically onward with a thunderous smash that soared deep into the left-field stands, Joe DiMaggio yesterday rocketed his current hitting streak beyond the all-time major league record.

For with that home-run clout, boisterously acclaimed by 8,682 sweltering fans in the sun-baked Yankee Stadium, DiMaggio the Magnificent extended his astounding string to forty-five consecutive games in which he has connected safely.

This surpassed by one the major league mark of 44 games set forty-four years ago by that famous mite of an Oriole, Wee Willie Keeler, who gained renown for his skill in "hitting them where they ain't." Yesterday DiMaggio shattered that mark by the simpler expedient of hitting one where they just couldn't get it.

**Clean Sweep of Series**

Jolting Joe's record-smashing blow was struck off Heber Newsome, freshman right-hander, in the fifth inning of a game which also saw the Yankees flatten the Red Sox, 8 to 4. That gave the Bronx Bombers a clean sweep of the three-game series, extended a new winning streak to six in a row and bolstered their hold on first place to three full games over the Indians.

But all this provided merely incidental music, for the crowd's attention remained riveted on the tall, dark-haired Yankee Clipper who, despite a warm and genial personality, seems to move so coldly aloof on a ball field.

The modern record of 41 games, set by George Sisler of the Browns in 1922, had already fallen by the wayside in last Sunday's double-header in Washington. Actually, there was no comparison between this new DiMaggio mark and the old record of Keeler's, for different rules prevailed in Wee Willie's day back in 1897. There was no foul strike rule hampering the hitter then so that DiMaggio, when he equaled the 41-game Keeler record on Tuesday, already seemed to have achieved a greater feat.

## Makes Leaping Catch

But, in order to preclude all further argument, Joe yesterday decided to smash the last remaining record and he certainly did it in the most emphatic manner possible. He almost broke the mark the first time up when he shot a sharp liner to right center which Stanley Spence for a moment misjudged. But the Boston right fielder righted his course just in time to make a leaping catch.

A snappy pick-up and throw by Third Baseman Jim Tabor on a difficult bouncing ball checked DiMaggio again in the third, but there was no stopping him in the fifth as he clubbed the ball into the left-field stand with Red Rolfe on base.

The shot came in the midst of a six-run rally which routed Newsome and enabled DiMaggio's bosom pal and roommate, Lefty Gomez, to chalk up his sixth mound victory of the year despite the fact that the heat forced Lefty to vacate in the next inning.

The DiMaggio clout was his eighteenth homer of the year, his thirteenth of the batting streak and his 100th hit of the season.

In the second inning Charlie Keller hit a homer for his No. 17 in addition to boosting his runs-batted-in total to 69, four above DiMaggio's current total.

## Second Nature With DiMaggio

Hitting in streaks seems almost to be a matter of second nature with DiMaggio. His mark of 61, which he set in 1933, still stands as the record in the Pacific Coast League.

And no longer ago than last Spring he set some sort of unofficial record by connecting safely in every exhibition game he played—a total of nineteen. As the championship campaign got under way he extended his string for weight more games before Lester McCrabb of the Athletics halted Joe for his first "horse collar" of the year.

DiMaggio, in fact, remained subdued for quite a time after that, for a period going into a terrific tailspin. But on May 15 he snapped out of it and nobody has stopped him since. In all, Jolting Joe has failed to hit safely in only eleven games this year.

Much as he also likes to collect his hits, Gomez simply couldn't get up the nerve to try for a base when he came up with two out and nobody on in the fourth. So he struck out on three listless swings.

But apparently that was just a "come on" for Jack Wilson to lob one over in the fifth, with the result that Lefty banged it right into center for two runs.

A souvenir hunter almost got away with a grand coup at the close of the game when he snatched DiMaggio's cap off his head and started dashing for the nearest exit like one of football's greatest open-field runners. But the Stadium's vigilant secondary defense of special guards finally nailed the culprit some twenty yards from his goal.

Although he is supposed to be suffering from a cracked rib which has had him reported as possibly out of the All-Star game, Jimmy Foxx emerged from the dugout in the ninth to serve notice on all and sundry that old Double XX still can nudge a few by coming up with a pinch single.

Today the McCarthymen will enjoy a brief respite from the heat prior to tackling the Senators in the holiday double-header at the Stadium which starts at 1:30 o'clock tomorrow.

The box score:

| BOSTON (A.) | ab | r. | h. | po. | a. | e. | NEW YORK (A.) | ab | r. | h. | po. | a. | e. |
|---|---|---|---|---|---|---|---|---|---|---|---|---|---|
| D. DiMag., cf | 5 | 1 | 0 | 1 | 0 | 0 | Sturm, 1b | 4 | 1 | 0 | 9 | 0 | 0 |
| Finney, 1b | 5 | 1 | 2 | 10 | 1 | 0 | Rolfe, 3b | 3 | 2 | 2 | 0 | 4 | 0 |
| Williams, lf | 3 | 1 | 1 | 1 | 0 | 0 | Henrich, rf | 5 | 0 | 3 | 3 | 0 | 0 |
| Cronin, ss | 2 | 1 | 1 | 0 | 1 | 1 | J. DiMag., cf | 5 | 1 | 1 | 3 | 0 | 0 |
| L.N'some, ss | 0 | 0 | 0 | 1 | 1 | 0 | Keller, lf | 4 | 2 | 2 | 4 | 0 | 0 |
| Spence, rf | 4 | 0 | 1 | 4 | 0 | 0 | Dickey, c | 3 | 1 | 0 | 3 | 0 | 0 |
| Tabor, 3b | 4 | 0 | 2 | 1 | 2 | 0 | Gordon, 2b | 5 | 1 | 0 | 2 | 3 | 0 |
| Doerr, 2b | 4 | 0 | 0 | 1 | 4 | 0 | Rizzuto, ss | 4 | 0 | 2 | 3 | 4 | 1 |
| Pytlak, c | 4 | 0 | 0 | 5 | 1 | 0 | Gomez, p | 3 | 0 | 1 | 0 | 1 | 0 |
| H. N'some, p | 2 | 0 | 1 | 0 | 0 | 0 | Murphy, p | 1 | 0 | 0 | 0 | 0 | 0 |
| Wilson, p | 0 | 0 | 0 | 0 | 0 | 0 | | | | | | | |
| Potter, p | 1 | 0 | 0 | 0 | 0 | 0 | | | | | | | |
| ªFoxx | 1 | 0 | 1 | 0 | 0 | | | | | | | | |
| Total | 35 | 4 | 9 | 24 | 10 | 1 | Total | 37 | 8 | 11 | 27 | 12 | 1 |

ªBatted for Potter in ninth.

| Boston | 000 | 003 | 100—4 |
|---|---|---|---|
| New York | 011 | 060 | 00..—8 |

Runs batted in—Keller, J. DiMaggio 3, Rolfe, Gomez 2, Spence 2, Tabor, Cronin.

Two-base hits—Rizzuto, Rolfe. Home runs—Keller, J. DiMaggio. Stolen base—Sturm. Double plays—Gomez, Rizzuto and Sturm; Rolfe, Gordon and Sturm. Left on bases—New York 11, Boston 7. Bases on balls—Off Gomez 2, H. Newsome 3, Wilson 1, Murphy 1, Potter 2. Struck out—By Gomez 2, H. Newsome 2, Wilson 1, Murphy 1, Potter 1. Hits—Off H. Newsome 6 in 4 1–3 innings, Wilson 1 in 2–3, Potter 4 in 3, Gomez 5 in 5 1–3, Murphy 4 in 3 2–3. Wild pitch—Gomez. Passed balls—Pytlak 2. Winning pitcher—Gomez. Losing pitcher—H. Newsome. Umpires—Rommell, Stewart, Summers and Roe. Time of game—2:22. Attendance—8,682.

### *DiMaggio Streak Shows 67 Hits for 124 Bases*

Although Willie Keeler compiled a greater total of hits in his string of 44 games back in 1897 than Joe DiMaggio collected in the 45 games which enabled him to surpass the old Oriole's mark yesterday, a comparison of the two records shows Jolting Joe to have excelled Keeler in the matter of total bases.

In his string of 45, DiMaggio has collected a total of 67 hits which includes 12 doubles, 3 triples and 13 homers for a total of 124 bases. Against this, Keeler's record of 44 games, though Wee Willie made 82 safe blows, shows only 113 total bases. The old Oriole hit 11 doubles and 10 triples, but failed to connect for a single home run.

A comparison of Keeler's 44-game hitting streak and DiMaggio's record-smashing string of 45 follows:

|           | AB. | H. | 2B. | 3B. | H.R. | P.C. |
|-----------|-----|----|-----|-----|------|------|
| Keeler    | 201 | 82 | 11  | 10  | 0    | .408 |
| DiMaggio  | 179 | 67 | 12  | 3   | 13   | .374 |

July 18, 1941

## *DiMaggio's Streak Ended at 56 Games, but Yanks Down Indians Before 67,468*

### SMITH AND BAGBY STOP YANKEE STAR

### DiMaggio, Up for Last Time in Eighth, Hits Into a Double Play With Bases Full

### M'CARTHYMEN WIN BY 4–3

### Stretch lead Over Indians to 7 Lengths before Biggest Crowd for Night Game

### By JOHN DREBINGER

*Special to* THE NEW YORK TIMES.

CLEVELAND, July 17—In a brilliant setting of lights and before 67,468 fans, the largest crowd ever to see a game of night baseball in the major leagues, the Yankees tonight vanquished the Indians, 4 to 3, but the famous hitting streak of Joe DiMaggio finally came to an end.

Officially it will go into the records as fifty-six consecutive games, the total he reached yesterday. Tonight in Cleveland's municipal stadium the great DiMag was held hitless for the first time in more than two months.

Al Smith, veteran Cleveland left-hander and a Giant cast-off, and Jim Bagby, a young right-hander, collaborated in bringing the DiMaggio string to a close.

Jolting Joe faced Smith three times. Twice he smashed the ball down the third-base line, but each time Ken Keltner, Tribe third sacker, collared the ball and hurled it across the diamond for a put-out at first. In between these two tries, DiMaggio drew a pass from Smith.

Then, in the eighth, amid a deafening uproar, the streak dramatically ended, though the Yanks routed Smith with a flurry of four hits and two runs that eventually won the game.

### Double Play Seals Record

With the bases full and only one out Bagby faced DiMaggio and, with the count of one ball and one strike, induced the renowned slugger to crash into a double play. It was a grounder to the shortstop, and as the ball flitted from Lou Boudreau to Ray Mack to Oscar Grimes, who played first base for the Tribe, the crowd knew the streak was over.

However, there were still a few thrills to come, for in the ninth, with the Yanks leading 4 to 1, the Indians suddenly broke loose with an attack that for a few moments threatened to send the game into extra innings and thus give DiMaggio another chance.

Gerald Walker and Grimes singled, and, though Johnny Murphy here replaced Gomez, Larry Rosenthal tripled to score his two colleagues. But with the tying run on third and nobody out the Cleveland attack bogged down in a mess of bad base-running and the Yanks' remaining one-run lead held, though it meant the end of the streak for DiMaggio, who might have come up fourth had there been a tenth inning.

## Started May 15

It was on May 15 against the White Sox at the Yankee Stadium that DiMaggio began his string, which in time was to gain nationwide attention. As the great DiMag kept clicking in game after game, going into the twenties, then the thirties, he became the central figure of the baseball world.

On June 29, in a double-header with the Senators in Washington, he tied, then surpassed the American League and modern record of forty-one games set by George Sisler of the Browns in 1922. The next target was the all-time major league high of forty-four contests set by Willie Keeler, famous Oriole star, forty-four years ago under conditions much easier then for a batsman than they are today. Then there was no foul-strike rule hampering the batter.

But nothing hampered DiMaggio as he kept getting his daily hits, and on July 1 he tied the Keeler mark. The following day he soared past it for game No. 45, and he kept on soaring until tonight. In seeking his fifty-seventh game, he finally was brought to a halt.

Actually, DiMaggio hit in fifty-seven consecutive games for on July 8 he connected safely in the All-Star game in Detroit. But that contest did not count in the official league records.

## Did Better on Coast

DiMaggio's mark ends five short of his own Pacific Coast League record of sixty-one consecutive games, which he set while with San Francisco in 1933. The all-time minor league high is sixty-seven, set by Joe Wilhoft of Wichita in the Western League in 1919.

The contest tonight was a blistering left-handed mound duel between Gomez and Smith, with Gomez going ahead one run in the first on Red Rolfe's single and Tommy Henrich's double.

A tremendous home run inside the park, which Walker outgalloped, tied the score in the fourth and the battle remained deadlocked until Joe Gordon untied it with his fifteenth homer of the year into the left-field stand in the seventh.

In the eighth the Yanks seemingly clinched victory when Charlie Keller rifled a triple to center past Roy Weatherly, who played the ball badly, needlessly charging in when he might just as well have played it safe for a single.

In its wake came singles by Gomez and Johnny Sturm. A double by Rolfe and two runs were in. Smith walked Henrich to fill the bases, and in this setting, with one out, the result of a harmless grounder by Phil Rizutto, Bagby stepped in to face the great DiMag. A moment later the streak was over.

### Traffic Snarl on Bases

The Indians were guilty of atrocious work on the bases in the ninth after Rosenthal had cracked Murphy for a triple to drive in two. Hal Trosky, pinch hitting, grounded out to first. Then Soup Campbell, batting for Bagby, splashed a grounder to Murphy. Rosenthal tried to score, was run down between third and home.

To make matters worse, Campbell, dashing past first base, never looked to see what was going on and so made no attempt to grab second during the run-up. Weatherly, amid no end of hoots and jeers, grounded out for the final play.

The victory was Gomez's eighth, his sixth in a row. It was the Yanks' seventeenth in their last eighteen games and thirty-first in their last thirty-six contests. Their lead over the thoroughly demoralized Tribe was stretched to seven games.

With 40,000 reserved-seat tickets disposed of in the advance sale, a banner crowd was assured before a fan showed up, and with ideal weather conditions prevailing, the unreserved sections lost no time clinching the matter.

A swing band, barricaded behind a wire screening just to the rear of home plate, provided entertainment for the early arrivals. And just to match the soutpaw efforts of Gomez and Smith the band leader also was left handed.

Although Bill Dickey has fully recovered from the charley horse which has kept him on the sidelines the past few days, Manager McCarthy decided to give his veteran backstop an additional day of rest inasmuch as Rosar has been thumping the ball at a merry clip.

Just before the game, Manager Peckinpaugh received an electric refrigerator, a gift from his admirers.


### D'MAGGIO SORRY IT'S OVER

#### Wanted to Go On Improving His Streak as Long as He Could

CLEVELAND, July 17 (AP)—Joe DiMaggio, whose hitting streak of fifty-six games was ended tonight, expressed regret that he had failed to extend the record.

After the game DiMaggio said:

"I can't say I'm glad it's over. Of course I wanted to go on as long as I could.

"Now that the streak is over, I just want to get out there and keep helping win ball games."

## YANKEE BOX SCORE

| NEW YORK (A.) | ab | r. | h. | po | .a. | e. | CLEVELAND (A.) | ab | r. | h. | po | .a. | e. |
|---|---|---|---|---|---|---|---|---|---|---|---|---|---|
| Sturm, 1b | 4 | 0 | 1 | 10 | 2 | 0 | Weatherly, cf | 5 | 0 | 1 | 4 | 0 | 0 |
| Rolfe, 3b | 4 | 1 | 2 | 2 | 3 | 0 | Keltner, 3b | 3 | 0 | 1 | 1 | 4 | 0 |
| Henrich, rf | 3 | 0 | 1 | 4 | 0 | 0 | Boudreau, ss | 3 | 0 | 0 | 0 | 2 | 0 |
| DiMaggio, cf | 3 | 0 | 0 | 2 | 0 | 0 | Heath, rf | 4 | 0 | 0 | 0 | 0 | 0 |
| Gordon, 2b | 4 | 1 | 2 | 0 | 1 | 0 | Walker, lf | 3 | 2 | 2 | 1 | 0 | 0 |
| Rosar, c | 4 | 0 | 0 | 5 | 1 | 0 | Grimes, 1b | 3 | 1 | 1 | 12 | 0 | 0 |
| Keller, lf | 3 | 1 | 1 | 0 | 0 | 0 | Mack, 2b | 3 | 0 | 0 | 4 | 7 | 0 |
| Rizutto, ss | 4 | 0 | 0 | 2 | 1 | 0 | a Rosenthal | 1 | 0 | 1 | 0 | 0 | 0 |
| Gomez, p | 4 | 1 | 1 | 2 | 1 | 0 | Hemsley, c | 3 | 0 | 1 | 5 | 1 | 0 |
| Murphy, p | 0 | 0 | 0 | 0 | 1 | 0 | b Trosky | 1 | 0 | 0 | 0 | 0 | 0 |
| | | | | | | | Smith, p | 3 | 0 | 0 | 0 | 0 | 0 |
| | | | | | | | Bagby, p | 0 | 0 | 0 | 0 | 0 | 0 |
| | | | | | | | cCampbell | 1 | 0 | 0 | 0 | 0 | 0 |
| Total | 33 | 4 | 8 | 27 | 10 | 0 | Total | 33 | 3 | 7 | 27 | 14 | 0 |

aBatted for Mack in ninth.
bBatted for Hemsley in ninth.
cBatted for Bagby in ninth.

| | | | |
|---|---|---|---|
| New York | 100 | 000 | 120—4 |
| Cleveland | 000 | 100 | 002—3 |

Runs batted in—Henrich, Walker, Gomez, Gordon, Rolfe, Rosenthal 2.

Two-base hits—Henrich, Rolfe. Three-base hits—Keller, Rosenthal. Home runs—Walker, Gordon. Sacrifice—Boudreau. Double play—Boudreau, Mack and Grimes. Left on bases—New York 5, Cleveland 7. Bases on balls—Off Smith 2, Bagby 1, Gomez 3. Struck out—By Gomez 5, Smith 4, Bagby 1. Hits—Off Smith 7 in 7 1–3 innings, Bagby 1 in 1 2–3, Gomez 6 in 8 (none out in ninth), Murphy 1 in 1. Passed ball—Hemsley. Winning pitcher—Gomez. Losing pitcher—Smith. Umpires—Summers, Roe and Stewart. Time of game—2:03. Attendance—67,468.

---

## DIMAGGIO'S RECORD STREAK

| Date | Opponent | ab. | r. | h. | 2b. | 3b. | hr. | Date | Opponent | ab. | r. | h. | 2b. | 3b. | hr. |
|---|---|---|---|---|---|---|---|---|---|---|---|---|---|---|---|
| May 15—White Sox | | 4 | 0 | 1 | 0 | 0 | 0 | June 17—White Sox | | 4 | 1 | 1 | 0 | 0 | 0 |
| May 16—White Sox | | 4 | 2 | 2 | 0 | 1 | 1 | June 18—White Sox | | 3 | 0 | 1 | 0 | 0 | 0 |
| May 17—White Sox | | 3 | 1 | 1 | 0 | 0 | 0 | June 19—White Sox | | 3 | 2 | 3 | 0 | 0 | 1 |
| May 18—Browns | | 3 | 3 | 3 | 1 | 0 | 0 | June 20—Tigers | | 5 | 3 | 4 | 1 | 0 | 0 |
| May 19—Browns | | 5 | 1 | 1 | 0 | 0 | 0 | June 21—Tigers | | 4 | 0 | 1 | 0 | 0 | 0 |
| May 20—Browns | | 5 | 1 | 1 | 0 | 0 | 0 | June 22—Tigers | | 5 | 1 | 2 | 1 | 0 | 1 |
| May 21—Tigers | | 5 | 0 | 2 | 0 | 0 | 0 | June 24—Browns | | 4 | 1 | 1 | 0 | 0 | 0 |

| Date | AB | R | H | 2B | 3B | HR | Date | AB | R | H | 2B | 3B | HR |
|---|---|---|---|---|---|---|---|---|---|---|---|---|---|
| May 22—Tigers | 4 | 0 | 1 | 0 | 0 | 0 | June 25—Browns | 4 | 1 | 1 | 0 | 0 | 1 |
| May 23—Red Sox | 5 | 0 | 1 | 0 | 0 | 0 | June 26—Browns | 4 | 0 | 1 | 1 | 0 | 0 |
| May 24—Red Sox | 4 | 2 | 1 | 0 | 0 | 0 | June 27—Athletics | 3 | 1 | 2 | 0 | 0 | 1 |
| May 25—Red Sox | 4 | 0 | 1 | 0 | 0 | 0 | June 28—Athletics | 5 | 1 | 2 | 1 | 0 | 0 |
| May 27—Senators | 5 | 3 | 4 | 0 | 0 | 1 | June 29—Senators | 4 | 1 | 1 | 1 | 0 | 0 |
| May 28—Senators | 4 | 1 | 1 | 0 | 1 | 0 | June 29—Senators | 5 | 1 | 1 | 0 | 0 | 0 |
| May 29—Senators | 3 | 1 | 1 | 0 | 0 | 0 | July 1—Red Sox | 4 | 0 | 2 | 0 | 0 | 0 |
| May 30—Red Sox | 2 | 1 | 1 | 0 | 0 | 0 | July 1—Red Sox | 4 | 0 | 2 | 0 | 0 | 0 |
| May 30—Red Sox | 3 | 0 | 1 | 1 | 0 | 0 | July 2—Red Sox | 5 | 1 | 1 | 0 | 0 | 1 |
| June 1—Indians | 4 | 1 | 1 | 0 | 0 | 0 | July 5—Athletics | 4 | 2 | 1 | 0 | 0 | 1 |
| June 1—Indians | 4 | 0 | 1 | 0 | 0 | 0 | July 6—Athletics | 5 | 2 | 4 | 1 | 0 | 0 |
| June 2—Indians | 4 | 2 | 2 | 1 | 0 | 0 | July 6—Athletics | | | | | | |
| June 3—Tigers | 4 | 1 | 1 | 0 | 0 | 1 | July 10—Browns | 2 | 0 | 1 | 0 | 0 | 0 |
| June 5—Tigers | 5 | 1 | 1 | 0 | 1 | 0 | July 11—Browns | 5 | 1 | 4 | 0 | 0 | 1 |
| June 7—Browns | 5 | 2 | 3 | 0 | 0 | 0 | July 12—Browns | 5 | 1 | 2 | 1 | 0 | 0 |
| June 8—Browns | 4 | 3 | 2 | 0 | 0 | 2 | July 13—White Sox | 4 | 2 | 3 | 0 | 0 | 0 |
| June 8—Browns | 4 | 1 | 2 | 1 | 0 | 1 | July 13—White Sox | 4 | 0 | 1 | 0 | 0 | 0 |
| June 10—White Sox | 5 | 1 | 1 | 0 | 0 | 0 | July 14—White Sox | 3 | 0 | 1 | 0 | 0 | 0 |
| June 12—White Sox | 4 | 1 | 2 | 0 | 0 | 1 | July 15—White Sox | 4 | 1 | 2 | 1 | 0 | 0 |
| June 14—Indians | 2 | 0 | 1 | 1 | 0 | 0 | July 16—Indians | 4 | 3 | 3 | 1 | 0 | 0 |
| June 15—Indians | 3 | 1 | 1 | 0 | 0 | 1 | | | | | | | |
| June 16—Indians | 5 | 0 | 1 | 1 | 0 | 0 | Total | 223 | 56 | 91 | 16 | 4 | 15 |

November 12, 1941

### *DiMaggio Most Valuable American League Player for Second Time in 3 Years*

## YANKEE ACE TOPS WILLIAMS POLL

### DiMaggio Gets 291 Points to 254 for Red Sox' Star, Who Hit .406 and 37 Homers

## 56-GAME STREAK DECISIVE

### Writers Influenced by Joe's Record Batting String That Led Team to Pennant

#### By JOHN DREBINGER

Ted Williams, lanky outfielder of the Boston Red Sox, whose blazing .406 average won the batting crown last Summer, became the first major leaguer to crash baseball's magic group of "four hundred" clouters since

Joe DiMaggio, Ted Williams and Dom DiMaggio, American League sluggers. (THE NEW YORK TIMES)

Bill Terry achieved the feat in 1930, but the most valuable player in the American League in 1941 was a fellow named Joe DiMaggio.

This was the decision, announced yesterday, of the special committee of the Baseball Writers Association of America, which, with this action, bestowed the coveted honor upon the world champion Yankees' brilliant center fielder for the second time in three years. DiMaggio first gained the award in 1939.

DiMaggio's total was 291 points, against 254 for Williams, who placed second. Third honors went to Bob Feller, fireball pitcher, who won twenty-five games for the Indians. Rapid Robert scored 174 points, and fourth place went to Thornton Lee, twenty-two-game winner of the White Sox, who polled 144.

### 14 Points for First Place

In the wake of these came Charlie Keller of the Yankees with 126 and Cecil Travis of the Senators, 101. These were all that scored more than 100 points in the balloting, in which each committee-man ranked ten players on his list, points being distributed on a basis of 14 for first place, 9 for second, 8 for third and so on down to 1 for tenth.

DiMaggio received 15 first place votes and was the second choice of the 9 remaining ballots. Williams drew 8 first place counts, 14 second and 2 third.

The only other player to receive a first place vote was Lee, who got 1. Feller drew 14 third-place votes, 6 fourth, 1 fifth, 2 sixth and 1 seventh.

Thus the writers made it clear that they considered DiMaggio's spectacular 56-game hitting streak, together with Joe's vastly superior defensive skill and base running ability, had more than offset Williams' impressive .408 average and 37 homers, though both these figures topped all others in the majors. The Yankee star, who had won the batting crown in 1929 and 1940, last Summer hit .357.

## Spurt Electrifies Nation

It was the fifty-six-game hitting streak, all-time high for the major leagues, which doubtless clinched the verdict.

It began on May 15 with a single off Edgar Smith of the White Sox. Then, sweeping into the discard the major league mark of the immortal Willie Keeler and the American League record of George Sisler, it continued until the memorable night game of July 17 in Cleveland Stadium, when 67,468, the largest crowd ever to attend a nocturnal battle, saw the combined pitching efforts of the Indians' Al Smith and Jim Bagby finally "horse collar" Jolting Joe.

But they didn't check the Great DiMag for long. For immediately after this setback he ripped off another hitting streak of sixteen games, so that in that long span from May 15 to Aug. 3 he set the even more astounding record of batting safely in seventy-two of seventy-three contests.

It was by far the most remarkable exhibition of sustained hitting the majors ever had seen and concurrently with DiMaggio's brilliant spurt ran the Yankees' irresistible sweep to the pennant.

The voting follows:

| | Points | | | Points |
|---|---|---|---|---|
| 1—Joe DiMaggio, Yankees | 291 | | 16—Ted Lyons, White Sox | 12 |
| 2—Ted Williams, Red Sox | 254 | | 17—Dick Siebert, Athletics | 10 |
| 3—Bob Feller, Indians | 174 | | 18—Lou Boudreau, Indians | 10 |
| 4—Tornton Lee, White Sox | 144 | | 19—Al Benton, Tigers | 8 |
| 5—Charlie Keller, Yankees | 126 | | 20—Phil Rizutto, Yankees | 7 |
| 6—Cecil Travis, Senators | 101 | | 21—Emil Leonard, Senators | 7 |
| 7—Joe Gordon, Yankees | 60 | | 22—Bruce Campbell, Tigers | 4 |
| 8—Jeff Heath, Indians | 37 | | 23—Rudy York, Tigers | 3 |
| 9—Heber Newsome, Red Sox | 32 | | 24—Frank Hayes, Athletics | 3 |
| 10—Roy Cullenbine, Browns | 29 | | 25—Taft Wright, White Sox | 2 |
| 11—Joe Cronin, Red Sox | 26 | | 26—Charles Ruffing, Yankees | 2 |
| 12—Sam Chapman, Athletics | 25 | | 27—Elden Auker, Browns | 1 |
| 13—Bill Dickey, Yankees | 18 | | 28—Frank Higgins, Tigers | 1 |
| 14—Tommy Henrich, Yankees | 16 | | 29—Dom DiMaggio, Red Sox | 1 |
| 15—Barney McCosky, Tigers | 12 | | | |

February 17, 1943

### *Joe DiMaggio Joins Army Today as Voluntary Inductee; Durocher Put in 1-A*

## YANKS' STAR GETS 'ACTION' ON COAST

# Frisco Draft Board Complies With DiMaggio's Desire to Join Army Immediately

## BARROW PRAISES DECISION

### Cites 13 Players on Club in Service—'He'll Make Good Soldier' Says McCarthy

#### By The Associated Press.

SAN FRANCISCO, Feb. 16—Joltin' Joe DiMaggio trades a $35,000 or better baseball job tomorrow for the $50 monthly play of a buck private.

The 28-year-old Yankee star reported today he had received permission from his draft board to become a volunteer inductee. The usual procedure is to assign San Francisco inductees to Monterey before sending them to training camp.

With a smile breaking his usual dead-pan expression, DiMaggio said he had no idea which branch of the service he would join.

"All I know is I'm to report for physical examination tomorrow at 7:30," he said.

For the past few weeks, DiMaggio had vacationed in Hollywood with his wife. She will reside there permanently, Joe said, with their infant son, Joe Jr.

As a married man with a child, DiMaggio had a draft status of 3-A. Under voluntary induction, tantamount to enlistment, he was reclassified 1-A.

DiMaggio, sold to the Yankees by San Francisco of the Pacific Coast League for $25,000, joined the American League club in 1936. He was voted the circuit's most valuable player in 1939 and 1941.

DiMaggio expressed the hope that baseball would be allowed to continue to function, "if war conditions permit. I think everybody wants it to go on," he said.

### Preliminary Examination Passed
*Special to THE NEW YORK TIMES.*

SAN FRANCISCO, Feb. 16—Joe DiMaggio, who already has passed his preliminary Army examination, revealed today that he had not received a 1943 contract from the Yankees, but said he "would only have sent it back anyway."

"I guess they didn't send me one because they figured I was serious about this Army business," he went on. "They know now."

"This desire to join the Army isn't anything recently born. I seriously entertained the thought immediately after the world series last Fall, but private and domestic troubles curved my mind a little away from the Army."

DiMaggio, who last season, his seventh with the Yankees, earned "in excess of $50,000," was asked whether he would prefer driving a tank, riding a jeep or manning a gun.

"I'll bet those jeep rides are O.K., huh?" he replied. "But they can put me where they think I'll do the most good. I haven't asked for anything special."

DiMaggio first approached his draft board about two or three weeks ago to ask for reclassification from 3-A to 1-A, according to Neal Callaghan, chairman. "He frankly stated that he wanted to get into the service and this was the only way open now that enlistments had been stopped." Mr. Callaghan related. "He wanted immediate action and we gave it to him."

After the war, DiMaggio promised he would be back with the Yankees. "Every hour on the diamond was a thrill for me," he told newspaper men. "I loved it and I'll love the Army, too."

### A Surprise to Barrow

News of Joe DiMaggio's impending induction into the Army came as something of a surprise yesterday to President Ed barrow of the Yankees. Confined to his home in Larchmont with a cold Barrow unhesitatingly approved the slugger's decision, however, and proudly pointed to the fact DiMaggio was the thirteenth Yankee to answer the nation's call.

---

BUFFALO, Feb. 16 (AP)—Informed that Joe DiMaggio had announced he was entering the Army tomorrow, Joe McCarthy, manager of the Yankees, said tonight: "God bless him, he'll make a good soldier."

November 28, 1947

### *Joe DiMaggio Named Most Valuable American League Player for Third Time*

#### YANKEE STAR LEADS WILLIAMS BY POINT

#### DiMaggio Selected for Player Award With Score of 202 by Baseball Writers

#### BOUDREAU IS RATED THIRD

#### Page is Fourth, Just Back of Indians' Manager, Despite Seven First-Place Votes

#### By JOHN DREBINGER

By the slender margin of a single point, Joe DiMaggio, star centerfielder of the Yankees has been named the American League's most valuable player for 1947, it was announced yesterday by the Baseball Writers Association of America.

In being voted the Kenesaw Mountain Landis Memorial award, Jolting Joe received 202 points in the poll of the scribes' twenty-four-man committee as against 201 for Ted Williams, Red Sox star slugger and winner of the prize last year.

Third ranking also was gained by only a single point with Lou Boudreau, manager-shortstop of the Indians,

Joe DiMaggio, his right arm in a cast following a recent operation, turns southpaw as he takes his turn at Thanksgiving dinner plate. (ASSOCIATED PRESS)

scoring 168 points to 167 for Joe Page, the tireless left-hander who did an amazing relief job for the Yankees last summer. Fifth place went to George Kell, Tiger third sacker, who scored 132.

### First Honored in 1929

It marked the third time that DiMaggio had finished on top, the Yankee clipper having first captured the award in 1939 and again in 1941. And for Williams it was the third time Boston's temperamental "problem child" had failed to win the prize despite a distinguished personal record.

In 1941 Williams hit .406, yet bowed to DiMaggio who that year had set his spectacular fifty-six-game hitting streak. In 1942 Williams again won the batting crown with .364 but trailed behind Joe Gordon, then with the Yanks, for the MVP award.

The past season again saw Williams lead individual batting as well as top the field in homers and runs batted in. But the scribes apparently estimated DiMaggio the more valuable team worker.

Jolting Joe polled eight first place ballots as against only three for Williams who drew most of his points from ten second place ratings. As in the National League vote, points were distributed on a basis of 14 points for first place, 9 for second, 8 for third and so on down to one for tenth.

### McQuinn Rated Sixth

Curiously Page, whom his manager, Bucky Harris, openly named as the year's most important factor in the Yanks' pennant victory, had the second highest first place votes to DiMaggio, the lefty appearing No. 1 in seven ballots.

George McQuinn, the veteran Mack cast-off, whose astonishing comeback at first base also played a strong role in the Yankee victory, received three first-place votes which helped him finish sixth with 77 points. In all eighteen of the twenty-four writers named a Yankee for the No. 1 spot. Eddie Jost of the Athletics got two of the remaining first ballot votes, while Boudreau got the other.

The Bombers, in fact, did exceptionally well, placing eight men among the thirty-four who received points. Tommy Henrich, Frank, Shea, Yogi Berra and Allie Reynolds are bunched between 33 and 18 points, while a little further down the line Bill Johnson appears with 9.

That it was a tough year for old favorites was indicated when Hal Newhouser, winner in 1944 and 1945, this year had to be satisfied with honorable mention, for which no points are awarded. But Joe Gordon, who as a Yank won in 1942, still was able to make a presentable showing as an Indian. He placed seventh with 59 points, one more than Cleveland's Bob Feller received.

The complete point score follows:

DiMaggio, Yankees, 202; Williams, Red Sox, 201; Boudreau, Indians, 168; Page, Yankees, 167; Kell, Tigers, 132; McQuinn, Yankees, 77; Gordon, Indians, 59; Feller, Indians, 58; Marchildon, Athletics, 47; Appling, White Sox, 43; Joost, Athletics, 35; McCosky, Athletics, 35; Henrich, Yankees, 33; Shea, Yankees, 23; Berra, Yankees, 18; Reynolds, Yankees, 18; Dillinger, Browns, 13; Pesky, Red Sox, 11; Pain, Athletics, 9; W. Johnson, Yankees, 9; Spence, Senators, 9; Hutchinson, Tigers, 8; Wynn, Senators, 7; Doerr; Red Sox, 6; Rosar, Athletics, 6; Christman, Browns, 4; McCahan, Athletics, 4; Mitchell, Indians, 4; Cullenbine, Tigers, 3; Dobson, Red Sox, 3; Heath, Browns, 1; Lopez, White Sox, 1; Stephens, Browns, 1; Wright, White Sox, 1.

Honorable Mention—Red Sox: D. DiMaggio, Murrell Jones. White Sox: Philley, Haynes, Tresh. Tigers: Newhouser, Evers, Overmire. Yankees: Rizzuto, Newsom, Keller, Stirnweiss, Lindell. Athletics: Valo, Suder, Majeski, Fowler. Browns: Lehner, Judnich. Senators: Vernon, Yost.

---

May 21, 1948

### *DiMaggio's 5 Blows Highlight Yank Victory; Dodgers, Giants Bow*

## BOMBERS CONQUER WHITE SOX BY 13–2

### DiMaggio Smashes 2 Homers, Triple, Double and Single to Top 22-Hit Attack

## LINDELL ALSO CONNETCS

### Drives 4-Bagger, Two Singles for Yanks—Raschi Coasts to His Third Victory

### By JAMES P. DAWSON

*Special to THE NEW YORK TIMES.*

CHICAGO, May 20—Inspired by the greatest batting day Joe DiMaggio has enjoyed since pre-war times, the Yankees touched record heights in the vital statistics department at Comiskey Field today when they overwhelmed the hapless White Sox, 13 to 2.

The Bombers from the Bronx slugged four of Ted Lyons' throwers for twenty-two hits, good for thirty-eight bases, exceeding their previous high in hits by six and their best previous accumulation of total bases by twelve. Their thirteen runs bettered by one the dozen accumulated in the season's opener April 19 against Washington, when they banged out sixteen hits, good for twenty-six bases.

In today's slugging orgy DiMaggio hammered out two homers, a triple, a double and a single. He pounded in six runs and was deprived of a "6 for 6" day when Ralph Hodgin backed to the left-field wall in the eighth to pull down what would have been another extra-base blow.

Big John Lindell exploded a homer and contributed two singles to the cannonade that rang about the ears of the futile Sox hurlers. Billy Johnson had a three-hit day, with one double. Bobby Brown stroked three singles. All told the Yanks got three homers, one triple, five doubles and thirteen singles in the explosion that entertained a meager 5,001 cash customers and brought immeasurable pain to Ted Lyons.

## Stirnweiss Is Hitless

Only George Stirnweiss failed to get a hit in this slugfest, and Ike Pearson was the only one of the five hurlers Lyons tossed into the fray to escape the barrage. The veteran right-hander got the call with two out in the four-run ninth, just in time to make Stirnweiss bang into a force play that dropped the curtain on the worst beating the Sox have absorbed this campaign.

Vic Raschi picked up his third straight triumph, though his performance held room for improvement. He walked in a run on four passes in the fourth. He was clubbed for three hits by Taft Wright, one a home run in the eighth, and allowed seven hits in all.

Lyons started Orval Grove, who got into trouble by messing up an easy double in the first and finished in the fifth after being clubbed for nine hits and five runs. Fred Bradley appeared with the sixth, but was hammered to shelter with one man away and four runs in. Earl Harrist checked the scoring without interfering with the hitting. And in the ninth the aging Earl Caldwell was moved out of the contest under a six-hit salvo that included Lindell's homer and produced four more runs.

## Both Wallops Off Grove

Grove was the victim of DiMaggio's two homers. Walloping Joe exploded the first with two aboard in the first inning. After the Yanks had added another run in the second on three hits, DiMaggio opened the fifth with his second homer, his sixth of the campaign. Singles by Raschi and Lindell with DiMaggio's triple finished Bradley quickly in the sixth, and a double by Yogi Berra greeted Harrist as the Yanks collected four more.

That was all until the ninth, when Bobby Brown singled, Cliff Mapes doubled, Lindell hit his homer with one on, DiMaggio doubled, Berra walked, Johnson doubled and George McQuinn singled, all for four more before Pearson came on to end the slaughter.

The home-run production boosted the Yankee total to thirty. Sox pitchers have now been clubbed for thirty-one this season.

Illustrating the sorry condition of Lyons' pitching squad is the fact that in twenty-four games, including a tie, the Southsiders have had sixty-nine in action.

Until today Grove enjoyed the distinction of being the only Sox hurler to go the route, in spring exhibitions and regular play.

The Yanks could do nothing wrong today. Contrarily nothing went right for the Sox.

Johnson tripped and fell under Luke Appling's pop in the seventh but stuck out his glove to make the catch while lying on the ground.

The box score:

| NEW YORK (A.) | ab | r. | h. | po. | a. | e. | CHICAGO (A.) | ab | r. | h. | po. | a. | e. |
|---|---|---|---|---|---|---|---|---|---|---|---|---|---|
| Brown, ss | 5 | 0 | 3 | 2 | 3 | 0 | Baker, 2b | 3 | 0 | 0 | 3 | 1 | 0 |
| Keller, lf | 4 | 2 | 1 | 1 | 0 | 0 | Lupten, 1b | 5 | 0 | 2 | 6 | 1 | 0 |
| Mapes, lf | 1 | 1 | 1 | 1 | 0 | 0 | Appling, 3b | 4 | 1 | 0 | 3 | 2 | 0 |
| Lindell, rf | 6 | 3 | 3 | 4 | 0 | 0 | Hodgin, lf | 3 | 0 | 1 | 3 | 2 | 0 |
| DiMa'io, cf | 6 | 4 | 5 | 3 | 0 | 0 | Wright, rf | 4 | 1 | 3 | 4 | 0 | 0 |
| Berra, c | 5 | 1 | 2 | 2 | 0 | 0 | Robinson, c | 3 | 0 | 1 | 3 | 1 | 0 |
| Johnson, 3b | 6 | 0 | 3 | 1 | 1 | 0 | Philley, cf | 3 | 0 | 0 | 3 | 0 | 0 |
| M'Qu'n, 1b | 4 | 0 | 2 | 10 | 1 | 0 | Michaeis, ss | 3 | 0 | 0 | 2 | 7 | 0 |
| Stirn'ss, 2b | 6 | 0 | 0 | 2 | 5 | 0 | Grove, p | 1 | 0 | 0 | 0 | 0 | 1 |
| Raschi, p | 5 | 2 | 2 | 1 | 1 | 0 | aKolloway | 1 | 0 | 0 | 0 | 0 | 0 |
| | | | | | | | Bradley, p | 0 | 0 | 0 | 0 | 0 | 0 |
| | | | | | | | Harrist, p | 0 | 0 | 0 | 0 | 0 | 0 |
| | | | | | | | bWallaesa | 1 | 0 | 0 | 0 | 0 | 0 |
| | | | | | | | Caldwell, p | 0 | 0 | 0 | 0 | 0 | 0 |
| | | | | | | | Pearson, p | 0 | 0 | 0 | 0 | 0 | 0 |
| | | | | | | | cWeigel | 1 | 0 | 0 | 0 | 0 | 0 |
| Total | 48 | 13 | 22 | 27 | 11 | 0 | Total | 32 | 2 | 7 | 27 | 14 | 1 |

aPopped out for Grove in fifth.
bFlied out for Harrist in seventh.
cGrounded out for Pearson in ninth.

| | | |
|---|---|---|
| New York | 310 014 004—13 |
| Chicago | 000 100 010—2 |

Runs batted in—DiMaggio 6, Keller, Lindell, 2. Philley, Berra, Wright, Johnson, McQuinn.

Two-base hits—McQuinn, Berra, Mapes, DiMaggio, Johnson. Three-base hits—DiMaggio. Home runs—DiMaggio 2, Wright, Lindell. Double plays—Johnson, Stirnweiss and McQuinn; Stirnweiss, Brown and McQuinn. Left on bases—New York 13, Chicago 10. Bases on balls—Off Grove 1, Bradley 1, Harrist 1, Caldwell 2, Raschi 7. Struck out—By Raschi 2, Harrist 1. Hits—Off Grove 9 in 5 innings, Bradley 3 in 1–3, Harrist 2 in 1 2–3, Caldwell 8 in 1 2–3, Pearson 0 in 1–3. Wild pitch—Grove. Losing pitcher—Grove. Umpires—Rommell, Passarella and Boyer. Time of game—2:26. Attendance—5,001.

### *DiMaggio Reported All-Time Top-Salaried Player With $90,000 Contract*

## CLIPPER ACCEPTS TERMS FOR A YEAR

### Figures of DiMaggio Pact Not Revealed but Yanks Admit He Got Big Increase

## DREW $70,000 FOR 1948

### New Stipend Believed Above Ruth's $80,000 Peak—Star Leaves on Mexican Trip

#### By JOHN DREBINGER

All further speculation on whether Joe DiMaggio would be in uniform when the Yankees open their spring training operations March 1 came to an end yesterday when the famed Clipper came to terms with his employers for the 1949 season.

Announcement of this came after an hour's conference at the club's Fifth Avenue offices between the star center fielder and Dan Topping, president of the Yanks, and General Manager George Weiss. It failed to disclose the actual salary figures. There was no further reference to this item of curiosity beyond the terse statement that it provided an increase.

To this DiMaggio added that it was "the best of the eleven contracts I have signed to date with the Yankees." Topping also produced a broad smile of satisfaction while a battery of press and newsreel photographers made it look as though the baseball writers were putting on an encore to their show of the previous night at the Waldorf-Astoria.

Most logical of various estimates was that the Clipper settled for a flat salary of about $90,000. That could be about correct, for it was understood DiMaggio had been asking for $100,000, an amount the Yankees were willing enough to pay if bonus arrangement based on attendance figures produced that amount. When DiMaggio steadfastly declined to accept a bonus contract such as he received last year, the $90,000 figure was accepted as a compromise.

#### Off for Mexican Retreat

Immediately after the signing the Clipper, who declared himself in fine physical trim except for being a few pounds underweight, packed his grips for two weeks' vacation trip and last night was winging by plane toward Acapulco, Mexico. He said he would be back Feb. 21 to spend a few more days in New York before heading for the St. Petersburg training camp.

Thus, the 34-year-old son of an Italian immigrant fisherman, who used to sell newspapers for a dollar and a half a day on the streets of San Francisco, became the highest salaried ball player in Yankee history and perhaps in all baseball, although this distinction cannot become official until the club sees fit to disclose the actual figures.

For in the day when Babe Ruth was soaring to his $80,000-per-annum peak in 1920 and 1931 Col. Jacob Ruppert, then the owner of the Bombers, made it a point to let in the public on the exact amount. Also, it is a certainty the late Bambino still holds the all-time high for "take home money," as the players call it, for there

Joe DiMaggio as he came to terms at the club's offices, February 7, 1949. Looking on are Dan Topping (left), one of the owners, and George Weiss, general manager. (THE NEW YORK TIMES)

was no staggering income tax slashes in those days. In addition, the Babe also drew a 10 per cent net from all exhibition game receipts.

The present Yankee regime, however, has always declined to reveal contract figures at the time of signing, and it was not until yesterday that admission was made that DiMaggio had received approximately $70,000 for 1948.

## Started at $7,500

At that, should the $90,000 be correct, the Clipper by next fall could bring his all-time earnings to about $475,000 as a Yankee, which isn't bad considering he started as a $7,500 rookie in 1936 and then "lost" three years in the Army, when his pay dropped to "sixty-a-month" as a corporal.

According to Arthur E. Patterson, the club's publicity director, the Yanks No. 1 Bomber has received about $345,750 in salary plus $40,809.20 in world series revenues, making a grand total of $386,559.20. Of his world series checks, seven were for actual series participation, the top figure being $6,471.10 which Joe drew as a winning Yank in the last all-New York series in 1937. Last year he drew a third-place share of $778.88.

Although he received regular boosts following his 1936 debut, DiMaggio's salary rises hit a snag with the war, which left him with a $48,750 contract for 1942. Under baseball law he had to accept this same figure when he returned in 1946, and when he encountered difficulty in regaining his earlier form in his first post-war season he settled for a similar amount in 1947.

## Drove a Hard Bargain

Because of his magnificent comeback last year, plus the fact that he always felt the Yanks had treated him rather shabbily in pre-war years, it is generally felt the Clipper this time drove a sharp bargain.

Before leaving for Mexico, DiMaggio said he had recovered completely from the operation performed on his right heel last November and that, barring mishaps, he expected to enjoy a good season.

"I never bother with any special exercises in winter," said Joe, "because I just naturally don't put on weight. In fact, I usually lose a little and am a few pounds off now which I'd like to put back on before reporting."

He said he scales at present about 193. His average weight through the last playing season was around 196.

## Henrich Confers With Topping

No sooner had the hubbub attending the DiMaggio ceremonies subsided than Tommy Henrich arrived in the Yankee offices, but there was no second contract signing. For after being closeted with Topping and Weiss, the Bombers' Old Reliable emerged without coming to terms. It was said that Tommy, on receiving the club's proposal, had asked for a few more days to think it over and would return Wednesday for another talk.

Henrich last summer had just about his best season with the Yanks, his hard hitting and versatile play both in the outfield and at first base ranking him second to DiMaggio as a valuable performer.

It is believed another celebrity came to terms in New York yesterday when Bill Veeck and Bob Feller, who had attended the writers' dinner the previous night, settled their salary differences. Feller is said to have agreed to a cut in his basic salary from $50,000 to $40,000. However, it is not likely there will be an official announcement of this until later in the week when Veeck puts on his own special tub-thumping act in Cleveland.

### *DiMaggio's Salary Record*

Following is a list of the estimated salaries and world series checks which Joe DiMaggio has received as a Yankee since 1936:

|          | **Estimated Salary** | **World Series Checks** |
| -------- | -------------------- | ----------------------- |
| 1936     | $7,500               | $6,430.55               |
| 1937     | 15,000               | 6,471.10                |
| 1938     | 25,000               | 5,782.76                |
| 1939     | 27,500               | 5,614.26                |
| 1940     | 32,000               | 546.59                  |
| 1941     | 37,500               | 5,943.31                |
| 1942     | 43,750               | 3,018.77                |
| 1943–44–45 | (Served in Army)   |                         |
| 1946     | 43,750               | 392.95                  |
| 1947     | 43,750               | 5,830.03                |
| 1948     | 70,000               | 778.88                  |
| Total    | $345,750             | $40,809.20              |

Grand total, $386,559.20

### *DiMaggio's 2-Run Homer Helps Yanks Win; Giants, Dodgers Victors*

## JOE IN FIRST START AS BOMBERS SCORE

## Red Sox Are Set Back by 5–4, Yankees' DiMaggio Hitting Home Run and a Single

## CLIPPER CATCHES 6 FLIES

## Bauer Smashes 4-Bagger With 2 Mates Aboard—Page Saves Reynolds in the Ninth

### By LOUIS EFFRAT

*Special to* THE NEW YORK TIMES.

BOSTON, June 28—Joe DiMaggio became a Yankee in good standing tonight. Too long was the wait for his official return and there were probably times during the sixty-five games he missed because of an ailing right heel that all concerned wondered if the Clipper ever would make it. But make it he did for the first time this season tonight—and how!

Before the season's biggest turnout and the largest after-dark attendance in Fenway Park history, 36,228 fans, DiMaggio started to earn the $90,000 he is being paid. Like the DiMaggio of old, he made the enemy cringe, as he carried his team to a thrilling 5–4 victory over the red-hot Red Sox.

Carried is the word, too. For Joltin' Joe, directly and indirectly had his hand in the scoring of all the New York runs. In his first time at bat, DiMaggio opened the second inning with a solid single to left center. The next two Yankees were fanned by Southpaw Maurice McDermott, so that if Joe had not hit, the visitors would have been retired.

### Drives Into the Screen

Given this life by DiMaggio, the Bombers remained alive and, after Johnny Lindell walked, Hank Bauer hit his third homer of the campaign, giving the New Yorkers a 3–0 bulge. Nor did DiMaggio stop there. In the third, with Phil Rizutto aboard via a single, DiMaggio came through with his first homer, a dynamic clout into the screen above the high left-field wall and it was 5–0.

Idle so long, in need of batting practice and facing a brilliant, 20-year-old lefthander, with a fair strikeout record, the Yankees Clipper was hitting 1.000 after his first two trips to the plate. In two other attempts, Joe grounded to the pitcher and walked, but he had provided the big punches that enabled his team to stave off Boston's strong closing bid.

This was a good game for the Yankees to capture. The Red Sox, with a 4-game winning streak and 10-out-of-11, had to be stopped by the leagues leaders. Casey Stengel entrusted Allie Reynolds with the pitching chores and, though he needed the help of Lefty Joe Page in the ninth, Reynolds notched his eighth triumph of the season against a single setback—thanks principally to Joe DiMaggio.

## Wears Special Shoe

Wearing a special shoe on his right foot—no spikes under the heel—DiMaggio patrolled center field flawlessly. He captured six flies and fielded three ground singles that came his way with his old-time grace. In the eighth, when Joe walked, Yogi Berra grounded to Bobby Doerr. DiMaggio was an easy force-out at second, but his take-out slide prevented Vern Stephens from completing a double play. In short, it was a tremendous night for the returning hero.

DiMaggio, with an assist from Bauer, supplied Reynolds with a big lead, which, at the finish proved barely sufficient. The Red Sox, who outhit the Yankees 11–8, retrieved two runs in the fourth when, with the bases loaded and one out, Reynolds passed Al Zarilla, forcing one over, and the other tallied after a fly to left by Matt Batts.

Doerr hit his sixth homer of the season in the eighth and in the ninth a triple by Batts and a pinch single by Birdie Tebbets brought Page to the rescue.

Dom DiMaggio sacrificed, placing the tying run—Lou Stringer ran for Tebbets—at second. Johnny Pesky then smashed a sizzler off Page's foot. However, the carom went to Jerry Coleman, who threw out Pesky, Stringer advancing to third.

This brought up Ted Williams, who earlier had achieved two scratchy singles. A hit here would have deadlocked the issue, a homer would have given it to Joe McCarthy's men. Williams swung hard and drove the ball nearly 400 feet to deep center, but DiMaggio—Joe—made the catch look easy, the Yankees were home free and McDermott was charged with his first defeat.

Rizutto and Pesky collided while the Scooter was making a double play at first. It appeared that Rizutto was hurt but after a couple of minutes he arose and continued the game.

If the Red Sox had a park large enough to accommodate all the fans who wanted to see this contest, about 100,000 would have been on hand.

The box score:

| NEW YORK (A.) | ab | r. | h. | po. | a. | e. | BOSTON (A.) | ab | r. | h. | po. | a. | e. |
|---|---|---|---|---|---|---|---|---|---|---|---|---|---|
| Coleman, 2b | 5 | 0 | 1 | 2 | 2 | 0 | D. Dmgio, cf | 4 | 0 | 0 | 4 | 0 | 0 |
| Rizutto, ss | 4 | 1 | 1 | 4 | 2 | 0 | Pesky, 3b | 5 | 0 | 2 | 1 | 0 | 0 |
| Henrich, 1b | 4 | 0 | 0 | 7 | 2 | 0 | Williams, lf | 5 | 1 | 2 | 2 | 0 | 0 |
| J. D'M'gio, cf | 3 | 2 | 2 | 6 | 0 | 0 | Stephens, ss | 4 | 0 | 1 | 2 | 4 | 0 |
| Berra, c | 4 | 0 | 0 | 4 | 1 | 0 | Doerr, 2b | 3 | 2 | 1 | 4 | 1 | 0 |
| Johnson, 3b | 3 | 0 | 0 | 0 | 1 | 0 | G'dman, 1b | 4 | 0 | 2 | 4 | 1 | 0 |
| Lindell, lf | 3 | 1 | 0 | 4 | 0 | 0 | Zarilla, rf | 3 | 0 | 1 | 1 | 0 | 0 |
| Woodling, lf | 0 | 0 | 0 | 0 | 0 | 0 | Batts, c | 3 | 1 | 1 | 9 | 0 | 0 |
| Bauer, rf | 4 | 1 | 3 | 0 | 0 | 0 | M'D'mott, p | 3 | 0 | 0 | 0 | 2 | 0 |
| Reynolds, p | 4 | 0 | 1 | 0 | 0 | 0 | ªTebbets | 1 | 0 | 1 | 0 | 0 | 0 |
| Page, p | 0 | 0 | 0 | 0 | 0 | 0 | ᵇStringer | 0 | 0 | 0 | 0 | 0 | 0 |
| Total | 34 | 5 | 8 | 27 | 8 | 0 | Total | 35 | 4 | 11 | 27 | 8 | 0 |

ªSingled for McDermott in ninth.
ᵇRan for Tebbets in ninth.

| | | | |
|---|---|---|---|
| New York | 032 | 000 | 000—5 |
| Boston | 000 | 200 | 011—4 |

Runs batted in—Bauer 3, J. DiMaggio 2, Zarilla, Batts, Doerr, Tebbetts.

Three-base hit—Batts. Home runs—Bauer, J. DiMaggio, Doerr. Sacrifice—D. DiMaggio. Double plays—Rizutto and Henrich; Berra and Coleman. Left on bases—New York 9, Boston 8. Bases on balls—Off Reynolds 3, McDermott 3. Struck out—By Reynolds 3, McDermott 9. Hits—Off Reynolds 11 in 8 innings (none out in 9th), Page 0 in 1. Winner—Reynolds (8–1), Loser—McDermott (2–1). Umpires—Summers, Stevens, Grieve and Honochirk. Time of game—2:28. Attendance—36,228.

---

June 30, 1949

### *DiMaggio Hits 2 Homers as Yanks Win; Dodgers, Giants Triumph*

## RED SOX OVERCOME BY BOMBERS, 9 TO 7

### Joe DiMaggio Twice Hits for Circuit, His Second Homer Deciding for Yanks

## BOSTON GAINS 7–1 MARGIN

### But Stengel's Men Draw Even in 7th Frame as Woodling Drives a 3-Run Double

#### By LOUIS EFFRAT

*Special to THE NEW YORK TIMES.*

BOSTON, June 29—Joe DiMaggio turned apparent defeat into a victory for the Yankees over the Red Sox at Fenway Park today, and in this hotbed of Red Sox rooters the crowd of 29,563 vociferously accorded the Jolter his due.

Playing in his second game of the season, Joe, hero of last night's triumph, repeated the role today, smashing two homers, his second and third, and driving in four runs as the Bombers beat the Bosox, 9–7.

The home side knocked out Tommy Byrne in the opening round and hammered Cuddles Marshall, his successor, until, as early as the fourth, Boston enjoyed a 7–1 advantage. With Ellis Kinder going for the Red Sox, it certainly looked like an easy conquest for Joe McCarthy's powerhouse. The Yankees appeared lethargic and quite ready to drop.

#### Inspires His Club

But DiMaggio aroused his mates in the fifth when, following passes to Phil Rizutto and Tommy Henrich, after two out, the Clipper drove a long four-bagger into the net in left center. This made it 7–4 and the New Yorkers were far from home, but the inspiration that Joe gave his club was precious.

Joe DiMaggio          203

In due time, the Yankees routed Kinder and tied the score at the expense of Tex Hughson with a three-run outburst in the seventh as Gene Woodling doubled with the bases filled. Thus, it was a 7–7 game when DiMaggio came up in the eighth. There were two out and none on when the Clipper struck the pay-off blow.

Here, at the Fenway, the left field wall is forty feet high. Also there is a twenty-foot net above it. DiMaggio, taking a fancy to Southpaw Earl Johnson's offering, promptly slammed it over the netting, into the street. This one was labeled "homer" from the instant of contact, a truly tremendous clout.

## Squeezes Johnston Home

The Yankees tallied another run in the ninth when, with the bases loaded and two out, Rizutto pushed a perfect bunt-single to the right of the mound, squeezing home Billy Johnson. The New Yorkers did not need that tally, but Lefty Joe Page, fourth and victorious hurler for Casey Stengel, was happy to have it.

Page, who followed Byrne, Marshall and Spec Shea on the firing line, took over at the start of the seventh and twirled three scoreless innings to achieve his sixth triumph of the campaign. Johnson, taking over for Boston in the eighth, was the loser.

The Yankees scored in the first on opening back-to-back doubles by Jerry Coleman and Rizutto, but the Red Sox rebounded with four as they greeted Byrne with successive doubles by Ted Williams, Vern Stephens and Bobby Doerr. Byrne was wild, too, walking three men before he was removed for Marshall.

In the second, Williams, taking advantage of the special shift, bunted safely, and Stephen followed with his seventeenth homer of the year. Coleman's wild throw helped the Sox to the run which made it 7–1 in the fourth. The situation was desperate, but before long DiMaggio asserted himself.

## Freak Double Play

A freak double play saved the Yankees in the first. With the bases filled, Kinder slammed a hot liner off Marshall's glove. The ball then hit second base, caromed off Coleman's glove and Rizutto scooped it up. The Scooter stepped on the bag and fired to Henrich for the twin killing.

Yogi Berra suffered a split nail on the little finger of his right hand in the second, the result of a foul tip by Billy Goodman. Yogi retired and Charley Silvera took over, but Berra is expected back tomorrow.

Rizutto, by the way, continues to field sensationally and contribute timely hits. He bobbed up with three gems today.

Aside from a bit of muscular stiffness, DiMaggio was all right following last night's sensational debut. . . . Bases on balls were cheap today, the Yankees getting ten and the Red Sox eight.

The box score:

| NEW YORK (A.) | | | | | | | BOSTON (A.) | | | | | | |
|---|---|---|---|---|---|---|---|---|---|---|---|---|---|
| | ab | r. | h. | po. | a. | e. | | ab | r. | h. | po. | a. | e. |
| Coleman, 2b | 5 | 1 | 1 | 2 | 4 | 1 | D. DiM'io, cf | 4 | 1 | 1 | 2 | 0 | 0 |
| Rizutto, ss | 4 | 2 | 3 | 3 | 4 | 0 | Pesky, 3b | 5 | 0 | 0 | 3 | 0 | 1 |
| Henrich, 1b | 5 | 1 | 0 | 12 | 1 | 0 | Williams, lf | 5 | 3 | 3 | 3 | 0 | 0 |
| J. DiM'gio, cf | 5 | 2 | 2 | 5 | 0 | 0 | Stephens, ss | 3 | 2 | 2 | 3 | 3 | 0 |

| | | | | | | | | | | | | | | |
|---|---|---|---|---|---|---|---|---|---|---|---|---|---|---|
| Berra, c | 1 | 0 | 0 | 0 | 0 | 0 | | Doerr, 2b | 5 | 1 | 2 | 4 | 3 | 0 |
| Silvera, c | 3 | 1 | 0 | 1 | 0 | 0 | | Goodman, 1b | 3 | 0 | 0 | 7 | 0 | 0 |
| W. J'nson, 3b | 4 | 2 | 2 | 0 | 2 | 0 | | Zarilla, rf | 4 | 0 | 1 | 3 | 0 | 0 |
| Woodling, lf | 3 | 0 | 2 | 1 | 0 | 0 | | Tebbets, ᶜ | 2 | 0 | 1 | 2 | 0 | 0 |
| Mapes, rf | 3 | 0 | 0 | 2 | 0 | 0 | | Kinder, p | 2 | 0 | 0 | 0 | 0 | 0 |
| Bauer, rf | 0 | 0 | 0 | 0 | 0 | 0 | | Hughson, p | 0 | 0 | 0 | 0 | 0 | 0 |
| Byrne, p | 0 | 0 | 0 | 0 | 0 | 0 | | ᶜHitchcock | 1 | 0 | 0 | 0 | 0 | 0 |
| Marshall, p | 2 | 0 | 0 | 0 | 3 | 0 | | E. Johnson, p | 0 | 0 | 0 | 0 | 1 | 0 |
| ᵃKeller | 1 | 0 | 0 | 0 | 0 | 0 | | | | | | | | |
| Shea, p | 0 | 0 | 0 | 0 | 0 | 0 | | | | | | | | |
| ᵇKryhoski | 0 | 0 | 0 | 0 | 0 | 0 | | | | | | | | |
| Page, p | 1 | 0 | 0 | 1 | 1 | 0 | | | | | | | | |
| Total | 37 | 9 | 10 | 27 | 15 | 1 | | Total | 34 | 7 | 10 | 27 | 7 | 1 |

ᵃFlied out for Marshall in sixth.
ᵇWalked for Shea in seventh.
ᶜFlied out for Hughson in seventh.

New York        100 030 311—9
Boston            420 100 000—7

Runs batted in—Rizzuto, 2, Williams, Stephens 3, Doerr, Tebbets, J. DiMaggio 4, Woodling 3.

Two-base hits—Coleman, Rizzuto 2, Woodling, Williams, Stephens, Doerr. Home runs—J. DiMaggio 2, Stephens. Stolen base—Tebbets. Sacrifices—Woodling, Kinder. Double plays—Marshall, Coleman, Rizzuto and Henrich; Coleman, Rizzuto and Henrich. Left on bases—New York 12, Boston 9. Bases on balls—Off Kinder 3, Hughson 5, E. Johnson 2, Byrne 3, Marshall 4, Shea 1. Struck out—By Kinder 1, Johnson 1. Hits—Off Kinder 6 in 5 innings (none out in sixth), Hughson 1 2, Johnson 3 in 2, Byrne 3 in 2-3, Marshall 6 in 4 2-3, Shea 0 in 1, Page 1 in 3. Wild pitch—Marshall. Passed ball—Berra. Winner—Page (6–3), Loser—E. Johnson (3–5). Umpires—Stevens, Grieve and Honochick and Summers. Time of game—3:05. Attendance—29,563.

---

July 1, 1949

### *DiMaggio's 4th Homer Beats Red Sox Again; Dodgers Bow: Giants Drop Two*

## DRIVE WITH TWO ON WINS FOR YANKS, 6–3

### DiMaggio's Blast Off Parnell in 7th Defeats Red Sox Third Time in Row

## RASCHI CAPTURES NO. 12

# Big Right-Hander Goes Route Although Reached for 12 Hits—Rizutto Hurt

## By LOUIS EFFRAT

*Special to THE NEW YORK TIMES.*

BOSTON, June 30—Proceeding on the theory that a homer-a-day will keep Dr. George E. Bennett away, Joltin' Joe DiMaggio, the no-longer-ailing pro of the Yankees, provided the winning margin today, as Casey Stengel's men made it three in a row over the Red Sox. With Big Vic Raschi in the box, the clean sweep of this vital set was completed with a 6–3 victory of the now thoroughly cooled-off Bosox at Fenway Park.

DiMaggio's contribution was a tremendous homer in the seventh, following successive singles by Snuffy Stirnweiss and Tommy Henrich. The three-run blow against Southpaw Mel Parnell was unquestionably his hardest-hit drive since DiMaggio, after missing sixty-five games, returned to the Yankees' line-up.

### Blasts 3-And-2 Pitch

The three four-bagger the Yankee Clipper fashioned in the first two games were tagged well enough, but these were dwarfed alongside his latest. With the count at 3-and-2, DiMaggio's vicious cut sent the ball screaming, a high liner to left. It cleared the net, rammed a light tower and bounced back on the field.

The Ladies' Day crowd (25,237 paid) voiced its admiration, if not approval of the homer, the importance of which was emphasized in the home half of the seventh, when the Red Sox tallied once. For prior to DiMaggio's wallop, the Yankees were clinging to a precarious 3–2 edge.

Raschi, earning his twelfth triumph of the year, fell behind in the first. Dom DiMaggio walked and stopped at second on Johnny Pesky's single to center. Ted Williams rapped into a double play, Dom reaching third, and scoring when Vern Stephens slashed a single off Billy Johnson's glove. The visitors tied it in the third, only because of Parnell's wildness. A walk, single and another walk, along with a wild pitch, netting a run.

### Parnell Falls Behind

Parnell, seeking his eleventh victory, was solved for two more in the fourth on Johnny Lindell's double, a run-scoring single by Hank Bauer, who went to second on the throw-in, and a single to center by Raschi. Billy Goodman's double and a single by Birdie Tebbetts brought the Red Sox to within a run of the leaders in the sixth.

Then the Jolter supplied the knockout punch. That Raschi needed this help was proved in the home half of the seventh, when singles by Dom DiMaggio, Pesky and Stephens produced a run. Bobby Doerr's single filled the bases, whereupon Goodman hit into a double play. The Red Sox vigorously protested that Goodman was safe at first but to no avail.

Raschi was reached for twelve hits, three more than the Yankees made against Parnell, Joe Dobson and Tex Hughson. However, Vic managed to keep Williams hitless in five trips. It was the first time this year Ted has gone 5-to-0 in a game.

And so the Yankees left Boston, convinced that they had done a good job, deflating the ambitious Red Sox, who had captured ten of eleven before the New Yorkers dropped into town.

1949 All-Star Game: Joe DiMaggio scores the second run for the American League on a single by Eddie Robinson of the Senators. The catcher is Andy Seminick of the Phillies. (THE NEW YORK TIMES)

## Rizutto Suffers Cramp

Phil Rizutto had a double-date with the doctors today. This morning he had his head X-rayed because of pains and dizziness which followed Tuesday night's collision with Pesky. The results were negative. Suddenly, in the last half of the first, the Scooter developed a cramp in his right wrist and forearm. He immediately went to Massachusetts General Hospital to be examined by Dr. William Sweet, neurologist specialist.

An electro-encephtogram disclosed no blood clot and Dr. Sweet said Rizutto's condition—he still had a tremor in his right arm—might be post-traumatic as a result of his collision with Pesky. Phil did not accompany the Yankees to Washington tonight. Instead, he returned to New York to be examined by the club physician, Dr. Sidney Gaynor. Whether Rizutto joins the team at Griffith Stadium will depend on Dr. Gaynor's findings.


This was quite an inaugural set for Joe DiMaggio. He slammed four homers and a single in eleven attempts, drove in nine runs and caught thirteen flies.


The box score:

| | ab | r. | h. | po. | a. | e. | | ab | r. | h. | po. | a. | e. |
|---|---|---|---|---|---|---|---|---|---|---|---|---|---|
| | \|**NEW YORK (A.)** | | | | | | \|**BOSTON (A.)** | | | | | |
| Cole'n, 2b | 5 | 0 | 2 | 3 | 2 | 0 | D. DiM'o, cf | 4 | 2 | 1 | 5 | 0 | 0 |
| Rizutto, ss | 1 | 0 | 0 | 0 | 0 | 0 | Pesky, 3b | 3 | 0 | 2 | 0 | 5 | 0 |
| Stirnw's, 2b | 3 | 1 | 1 | 4 | 4 | 0 | Williams, lf | 5 | 0 | 0 | 1 | 0 | 0 |
| Henrich, 1b | 4 | 1 | 1 | 0 | 1 | 0 | Stephens, ss | 4 | 0 | 2 | 3 | 2 | 0 |
| J. DiMag'o, cf | 3 | 1 | 1 | 2 | 0 | 0 | Doerr, 2b | 4 | 0 | 2 | 6 | 4 | 0 |
| Johnson, 3b | 4 | 0 | 0 | 1 | 2 | 0 | Goodman, 1b | 4 | 1 | 2 | 8 | 0 | 0 |
| Lindell, lf | 3 | 1 | 2 | 3 | 0 | 0 | Zarilla, rf | 4 | 0 | 1 | 1 | 0 | 0 |
| Woodling, lf | 0 | 0 | 0 | 0 | 0 | 0 | Tebbets, c | 4 | 0 | 1 | 3 | 1 | 0 |
| Bauer, rf | 3 | 1 | 1 | 1 | 0 | 0 | Parnell, p | 3 | 0 | 1 | 0 | 2 | 0 |
| Mapes, rf | 1 | 0 | 0 | 0 | 0 | 0 | Dobson, p | 0 | 0 | 0 | 0 | 0 | 0 |
| Silvera, c | 4 | 0 | 0 | 4 | 0 | 0 | [a]Hitchcock | 1 | 0 | 0 | 0 | 0 | 0 |
| Raschi, p | 3 | 1 | 1 | 0 | 1 | 0 | Hughson, p | 0 | 0 | 0 | 0 | 0 | 0 |
| Total | 34 | 6 | 9 | 27 | 10 | 0 | Total | 36 | 3 | 12 | 27 | 14 | 0 |

[a]Lined out for Dobson in eighth.

New York        001 200 300—6
Boston          100 001 100—3

Runs batted in—Stephens 2, Bauer, Raschi, Tebbetts, J. DiMaggio 3.

Two-base hits—Goodman, Zarilla, Lindell. Home run—J. DiMaggio. Stolen base—Coleman. Double plays—Henrich, Coleman and Henrich; Stirnweiss and Henrich; Stirnweiss, Coleman and Henrich; Stephens, Doerr and Goodman 2. Left on bases—New York 8, Boston 10. Bases on balls—Off Parnell 6, Raschi 4. Struck out—By Parnell 3, Dobson 1, Raschi 4. Hits—Off Parnell 9 in 6 1–3 innings, Dobson 0 in 1 2–3, Hughson 0 in 1. Hit by pitcher—By Parnell (J. DiMaggio). Wild pitches—By Parnell, Raschi. Winner—Raschi (12–2), Loser—Parnell (10–1). Umpires—Grieve, Honochick, Summers and Stevens. Time of game—2:36. Attendance—25,257.

October 2, 1949

### YANKS WIN, 5–4, GO INTO FINAL DAY EVEN WITH RED SOX; DODGERS BEATEN BUT ARE SURE OF TIE AS CARDS LOSE; COLUMBIA DEFEATS HARVARD, 14–7; NAVY TOPS PRINCETON

## HOME RUNS DECIDES

### Lindell's Clout in the 8th Sets Back Boston Before 69,551 in Stadium

# YANKS ONCE TRAIL BY 4–0

## Page Pitches Brilliantly in Relief after Wobbly Start—DiMaggio Doubles, Singles

### By JOHN DREBINGER

And so, it develops, those battered Bombers with their countless aches and bruises, weren't ready to be rolled into a boneyard after all.

At least, on this, the final day of the American League championship season, they are still standing, and what is more, they are standing as well as their formidable rivals, the hale and hearty Bosox.

For, with Johnny Lindell exploding an eighth-inning homer to break a four-all tie, Casey Stengel's Yankees brought down Joe McCarthy's Red Sox in the penultimate encounter of the campaign in the stadium yesterday by a score of 5 to 4, and with that the raging pennant race once more goes into deadlock.

Both the Yanks and Bosox stand tied this morning at 96 victories against 57 defeats and everything now hangs on the slender thread of a single game which these two keen foes will play this afternoon. Vic Raschi, the Bombers' 20-game winner, will oppose Ellis Kinder, Boston's 23-game hurler.

### Soul-Stirring Spectacle

It was a soul-stirring spectacle those Bombers put on display yesterday to electrify a gathering of 69,551 and bring to an almost story-book climax baseball's long awaited Joe DiMaggio day.

In an amazing hour-long ceremony before the game, close to $50,000 in gifts had been showered upon Joltin' Joe, and the Clipper, in response to this overwhelming tribute, forgot all about his convalescence and played the full nine innings.

He played them well, too, despite the fact that he is still far from having recovered from the siege of virus infection which laid him down three weeks ago.

He paced the first Yankee tally home in the fourth inning with a double, and then contributed a single in a rousing fifth-inning rally in which the Bombers scored twice to route McCarthy's redoubtable 25-game winner, Mel Parnell, and plunge the battle into a deadlock.

But in the end it was that most extraordinary relief specialist, perhaps of all time, Joe Page, and the unsung Johnny Lindell who were the heroes of this epic struggle that now enables the Yanks to carry the flag fight right down to the final day.

Coming to Allie Reynolds' relief in the third inning, the famed southpaw for a few moments threatened to envelop the entire show in complete disaster. For though the mighty Bosox came up with only four hits for the complete game, they almost duplicated their extraordinary performance of Friday in Washington when they brought down the Senators, 11 to 9, although outhit, 18 to 5.

They had clipped Reynolds for a run in the first inning and in the third they made off with three more tallies on just one puny single and five walks. Reynolds gave up three of these, along with the hit, while Page yielded the last two, which forced in the second and third runs of the inning.

That gave the Bosox a 4-to-0 lead behind their flashy southpaw Parnell, but with the fourth the Yanks ripped into the lefty for two runs. They grabbed two more in the fifth with an outburst that brought Joe Dobson to the mound.

And there the struggle hung until the strapping Lindell leaned into a fast ball to send the white pill hurtling into the left field stands in the eighth inning.

There were two out and the bases empty as Long John came to the plate in the last of the eighth. Wallowing in a season-long slump with a meager .229 batting average, the big fellow never had rated very high in Stengel's book throughout the summer.

In fact, he only started in left field in this game because the opposition was pitching a southpaw, and usually when a right-hander appears Lindell vanishes.

But Stengel, riding perhaps a hunch, allowed him to remain when Dobson replaced Parnell. Then, too, the big good-natured Californian had shown earlier in the day he was out to make amends for a lack-luster season by connecting with two sharp singles, one of which helped in the fourth-inning scoring.

And then, all in a twinkling of an eye, Lindell was to put all his power into a drive that eventually was to carry the day. It was only his sixth homer of the year and the first since July 31, but to this hour it was easily the most important blow yet delivered by a Yankee.

Fortified behind this margin, Page then was to turn on some of his most dazzling relief hurling of the year. He already had, in fact, made an astonishing about-face after his wabbly start in the third. For, from the point of those two run-scoring passes, the southpaw was to allow only one hit to the Bosox the rest of the way.

## Keeps Williams in Check

The renowned Ted Williams, whose single had helped the Sox to their first inning tally, got nothing but two pop-ups off Joe's tricky delivery, although the second one was a pop that carried Li'l Phil Rizutto almost into left field before the indomitable Yankee shortstop snared the ball.

It was Page's sixtieth mound appearance of the year and the victory was his thirteenth against eight setbacks. Needless to say, he'll be ready to do it again today if exigencies demand it.

Of the games in which Page has appeared this year the Yankees have triumphed in forty-two, lost seventeen and tied one. And his relief job yesterday of six and two-thirds innings was his longest stretch of the year.

They had scarcely cleared away the carloads of gifts that had been showered upon DiMaggio than the Red Sox, even though they had joined in the ceremonies honoring their distinguished adversary, served notice that from now on they meant strictly business.

They grabbed a tally in the opening round, although it was a peculiar lapse in control on the part of Reynolds that gave the Bosox a material lift. Wahoo, though he issued no walks in the round, did unfurl two wild pitches and the first of these proved very costly.

Dom DiMaggio opened by slicing a single into right. He was forced by Johnny Pesky, who slapped a grounder squarely into Reynolds' hands. But there was no checking Ted Williams, who banged a single down the first-base line.

In fact, luck rode here a bit with the Yanks on this play. For as the ball skimmed off Tommy Henrich's outstretched glove, it collided with the huge frame of first-base umpire Cal Hubbard and that stopped traffic in all directions.

Had this not happened the ball likely would have gone on down the foul line for a possible double with Pesky surely reaching third. Instead, Johnny had to pull up at second.

## Advances the Runners

However, Reynolds spoiled all the advantage of himself when he cut loose with a wild pitch in tossing to Vern Stephens. That one did advance the runners to second and third, and a moment later Pesky tallied as Stephens lifted a long fly to Johnny Lindell in left.

On the heels of that came still another wild pitch that advanced Williams to third, but Reynolds finally got a grip on the situation and fanned Bobby Doerr for the third out.

In the same inning the Yanks threatened briefly to get this tally back when Phil Rizutto worked Parnell for a pass and moved around to third on successive infield outs by Henrich and Yogi Berra.

Then DiMaggio, J., stepped to the plate and the cheers that greeted the Clipper earlier during the fan day ceremonies were as nothing compared with the thunderous welcome that attended his official return to action.

It was Jolting Joe's first appearance in the Yankee line-up since Sept. 18, when he was felled by a virus infection that was to take him out just when the race was reaching its most critical stage.

The Clipper tried hard to give it all he had, but two afternoons of light batting practice was all he had had to prepare himself for this big test and apparently he wasn't quite ready yet. He wound up striking out.

Then, after an uneventful second inning, came a harrowing third, when the Bombers practically stood helplessly in the field while the pitching of Reynolds and Page went completely haywire. Five bases on balls, surrounding one puny little pop fly single, gave the Bosox three more runs.

With one down, Reynolds walked Pesky, Williams and Stephens to fill the bases. Then Doerr lifted a pop fly in short right that fell just beyond Jerry Coleman's reach for a single and Pesky tallied while the bases still remained jammed.

That was all for Reynolds and Page emerged from the bullpen. But the tireless southpaw, whose magic skill suddenly seemed to leave him several weeks ago when he bogged down with three damaging defeats, still seemed to experience trouble getting back on the beam.

While Stengel and practically every Yankee fan in the packed arena squirmed in agony, Page walked Al Zarilla to force one run in. Then he delivered four successive balls to Bill Goodman to push over another.

With that he finally squared off to fan Birdie Tebbetts and Parnell, ending the long-drawn-out inning, but the Yanks were now four runs in arrears and, with Parnell zooming along nicely, the situation looked pretty hopeless.

## The Bombers Lash Back

However, the Bombers weren't folding by any means, and in the fourth they lashed back to score two runs on three solid hits. Fittingly, though, Joe DiMaggio launched this assault on Parnell with a line drive that went into the right-field stands on one hop for a ground-rule-double.

Billy Johnson struck out, but Hank Bauer slammed a single into left, scoring the Clipper. Then Lindell, who had come up with the first Yankee hit in the second, followed with another line single and Bauer tore around to third. Coleman followed with a fly to Dom DiMaggio in center and Bauer counted.

Half of Parnell's lead had been shot away. In the fifth the other half went and with it went Parnell as well. Sharp and swift moved the Yankee attack in this round.

Rizutto opened with a single to center. Henrich hammered one over second and when Berra rifled another one-baser into center Rizutto streaked over the plate. McCarthy here called a halt and waved Dobson up from the bullpen.

## Roar of Fans Deafening

Joe DiMaggio greeted the veteran right-hander with a hard slam to the mound that caromed off Dobson's glove for the Yank's fourth successive single. It filled the bases with still nobody out and the noise in the arena at this point was deafening.

But Dobson still was to prove a rugged opponent. He got Johnson to ground into a twin-killing, Doerr to Stephens to Goodman, and though Berra winged home with the tying run of the battle, the double-play did wreck the rally. For Bauer went out on a long fly to Dom DiMaggio in center and the inning was over.

The box score:

| | BOSTON (A.) | | | | | | | NEW YORK (A.) | | | | | |
|---|---|---|---|---|---|---|---|---|---|---|---|---|---|
| | ab | r. | h. | po. | a. | e. | | ab | r. | h. | po. | a. | e. |
| D. DiMag., cf | 5 | 0 | 1 | 5 | 0 | 0 | Rizutto, ss | 2 | 1 | 1 | 4 | 5 | 0 |
| Pesky, 3b | 3 | 2 | 0 | 0 | 2 | 0 | Henrich, 1b | 3 | 1 | 1 | 8 | 0 | 0 |
| Williams, lf | 3 | 1 | 1 | 1 | 0 | 0 | Berra, c | 4 | 0 | 2 | 8 | 0 | 0 |
| Stephens, ss | 2 | 1 | 0 | 2 | 2 | 0 | J. DiMag., cf | 4 | 1 | 2 | 2 | 0 | 0 |
| Doerr, 2b | 4 | 0 | 2 | 2 | 1 | 0 | Johnson, 3b | 3 | 0 | 0 | 1 | 2 | 0 |
| Zarilla, rf | 2 | 0 | 0 | 0 | 0 | 0 | Brown, 3b | 1 | 0 | 0 | 0 | 0 | 0 |
| G'man, 1b | 3 | 0 | 0 | 7 | 0 | 0 | Bauer, rf | 3 | 1 | 1 | 2 | 0 | 0 |
| Tebbetts, c | 3 | 0 | 0 | 7 | 0 | 0 | Mapes, rf | 1 | 0 | 0 | 0 | 0 | 0 |
| Parnell, p | 2 | 0 | 0 | 0 | 2 | 0 | Lindell, lf | 4 | 1 | 3 | 2 | 0 | 0 |
| Dobson, p | 1 | 0 | 0 | 0 | 1 | 0 | Coleman, 2b | 4 | 0 | 1 | 0 | 2 | 0 |
| ªBatts | 1 | 0 | 0 | 0 | 0 | 0 | Reynolds, p | 0 | 0 | 0 | 0 | 1 | 0 |
| | | | | | | | Page, p | 4 | 0 | 1 | 0 | 1 | 0 |
| Total | 29 | 4 | 4 | 24 | 8 | 0 | Total | 33 | 5 | 12 | 27 | 11 | 0 |

ªGrounded out for Dobson in ninth.

| Boston | 103 000 000—4 |
|---|---|
| New York | 000 220 01×—5 |

Runs batted in—Stephens, Doerr, Zarilla, Goodman, Bauer, Coleman, Berra, Lindell.

Two-base hits—J. DiMaggio. Home run—Lindell. Sacrifice—Rizutto. Double plays—Parnell, Stephens and Goodman; Coleman, Rizutto and Henrich; Doerr, Stephens and Goodman; Rizutto and Henrich. Left on bases—Boston 6, New York 7. Bases on balls—Off Parnell 2, Reynolds 4, Page 3. Struck out—By Reynolds 2, Page 5, Parnell 4, Dobson 3. Hits—Off Reynolds 3 in 2 1–3 innings, Page 1 in 6 2–3, Parnell 8 in 4 (none out in 5th), Dobson 4 in 4. Hit by pitcher—By Page (Zarilla). Wild pitches—Reynolds 2. Winner—Page (13–8), Loser—Dobson (14–12). Umpires—Summers, Hubbard, Rommel, Berry, Hurley and Honochick. Time of game—2:30. Attendance—59,551.

# DIMAGGIO HONORED BY FANS, PLAYERS

## Yanks Star Gets Many Gifts—Thousands of Dollars Go to Heart, Cancer Funds

### By LOUIS EFFRAT

A great day for a great guy, that's what it was, as his friends in the stands and his rivals on the field paid tribute to Joe DiMaggio yesterday at the Stadium. For a solid hour before the game the Yankee Clipper, wan and weak after his recent siege, heard himself extolled and found himself surrounded by a small mountain of gifts, ranging from 300 quarts of ice cream to a super-special speedboat.

It was "Joe DiMaggio day" and a memorable occasion it was. Certainly, the Clipper, himself, will never forget it. Nor will the unfortunates who will benefit from the cash contributions. Mel Allen, the master-of-ceremonies, and Mayor William O'Dwyer explained that, on Joltin' Joe's insistence, all money gifts will be donated to the New York Heart Fund and the Damon Runyon Memorial Cancer Fund. Some $7,500 with more rolling in, will be turned over to these agencies.

## Tribute to His Mates

A warm, humble man, who long ago won the admiration of the entire baseball world, DiMaggio would have given anything to have been able to stand aside, honoring another player. Those who know him know that this is not an affectation, but a true picture of the man.

But he had to go through with the ceremonies and, like the champion he is, handled himself admirably.

With simple eloquence, DiMaggio told how proud, how happy he was and lucky he was to be a Yankee.

"When I was in San Francisco Lefty O'Doul told me: 'Joe, don't let the big city scare you. New York is the friendliest town in the world.' This day proves it. I want to thank my fans, my friends, my manager, Casey Stengel, and my team-mates, the gamest, fightingest bunch that ever lived. And I want to thank the good Lord for making me a Yankee."

All the Yankees and Red Sox were assembled at home plate and one of the surprise gifts was a plaque, autographed by all the Red Sox. This was especially appreciated by the Clipper and the crowd, and Joe did not forget them. Of Joe McCarthy and his charges, DiMaggio said:

"They're a great bunch, too, and if we don't win the pennant I'm happy that they will."

Now grab a chair, and listen, but don't dare hold your breath until the list—partial at that—of DiMaggio's gifts is completed:

## A list of the Gifts

An automobile, a boat, two watches, chain, knife, wallet, cuff links, gold buckle, tie pin and cuff links, art work, trophy, two television sets, rifle, bronze plaque, $100 hat, golf bag, electric blanket, radio, thermos jug set, gold key chain, silver loving cup, phonograph records, driving glasses, sun glasses, candy, shirts, clock, oil painting, carpeting, roaster, gold money clip, Medal of Honor, statuette, neckerchief and clip, mattress and springs, cheese, potatoes, oranges, walnuts, lemonade, lima beans, paper weight, wallet, metal elephant, portrait, dozen golf balls, ash tray, tote bag, cocker spaniel, traveling bag, alarm clock, silver money clip, many ties, taxi service.

One deserving youth, to be selected from among the thousands of Yankee juniors, will be awarded a four-year scholarship to any New York university, another donation from "Joe DiMaggio Day."

Ovations for DiMaggio were tremendous throughout the day, but none was bigger than the one that greeted his fourth-inning two-bagger to right. That was the blow that started a Yankee two-run rally.

Mrs. Rosalie DiMaggio, Joe's mother, here from San Francisco, was not forgotten; she received an automobile and flowers. Little Joe, the Clipper's son, got a bike, electric trains and other gifts. In all, it was estimated, about $50,000 might cover the cost of everything.

Little Joe was indeed proud of his famous dad. But the youngster could hardly keep his eyes off the new bike. And who could blame the lad?

Mayor O'Dwyer spoke and Phil Brito and Ethel Merman sang and a good time was had by all.

Many may be wondering what DiMaggio is going to do with the 300 quarts of ice cream. It will be sent to a children's institution.

### Gets Ball From Schulte

Before the game, Little Joe approached John Schulte, former Yankee coach, now with the Red Sox. "Aw, why did you have to leave the Yankees?" he frowned, and in the next breath, "Could I have a ball?" He got it.

The press box was overloaded with correspondents from everywhere. Arlie Latham, in charge of the box, was asked admittance by a Japanese writer. This was all right with Arlie, until the gentleman wanted to bring his interpreter along.

Nine-year-old Allen Levy, up from Miami, represented the National Children's Cardiac Home, one of DiMaggio's favorite charities. In fact, the Jolter is honorary Mayor of Mending Hearts Village, home site of the institution.

June 21, 1950

## *Dodgers Rout Reds, Take First Place Undisputed; Giants, Yanks Win*

*Bombers Crush Indians, 8 to 2, DiMaggio Smashing 2,000 Hit*

### Single Sends In Woodling With Yanks' 7th Run—Lopat Registers Eighth Triumph, Halting Cleveland's 6-Game Streak

#### By ROSCOE McGOWEN

*Special to* THE NEW YORK TIMES.

CLEVELAND, June 20—The long-time mastery of chubby Ed Lopat over Cleveland still functioned to-night as he pitched the Yankees to an 8–2 victory for his eighth of the season, his third over the Indians this year and his twenty-fifth against them during his career.

Altogether, it was a lovely night for the Bombers, though not so enjoyable for the 52,733 fans who crowded the Cleveland stadium to see the affair.

In addition to snapping a six-game winning streak for Lou Boudreau's men, the New Yorkers' own Joe DiMaggio punched out the two-thousandth hit of his great career. The blow was a clean single through to left center off Marino Pieretti, third pitcher summoned by Boudreau, drove Gene Woodling home with the Yanks' seventh run in the seventh inning, and the ball was fielded by Larry Doby.

## Mapes Draws Pass

Joe walked home with the eighth run a little later, after Pieretti had walked two more Yankees and pitched two balls to Cliff Mapes. Big Al Benton completed the pass, which was charged to Pieretti.

Mapes came through with the first big blow of the game in the second inning when he whacked his fifth homer of the campaign over the right field fence in the wake of a single by Yogi Berra to give the Yankees a 2–0 lead.

Bob Lemon, ace of the Indians' staff, was the victim and Bob was knocked out in the third inning by DiMaggio's 1,999th hit, a looping single to center that drove in two runs of the four the Yankees scored in that frame.

The inning also produced two big rhubarbs, the first by the Indians, the second by the Yankees. Boudreau, Lemon and Jim Hegan all argued violently that DiMag had swung at a third strike, which Umpire Ed Hurley called a ball.

If Hurley was wrong, as the Indians claimed, it was a costly call, considering what DiMaggio did immediately thereafter. Joe's hit had been preceded by an opening pass to Lopat, singles by Phil Rizutto and Gene Woodling and a pass to Joe Collins.

After Dick Weik replaced Lemon, Berra dropped a pop fly safely into right center field for a single and Bobby Brown, after failing to bunt, looked at a third strike.

## Woodling Gets Double

Here came the second rhubarb. Mapes pulled back and hit a soft bounder toward the right of second base. Berra, directly in front of Joe Gordon, was charged with interference and called out, thus bringing Bill Dickey, Frankie Crosetti and Casey Stengel storming after Bill McKinley, who made the call.

After the argument, Weik went on to stop the Yankees until the end of the sixth, when he left for a pinch-hitter. Woodling doubled to left center off Pieretti and, with two out, scored on the historic DiMaggio single.

Lopat had little difficulty, stifling all Cleveland threats until two were out in the fifth. Then Bob Kennedy whaled his sixth homer of the season over the left center field fence for the first Indian run. They scored one in the sixth after having the bases filled with one out on Doby's opening single, a bad fielder's choice by brown and a pass to Ray Boone.

The run came in as Hegan grounded to Collins for the second out. Then Allie Clark, batting for Weik, fouled to Collins on the first pitch.

A small boy created a pleasant diversion as the Yankees took the field in the eighth. He ran out to center field, apparently got DiMaggio's autograph, then raced back, eluding a policeman, and ran into the Yankee dugout where the players welcomed him. The cop gave up the chase.

Lopat was Lemon's opponent in New York on June 4 when Eddie hurled a six-hit shutout.

Johnny Mize and Tommy Henrich returned from their visit to Phog Allen in Lawrence, Kan., some time

Joe DiMaggio being congratulated at the plate by Yogi Berra and Johnny Mize (36) after a first-inning homer, 1950. (ERNEST SISTO/THE NEW YORK TIMES)

before the game. Henrich said Allen had "found something," and had worked on him and "it felt better," but wasn't sure whether what the Kansas osteopath had discovered was in his knee or elsewhere.

Coach Jim Turner's father took a turn for the worse and Jim wasn't on hand as expected, remaining in Nashville, Tenn.

| NEW YORK (A.) | | | | | | | CLEVELAND (A.) | | | | | | |
|---|---|---|---|---|---|---|---|---|---|---|---|---|---|
| | ab. | r. | h. | po. | a. | e. | | ab. | r. | h. | po. | a. | e. |
| Rizutto, ss | 5 | 1 | 2 | 0 | 4 | 0 | Mitchell, lf | 5 | 0 | 2 | 1 | 0 | 0 |
| W'dling, lf | 5 | 2 | 2 | 4 | 0 | 0 | Kennedy, rf | 4 | 1 | 1 | 2 | 0 | 0 |
| Collins, 1b | 4 | 1 | 1 | 10 | 1 | 0 | Easter, 1b | 4 | 0 | 0 | 12 | 0 | 0 |
| DiM'gio., cf | 5 | 1 | 2 | 4 | 0 | 0 | Doby, cf | 2 | 1 | 1 | 2 | 0 | 1 |
| Berra, c | 4 | 1 | 2 | 4 | 0 | 0 | Rosen, 3b | 4 | 0 | 1 | 0 | 1 | 0 |
| Brown, 3b | 3 | 0 | 0 | 0 | 2 | 0 | Gordon, 2b | 3 | 0 | 0 | 3 | 7 | 0 |
| Mapes, rf | 3 | 1 | 2 | 1 | 0 | 0 | Boone, ss | 3 | 0 | 2 | 1 | 2 | 0 |
| Coleman, 2b | 4 | 0 | 1 | 3 | 5 | 0 | Hegan, c | 4 | 0 | 0 | 6 | 1 | 0 |
| Lopat, p | 3 | 1 | 0 | 1 | 0 | 0 | Lemon, p | 1 | 0 | 0 | 0 | 0 | 0 |
| | | | | | | | Welk, p | 1 | 0 | 0 | 0 | 0 | 0 |
| | | | | | | | a Clark | 1 | 0 | 0 | 0 | 0 | 0 |
| | | | | | | | Pieretti, p | 0 | 0 | 0 | 0 | 0 | 0 |
| | | | | | | | Benton, p | 0 | 0 | 0 | 0 | 0 | 0 |
| | | | | | | | b Murray | 1 | 0 | 0 | 0 | 0 | 0 |
| Total | 36 | 8 | 12 | 27 | 12 | 0 | Total | 33 | 2 | 7 | 27 | 12 | 1 |

[a]Fouled out for Welk in sixth.
[b]Grounded out for Benton in ninth.

| New York | 024 000 200—8 |
|----------|---------------|
| Cleveland | 000 011 000—2 |

Runs batted in—Mapes 3, Woodling, DiMaggio 4, Berra, Kennedy, Hegan.

Two-base hits—Woodling. Home runs—Mapes, Kennedy. Double plays—Gordon, Boone and Easter; Coleman, Rizutto, Coleman and Collins 2; Rosen, Gordon and Easter. Left on bases—New York 6. Cleveland 9. Bases on balls—Off Lopat 5, Lemon 2, Pieretti 3. Struck out—By Lopat 2, Lemon 1, Welk 4, Benton 1. Hits—Off Lemon 5 in 2 innings (none out in third), Welk 4 in 4, Pieretti 2 in 2–3, Benton 1 in 2 1–3. Winning pitcher—Lopat (8–4). Losing pitcher—Lemon (8–4). Umpires—Hurley, Honochick, McKinley and McGowan. Time of game—2:40. Attendance—52,733.

---

October 6, 1950

## *Yanks Beat Phils, 2–1, in 10th On a Home Run by DiMaggio*

### Reynolds Hurls Bombers Into 2–0 Lead in Games, Missing Shutout on Bad Hop—Series Shifts to Stadium Today

#### By JOHN DREBINGER

*Special to* THE NEW YORK TIMES

PHILADELPHIA, Oct. 5—For nine innings today under a cloudless sky, Ed Sawyer's Whiz Kids matched the mighty Yankees move for move and for a time it looked as if they did have all the world series answers. But in an unguarded moment, they overlooked the Bombers' mightiest weapon.

With the score deadlocked at 1–all, Joe DiMaggio, first up in the tenth inning and still seeking his first hit in the classic, leaned into a pitch delivered by Robin Roberts.

The ball streaked on a line into the upper deck of the densely packed left-field pavilion of Shibe Park and on the wings of that shot Casey Stengel's American League champions, behind fast-balling Allie Reynolds, brought down the Phillies in the second encounter of the series, 2 to 1.

It was a jolt that plunged the majority in a crowd of 32,660 deep in grief since it gave the vaunted Bombers a 2-to-0 lead in games as the series now swings to New York, where tomorrow at Yankee Stadium the third engagement will be played.

It was, though, again a low scoring mound duel, a far more rugged contest than yesterday's 1–0 opener. For where Vic Raschi had held the Phils virtually helpless with his two-hitter, they gave Reynolds a far more robust battle.

They clipped the Chief for seven hits, including a triple and three doubles, and several times appeared on the verge of breaking through. But the deeply tanned Oklahoman, a part Creek Indian, stoically held on to the end to nail down the victory and he even would have accomplished it in nine innings except for a crazily bounding ball that helped the Phils to their run.

A year ago Reynolds had tossed that sparkling two-hitter at the Dodgers to win the opener. Though not quite that sparkling, the Chief pitched perhaps an even more important triumph. For with two games in the sack, the New Yorkers are now halfway to the goal line and need only two more to stalk off with their thirteenth world series title.

Roberts, handsome dark-haired youth who last Sunday had pitched the Phils to the National League pennant over the Dodgers, did a stout job, too. The 24-year-old bonus righthander yielded ten blows, but none really hurt until the Clipper, with the count at two balls and one strike, rifled that shot into the stands with the deadly accuracy of a billiard expert banging the winning ball into a side pocket.

So amazingly did young Robin pitch that his team-mates made only four assists in the ten innings, one more than the world series record of three. Almost everything the Bombers hit went into the air, but one shot went just a little too far into the ether.

That was the one DiMaggio exploded for his seventh world series homer with startling effect. For in his first four trips to the plate the Clipper not only had failed to deliver a safe blow but never had got the ball beyond reach of the infield. Twice he had popped to the second baseman, the third time to the third sacker and his fourth attempts had ended in a foul pop-up into the first baseman's glove.

## Yanks Score in Second

Until that slip, Roberts fought back grimly. He had fallen a run behind in the second inning when a pass to Jerry Coleman and singles by Reynolds and Gene Woodling produced the first Yankee tally.

In the fifth the Phils, amid thunderous cheers, drew even with their first marker of the series on singles by Mike Goliat and Eddie Waitkus, the latter's a lucky shot that bounced over Coleman's head, and a long fly by Richie Ashburn. But once the DiMaggio circuit clout had put them behind again in the tenth the Philadelphians had nothing in rebuttal.

Jack Mayo, first up in the tenth as pinch-hitter for Roberts, drew a pass, the third off Reynolds. Though Waitkus advanced the runner on a sacrifice, that one more needed blow never was struck. Ashburn fouled out back of first and Dick Sisler, hero of that Sunday Flatbush triumph, went down swinging on a bad strike to round out his second hitless afternoon in the series.

As in the opener, the Yanks again made threatening gestures in the first inning without, however, accomplishing anything beyond giving the home folks a bit of a scare. Woodling led off by outgalloping an infield hit and after Phil Rizutto had fouled out behind the plate, Yogi Berra sliced a single into left for his first hit of the series.

That blow sent Woodling sprinting around to third, but Gene might just as well have pulled up a chair and sat it out. DiMaggio popped weakly to Goliat behind second base and Johnny Mize didn't even get it that far. His lofty shot was caught no farther than about ten feet from the plate by Andy Seminick.

## Phils Also Threatens Early

That left the crowd chortling with glee and in the lower half of the first there were more cheers when the Phils, who yesterday hadn't so much as put a runner on base before the fifth inning, had a fellow in scoring position with the second batter.

After Waitkus had grounded out, Ashburn lifted a pop fly in short right center. Since DiMaggio no longer races in for these with the speed of old, Hank Bauer tore over the turf and, with a last second slide, tried to make a sitting catch. Hank couldn't hold the ball and before he could unravel himself the fleet Ashburn was on second with a double.

Richie, however, might have saved himself the trouble, as he never got beyond the midway post, Sisler fanned and Del Ennis ended it with a grounder to the sure-handed Coleman.

In the second the Yanks struck for their first run and virtually did it from ambush. Roberts scarcely could have suspected anything when, with two out, he walked Coleman, for Reynolds was the next batter.

But the Yankee hurler confounded the Philly board of strategy no little when he slammed a single down the right field line, sweeping Coleman around to third. A moment later Woodling again came through with an infield hit to deep short.

## Hamner Tries for Forceout

Granny Hamner tried hard to flip the ball to second for a force play on Reynolds but it failed to arrive in time and with Coleman skimming over the plate the Bombers again were off to a one run lead.

In the same round the Phils tossed the gathering into a dither. With one down Hamner, who had finished out the regular season 21 for 0 and was seeking his first hit of the series, drove a triple into right center. DiMaggio retrieved the ball off the wall beneath the scoreboard.

It marked the first time in the series the Phils had advanced a runner to that outpost, but it again got them nothing. With the infield playing close, Reynolds induced Seminick to ground to Coleman for a putout at first, while Hamner remained glued to third, and Goliat ended the threat with an easy drive to DiMaggio in center.

Almost the same exasperating thing happened in the third when, again with only one out, Waitkus bashed a double to right, the ball landing squarely on the foul line. Ashburn this time fouled out to Berra and Sisler grounded to Coleman.

The Phils up to then had three clouts for a total of seven bases, yet they couldn't have kept themselves farther from a score had they remained in their hotel quarters.

But the Yanks were to get a taste of the same in the fourth. With one out of the way, Coleman doubled down the center of the fairway and Roberts, after running the count to Reynolds to three and two, lost him with a fourth ball.

Though the Yanks had the top of their batting order up, they also were to run into a stone wall of superlative pitching. Woodling lifted a high foul which Sisler hauled down in front of the left-field seats, Rizzuto lined to Ennis and this round was out of the way.

Still and all, the Yanks were in front and it wasn't until the fifth that the Phils gave the National League cohorts their first big moment of cheer when they broke through to deadlock the score at 1–all, with the gods of fortune lending a helping hand.

After Gehrig had opened with an infield hit on which the acrobatic Coleman made a spectacular stop, Roberts stalled the attack by popping into Reynolds' hands on an attempted sacrifice.

But Waitkus came through with his second hit in a row, a sharp grounder to Coleman which struck some obstruction and bounced over his head. It went for a single to right that hustled Goliat around to third and when Ashburn followed with a robust fly to left one might have thought that, from the terrific din, the blow had knocked William Penn's hat off down at City Hall.

## Goliat Streaks Over Plate

Actually, it was an easy catch for Woodling, but too far out for even the mightiest arm to prevent a score and as Goliat streaked for home the folks went wild with joy. The Phils had finally broken the ice and were standing on even terms with their formidable adversaries.

Joe DiMaggio        219

Also, it marked the first run off Reynolds in 16⅓ innings of world series competition, the Chief having blanked the Dodgers in 12⅓ innings last October.

From then on one could fairly fell the tension. In the sixth an expectant roar went up as Ennis, still hitless in the series, lifted a towering shot toward the wall in deep center, but DiMaggio, after a hard run, hauled down the ball at the base of the light tower 400 feet away.

In the eighth the Yanks produced shivers through the stands as they tore off two successive singles. With one down, Bobby Brown and Bauer smacked one-basers to left, putting runners on first and second, but though Stengel made one of his characteristic strategic moves, calling on Johnny Hopp to run for Brown, Johnny-the-Hopp didn't run far. He moved up to third and Bauer to second while Coleman was being retired at first and then just expired as Roberts coolly slipped a third strike past Reynolds for the third out.

## Hopes Rise in Ninth

Philly hopes rose in the ninth when, with one down, Hamner got his second extra base clout, a double to right center.

The next scheduled hitter was Ken Silvestri, second string receiver who had gone into the game after Seminick had vacated for a pinch-runner in the seventh. Sawyer, however, had other ideas and called on Dick Whitman to bat for his light hitting catcher.

But Stengel had a move to match this. He ordered the former Dodger intentionally passed and the Yanks' stonewall inner defense did the rest. Goliat drilled into a double play, Rizzuto to Coleman to Hopp, who was then covering first, and the Phils found themselves frustrated again.

Then came the Clipper's electrifying shot in the tenth and in a few minutes it was all over.

Outstanding, too, in the Yankee triumph was a spectacular play by Rizzuto that stalled a desperate Philadelphia bid for a run in the eighth. With Ashburn on first, the result of a bunt hit, Sisler also bunted for a sacrifice attempt.

Reynolds pounced on the ball and in a daring play fired to second for a force out. The throw was off to the right, but li'l Phil stretched himself for his full 5-feet 6-inches and froze to the peg just as Ashburn crashed into the bag.

It was an eyelash play, so when Umpire Charlie Berry called the Philly runner out Richie kicked and the fans booed. Nor was their temper improved when Ennis a moment later ended the inning by slapping into a double play.

So tonight, in a setting all too familiar to the harried National League adherents, the Bombers roared back to New York poised to move in on the kill of another World Series triumph. Having made off with the first two encounters with his right-handed aces, Raschi and Reynolds, Stengel tomorrow will switch to his crafty southpaw, Eddie Lopat, in the hope of rolling up the third straight.

Sawyer, on the other hand, having lost with two well-pitched games from his surprise opening starter, Jim Konstanty, and the stalwart Roberts, seemed undecided what to try. It may be another youngster, Bob Miller, only recently recovered from an ailing arm. More likely, it will be the veteran southpaw, Ken Heintzelman.

# SERIES BOX SCORE

## SECOND GAME

| NEW YORK YANKEES | AB. | R. | H. | PO. | A. | E. | PHILADELPHIA PHILLIES | AB. | R. | H. | PO. | A. | E. |
|---|---|---|---|---|---|---|---|---|---|---|---|---|---|
| Woodling, lf | 5 | 0 | 2 | 2 | 0 | 0 | Waitkus, 1b | 4 | 0 | 2 | 8 | 0 | 0 |
| Rizzuto, ss | 4 | 0 | 0 | 2 | 1 | 0 | Ashburn, cf | 5 | 0 | 2 | 4 | 0 | 0 |
| Berra, c | 5 | 0 | 1 | 7 | 0 | 0 | Sisler, lf | 5 | 0 | 0 | 3 | 0 | 0 |
| DiMaggio, cf | 5 | 1 | 1 | 3 | 0 | 0 | Ennis, rf | 4 | 0 | 0 | 1 | 0 | 0 |
| Mize, 1b | 4 | 0 | 1 | 6 | 0 | 0 | Jones, 3b | 4 | 0 | 0 | 3 | 0 | 0 |
| Johnson, 3b | 1 | 0 | 0 | 0 | 2 | 0 | Hamner, ss | 3 | 0 | 2 | 2 | 2 | 0 |
| Brown, 3b | 4 | 0 | 2 | 0 | 0 | 0 | Seminick, c | 2 | 0 | 0 | 5 | 0 | 0 |
| Hopp, 1b | 1 | 0 | 0 | 3 | 0 | 0 | [a]Caballero | 0 | 0 | 0 | 0 | 0 | 0 |
| Bauer, rf | 5 | 0 | 1 | 1 | 0 | 0 | Silvestri, c | 0 | 0 | 0 | 1 | 0 | 0 |
| Coleman, 2b | 3 | 1 | 1 | 5 | 6 | 0 | [b]Whitman | 0 | 0 | 0 | 0 | 0 | 0 |
| Reynolds, p | 3 | 0 | 1 | 1 | 2 | 0 | Lopata, c | 0 | 0 | 0 | 1 | 0 | 0 |
| | | | | | | | Goliat, 2b | 4 | 1 | 1 | 2 | 2 | 0 |
| | | | | | | | Roberts, p | 2 | 0 | 0 | 0 | 0 | 0 |
| | | | | | | | [c]Mayo | 0 | 0 | 0 | 0 | 0 | 0 |
| Total | 40 | 2 | 10 | 30 | 11 | 0 | Total | 33 | 1 | 7 | 30 | 4 | 0 |

[a]Ran for Seminick in seventh.
[b]Intentionally walked for Silvestri in ninth.
[c]Walked for Roberts in tenth.

| New York (A.) | 010 | 000 | 000 | 1—2 |
|---|---|---|---|---|
| Phila. (N.) | 000 | 010 | 000 | 0—1 |

Runs batted in—Woodling, Ashburn, DiMaggio.

Two-base hits—Ashburn, Waitkus, Coleman, Hamner. Three-base hit—Hamner. Home run—DiMaggio. Stolen base—Hamner. Sacrifices—Roberts, Waitkus. Double plays—Johnson, Coleman and Hopp; Rizzuto, Coleman and Hopp. Left on bases—New York 11, Philadelphia 8. Bases on balls—Off Roberts 3 (Coleman, Reynolds, Rizzuto); Reynolds 4 (Seminick, Hamner, Whitman, Mayo). Struck out—By Reynolds 6 (Sisler 2, Jones, Roberts, Ennis, Seminick); Roberts 5 (Berra, Mize, Reynolds 2, Johnson). Winning pitcher—Reynolds. Losing pitcher—Roberts.

Umpires—Bill McGowan (A.) plate; Dusty Boggess (N.), first base; Charlie Berry (A.), second base; Bill McKinley (A.), left field foul line; AL Barlick (N.), right field foul line. Time of game—3:06. Attendance—32,660.

*Game-Winning Wallop Brought Biggest Thrill of His Career, Says DiMaggio*

## LOW, INSIDE PITCH BELTED FOR CIRCUIT

### DiMaggio 'Knew It Was Gone When I Saw It Sailing'—Lauds Rival Pitchers

## REYNOLDS FELT 'STRONG'

### At Best When He Struck Out Sisler to End Game—Phils Still Tough, Says Stengel

By JAMES P. DAWSON

*Special to* THE NEW YORK TIMES

PHILADELPHIA, Oct. 5—"I never hit a better one in my life. That was the greatest homer of my career. Any 4-bagger that wins a ball game carries a thrill. But this one tops any that I can remember."

Joe DiMaggio was talking in the Yankee clubhouse after today's thrilling 2-to-1, ten-inning victory that made the American League champions 2-up on the Fighting Phillies.

He was trying to answer a flood of questions and at the same time grab a smoke, quench the thirst that only a tense ball game can bring, get out of his playing togs and shower before donning his street clothes for the run to the 5:14 P.M. train which was to carry a triumphant Yankee squad back to New York.

Joe was doing a pretty good job as reporters crowded about him and photographers yelled for his picture in front of his 2 × 4 locker. But he was taking it all good-naturedly.

"It was a long time coming," said the Yankee slugger. "They (the Phils' pitchers) haven't been giving us much to hit at. In fact, what I got hold of today wasn't much either. It was a low, inside slider. But, I just managed to get enough of it. As I watched it sail I knew it was a big one."

### Big Thrill for the Team

All the Yankees got a big thrill out of this second victory.

"How about that one, yeah!" the voice of Coach Bill Dickey could be heard above the din and clatter as the players, out of sight of the crowds crowded through the small clubhouse door to start a session of back-slapping and yelling.

Allie Reynolds got his share of the pummeling. DiMaggio was congratulated on all sides. Phil Rizzuto was mobbed for a great catch he made of Reynolds' high throw to second that forced Richie Ashburn in the eighth after Ashburn's bunt had gone for a clean single.

Despite their joy the Yanks were forgetting the tight squeezes they faced in the first two games.

## Old Casey Sums Up

Manager Casey Stengel summed up:

"Good pitching, that's what it was today, just as it was yesterday," said the grey-haired Yankee leader. "The pitching has been great in this series, and that was no surprise to us. We knew we had good pitching to stand them off and we expected good pitching from them.

"When you get top pitching you can't blame the hitters. They don't get much to hit at. Reynolds was great today. So was that Roberts. But good, old Joe came back and it was like old times. That's all there was to it. I'm glad he came to life. Just at the right moment, too, hey?"

Somebody made bold to ask if old Casey would say four-in-a-row.

"Not on your life," yelled the Yankee pilot. "How can you even think four in a row with what we've faced so far. Their pitching is good. If it wasn't they wouldn't be fooling my big men the way they have. No, we'll just go along; we'll take 'em all if we can, and we'll be aiming that way. But their club is far from a push-over."

DiMaggio, with becoming modest, gave full credit to Reynolds, who was pretty happy about it all. He had come into the club-house for a smoke while the Yanks were batting in the tenth and, after DiMaggio's wallop, he strode out there grimly determined to blow down the Phillies in their tenth. He did, after walking pinch hitter Jack Mayo.

## Mixed Curves, Fast Ones

"I felt strong and worked the way I wanted all through the game," said Allie. "I had them in hand with fast pitches and curves mixed up. They were shut out but for that hopper by Waitkus which bounced unexpectedly over Coleman's head in the fifth and put their run in scoring position. That was just one of those breaks. But you can't control those things. They were hitting sliders for those extra-base hits early. But I saw to it they didn't do them much good."

Yogi Berra said Reynolds was fast and that his curve was breaking sharply, although he said he had seen the big right-hander faster. He was satisfied Reynolds never was faster than with those three pitches with which he fanned Dick Sisler to end the game.

Not necessarily emphasizing the Yankee victory, but paying tribute to a great competitor, Bill Dickey was lavish in his praise of Robin Roberts. "There's the best young pitcher in either league," said Dickey. "He had everything out there this afternoon, fast stuff, slow stuff, curves, sliders. He's a great pitcher."

As a parting shot, Stengel said: "I'll throw Eddie Lopat tomorrow and after that it'll be Whitey Ford."

So the Phillies are in for some conk-hand flipping in New York.

### *Joe DiMaggio Retires as Player; Stanky Signs to Manage Cardinals*

Joe DiMaggio announced his retirement as a player yesterday in one of two big developments in the baseball front. In the other, Eddie Stanky, second baseman of the Giants for the past two seasons, was officially named player-manager of the Cardinals.

In telling of his retirement at the Yankee office, DiMaggio said he was not ready to reveal his plans but that he expected to remain in the organization of the world champions. It is generally believed that the centerfielder, who received an estimated $100,000 in salary for each of the last three seasons, will devote his future activities to radio and television. The job of television announcer at Yankee Stadium games, recently vacated by Dizzy Dean, would alone bring him about $50,000.

Stanky, a dashing player who helped spark the Dodgers to a pennant in 1947, brought another to the Braves in 1948 and then played so spectacular a role in the Giants' flag triumph this year, signed a two-year contract for Fred Saigh, cardinal owner, at a reported salary of $37,000 a season.

This sealed a deal in which the Giants will receive max Lanier, veteran southpaw hurler, and Chuck Diering, an outfielder.

### *DiMaggio Retires as Player but Expects to Remain in Yankee Organization*

## CLIPPER GIVES HINT OF TELEVISION JOB

### DiMaggio, After 13 Seasons With Yankees, Says He Is Through as a Player

## NO AMBITION TO MANAGE

### Decision, Made Last Spring, Laid to Age and Injuries—Mantle Due for Post

#### By JOHN DREBINGER

The Yankee Clipper has made his last graceful catch and taken his last cut at the ball.

Amid a fanfare without precedent in the retirement of a player, Joe DiMaggio yesterday told the Bombers and the world that he was retiring as an active performer and that nothing could ever persuade him to play again.

As newsreel cameras clicked, light bulbs flashed and photographers and reporters jammed every inch of the Yankees' Fifth Avenue suite in the Squibb Tower, the son of an Italian immigrant who rose from the wharves of San Francisco to a position of eminence and an accumulation of more than $700,000 in baseball earnings quietly revealed that he alone had made the decision.

## No Longer Has 'It'

It was prompted, he said, by advancing years—he was 37 on Nov. 25—physical injuries and the conviction that as a player "I no longer have it." He said also night baseball was partly to blame and was convinced it had shortened his career by at least two years. DiMaggio started his major league career in 1936, and was with the Yankees for thirteen seasons, with three years out for Army service.

What were his future plans? These, he said, he was not prepared to reveal, but hinted that they likely would bring him into radio and television. He revealed also that for the present, at least, his plans were to remain with the Yankee organization, but in what capacity he would not say.

His new post would not be in connection with any field work or managing. Asked whether he aspired to managing the Yankees, DiMaggio replied, "That one I have answered many times. I never wanted to be a manager and never will."

Asked why he felt so strongly on this point, he answered with a wry smile, "because I had enough to do with my own troubles without worrying about the troubles of twenty-five other players."

## Television Job Likely

The general belief is that part of DiMaggio's future activities will see him engaged as the Yankee television broadcaster at a salary of about $50,000. As a player he is reputed to have received $100,000 for each of the past three season.

Dan Topping, who was present with his co-owner Del Webb and Manager Casey Stengel, said that up to the last he had hoped to persuade DiMaggio to change his mind. But the Clipper's mind had been made up long ago.

DiMaggio said he knew last spring this would be his last year. The Clipper said he regretted having hinted at his retirement then, for he realized later his remarks had been ill-timed.

"But I knew my mind was made up, although I never mentioned it again until after the world series and then only to Topping," said DiMaggio. "He asked me to think it over a while longer and in fairness to him I decided this was the only thing to do. I never mentioned it to another soul and not even my brother Dominic knew what my decision would be today."

## 'What Is There to Say'

The usual loquacious Stengel had little to say.

"What is there to say?" said Casey, "I just gave the Big Guy's glove away and it is going to the Hall of Fame, where Joe himself is certain to go. He was the greatest player I ever managed and right now I still say there isn't another centerfielder in baseball his equal."

Concerning a replacement, Stengel said the job would be "wide open," with Mickey Mantle, rookie star of the past season, receiving first call, closely followed by Jackie Jensen.

As the appointed hour of 2 P.M. arrived, Arthur (Red) Patterson, in charge of the ceremonies and striving to keep reporters from choking on sandwiches and stumbling over newsreel wires, issued a typed statement for DiMaggio.

Joe DiMaggio, center, as he talked with newsmen about his retirement at the Yankee offices. With him, left to right, are General Manager George Weiss, Manager Casey Stengel and owners Del Webb and Dan Topping [not shown]. (ASSOCIATED PRESS)

"I told you fellows last spring," the statement read, "I thought this would be my last year. I only wish I could have had a better year, but even if I had hit .350, this would have been the last year for me.

"You all know I have had more than my share of physical injuries and setbacks during my career. In recent years these have been much too frequent to laugh off. When baseball is no longer fun, it's no longer a game.

"And so, I've played my last game of ball.

"Since coming to New York, I've made a lot of friends and picked up a lot of advisers, but I would like to make one point clear—no one has influenced me in making this decision. It has been my problem and my decision to make.

"I feel that I have reached the stage where I can no longer produce for my ball club, my manager, my teammates and my fans the sort of baseball their loyalty to me deserves.

"In closing, I would like to say that I feel I have been unusually privileged to play all my major league baseball for the New York Yankees.

"But it has been an even greater privilege to be able to play baseball at all. It has added much to my life. What I will remember most in days to come will be the great loyalty of the fans. They have been very good to me."

After fulfilling his obligations to the photographers and radio commentators, the Clipper drifted back to the press room, where he answered a barrage of questions.

When did he first realize he was slipping? About three years ago.

What ailments bothered him most?

"My right knee," he replied. "It kept buckling under me every little while. Also both shoulders. These have bothered me for a long time and finally retarded my swing so much I simply couldn't hit in front of the plate as I used to. Right now, though, I feel fine, and have no intention of going near a doctor. But I know I couldn't do it again on the ball field."

What were his biggest thrills in his major league career?

"Well, I guess the fifty-six game hitting streak in 1941," he said. "And then there was that series up in

Boston in 1949 when, after missing the first sixty-five games because of my heel operation, I belted a couple of home runs."

In that series, the Clipper exploded for four home runs in three games, drove in nine runs and virtually wrecked the Red Sox for the rest of the campaign.

Who was the toughest pitcher he ever faced?

"When I first came up, Mel Harder. But last season," he added with a chuckle, "they all were pretty tough."

What was his greatest fielding play?

"I guess the one I made off Hank Greenberg back in 1938 or 1939, out by the flagpole in the Stadium just in front of the 461-foot mark. Don't know yet how I made it. Just stuck my glove up the last moment and there was the ball.

## Failed to Get Averill

"But actually I also pulled a rock on that one," the Clipper reminisced. "Earl Averill was on first at the time and there was only one out. When I caught the ball Averill was almost to third and I should have doubled him up easily. But in the excitement I thought the catch retired the side and before I woke up Averill was back on first."

In addition to being a powerful hitter, DiMaggio displayed great fielding skill and was an excellent base runner.

Having started as a professional player with the San Francisco Seals in 1932, DiMaggio appeared in three games that season as a shortstop but the next year became an outfielder and since has not played anywhere else.

He first attracted attention in the East when, still with the Seals, he compiled a sixty-one-game hitting streak. The Yankees, then owned by the late Col. Jacob Ruppert and directed by Ed Barrow, bought DiMaggio for $25,000 for delivery in the spring of 1936. Throughout 1935 there was considerable apprehension when the youngster was believed suffering from a trick knee.

The San Francisco Club even offered to cancel the deal, but the Yanks, acting on the advice of their Coast scouts, decided to stay with it and never regretted it. For with Babe Ruth already gone from the Stadium and Lou Gehrig destined to carry on for only a few more seasons, DiMaggio was to give the Bombers still another diamond immortal who was to draw thousands through the turnstiles.

Few rookies ever had to respond to so great a ballyhoo as accompanied DiMaggio eastward in the spring of 1936. But his place in stardom was established almost from the start. Manager Joe McCarthy needed only one look to realize that he had the player of the generation.

And with the rise of DiMaggio, the Yanks rode to great triumphs. In his first four years, from 1936 through 1939, the Yanks won four pennants, and world titles. In all, DiMaggio played in ten world series and nine times was with the winner. And in his final game last October, he ran his total of series games to fifty-one, one above the previous record held by Frankie Frisch.

Most impressive was his achievement in 1941, when he hit safely in fifty-six consecutive games for a major league record. The streak began on May 15. It ended in a night game on July 17 in Cleveland and it took two great fielding plays, one by Ken Keltner, the other by Lou Boudreau, to turn the trick.

In each of his thirteen active seasons, DiMaggio was picked for the All-Star Game, but twice, in 1946 and 1951, he was sidelined because of injuries.

Starting with $8,000 in his first season and continuing until his salary reached $100,000 for each of the last three, DiMaggio received an estimated $646,250 in pay from the Yankees. World series shares raised this by $58,519.17 for an over-all total of $704,769.71. To this must be added about $250,000 received for radio and television appearances and for endorsements of products.

Despite this income, DiMaggio, when asked if he would like to loaf for a year, replied with a grim smile:

"Yes, I would like to loaf, but I'm afraid I'm not that well fixed."

The star outfielder is hailed by his team-mates as he returns to the dugout after a home run in Game 4 of the 1951 World Series. (THE NEW YORK TIMES)

## Named Most Valuable

DiMaggio was named the most valuable player in the American League in 1939, 1941 and again in 1947. Three years in service kept him out of play from 1943 through 1945. He led the league in runs batted in in 1941; was twice the circuit's home-run king, with forty-six in 1937 and thirty-nine in 1948, and captured two batting crowns, his top average the .381 that won him the crown in 1939.

Despite a falling off to a meager .263 average the past season for 116 games, he completed his career with a lifetime average of .325. Also, his lifetime total of home runs, 361, tops that of any active player in the game today.

Yet, when asked yesterday who he considered the greatest of present-day hitters, DiMaggio replied, "Ted Williams. He is by far the greatest natural hitter I ever saw."

The Clipper joined the 2,000-hit group on June 20, 1950, and when he drove in five runs against the White Sox on July 29 last, he raised his RBI total to the 1,500 mark.

Small wonder Stengel ponders when and with whom he will ever plug the gap in centerfield. It was obvious, too, that Casey and the other Yanks had been hopeful to the last that the Clipper might change his mind. He undoubtedly recalled that though DiMag had gone hitless in the first three games of last October's world series, he exploded six blows in the final three, including a resounding homer.

## Seldom Argued Decision

DiMaggio rarely complained to an umpire. In striking contrast with the flamboyant Babe Ruth, the Clipper lacked utterly in glamour, yet by his quiet demeanor in time developed a fascinating hold upon the fans throughout the nation.

Shy as a rookie, his attitude developed into an aloofness that seldom relaxed except among close friends. He greeted his fellow players with a reserved cordiality but "palled" with few—for a time Lefty Gomez, later Joe Page.

DiMaggio expects to return Friday to California, where he plans to make his permanent home. Within one week or so, he said, he will be ready to reveal his future activities.

## Clipper's Earnings Since 1936 Placed at 704,769

Joe DiMaggio earned an estimated $704,169.71 during his major league baseball career. Here are the financial figures, including newspaper estimates of the Yankee Clipper's salary and his world series shares:

|         | Estimated Salary | World Series Checks |
|---------|------------------|---------------------|
| 1936    | $8,000           | $6,430.55           |
| 1937    | 15,000           | 6,471.10            |
| 1938    | 25,000           | 5,782.76            |
| 1939    | 27,500           | 5,614.26            |
| 1940    | 32,000           | 3d pl.   546.59     |
| 1941    | 37,500           | 5,943.31            |
| 1942    | 43,750           | 3,018.77            |
| 1943–45 | Military Service |                     |
| 1946    | 43,750           | 3d pl. 392.95       |
| 1947    | 43,750           | 5,830.03            |
| 1948    | 70,000           | 3d pl. 778.88       |
| 1949    | 100.000          | 5,526.47            |
| 1950    | 100.000          | 5,737.95            |
| 1951    | 100.000          | 6,446.09            |
| Total   | $646,250         | $58,519.17          |

Total earning—$704,769.71.

Joe DiMaggio announcing his retirement from baseball, Dec. 11, 1951. He stops for a moment outside the Yankee office after making the announcement. (THE NEW YORK TIMES)

### 56-Game Batting Streak In 1941 Set New Record

Joe DiMaggio set a major league record in 1941 by batting safely in fifty-six consecutive games. The details of his streak follow:

| Date—Opponent | Ab | r | h | 2b | 3b | hr | rbi |
|---|---|---|---|---|---|---|---|
| **May** | | | | | | | |
| 15—Chicago | 4 | 0 | 1 | 0 | 0 | 0 | 1 |
| 16—Chicago | 4 | 2 | 2 | 0 | 1 | 1 | 1 |
| 17—Chicago | 3 | 1 | 1 | 0 | 0 | 0 | 0 |
| 18—St. Louis | 3 | 3 | 3 | 1 | 0 | 0 | 0 |
| 19—St. Louis | 3 | 0 | 1 | 1 | 0 | 0 | 0 |
| 20—St. Louis | 5 | 1 | 1 | 0 | 0 | 0 | 1 |
| 21—Detroit | 5 | 0 | 2 | 0 | 0 | 0 | 1 |
| 22—Detroit | 4 | 0 | 1 | 0 | 0 | 0 | 1 |
| 23—Boston | 5 | 0 | 1 | 0 | 0 | 0 | 2 |
| 24—Boston | 4 | 2 | 1 | 0 | 0 | 0 | 2 |
| 25—Boston | 4 | 0 | 1 | 0 | 0 | 0 | 0 |
| 27—Washington | 5 | 3 | 4 | 0 | 0 | 1 | 3 |
| *28—Washington | 4 | 1 | 1 | 0 | 1 | 0 | 0 |
| 29—Washington | 3 | 1 | 1 | 0 | 0 | 0 | 0 |
| 30—Boston | 2 | 1 | 1 | 0 | 0 | 0 | 0 |
| 30—Boston | 3 | 0 | 1 | 1 | 0 | 0 | 0 |

## June

| | | | | | | | |
|---|---|---|---|---|---|---|---|
| 1—Cleveland | 4 | 1 | 1 | 0 | 0 | 0 | 0 |
| 1—Cleveland | 4 | 0 | 1 | 0 | 0 | 0 | 0 |
| 2—Cleveland | 4 | 2 | 2 | 1 | 0 | 0 | 0 |
| 3—Detroit | 4 | 1 | 1 | 0 | 0 | 1 | 1 |
| 5—Detroit | 5 | 1 | 1 | 0 | 1 | 0 | 1 |
| 7—St. Louis | 5 | 2 | 3 | 0 | 0 | 0 | 1 |
| 8—St. Louis | 4 | 3 | 2 | 0 | 0 | 2 | 4 |
| 8—St. Louis | 4 | 1 | 2 | 1 | 0 | 1 | 3 |
| 10—Chicago | 5 | 1 | 1 | 0 | 0 | 0 | 0 |
| *12—Chicago | 4 | 1 | 2 | 0 | 0 | 1 | 1 |
| 14—Cleveland | 2 | 0 | 1 | 1 | 0 | 0 | 1 |
| 15—Cleveland | 3 | 1 | 1 | 0 | 0 | 1 | 1 |
| 16—Cleveland | 5 | 0 | 1 | 1 | 0 | 0 | 0 |
| 17—Chicago | 4 | 1 | 1 | 0 | 0 | 0 | 0 |
| 18—Chicago | 3 | 0 | 1 | 0 | 0 | 0 | 0 |
| 19—Chicago | 3 | 2 | 3 | 0 | 0 | 1 | 2 |
| 20—Detroit | 5 | 3 | 4 | 1 | 0 | 0 | 1 |
| 21—Detroit | 4 | 0 | 1 | 0 | 0 | 0 | 1 |
| 22—Detroit | 5 | 1 | 2 | 1 | 0 | 1 | 2 |
| 24—St. Louis | 4 | 1 | 1 | 0 | 0 | 0 | 0 |
| 25—St. Louis | 4 | 1 | 1 | 0 | 0 | 1 | 3 |
| 26—St. Louis | 4 | 0 | 1 | 1 | 0 | 0 | 1 |
| 27—Philadelphia | 3 | 1 | 2 | 0 | 0 | 1 | 2 |
| 28—Philadelphia | 5 | 1 | 2 | 1 | 0 | 0 | 0 |
| 29—Washington | 4 | 1 | 1 | 1 | 0 | 0 | 0 |
| 29—Washington | 5 | 1 | 1 | 0 | 0 | 0 | 1 |

## July

| | | | | | | | |
|---|---|---|---|---|---|---|---|
| 1—Boston | 4 | 0 | 2 | 0 | 0 | 0 | 1 |
| 1—Boston | 3 | 1 | 1 | 0 | 0 | 0 | 1 |
| 2—Boston | 5 | 1 | 1 | 0 | 0 | 1 | 3 |
| 6—Philadelphia | 5 | 2 | 4 | 1 | 0 | 0 | 2 |
| 6—Philadelphia | 4 | 0 | 2 | 0 | 1 | 0 | 2 |
| *10—St. Louis | 2 | 0 | 1 | 0 | 0 | 0 | 0 |
| 11—St. Louis | 5 | 1 | 4 | 0 | 0 | 1 | 2 |
| 12—St. Louis | 5 | 1 | 2 | 1 | 0 | 0 | 1 |
| 13—Chicago | 4 | 2 | 3 | 0 | 0 | 0 | 0 |
| 14—Chicago | 3 | 0 | 1 | 0 | 0 | 0 | 0 |
| 15—Chicago | 4 | 1 | 2 | 1 | 0 | 0 | 2 |
| 16—Cleveland | 4 | 3 | 3 | 1 | 0 | 0 | 0 |
| **Total** | **223** | **56** | **91** | **18** | **4** | **15** | **55** |

*Night Games
Batting average—.408.

## Joe DiMaggio Weds Marilyn Monroe

*Special to The New York Times.*

SAN FRANCISCO, Jan. 14—Marilyn Monroe, the motion-picture actress, and Joe DiMaggio, former outfielder of the New York Yankees baseball club, were married here today at the City Hall.

Municipal Court Judge Charles S. Peery performed the ceremony in his chambers after clearing the room of reporters and photographers who had awaited the couple's arrival. The bride had telephoned her studio in Hollywood that the wedding would take place at 1:30 P.M.

Reno Barsocchini, Mr. DiMaggio's partner in his Fishermen's Wharf Restaurant, served as best man and Mrs. Barsocchini was matron of honor. The bride wore a dark brown broadcloth suit with an ermine collar.

The couple answered questions and posed for pictures before the ceremony. The picture-taking was resumed after the wedding, when Judge Peery had the doors unlocked.

Mr. DiMaggio retired from baseball in 1951 and now stars on a television show produced for children. The bride said she would continue her movie career.

This was the second marriage for both. Mr. DiMaggio was divorced in 1944 from the former Dorothy Arnold, an actress. Miss Arnold has custody of their son, Joe, Jr. Miss Monroe was married at 16 to a merchant seaman. The marriage lasted two years.

March 9, 1999

## Joe DiMaggio, Yankee Clipper, Dies at 84

### BY JOSEPH DURSO

HOLLYWOOD, Fla., March 8—Joe DiMaggio, the flawless center fielder for the New York Yankees who, along with Babe Ruth and Mickey Mantle, symbolized the team's dynastic success across the 20th century and whose 56-game hitting streak in 1941 made him an instant and indelible American folk hero, died early today at his home here. He was 84 years old.

DiMaggio died shortly after midnight, nearly five months after undergoing surgery for cancer of the lungs. He had spent 99 days in the hospital while battling lung infections and pneumonia, and his illness generated a national vigil as he was reported near death several times. He went home on Jan. 19, alert but weak and with little hope of surviving. Several family members and close friends were at his bedside this morning.

DiMaggio's body was flown to Northern California for a funeral Thursday and for burial in San Francisco, his hometown.

In a country that has idolized and even immortalized its 20th century heroes, from Charles A. Lindbergh to Elvis Presley, no one more embodied the American dream of fame and fortune or created a more enduring legend than Joe DiMaggio. He became a figure of unequaled romance and integrity in the national mind because of his consistent professionalism on the baseball field, his marriage to Hollywood star Marilyn Monroe, his devotion to her after her death, and the pride and courtliness with which he carried himself throughout his life.

DiMaggio burst onto the baseball scene from San Francisco in the 1930's and grew into the game's most gallant and graceful center fielder. He wore No. 5 and became the successor to Babe Ruth (No. 3) and Lou Gehrig (No. 4) in the Yankees' pantheon. DiMaggio was the team's superstar for 13 seasons, beginning in 1936 and ending in 1951, and appeared in 11 All-Star Games and 10 World Series. He was, as the writer Roy Blount Jr. once observed, "the class of the Yankees in times when the Yankees outclassed everybody else."

He was called the Yankee Clipper and was acclaimed at baseball's centennial in 1969 as "the greatest living ballplayer," the man who in 1,736 games with the Yankees had a career batting average of .325 and hit 361 home runs while striking out only 369 times, one of baseball's most amazing statistics. (By way of comparison, Mickey Mantle had 536 homers and struck out 1,710 times; Reggie Jackson slugged 563 homers and struck out 2,597 times).

But DiMaggio's game was so complete and elegant that it transcended statistics; as the New York Times said in an editorial when he retired, "The combination of proficiency and exquisite grace which Joe DiMaggio brought to the art of playing center field was something no baseball averages can measure and that must be seen to be believed and appreciated."

DiMaggio glided across the vast expanse of center field at Yankee Stadium with such incomparable grace that long after he stopped playing, the memory of him in full stride remains evergreen. He disdained theatrical flourishes and exaggerated moves, never climbing walls to make catches and rarely diving headlong. He got to the ball just as it fell into his glove, making the catch seem inevitable, almost preordained. The writer Wilfred Sheed wrote, "In dreams I can still see him gliding after fly balls as if he were skimming the surface of the moon."

His batting stance was as graceful as his outfield stride. He stood flatfooted at the plate with his feet spread well apart, his bat held still just off his right shoulder. When he swung, his left, or front, foot moved only slightly forward. His swing was pure and flowing with an incredible follow-through. Casey Stengel, the Yankee manager for DiMaggio's last three seasons, said, "He made the rest of them look like plumbers."

At his peak, he was serenaded as "Joltin' Joe DiMaggio" by Les Brown and saluted as "the great DiMaggio" by Ernest Hemmingway in "The Old Man and the Sea." He was mentioned in dozen of films and Broadway shows; the sailors in "South Pacific" sing that Bloody Mary's skin is "tender as DiMaggio's glove." Years later, he was remembered by Paul Simon, who wondered with everybody else: "Where have you gone, Joe DiMaggio? A Nation turns its lonely eyes to you."

Sensitive to anything written, spoken or sung about him, he confessed that he was puzzled by Simon's lyrics and sought an answer when he met Simon in a restaurant in New York. "I asked Paul what the song means, whether it was derogatory," DiMaggio recalled. "He explained it to me."

When injuries eroded his skills and he no longer could perform to his own standard, he turned his back on his $100,000 salary—he and his rival Ted Williams of the Boston Red Sox then drew the largest paychecks in sports—and retired in 1951 with the dignity that remained his hallmark.

His stormy marriage to Marilyn Monroe lasted less than a year, but they remained one of America's ultimate romantic fantasies: the tall, dark and handsome baseball hero wooing and winning the woman who epitomized Hollywood beauty, glamour and sexuality.

He was private and remote. Even Monroe, at their divorce proceedings, said he was given to black moods and would tell her, "Leave me alone." He once said, with disdain, that he kept track of all the books written about his storied life without his consent, and by the later 1990's knew that the count had passed 33.

Yet he could be proud, reclusive and vain in such a composed, almost studied way that his reclusiveness contributed to his mystique. In the book "Summer of '49," David Halberstam wrote that DiMaggio "guards his special status carefully, wary of doing anything that might tarnish his special reputation. He tends to avoid all those who might define him in some way other than the way he defined himself on the field."

## Quietly Doing It All For 13 Seasons

DiMaggio joined the Yankees in 1936, missed three years while he served in the Army Air Forces in World War II, then returned and played through the 1951 season, when Mickey Mantle arrived to open yet another era in the remarkable run of Yankee success. In his 13 seasons, DiMaggio went to bat 6,821 times, got 2,214 hits, knocked in 1,537 runs, amassed 3,948 total bases and reached base just under 40 percent of the time.

For decades, baseball fans argued over who was the better pure hitter, DiMaggio or Williams. Long after both had retired, Williams said: "In my heart, I always felt I was a better hitter than Joe. But I have to say, he was the greatest baseball player of our time. He could do it all."

And he did it all with a sureness and coolness that seemed to imply an utter lack of emotion. DiMaggio was once asked why he did not vent his frustrations on the field by kicking a bag or tossing a bat. The out-fielder, who chain-smoked cigarettes and had suffered from ulcers, replied: "I can't. It wouldn't look right."

But he betrayed his sensitivity in a memorable gesture of annoyance in the sixth game of the 1947 World Series after his long drive was run down and caught in front of the 415-foot sign in left-center field at Yankee Stadium by Al Gionfriddo of the Brooklyn Dodgers. As DiMaggio rounded first base, he saw Gionfriddo make the catch and, with his head down, kicked the dirt.

The angry gesture was so shocking that it made headlines.

In the field, DiMaggio ran down long drives with a gliding stride and deep range. In 1947, he tied what was then the American League fielding record for outfielders by making only one error in 141 games.

He also had one of the most powerful and precise throwing arms in the business and was credited with 153 assists in his 13 seasons.

His longtime manager, Joe McCarthy, once touched on another DiMaggio skill. "He was the best base run-ner I ever saw," McCarthy said. "He could have stolen 50, 60 bases a year if I let him. He wasn't the fastest man alive. He just knew how to run bases better than anybody."

Three times DiMaggio was voted his league's most valuable player: in 1939, 1941 and 1947. In 1941, the magical season of his 56-game hitting streak, he won the award even though Williams batted .406.

In each of his first four seasons with the Yankees, DiMaggio played in the World Series, and the Yankees won all four. He appeared in the Series 10 times in 13 seasons over all, and nine times the Yankees won. And although he failed to get enough votes to make the baseball Hall of Fame when he became eligible in 1953, perhaps because his aloofness had alienated some of the writers who did the voting, he sailed into Coopers-town two years later.

Whitey Ford was a rookie pitcher in 1950 when he first saw DiMaggio, and he later remembered, "I just stared at the man for about a week."

## Baseball Blood In a Fisherman's Family

Joseph Paul DiMaggio was born on Nov. 25, 1914, in Martinez, Calif., a small fishing village 25 miles northeast of the Golden Gate. He was the fourth son and the eighth of nine children born to Giuseppe Paolo and Rosalie DiMaggio, who had immigrated to America in 1898 from Sicily. His father was a fisherman who moved his family to North Beach, the heavily Italian section near San Francisco waterfront, the year Joe was born.

The two oldest sons, Tom and Michael, joined their father as fishermen; Michael later fell off a boat and drowned. But the three other sons became major league outfielders by way of the sandlots of San Francisco. Vince, four years older than Joe, played 10 seasons with five teams and led the National League in strikeouts six times. Dominic, three years younger than Joe, was known as the Little Professor because he wore eyeglasses when he played 11 seasons with the Boston Red Sox, hitting .298 for his career. Of the three, Joe was the natural.

He started as a shortstop in the Boys Club League when he was 14, dropped out of Galileo High School after one year and joined Vince on the San Francisco Seals of the Pacific Coast League, the highest level of minor league baseball. It was 1932, and Joe was still 17 years old.

The next year, in his first full season with the Seals, he hit .340 with 28 home runs and knocked in 169 runs in 187 games. He also hit safely in 61 games in a row, eight years before he made history in the big leagues by hitting in 56. He tore up the league during the next two seasons, hitting .341 and .398. But he injured his left knee stepping out of a cab while hurrying to dinner at his sister's house after a Sunday doubleheader and was considered damaged goods by most of the reams in the big league.

He got his chance at the majors because two scouts, Joe Devine and Bill Essick, persisted in recommending him to the Yankees. The general manager, Ed Barrow, talked it over with his colleagues. And for $25,000 plus five players, the Yankees bought him from the Seals.

DiMaggio was left in San Francisco for the 1935 season to heal his knee and put the finishing touches on his game, then was brought up to New York in 1936 to join a talented team that included Lou Gehrig, Bill Dickey, Tony Lazzeri, Red Rolfe, Red Ruffing and Lefty Gomez. It was two years after Babe Ruth had left, and an era of success had ended.

But now, the rookie from California was arriving with a contract for $8,500, and a new era was beginning. It was delayed because of a foot injury, but DiMaggio made his debut on May 3 against the St. Louis Browns. He went on to play 138 games, got 206 hits with 29 home runs, batted .323 and drove in 125 runs. In the fall, the Yankees made the first of four straight trips to the World Series—they would go on to play in 22 out of 29 Series through 1964—and the rookie hit .346 against the Giants and made a spectacular catch in deepest center field in the Polo grounds before a marveling crowd of 43,543, including President Franklin D. Roosevelt.

DiMaggio's luster was sometimes dimmed by salary disputes. In 1937 he hit .346 with 46 home runs and 167 r.b.i. and the following year he held out for $40,000 but was forced to sign for $25,000. DiMaggio's holdout lasted a couple of weeks into the season; when he returned, he was booed. When he began the 1941 season, he had missed four of his first five openers because of injury or salary fights, and many fans resented it. "He got hurt early in his career, more than he ever let on," Phil Rizutto once said.

He also had to endure the casual bigotry that existed when he first came up. Life magazine, in a 1939 article intending to compliment him, said: "Although he learned Italian first, Joe, now 24, speaks English without an accent, and is otherwise well adapted to most U.S. mores. Instead of olive oil or smelly bear grease he keeps his hair slick with water. He never reeks of garlic and prefers chicken chow mein to spaghetti."

But he energized the fans by leading the league in hitting in 1939 (at .381) and again in 1940 (.352). Then in 1941, he put together what has since been known simply as the Streak, and fashioned perhaps the most enduring record in sports. Streaks were nothing new to DiMaggio. He had hit in those 61 straight games for the Seals, in 18 straight as a rookie with the Yankees, in 22 straight the next year and in 23 straight the year after that. In fact, in 1941, he hit safely in the last 19 games in spring training, and he kept hitting for eight more games after the regular season opened.

The Streak began on May 15, 1941, with a single in four times at bat against the Chicago White Sox. The next day, he hit a triple and a home run. Two weeks later, he had a swollen neck but still hit three singles and a home run in Washington. The next week against the St. Louis Browns, he went 3 for 5 in one game, then 4 for 8 in a doubleheader the next day with a double and three home runs. His streak stood at 24.

On June 17, he broke the Yankees' club record of 29 games. On June 26, he was hitless with two out in the eighth inning against the Browns, but he doubled, and his streak reached 38. On June 29, in a doubleheader against Washington, DiMaggio lined a double in the first game to tie George Sisler's modern major league record of hitting in 41 straight games and then broke Sisler's record in the second game by lining a single. On July 1, with a clean single against the Red Sox at Yankee Stadium, he matched Willie Keeler's major league record of 44 games, set in 1897 when foul balls did not count as strikes. The next day he broke it with a three-run homer.

As DiMaggio kept hitting safely, radio announcers kept an excited America informed. Bojangles Robinson danced on the Yankee dugout roof at the Stadium for good luck, and Les Brown recorded "Joltin' Joe DiMaggio . . . we want you on our side."

## The Streak Ends, But Not the Heroics

The Streak finally ended on the steamy night of July 17 in Cleveland, before 67,468 fans at Municipal Stadium. The Cleveland pitchers were Al Smith and Jim Bagby Jr., but the stopper was the Indians' third baseman, Ken Keltner, who made two dazzling backhand plays deep behind third base to rob DiMaggio of hits. It is sometimes overlooked that DiMaggio was intentionally walked in the fourth inning of that game, and that he promptly started a 16-game streak the next day.

In 56 games, DiMaggio had gone to bat 223 times and delivered 91 hits for a .408 average, including 15 home runs. He drew 21 walks, twice was hit by pitched balls, scored 56 runs and knocked in 55. He hit in every game for two months, and struck out just seven times.

The Yankees, fourth in the American League when the streak began, were six games in front when it ended, and won the pennant by 17.

DiMaggio was passing milestones in his personal life, too. In 1939, he married an actress, Dorothy Arnold. In October 1941, his only child, Joseph Jr., was born. In addition to his son, he is survived by his brother Dominic; two granddaughters, Paula and Cathy; and four great-grandchildren.

On Dec. 3, 1942, DiMaggio enlisted in the Army Air Forces and spent the next three years teaching baseball in the service. Along with other baseball stars like Bob Feller and Williams, he resumed his career as soon as the war ended, returning to the Yankees for the 1946 season and a year later leading them back into the World Series.

His most dramatic moments came in the season of 1949, after he was sidelined by bone spurs on his right heel and did not play until June 26. Then he flew to Boston to join the team in Fenway Park, hit a single and home run the first two times he went to bat, hit two more home runs the next day and another the day after that.

The Yankees entered the final two days of that season trailing the Red Sox by one game. They had to sweep two games in Yankee Stadium to win the pennant, and they did. There were poignant moments before the first game when 69,551 fans rocked the stadium and cheered their hero, who was being honored with a Joe DiMaggio Day. He was almost too weak to play because of a severe viral infection, but he did, and he hit a single and double before removing himself from center field on wobbly legs.

After the Yankees won yet another World Series in 1951, he retired and eased into a second career as Joe DiMaggio, the legend. It included cameo roles as a broadcaster, a spring training instructor with the Yankees and a coach with the Oakland Athletics, appearances at old-timers' games, where he was invariably the last player introduced, and a larger role, with surprising impact, as a mellow and credible pitchman on television commercials.

He had long since created an image of a loner both on and off the playing field, particularly in the 1930's and 1940's when he lived in hotels in Manhattan and was considered something of a man about town. He once was characterized by a teammate as the man "who led the league in room service." But he spent many evenings at Toots Shor's restaurant in Manhattan, where he hid out at a private table far in the back while Shor protected him from his public.

But his legend took a storybook turn in 1952, the year after he retired from the Yankees, when DiMaggio, whose marriage to Dorothy Arnold had ended in divorce in 1944, arranged a dinner date with Marilyn Monroe in California. They were married in San Francisco on Jan. 14, 1954, and spent nine months trying to reconcile their differences before they divorced in October. DiMaggio always seemed tortured by Monroe's sex goddess image. He protested loudly during the making of Billy Wilder's "The Seven Year Itch" when the script called for her to cool herself over a subway grate while a sudden wind blew her skirt up high.

But when the actress seemed on the verge of an emotional collapse in 1961, DiMaggio took her to the Yankees' training camp in Florida for rest and support. And when she died of an overdose of barbiturates at age 36 on Aug. 4, 1962, he took charge of her funeral, and for the next 20 years he sent roses three times a week to her crypt in the Westwood section of Los Angeles.

### Finally at Ease In the Spotlight

When DiMaggio made an unexpected and dramatic return to the public scene in the 1970's as a television spokesman for the Bowery Savings Bank of New York and for Mr. Coffee, a manufacturer of coffee makers, he did it with remarkable ease for a man who had been obsessed with privacy, who had once confided that he always had "a knot" in his stomach because he was so shy and tense.

Gone was the stage fright that had rattled him during earlier sorties into broadcasting. Instead, he was the epitome of credibility, the graying and trustworthy hero who had hit his home runs and was now returning to extol the virtues of saving money and brewing coffee. He soon became a familiar and comforting presence for a generation of baseball fans who never saw him play.

For some years, he lived in San Francisco with his widowed sister Marie in a house in the Marina District that he had bought for his parents in 1939 and that he and his sister had shared with Marilyn Monroe. When the damp San Francisco climate troubled the arthritis in his back, he began to spend most of his time in Florida, where he established his home. He played golf and made selected excursions to Europe and the Far East, where the demand for his appearance and his autograph returned high dividends.

But he seemed to take the most pleasure in establishing a children's wing, called the Joe DiMaggio Children's Hospital, at Memorial Regional Hospital in Hollywood, Fla. And he seemed to relish the invitations back to Yankee Stadium, where he frequently threw out the first ball on opening day, tall but slightly stooped, dressed elegantly, as always, in a dark business suit, walking to the mound and lobbing one to the catcher.

It was there on the day the season ended last year, as the Yankees set a team record with their 114th victory, that he was acclaimed on yet another Joe DiMaggio Day, the timeless hero and the symbol of Yankee excellence, acknowledging the cheers of Yankee players and fans.

It was the kind of cheering that accompanied him through life and that he had quietly come to expect. It recalled the time when he and Monroe, soon after their wedding, took a trip to Tokyo. She continued on to entertain American troops in Korea, and said with fascination when she returned, "Joe, you've never heard such cheering."

And Joe DiMaggio replied softly, "Yes, I have."

## REGULAR SEASON STATISTICS

|  | AB | R | H | SO | HR | RBI | AVG. |
|---|---|---|---|---|---|---|---|
| '36 | 637 | 132 | 206 | 39 | 29 | 125 | .323 |
| '37 | 621 | 151 | 215 | 37 | 46 | 167 | .346 |
| '38 | 599 | 129 | 194 | 21 | 32 | 140 | .324 |
| '39 | 462 | 108 | 176 | 20 | 30 | 126 | .381 |
| '40 | 508 | 93 | 179 | 30 | 31 | 133 | .352 |
| '41 | 541 | 122 | 193 | 13 | 30 | 125 | .357 |
| '42 | 610 | 123 | 186 | 36 | 21 | 114 | .305 |
| '43–5 In military service | | | | | | | |
| '46 | 503 | 81 | 146 | 24 | 25 | 95 | .290 |
| '47 | 534 | 97 | 168 | 32 | 20 | 97 | .315 |
| '48 | 594 | 110 | 190 | 30 | 39 | 155 | .320 |
| '49 | 272 | 58 | 94 | 18 | 14 | 67 | .346 |
| '50 | 525 | 114 | 158 | 33 | 32 | 122 | .301 |
| '51 | 415 | 72 | 109 | 36 | 12 | 71 | .263 |
| TOT | 6,821 | 1,390 | 2,214 | 369 | 361 | 1,537 | .325 |

## WORLD SERIES TOTALS

| YRS | AB | R | H | SO | HR | RBI | AVG. |
|---|---|---|---|---|---|---|---|
| 10 | 199 | 27 | 54 | 23 | 8 | 30 | .271 |

March 9, 1999

## GEORGE VECSEY

*Sports of The Times*

### DiMaggio Left a Mark In the Sands

It was a warm afternoon in early summer of '49, and all of New York was jammed into Jones Beach, blanket to blanket, shoulder to shoulder. The triumphal bellow of Mel Allen, emanating from rudimentary portable radios, drowned out the waves themselves.

It seemed that all of New York was tuned into the return of Joe DiMaggio, the aging Yankee Clipper, who had missed nearly three months because of a heel spur.

The Streak: Joe DiMaggio drew throngs of fans during the 56-game hitting streak that made him a folk hero in 1941. A crowd in Washington watched the Yanks play the Senators. (UNITED PRESS INTERNATIONAL/BETTMANN NEWSPHOTOS)

This was the age when baseball players were the princes of American sports, along with heavyweight boxers and Derby horses and the odd galloping ghost of a running back from down South or the occasional lanky baseball player in short shorts.

Baseball players were the souls of their cities—Stan the Man in St. Louis, The Kid in Boston, Pee Wee and Jackie in Brooklyn, and Giants fans waiting for Willie Mays to arrive on his magic spaceship.

These were times of innate sportsmanship, none of those ugly chants that you hear today. Dodger fans accepted Musial's doubles, Midwesterners took their children to see Williams put dents in the walls and fans everywhere worshiped Joseph Paul DiMaggio, long and slender, like a holy man in an El Greco painting.

Brooklyn fans did not love him the way perhaps they loved Musial or Mays, if they admitted the secret of their hearts, but they respected DiMaggio. They did not wish him harm.

Nowadays the baseball players are just dunking each other into submission, and the hockey players are toting the Stanley Cup in the slush of late June. But back then, DiMaggio was quite noticeably three months late in the most important sporting season.

On that afternoon on June 28, 1949, with the Northeast celebrating the arrival of summer, the papers were full of speculation about whether DiMaggio would hold up, and why should he begin in Boston of all places?

He answered the questions across the sands of Jones Beach, the boardwalks of Coney Island, the roofs of Tar Beach, the towns of Jersey, the villages upstate, the hills of Connecticut—a weekend of baseballs soaring toward distant fences, the blare of Mel Allen gleefully announcing four homers in three games.

The Yankees won the World Series that year, and they won it again in 1950, and they won it again in 1951, and then DiMaggio retired at the age of 36. He had a great sense of self, and he knew it was time to go.

He left two of the greatest statistics in the history of baseball. Everybody knows about the 56-game hitting streak in 1941, but Frank Robinson, a great player of later generations, says he is awed by DiMaggio's career totals of 361 home runs and only 369 strikeouts, a staggering blend of power and self-control. Robinson, by contrast, hit 586 home runs and struck out 1,532 times, nearly a 1–3 ratio.

DiMaggio was poised off the field as well. His journey is surely not to be compared to that of Jackie Robinson, but Italian-Americans became bank presidents and college professors a bit more easily in the wake of this well-dressed and mannered son of a fisherman.

He effortlessly worked at never being embarrassed. It is quite possible that he knew he did not have much to say, so he did not say it, an exact opposite of the twits who cannot wait to tell their dismal stories to Barbara Walters or Jerry Springer. I suspect he would have held his counsel even if he were not shielding a terrible pain over Marilyn Monroe.

Only once did I ever see him look foolish—as a coach in the garish green and gold uniform of Charles O. Finley's Oakland A's. It was like displaying an El Greco in El Rastro, the flea market of Madrid, instead of the Prado.

He had a long time for other roles, as pitchman or citizen. At the 1983 World Series in Philadelphia, an elevator operator closed the door on DiMaggio, snapping, "Press only!" Asked if she knew who that was, she replied, "Sure, Mr. Coffee." And in the wake of the Bay Area earthquake in 1989, DiMaggio visited an emergency center in the Marina District to discover where his sister had been relocated. He stood in line, I am told, like any other worried relative.

Normally, the Yankee Clipper did not suffer strangers easily. He could ice you if you approached him at the wrong moment. Burned by the Yankees when he held out as a young player, he set the conditions for his appearances on Old-Timers' Day. He was always introduced last, always described as "the greatest living ballplayer," which was, of course, always true, right up until yesterday.

March 9, 1999

## Amid Crumbling Records, A Streak That Will Endure

### By MURRAY CHASS

Tommy Henrich walked toward home plate. It was the second game of a doubleheader in 1941, and the Yankees' right fielder was preparing to face Jack Wilson, the Boston Red Sox right-hander. Suddenly, Henrich heard a voice behind him. "Joe comes out," Henrich related, "and the first time in his life he shouted at me, 'Tom, you got my ball bat?' I said, 'I got one of your bats, but it's the one I've been using.' He looked at it and said, 'Someone stole my ball bat.'"

Two days before, against the Washington Senators, DiMaggio had broken George Sisler's American League record by hitting his 42d consecutive game. Now he was a hit away from tying Willie Keeler's major league record of 44 in a season, but he didn't have his game bat, his 36-ounce, 36-inch weapon of choice.

In his first trip up against Wilson, using another of his bats, DiMaggio lashed a line drive to right-center field that was caught. "If it had been my ball bat," he said to Henrich as they went to the outfield, "it would have been in there."

Henrich suggested to DiMaggio that he use the bat Henrich had been using. DiMaggio took it in his hands but said, "I don't want to use your bat." After making another out in his second time up, though, DiMaggio relented.

"The third time he batted," Henrich said, "he used it and got a hit."

About a week later, Henrich recalled, some fans in Newark discovered that a young man from their city had somehow stolen the bat. They reclaimed it and returned it to DiMaggio, and he used it for the rest of the most famous streak in sports history.

On July 17 in that fabled season of 1941, Al Smith and Jim Bagby Jr. of Cleveland held DiMaggio without a hit, stopping the streak at 56 games. For all his greatness during his 13-year career, DiMaggio, who died yesterday at age 84, will be remembered many years into the future for a record many people in baseball believe will never be broken.

Babe Ruth's career record of 714 home runs was broken, his season record of 60 and Roger Maris's of 61, too. Someone even came along and surpassed Lou Gehrig's consecutive games streak of 2,130, which people were convinced would never even be approached.

But DiMaggio's 56-game hitting streak? Come back at the end of the next millennium, many believe, and the line will still be in the record books: Most Games, Consecutive, 1 or more hits . . . 56, Joe DiMaggio, New York May 15–July 16, 1941.

"It seems that one's going to stand the test of time," said Tony Gwynn, the best hitter of this time. "But all records are made to be broken. Someone's going to come along and get on a roll, at least get close enough to mention Joe DiMaggio."

When Pete Rose hit in 44 consecutive games in 1978, DiMaggio's name was mentioned all right, and the challenge proved too great for Rose, who would end his career with the most hits in history.

In 20 seasons since then, only seven players have reached 30 games, including three the last two

## THROUGH THE SEASONS

As he batted and fielded his way to the Hall of Fame in a 13-season career with the Yankees, Joe DiMaggio could look back at 10 pennants and 9 World Series championships. But that was not all there was.

### 1936
**MAY 3** In his first major league game, playing left field and batting third, DiMaggio singles twice, triples and scores three runs in a 14–5 rout of the St. Louis Browns.
**JULY 7** DiMaggio becomes the first rookie to start an All-Star Game.
**WORLD SERIES** The Yankees' rookie center fielder bats .346 with nine hits in helping beat the Giants in six games.
*DiMaggio shares the American League leadership in triples with 15.*

### 1937
**JUNE 13** Three homers in a row by DiMaggio in the second game of a doubleheader against the Browns fail to bring the Yankees more than an 8–8 tie.
*DiMaggio leads league in homers with 46 and runs scored with 151*

### 1938
**WORLD SERIES** Yankees sweep Cubs, making it 3 for 3 for DiMaggio.

### 1939
**WORLD SERIES** Yanks sweep Reds, making it 4 for 4 for DiMaggio, who bats .313.
*DiMaggio is batting champion with career high .381 average.*

### 1940
**JULY 13** Against the Browns, DiMaggio has 4 hits and 7 r.b.i. in the opener and a two-run homer in Game 2.
*Another batting title, .352, but finally no World Series.*

### 1941
**MAY 15** The hitting streak starts in a 13–1 loss to the White Sox.

**JULY 1** DiMaggio matches (Wee) Willie Keeler's major league mark of 44 straight with a single against Boston.

**JULY 17** The arms of Al Smith and Jim Bagby Jr. combine with the glove of Ken Keltner to stop the hitting streak after 56 games and a month of national fascination.

**JULY 18** DiMaggio begins a hitting streak that lasts 16 games.

**WORLD SERIES** Another ring.

*DiMaggio leads league in r.b.i., 125 and total bases, 348.*

### 1942

**WORLD SERIES** The Cardinals win in five, DiMaggio's only Series loss.

### 1946

No World Series or .300 average in first year back from the service.

### 1947

**WORLD SERIES** Back to the Series, and back, back, back goes Al Gionfriddo of the Dodgers to foil him with a legendary catch in left-center at Yankee Stadium, the pivotal point of Game 6. The Yankees pull out Game 7 for DiMaggio's sixth ring.

*Though leading in no category, DiMaggio earns third m.v.p. award.*

### 1948

**MAY 23** Bob Feller of the Indians is victimized twice as DiMaggio homers three times in a 6–5 victory.

*No World Series but no chopped liver either; DiMaggio leads A.L. in homers, 39, r.b.i., 155, and in total bases, 355.*

### 1949

**JUNE 28–30** After missing the first 65 games of the season with injuries, DiMaggio breaks out in Boston with 4 homers and 9 r.b.i. in a three-game sweep that shocks the front-running Red Sox.

**WORLD SERIES** DiMaggio's seventh title in 11 years, in five games over the Dodgers.

### 1950

**WORLD SERIES** Game 2 goes to the Yankees, 2–1, when DiMaggio homers off Robin Roberts

years—Eric Davis, Sandy Alomar Jr. and Normar Garciaparra. All three were stopped at precisely 30. Only one player since Rose has gone beyond 34, and that was Paul Molitor with 39 in 1987.

"It was unbelievable to watch him and see how he handled himself," Jay Bell said of Molitor. "If anybody was going to be able to catch Rose and then DiMaggio, it was going to be Molly, and he fell short."

Bell, now with the Arizona Diamondbacks, knows about hitting streaks because in 1992, with the Pittsburgh Pirates, he had the National League's longest streak. But it was only 22 games long.

"Twenty-two was hard enough, Bell said. "I can't even think of what it would be like to do 30. If Molly couldn't do it and Rose couldn't, I don't know that anybody can do it. I can't imagine that one being broken. It will be tough to do."

No one on the Yankees paid much attention to DiMaggio's streak until he had reached 30, Henrich recalled. Then they took it seriously.

"He was up to 37," Henrich related as if it were yesterday, "and we were facing Eldon Auker. We were ahead by two runs in the last of the eighth, and DiMaggio is the fourth hitter. Johnny Sturm is already out, and Red Rolfe is at bat."

The thought struck Henrich that if Rolfe reached base, he could hit into a double and DiMaggio, who had not had a hit in his first three times up, would not bat again.

"I went to Joe McCarthy and said, 'If Rolfe gets on, is it O.K. if I bunt?' " Henrich recounted. "McCarthy thought for about three or four seconds and said O.K. Rolfe got a base on balls, and I bunted. DiMaggio came up and hit a line drive to right field. That got him past 37."

Gwynn, and eight-time batting champion, has never got past 25. "And that happened my second year in the big leagues," he said.

Hitting streaks are unforgiving. Fail to hit in one game, the batter starts over. For a player to match DiMaggio's feat, he has to get at least one hit in 56 consecutive games.

On his way to a mind-boggling 70 home runs last season, Mark McGwire went nine games without hitting a home run in late July and early August, and he hit only two home runs in a longer span of 19 games in that period. But then he hit 15 home runs in the next 22 games, breaking Maris's record with the 15th.

Hitting streaks don't allow make-ups. "You can't have an off day," Gwynn said.

A hitter, Bell said, "can have four great at-bats during the course of a game, sting the ball four consecutive times and still make four outs, so there has to be some luck involved."

If a game is rained out after five innings and the streaker doesn't have a hit in two at-bats, his streak is finished because the game is official.

of the Phillies in 10th inning as Yanks sweep Philadelphia.
*DiMaggio tops A.L. in slugging again with a .585 average.*

**1951**
WORLD SERIES in DiMaggio's final career at-bat, he doubles off Larry Jansen and the Yankees beat the Giants in six games—as they did in DiMaggio's rookie season 15 years earlier.

A home run hitter doesn't have to hit a home run in that game; he has the next game and more games after that. A player in a consecutive-games playing streak doesn't have to get a hit; he just has to show up during the game. Rain-shortened games don't work against him as long as he is in the lineup.

"Eventually a guy will come along who may possibly break it," Gwynn said, "but the game I see on an everyday basis, I don't see anyone doing it. The game is so specialized now. If you don't get it the first at-bat, you see the long man, the setup guy, the closer. That plus the scrutiny you have to go through if you're fortunate enough to get close."

Indeed, DiMaggio didn't have a slew of reporters, microphones and cameras dogging his every step before and after every one of those 56 games. Sammy Sosa seemed to thrive on the attention during the home run race last season; McGwire did not.

"They barely talk about it until you get to 30," Gwynn said. "Then when you get to 30, they talk about it every day. It's going to take a guy who's mentally tough, who'll talk about it before the game and after the game."

DiMaggio didn't talk about the streak. "He never mentioned it," Henrich said. "He wouldn't do that. Certainly he was proud of what he was doing, but he didn't show it. We didn't talk to him about it, either. DiMaggio wasn't that type of fellow."

If there was pressure on DiMaggio during the streak, Henrich said, it was when it reached the low 40's, as he approached the records. Henrich wondered how pitchers today would treat a player threatening DiMaggio's record.

"I wonder if some pitcher would do what Johnny Babich was going to do," Henrich said. "Babich said, 'I'll stop him.' He did it by not throwing the ball over the plate. But McCarthy gave him the hit sign on 3–0, and he hit a line drive to center and kept it going. I don't think any pitcher would have the gall not to pitch to a guy and live with that for the rest of his life."

DiMaggio's life has ended, but his streak will live long after him.


**REACHING 56**

**May 15** Single Singles off Ed Smith of the Chicago White Sox to begin streak.
**June 29** Extends streak to 42 games to pass George Sisler's A.L. record.
**July 2** Streak reaches 45 games, surpassing Willie Keeler's all-time record.
**July 17** Streak ends in Cleveland.

## Today's Yankees Mourn a Timeless Hero

### By BUSTER OLNEY

TAMPA, Fla., March 8—They began paying tribute to Joe DiMaggio here early this morning, fans old and young visiting the pinstriped plaque erected in his name outside Legends Field, many of them wearing Yankees caps. A few brought flowers, others took pictures, some prayed.

The Yankee players, too, honored the man introduced as "the greatest living ballplayer" at Yankee Stadium every year. Before tonight's exhibition game with Philadelphia, they emerged from their dugout, hats off, for a moment of silence, DiMaggio's No. 5 sewn onto the left sleeve of each uniform. Bob Cucuzza, the Yankees' equipment manager, had brought 300 of the emblems to Florida, just in case; he had hoped he would not have to use them.

When a highlight reel was shown on the video scoreboard, the fans all stood before anybody asked them to. "It's a sad day here," David Cone said.

Derek Jeter said, "There was a mystique about him, the way he played."

George Steinbrenner said, "It was the class and dignity with which he led his life that made him part of us."

Jeter learned of DiMaggio's death when the news crawled across the bottom of his television screen. To Jeter and to most of the other Yankees, DiMaggio was royalty who passed through the clubhouse once or twice a year: you never initiated conversation with him.

You could joke and laugh and swap stories with Whitey Ford and Reggie Jackson and other Yankees greats; with DiMaggio, most of the Yankees remained silent until he spoke to them. Jeter, Daryl Strawberry, Cone and others mentioned how they never had the intestinal fortitude to ask DiMaggio for an autograph; you heard stories, Andy Pettitte said, about how he refused autograph requests. Cone, in fact, bought a dozen balls autographed by DiMaggio, rather than ask him.

But DiMaggio repeatedly surprised them. Someone apparently mentioned to DiMaggio that right fielder Paul O'Neill had a collection of autographed bats, and before an Old-Timers' Day game, DiMaggio approached O'Neill and asked, "You have that bat for me to sign?" That bat, O'Neill said, is encased in his basement, "and always will be."

DiMaggio came face-to-face with Cone once, told him he had seen him pitch on many occasions. "Sometimes you look unhittable," DiMaggio said, "and sometimes you look very hittable."

Cone laughed today, recalling the exchange. "I didn't know what to make of it," Cone said. "I walked away with my tail between my legs."

Andy and Laura Pettitte attended a team dinner following the 1996 World Series victory and DiMaggio happened by, looking for a place to sit. He took a chair next to the pitcher and chatted amiably throughout the meal. "He really was very nice," Pettitte said. DiMaggio once paused to compliment Bernie Williams, the latest heir in the Yankees' long line of superlative center fielders. The praise stunned Williams, so much so that he does not recall anything else DiMaggio said to him.

David Wells, traded to Toronto less than three weeks ago, may have had the most extensive contact with DiMaggio. Before DiMaggio was honored before the final game of last season, on Joe DiMaggio Day, he congratulated Wells for his perfect game. Wells was so fidgety during the game that Manager Joe Torre facetiously suggested that he go bother DiMaggio—and Wells did, taking the elevator to Steinbrenner's office.

Wells joined DiMaggio, Phil Rizzuto and Steinbrenner, gabbing and laughing. Wells asked DiMaggio—"Mr. DiMaggio," Wells called him—for an autograph and the Yankees' legend obliged him. "When he showed up at the Stadium, George treated him like a king," Wells said today. "He'd roll out the red carpet, and rightfully so."

Before he threw out the first ball on opening day or on Old-Timers' Day, DiMaggio shook hands with players in the dugout, then strolled onto the field, ball in hand. O'Neill was struck by the way DiMaggio moved in his 80's, his stride even and graceful. You could see what a wonderful athlete he was, O'Neill said. Not until recent years did DiMaggio concede to age and move forward from the mound to shorten his toss to the catcher, and his throw usually was right on target; some of the Yankees were sure that he practiced.

After throwing the first ball, he would move forward and shake hands with the catcher—Joe Girardi last April—and say, "Good luck." And then he walked off steadily into the dugout, disappearing.

The daylight waned. Approaching DiMaggio's plaque, Pete Mastrobono, 86, removed his blue Yankees cap and covered his heart, silent words moving his lips. Now of Zephyr Hills, Fla., Mastrobono grew up in Westchester County and went to Yankee Stadium on Sundays with his friends, to watch DiMaggio with $2 tickets. Mastrobono remembered, in his mind's eye, how DiMaggio slammed home runs, the way he slowed gracefully after rounding first base once he knew the ball had cleared the fence.

Mastrobono had a ticket to tonight's game, a birthday present from neighbors who share his love for the Yankees and looked out for him in recent years, after Mastrobono's wife passed away. Ralph Zito—a Yankees zealot reared in Newark—invites Mastrobono to watch games with his family, including his daughter, Ginger, 14 and freckled; she inherited the Yankees gene, and has a particular affinity for Jeter. Italian meal before the World Series games, and every play seemed to spur memories and Mastrobono would tell stories until the Zitos would smile at each other and ask him to lower his voice. Ssshh, Jeter is batting.

Mastrobono backed away from DiMaggio's plaque before removing his Yankees cap. His aged eyes bright, Mastrobono smiled and said, "I just said hi to old Joe."

March 9, 1999

## Coast Friends Recall DiMaggio as a Loner

### By EVELYN NIEVES

SAN FRANCISCO—No matter where he lived, Joe DiMaggio's home was always North Beach, where people knew him when he lived in a rented flat on Taylor Street with eight brothers and sisters and played sandlot ball in hand-me-downs, same as everybody else.

In old North Beach, people know that DiMaggio was a brooder, always had been, and let him be. True, most of that world is gone—at least compared to the days when North Beach was all Italian and everybody's father was a fisherman. There are trendy restaurants there now, and the nightclubs, and tourists on the streets. In the end, DiMaggio's movements around town became as exquisitely predictable as his swing.

He ate at the same few restaurants, nursed his beers at the same few pubs, visited the same few friends. Sometimes he would pass by the San Francisco Italian Athletic Club, across the park from the church, SS.

Peter and Paul, where he married his first wife, Dorothy Arnold. Or he would take a turn by the New Pisa restaurant and drink black coffee at the bar, his back to the aging photos of himself along the wall. He would retreat for the day to the house overlooking the Marina that he bought for his parents the year he starred in his fourth consecutive World Series, 1939.

He almost never made public appearances, unless you count his occasional stops at Liverpool Lil's, a dark, cozy neighborhood bar not far from the Marina. Here, he drank working-Joe beers—Pabst, until the bar no longer carried it, then Budweiser—at a small table near the door. The table sat under two photos of DiMaggio: a framed Time magazine cover with him in the middle of that balletic swing, and a black-and-white picture of him leaning against the field-box railing, signing a ball. Sitting at that table, he never looked less than his best, in a crisp shirt, well-cut jacket and spit-shined shoes.

"He could be gruff or cranky," said Christy Witherspoon, Liverpool Lil's manager, who always brought honey-roasted peanuts for DiMaggio to have with his beers. "It just depended. It was funny. He liked to get some attention, but not too much. He wanted it when he wanted it."

It sometimes seemed as though he could not help enjoying the buzz his presence created, especially among women. "The ladies would go bananas when he came in," Witherspoon said. "Sometimes, someone would approach him, and he could be pleasant." But the smiles turned to stone whenever anyone mentioned Marilyn Monroe, "he would just hustle out of here," Witherspoon said.

His friends were amazed that DiMaggio landed Monroe, whom he married here at City Hall in 1954, showing her off afterward at his brother Tom's restaurant on Fisherman's Wharf. What was so remarkable about the union was that even after he became Joltin' Joe, American hero, he was still Joe DiMaggio of North Beach: shy, bashful and awkward around women.

"But he had taste," said Dante Benedetti, who runs the new Pisa restaurant. "I guess he went for the ones who led the team in hitting."

Benedetti, 79, was a part of baseball-crazed North Beach in the 1930's, when it was producing seven major league players, including three DiMaggio boys. In those days, Joe and his brothers—Tom and Mike, who never pursued the game, and Vince and Dom, who did—were the stars of the diamond.

There were a lot of kids, Benedetti said, and they would choose up sides. "If Joe was sitting there, he'd be picked first."

But often, DiMaggio was not waiting to play ball. He was selling newspapers on the street. "Joe was not a guy to pal around with," Benedetti said. "He had his own way."

The veterans of the Italian club, who went back more than 70 years with DiMaggio, remember him the same way. Mario Vigo, 91, remembers when the two played in an organized league together, before DiMaggio joined his brother Vince with the San Francisco Seals of the Pacific Coast League. "He played with the Jolly Knights team, and I played with him, and against him," Vigo said of Joe. "I didn't really pal around with him. He was just a regular guy, more of a loner, very quiet."

DiMaggio was never one to flaunt his status. In fact, some of the guys at the club said DiMaggio had zippers on his pockets, that he was tight with a dollar. But Benedetti said DiMaggio simply remembered what it was like to be poor. "He was brought up in a fisherman's family. He just happened to become a great ballplayer."

Benedetti remembers the time he asked DiMaggio why he didn't get out and show himself off to his public more. "He told me, 'Believe me, Dante, you'd get tired of it too,'" Benedetti said.

That made DiMaggio's appearance at the dedication of a field named for Dante Benedetti at the University of San Francisco all the more spectacular. Benedetti had been baseball coach at the university for 26 years, and the dedication, on March 2, 1985, had been announced in the San Francisco Chronicle. Since DiMaggio for years ignored all requests to appear at ceremonies, his homage to Benedetti at the dedication was a complete surprise.

"If they had written Joe a letter and asked him to come and talk the day they named the field for me," Benedetti said, "he never would have come. But on his own, he did it."

## Contemporaries Remember Him As the Best Baseball Had to Offer

### By JACK CURRY

They remembered Joe DiMaggio fondly and sadly yesterday and with the familiar words that had become forever linked with the player who treated center field at Yankee Stadium like his own playground. Class. Grace. Dignity. Greatness. The men who played with and against DiMaggio took deep breaths, forced their minds to rewind and spoke in reverential tones about perhaps the greatest all-around baseball player.

A day does not vanish without Al Gionfriddo being remembered by someone, anyone, of his wondrous catch against DiMaggio in the 1947 World Series. A fly ball does not sail into the gap without Bobby Brown telling himself that DiMaggio would have grabbed it, and without diving. A discussion with Yogi Berra about the most awe-inspiring dinner he ever had focuses on one of the meals that he shared with DiMaggio and Marilyn Monroe. A dialogue with Stan Musial about superb hitters is incomplete unless DiMaggio is prominently mentioned.

"Joe was the pride of the Yankees," Musial said. "He was the pride of baseball. He was a great, great player and a classy guy. He was a really classy guy. But, in our era, a lot of folks are passing on. It's part of life."

Berra was stymied for a moment when asked to describe DiMaggio's legacy with the Yankees before raising his hands and saying: "He's gotta be like Babe Ruth. The both of them. They were great."

Whether it was Whitey Ford getting misty about how he fell in love while watching DiMaggio as a 9-year-old attending his first game at the Stadium, Jerry Coleman chuckling as he discussed how DiMaggio told the second baseman to get out of the way if he heard him chasing a baseball or Hank Bauer revealing that the first time he went out for a drink with DiMaggio was 20 years after they first became teammates on the Yankees, splendid tales about DiMaggio abounded. There was so much to recall about DiMaggio, whose contemporaries referred to him as baseball's Sinatra.

"I think some people have a hard time understanding how much of a hero he was," said Brown, who played six years with DiMaggio. "The difference between then and now is the coverage on TV. Most of his career, there was no TV, or TV was in its earliest stages, so what people knew about him was not from a television image. It was the real thing. Once you saw him play and saw the way he carried himself, it was something that you didn't forget."

Not even if a player was wearing the same uniform.

"Right off the bat, he was my hero," Ford said. "He was the first player that I noticed as a kid. When I got the chance to play with him, I couldn't believe I was on the mound and he was in center field."

Coleman added: "He was the icon of baseball and in all sports in his day. There were people who dominated the sports pages like Dempsey and Tunney and Louis, but he dominated them all."

What did opponents think of facing DiMaggio?

"That we had Joe DiMaggio and they didn't," Berra said.

And what did Berra think of dining with DiMaggio and Monroe?

"It was Marilyn Monroe," Berra answered incredulously. "That was great."

Gionfriddo defeated DiMaggio for one moment more than 50 years ago when he retreated to the fence at Yankee Stadium to make a one-hand grab on DiMaggio's 415-foot blast in Game 6 of the World Series. The black-and-white footage of DiMaggio kicking at the dirt after the catch is a rare moment when he displayed any emotion. While Gionfriddo never played in another game after the Dodgers lost the series in seven games, the 5-foot-6-inch left fielder remained linked with DiMaggio for more than half a century.

"I had my moment in the sun, I guess," Gionfriddo said, almost apologetically.

Two years ago, DiMaggio and Gionfriddo attended a baseball card show together, and Gionfriddo asked DiMaggio to autograph a picture of the famous catch. DiMaggio wrote, "Al, 49 years have passed. But it hasn't passed. Joe DiMaggio."

Of course, the record that is synonymous with the great DiMaggio is his 56-game hitting streak in 1941. It is a record that Musial, a Hall of Famer who accumulated 3,630 career hits, gushed over. "What Joe did in baseball will never be equaled," Musial said. "No one has ever come close to 56 games, and no one will."

Musial recalled how the Cardinals and Yankees shared spring training facilities in St. Petersburg, Fla., during his rookie season in 1942 and how impressive DiMaggio was in person. Coleman visited troops in Vietnam with DiMaggio, Tony Conigliaro and Peter Rose in 1967 and said the other men "might as well have been invisible."

The men who played with and against DiMaggio watched the news stations for updates on his condition and were buoyed when he was released from the hospital. They hoped it was a good sign. That routine of waiting for positive news ended yesterday.

"When you see these things, you remember how young someone like DiMaggio used to be and how you used to think that they were indestructible," Brown said. "You always find that we're human. It's a stark feeling. No one is immune to aging. You wish that some were. There are people who we'd like to keep the way that we remember them forever."

# DAVE ANDERSON

## *Sports of The Times*

### 60 Years In Public's Eye: His Privacy, Pride, Ego and Dignity

For years, Joe DiMaggio had fresh flowers placed at Marilyn Monroe's grave; now he takes her memory to his grave. During the baseball memorabilia boom, he sold himself as an icon for the millions of dollars he never made as a player, but he never sold his memories of the Hollywood goddess he was married to for 274 days.

Whenever a book publisher talked about him writing his autobiography, he declined.

"They want me to write about Marilyn," he once said. "I don't want to do that. I'll never do that."

That's maintaining your privacy, which Joe DiMaggio did even better than he played baseball.

You can still see him on television in grainy black-and-white newsreel film, but only today's old-timers really saw him swing a bat with that sweeping follow-through and really saw him run down deep fly balls in Yankee Stadium in the days when center field was much bigger than it is now.

"He did everything so easily," his first Yankee manager, Joe McCarthy, once said. "You never saw him make a great catch. You never saw him dive for a ball. He didn't have to. He was already there to catch it."

He inspired songs. His 56-game hitting streak in 1941 prompted Les Brown's band to record "Joltin' Joe

DiMaggio." Paul Simon sang "Where have you gone, Joe DiMaggio? A nation turns its lonely eyes to you."

He even inspired literature. In Ernest Hemmingway's "Old Man and the Sea," the old Cuban fisherman says: "I would like to take the great DiMaggio fishing. They say his father was a fisherman. Maybe he was as poor as we are and would understand."


DiMaggio's father had come over from Sicily and settled in Martinez, Calif., where the great DiMaggio was born across the bay from San Francisco. He would have a 61-game hitting streak as an 18-year-old outfielder for the San Francisco Seals in the Pacific Coast League before joining the Yankees in 1936.

"My father would get The San Francisco Chronicle at 5 in the morning," he once said. "If I had a good day, he'd wake my mother up. If I didn't, he'd let her sleep."

His mother was usually awakened. In 13 seasons interrupted by three years in the Army for World War II, he batted .325 with 361 homers and 1,573 runs batted in as the Yankees won 10 American League pennants and nine World Series.

"When he walked into the clubhouse, the lights flickered," Peter Sheehy, the legendary Yankee clubhouse man, often said. "Then he'd turn to me an say, 'Half a cup.'"

He meant half a cup of coffee. Years later he emerged as "Mr. Coffee," shilling for a coffee maker, and as a longtime spokesman for the Bowery Savings Bank. Although not yet 37 after the 1951 season, he had turned down the Yankees' offer to continue his $100,000 salary even as a part-time player.

"I'm no longer Joe DiMaggio," he said.

That's maintaining your pride, as he did the night his 56-game hitting streak was stopped in Cleveland when Ken Keltner played a deep third base for the Indians.

"Keltner was daring me to bunt," he once said. "I hadn't bunted during the streak."

And he didn't bunt that night as Keltner turned two sizzling grounders into outs.

In the years when the St. Louis Browns were in the American League, DiMaggio was sitting in the dugout at the steaming Sportsman's park before a Sunday afternoon doubleheader when he was asked how he was always able to perform at such a high level. He gestured toward the grandstand.

"Maybe some of these people," he said quietly, "never saw me play before."

That's maintaining your ego, which all the great ones have, with dignity. His teammate Bobby Brown, later the American League president, best described DiMaggio's blend of ego with dignity.

"Joe goes through life scared to death people will ask for his autograph," Brown said. "And scared to death they won't."


He could laugh, too. He often told about the time he hit a home run off Bobo Newsom's fastball. Connie Mack, the Philadelphia A's manager, ordered Newsom never to throw DiMaggio a fastball again. His next time up, he hit a curveball for another homer.

"As I rounded third base," he remembered, "I heard Bobo yell, 'Hey, Mr. Mack, he hit yours farther than he hit mine.'"

But now Joe DiMaggio, fulfilling Paul Simon's song, has really "left and gone away." And taken Marilyn Monroe with him.

# MICKEY MANTLE

Mickey Mantle, 1951, picks a bat at Yankee Stadium. (THE NEW YORK TIMES ARCHIVES)

### *Yanks Blank Red Sox in First Game Before 44,860; Giants Shut Out Braves*

## RASCHI AND JENSEN SPARK 5–0 TRIUMPH

### Yankee Ace Holds Red Sox to 6 Singles—Outfielder Gets a 2-Run Homer in Third

## THEN HE DOUBLES IN SIXTH

### 3 Tallies Follow to Rout Wight—Bombers Honored by Many Awards Before Contest

### By JOHN DREBINGER

Amid the usual pomp of a Stadium inaugural, the Yankees launched the 1951 American League season yesterday in much the same manner that they had closed the 1950 campaign last October.

They unfurled their world series banner in the snappy breeze and then, to the thunderous cheers of 44,860 paying eye witnesses, those extraordinary Bombers proceeded to take that first long stride toward another flag by convincingly drubbing those perennial spring favorites, the Red Sox.

The score of 5 to 0 scarcely begins to describe the disparity that appeared to exist between the two clubs of this important day at least.

Vic Raschi, the big wheel of Casey Stengel's mound staff, hurled the shut-out, scattering six hits, all singles, across as many innings.

Behind this effective hurling, Jackie Jensen, the blond thatched outfielder, was the surprise entry to steal the thunder of the performance. Named to play left field because Hank Bauer was sidelined with a charley horse, the bonus freshman of last year opened the scoring with a two-run homer in the third inning that sailed into the right-field stand.

## Californian Doubles in Sixth

In the sixth, the husky Californian led off with a two-bagger against Southpaw Bill Wight, among the latest of Boston acquisitions the past winter. In the wake of that double came solid singles by Mickey Mantle, tagged as the rookie sensation of 1951, the venerable Joe DiMaggio and Yogi Berra.

The broadside, following a slight fielding miscalculation on the part of Steve O'Neill's minions, sent three tallies skipping over the plate. It routed Wight and just about completed the day's work for both sides.

Just once did the Bosox so much as offer a threatening gesture. That was right at the start and ironically the elder DiMaggio wrecked the effort.

The spectators had just settled back into their seats after a long series of presentations when Dom DiMaggio ripped one of Raschi's offerings into right-field for a single. Bill Goodman followed with a blooper into short center that appeared tagged as another single.

From deep center, DiMaggio, J., admittedly not the nimble footed performer of old, turned back the clock as he streaked over the freshly seeded turf and snared the ball inches off the ground.

## Little Professor Gets a Lesson

Since the Yankees trained on the Pacific coast this year and the Red Sox in their familiar Sarasota lair, somebody must have slightly misinformed brother Dom on just how far back brother Joe had gone in his fielding. For the little professor was virtually at second base when the Clipper made that amazing catch, so the latter almost could have walked to first base to complete the double play.

With that twin killing, which the Clipper made with the conventional toss to Johnny Mize at first, one could hear the lock on the iron door click once again on Boston hopes. Only two men had batted, but one could sense the end was written for another day, and perhaps another season, even though Ted Williams did follow resolutely with a single.

As in the past, the Tom Yawkey entry reached the Stadium loaded with additional strength. At short it had the talented Lou Boudreau and the former Cleveland skipper acquitted himself well. He got one of the six singles and, though he fumbled one ball for an inconsequential error, aided in the making of two sharp double plays.

## Stephens Still in Line-up

But force of habit seems to exert an astounding influence upon a Red Sox manager, whether he be the capable O'Neill or the retired Joe McCarthy. Despite all the spring warnings that Vern Stephens, the strictly Fenway Park player, would not appear in a Boston line-up on the road and that Johnny Pesky would be the third sacker, Junior occupied the hot corner in the line-up and batted in the clean-up spot.

In that important post he got no hits, slapped into a double play and ironically in the field committed a mental slip at third that paved the way for the Yanks' decisive thrust in the sixth.

To young Jerry Coleman went the distinction of the first Yankee hit, a single to left in the third. Raschi sacrificed and a moment later Jensen, a right-handed batter, stroked a hefty shot into the right-field stand.

Coleman almost did it again for the Yanks in the fifth when he singled to right behind a pass to Bill Johnson, but a fine peg by Goodman nipped Buffalo Bill at third. There was no checking the Bombers in the sixth, though. Following Jensen's double, also to right, Phil Rizzuto bunted.

As a bunt it wasn't up to Li'l Phil's best. It was tapped pretty hard and almost into pitcher Wight's hands. A put-out at third appeared simple, but Stephens failed to get back in time, missed the tag and the Yanks had runners on first and third.

Mantle, making his debut as a Yankee, lashed a single into left and Jensen scored. DiMaggio, J., followed with another to the same spot and Rizzuto scored. Berra slammed one into center for the third run and Wight was through.

Ellis Kinder checked the drive, gave way to a pinch-hitter and then Maurice McDermott blanked the Bombers the rest of the way.

Only two Boston runners got to second. None reached third.

In the sixth Williams drew a pass, but Rizzuto made an electrifying stop on Stephens' grounder in deep short and started a twin killing. In the eighth Goodman singled, only to be forced by Williams. After Walt Dropo had singled in the ninth the battle ended as that matchless pair, Rizzuto and Coleman, turned on one more eye-filling double play.

### YANKEES' BOX SCORE

| BOSTON (A.) | ab | r. | h. | po. | a. | NEW YORK (A.) | ab | r. | h. | po. | a. |
|---|---|---|---|---|---|---|---|---|---|---|---|
| D. DiMag'o., cf | 3 | 0 | 2 | 1 | 0 | Jensen, lf | 4 | 2 | 2 | 3 | 0 |
| Goodman, rf | 3 | 0 | 1 | 2 | 1 | Rizzuto, ss | 3 | 1 | 0 | 1 | 3 |
| Williams, lf | 3 | 0 | 1 | 1 | 0 | Mantle, rf | 4 | 1 | 1 | 3 | 0 |
| Stephens, 3b | 4 | 0 | 0 | 2 | 2 | J. DiMag'o., cf | 4 | 0 | 1 | 2 | 1 |
| Dropo, 1b | 4 | 0 | 1 | 10 | 0 | Berra, c | 2 | 0 | 1 | 6 | 0 |
| Doerr, 2b | 4 | 0 | 0 | 3 | 2 | Mize, 1b | 3 | 0 | 0 | 8 | 0 |
| Boudreau, ss | 4 | 0 | 1 | 1 | 3 | Collins, 1b | 0 | 0 | 0 | 1 | 0 |
| Rosar, c | 2 | 0 | 0 | 4 | 1 | Johnson, 3b | 2 | 0 | 0 | 1 | 1 |
| Wight, p | 2 | 0 | 0 | 0 | 2 | Coleman, 2b | 3 | 1 | 2 | 2 | 4 |
| Kinder, p | 0 | 0 | 0 | 0 | 0 | Raschi, p | 2 | 0 | 0 | 0 | 1 |
| [a]Maxwell | 1 | 0 | 0 | 0 | 0 | | | | | | |
| McDerm'tt, p | 0 | 0 | 0 | 0 | 1 | | | | | | |
| Total | 30 | 0 | 6 | 24 | 12 | Total | 27 | 5 | 7 | 27 | 10 |

[a]Batted for Kinder in seventh.

| Boston | 000 | 000 | 000—0 |
|---|---|---|---|
| New York | 002 | 003 | 00..—5 |

Error—Boudreau.

Runs batted in—Jensen 2, Mantle, J. DiMaggio, Berra.

Two-base hit—Jensen. Home run—Jensen. Sacrifices—Raschi, Rizzuto. Double plays—J. DiMaggio and Mize; Rizzuto, Coleman and Mize; Wight, Boudreau and Dropo; Boudreau, Doerr and Dropo; Rizzuto, Coleman and Collins. Left on bases—New York 2, Boston 7. Bases on balls—Off Wight 2, Raschi 4. Struck out—By Raschi 6, Wight 1, McDermott 1. Hits—Off Wight 7 in 5 innings; McDermott 0 in 2, Kinder 0 in 1. Winning pitcher—Raschi (1-0). Losing pitcher—Wight (0-1). Umpires—McGowan, McKinley, Honochick and Soar. Time of game—2: 12. Attendance—44,860.

## Pre-Game Awards Numerous

In the pre-game ceremonies, which opened with the traditional parade to the center-field flagpole behind Major Francis Sutherland's Seventh Regiment Bans, prizes and awards were tossed about at home plate as if it were bank night at the lodge.

Dick Butler, deputy for the absent baseball commissioner, Albert B. Chandler, presented to all the Yankee players their individual world series emblems in the form of rings and wrist watches.

President Will Harridge of the American League bestowed upon Rizzuto the Kenesaw Mountain Landis award as the circuit's most valuable player and to the youthful Coleman went the New York Baseball Writers' Babe Ruth memorial plaque as the outstanding player in the 1950 world series.

Biggest prize of all was the three-and-a-half-foot trophy given to Mel Allen by the Sporting News as the foremost baseball broadcaster of 1950. Sporting News awards also went to Rizzuto as the year's No. 1 player and to George M. Weiss, Yankee general manager, as baseball's outstanding executive.

In the parade were Police Commissioner Thomas F. Murphy, easily recognizable as he towered above everyone else in his familiar bowler hat, and Fire Commissioner George P. Monaghan. Others to march, along with the players of both clubs, were James L. Lyons, Bronx Borough President, and the Yanks' official family, President Dan Topping, Vice President Del Webb and Weiss.

In the center-field flagpole ceremonies, Miss Lucy Monroe sang the Star Spangled Banner to the raising of the American flag, accomplished by three strong-armed young marines, after which Stengel, in a Mighty Casey solo act, raised the world series pennant all by himself.

As a reminder of last year, Eddie (Whitey) Ford, freshman star of 1950, but now a rookie in the Army, tossed out the first ball.

October 6, 1951

## *Yanks Win, 3 to 1, Tie Series; Lopat Holds Giants to 5 Hits*

### By JOHN DREBINGER

The Polo Grounds express that so fantastically had thundered into a National League pennant and then bowled over the Yankees in the opening clash of the 1951 world series, ran out of fuel at the Stadium yesterday.

As it came to a dead stop a lot of things caught up with Leo Durocher and his Giants very fast, including a 3–1 defeat which Casey Stengel's Bombers expertly slapped on them in the second game. That squared the struggle at a victory apiece as it moves into the Polo Grounds for the third game this afternoon.

For days on end the baseball world had been hearing and reading about those amazing Giants. But yesterday it was largely the Giants, as well as a majority in a gathering of 66,018, who were amazed.

Eddie Lopat baffled them with his weird assortment of left-handed "nothing ball" deliveries. Even more bewildering was the versatility of the Yankee attack which, skillfully manipulated by Professor Stengel, toppled the Giants' own talented right-hander, Larry Jansen, primed as the latter was to hurl perhaps one of the best games of his career.

## Drives Across Final Tally

A couple of fancy bunts and a pop fly single gave the American League champions a run in the first inning. In the second Joe Collins popped a home run into the seats in right field and, in the eighth, by way of demonstrating that there is no telling which end of the Yankee batting order carries the dynamite, Lopat himself drove in the third and final Bomber tally with a single. Relief Pitcher George Spencer was the victim of that one.

It was all done neatly and quietly. In contrast with the tempestuous and nerve-tingling battles that the fans had been witnessing of late, this one, indeed, was a rather drab affair for all that the weather was perfect for something infinitely more exciting.

As for the Giants offensive, it spluttered fitfully all day, managed to jam one run across in the seventh when pinch hitter Bill Rigney hit a fly ball with the bases full and then petered out completely.

Indeed, only one Giant stood out today as Lopat handcuffed the National Leaguers on five hits. That was the still rampant Monte Irvin, who got three of the Polo Grounders' blows.

All of them were singles, the second one pacing the Giants to their one tally in the seventh. The three, together with the four safeties he got in Thursday's opener, brought his world series total to seven, a start that could see this Negro star set a new series record for total hits.

The present mark is twelve, held jointly by four players. Two of these, Edgar Rice and Pepper Martin, made it in seven games. Two others, Buck Herzog and Joe Jackson required eight.

## Still Seeks First Hit

About the only damaging Giant spot came in the fifth when Willie Mays, still seeking his first hit in the series, lifted a high fly in right center. It resulted in an easy out for Joe DiMaggio but, through a rather freakish mishap, eliminated another Yankee player. Dashing over from right field, Mickey Mantle, fleet-footed outfielder, in some unaccountable manner tripped as he came near DiMaggio and fell flat. He had to be carried off the field on a stretcher and later it was revealed by Dr. Sidney Gaynor, Yankee physician, that the youngster had suffered a sprained right knee that would sideline him for the remainder of the series.

Perhaps the only genuinely exciting moments of the entire day came in the first inning when the Stengeleers craftily opened with their bunting attack that all but had the Giants bumping their heads.

The crowd, which, though slightly larger than for Thursday's opener showed slightly less in receipts with $310,215, had just finished straggling into the arena when the fun began. Mantle pushed a swinging bunt toward the right side of the mound and, as Jansen sought to collar it, the tall Oregonian went sprawling head over heels.

Brushing himself off, Larry returned to the mound to pitch to Phil Rizzuto and promptly had his composure upset again as Li'l Phil followed with another perfectly executed swinging bunt to the right of the mound.

## Lockman's Throw Wide

This one had Jansen, First Baseman Whitey Lockman and even such an old hand as Second Baseman Eddie Stanky running in all directions. Lockman finally caught up with it and threw the ball to Stanky, who by now had headed to first base. But the peg went wide and Mantle wound up on third on the error.

Both bunts were breathtaking affairs and perhaps, on his own say so, no one was more surprised than Stengel himself, Casey later insisting that he had not conceived this part of the attack.

At all events, it did have the Giants rattled. Gil McDougald then lifted a rather feeble pop fly in short right. Henry Thompson, subbing for the injured Don Mueller, came tearing in for it and, for a few fleeting moments, it looked as if he would catch it. But Mr. Henry couldn't quite make it and, as the ball fell in front of him, Mantle streaked over the plate.

Curiously, the Yankee attack folded here as swiftly as it had flared up, for Jansen now really began to pitch in earnest. DiMaggio might have dealt the Giants a devastating blow, but the old Clipper, who was to put in another hitless afternoon, broke up this rally by drilling into a double play, while Yogi Berra brought it to a stop by striking out. Still, the Yanks had one tally, and that was to prove a mighty tough break for Jansen. For the tall Northwesterner was to allow only one more Bomber to get on base in his five remaining rounds on the hill.

## Back Against Field Boxes

That was Collins and Joe not only got on base but touched all the bases. Jansen had just retired Gene Woodling and Bobby Brown in the last of the second when Collins lifted a towering fly toward right. His back to the field boxes, Thompson was all set to catch it, but unhappily for Mr. Henry he was still about two rows away. It fell into the seats, and the jubilant Yankees were two up.

Thirteen Yankees went out in a row before Jansen's air-tight pitching after Collins had squeezed out that homer. Had the Giants been able to squeeze just one more run out of their counteroffensive in the top of the seventh, Larry might have fared better on the day. But when that all-out bid by Durocher for a second tally failed it settled the issue for the day.

For six innings exactly three Giants got on base, so adroitly did Lopat manipulate the strings. In the second inning, Irvin opened with his first single, a solid shot to center. Monte even stole second, much to the annoyance of Berra, but not one of the next three could push the ball out of the infield. In the third Stanky walked.

Not another Giant got on until, with two out in the sixth, Alvin Dark singled to left. But Bobby Thomson, another of the series' headliners who had to spend a hitless afternoon, had nothing better to offer than a high fly which DiMaggio smothered in center. Finally, in the seventh, the Giants got to moving and the crowd, which ever since the second, had sat in almost dead silence, began to perk up.

Again it was Irvin who strove to spark the Polo grounders into action. He singled to left and, when Lockman followed with a sharp single to center, the Giants had runners on first and second. They might even have had one of them on third, for it looked as though Irvin, with his great speed, might easily have made that bag on the Lockman hit.

## Takes Prudent Course

But he was apparently flagged down by Durocher. Leo, two runs behind and realizing he was struggling against tough pitching, doubtless decided on a more prudent course. DiMaggio still can throw when occasion demands. In the end, however, it really didn't make much difference.

For a moment the rally stalled when Willie Mays, once again hitless, bunted into a force play at second and that removed Lockman. But when Wes Westrum drew a pass, Lopat's second and last of the day, the bases were filled.

Durocher now started to stir things up by firing into the fray a profusion of pinch operators. He sent Hank Schenz in to run for Westrum and Rigney was assigned to bat for Thompson.

The moves produced some measure of result, for Rigney lifted a substantial fly to Hank Bauer, Mantle's replacement in right, and Irvin dashed home with the run.

But that's how far the Giants got even though Durocher made one more switch. He called Ray Noble, his Negro second-string catcher, to bat for Jansen, a tough decision to make, considering how smoothly Larry was pitching.

But a hit, not pitching, was something the Giants in this tense moment needed most, and the blow never came. For Noble's mightiest cut at the ball resulted in nothing more than a pop foul that Berra caught behind the plate.

## His Effort in Vain

And with that the Giants as good as folded for the day. Durocher had made one desperate effort to get his Polo Grounds express going but something clogged the machinery and that's as far as it went.

To make the Giants cause even more hopeless, the Yanks in the last of the eighth picked up one more run. Spencer, who, replacing Jansen in the last of the seventh, had kept the bases clear in that round, had Brown greet him with a single to open the last of the eighth. After Billy Martin had been sent in to run for the doctor, Collins bounced an easy grounder to Thomson. Bobby fielded the ball neatly and with the best of intentions of starting a double play by way of second.

But Dark and Stanky somehow left the keystone sack uncovered and, with nobody at second to receive his throw, Thomson finally fired the ball to first for the put-out on the batter. It seemed trivial at that, but it was to cost the Giants another run. For Martin was now on second and, a moment later, Billy was over the plate as Lopat smacked a single into center field.

Lopat never gave the Giants another chance after the seventh. The irrepressible Irvin opened the ninth with a single to center. But this time Lockman forced him at second. Mays also slapped into a force play and Clint Hartung, who had come into the fray as a right fielder, ended it with a grounder to Collins, who deftly tossed the ball to Lopat at first for the final putout.

Thus, Stengel and Durocher stand all square at a victory apiece and today, as the conflict moves over to the Polo Grounds, which is to be the scene of action for the next three games, it will be Jim Hearn, the tall right-hander who downed the Dodgers in the first game of the National League play-off series on Monday against Vic Raschi, right-handed twenty-one game winner of the Bombers.

## The Box Score

### SECOND GAME

| NEW YORK GIANTS | | | | | | | NEW YORK YANKEES | | | | | | |
|---|---|---|---|---|---|---|---|---|---|---|---|---|---|
| | AB. | R. | H. | PO. | A. | E. | | AB. | R. | H. | PO. | A. | E. |
| Stanky, 2b | 3 | 0 | 0 | 1 | 4 | 0 | Mantle, rf | 2 | 1 | 1 | 0 | 0 | 0 |
| Dark, ss | 4 | 0 | 1 | 0 | 4 | 0 | Bauer, rf | 2 | 0 | 0 | 1 | 0 | 0 |
| Thomson, 3b | 4 | 0 | 0 | 2 | 3 | 0 | Rizzuto, ss | 4 | 0 | 1 | 2 | 2 | 0 |
| Irvin, lf | 4 | 1 | 3 | 3 | 0 | 0 | McDougald, | 3 | 0 | 1 | 2 | 3 | 0 |

| Lockman, 1b | 4 | 0 | 1 | 11 | 0 | 1 | 2b., 3b | | | | | |
| Mays, cf | 4 | 0 | 0 | 2 | 0 | 0 | DiMaggio, cf | 3 | 0 | 0 | 4 | 0 | 0 |
| Westrum, c | 2 | 0 | 0 | 5 | 0 | 0 | Berra, c | 3 | 0 | 0 | 2 | 0 | 0 |
| bSchenz | 0 | 0 | 0 | 0 | 0 | 0 | Woodling, lf | 3 | 0 | 0 | 4 | 0 | 0 |
| Hartung, rf | 1 | 0 | 0 | 0 | 0 | 0 | Brown, 3b | 3 | 0 | 1 | 0 | 4 | 0 |
| Thompson, rf | 2 | 0 | 0 | 0 | 0 | 0 | cMartin | 0 | 1 | 0 | 0 | 0 | 0 |
| aRigney | 1 | 0 | 0 | 0 | 0 | 0 | Coleman, 2b | 0 | 0 | 0 | 1 | 0 | 0 |
| Spencer, p | 0 | 0 | 0 | 0 | 0 | 0 | Collins, 1b | 3 | 1 | 1 | 9 | 2 | 0 |
| Jansen, p | 2 | 0 | 0 | 0 | 0 | 0 | Lopat, p | 3 | 0 | 1 | 2 | 2 | 0 |
| Noble, c | 1 | 0 | 0 | 0 | 0 | 0 | | | | | | | |
| Total | 32 | 1 | 5 | 24 | 11 | 1 | Total | 29 | 3 | 6 | 27 | 13 | 0 |

aFlied out for Thompson in seventh.

bRan for Westrum in seventh.

cRan for Brown in eighth.

| Giants | 000 000 100—1 |
| Yankees | 110 000 01..—3 |

Runs batted in—McDougald, Collins, Rigney, Lopat.

Home run—Collins. Stolen base—Irvin. Left on bases—Giants 6, Yankees 2. Bases on balls—Off Lopat 2 (Stanky, Westrum). Struck out—By Lopat 1 (Thompson); Jansen 5 (Berra, Mantle, DiMaggio, Lopat, McDougald). Hits and runs— Off Jansen 4 and 2 in 6 innings; Spencer 2 and 1 in 2. Double play—Dark, Stanky and Lockman. Winning pitcher—Lopat. Losing pitcher—Jansen. Umpires—Lee Ballafant (N.), plate; Joe Paparella (A.), first base; Al Barlick, (N.) second base; Bill Summers (A.), third base; Art Gore (N.), left field; John Stevens (A.), right field. Time of game—2:05. Attendance— 66,018.

---

October 6, 1951

### *Yanks Joy Over Triumph Is Tempered by Loss of Mantle for Remaining Games*

## NEW LEAD-OFF MAN STENGEL PROBLEM

### Pilot Considering Rizzuto and Woodling for Top Spot to Replace Injured Mantle

## EXPLAINS BUNTING ATTACK

### Says Yankee Players Acted on Their Own—Lopat Praises Irvin's Hitting Prowess

#### By JAMES P. DAWSON

The Yankees were happy yesterday, but not excessively so. They were noisy, but in a restrained way. Casey Stengel was giving out with the big wink as he led his triumphant squad up the dugout runway to the clubhouse. But only the muscles about his eyes moved. There was no smile. Rather, the impression was that the Yankee pilot was more relieved than enthusiastic about this 3-to-1 victory over the Giants which deadlocked the series at a game apiece.

For the triumph was costly. The Yanks lost their service of the highly publicized high school boy, Mickey Mantle, for the remainder of the series.

Dr. Sidney Gaynor, the Bombers' physician, made this announcement. He diagnosed Mantle's trouble as a sprained muscle on the inside of the right knee, sustained when Mickey crashed in some mysterious manner in the fifth inning under a fly raised by the Giants' Willie Mays.

Carried off the field on a stretcher as Hank Bauer took over in right field, Mantle was ruefully appraising a right leg encased in a splint and bandages when his mates barged into the clubhouse. With difficulty Mantle got into his street clothes, after answering solicitous inquiries. He hobbled, painfully into Trainer Gus Mauch's room.

With a wan smile Mickey responded to the good-natured "ribbing" of Lefty Ed Lopat, whose superb pitching throttled the National League champions; Joe Collins, whose home run sealed the doom of the Giants, and Frank Shea, relief pitcher who has an infection of the little finger of his left hand.

## Unable to Explain Accident

Mantle was concerned with his misfortune, sorrowed by an accident he could not explain, which abruptly took him out of his first world series before he really had a chance to shine.

Mickey's loss posed a problem for Manager Stengel. This emergency could very well explain the attitude, almost of reserve, with which the Yankee skipper reviewed the triumph of his club over Larry Jansen.

Stengel must re-align his squad. He must assign a new lead-off man. He gave it all the implication of a weighty problem. And it is. The pilot can lead off with Phil Rizzuto or with Gene Woodling. His outfield for the rest of the series appears to be Woodling, Joe DiMaggio and Bauer, regardless of right or left handed rival pitching. The prospects of shifting an infielder to the outfield—say, putting Joe Collins on the picket line and inserting Big Jawn Mize in the line-up—are not encouraging. Although Stengel professed uncertainty on the point, Mize has a back and leg condition which, Big Jawn said, makes it difficult for him to play first. The complaints, however, do not eliminate him as a pinch hitter.

## Sees Possible Mistake

"I don't know who I'll make lead off," said Stengel, "I'll play Bauer in right, but I must give the line-up for tomorrow's game overnight consideration. It may be Woodling or it may be Rizzuto in the top spot. All I know now is that I'll pitch Vic Raschi tomorrow. I haven't given a thought to the pitching situation beyond tomorrow's game. I'll have to be guided by what happens tomorrow in the Polo Grounds.

"That game today makes this a good series now. I thought we played better ball today than yesterday. For one thing, our pitching was better. Maybe losing the opener pepped the boys up a little. Mantle and Rizzuto were bunting on their own with those two stabs that brought our first run. They're drilled to do that whenever they think they can get away with it. They got away with it both times.

"Maybe I made a mistake myself in that first. Maybe I should have had my guys running after McDonald's blooper scored Mantle, with DiMaggio up there and none out. I never gave a thought to Joe bunting. Nobody ever has to tell that fellow what to do when he's up there. He knows, and, whatever he thinks necessary he does.

"I thought we might have got some more runs in the first, but that's one of those things. Collins' homer in the second made it easier. Lopat pitched a great game out there, a smart game. Then Jansen was real good, too. He throws a fast ball four places. He's here, there and all over with it, giving you plenty of trouble. Both clubs are fast, too. They've proved that. Billy Martin got a break when they gummed up a double play in the eighth, and he had just enough lead to come in ahead of a great throw by that Mays. There's a fast guy who can throw."

## Lopat Asks Question

Manager Stengel said he had no intention of dropping a hitless DiMaggio lower in the batting order. He said, without intending reflection on his hitters, that he has encountered trouble finding a clean-up man and plans to go along with Wallopin' Joe in the old, familiar slot.

"Where are those fellows who are going to murder left-handed pitching. I thought the Giants were southpaw killers."

The flame-haired Lopat let loose with that shout, circulating among his mates, acknowledging compliments and extending congratulations to Collins, Bobby Brown, Mantle, Rizzuto and Gil McDougald, the hitters who gave him the runs he needed.

"That Irvin gave me some trouble with his three hits. He's a real, good hitter. Jansen didn't make it any easier for me, either. He pitched swell ball. But my plan was to keep them off balance; tip them this way and that. I gave them a lot of screw balls, knucklers, curves and my 'fast' stuff. I think I should have had Irvin's hit in the seventh. In fact, I thought I had it. Then it skipped by me.

"But, I wasn't worried out there when they got three runs and had the bases loaded. I fed Rigney two screw balls and then got him to lift a fly on a fast ball. I fed Noble screw balls until he fouled out."

Joe Collins said he made his homer off a low curve. "I fell into it," he said, with a smile. But, with that thrust, Jansen and the Giants fell in defeat.

April 18, 1953

## *Giants Divide With Dodgers; Mantle's 565-Foot Home Run Helps Yankees Win*

### *Towering Drive by Yank Slugger Features 7–3 Defeat of Senators*

### *Mantle's 565-Foot Homer at Capital Surpassed Only by Mighty Ruth Wallops*

### By LOUIS EFFRAT

*Special to* THE NEW YORK TIMES.

WASHINGTON, April 17—Unless and until contrary evidence is presented, recognition for the longest ball ever hit by anyone except Babe Ruth in the history of major league baseball belongs to Mickey Mantle of the Yankees. This amazing 21-year-old athlete today walloped one over the fifty-five-foot high left-field wall at Griffith Stadium. That ball, scuffed in two spots, finally stopped in the backyard of a house, about 565 feet away from home plate.

This remarkable homer, which helped the Yankees register a 7–3 victory over the Senators, was Mickey's first of the season, but he will have to go some, as will anyone else, to match it.

Chuck Stobbs, the Nat southpaw, had just walked Yogi Berra after two out in the fifth, when Mantle strode to the plate. Batting right-handed, Mantle blasted the ball toward left center, where the base of the front bleachers wall is 391 feet from the plate. The distance to the back of the wall is sixty-nine feet more and then the back wall is fifty feet high.

## Bounces Out of Sight

Atop that wall is a football scoreboard. The ball struck about five feet above the end of the wall, caromed off the right and flew out of sight. There was no telling how much farther it would have flown had the football board not been there.

Before Mantle, who had cleared the right-field roof while batting right-handed in an exhibition game at Pittsburgh last week (only Babe Ruth and Ted Beard had ever done that) had completed running out the two-run homer, Arthur Patterson of the Yankees' front-office staff was on his way to investigate the measure.

Patterson returned with the flowing news:

A 10-year-old had picked up the ball. He directed Patterson to the backyard of 434 Oakdale Street and pointed to the place where he had found it, across the street from the park. The boy, Donald Dunaway of 343 Elm Street N.W., accepted an undisclosed sum of money for the prize, which was turned over to Mantle. The Yankee was to send a substitute ball, suitably autographed to the boy.

Until today, when Mantle made it more or less easy for lefty Ed Lopat, who worked eight innings to gain his first triumph, no other batter had cleared the left-field wall here. Some years ago, Joe DiMaggio bounced a ball over, but Mickey's accomplishment was on the fly.

## Longest Bunt as Well

Later in the contest, Mickey dragged a bunt that landed in front of second base and he out-sped it for a single. Thus, in the same afternoon, it would appear, the young man from Commerce, Okla., fashioned one of the longest homers and the longest bunt on record. Everything else that occurred in this contest was dwarfed by Mantle's round-tripper, which traveled 460 feet on the fly. There was a third-inning homer by Bill Martin, which gave the Yankees the lead.

The Nats tied it against Lopat in the same frame on a single by Wayne Terwilliger, a sacrifice by Stobbs and Eddie Yost's single to left.

However, Hank Bauer doubled and counted on a single by Joe Collins for a 2–1 edge in the fourth, then it was that Mickey connected with a fast ball and wrote diamond history. Other things happened, including Tom Gorman's appearance for the last inning, but no one appeared to be interested.

## Gone With The Wind

It is true that a strong wind might have helped Mantle, but if the A.A.U. will not recognize the homer, all of baseball will.

Casey Stengel was telling before the game about the great young catching prospect the Yankees have at Kansas City. "Everyone is raving about Elston Howard," Casey said. Howard is a Negro, who after having come out of the service last summer, played at Muskegon in the Michigan State League.

There is no connection with Stengel's mention of Howard and the fact that Berra, who fanned only a dozen times last season, already has struck out four times this year. Barring injury, it will be quite some time before anyone takes away Yogi's job.

The charley horse in Mantle's left leg did not seem to hamper the lad during batting practice. He put on an electrifying show, hitting against Whitey Ford. Bauer, too, and Jackie Jensen for the Senators smashed long drives into the bleachers.

## RUTH HIT HOMER 600 FEET

### Detroit Scene of 1926 Blast—Exhibition Drive Went 587

Mickey Mantle's home run in Griffith Stadium yesterday failed by about thirty-five feet to match the homer Babe Ruth hit in Briggs Stadium at Detroit in 1926, according to The Associated Press.

Ruth's blow is considered the longest home run ever hit in a major league game. At the time, H.G. Salsinger, sports editor of The Detroit News, obtained an affidavit from several witnesses, who said the ball landed about 600 feet from home plate.

The Babe also is credited with a 587-footer in a 1919 exhibition game at Tampa, Fla., where Ken Silvestri, now with the Phillies, hit one 538 feet in 1941.

Until Mantle's blast yesterday, Ralph Kiner of the Pirates held second place in regular-season competition. He hit one about 560 feet against Cincinnati at Pittsburgh April 22, 1950.

## THE BOX SCORE

| NEW YORK (A.) | ab. | r. | h. | po. | a. | WASHINGTON (A.) | ab. | r. | h. | po. | a. |
|---|---|---|---|---|---|---|---|---|---|---|---|
| Martin, 2b | 4 | 1 | 2 | 3 | 4 | Yost, 3b | 5 | 0 | 2 | 1 | 4 |
| Rizzuto, ss | 5 | 0 | 1 | 3 | 3 | Busby, cf | 4 | 0 | 1 | 4 | 1 |
| Berra, c | 4 | 1 | 1 | 2 | 2 | Vernon, 1b | 3 | 0 | 0 | 13 | 1 |
| Mantle, cf | 3 | 1 | 2 | 0 | 0 | Jensen, rf | 4 | 0 | 0 | 3 | 0 |
| Bauer, rf | 4 | 2 | 1 | 2 | 0 | Runnels, ss | 3 | 1 | 1 | 0 | 2 |
| Woodling, lf | 5 | 1 | 2 | 5 | 0 | Wood, lf | 4 | 0 | 1 | 2 | 0 |
| Collins, 1b | 4 | 0 | 1 | 11 | 1 | Ter'liger, 2b | 4 | 3 | 2 | 3 | 5 |
| Carey, 3b | 4 | 1 | 1 | 1 | 1 | Peden, c | 4 | 0 | 1 | 0 | 1 |
| Lopat, p | 4 | 0 | 1 | 0 | 4 | Stobbs, p | 1 | 0 | 0 | 2 | 1 |
| Gorman, p | 0 | 0 | 0 | 0 | 0 | [a]Hoderlein | 1 | 0 | 1 | 0 | 0 |
| | | | | | | Moreno, p | 0 | 0 | 0 | 0 | 0 |
| | | | | | | [b]Verble | 1 | 0 | 0 | 0 | 0 |
| Total | 37 | 7 | 12 | 27 | 15 | Total | 34 | 3 | 10 | 27 | 15 |

[a]Singled for Stobbs in seventh.

[b]Flied out for Moreno in ninth.

Off to a Good Start: Mickey Mantle of the Yankees being greeted by the next man up, Hank Bauer (9), and the bat boy after hitting a home run in the first inning of a game with the Chicago White Sox at the Stadium. (ERNEST SISTO/THE NEW YORK TIMES)

New York        001 120 031—7
Washington      001 000 110—3

Errors—None

Runs batted in—Martin 2, Yost, Collins, Mantle 2, Hoderlein, Carey, Woodling Terwilliger. Two-base hits—Bauer, Terwilliger, Woodling. Home run—Martin, Mantle. Stolen base—Mantle. Sacrifice—Stobbs. Double play—Lopat, Martin and Collins. Left on bases—New York 9, Washington 8. Bases on balls—Off Stobbs 4, Lopat 3, Moreno 2. Struck out—By Lopat 2. Hits—Off Lopat 10 in 8 innings, Stobbs 7 in 7, Gorman 0 in 1, Moreno 5 in 2. Runs and earned runs—Stobbs 4 and 4, Lopat 3 and 3, Moreno 3 and 3. Winning pitcher—Lopat (1–0). Losing pitcher—Stobbs (0-1). Umpires—Honochick, McGowan, Paparella and McKinley. Time of game—2:27. Attendance—4,206.

---

May 14, 1955

### *Yanks Beat Tigers on Mantle's 3 Homers; Giants Down Cards; Dodgers Win*

## MICKEY BATS IN 5 FOR 5–2 TRIUMPH

### Mantle Adds Run-Producing Single to 3 Homers for Yanks Against Tigers

#### By JOSEPH M. SHEEHAN

Mickey Mantle went on a batting rampage yesterday to pace the Yankees to a 5–2 victory over the Detroit Tigers. The muscular 25-year-old center fielder clouted three home runs and a single to drive in all the Bomber runs.

His homers all carried into the Stadium's center-field bleachers. So far as could be determined, that multiple feat had not been accomplished previously. Nor was there any prior documented evidence of an American League-player's having hit homers from both sides of the plate in the same game.

Mickey crashed his first and second homers swinging left-handed against Steve Gromek, a right-hander. He hit his third from the right side of the plate against Bob Miller, a southpaw.

All were titanic blows. End to end they would have measured in the neighborhood of 1,300 feet. The first was a screaming line drive that cleared the bleacher wall above the auxiliary scoreboard to the left of the Yankee bullpen with something to spare.

## Bigger and Better

The second was a towering fly that carried well into the seats just to the right of the 407-foot sign on the bleacher wall in right center. The third was the best tagged of all, a tremendous thrust that traveled faster, slightly higher and farther along the course followed by No. 1.

Andy Carey was on base as a result of a bunt single when Mantle connected in the first inning. The bases were empty on his subsequent clouts, in the fifth and eighth innings. His third-inning single through the middle sent Hank Bauer home from second base. Mickey has provided headlines with his distance clouting on several other occasions during his five-year career as a Yankee. Early in 1953 he made history by becoming the first player to hit a ball over the left-field wall in Washington's Griffith Stadium. That wallop was measured at 565 feet.

But it was the first time he had three homers in one game. He was the eighth Yankee to turn the trick. Joe DiMaggio and Lou Gehrig each did it three times. Tony Lazzari twice and Babe Ruth, Bill Dickey, Charlie Keller and Johnny Mize once each.

The three-homer feat has been accomplished 108 times in the major leagues. Mize performed it in five games. Detroit's Al Kaline, who hit three homers against Kansas City in Detroit on April 17, was the last before Mantle to do it.

## Elite Ambidextrous Club

The evidence is that Jim Russell of the Dodgers, against the Cardinals at Ebbets Field on July 26, 1950, and Red Schoendienst of the Cardinals, against the Pirates at Pittsburgh on July 8, 1951, are the only previous players to have hit home runs from both sides of the plate in the same game.

In the excitement occasioned by Mantle's lustrous performance, another happy Yankee development was all but overlooked. Whitey Ford, who had turned sour after three impressive outings, snapped back into his best pitching form.

The southpaw ace of the Bombers held the Tigers hitless for four and one-third innings and runless for six and two-thirds innings. Ray Boone clipped him for a two-run homer at that stage.

A blister on the middle finger of Ford's pitching hand forced him to retire after the seventh. Tom Morgan preserved Whitey's fourth victory in five decisions with another strong relief job.

## Mantle Shares Homer Lead

With ten homers, Mantle moved into a tie with Kansas City's Guz Zernial for the major league leadership. . . . Incidentally, his eighth-inning blast was Mickey's first right-handed homer of the season.

The Yankees twice bunted for hits and twice sacrificed successfully against Gromek. . . . Bucky Harris sent nine right-handed hitters into action against Ford. . . . The Tiger manager has an infected little finger on his right hand, so he had one of the Detroit newspapermen fill out the line-up cards that are presented to the umpires. It seems this formula had worked before a winning Tiger game in Washington.

The Tigers vainly claimed interference by Carey when Bauer stole second in the third inning.

The box score:

| DETROIT (A.) | ab. | r. | h. | po. | a. | NEW YORK (A.) | ab. | r. | h. | po. | a. |
|---|---|---|---|---|---|---|---|---|---|---|---|
| Kuenn, ss | 3 | 0 | 0 | 0 | 2 | Bauer, rf | 4 | 1 | 2 | 3 | 0 |
| Tuttle, cf | 3 | 0 | 1 | 2 | 0 | Carey, 3b | 3 | 1 | 1 | 0 | 2 |
| Kaline, rf | 4 | 0 | 0 | 3 | 0 | Mantle, cf | 4 | 3 | 4 | 1 | 0 |
| Porter, 1b | 4 | 1 | 0 | 10 | 1 | Berra, c | 4 | 0 | 0 | 3 | 0 |
| Boone, 3b | 3 | 1 | 2 | 0 | 2 | Collins, 1b | 4 | 0 | 0 | 13 | 1 |
| B. Phillips, lf | 3 | 0 | 0 | 3 | 0 | Noren, 1b | 4 | 0 | 1 | 1 | 0 |
| Wilson, c | 3 | 0 | 0 | 4 | 0 | McDoug'd, 2b | 3 | 0 | 1 | 4 | 3 |
| Malmb'g, 2b | 2 | 0 | 0 | 1 | 3 | Hunter, ss | 2 | 0 | 0 | 1 | 7 |
| bHatf'ld, 2b | 0 | 0 | 0 | 0 | 0 | Ford, p | 2 | 0 | 0 | 0 | 2 |
| Gromek, p | 1 | 0 | 0 | 1 | 1 | dHoward | 1 | 0 | 0 | 0 | 0 |
| aFain | 1 | 0 | 0 | 0 | 0 | Morgan, p | 0 | 0 | 0 | 1 | 1 |
| Abner, p | 0 | 0 | 0 | 0 | 0 | | | | | | |
| cDelsing | 0 | 0 | 0 | 0 | 0 | | | | | | |
| Miller, p | 0 | 0 | 0 | 0 | 0 | | | | | | |
| Total | 27 | 2 | 3 | 24 | 9 | Total | 31 | 5 | 9 | 27 | 16 |

aGrounded out for Gromek in sixth.
bHit by pitcher for Malmberg in eighth.
cWalked for Aber in eighth.
dFlied out for Ford in seventh.

| Detroit | 000 | 000 | 200—2 |
|---|---|---|---|
| New York | 201 | 010 | 01..—5 |

Error—Wilson.

Runs batted in—Boone, 2, Mantle 5.

Home runs—Boone, Mantle 3. Stolen base—Bauer. Sacrifice—Carey, Hunter. Double plays—McDougald and Collins; Hunter, McDougald and Collins. Left on bases—Detroit 3. New York 4. Bases on balls—Off Ford 2, Morgan 2. Struck out—By Abner 2, Miller 1, Ford 3. Hits—Off Gromek 7 in 5 innings, Abner 1 in 2, Miller 1 in 1, Ford 3 in 7, Morgan 0 in 2. Runs and earned runs—Off Gromek 4 and 4, Abner 0 and 0, Miller 1 and 1, Ford 2 and 2, Morgan 0 and 0. Hit by pitcher—By Morgan (Hatfield). Winning pitcher—Ford (4–1). Losing pitcher—Gromek (5–2). Umpires—Paparella, Honochick, Umont and Rommel. Time of game—2:02. Attendance—7,177.

### *Mantle Swings From Both Sides of Plate With Borrowed Bats in His Big Day Here*

Prodding by Manager Casey Stengel, conscientious extra practice under Coach Bill Dickey and a couple of borrowed bats figured in Mickey Mantle's homerun explosion of yesterday.

Since the start of the season, Stengel has been urging Mantle to cut down on his swing and concentrate on meeting the ball with accentuated wrists action.

Whenever he knew Mickey was in earshot, Casey would proclaim, "I've got a feller on my team who thinks he should hit a homer every time and gets mad when the other pitchers won't let him.

"If he'd just fling his bat at the ball, like this," Stengel would add, with appropriate wrist-snapping gestures, "he'd hit it just as far and maybe wouldn't strike out so much and get so mad."

That Casey's pointed remarks hit the target is attested by the fact that through this Yankee home stand, Mantle has been reporting to the Stadium at 10:30 A.M., for batting seminars with Dickey.

"Yes, I'm trying to shorten my swing," admitted Mickey after his big splash against the Tigers. "And I think I'm getting the idea. At least it worked today. Now if only I don't go 5-for-0 tomorrow. That's usually what happens after you have a big day."

The Yankee center-fielder revealed he had hit his two left-handed homers with a bat discarded by Enos Slaughter, sold to Kansas City by the Yankees last Wednesday. His tremendous right-handed wallop was struck with one of Bill Skowron's sticks. He said in each instance he had hit a fast ball. "You never know," he added. "I generally don't have much luck against Gromek. He got me out with the same pitches in Detroit a couple of weeks ago."

### *Mantle Hits 19th and 20th Homers to Help Yankees Defeat Senators Twice*

## BOMBERS RECORD 4–3, 12–5 VERDICTS

### Mantle's First-Game Homer 18 Inches Short of Going Over Roof at Stadium

#### By JOSEPH M. SHEEHAN

Mickey Mantle clouted two homers, including one of colossal proportions, as the Yankees, with five four-baggers in all, downed the Washington Senators, 4–3, and 12–5, before a throng of 29,825 at the Stadium yesterday.

As a result of their double triumph, Casey Stengel's rampaging Bombers stretched to six games their lead over the second-place White Sox, who beat the Indians twice.

No more than eighteen inches of elevation kept the muscular Mantle from achieving the distinction of being the first player to hit a fair ball out of the Stadium.

Back in Business at the Same Old Stadium: Mickey Mantle watches his home-run ball in flight in the fourth inning of a game against Philadelphia. Catcher is Stan Lopata. The Phillies won by a 3–2 score. (THE NEW YORK TIMES)

## Mantle Connects in Fifth

Mickey's nineteenth homer, hit off Pedro Ramos on a 2–2 count in the fifth inning of the opener, was a skyscraper wallop to right that just hit below the top of the roof cornice high above the third deck.

Even though Mantle did not quite get enough loft to clear everything, he reached previously unplumbed territory with his mighty drive. No one previously got close to hitting the roof facade at the home of champions.

A check of Stadium blueprints disclosed that the ball struck at a point about 370 feet from the plate some 117 feet above the ground. While it obviously was descending when it hit the cornice, it retained enough velocity to rebound on to the field.

"I've never seen anything like it before," the Yankees said between games.

Mickey allowed, "It was the best I ever hit a ball left-handed."

There was nothing modest, either, about the dimensions of Mantle's twentieth homer, which he clouted off Pascual in the fifth inning of the nightcap. It carried halfway up into the right-field bleachers, just to the left of the bullpen.

## 16 Homers for Month

With sixteen homers in this merry month of May, Mickey is eleven games ahead of Babe Ruth's record sixty-homer pace of 1927. The Babe hit No. 20 in his fifty-second game on June 11, and had only fourteen on Memorial Day.

By way of demonstrating his versatility, Mantle also contributed a nifty third-strike drag bunt single, a right-handed line single, a stolen base and a rifle throw in the first game and drew a pass in the second game.

Excused after seven innings of the second game, Mantle ended the day leading the majors in six offensive departments: runs (45), hits (65), total bases (135), homers (20), runs batted in (50), and batting average (.425).

Hank Bauer and Eddie Robinson joined Mantle as homer hitters in the second game, in which the Bombers pounded Camilo Pascual, Bunky Stewart and Truman Clevenger for thirteen hits. Hank hit two, No. 10 leading off in the first, and No. 11, inside-the-park in the eighth. Eddie rapped his second leading off in the second.

Mantle's fifth-inning homer put the Bombers ahead to stay and they settled matters with a five-run outburst in the sixth, marked by Joe Collins' three-run double.

Bob Turley was the beneficiary of this assorted slugging. However, Bob became wild and needed help from Tom Sturdivant to bag the victory.

Besides being a conversation piece, Mantle's homer was the chief factor in the Yankee's opening-game victory. Mickey touched off his big blast with two mates aboard to erase a 1–0 lead Washington had taken on Johnny Kucks in the second.

The Bombers added a tally in the sixth on a single by Kucks and Hank Bauer's long double to center. However, Kucks apparently cooked himself scoring from first on Bauer's blow.

The Senators ripped into Johnny for three hits and two runs in the seventh. When Kucks got into further difficulties in the eighth, Casey Stengel called in Tom Morgan to preserve the youngster's sixth victory.


### Dickey Hit by Ball

Bill Dickey, the Yankee first base coach, was so painfully cracked on the right shin by a sharp foul off the bat of Joe Collins in the sixth inning of the opener that he relinquished his post to Jim Turner for the rest of the game. "I was still thinking about that ball Mickey hit and didn't react fast enough," explained Dickey.

Empire Bill Summers ejected Lou Berberet, Washington's catcher, for protesting a ball call to Gil McDougald in the fifth inning of the first game.

Yogi Berra made a brilliant diving catch of a foul pop by Harmon Killebrew in front of the Yankee dugout in the eighth inning of the opener.

The first game started and ended in a spatter of rain.

Before the double-header, there was a brief ceremony honoring this nation's war dead. The players of both teams and a Marine Corps color guard participated.

## FIRST GAME

| WASHINGTON (A.) | ab. | r. | h. | po. | a. | NEW YORK (A.) | ab. | r. | h. | po. | a. |
|---|---|---|---|---|---|---|---|---|---|---|---|
| Yost, 3b | 4 | 0 | 0 | 1 | 1 | Bauer, rf | 4 | 1 | 1 | 1 | 0 |
| Luttrell, ss | 4 | 0 | 2 | 5 | 5 | McD'g'd, ss | 3 | 1 | 1 | 2 | 5 |
| Herzog, lf | 3 | 0 | 1 | 3 | 0 | Mantle, cf | 4 | 1 | 3 | 3 | 0 |
| Sievers, 1b | 4 | 0 | 0 | 10 | 0 | Berra, c | 2 | 0 | 0 | 6 | 1 |
| Lemon, rf | 2 | 0 | 0 | 2 | 0 | Collins, lf | 3 | 0 | 0 | 2 | 1 |
| K'brew, 2b | 4 | 1 | 0 | 1 | 1 | bHoward, lf | 1 | 0 | 0 | 0 | 0 |
| Olson, cf | 4 | 1 | 3 | 1 | 0 | Rob'son, 1b | 3 | 0 | 0 | 6 | 0 |
| Berberet, c | 2 | 0 | 0 | 1 | 0 | Martin, 2b | 4 | 0 | 0 | 7 | 2 |
| Courtney, c | 2 | 0 | 1 | 0 | 1 | Carey, 3b | 4 | 0 | 1 | 0 | 3 |
| Ramos, p | 2 | 0 | 0 | 0 | 0 | Kucks, p | 2 | 1 | 1 | 0 | 0 |
| aRunnels | 1 | 1 | 1 | 0 | 0 | Morgan, p | 1 | 0 | 0 | 0 | 0 |
| Stewart, p | 0 | 0 | 0 | 0 | 0 | | | | | | |
| cPaula | 1 | 0 | 0 | 0 | 0 | | | | | | |
| Total | 33 | 3 | 8 | 24 | 8 | Total | 31 | 4 | 7 | 27 | 12 |

aTripled for Ramos in seventh.
bGrounded out for Collins in seventh.
cFlied out for Stewart in ninth.

Washington      0 1 0   0 0 0   3 0 0—3
New York        0 0 0   0 3 1   0 0..—4

Errors—Killebrew, Martin.

Runs batted in—Berberet, Runnels, Lutrell, Mantle 3, Bauer.

Two-base hits—Lutrell, Bauer. Three-base hits—Herzog, Runnels. Home run—Mantle.

Stolen base—Mantle. Sacrifice—Herzog. Double play—Martin, McDougald and Robinson. Left on bases—Washington 7, New York 8. Bases on balls—Off Ramos 5, Kucks 3. Struck out—By Ramos 1, Kucks 4. Hits—Off Ramos 5 in 6 innings, Kucks 7 in 7 1–3, Stewart 2 in 2, Morgan 1 in 1 2–3. Runs and earned runs—Off Ramos 4 and 4, Kucks 3 and 3. Winning pitcher—Kucks (6–2). Losing pitcher—Ramos (3–2). Umpires—Summers, McKinley, Flaherty and Rice. Time—2:36.

## SECOND GAME

| WASHINGTON (A.) | ab. | r. | h. | po. | a. | NEW YORK (A.) | ab. | r. | h. | po. | a. |
|---|---|---|---|---|---|---|---|---|---|---|---|
| Yost, 3b | 2 | 0 | 1 | 2 | 3 | Bauer, rf | 6 | 3 | 3 | 2 | 0 |
| Luttrell, ss | 3 | 0 | 1 | 0 | 0 | Martin, 2b | 3 | 1 | 1 | 4 | 2 |
| Herzog, 1f | 5 | 0 | 2 | 1 | 1 | ᶜ J. C'man, 2b | 1 | 0 | 0 | 1 | 0 |
| Sievers, 1b | 4 | 0 | 0 | 5 | 0 | Mantle, cf | 4 | 1 | 1 | 0 | 0 |
| Courtney, c | 3 | 2 | 1 | 7 | 0 | Howard, 1f | 1 | 0 | 0 | 0 | 0 |
| Olson, cf | 5 | 0 | 1 | 3 | 0 | Berra, c | 3 | 1 | 2 | 6 | 1 |
| Lemon, rf | 2 | 1 | 0 | 3 | 0 | Col'ns, 1f cf | 4 | 1 | 1 | 2 | 1 |
| Kill'brew, 2b | 3 | 1 | 1 | 3 | 2 | Robi'son, 1b | 4 | 2 | 1 | 10 | 0 |
| Pascual, p | 2 | 1 | 1 | 0 | 0 | M'D'gald, ss | 3 | 1 | 1 | 0 | 4 |
| ᵃPaula | 1 | 0 | 0 | 0 | 0 | Carey, 3b | 3 | 2 | 1 | 1 | 3 |
| Stewart, p | 0 | 0 | 0 | 0 | 0 | Turley, p | 4 | 0 | 2 | 1 | 2 |
| ᵇOravetz | 0 | 0 | 0 | 0 | 0 | Stur'vant, p | 1 | 0 | 0 | 0 | 0 |
| Clev'nger, p | 0 | 0 | 0 | 0 | 1 | | | | | | |
| Total | 30 | 5 | 8 | 24 | 7 | Total | 37 | 12 | 13 | 27 | 13 |

ᵃFouled out for Pascual in seventh.
ᵇWalked for Stewart in eighth.
ᶜGrounded out for Martin in eighth.

```
Washington      0 1 1   1 0 0   0 2 0—5
New York        1 2 0   0 1 5   0 3 ..—12
```

Errors—Sievers, Lemon.

Runs batted in—Bauer 3, Lemon, Robinson 2, Mantle 2, Herzog, Killebrew, Collins 3, Turley, Oravetz, Yost, Carey.

Two-base hits—Yost, Berra, McDougald, Collins, Carey. Home runs—Bauer 2, Robinson, Killebrew, Mantle. Stolen bases—Carey 2. Sacrifice—Lutrell. Sacrifice fly—Lemon. Double plays—Berra and Martin; McDougald, Martin and Robinson. Left on bases—Washington 10, New York 12. Bases on balls—Off Turley 9, Pascual 9, Stewart 1, Sturdivant 1, Clevenger 1. Struck out—By Turley 6, Pascual 6. Hits—Off Pascual 10 in 6 innings, Stewart 1 in 1, Clevenger 2 in 1, Turley 7 in 7 2–3, Sturdivant 1 in 1 1–3.

Runs and earned runs—Off Pascual 9 and 7, Turley 5 and 5, Clevenger 3 and 3. Wild pitch—Turley. Winning pitcher—Turley (2–2). Losing pitcher—Pascual (2–6).

Umpires—McKinley, Flaherty, Rice and Summers. Time—3:10. Attendance: 26,625.

*Sports of The Times*

# BY ARTHUR DALEY

## The Boy Grew Older

---

MICKEY MANTLE was leaning against the batting cage in St. Pete one bright morning this spring. He stared admiringly out on the diamond, where a slew of brilliant rookie prospects moved around in eye-catching fashion.

"We sure have a lot of fine-looking kids," he said.

The significance of that remark was not immediately apparent. But it is now beginning to register. Perhaps it explains why Master Mickey is slamming home runs at a faster clip than Babe Ruth and is slashing out hits at a pace worthy of Ty Cobb.

For the first time since he joined the Yankees five years ago, Mantle no longer regards himself as a kid. He speaks and acts with the assurance of an old-timer. The once awed and frightened youngster from Commerce, Okla., has finally left boyhood behind and has flowered to full maturity at long last.

## Big Leap

A ballplayer with the rare intelligence, adaptability and poise of a Tommy Henrich might have done it in a few months. But even an uncommon operative such as Old Reliable would not have found it easy. Mantle was yanked from the sleepy seclusion of Commerce (pop. 2,422) and was playing in the world series at the age of 19. He was lionized and subjected to the most extravagant raves. It was a bewildering, head-spinning process, particularly to a fundamentally shy introvert like Mantle.

Each spring experts would predict: "This would be the year when Mantle will cash in on his potentialities and reach greatness."

Mickey tried for all he was worth, but he never quite made it. The fans booed him constantly—and unfairly, it might be added—and that didn't help any. The burden of succeeding Babe Ruth and Joe DiMaggio as the Yankee superstar was too much of a burden.

"I'd say that Mickey attained maturity on opening day this season," said Jerry Coleman, the most articulate and shrewdest analyst among the Yankees. "It was—boom! boom!—and he had two tremendous homers without even trying. It gave him confidence. I've noticed since that he's giving in to the pitchers. It they pitch him outside, he'll slice to the opposite field. Last year he'd have tried to overpower them by pulling the ball away. The boy has come of age."

## All in Stride

The change in the Oklahoma kid also appears in more subtle ways. Interviewers and cameramen now give him no peace. He once would have fled in terror from them. Now he talks without stammering to the one and poses uncomplainingly for the other, totally oblivious of the jeers of his mates and no longer squirming in embarrassment. Patiently, he endured the glare of bright lights for movie cameras in the dressing room the other day.

"Aren't you afraid of getting klieg in eyes?" asked this visitor.

"I oughta go to Hollywood and get it over with," said Mickey with a broad grin.

As a wisecrack, it was only passable. But the Mantle of a year ago would neither have thought of it nor dared make it.

Still sharp in memory is an incident that is highly personal, but too illustrative to be ignored. It happened during the world series of Master Mickey's freshman year with the Yankees. All that season we'd exchanged only a few polite pleasantries, Mickey being too ill at ease with the press to make conversation profitable.

Before the opening game, a hundred out-of-town newspaper men wandered behind the batting cage. Most of these strangers seemed to descend on Mantle and there was a look of panic in his eyes as he searched for a friendly face. As soon as he saw this reporter watching in amusement, he rushed over, addressed me by first name for the first time and talked my ear off for fifteen minutes. It was, as they say, the start of a beautiful friendship.

## Nature Boy

The scared, confused kid has given way at long last to the reasonably poised man. Just being in the big league had floored him originally. The shrewd Henrich had once remarked, "Mantle's biggest handicap is that he comes from Commerce, Okla." In those days, Mickey played ball by merely "doin' what comes natcherally." Now he studies the pitchers and the other hitters.

"Mick knows what's goin' on," says Yogi Berra with a knowing wink.

Casey Stengel just smiles smugly and says nothing. Master Mickey had been both his despair and his delight. Casey wanted Mantle to be his greatest star, and that wish may yet be realized.

Mantle can't explain his sudden emergence as a superstar any more than he can explain the fact that he uses Hank Bauer's thirty-two-ounce bat when swinging left-handed and Bill Skowron's thirty-six-ouncer when swinging righty.

"I dunno," he says. "It just feels better that way."

At the age of 24, Mickey Mantle has reached maturity. His batting feats would seem to prove it.

October 1, 1956

### *Mantle Heads Both Leagues in Homers, Runs Batted In and Batting Percentage*

―――――――――

## YANKEE FINISHES WITH .353 MARK

―――――――――

### Mantle, in Pinch Role, Drives in Run as Bombers Lose to Red Sox in 10th, 7–4

―――――――――

#### By WILLIAM J. BRIORDY

Mickey Mantle yesterday became the fourth player to win the major league triple batting crown.

The switch-hitting centerfielder of the Yankees closed the 1956 season with a batting percentage of .353, fifty-two homers and 130 runs batted in. Mantle drove in one run as the American League's champion Yankees ended their regular campaign by bowing to the Boston Red Sox, 7 to 4, in ten innings at the Stadium.

Since the Cleveland Indians lost to the Detroit Tigers, the Bombers completed their 154-game schedule nine games in front of the pack.

The fact that the Red Sox pushed three runs over the plate in the top of the tenth to beat the Yankees was secondary. Mantle commanded the news as he became the first Yankee to perform the batting feat for both leagues since Lou Gehrig turned the trick in 1934. The last player to take the three championships in the majors was Ted Williams of Boston. He headed both leagues in 1942. Williams also led the American League in the three divisions in 1947.

Rogers Hornsby, with the Cards in 1925, was the first to [win?] honors in both leagues. Mantle, who will be 25 on Oct. 20, had already clinched the laurels in the home run department. On Saturday he had virtually sewed up the batting honors in his fight with Williams.

## Kaline Closest Rival

The only man who had a chance to beat the Oklahoman for the runs-batted-in title was Detroit's Al Kaline. Kaline batted two runs across yesterday to finish with 128. Mantle had every intention to start yesterday's game, but Manager Casey Stengel saw it otherwise. Mickey, bothered by a pulled groin muscle, was kept on the bench until the ninth inning.

Stengel and the tenants of the Stadium press box had been receiving up-to-the minute reports on Kaline's progress. The Ol' Professor said earlier in the day that in the event Mantle's runs-batted-in title was in jeopardy, he planned to send the Oklahoman in as a pinch-hitter.

Casey did just that. Mantle hit for Jim Coates, a rookie right-hander, in the ninth. With Jerry Lumpe stationed at third base, Mantle's grounder to third brought in the run that tied the score, at 4–4.

Tom Morgan, the fourth Yankee pitcher, was clubbed for three hits and three runs as nine Red Sox went to the plate in the top of the tenth.

Dave Sisler, Red Sox right-hander, pitched well in beating the Bombers for a second time this year. He yielded three runs and five of the Bombers' nine hits in the first two innings. Then he applied the clamps to gain his ninth victory against eight defeats.

The Yankees went ahead in the first when Yogi Berra smashed his thirtieth homer into the lower right field seats.

Berra, who matched his major league high for homers, connected behind Norm Siebern's double with two out.

## Mantle 'Isn't Right'

Stengel said before the game that Mantle "isn't right." After the game, Mantle said he would be ready for the world series opener against the Dodgers. Last year Mantle was hobbled by a knee injury and saw limited service in the Yanks' losing fight to the Brooks.

The Yanks, poised for another shot at the Dodgers, will drill this morning at 11 o'clock. It will be chiefly a batting workout.

Stengel won't commit himself regarding his starting pitcher for the first world series game, but it could be his ace left-hander, Whitey Ford. Ford and Don Larsen, the right-hander who pitched four four-hit games this month, saw the Dodgers win the National League flag.

Statistics Department: Williams wound up with a .345 batting average. He hit only .196 (11 for 56) against New York this year. . . . Mantle's 132 runs scored topped the American League. . . . When Berra hit his homer in the first it brought the Yanks' 1956 total to 190, tops in the league. . . . The 18,587 paying fans brought the Yanks' home attendance to 1,491,844. The Bombers drew 1,713,912 on the road for a total of 3,205,756. Those figures surpassed the 1955 aggregates.

| BOSTON (A.) | ab. | r. | h. | po. | a. | NEW YORK (A.) | ab. | r. | h. | po. | a. |
|---|---|---|---|---|---|---|---|---|---|---|---|
| Bolling, 3b | 4 | 2 | 1 | 1 | 1 | Bauer, rf | 3 | 0 | 1 | 1 | 0 |
| Klaus, ss | 4 | 0 | 1 | 4 | 3 | Wilson, rf | 2 | 0 | 0 | 0 | 0 |
| Williams, lf | 0 | 0 | 0 | 0 | 0 | Siebern, lf | 4 | 1 | 1 | 3 | 0 |
| aSthps, lf, cf | 5 | 0 | 1 | 5 | 0 | cSlaughter | 1 | 0 | 0 | 0 | 0 |
| Zauchin, 1b | 3 | 1 | 0 | 8 | 0 | Cerv, cf | 5 | 0 | 1 | 5 | 1 |
| Thrnbry, rf | 5 | 1 | 2 | 2 | 0 | Berra, c | 4 | 1 | 1 | 8 | 0 |
| Piersall, cf | 1 | 0 | 0 | 0 | 0 | Skowron, 1b | 3 | 0 | 1 | 2 | 0 |
| Gernert, lf | 2 | 1 | 0 | 0 | 0 | Noren, 1b | 2 | 0 | 0 | 4 | 1 |
| Consolo, 2b | 4 | 1 | 1 | 1 | 3 | McDougd, ss | 3 | 0 | 0 | 1 | 1 |
| Daley, c | 4 | 1 | 3 | 8 | 0 | Hunter, ss | 1 | 0 | 0 | 0 | 1 |
| Sisler, p | 3 | 0 | 0 | 1 | 1 | Martin, 2b | 3 | 1 | 1 | 2 | 0 |
| | | | | | | Coleman, 2b | 1 | 0 | 0 | 3 | 3 |
| | | | | | | Carroll, 3b | 2 | 0 | 1 | 0 | 0 |
| | | | | | | Lumpe, 3b | 2 | 1 | 1 | 1 | 1 |
| | | | | | | Turley, p | 2 | 0 | 0 | 0 | 0 |
| | | | | | | McDrmt, p | 1 | 0 | 1 | 0 | 0 |
| | | | | | | Coates, p | 0 | 0 | 0 | 0 | 0 |
| | | | | | | bMantle | 1 | 0 | 0 | 0 | 0 |
| | | | | | | Morgan, p | 0 | 0 | 0 | 0 | 2 |
| Total | 35 | 7 | 9 | 30 | 8 | Total | 40 | 4 | 9 | 30 | 10 |

aRan for Williams in first.
bGrounded out for Coates in ninth.
cFouled out for Siebern in tenth.

| Boston | 1 0 0 | 2 1 0 | 0 0 0 | 3—7 |
|---|---|---|---|---|
| New York | 2 1 0 | 0 0 0 | 0 0 1 | 0—4 |

Errors—Sisler, Stephens.

Runs batted in—Zauchin, Berra 2, Bauer, Daley 4, Throneberry, Mantle, Klaus. Two-base hits—Siebern, Martin, Bauer, Daley. Home run—Berra. Sacrifices—Sisler 2, Gernert. Double plays—Cerv and McDougald. Left on bases—Boston 11, New York 7. Bases on balls—Off Turley 5, Coates 2, Morgan 3, Sisler 1. Struck out—By Turley 6, McDermott 1, Sisler 7. Hits—Off Turley 5 in 5 innings, McDermott 1 in 3, Coates 0 in 1, Morgan 3 in 1. Runs and earned runs—Off Turley 4 and 4, Morgan 3 and 3, Sisler 4 and 3. Wild pitch—Coates. Winning pitcher—Sisler (9–8). Losing pitcher—Morgan (6–7). Umpires—Paparella, Hurley, McKinley and Chylak. Time of game—2:30. Attendance—18,587.

## *Yanks Crush Pirates, 16–3. In 2d Game and Tie Series*

### By JOHN DREBINGER

*Special to The New York Times.*

PITTSBURGH, Oct. 6—Unloading a violent offensive, surpassed only once in world series history, the Yankees today crushed the Pittsburgh Pirates, 16 to 3, in the second game at Forbes Field.

The overwhelming triumph, which stunned a crowd of 37,308, deadlocked the series at a victory apiece. It now moves to New York, where the third game will be played in the Yankee Stadium on Saturday.

Two tremendous home runs by Mickey Mantle, the first a 400-foot smash, the second a 450-foot blast over the center-field wall, accounted for five tallies. The aroused New Yorkers battered six pitchers for nineteen hits.

The sixteen runs left Casey Stengel's sluggers only two behind the Yanks' old world series record of eighteen for one game, piled up against the New York Giants in 1936. And their nineteen assorted blows were just one short of their own series record of twenty set in that same game.

The Yanks, already enjoying a 5–1 lead, virtually tore the game apart with a bruising seven-run demonstration in the sixth. This matched their own—though not a series—record of seven runs in one inning which they heaped on the Giants in 1936 and again in 1937.

Behind all this cannonading, it was a comparatively simple task for Bob Turley, the Yanks' burly and at times erratic right-hander, to gain the pitching victory. Apparently more tired from sitting around than from anything the Pirates did to him, Turley couldn't finish the ninth.

### Double Play Ends Game

He ran into a squall when the Bucs scored twice on three singles and a misplay and little Bobby Shantz collected the final two outs. This the lefty did on one play as Don Hoak rammed into a twin killing.

Bob Friend, the Bucs' No. 2 right-hander led the Pirates' parade of pitchers. Oddly, he did not pitch badly and was trailing by only 3–1 when asked to vacate for a pinch-hitter in the fourth. Ironically, as such things will happen, the hitter did nothing and the succeeding pitchers failed.

To make matters worse for the disheartened National League fans, a gloomy morning of rain, which threatened to cause a postponement, gave way to a brilliant sunny afternoon. That made the harrowing details of the struggle reveal themselves even more garishly. The uncertain weather had Baseball Commissioner Ford C. Frick up at the crack of dawn. If there had to be a postponement, the decision was his to make. He had some anxious moments, for it had rained quite heavily through the night while misty drizzle fell intermittently through the morning.

However, before noon it cleared sufficiently to permit both teams to have batting practice. The Pirates also got in their fielding drill before the drizzle returned.

That had the ground crew covering the infield again with its mechanical roller. It also deprived the Yanks of their fielding practice, which brought a growl from Stengel. "From the way we played yesterday," he grumbled, "I'd say we need that more than anything else."

Finally, along about 12:45 P.M., the weather relented. The drizzle ceased, the sun strove valiantly to break through the haze and at 1:01 the encounter got on the way. Stengel, who hadn't been overly strong this year in producing surprises, showed he hadn't lost his touch. Because Elston Howard had hit a ninth-inning pinch homer in the first game, Casey Stengel had Howard behind the plate, with Yogi Berra shifted to left field.

It marked the first time since his rookie year in 1947 that Yogi had played any position except catcher in a world series game.

Manager Danny Murtaugh also did some last-minute shifting in the Pittsburgh battlefront when Bob Skinner, his left fielder, bobbed up this morning with a swollen left thumb, a memento of his slide into third base in the fifth inning yesterday.

This induced Murtaugh to meet the emergency with a double shift. He called on Gino Cimoli to play left and, since the defection of Skinner deprived him of a valuable left-handed batsman, replaced Dick Stuart at first base with Rocky Nelson, a left-handed swinger.

The master-minding on both sides worked smoothly enough in the first two innings, though Stengel's attempt to baffle the opposition with a first-inning running attack such as the Bucs used successfully yesterday, didn't pay off. After Tony Kubek had opened with a single, he was out trying to steal second on a fine peg by Smokey Burgess. So the bases were empty when Roger Maris singled for his fourth hit of the series.

However, the situation improved sharply for the Bombers in the third. Friend, who had fanned Mantle in the first and had picked up two more strikeouts—Bill Skowron and Howard—in the second, opened the third by walking Bobby Richardson. Turley sacrificed. Then two swift, decisive blows had the Yanks in front with two tallies.

Kubek stroked the first, a single to center that scored Richardson, Gil McDougald, at third in place of Cletis Boyer, nudged a two-bagger barely inside the left-field line. This shot scored Kubek all the way from first.

In the fourth, Friend fanned both Skowron and Howard a second time before Richardson poked a single into center. Although a short passed ball enabled Bobby to reach second, the situation didn't appear threatening.

## Turley Bats in Richardson

For the batter was Turley. But Bullet Bob jarred his Hoosier mound adversary by belting a single into left center that drove in Richardson and the Yanks were three in front.

Meanwhile Turley was breezing along smoothly. In the fourth, however, the Bucs kicked up another high wind and for a few minutes it looked as if this one would blow Turley right off the mound.

Cimoli singled to right, Burgess singled to right and when Don Hoak doubled to the same sector the Pirates had one tally in, runners on second and third and nobody out. This had Stengel going to the mound, bent on stalling matters for a time.

For the attack had struck with such swiftness there had been little activity in the Yankee bullpen. But Turley soon put Casey's mind at ease.

Mazeroski ran into a tough break when his line drive down the third base line landed squarely in McDougald's glove and Bill Virdon ended it grounding out.

So one tally was all the Bucs extracted from their inviting start in the round and from there the National Leaguers went downhill rapidly. Fred Green, a tall rookie left-hander who had done excellent relief work during the regular season, brought no relief as he went to the mound in the fifth.

After walking McDougald, Green got Maris to slap into a force play at second. Then Mantle, still seeking his first series hit and doubtless boiling because in two games he had fanned three times, batted.

The Switcher, batting right-handed, smacked a powerful home-run drive into the lower stand in right center some 400 feet away for two tallies.

Green got the side out, only to plunge into deeper difficulty in the sixth, when the Bombers exploded for seven runs. Howard opened with a triple off the base of the light tower beside the 436-foot mark in center.

Richardson doubled and that was all for Green. He was replaced by Clem Labine, a right-hander who, as a Dodger, had opposed the Yanks in many world series games. The 34-yeart-old Labine ran into heavy going this time.

He retired Turley on a tap to the mound and would have fared better had not Dick Groat fumbled Kubek's grounder. Behind that slip the Bombers simply poured it on.

About all the harried Labine accomplished was to slip over a third strike on Mantle. Just before that McDougald singled and Maris walked. Singles by Berra (with bases full) and Skowron followed.

George Witt, a right-hander, replaced Labine, and got tagged for singles by Howard and Richardson, which accounted for the sixth and Seventh runs. Only two of the runs were earned.

Joe Gibbon, a rookie left-hander, went in for the Bucs in the seventh. Singles by Kubek and Joe DeMaestri (Stengel now was really showing off his bench strength) greeted this young southpaw.

Gibbon possibly lulled himself into a feeling of false security when he fanned Maris, but Mantle swiftly disillusioned him.

The Switcher really put "the good wood" to this one. The ball soared down the center of the field and surely would have split the goal posts had there been any. Even the stunned Pittsburgh fans gave Mantle a hand.

Meanwhile Turley, staggering from inning to inning though still holding the Bucs to one tally, finally folded in the ninth. He allowed thirteen hits before giving way to Shantz and this gave the Corsairs one comfort.

The thirteen blows, added to the Yankees' nineteen, set a world series record of thirty-two hits for both clubs in one game. The former mark of twenty-nine had been set by the St. Louis Cardinals and Boston Red Sox in 1946.

While the series stands even, the advantage now seems to rest with the Bombers, who will play the next three games on their home field. Also there remains the question of how well the battered Bucs can recover from the psychological blow of the second-game rout.

## Yanks' Big Sixth Inning

Howard tripled off the center-field wall, near the 436-foot mark. Richardson doubled to left, scoring Howard. Labine replaced Green on the mound for Pittsburgh, Richardson took third on a passed ball. Turley grounded out, pitcher to first base, Richardson holding third. Kubek reached first when Grout bobbled his grounder, Richardson still holding third. McDougald singled to left, scoring Richardson and sending Kubek to second. Maris walked, filling the bases, Mantle took a called third strike. Berra singled to left center, scoring Kubek and McDougald and sending Maris to third. Skowron singled to left center, scoring Maris and sending Berra to third. Witt replaced Labine on the mound for Pittsburgh. Howard singled to left, scoring Berra and sending Skowron to second. Richardson singled to center, scoring Howard as Skowron stopped at second. Turley flied to center. Seven runs, seven hits, one error, two left.

### *Yankees Stress Defense in Sixth Inning Despite a Lead of Eleven Runs*

## SHIFTS DESIGNED TO THWART RALLY

## Kubek Moves to Left Field, DeMaestri and Boyer Play Infield in Late Innings

### By Louis Effrat

*Special to The New York Times.*

PITTSBURGH, Oct. 6—What, in a world series game, constitutes a reasonably safe lead? There were the Yankees, fresh from a seven-run assault in the top of the sixth inning and holding a 12–1 bulge when Casey Stengel made some changes at Forbes Field.

The New York manager removed Yogi Berra from left field (a surprise that he was there in the first place) and switched Tony Kubek from shortstop to the outfield. He sent Joe DeMaestri in at shortstop and substituted Cletis Boyer for Gil McDougald at third base. Why?

"Defense," was Casey's explanation in the dressing room, shortly after the Bombers had sealed their 16–3 walkover. "Defense," he repeated.

The 70-year-old strategist went no farther. He muttered something about giving Kubek more experience in left and he nodded when someone suggested he might have been giving Berra a breather, but one Yankee disclosed that Stengel, hardly one who takes anything for granted, had been urging his players to "pour it on—don't let 'em up."

Bob Turley, the victorious no-windup right-hander, was happy enough over his victory, but he felt he had pitched better games. "I had trouble with my curve," he said. "It was breaking all over, high, low, inside and outside, but not exactly where I wanted it to break. So I relied mostly on my fast ball. That wasn't bad."

### Howard Praises fast Ball

"Wasn't bad," Elston Howard, who was Turley's catcher, half-shouted. "Turley's fast ball was alive and jumping all through the game."

Turley made 141 pitches (according to Eddie Lopat, the pitching coach) before Bobby Shantz relieved in the ninth and threw four straight curves to Don Hoak. The Pirate bounced to Shantz, who started the game-ending double play. The left-handed Shantz said each of the curves he delivered was at a different speed.

"I once threw 200 pitches in a game and won," Turley said, "so I wasn't tired. Well, I wasn't exhausted, let's say. The danger spot for me was in the fourth inning when Gino Cimoli and Smoky Burgess singled and Hoak doubled.

"Casey came out and told me to try and get my pitches lower. Bill Mazeroski and Gene Baker were big outs of the game for me. You know, the drive that Mazeroski hit to Gil (McDougald) may have sounded hard, but it really wasn't. Mazeroski hit an outside curve at the end of his bat."

McDougald said it was not too difficult a chance. "The reason I went to my knee was that the ball was hit low," the third baseman said. "For an instant I was afraid I would lose sight of it in the background, but once I saw the ball I had no trouble catching it."

Stengel revealed that he had no idea of removing Turley when he walked to the mound after Hoak's first of two doubles had cut the Bucs' deficit to 3–1, with none out in the fourth.

## Stengel Explains Situation

"I had the infield playing back, ready to give one run on a slow grounder, if necessary," the manager said, "but I had no intention of removing the pitcher. Not then. Of course, if the feller (Mazeroski) had got a hit, I was making, in my mind, different preparations."

Berra declined to state his preference in any defensive alignment Stengel might have for him in the remainder of the series. "I don't care," the sometimes catcher, left fielder and right fielder said. "If Casey tells me to play third base, I'll do that, too. It's up to him."

Mickey Mantle's two homers were well belted, although the Oklahoman thought these were not quite the longest he had hit this year. He was asked whether he had aimed for the fences. "I was only trying not to strike out," he said.

As for Babe Ruth's world series record of fifteen homers—Mantle is now two short—the slugger has a definite opinion. "I think I have a good shot at it, especially if they pitch left-handers. I haven't been hitting too good against right-handers," he said.

Over-all, the scene in the winning clubhouse was one of controlled elation. Not one Yankee said he felt sorry for the solidly beaten Bucs.

## The Box Score

### SECOND GAME

| NEW YORK YANKEES | ab. | r. | h. | rbi. | po. | a. | PITTSBURGH PIRATES | ab. | r. | h. | rbi. | po. | a. |
|---|---|---|---|---|---|---|---|---|---|---|---|---|---|
| Kubek, ss, lf | 6 | 3 | 3 | 1 | 2 | 3 | Virdon, cf | 5 | 0 | 0 | 0 | 2 | 0 |
| McDougald, 3b | 3 | 1 | 2 | 2 | 1 | 0 | Groat, ss | 4 | 0 | 1 | 0 | 1 | 0 |
| DeMaestri, ss | 2 | 1 | 1 | 0 | 0 | 0 | Gibbon, p | 0 | 0 | 0 | 0 | 1 | 0 |
| Maris, rf | 5 | 2 | 1 | 0 | 3 | 0 | Cheney, p | 0 | 0 | 0 | 0 | 0 | 1 |
| Mantle, cf | 4 | 3 | 2 | 5 | 4 | 0 | cChristopher | 0 | 1 | 0 | 0 | 0 | 0 |
| Berra, lf | 4 | 1 | 1 | 2 | 1 | 0 | Clemente, rf | 5 | 0 | 2 | 0 | 1 | 0 |
| Boyer, 2b | 2 | 0 | 1 | 0 | 0 | 0 | Nelson, 1b | 5 | 1 | 2 | 0 | 4 | 3 |
| Skowron, 1b | 6 | 1 | 2 | 1 | 11 | 0 | Cimoli, lf | 4 | 1 | 2 | 1 | 2 | 0 |
| Howard, c | 5 | 1 | 2 | 1 | 1 | 0 | Burgess, c | 4 | 0 | 2 | 0 | 11 | 1 |
| Richardson, 2b | 4 | 3 | 3 | 2 | 4 | 6 | Hoak, 3b | 4 | 0 | 2 | 1 | 0 | 0 |
| Turley, p | 4 | 0 | 1 | 1 | 0 | 2 | Mazeroski, 2b | 5 | 0 | 1 | 0 | 2 | 2 |
| Shantz, p | 0 | 0 | 0 | 0 | 0 | 1 | Friend, p | 1 | 0 | 0 | 0 | 1 | 1 |
| | | | | | | | aBaker | 1 | 0 | 0 | 0 | 0 | 0 |
| | | | | | | | Green, p | 0 | 0 | 0 | 0 | 0 | 0 |
| | | | | | | | Labine, p | 0 | 0 | 0 | 0 | 0 | 1 |
| | | | | | | | Witt, p | 0 | 0 | 0 | 0 | 0 | 0 |
| | | | | | | | bSchofield, ss | 1 | 0 | 1 | 0 | 2 | 0 |
| Total | 45 | 16 | 19 | 15 | 27 | 12 | Total | 39 | 3 | 13 | 2 | 27 | 9 |

aPopped out for Friend in fourth.
bSingled for Witt in sixth.
cHit by pitch for Cheney in ninth.

| | | |
|---|---|---|
| New York | 002 127 301—16 |
| Pittsburgh | 000 100 002— 3 |

Errors—Groat, Richardson. Double play—Shantz, Richardson and Skowron. Left on bases—New York 8, Pittsburgh 13.

Two-base hits—Mazeroski, McDougald, Hoak 2, Richardson, Boyer. Three-base hit—Howard. Home runs—Mantle 2. Sacrifice—Turley.

| | IP. | H. | R. | ER. |
|---|---|---|---|---|
| Friend (L.) | 4 | 6 | 3 | 2 |
| *Green | 1 | 3 | 4 | 4 |
| Labine | ⅔ | 3 | 5 | 0 |
| Witt | ⅓ | 2 | 0 | 0 |
| Gibbon | 2 | 4 | 3 | 3 |
| Cheney | 1 | 1 | 1 | 1 |
| Turley (W.) | 8⅓ | 13 | 3 | 2 |
| Shantz | ⅔ | 0 | 0 | 0 |

*Faced two batters in sixth.

Bases on balls—Off Friend 2 (Richardson, Mantle), Green 1 (McDougald), Labine 1 (Maris), Cheney 1 (Mantle), Turley 3 (Cimoli, Burgess, Schofield). Struck out—By Friend 6 (McDougald, Mantle, Skowron 2, Howard 2), Labine 1 (Mantle), Gibbon 2 (Maris, Turley), Cheney 2 (DeMaestri, Maris). Hit by pitcher—By Turley (Christopher). Wild pitch—Cheney. Passed ball—Burgess 2.

Umpires—Stevens (A.), plate; Jackowski (N.), first base; Chylak (A.), second base; Boggess (N.), third base; Landes (N.), left field; Honochick (A.), right field. Time of game—3:14.

---

July 27, 1961

### *Blanchard Hits 2 Homers and Mantle Poles No. 39 as Yanks Beat White Sox*

## SHELDON IS VICTOR WITH 4-HITTER, 5–2

### Blanchard Runs Home Run Streak to Four—Boyer Connects as Yanks Win

#### By ROBERT L. TEAGUE

Whatever the task confronting them, the Yankees rely on the same crude all-purpose tools—blunt instruments that make baseballs and rival pitchers disappear.

Yesterday's job at the Stadium was to dig in and consolidate their position atop the American League standing. This they accomplished by slugging four home runs, which felled the Chicago White Sox, 5–2.

As foreman of the operation, Johnny Blanchard drove $7 worth of baseballs into the right-field seats on his first two trips to the plate. He thus extended his home run streak to four in as many at-bats, tying major league record.

The New York catcher had started the streak in Boston last week-end, when he connected twice in successive pinch-hitting roles.

Mickey Mantle and Cletis Boyer belted the other homers yesterday. The four drives cost the team $14 but that sum was easily offset by the 22,366 customers who paid to see Major Ralph Houk's home run circus. The crowd also was treated to a four-hit hurling performance by Roland Sheldon.

## Mantle One Behind

Mantle's clout was his thirty-ninth of the season. It put him one behind his equally destructive team-mate, Roger Maris, the major league home run leader.

Although Maris did not participate in the latest Yankee slugging bee, the assault on Ray Herbert seemed rather fulsome in view of Sheldon's knowledgeable handling of the White Sox.

After yielding an innocuous ground single to Al Pilarcik in the second inning, the rookie right-hander retired fourteen in a row. His shutout ended in the seventh. Here, a walk to Minnie Minoso, plus Roy Sievers' double to the running track in right center, put two men in scoring position with none out.

Joe Martin delivered both with a single through the middle. By that time, the Yankee bludgeons already had accounted for fiver runs and Sheldon thwarted the Chicago batters without notable incident thereafter.

Major Houk's wrecking crew literally got off to a pedestrian start, with Bobby Richardson leading off the first inning with a walk. He presently trotted home as Mantle lofted his homer about fifteen rows deep in the right-center field bleachers, scattering a covey of shirtless sunbathers.

## Statistics on Homers

That was Mickey's twenty-ninth circuit blast since May 29. A Yankee statistician was quick to point out that if the husky outfielder continued at that rate, he would finish the season with seventy-two homers. At the moment, he is twenty-two games ahead of Babe Ruth's pace of 1927, when the great Bambino clouted a record total of sixty. Maris is twenty-three games ahead.

Immediately following Mantle's drive, Blanchard stroked one into the right-field stand. That aforementioned Yankee statistician then reported that if Blanchard maintained his impossible pace he would wind up with 113 home runs this year.

Herbert was not molested again until he faced Blanchard in the fourth. This time Johnny knocked one into the upper deck in right, his thirteenth homer of the season.

Two outs later, Boyer pulled his seventh homer into the left-field seats, just beyond the 402-foot marker.

That closed the Yankee scoring. They got just one more hit off Herbert and none off Turk Lown, who replaced him in the eighth. The Bombers totaled only six hits, but these were good for nineteen bases.

## Turley's Elbow Inflamed

The Yanks requested permission from the American League to put Bob Turley on the disabled list. The right-handed pitcher is suffering from an inflammation of the elbow on his throwing arm.

X-rays indicated that the best treatment would be a prolonged rest for Turley. At present, there is no plan to bring up another pitcher to replace him. Turley has won three games and lost five.

Blanchard narrowly missed hitting a fifth consecutive homer. In the sixth inning, his long fly to right was caught by Floyd Robinson a few feet from the barrier.

| CHICAGO (A.) | ab. | r. | h. | rbi. | NEW YORK (A.) | ab. | r. | h. | rbi. |
|---|---|---|---|---|---|---|---|---|---|
| Robinson, rf | 4 | 0 | 0 | 0 | Rich'dson, 2b | 3 | 1 | 0 | 0 |
| Fox, 2b | 4 | 0 | 0 | 0 | Kubek, ss | 3 | 0 | 0 | 0 |
| Minoso, lf | 2 | 1 | 0 | 0 | Maris, rf | 3 | 0 | 0 | 0 |
| Sievers, 1b | 4 | 1 | 1 | 0 | Mantle, cf | 4 | 1 | 1 | 2 |
| Martin, 3b | 4 | 0 | 1 | 2 | Blanchard, c | 4 | 2 | 2 | 2 |
| Pilarcik, cf | 3 | 0 | 1 | 0 | Skowron, 1b | 3 | 0 | 0 | 0 |
| Aparicio, ss | 3 | 0 | 0 | 0 | Lopez, lf | 3 | 0 | 1 | 0 |
| Lollar, c | 3 | 0 | 0 | 0 | Boyer, 3b | 3 | 1 | 2 | 1 |
| Herbert, p | 2 | 0 | 0 | 0 | Sheldon, p | 3 | 0 | 0 | 0 |
| ªGoodman | 1 | 0 | 1 | 0 | | | | | |
| Lown, p | 0 | 0 | 0 | 0 | | | | | |
| Total | 30 | 2 | 4 | 2 | Total | 29 | 5 | 6 | 5 |

ªSingled for Herbert in 8th.

| | | | |
|---|---|---|---|
| Chicago | 000 | 000 | 200—2 |
| New York | 300 | 200 | 00..—5 |

E—Aparicio. DP—Sievers, Aparicio, Sievers. LOB—Chicago 3, New York 3.

PO—Chicago 24: Robinson 3, Sievers 10, Martin, Pilarcik 2, Aparicio 3, Lollar 3, Herbert 2. New York 27: Richardson 2, Kubek, Maris, Mantle 6, Blanchard 4, Skowron 11, Lopez, Boyer. A—Chicago 12: Sievers 3, Martin 4, Aparicio 5. New York 10: Richardson 2, Kubek 4, Boyer 3, Sheldon.

2B Hits—Boyer, Sievers. HR—Mantle, Blanchard 2, Boyer. Sacrifice—Kubek.

| | IP. | H. | R. | ER. | BB. | SO. |
|---|---|---|---|---|---|---|
| Herbert (L. 7–9) | 7 | 6 | 5 | 5 | 1 | 3 |
| Lown | 1 | 0 | 0 | 0 | 1 | 0 |
| Sheldon (W. 7–3) | 9 | 4 | 2 | 2 | 2 | 4 |

Umpires—Umony, Stewart, Berry, Linsalata.
Time—2:06. Attendance—22,366.

## *YANKEES BEAR INDIANS, 3–2, IN 10TH; FORD WINS 21ST; MEXICO LEADS U.S. IN TENNIS; DIVINE COMEDY VICTOR*

### ARROYO RELIEVES

### Howard's Hit Wins—Maris and Mantle Fail to Connect

### BY JOHN DREBINGER

*Special to The New York Times.*

CLEVELAND, Aug. 19—Once again the Yankees' two most destructive bombs, Roger Maris and Mickey Mantle, were silenced by slick Cleveland pitching today, but Ralph Houk and his Yanks revealed they had other means with which to finish on top in the American League flag race.

There was the indomitable spirit of Whitey Ford and there was a timely clutch single by Elston Howard in the tenth inning. That blow drove in a run that broke a 2–2 tie and presently gave the Bombers a 3–2 ten-inning victory over the Indians.

A special Ladies and Children's Day gathering of 58,557 was on hand. The paid attendance was 23,398, quite a windfall in itself.

The triumph was Ford's twenty-first of the season against only three defeats. It was, indeed, a stout-hearted performance by the Yanks' compact left-hander who, this time, needed his ubiquitous side, Luis Arroyo, for just one-third of an inning.

#### Piersall Grounds Out

With two out in the last of the tenth, the embattled Indians were still striving to draw even again and Ken Aspromonte came through with a double. But Arroyo, who may go down in Yankee history as one of the great relievers, retired Jimmy Piersall on a sharp grounder to third and that was it.

Although the Tigers also won, the victory kept the Bombers three games in front. Ford might have locked this one up in nine innings. In the eighth, though, with the Yanks leading 2–1, a wild pitch with two out and the bases filled allowed an Indian to scamper home with the tying run.

The Yanks had scored their first two runs off Barry Latman in the fourth while the Indians had scored only on a homer by John Romano in the fifth.

With their lead gone, the Yanks had to win it all over again. This they did in the tenth, which Billy Gardner opened with a double off Bobby, Locke. Locke had replaced Latman in the ninth.

Here, Maris, hitless for the third successive game, grounded out. It was his fifth time at bat without a hit, and extended his sudden hitless string to thirteen times at bat.

Then, Mantle, with a single and a walk in four previous times up, fanned for the second time amid delirious screams from the crowd.

Bow, however, Manager Jimmy Dykes, invoked some strategy that backfired. He ordered the still profoundly respected Yogi Berra intentionally passed in the hope that Howard for all his .353 batting average, would supply the third out. Instead, Howard singled sharply to right to drive in the run that won the game.

August 20, 1961

## *The Lively Bat Becomes a Livelier Issue*

### *Light Weapon Used in Race to Topple Ruth Homer Mark*

### By JOSEPH M. SHEEHAN

It takes two to tango. It also takes a bat as well as a ball to bring about a home run.

All unsubstantiated claims of a lively ball to the contrary notwithstanding, the bat remains the active agent in baseball's biggest hit. The ball is merely a passively motive object until struck squarely and violently by the barrel of a tapered cylindrical stick fashioned from seasoned second-growth northern white ash.

A second go-around on a pioneer research tour taken several years ago has strengthened the conviction that the current rash of homer hitting is attributable to revised qualities of the bat, rather than the ball.

Roger Maris and Mickey Mantle of the Yankees are having a rousing go at Babe Ruth's revered 1927 record of sixty home runs. More significantly, more players in both major leagues are hitting more homers than ever before.

Why so? Simply because most of today's players are taking heavier swings with lighter bats at more or less the same old ball.

Babe Ruth customarily used a forty-two-ounce bat. A big man—6 feet 2 inches and 215 pounds, according to the book—the Babe could handle that bludgeon. And from 1920, when he was traded from the Red Sox to the Yankees and gave up serious pitching, Ruth swung unabashedly for the fences. They paid him for that—at the apex of his career he received a bigger salary than the President of the United States.

Today's prime challengers of Ruth's record—Maris and Mantle—shoot at the barriers with lighter weapons. But for that very reason, their guns have higher muzzle velocity. Eventually, if not this season, one of them—or some other slugger—is going to break the Ruthian record.

With significant differences in conformation, the bats with which Maris and Mantle have been hitting homers like sixty measure thirty-five inches long and weigh a modest thirty-three ounces.

Roger's bat is relatively thick-handles, tapering gradually from barrel to gripping knob. Mickey uses a thin-handled bat, with more of its weight concentrated in the striking surface.

When he first joined the Yankees ten years ago, Mantle, an explosively powerful, heavily muscled 200-pounder who stands an even 6 feet, used a thirty-six-ounce bat. Maris, less conspicuously of approximately the same physical proportions, started out in the majors in 1957 using a thirty-three-ounce bat, went in his second year to a thirty-four, then returned to a thirty-three.

## Got to Have That Swing

"The weight of the bat isn't the most important thing," says Maris. "What counts more is how you swing."

To keep the quote in context, Roger was talking as much about Ruth and the Babe's preference for a heavier bat as about his own choice of weapons.

He was getting across the point that, at least as much as implements, intent underlies today's outcrop of homers. Keenly aware of the diamond solecism that "home run hitters drive Cadillacs," an increasing number of players "go for the pump" every time they swing.

"In our days, we weren't averse to taking a good rip now and then," says Wally Moses, the Yankee batting coach. Wally got a lot of base hits (2,138) but relatively few homers (eighty-nine) for the old Philadelphia Athletics, Chicago White Sox and Boston Red Sox from 1935 through 1951.

"With two strikes against us," he pointed out, "most of us would concentrate on guarding the plate and meeting the ball. That's where the big difference comes in now. Today, the guys keep swinging from their heels, regardless of the count."

It's a which-comes-first, the-chicken-or-the-egg type of proposition but the lighter bats in vogue today represent a vital component of this changed baseball philosophy.

Through constant experimentation, the players have discovered that the faster they can whip their bats into the ball, the farther it will carry. The lighter bat has emerged as the solution to the quest for more swinging speed and more distance. This is not opinion or conjecture. There are solid facts to support the thesis.

The Hillerich and Bradsby Company of Louisville, Ky., which manufactures the popular Louisville Slugger bat, reports that thirty-one and thirty-two-ounce bats are in greatest demand today. Ten years ago, the average weigh of the company's major league models was thirty-four–thirty-five ounces.

Going farther back, the company did most of its business in bats weighing thirty-six ounces and upward. Frank Ryan, the manager of H. & B.'s professional baseball division, supplies some interesting evidence on this score.

He reports:

"We have an old order on file from the Yankees for fifty-two-ounce bats for Ruth. Frankly, I doubt if the Babe ever used them. Our records show he favored a forty-two-ounce bat in his prime and never used one that weighed less than thirty-eight ounces.

"Many other players of that era also preferred heavy bats. Ty Cobb swung a real piece of lumber—it was only thirty-four and one half inches long but weighed forty-two ounces. Of our regular models, the heaviest I know of was Edd Roush's forty-eight-ouncer.

"Today our bats range from twenty-eight to thirty-six ounces. Billy Goodman, I believe, is alone in using the twenty-eight-ounce model. The thirty-six-ounce bat had a strange mixture of users. Among them are sluggers like Ted Kluszewski and Steve Bilko and slap-hitters like Johnny Temple and Dick Groat, who won the National League batting title with one last year."

Hal Schumacher, the former New York Giant pitcher who turned traitor to his class by becoming executive vice president of Adirondack Bats, Inc. of Dolgeville, N.Y., another principal major league supplier, concurred that the trend was toward lighter bats.

"The big demand now is for thirty-one to thirty-three-ounce bats as against thirty-three to thirty-six-ounce bats ten years ago," says Schumacher.

"With mixed feelings as an ex-pitcher, I understand the thinking that you can hit the ball farther with these lighter bats. But I think we've about reached the limit.

"Below, say, thirty ounces, you can't construct a bat that has real driving power. There just isn't enough good wood in it."

In trend with the times, Yankee players generally and most of the men on other major league clubs are using lighter bats than they started out with as baseball pros.

### Howard Exception to Rule

There's one glowing exception on the Bombers. Elston Howard, having his best year, is swinging "to meet the ball and hit it through the middle" with a thirty-five-ounce bat. In previous seasons, he tried for distance with erratic results with a thirty-three-ounce bat.

"Maybe with the change I won't hit as many homers as before, but if I can keep my batting average up around .350 I shouldn't have nay transportation problems either," says the Yankee catcher.

Ball clubs have double reason to be conscious of the lighter bats. Thinner-handled for the most part, they break more easily and have to be replaced more frequently. The Yankee bill for hitting lumber (at the stable price of $3 per bat) rose from $1,546 in 1950 to $2,250 in 1960.

However, if Maris, Mantle and company keep poling the ball into packed seats at home and on the road, there'll be no complaints if the heavier cost for lighter bats keep rising.

September 4, 1961

### *Mantle Makes It 49 and 50 and Yanks Make It Three Straight Over Tigers*

## HOWARD'S HOMER CAPS 8–5 VICTORY

### Drive in 9th Defeats Tigers After Mantle Ties Score—55,676 See Game

### By JOHN DREBINGER

Mickey Mantle, who hadn't been expected to play, treated himself, the Yankees and 55,676 fans to a pair of homers yesterday. They were his forty-ninth and fiftieth of the season and they readied things for an 8–5 Bomber victory.

The first homer, coupled with one by Yogi Berra, had put the Yankees into a 3–2 lead in the first inning. But that lead failed to stand up and the Yanks were trailing 5–4, in the ninth when Mantle hit his second drive.

Minutes later, with two Yanks aboard the bases, Elston Howard sent his No. 15 crashing into the left-field stand for the cluster of runs that ended the game.

## Lead Is 4½ Games

Thus, Ralph Houk's mighty Bombers swept the three-game series with second-place Detroit and moved into a four-and-a-half-game lead. Bob Scheffing's Bengals trail by five games in the loss column.

Mantle was a surprise starter after straining a muscle in the left forearm Saturday. Houk had feared his star would be out for three or four days, but Mickey slammed his way back into the dizzy scramble for Babe Ruth's thirty-four-year-old home run record of sixty.

Roger Maris, leading at fifty-three, was held to a single in four trips to the plate. He is eight games ahead of Ruth's record pace of 1927. Mantle is three games ahead.

The two have nineteen games remaining to reach or surpass the record within the 154-game limit set by Commissioner Ford Frick. Twenty-seven games in all that remain on the Yankee schedule.

Tense as was Friday's 1–0 opener, yesterday's encounter was the most thrilling of the series. With Bill Stafford opposing Jim Bunning at the start, the Yanks held a 4–2 lead as the struggle moved into the eighth. Back in the sixth Norm Cash had hit his thirty-third homer for the Tigers.

## Stafford Goes 7 Innings

But Stafford gave way in the heat and retired for a pinch-hitter in the seventh. And as the eighth opened, the incomparable Luis Arroyo stepped to the mound to play one of his most dramatic roles. It almost engulfed him in disaster.

Arroyo started out with three pitches. They produced an astounding result.

Bill Bruton singled on the first. Al Kaline singled on the second and sent Bruton to third. Rocky Colavito slapped the next one into a double play that scored Bruton, and the Yankee lead was shaved to 4–3. The next three pitches were strikes that fanned Cash for the third out.

In the ninth came more trouble. Dick McAuliffe walked and, after Chico Fernandez had struck out, Dick Brown topped a ball in front of the plate. Arroyo pounced on it and fired to first. But the ball slithered off Bill Skowron's glove for an error and the runners wound up on second and third.

At first Luis was charged with the error, but the official scorer later changed this and gave it to Skowron.

Arroyo issued an intentional pass then to Bubba Morton, a pinch-hitter, and filled the bases. But Jake Wood wrecked this strategy by hitting a single to left that scored two runs. And that had the Tigers in front, 5–4.

## Colavito Starts It Again

Mantle wiped that out in a jiffy in the last of the ninth. With Gerry Staley coming to the mound as the fourth Tiger pitcher, Mickey stroked a drive into the right-field bleachers alongside the bullpen.

Berra followed with a single and Ronnie Kline replaced Staley. Arroyo sacrificed Yogi to second.

Scheffing ordered an intentional walk to Skowron and the second out followed as Cletis Boyer flied to right. But Howard, with the count at one strike, clubbed the next pitch into the seats in left and that was it.

The victory was Arroyo's thirteenth in relief against only three defeats and his eleventh triumph in a row.

As on Saturday, Colavito again sent the Tigers off to a first-inning lead. This time, though, it was only for a single run. Wood opened with a single to left and was forced by Bruton, who then stole second. After Kaline had fouled out Colavito plunked a single into left that sent Bruton home.

The lead, however, endured for only two outs in the first. Maris singled and Mantle, with the count three and two, drove the ball deep in the lower right-field stand.

Like an echo of this shot Berra weighed in with a powerful smash that cleared the inner high gate in the Yankee bullpen in right center. It was No. 19 for Yogi.

Bunning steadied down after this, but in the fifth a couple of lesser lights in the Yankee battlefront nudged him for a run.

With one down Boyer singled, advanced on Stafford's sacrifice and galloped home on Bobby Richardson's second single in the afternoon.

That tally was to come in handy when Cash unloaded his homer in the sixth. Luckily for Stafford the bases were empty. Though Kaline had opened the inning with a single, Colavito, who on Saturday had hit his fortieth homer, cleared the bases this time by drilling into a double play.

And that was the way matters stood when the real fireworks began to explode in the eighth.

Mantle's two homers give him a lifetime total of 370 and sent him into eighth position in the homer list. Ralph Kiner had held the spot with 369.

## 171,503 at 3 Games

The crowd lifted the three-game total attendance to 171,503, a stadium record for a three-game series. The previous high—165,268—also was drawn by the Tigers, in July of 1950. The nine games with the Tigers here drew 328,309.

The Yanks won six of the nine. But in Detroit, where four games will be played later this month, the Bengals lead, three games to two.

Maris and Mantle have a combined home run total of 103. This leaves them four behind the two-man record set by Ruth and Lou Gehrig in 1927. Maris and Mantle are the only two players ever to hit fifty or more homers for one club in the same season. In '27, Gehrig hit forty-seven to Ruth's sixty.

Scheffing won't buy the idea that the Yankees are just plain lucky.

"There's nothing lucky about that club," says the Tiger skipper. "They represent one of the best balanced club we've ever seen. No matter who gets hurt they've got the bench to keep right on going.

"Imagine a club with a hitter like Skowron batting seventh. Skowron can be fooled at the plate, but let a pitcher be a little off in his control and the ball winds up in the seats."

## Mantle Elects to Play

Houk expected to make a shift in center field. But then Mantle belted a few his first time up in batting practice and told his skipper that he intended losing no more ground in the home run derby by sitting in the dugout.

Arroyo, portly, gray haired and distinguished looking, does not look like a ballplayer when in street attire. He delights in strolling among crowds unnoticed while listening "to what they have to say about Luis." For relaxation he enjoys nothing better than a fine cigar. "I can afford them," he says, "because I have no other pleasures."

Every time a Yankee hits a homer he adds to the American League club record the Bombers set a couple of days ago. The total now stands at 201. The major league mark, 221, was set by the Giants in 1947 and tied by the Reds in 1956.

# YANKS' SCORE

| DETROIT (A.) | ab. | r. | h. | rbi. | NEW YORK (A.) | ab. | r. | h. | rbi. |
|---|---|---|---|---|---|---|---|---|---|
| Wood, 2b | 5 | 0 | 2 | 2 | Richardson, 2b | 4 | 0 | 2 | 1 |
| Bruton, cf | 4 | 2 | 1 | 0 | Kubek, ss | 4 | 0 | 0 | 0 |
| Kaline, rf | 5 | 0 | 2 | 0 | Maris, rf | 4 | 1 | 1 | 0 |
| Colavito, lf | 4 | 0 | 1 | 1 | Mantle, cf | 4 | 2 | 2 | 3 |
| Cash, 1b | 4 | 1 | 2 | 1 | Berra, lf | 4 | 2 | 3 | 1 |
| McAuliffe, 3b | 3 | 1 | 1 | 0 | Blanchard, c | 2 | 0 | 0 | 0 |
| Fernandez, ss | 3 | 0 | 0 | 0 | cTresh | 0 | 0 | 0 | 0 |
| Roarke, c | 2 | 0 | 0 | 0 | Arroyo, p | 0 | 0 | 0 | 0 |
| aOsborne | 1 | 0 | 0 | 0 | Skowron, 1b | 3 | 1 | 0 | 0 |
| Brown, c | 1 | 0 | 0 | 0 | Boyer, 3b | 4 | 1 | 1 | 0 |
| fBertola | 0 | 1 | 0 | 0 | Stafford, p | 1 | 0 | 0 | 0 |
| House, c | 0 | 0 | 0 | 0 | dHoward | 2 | 1 | 1 | 3 |
| Bunning, p | 2 | 0 | 0 | 0 | | | | | |
| bMaxwell | 1 | 0 | 0 | 0 | | | | | |
| Regan, p | 0 | 0 | 0 | 0 | | | | | |
| Fox, p | 0 | 0 | 0 | 0 | | | | | |
| eMorton | 0 | 0 | 0 | 0 | | | | | |
| Staley, p | 0 | 0 | 0 | 0 | | | | | |
| Kline, p | 0 | 0 | 0 | 0 | | | | | |
| Total | 35 | 5 | 9 | 4 | Total | 32 | 8 | 10 | 8 |

aGrounded out for Roarke in 7th; bStruck out for Bunning in 7th; cRan for Blanchard in 7th; dStruck out for Stafford in 7th; ePurposely walked for Fox in 9th; fRan for Brown in 9th.

| | | | |
|---|---|---|---|
| Detroit | 100 | 001 | 012—5 |
| New York | 300 | 010 | 004—8 |

Two out when winning run was scored.

E—Skowron. DP—Cash, Fernandez, Cash; Kubek, Richardson, Skowron. LOB—Detroit 7, New York 2.

PO—Detroit 26: Wood 4, Bruton 2, Kaline 4, Colavito, Cash 2, Fernandez 3, Roarke 7, Brown 3, New York 27: Richardson 2, Kubek 2, Mantle, Berra 3, Blanchard 2, Skowron 12, Boyer 3, Howard 2. A—Detroit 5: McAuliffe, Fernandez, Cash, Bunning, Roarke. New York 16: Richardson 5, Kubek 5, Boyer 6.

2B Hit—Cash. HR—Mantle 2, Berra, Howard. SB—Bruton. Sacrifices—Stafford, Arroyo.

| | IP. | H. | R. | ER. | BB. | SO. |
|---|---|---|---|---|---|---|
| Bunning | 6 | 6 | 4 | 4 | 0 | 7 |
| *Regan | 0 | 1 | 0 | 0 | 1 | 0 |
| Fox | 2 | 0 | 0 | 0 | 0 | 3 |
| †Staley (L. 2-5) | 0 | 2 | 2 | 2 | 0 | 0 |
| Kline | 2/3 | 1 | 2 | 2 | 1 | 0 |
| Stafford | 7 | 6 | 2 | 3 | 2 | 1 |
| Arroyo (W. 13-3) | 2 | 3 | 3 | 2 | 2 | 2 |

*Faced 2 batters in 7th; †Faced 2 batter in 9th. Umpires—Chylak, Drummond, Paparella, Runge. Time—2:42. Attendance—55,676.

### *Mantle Hits Homer No. 52 as Yanks Downs Indians Before 41,762 at Stadium*

## BOMBERS CAPTURE NINTH IN ROW, 9–1

### Stafford Hurls 7-Hitter and Belts Triple and Single—Kubek Clouts Homer

#### By ROBERT L. TEAGUE

One of Gary Bell's pitches hovered a split second too long in Mickey Mantle's strike zone last night at the Stadium. Before the Cleveland right-hander had time to say "Shucks, there goes No. 52," it was gone. A crowd of 41,752 watched its flight. Other Yankees had pasted the usual "losing pitcher" label on Bell long before that juncture. Mantle's homer merely raised the count to 6–1 against the Indians. By the time Bill Stafford collected the final putout of his thirteenth victory, the scoreboard read 9–1. From his defensive station, Stafford held the Tribesmen to seven well-spaced hits. From the batter's box, he tormented them further with a triple and a two-run single.

Stafford's route-going performance was the fifth in a row by a New York hurler. It helped the American League leaders extend their winning streak to nine—matching their longest of the 1961 season.

#### A Lofty Trajectory

Mantle's blast in the fifth inning landed among roaring souvenir hunters in the lower right-field stand. It followed an extremely lofty trajectory—seeming twice as high as the arc traces about a minute earlier by Tony Kubek's seventh round-tripper of the year. With fifty-two homers after 141 games, Mantle now is one game behind the pace set by Babe Ruth in 1927, when the Bambino clouted a record total of sixty.

Roger Maris went hitless in four trips to the plate last night, but the Yankee outfielder still leads the home run derby with fifty-five. He is seven games ahead of Ruth, who poled his fifty-fifth in game No. 148.

After drawing a base on balls in the eighth, Mantle left the game because of a self-inflicted injury. He fouled off a pitch that struck him on the foot.

As matters finally turned out in the game, the issue actually was decided in the first inning, when eight Yankees batted and three scored.

One tallied as Maris grounded out. John Blanchard singled home the next run, following an intentional walk to Mantle. Elston Howard produced the third with a single to left.

#### Mantle Equals His Mark

Stafford's triple to left center preceded Kubek's clout in the fifth. One out later, Mantle connected and equaled the highest home run total of his career. He also belted fifty-two in 1956.

Mickey's drive lifted the M Squad's aggregate to 107 for the season, equaling the major league record for two team-mates, set by Ruth and Lou Gehrig thirty-four years ago. Gehrig hit forty-seven homers in 1927.

The total number of homers by Mantle and Maris now exceeds the output of the remainder of the Yanks by one.

Bob Allen and Frank Funk shared the responsibility for New York's final offensive—a three-run outburst in the eighth. Walks to Mantle and Blanchard started it. Howard's third single made the score 7–1.

After Cletis Boyer had been walked purposely, filling the bases, Stafford confounded the Indians by bouncing his two-run single through the box.

The set-back was Cleveland's fifteenth straight at the Stadium over a two-season span. The Tribe's run was scored in the third inning as Vic Power struck out on a wild pitch that bounced over the catcher's head. The bases were filled at the time.

## Methods Are Varied

In calculating the missile gap between the M Squad and Ruth, some statisticians include the tie games played by the 1927 Yanks and the current team. Others ignore the deadlocks when computing the number of games played because none of the dramatis personae hit a homer in either of the deadlocks anyway.

However, when the Yanks and Baltimore Orioles attempted to replay their 1961 tie several weeks ago, Mantle and Maris each connected for the circuit. Rain prevented the completion of the minimum number of innings, though, and so the homers were washed out.

Obviously, that natural catastrophe will be the subject of some heated debate around the hot stove league next winter if Mantle and Maris winds up the season one short of sixty home runs.

The 1927 Yanks played a tie in their third start of the season, thereby increasing their season game total to 155. Similarly, the 1961 Bombers will play 163 games—one more than the schedule requires since the league's expansion from eight to ten teams.

Cleveland's catcher, Johnny Romano, was honored by fans from his native Hoboken, N.J., before the game. His gifts included a 1962 Cadillac coupe.

Jack Reed, an outfielder with the Richmond (Va.) club of the International League was recalled by the Yankees yesterday. Reed, who batted .269 with the minor league team this season, will join the New York club next Tuesday in Chicago.

The Yankees also asked eight players who are on option with three farm teams to join them when the training season opens at Fort Lauderdale, Fla., next season.

| CLEVELAND (A.) | ab. | r. | h. | rbi. | NEW YORK (A.) | ab. | r. | h. | rbi. |
|---|---|---|---|---|---|---|---|---|---|
| Temple, 2b | 4 | 1 | 2 | 0 | Richardson, 2b | 4 | 1 | 1 | 0 |
| Francona, lf | 3 | 0 | 1 | 0 | Kubek, ss | 5 | 2 | 2 | 2 |
| Dillard, cf | 4 | 0 | 0 | 0 | Maris, rf, cf | 3 | 0 | 0 | 1 |
| Kirkland, rf | 4 | 0 | 0 | 0 | Mantle, cf | 2 | 2 | 1 | 1 |
| Power, 1b | 4 | 0 | 2 | 0 | cLopez, rf | 0 | 1 | 0 | 0 |
| Romano, c | 4 | 0 | 1 | 0 | Blanchard, lf | 3 | 1 | 2 | 1 |
| Held, ss | 4 | 0 | 0 | 0 | Howard, c | 4 | 1 | 3 | 2 |
| Phillips, 3b | 1 | 0 | 0 | 0 | Skowron, 1b | 4 | 0 | 0 | 0 |
| aDe la Hoz, 3b | 2 | 0 | 0 | 0 | Boyer, 3b | 3 | 0 | 0 | 0 |
| Bell, p | 2 | 0 | 0 | 0 | Stafford, p | 4 | 1 | 2 | 2 |
| bBond | 1 | 0 | 0 | 0 | | | | | |
| Allen | 0 | 0 | 0 | 0 | | | | | |
| Funk, p | 0 | 0 | 0 | 0 | | | | | |
| dNieman | 1 | 0 | 1 | 0 | | | | | |
| Total | 34 | 1 | 7 | 0 | Total | 32 | 9 | 11 | 9 |

aGrounded out for Phillips in 6th; bFlied out for Bell in 6th; cRan for Mantle in 8th; dSingled for Funk in 9th.

| Cleveland | 001 | 000 | 000—1 |
|---|---|---|---|
| New York | 300 | 030 | 03..—9 |

E—Richardson. DP—Stafford, Kubek, Skowron; Temple, Held, Power; Temple, Held, Power; Boyer, Richardson, Skowron. LOB—Cleveland 9, New York 5. PO—Cleveland 24: Temple, 4, Francona, Dillard 2, Power 8, Romano, Held 7, Bell. Yankees 27: Kubek 3, Maris 5, Mantle 3, Blanchard 2, Howard 5, Skowron 8, Boyer. A—Cleveland 16: Temple 6, Power, Held 7, Phillips, de la Hoz. Yankees 10: Richardson, Kubek 3, Skowron, Boyer, Stafford 4. 3B Hit—Stafford. HR—Kubek, Mantle.

| | IP. | H. | R. | ER. | BB. | SS. |
|---|---|---|---|---|---|---|
| Bell (L. 9–15) | 5 | 8 | 6 | 6 | 3 | 0 |
| Allen | 2⅓ | 3 | 3 | 3 | 3 | 1 |
| Funk | ⅔ | 0 | 0 | 0 | 0 | 0 |
| Stafford (W. 13–7) | 9 | 7 | 1 | 0 | 2 | 6 |

HBP—By Stafford (Phillips). Wild pitch—Stafford. Umpires—Stewart, Berry, Umont, Linsalata. Time—2:29. Attendance—41,762.

### Penn State Rally Downs Navy, 20–10; Army Wins; Mantle Hits 54th Homer; Reds Defeat Giants, 10–6

#### Yanks 8–3 Victors

#### Ford Stops Red Sox for 25th Triumph—Mantle Connects

#### By JOHN DREBINGER

*Special to The New York Times.*

BOSTON, Sept. 23—Mickey Mantle, who had almost become the forgotten man in 1961's rousing home run derby, crashed back into contention today.

The Switcher, appearing in the Yankee starting line-up for the first time since Sept. 17, hit his fifty-fourth homer. The blow, struck off the Red Sox' rookie star, Don Schwall, came in the first inning with two aboard and paved the way for an 8–3 Bomber triumph.

The home run also helped Whitey Ford to gain his twenty-fifth victory of the season against only four defeats. It also put Mantle within five homers of the fellow who had been overshadowing him for the past two weeks. Roger Maris again drew a blank today. This leaves Roger, at fifty-nine, still one shy of Babe Ruth's 154-game record although the Yankees in their expanded schedule have now played 156 to a decision. They have only six more games remaining.

Mantle, just recovered from a bout with virus, also connected for a single in four times at bat. Maris, in his five trips to the plate, walked twice and got a single.

#### Howard, Cerv Connect

Homers by Elston Howard and Bob Cerv also helped the Yanks to roll to a comparatively easy triumph despite the fact they were outhit by Boston, 11 to 7.

Ford, who pitched only five innings, scarcely could be said to have put on one of his better performances. He was buffeted for nine hits, including homers by Don Gile and Carl Yastrzemski.

Whitey was leading by a slender 4–3 margin when he stepped out. Jim Coates, who took over in the sixth, and the matchless Luis Arroyo, who hurled the ninth, held the Sox to the end, however. It was Luis' sixty-first relief appearance, which sets another Yankee record. The former mark, sixty, was held by Joe Page.

The first four innings presented an unusual contrast in offensive efficiency. Though the Yanks connected for only two hits, they picked up three runs—and one of the hits played no part in the scoring.

Meanwhile, the Sox peppered Ford for nine blows in those four innings, but had to be content with the same total—three. It took two homers to account for two of those runs.

Young Schwall set up the Yanks' runs in the first inning when he hit Bobby Richardson with a pitched ball. Bobby went to second on Tony Kubek's sharp drive to the mound that Schwall stopped with his bare hand and then recovered in time for a putout at first.

Maris got on when Gile, the Sox first baseman, fumbled his grounder. Then Mantle belted his fifty-fourth homer into the bull pen some 300 feet away. That gave the Yanks three runs and they didn't get their second hit until Cletis Boyer singled in the fourth. Meanwhile, the Sox swarmed all over the base paths until they reached third. Then, somehow, they would go astray.

## Scoring the Hard Way

In the first inning, they got to Whitey for three singles and a walk, but scored only once. The first hit, a single by Chuck Schilling, was wiped right out when Carroll Hardy hit into a double play.

Jackie Jensen then walked and it took two more singles, by Frank Malzone and Jim Pagliaroni, to bring Jackie home. The inning ended on a most excruciating note for the Sox, when Pagliaroni got himself picked off first base for the third out.

The second inning was even stranger. Here the Red Sox came up with four hits, one a homer, but again had to settle for one run.

After Pumpsie green had opened with a single, Yastrzemski banged into a double play. The bases, therefore, were empty when Gile, a rookie recently recalled from Seattle, belted one high over the left-field barrier. This not only was Gile's first major league homer, it was his first hit.

Two singles followed that homer, but Hardy ended the inning by grounding into a force play for the third out.

In the fourth, the Sox made two more hits off Ford, but only one counted. That was Yastrzemski's eleventh homer. Because it preceded Gile's single, the Sox again had to be satisfied with a single run, but at least they had tied the score.

## One Run on No Hits

However, the deadlock lasted only until the fifth, when the Yanks scored a run without any hits. After Maris had walked, Mantle struck out. An infield out advanced Roger to second, and a wild pitch put him on third and, when Frank Malzone threw wide to first on Elston Howard's grounder, Maris scored.

In the seventh, the Yanks connected for two singles, but again it was a helping hand from the opposition that gave them a run. Mantle singled to right and then stepped out for a pinch-runner, Tom Tresh, who ran very well indeed. He advanced to second on a wild pitch and came in on Yogi Berra's single to right.

With Arnold Early on the mound for the Sox in the eighth, the Yanks picked up two more runs, although their only hit in this inning was a single by Maris.

After a walk and a two-base error on a sacrifice attempt had put runners on second and third, one run came in on a fielder's choice, the other on Maris' single.

Meanwhile, the Bosox attack faded out completely. Ford, before vacating for a pinch hitter in the sixth, allowed no hits in the fifth. Coates and Arroyo held sway the rest of the way.

There was a mild flare-up in the seventh when Jensen headed for the mound after Coates had brushed him back with a close pitch. The plate umpire, Harry Schwartz, quickly stepped in before matters got out of hand, however.

Then the Yanks picked up two more runs in the ninth on two hits. Both were homers. Howard belted the first one, his twenty-first and Cerv, a pinch-hitter for Coates, hit his eighth.

## Turley to Face Surgery

Bob Turley said that he plans to have an operation to remove bone chips in his right elbow as soon as the world series is over. Bullet Bob, who was one of baseball's best pitchers in 1958 and never knew the meaning of a sore arm until this year, has been of little help to the Bombers this season.

| NEW YORK (A.) | ab | r. | h. | rbi. | BOSTON (A.) | ab | r. | h. | rbi. |
|---|---|---|---|---|---|---|---|---|---|
| Richardson, 2b | 4 | 1 | 0 | 0 | Schilling, 2b | 5 | 0 | 2 | 0 |
| Kubek, ss | 4 | 0 | 0 | 1 | Hardy, cf | 4 | 0 | 0 | 0 |
| Maris, rf, cf | 3 | 2 | 1 | 1 | Early, p | 0 | 0 | 0 | 0 |
| Mantle, cf | 4 | 1 | 2 | 3 | cClinton | 1 | 0 | 0 | 0 |
| bTresh | 0 | 0 | 0 | 0 | Jensen, rf | 2 | 1 | 0 | 0 |
| Blancahrd, rf | 1 | 0 | 0 | 0 | Malzone, 3b | 4 | 0 | 1 | 0 |
| Berra, lf | 4 | 0 | 1 | 0 | Pagliaroni, c | 3 | 0 | 2 | 1 |
| Howard, c | 5 | 0 | 0 | 0 | Green, ss | 4 | 0 | 1 | 0 |
| Skowron, 1b | 5 | 1 | 1 | 1 | Yastr'mski, lf | 3 | 1 | 1 | 1 |
| Boyer, 3b | 3 | 1 | 1 | 0 | Gile, 1b | 3 | 1 | 2 | 1 |
| Ford, p | 1 | 0 | 0 | 0 | Geiger, cf | 1 | 0 | 0 | 0 |
| aHale | 1 | 0 | 0 | 0 | Schwall, p | 2 | 0 | 1 | 0 |
| Coates, p | 0 | 1 | 0 | 0 | Runnels, 1b | 2 | 0 | 1 | 0 |
| dCerv | 1 | 1 | 1 | 1 | | | | | |
| Arroyo, p | 0 | 0 | 0 | 0 | | | | | |
| Total | 36 | 8 | 7 | 7 | Total | 34 | 3 | 11 | 3 |

aSafe on fielders' choice for Ford in 6th; bRan for Mantle in 7th; cSingled for Schwall in 7th, dHit homer for Coates in 9th; struck out for Early in 9th.

| New York | 300 | 010 | 022–8 |
|---|---|---|---|
| Boston | 110 | 100 | 000–3 |

E—Gile, Malzone, Green, Early. DP—Kubek, Skowron; Richardson, Kubek, Skowron 2; Green, Schilling, Gile. LOB—New York 11, Boston 8.
PO—New York 27: Richardson 2, Kubek 2, Maris, Berra 4, Howard 2, Skowron 9, Boyer. Boston 27: Schilling 4, Hardy, Jensen 2, Pagliaroni 8, Yastrzemski, Gile 9, Runnels 2. A—New York 13: Richardson 4, Kubek 5, Skowron, Boyer 2, Ford. Boston 15: Schilling 2, Malzone, Pagliaroni 2, Green 6, Gile, Schwall 2.

Home runs—Mantle, Gile, Yastrzemski, Howard, Cerv. Sacrifice—Ford, Richardson, Coates.

| | IP. | H. | R. | ER. | BO. | SO. |
|---|---|---|---|---|---|---|
| Ford (W 25–4) | 5 | 9 | 3 | 3 | 2 | 2 |
| Coates | 3 | 2 | 0 | 0 | 2 | 3 |
| Arroyo | 1 | 0 | 0 | 0 | 0 | 2 |
| Schwall (L 15–6) | 7 | 4 | 4 | 2 | 1 | 1 |

HBP—By Schwall (Richardson). Wild Pitch—Schwall 2, Coates. Umpires—Schwartz, Napp, Haller and Stevens. Time—2:30. Attendance—28,126.

### *Mantle Wins Most-Valuable-Player Award Third Time; Richardson Second*

## SELECTORS OMIT MARIS IN VOTING

### Winner Last 2 Years Yields to Mantle, Yank Teammate—Killebrew is Third

### By JOHN DREBINGER

Mickey Mantle, beaten by narrow margins the last two years in controversial contests for the American League's annual most-valuable-player award, yesterday won one that doubtless came as a surprise even to him.

The renowned 31-year-old slugger of the world champion Yankees, shackled for almost a third of the season with injuries, nevertheless scored a decisive victory for the league's 1962 award with a total of 234 points.

Bobby Richardson, the Yankees crack second baseman and generally regarded as a strong favorite for the prize, placed second with 152 points in the poll of the 20-man committee of the Baseball Writers Association of America.

Harmon Killebrew of the Minnesota Twins, who led the league in homers with 48 despite a .243 batting average finished third with 99 points. Leon Wagner, the distance-hitting outfielder of the Los Angeles Angels, was fourth with 85.

Roger Maris, who had defeated Mantle in the 1960 and 1961 photo finishes, finished nowhere at all, although he did hit 33 home runs. The Yankee outfielder, who last year had topped Babe Ruth's 60-home run record with 61, didn't get a point this year.

### Third Yankee Triple

Points are scored on a basis of 14 points for the first place, 9 for second, 8 for third and down to 1 for tenth.

For Mantle this marked the third most-valuable award. The Switcher won it in 1956 with a perfect 336 score and repeated in 1957 with 233. Mickey thus joins two other Yanks—Joe DiMaggio and Yogi Berra—and Jimmy Foxx as the only three-time winners in the American League.

In 1960, Maris topped Mantle, 202 points to 198, although Mantle had nipped Maris for the home run title, 40 to 39. Many disagree loudly with this result.

Last year the contest was even closer, despite Maris's record feat. The Roger won this one, 225 to 222, and again the result brought sharp criticism.

Mantle's tremendous value to the Yankees, of course, was never denied over the past season when he was physically fir to play. He batted .321, finishing second to Peter Runnels's league-leading 326, and he hit 30 home runs.

However, because of repeated injuries he was able to appear in only 123 of the Yankees' 162 games and in more than a dozen of these he appeared only as a part-time player or pinch-hitter. He also slumped badly in the World Series, although World Series play doesn't count in the most valuable voting.

## Richardson the Reliable

Richardson, on the other hand, was the solid man of the Yanks throughout the campaign. He missed only one game and in addition to his brilliant play at second base, batted .301. Most important of all, he compiled 209 hits, becoming the first Yankee to reach the 200-hit mark since Phil Rizzuto in 1950.

Discussing the outlook for the most-valuable vote during the World Series last month, Mantle conceded that he thought Richardson would win it. "I hope he gets it," said Mickey. "He certainly deserves it."

Manager Ralph Houk at the time seemed to share similar views.

"With our big sluggers not hitting the homers the way they did last year," said the skipper, "there is no denying that Bobby's steady hitting, especially with those time two-baggers, played a tremendous role in putting us over the top." Bobby led the club in doubles with 38.

However, the home run still holds sway, and Mantle's 30, against only eight for Richardson, apparently carried the vote for Mickey.

Mantle was named on all 20 ballots with 13 first-place votes, two seconds, three thirds and two sixths. Richardson had only five first-place votes and was named on 16 of the 20 ballots. He picked up three seconds, four thirds, two fourths, one fifth and one eighth.


## A Yankee Habit

Nine Yankees have now won the most-valuable-player award. These nine have totaled seventeen such awards, which far surpasses the figure of any other club. This also marked the third straight year the Yanks had run one, two in the balloting.

However, apart from Mantle and Richardson, only three other Bombers are to be found among the thirty-three players who scored points this year. The Yankee rookie star, Tom Tresh, placed 12th with 30 points and one first-place ballot. Ralph Terry finished 14th with 19 and Whitey Ford was 28th with 6.

Dick Donovan of the Cleveland Indians led the pitchers with 64 points, placing fifth over all. Killebrew drew the only first-place ballot.

# MOST VALUABLE PLAYERS
## AMERICAN LEAGUE

1931—Lefty Grove, Philadelphia
1932—Jimmy Foxx, Philadelphia
1933—Jimmy Foxx, Philadelphia
1934—Mickey Cochrane, Detroit
1935—Hank Greenberg, Detroit
1936—Lou Gehrig, New York
1937—Charlie Gehringer, Detroit
1938—Jimmy Foxx, Boston
1939—Joe DiMaggio, New York
1940—Hank Greenberg, Detroit
1941—Joe DiMaggio, New York
1942—Joe Gordon, New York
1943—Soud Chandler, New York
1944—Hal Newhouser, Detroit
1945—Hal Newhouser, Detroit
1946—Ted Williams, Boston

1947—Joe Gordon, New York
1948—Lou Boudreau, Cleveland
1949—Ted Williams, Boston
1950—Phil Rizzuto, New York
1951—Yogi Berra, New York
1952—Bobby Shantz, Philadelphia
1953—Al Rosen, Cleveland
1954—Yogi Berra, New York
1955—Yogi Berra, New York
1956—Mickey Mantle, New York
1957—Mickey Mantle, New York
1958—Jackie Jensen, Boston
1959—Nellie Fox, Chicago
1960—Roger Maris, New York
1961—Roger Maris, New York
1962—Mickey Mantle, New York

# THE MOST-VALUABLE VOTE
## (FIRST PLACES IN PARENTHESES)

| | Pts. | | Pts. |
|---|---|---|---|
| Mantle, New York (13) | 234 | Cunningham, Chicago | 9 |
| Richardson, New York (5) | 152 | Runnels, Boston | 9 |
| Killebrew, Minnesota (1) | 99 | Yastrzemski, Boston | 9 |
| Wagner, Los Angeles | 85 | Power, Minnesota | 8 |
| Donovan, Cleveland | 64 | Radaiz, Boston | 8 |
| Kaline, Detroit | 58 | Bunning, Detroit | 8 |
| Siebern, Kansas City | 53 | Versalles, Minnesota | 8 |
| Rollins, Minnesota | 47 | Lumpe, Kansas City | 7 |
| B. Robinson, Baltimore | 41 | Bressud, Boston | 6 |
| F. Robinson, Chicago | 33 | Rodgers, Los Angeles | 6 |
| L. Thomas, Los Angeles | 32 | Ford, New York | 6 |
| Tresh, New York (1) | 30 | Herbert, Chicago | 5 |
| Moran, Los Angeles | 29 | Hinton, Washington | 5 |
| Terry, New York | 19 | Maizone, Boston | 3 |
| Pascual, Minnesota | 14 | Cash, Detroit | 3 |
| Colavito, Detroit | 13 | Smith, Chicago | 1 |
| Aguirre, Detroit | 10 | | |

### *Hodges Named Senators' Manager; Yanks Win; Mets Bow*

---

## MANTLE'S HOMER SUBDUES A'S, 8–7

---

### Clout in 11th Almost Clears Stadium—Two-Out Drive in 9th Ties Yankees

---

#### By JOHN DREBINGER

The Yankees brought down the Kansas City Athletics, 8–7, in a torrid 11-inning struggle at the Stadium last night as Mickey Mantle belted one of the most powerful home run drives of his spectacular career.

First up in the last of the 11th with the score deadlocked at 7–all and a count of two balls and two strikes, the famed Switcher leaned into one of Carl Fisher's fast ones and sent the ball soaring. It crashed against the upper façade of the right-field stand, which towers 108 feet above the playing field.

A little higher and it would have become the first fair ball ever to sail out of the Stadium. Once before, Mantle came that close. That was on May 30, 1956, off Pedro Ramos, then with the Senators.

#### 'The Hardest I Ever Hit'

"It was the hardest ball I ever hit," said Mantle later, "but though I knew it would be well up there I didn't think it would go out of the park."

Routing the A's left-hander, Ted Bowsfield, in the second inning with a seven-run barrage, the Yanks looked to have this one all wrapped up as late as the start of the eighth, by which time Bill Stafford still had a three-hit shutout going.

But here a strange thing happened. In the crowd of 9,727 there appeared to be liberal sprinkling of Polo Grounds' enthusiasts. Finding the show rather boring at this point they set up the chant "Let's go Mets, Let's go Mets."

This had such an electrifying effect on the A's they suddenly reared up, routed Stafford and Marshall Bridges, and they even had Houk calling on Ralph Terry before a six-run splurge could be halted. And in the ninth Ed Charles hit a homer to tie the score.

It then remained for Steven Hamilton, 6-foot-7-inch left-hander, to hold the A's in check until Mantle's mighty smash ended it. It was Mickey's ninth homer.

#### Cimoli Hits a Homer

The league's leading hitter, Wayne Causey, hitless up to here, started the A's on their wild eighth inning with a single. Gino Cimoli hit a homer and two were in. Jerry Lumpe grounded out but Norm Siebern doubled, and when Cletis Boyer fumbled Charles's grounder, Houk removed Stafford and called in Marshall Bridges.

Although the Sheriff retired George Alusik for the second out, he walked Bobby Del Greco, filling the bases. When he served up two more balls to Frank Sullivan, Houk waved in his ace right-hander, Terry. But that didn't save the situation, for Terry walked Bobby and that forced in a third run.

Tony Kubek booted a grounder hit by Dick Howser as a pinch-batter and the fourth tally scored. Causey then hit his second single and two more came in. That made it six and the Yanks were gasping as Cimoli finally flied out, ending the inning.

But the Yanks weren't yet home free. Held scoreless in the last of the eighth by Bill Fischer, they saw Charles belt Terry for a homer and a tied game in the ninth. In the 10th Yogi Berra batted for Terry and delivered a pinch single. But the Yanks couldn't cash in.

The Yanks' big inning got off to an odd start when Roger Maris lifted a high fly down the right-field line. Both Roger and Many Jimenez marked time, waiting to see whether it would drop into the stand fair or foul.

It fell on the field just inside the foul line and Maris put on a full head of steam to make it for a double. Then things really began to pop.

Joe Pepitone, out to prove once again that left-handers no longer hold any terrors for him, slammed a single to right. Tony Kubek and Stafford did likewise and three runs were in. Cletis Boyer forced Stafford at second and a moment later made it to third when the badly rattled Bowsfield unfurled a wild pitch. A triple by Bobby Richardson drove in Boyer with the fourth run and when Tom Tresh walked, Bowsfield bowed out.

He was replaced by Dave Thies, a righthander, who plunged into deeper difficulties. He walked Mickey Mantle, filling the bases, then hit Elston Howard, forcing in a fifth run.

Maris, up for the second time, got another break when the catcher, Haywood Sullivan, dropped his pop foul behind the plate. Maris followed with a sacrifice fly to right that scored Tresh. However, Tresh and Mantle would have scored anyway on Pepitone's second single.

| KANSAS CITY (A.) | ab. | r. | h. | rbi. | NEW YORK (A.) | ab. | r. | h. | rbi. |
|---|---|---|---|---|---|---|---|---|---|
| Causey, ss | 5 | 1 | 2 | 2 | Boyer, 3b | 6 | 1 | 0 | 0 |
| Cimoli, 1f | 6 | 1 | 2 | 2 | Richardson, 2b | 6 | 1 | 2 | 1 |
| Lumpe, 2b | 6 | 0 | 0 | 0 | Tresh, 1f | 4 | 1 | 1 | 0 |
| Siebern, 1b | 4 | 1 | 1 | 0 | Mantle, cf | 3 | 2 | 1 | 1 |
| Charles, 3b | 5 | 2 | 1 | 1 | Howard, c | 3 | 0 | 0 | 1 |
| Jiminez, rf | 3 | 0 | 1 | 0 | Maris, rf | 3 | 1 | 1 | 1 |
| bAlusik, rf | 2 | 0 | 0 | 0 | Pepitone, 1b | 5 | 1 | 3 | 1 |
| Del Greco, cf | 4 | 1 | 0 | 0 | Kubek, ss | 4 | 1 | 1 | 1 |
| Sullivan, c | 3 | 1 | 1 | 1 | Stafford, p | 3 | 0 | 1 | 2 |
| Bowsfield, p | 0 | 0 | 0 | 0 | Bridges, p | 0 | 0 | 0 | 1 |
| Thies, p | 2 | 0 | 0 | 0 | Terry, p | 0 | 0 | 0 | 0 |
| aEssegian | 1 | 0 | 0 | 0 | dBerra | 1 | 0 | 1 | 0 |
| Willis, p | 0 | 0 | 0 | 0 | eLinz | 0 | 0 | 0 | 0 |
| cHowser | 1 | 0 | 0 | 0 | Hamilton, p | 0 | 0 | 0 | 0 |
| Fischer, p | 1 | 0 | 0 | 0 | | | | | |
| Total | 43 | 7 | 8 | 6 | Total | 38 | 8 | 11 | 8 |

aFlied out for Thies in 7th; bFlied out for Jiminez in 8th; cSafe on error for Willis in 8th; dSingled for Terry in 10th; eRan for Berra in 10th.

Kansas City       000   000   061   00–7
New York        070   000   000   01–8

One out when winning run was scored.

E—Sullivan, Boyer, Kubek. A—Kansas City 11, New York 10. LOB—Kansas City 10, New York 11.

2B Hits—Maris, Siebern. 3B—Tresh, Richardson. HRS—Cimoli, Charles, Mantle.

Sacrifice—Howard.

|  | IP. | H. | R. | ER. | BB. | SO. |
|---|---|---|---|---|---|---|
| Bowsfield | 1⅓ | 6 | 6 | 6 | 2 | 1 |
| Thies | 4⅔ | 2 | 1 | 1 | 3 | 2 |
| Willis | 1 | 1 | 0 | 0 | 0 | 0 |
| *Fischer (L, 6–1) | 3 | 2 | 1 | 1 | 2 | 1 |
| Stafford | 7⅓ | 6 | 4 | 2 | 3 | 2 |
| Bridges | ⅓ | 0 | 2 | 0 | 2 | 0 |
| Terry | 2⅓ | 2 | 1 | 1 | 1 | 2 |
| Hamilton (W, 2–11) | 1 | 0 | 0 | 0 | 1 | 1 |

*Faced 1 batter in 11th.

HBP—By Thies (Howard), by Willis (Kubek). Wild Pitch—Bowsfield. Umpires—Dimuro, Carrigan, Flaherty, Hurley. Time—3:13. Attendance—9,727.

---

August 5, 1963

## Mantle's Heroics Prove Cheers For Slugger Are Well Deserved

At 7:31 last night Mickey Mantle returned to action at Yankee Stadium, swung his bat in anger for the first time in 61 games, and received two of the loudest cheers that have reverberated through the cool, green arches of the House That Ruth Built in a long time.

The first came when the powerful Yankee slugger appeared on the field as a pinch-hitter in the seventh inning of the second game of the Yanks' double-header with the Orioles. The second came a moment later when Mantle drove a pitch into the left-field stands for a home run.

The homer, Mantle's 12th, came just two months after his 11th, which was hit against the Orioles in Baltimore on June 4.

The next day Mantle broke a bone in his left foot trying to make a catch in the outfield. He was put on the disabled list on June 7 and returned to active status on July 12. In all, Mantle has played in only 37 of the Yanks' 107 games. His home run raised his batting average 6 points to .316.

The Yanks, who have a record of 27 victories and 25 defeats on the road, will start Whitey Ford and Stan Williams against the Senators in Washington tomorrow night. From Washington, the world champions will move on to Los Angeles, Boston and Chicago.

Despite the prospect of having to go from Los Angeles to Boston and then back to Chicago, Manager Ralph Houk thinks baseball players have life easier these days than they did when they traveled by train.

"There's no doubt about it. Players get more rest now than they did in the old day," Houk says. "People think the schedule is tougher because of the distances involved. With planes it's a question of time, not miles."

Harry Brecheen, the Orioles coach, pitched batting practice before the game. Looking almost as lean and sharp as he did when he was with the St. Louis Cardinals, the left-hander sent a number of hitters out of the cage with thoughtful looks on their faces.

August 5, 1963

### *Yanks Bow, 7–2, Then Beat Orioles, 11–10, on Berra's Sacrifice Fly in 10th*

---

## MANTLE'S HOMER TIES SCORE IN 7TH

---

### Bomber Star Clicks in First Appearance Since June 5—Terry Beaten in Opener

---

### By Will Bradbury

The New York Yankees, in an intriguing reversal of roles, lost with a minimum of effort and then won with a maximum of difficulty yesterday as they divided a double-header with the Baltimore Orioles before 39,432 at Yankee Stadium.

First, the Bombers slipped quietly to a 7–2 defeat at the hands of Steve Barber and Dick Hall in the opener. Then, with a dramatic assist from Mickey Mantle, they kept hope alive for nine innings and rallied for a run in the 10th to win the second game, 11–10.

Mantle, appearing for the first time in 61 games, batted in the seventh inning of the finale with the Yanks a run behind after six unattractive, walk-filled innings of hit-and-miss baseball.

The big slugger, idle since June 5, took a strike. Then he blasted a fast ball into the left-field stand against George Brunet, the fifth of six Oriole pitchers. The homer tied the score at 10–10, and that was the way matters stood until the Yanks batted in the 10th.

#### Kubek Opens Winning Rally

Hal Reniff, who picked up the victory in relief, struck off as leadoff man in the 10th. Tony Kubek followed with a single to right, and Bobby Richardson neatly punched a hit through short as Luis Aparicio moved to cover against Kubek, who was running on the play.

Manager Billy Hitchcook of the Orioles then ordered Tom Tresh intentionally walked, and Manager Ralph Houk of the Yanks sent up Yogi Berra to hit against Stu Miller, a right-hander. Berra hit a fly to right field on a 0-and-2 pitch, and Kubek raced across the plate with the winning run.

The victory, the Yanks' 13th of the 18-game home stand that ended yesterday, kept the league-leading Bombers seven and a half games ahead of the Chicago White Sox. The Orioles, in third place, are nine games behind.

From the first inning on, the second game careened along out of control like a runaway bus. The Orioles, aided by the first of three Yankee errors, picked up two runs in the first inning and then stood around helplessly while the Yanks sent nine men to the plate and scored four runs.

## 2 Innings Last 75 Minutes

The second inning was no improvement as the Orioles added three runs, all unearned, and the Yanks turned four walks, a single to center by Harry Bright and a sacrifice into three more. The first two innings accounted for 1 hour 15 minutes of the 3-hour-44-minute game.

In the fourth, the Orioles tied the score with two runs on three walks and a single and then went ahead with three in the sixth against Bill Stafford and Steve Hamilton. A two-run homer by Brooks Robinson capped the inning, which included a triple, double and bunt single.

Howard's 20th home run, with Tresh on base, cut the Oriole lead to 10–9 in the sixth and set the stage for Mantle's blow.

The defeat of the Yanks—and Ralph Terry—in the first game was uncomplicated and prosaic. Against Barber and Hall, who relieved in the seventh, the world champions struck out seven times, left seven men on base and never really seemed interested.

## Pepitone Belts 19th Homer

A home run by Joe Pepitone, his 19th of the year, gave the Yanks a run in the second and John Powell, the Orioles' left fielder, gave them another in the fifth. Kubek opened the fifth with a single and then Powell, who hits better than he runs, let a sinking liner by Elston Howard bounce under his glove for a triple that scored Kubek.

The Orioles, on the other hand, performed dutifully from beginning to end. They salted their 12 hits with home runs by Barber, Powell and John Orsino, knocked Terry out in the sixth and then provided Tom Metcalf with a grim introduction to life in the major leagues.

The Yanks were trailing, 4–2, when Metcalf, recently brought up from Richmond, entered the game in the eighth. He replaced Hamilton, who replaced Terry.

Russ Snyder, the first major league hitter to face Metcalf, blooped a double to left. After Powell had flied to center, Orsino slammed his home run into the left-field seats. A double by Jerry Adair and two singles gave the Orioles their final run.

Hall, who took over from Barber, saved Metcalf from further indignities.

In the sixth, Powell's homer and a single by Orsino ended Terry's tour on the mound. In the previous inning the slender right-hander had given two runs on a double and two singles. A throwing error by Kubek allowed Luis Aparicio to reach third base after the runs had scored, but Terry struck out Snyder to end the inning.

Hall, who took over for Barber with one out in the seventh, was superb. He retired the last eight men in order to protect the left-hander's 15th victory in 23 decisions. Terry has won 12 games and lost 11.

## Yanks' Score

### FIRST GAME

| BALTIMORE (A.) | ab. | r. | h. | rbi. | NEW YORK (A.) | ab. | r. | h. | rbi. |
|---|---|---|---|---|---|---|---|---|---|
| Aparicio, ss | 5 | 0 | 2 | 2 | Kubek, ss | 3 | 1 | 1 | 0 |
| Snyder, rf | 5 | 1 | 1 | 0 | Rich'son, 2b | 3 | 0 | 0 | 0 |
| Powell, lf | 4 | 1 | 1 | 1 | Tresh, c | 4 | 0 | 1 | 0 |
| Saverine, cf | 0 | 0 | 0 | 0 | Howard, cf | 4 | 0 | 1 | 1 |
| Orsino, c | 4 | 1 | 3 | 2 | Bright, 1f | 4 | 0 | 1 | 0 |
| Gentile, 1b | 4 | 0 | 0 | 0 | Pepitone, 1b | 4 | 1 | 1 | 1 |
| Robinson, 3b | 4 | 0 | 0 | 0 | Lopez, lf | 4 | 0 | 0 | 0 |
| Brandt, cf, 1f | 4 | 1 | 1 | 0 | Boyer, 2b | 3 | 0 | 1 | 0 |
| Adair, 2b | 4 | 2 | 2 | 0 | Terry, p | 2 | 0 | 0 | 0 |
| Barber, p | 3 | 1 | 1 | 1 | Hamilton, p | 0 | 0 | 0 | 0 |
| Hall, p | 1 | 0 | 1 | 1 | ªLinz | 1 | 0 | 0 | 0 |
| | | | | | Metcalf, p | 0 | 0 | 0 | 0 |
| | | | | | ᵇBlanchard | 1 | 0 | 0 | 0 |
| Total | 38 | 7 | 12 | 7 | Total | 33 | 2 | 6 | 2 |

ªGrounded out for Hamilton on 7th; ᵇGrounded out for Metcalf in 9th.

| | | | | | |
|---|---|---|---|---|---|
| Baltimore | 001 | 021 | 021—7 | | |
| New York | 010 | 010 | 000—2 | | |

E—Boyer. A—Baltimore 11, New York 13. DP—Richardson, Kubek, Bright. LOB—Baltimore 4, New York 7.

2-B Hits—Orsino, Bright, Adair 2, Snyder. 3-B—Howard. HR—Pepitone, Barber, Powell, Orsino.

| | IP. | H. | R. | ER. | BB. | SO. |
|---|---|---|---|---|---|---|
| Barber (W, 15-8) | 6⅓ | 6 | 2 | 2 | 2 | 5 |
| Hall | 2⅓ | 0 | 0 | 0 | 0 | 1 |
| *Terry (L, 12-11) | 5 | 7 | 4 | 4 | 0 | 2 |
| Hamilton | 2 | 0 | 0 | 0 | 0 | 0 |
| Metcalf | 2 | 5 | 3 | 3 | 0 | 0 |

*Faced two batters in 6th.
Umpires—Smith, Paparella, Haller, Honochick. Time of game—2:19.

## SECOND GAME

| BALTIMORE (A.) | ab. | r. | h. | rbi. | | NEW YORK (A.) | ab. | r. | h. | rbi. |
|---|---|---|---|---|---|---|---|---|---|---|
| Aparicio, ss | 6 | 1 | 0 | 0 | | Kubek, ss | 5 | 2 | 1 | 0 |
| Snyder, rf | 6 | 3 | 2 | 0 | | Richards'n, 2b | 5 | 2 | 2 | 0 |
| Powell, lf | 3 | 1 | 1 | 2 | | Tresh, c | 4 | 3 | 3 | 0 |
| Saverine, cf | 0 | 0 | 0 | 0 | | Howard, c | 5 | 1 | 1 | 3 |
| Gentile, 1b | 5 | 1 | 3 | 3 | | fBerra | 0 | 0 | 0 | 1 |
| Brandt, cf, 1f | 5 | 1 | 2 | 3 | | Bright, 1b | 1 | 1 | 1 | 2 |
| Robinson, 3b | 5 | 1 | 2 | 2 | | bBlanchard, rf | 3 | 0 | 0 | 0 |
| Adair, 2b | 6 | 0 | 1 | 0 | | Pepitone, rf, 1b | 3 | 1 | 0 | 0 |
| Brown, c | 3 | 1 | 1 | 0 | | Lopez, 1f | 5 | 0 | 1 | 2 |
| dOrsino, c | 0 | 0 | 0 | 0 | | Boyer, 3b | 4 | 0 | 1 | 1 |
| McNally, p | 0 | 0 | 0 | 0 | | Bouton, p | 1 | 0 | 0 | 0 |
| Stock, p | 0 | 0 | 0 | 0 | | Stafford, p | 0 | 0 | 0 | 0 |
| aValentine | 0 | 1 | 0 | 0 | | Hamilton, p | 0 | 0 | 0 | 0 |
| McCormick, p | 0 | 0 | 0 | 0 | | c Mantle | 1 | 1 | 1 | 1 |
| Starrett, p | 1 | 0 | 0 | 0 | | Reniff, p | 1 | 0 | 0 | 0 |
| Brunet, p | 0 | 0 | 0 | 0 | | | | | | |
| eSmith | 1 | 0 | 0 | 0 | | | | | | |
| Miller, p | 0 | 0 | 0 | 0 | | | | | | |
| Total | 41 | 10 | 12 | 10 | | Total | 38 | 11 | 11 | 10 |

aWalked for Stock in 2d; bPopped out for Bright in 4th; cHit homer for Hamilton in 7th; dWalked for Brown in 8th; eStuck out for Brunet in 8th; fHit sacrifice fly for Howard in 10th.

```
Baltimore    230  203  000  0—10
New York     430  002  100  1—11
```

Two out when winning run was scored.

E—Bright 2, Pepitone, Brown. A—Baltimore 11, New York 12. DP—Boyer, Richardson, Pepitone. LOB—Baltimore 12, New York 9.

2B Hits—Gentile, Tresh, Adair. 3B—Brandt, Snyder. HR—Robinson, Howard, Mantle. Sacrifices—Starell, Brandt, Stafford. SF—Berra.

| | IP. | H. | R. | ER. | BB. | SO. |
|---|---|---|---|---|---|---|
| McNally | ⅔ | 3 | 4 | 4 | 2 | 0 |
| Stock | ⅓ | 1 | 0 | 0 | 0 | 1 |
| McCormick | ⅓ | 1 | 3 | 2 | 4 | 1 |
| †Starrett | 3⅔ | 3 | 2 | 2 | 1 | 1 |
| Brunet | 2 | 1 | 1 | 1 | 0 | 1 |
| Miller (L, 4-5) | 2⅓ | 2 | 1 | 1 | 1 | 4 |
| Bouton | 1⅔ | 4 | 5 | 0 | 0 | 2 |
| *Stafford | 3⅓ | 3 | 3 | 3 | 3 | 0 |
| Hamilton | 2 | 3 | 2 | 2 | 1 | 1 |
| Reniff (W, 3-2) | 3 | 2 | 0 | 0 | 3 | 2 |

*Faced 1 batter in 6th, †Faced 2 batters in 6th.

HBP—By Starrett (Stafford). Umpires—Paparella, Haller, Honochick, Smith. Time of game—3:44. Attendance—38,555.

---

## *Yanks Down White Sox, 7–3, on Stottlemyre's 7-Hitter; Pirates Top Mets, 5–4*

### MANTLE WALLOPS 500-FOOT HOMER

### Connects Twice As Yankee Hurler Checks Chicago in Debut in Big Leagues

### By JOSEPH DURSO

The New York Yankees snapped out of it yesterday with four booming home runs that upended the Chicago White Sox, 7-3, and made the major league debut of Mel Stottlemyre a total success.

One of the home runs was a monumental, fourth-inning drive by Mickey Mantle that cleared the black backdrop screen shielding the center-field bleachers and landed over 500 feet from home plate for one of the longest home runs ever hit in Yankee Stadium. Four innings later Mantle switched to the right side of the plate and hit a more prosaic shot that traveled 350 feet into the right-field grandstand. Cletis Boyer reached the left-field stand with the third Yankee homer of the day and Roger Maris bombed the fourth into the right-field mezzanine.

The cannonading was enriched with two doubles and six singles for a total of 12 hits off four Chicago pitchers.

### Rookie Throws 116 Pitches

In the midst of all the power hitting, Stottlemyre threw 116 pitches in his first major league game 24 hours after arriving from the Yankee farm at Richmond.

Seven pitches were hit safely by the White Sox, one for a triple by Pete Ward, one for a double by Ward and five for singles. More significantly, though, 21 Chicago batters hit ground balls—two of which the Yankees turned into errors, but 19 of which they turned into outs.

Stottlemyre, who said later his curve ball was not especially sharp, also walked only one batter, who thereupon scored the first run off him.

This occurred with two out in the third inning as the 22-year-old right-hander opposed Ray Herbert, who was shooting for his fifth straight victory. Mike Hershberger received the base on balls, stole second and scored when Tony Kubek hurriedly threw Don Buford's grounder on one hop past Joe Pepitone.

## Boyer Clouts No. 8

The Yankees promptly got this run back, though, when they unloaded their first home run half an inning later. Boyer hit this one, his eighth of the season, with the bases empty. As a postscript, Stottlemyre then hit the first pitch thrown to him for a single to center, but the real slugging was yet to come.

It came after Ward had tripled to the base of the 457-foot sign in center field, and, after two ground-ball outs, had scored on Ron Hansen's single to left for a 2–1 lead.

Then Mantle led off the fourth inning against Herbert batting left-handed. With a count of three balls and one strike, he powered a tremendously high fly to straightaway center field that Gene Stephens chased to the bleacher wall. It cleared the wall and the black screen on top of it and dropped 15 rows behind the 461-foot sign for Mantle's 24th home run and the 443d of his 14-year career.

When Bobby Richardson singled to left in the sixth, Don Mossi replaced Herbert. Maris at once further exploded the theory that he can't hit left-handers by exploding his 18th home run of the season into the second deck.

Mantle, batting right-handed, then lined a single to left, slid into third on Joe Pepitone's single to center and slid across the plate after Buford had chased, clutched, then dropped John Blanchard's fly into short center.

## Stormy Inning for Mossi

That finished Mossi after one-third of a stormy inning and brought Eddie Fisher to the mound for the most successful moment the Chicago pitching staff managed—two batters, two strike-outs.

However, in the eighth, after the White Sox had narrowed the score to 5–3, Frank Baumann was pitching and Mantle was hitting.

Leading off, as he had in the fourth, Mickey again hit an authoritative home run. This one was struck right-handed to the opposite field and landed in the lower stand in right for No. 25 of the year. Tom Tresh doubled, went to third after a long fly and scored after Blanchard's fly to right, and Stottlemyre was on top, 7–3.

| CHICAGO (A.) | ab. | r. | h. | rbi. | NEW YORK (A.) | ab. | r. | h. | rbi. |
|---|---|---|---|---|---|---|---|---|---|
| Herschbrgr, rf | 4 | 1 | 0 | 0 | Kubek, ss | 4 | 0 | 0 | 0 |
| Buford, 2b | 4 | 0 | 0 | 0 | Richardson, 2b | 4 | 1 | 3 | 0 |
| Robinson, 1f | 4 | 0 | 1 | 0 | Maris, rf | 4 | 1 | 1 | 2 |
| Ward, 3b | 4 | 2 | 2 | 0 | Mantle, cf | 4 | 3 | 3 | 2 |
| Skowron, 1b | 4 | 0 | 1 | 1 | Lopez, 1f | 0 | 0 | 0 | 0 |
| Stephens, cf | 4 | 0 | 0 | 0 | Tresh, 1f, cf | 4 | 1 | 2 | 0 |
| Hansen, ss | 4 | 0 | 1 | 1 | Pepitone, 1b | 4 | 0 | 1 | 0 |
| Martin, c | 4 | 0 | 1 | 0 | Blanchard, c | 3 | 0 | 0 | 1 |
| Herbert, p | 2 | 0 | 0 | 0 | Boyer, 3b | 4 | 1 | 1 | 1 |
| Peters, ph | 1 | 0 | 0 | 0 | Stottlemyre, p | 3 | 0 | 1 | 0 |
| Weis, ph | 1 | 0 | 1 | 0 | | | | | |
| Total | 36 | 3 | 7 | 2 | Total | 34 | 7 | 12 | 6 |

| | | | | | | |
|---|---|---|---|---|---|---|
| Chicago | 001 | 100 | 010—3 | | | |
| New York | 001 | 103 | 02..—7 | | | |

E—Buford, Kubek 2. DP—Chicago 2. LOB—Chicago 7, New York 4. 2B—Ward, Richardson, Tresh. 3B—Ward. HR—Boyer (8), Mantle (24, 25), Maris (18). SB—Hershberger. SF—Blanchard.

| | IP. | H. | R. | ER. | BB. | SO. |
|---|---|---|---|---|---|---|
| Herbert (L, 5—4) | *5 | 6 | 3 | 3 | 0 | 0 |
| Mossi | ⅓ | 3 | 2 | 1 | 0 | 0 |
| Fisher | ⅔ | 0 | 0 | 0 | 0 | 2 |
| Baumann | 2 | 3 | 2 | 2 | 0 | 0 |
| Stottlemyre | 9 | 7 | 2 | 1 | 1 | 1 |
| (W, 1—0) | | | | | | |

*Faced 1 batter in 6th. T—2:09. A—16,945.

August 13, 1964

## Mantle Measures Up to History

*Long Homer Adds to His Records at Yankee Stadium*

## 2 of His Clouts in Past Came Close to Leaving Park

Only two home runs have been hit into the bleachers in dead center field since Yankee Stadium was built in 1923—one by Mickey Mantle on June 21, 1955, and an even longer one by Mantle in the fourth inning yesterday.

The one nine years ago, struck off Alex Kellner of the Kansas City Athletics, landed nine rows back and 486 feet from home plate.

The one yesterday, hit off Ray Herbert of the Chicago White Sox, cleared the bleacher screen and a black "visibility" screen 22 feet 5 inches tall, and landed in the 15th row behind the 461-foot sign on the center-field wall.

It was the 24th home run of the season for Mantle and the 443d—but not the farthest or hardest—of his 14-year career. In fact, Mantle said in the clubhouse after the game, "I thought it was going to be caught."

After the ball had sailed into the bleachers, the Yankees' public-address announcer told the crowd of 16,945 with controlled wonder in his tone that "efforts are being made to compute the distance."

An hour later the distance was computed at "just over 500 feet," making it the longest home run actually tracked in the stadium, though probably not the longest ever hit there. The longest are to be two that Mantle nearly hit out of the stadium, one on May 30, 1956, off Pedro Ramos of Washington and one on 21, 1963, off Billy Fisher of Kansas City.

Both balls hit the façade of the third deck in right field, 106 feet above the ground. The one off Fisher was still rising when it struck and was, Mantle said, "the hardest ball I ever hit."

Neither, though, actually left the stadium. That has never been achieved by any hitter. As for the other sections of the bleachers in Yankee Stadium, 16 hitters have driven home runs into those in left field while many have reached those in right field, including Mantle three times in one game on May 13, 1955.

The longest home run in history was a 600-footer that Babe Ruth belted in Detroit in 1926, while Mantle's record is 565 feet at Griffith Stadium, Washington.

Yesterday's homer, hit left-handed, was followed by one in the eighth inning right-handed. It was the 10th time in his career that Mantle has hit home runs from both sides of the plate in one game.

He also had hit one in the ninth inning Tuesday night, giving him three homers in his last five times at bat and six hits in 11 times up since going hitless on 17 previous trips. Mantle, who will be 33 years old in October, listened attentively to a description of his home run after yesterday's game and then commented with a grin:

"I wouldn't care if it hit the back of the screen—coming down."

September 2, 1963

### *Mets Top Braves, 6–4, on Harkness's Homer in 16th; Yanks Down Orioles, 5–4*

---

## 2 HOMERS IN 8TH WIN FOR BOMBERS

---

### Mantle, as a Pinch-Hitter, and Tresh Connect With One Man on Base

---

### By JOHN DREBINGER

*Special to The New York Times*

BALTIMORE, Sept. 1—The Yankees, so coldly efficient, some complain, that they take all the thrill out of baseball, can still pour on the dramatics when the occasion calls for it. They certainly poured it on today as a pair of two-run homer in the eighth inning enabled them to beat the Orioles, 5–4, for a sweep of the three-game series.

Mickey Mantle, in the role of pinch-hitter, smacked the first of these on the first pitch that left-handed Mike McCormick served him, and Tom Tresh hit the second. Tresh, who had hit a base-empty homer in the seventh, connected off Dick Hall, a right-hander who had just relieved McCormick. That was the blow that flattened Billy Hitchcock, his Orioles and their sympathizers in the crowd of 24,073.

For the Yanks, however, there was one regrettable note. Ralph Terry, seeking his 16th victory and a place in the 20-game winner derby, yielded three runs in the third inning and failed to last the fifth.

It now looks as if Whitey Ford, who goes for No. 20 in Detroit tomorrow, and Jim Bouton, who bagged No. 19 last night, will be the only Yanks to make it.

## Orsino Clouts Homer

McCormick started the rush on Terry in the third with a single. A double by Russ Snyder and an infield out followed for the first run. Then John Orsino drove in two more with his 15th homer and second in two games.

The Birds added a run in the seventh. Jim Gentile drove it in with a single off the rookie, Tom Metcalf.

In the same inning, the Yanks registered their first score as Tresh, batting right-handed against McCormick, hit homer No. 1 into the left-field bull pen.

A single by Cletis Boyer lighted the Yanks' fuse in the eighth. As Mantle walked out to hit for Metcalf amid some lusty cheers, Hitchcock strode to the mound to advise McCormick.

Whatever the advice was, it met with Mantle's consent. Mickey, batting right-handed, lifted the first pitch over the left-field barrier. It was his 13th homer of the year and second since he began his role of an occasional pinch-hitter against the Orioles on Aug. 4.

With two out, Bobby Richardson singled and that inspired Hitchcock to make another master move. He called in Hall, and Tresh, batting left-handed, smacked his 23d homer of the year into the right-field bleachers.

It was the first time as a Yankee that Tresh had hit homers from both sides of the plate in one game. He also became the ninth major-league player ever to do so.

That shot put the Yanks in front, and there they remained as Hal Reniff, who bailed out Bouton in the ninth last night, nailed down this one by snuffing out six Orioles in the last two innings.

As Metcalf was the pitcher of record when the Yanks shot ahead, the young right-hander received credit for the victory, his first as a Yankee.

## Maris Sits One Out

Roger Maris, who returned to the line-up Saturday night for the first time since Aug. 14, was on the bench again. It was only because Ralph Houk is not of a kind to rush things. With a left-handed starting, the Major decided it probably would be better if Roger sat out another day.

| NEW YORK (A.) | ab. | r. | h. | rbi. | | BALTIMORE (A.) | ab. | r. | h. | rbi. |
|---|---|---|---|---|---|---|---|---|---|---|
| Kubek, ss | 4 | 0 | 1 | 0 | | Aparicio, ss | 5 | 2 | 2 | 0 |
| Rich'son, 2b | 4 | 1 | 2 | 0 | | Snyder, cf, rf | 5 | 1 | 1 | 0 |
| Tresh, cf | 3 | 2 | 3 | 3 | | Powell, lf | 4 | 0 | 2 | 1 |
| Howard, c | 4 | 0 | 1 | 0 | | Orsino, c | 3 | 1 | 1 | 2 |
| Pepitone, 1b | 4 | 0 | 1 | 0 | | Gentile, 1b | 4 | 0 | 1 | 1 |
| Lopez, lf | 4 | 0 | 0 | 0 | | Smith, rf | 4 | 0 | 0 | 0 |
| Linz, rf | 3 | 0 | 0 | 0 | | Saverine, cf | 0 | 0 | 0 | 0 |
| Reed, rf | 1 | 0 | 1 | 0 | | Robinson, 3b | 4 | 0 | 0 | 0 |
| Boyer, 3b | 4 | 1 | 1 | 0 | | Johnson, 2b | 4 | 0 | 1 | 0 |
| Terry, p | 1 | 0 | 0 | 0 | | McCormick, p | 3 | 0 | 1 | 0 |
| Hamilton, p | 0 | 0 | 0 | 0 | | Hall, p | 0 | 0 | 0 | 0 |
| ᵃBright | 1 | 0 | 0 | 0 | | ᶜValentine | 1 | 0 | 0 | 0 |
| Metcalf, p | 0 | 0 | 0 | 0 | | Miller, p | 0 | 0 | 0 | 0 |
| ᵇMantle | 1 | 1 | 1 | 2 | | | | | | |
| Reniff, p | 1 | 0 | 0 | 0 | | | | | | |
| Total | 35 | 5 | 11 | 5 | | Total | 37 | 4 | 9 | 4 |

ᵃFlied out for Hamilton in 6th; ᵇHit homer for Metcalf in 8th; ᶜStruck out for Hall in 8th.

| | | | |
|---|---|---|---|
| New York | 000 | 000 | 140—5 |
| Baltimore | 003 | 000 | 100—4 |

E—Lopez.—A—New York 11, Baltimore 11. DP—Robinson, Johnson, Gentile; Aparicio, Gentile. LOB—New York 4, Baltimore 8.

2B Hits—Snyder, Reed. HR—Orsino, Tresh 2, Mantle. SB—Aparicio, Reed.

| | IP. | H. | R. | ER. | BB. | SO. |
|---|---|---|---|---|---|---|
| Terry | 4⅔ | 6 | 3 | 3 | 0 | 1 |
| Hamilton | ⅓ | 0 | 0 | 0 | 0 | 1 |
| Metcalf (W, 1–0) | 2 | 3 | 1 | 1 | 1 | 1 |
| Reniff | 2 | 0 | 0 | 0 | 0 | 3 |
| McCormick | 7⅔ | 8 | 4 | 4 | 1 | 3 |
| Hall (L, 5–5) | ⅓ | 2 | 1 | 1 | 1 | 0 |
| Miller | 1 | 1 | 0 | 0 | 0 | 2 |

HBP—By Terry (Orsino). Balk—Metcalf. Umpires—Kinnamon, Soar, Paparella, Stewart. Time—2:27. Attendance—24,073.

The Clincher: Mickey Mantle connects in the bottom of the ninth inning of the third World Series game, 1964. (UNITED PRESS INTERNATIONAL)

October 11, 1964

## *YANKS BEAT CARDS, 2–1, ON MANTLE'S HOMER IN NINTH; OLYMPIC GAMES START; PENN STATE DEFEATS ARMY, 6–2*

### 3d-Tier Drive Off Schultz Provides 2–1 Series Lead

### By Leonard Koppett

Mickey Mantle's 16th World Series home run broke a tie, a record and Barney Schultz's heart at Yankee Stadium yesterday. Coming on the first pitch of the last half of the ninth inning, Mantle's drive into the third deck in right field gave the New York Yankees a 2–1 victory over the St. Louis Cardinals and a 2–1 lead in the four-of-seven-game series. The record Mantle broke was one of the most distinguished in baseball's volumes of statistics.

Babe Ruth had hit 15 home runs in 41 games in 10 series. Last October Mantle caught up, with a home run off Sandy Koufax in the fourth game. Yesterday Mantle moved ahead in his 61st World Series game.

Only one other player has hit as many as 12 homers in Series competition—Lawrence P. (Yogi) Berra, yesterday's winning manager.

This dramatic ending to a sparkling game, which had a crowd of 67,101 in a state of steadily mounting excitement, snatched attention away from the pitching duel that preceded it.

## Many Narrow Escapes

Jim Bouton, the 25-year-old Yankee right-hander, and Curt Simmons, the 35-year-old Cardinal left-hander, engaged in it. Simmons was tougher, but Bouton was more exciting as he escaped from one threatening situation after another.

But Simmons had to be removed for a pinch-hitter in the ninth because the Cards had a chance to score and, as the visiting team, could not risk passing it up. Bouton stopped them again, however, and Schultz, the 38-year-old knuckleball specialist who had done so much to pitch the Cards to the National League pennant, took over.

His first pitch, in his own words, "had to be a knuckleball." It was, but not a good one. According to Mantle, "It didn't quite knuckle."

At any rate, Mantle took one big swing from the left side of the plate—the side from which he doesn't hit so well because of the pressure on his weakened legs. The sound that resulted was more of a "click" than a "crack," but once the ball was airborne, it was clearly a home run. It landed in the third-tier boxes, about 40 feet in front of the foul line, about 60 feet above the ground, about 360 feet from home plate.


## Company on Bases

As Mantle trotted around the bases, a stream of young fans raced across the outfield from the left-field bleachers. As Mantle rounded third, Coach Frank Crosetti joined him and they crossed home plate almost in step. Mick's enthusiastic welcome by teammates was a departure from traditional Yankee calm.

As for Schultz, he strode off the field and into the clubhouse, where he sat alone in front of his locker. He was so dejected that neither teammates nor interviewers would approach him at first. After 20 years of professional pitching, almost all of it in the minors and usually with little reward, Schultz had joined the Cardinals in August and had allowed only one home run in 30 National League appearances.

Wednesday, he pitched the last three innings of the Cardinal victory in the opening game and sat atop the baseball world. Thursday, he relieved with the Cardinals already behind and was tagged for a home run by Phil Linz.

Yesterday, he sat alone in front of his locker—which happened to be adjacent to Simmons's.

Simmons, who has been a major leaguer for 18 years and knew only a couple of months of minor league life, had never before been given the opportunity to pitch in the World Series.

When the chance finally came, he produced the most thoroughly professional job imaginable. He threw his curves and assorted slow pitches to the spots he wanted. He drove in the only run his team scored. He bunted perfectly when a sacrifice was needed. And he fielded his position with total competence, covering first base twice and handling a tricky ball hit back at him.

In eight innings, Simmons allowed only four hits. He struck out two and one of the three walks he issued was intentional.

He did not reap the reward of victory, however, because the Cardinal batters could never break through Bouton under their own power. The run that scored was unearned, since an error by Mantle moved it into scoring position.

Bouton gave six hits in nine innings, struck out two and walked three, one intentionally. But two Yankee errors complicated his task and he had to leave nine St. Louis base-runners stranded to avoid defeat. Four times he got the third out with men in scoring position.

The Yankees scored first. With one out in the second inning, Elston Howard bounced a single to center. After Tom Tresh had fouled out, Simmons tried to pitch to Joe Pepitone tight, sending him sprawling with the first pitch. Then he couldn't find the plate and walked Pepitone on four pitches.

Clete Boyer was the next batter—a .218 hitter, but not against soft-stuff left-handers. Boyer lined a double into left corner, and the Yankees led, 1–0.

Bouton had no real trouble until the fifth, when he lost the lead. Tim McCarver led off with a single to right and wound up at second when Mantle let the ball go through. A liner to Mantle retired Mike Shannon, and Dal Maxvill's grounder to Bobby Richardson moved McCarver to third.

Simmons, who is a capable hitter for a pitcher, promptly lined a hit off Boyer's glove. Playing shallow, Boyer made a remarkable dive to his right to touch the ball, but he couldn't keep it from trickling behind him and McCarver came in with the tying run. In the next inning, both Bouton and Simmons pitched out of bases-filled situations that arose in nearly identical fashion, while the tension increased.

In the Cardinal half, Bill White beat out a high bouncer to Boyer with one out; Ken Boyer, a home run threat, flied out; Dick Groat doubled to left, with Tresh making a good play to keep White from going beyond third, and McCarver was purposely passed. Bouton then made Shannon hit to Linz for a force-out at second.

In the Yankee half, Richardson singled to center with one out; Roger Maris, the home run threat, flied out; Mantle lined a double against a defense that was shifted left, and Howard was purposely passed. Then Tresh, lunging at a high curve, popped the first pitch to White.

No other Yankee reached base against Simmons, but Bouton had plenty of trouble ahead. Maxvill opened the seventh with a double to right center and Simmons sacrificed—but Bouton made Curt Flood pop to Maris in short center (too short for a scoring attempt) and got Lou Brook on a bouncer to Boyer.

The ninth began with McCarver skimming a grounder right at Linz—and Linz let it go right through for an error. Shannon immediately sacrificed, and Carl Warwick, who had hit safely as a pinch-hitter in each of the first two games, batted for Maxvill.

Standard strategy called for an intentional pass, since the next scheduled hitter was Simmons. If Warwick drove in the run, the Cards would be ahead and Simmons would stay in to pitch, but if Simmons had to bat with the score still tied, a pinch-hitter would have to be used for him. Walking Warwick, therefore, would either force Simmons out of the game or give the Yankees a chance for a double play if Simmons did bat.

Warwick walked—but not intentionally. Bouton tried to get him to swing at a bad pitch, and when the count was 3–0, threw a strike. But finally Warwick walked; and Simmons was out.

Bob Skinner, a left-handed batter, was the pinch-hitter. He sent a 400-foot fly to right center that Maris was able to catch, and McCarver moved to third. But Flood, after he had chopped a foul that would have been a hit had it stayed fair, flied to Mantle in right and Bouton was safe again.

Bouton had thrown 123 pitches, Simmons 111.

Schultz threw one.

## BOX SCORE OF THIRD SERIES GAME

| ST. LOUIS (N.) | AB. | R. | H. | RBI. | PO. | A. | NEW YORK (A.) | AB. | R. | H. | RBI. | PO. | A. |
|---|---|---|---|---|---|---|---|---|---|---|---|---|---|
| Flood, cf | 5 | 0 | 0 | 0 | 1 | 0 | Linz, ss | 4 | 0 | 0 | 0 | 0 | 3 |
| Brock, lf | 4 | 0 | 0 | 0 | 2 | 0 | B. Rich'dson, 2b | 4 | 0 | 1 | 0 | 4 | 3 |
| White, 1b | 4 | 0 | 1 | 0 | 12 | 2 | Maris, cf | 4 | 0 | 0 | 0 | 4 | 0 |
| K. Boyer, 3b | 4 | 0 | 0 | 0 | 1 | 3 | Mantle, rf | 3 | 1 | 2 | 1 | 3 | 0 |
| Groat, ss | 4 | 0 | 1 | 0 | 1 | 4 | Howard, c | 2 | 1 | 1 | 0 | 2 | 0 |
| McCarver, c | 2 | 1 | 1 | 0 | 3 | 0 | Tresh, lf | 3 | 0 | 0 | 0 | 4 | 0 |
| Shannon, rf | 3 | 0 | 1 | 0 | 1 | 0 | Pepitone, 1b | 2 | 0 | 0 | 0 | 8 | 0 |
| Maxvill, 2b | 3 | 0 | 1 | 0 | 1 | 2 | C. Boyer, 3b | 3 | 0 | 1 | 1 | 1 | 3 |
| ªWarwick | 0 | 0 | 0 | 0 | 0 | 0 | Bouton, p | 3 | 0 | 0 | 0 | 1 | 0 |
| Buchek, 2b | 0 | 0 | 0 | 0 | 0 | 0 | | | | | | | |
| Simmons, p | 2 | 0 | 1 | 1 | 2 | 0 | | | | | | | |
| ᵇSkinner | 1 | 0 | 0 | 0 | 0 | 0 | | | | | | | |
| Schultz, p | 0 | 0 | 0 | 0 | 0 | 0 | | | | | | | |
| Total | 32 | 1 | 6 | 1 | *24 | 11 | Total | 28 | 2 | 5 | 2 | 27 | 9 |

*None out when winning run was scored. ªWalked for Maxvill in 9th. ᵇFlied out for Simmons in 9th.

St. Louis Cardinals    000 010 000—1
New York Yankees    010 000 001—2

Errors—Mantle, Linz. Double play—Maxvill, Groat and White. Left on bases—St. Louis 9, New York 5.

Two-base hits—C. Boyer, Groat, Mantle, Maxvill. Home run—Mantle. Sacrifice—Simmons, Shannon.

| | IP. | H. | R. | ER. | SS. | SO. | HBP. | WP. | Balks |
|---|---|---|---|---|---|---|---|---|---|
| Simmons | 8 | 4 | 1 | 1 | 3 | 2 | 0 | 0 | 0 |
| *Schultz (L) | 0 | 1 | 1 | 1 | 0 | 0 | 0 | 0 | 0 |
| Bouton (W) | 9 | 6 | 1 | 0 | 3 | 2 | 0 | 0 | 0 |

*Faced one batter in 9th.

Bases on balls—Off Simmons 3 (Pepitone, Mantle, Howard), Bouton 3 (McCarver 2, Warwick). Struck out—By Simmons 2 (C. Boyer, Maris), Bouton 2 (Groat, Simmons). Umpires—Burkhart (N.), plate; Soar (A.), first base; V. Smith (N.), second base; A. Smith (A.), third base; Secory (N.), left field; McKinley (A.), right field. Time of game—2:16. Attendance—67,101.

Spring training 1967: Mickey Mantle and Joe DiMaggio, at Yankee camp, share their feelings on infield duty. (THE NEW YORK TIMES)

May 14, 1967

## Mantle a Superstar to Teammates

*Humor and Modesty Are a Few Traits of Yankee Ace*

*But He Is Reticent and Impatient Off Field*

### By LEONARD KOPPETT

As the spotlight continues to blaze unrelentingly on Mickey Mantle, for the 17th year of his 35-year-old life, one facet of his nature remains generally unappreciated by the public.

Among the superstars of his era—Joe DiMaggio, Ted Williams, Stan Musial, Willie Mays, Sandy Koufax, Warren Spahn and Bob Feller—Mickey has been the least distant from his teammates, the most enjoyed by them, and in this sense, the most humble. To single Mantle out in this way is not to disparage the others, nor to minimize the respect other players felt for them. DiMaggio, by his nature, was silent and aloof; Williams was moody, extremely charming at times, difficult at others; Feller and Spahn, and to a degree Koufax, were self-absorbed men, properly open and giving to their teammates but also somewhat reserved; Musial, the most genial of men, also had his quiet side and in his later years was more a benign presence in the clubhouse than "one of the boys."

Even Mays, everybody's pet and the butt of everyone's jokes as a youngster, became more self contained as he matured, always friendly and eventually a leader, in his own way an elder statesman.

But with Mickey, even at this stage of his eminence, a sort of boyish, unassuming warmth pervades his relations with other players, on his own and other teams.

Three of the elements in Mantle's manner are humor, a sincere and obvious desire that others do well, and a modesty that borders on an inferiority complex.

No one enjoys sharing a joke more than Mantle, and whatever funny stories are currently circulating, Mickey can always be found in the center, telling or hearing them. More striking, however, is his own sharp sense of spontaneous humor, the laugh-provoking remark or insight that brightens up a club, bench or trip.

Through all his humor, which is "country" rather than "slick," there runs a self-deprecating element that underlines his common humanity. Nine years ago, when the Yankees had fallen behind in the World Series three games to one, to the Milwaukee Braves, it was Mantle who showed up in the clubhouse with a trick arrow, one of those that can be strapped to the head so that it appears to go in one ear and out the other.

"We're in tough shape, boys," Mantle announced, making one of his cross-eyed, tongue-sticking-out faces, and a lot of tension suddenly vanished. That's not the reason the Yankees won the next three games in the series, but it didn't hurt.

Only last week, Mantle walked around with his first baseman's mitt strapped to his shoulder.

"I'm strictly leather, now," he declared, "a glove man. The way I'm hitting, I can't afford to lose that glove."

This was a man trying for his 500th home run, supposedly overcome with tension. Most of the superstars play down their achievements when going good, but few kid themselves so pointedly when going bad.

And then Mantle turned to Bill Robinson, the highly touted rookie, who is hitting .119.

"You better do that to your glove, too, the way you're going," Mantle advised with a grin. In context, it wasn't a needle, but an inclusion: The message was, we're all human—and fallible—together, and let's get some fun out of it.

So, when a new young man comes to the Yankees, it is Mantle who goes out of his way to make the first contact easy. Most people (not only players) who meet him are awestruck by his identity; with a 19-year-old teammate, Mantle is likely to introduce himself first, and then talk baseball or tell a joke with an air of instant equality.

On the bench, during a game, few players cheer and urge a team on more wholeheartedly than Mickey. When a player hits a home run or some other important hit, Mickey is one of the first hand-pumpers.

More quietly, in the day to day life of the team, the degree to which Mantle is pulling for everybody, offering little advice if asked, really sympathizing with trouble, can't be missed.

His leadership qualities, therefore, are much more than mere example. That he has played as well as he has, crippled as he has been, is something other players never cease marveling at. But to his own teammates, he is also, at times, a direct inspiration, or a goad, or a comfort.

All this rarely shows outside the privacy of club life. To interviewers, Mantle is usually reticent; perhaps polite, perhaps not, but almost always distant and impatient. To the autograph-hounding public, Mantle tries to act responsibly but could never be called friendly. In more formal public appearances he is surprisingly warm, but within himself uncomfortable.

But among ballplayers—he's with his own. He's one of them, completely, heart and soul, and totally indifferent to rank—theirs or his.

So if anyone thinks Mantle never succeeded in fully projecting the Idol image, the reason is simple: He's too human.

All this rarely shows outside the privacy of club life. To interviewers, Mantle is usually reticent; perhaps polite, perhaps not, but almost always distant and impatient. To the autograph-hounding public, Mantle tries to act responsibly but could never be called friendly. In more formal public appearances he is surprisingly warm, but within himself uncomfortable.

But among ballplayers—he's with his own. He's one of them, completely, heart and soul, and totally indifferent to rank—theirs or his.

So if anyone thinks Mantle never succeeded in fully projecting the Idol image the reason is simple: He's too human.

May 15, 1967

## *Mantle's 500th Homer Beats Orioles, 6–5; Mets Top Gibson of Cards 3–1*

### YANKEE CONNECTS OFF MILLER IN 7TH

### Mantle, Nervous After Feat and Fans' Ovation, Makes Error in Next Inning

### By LEONARD KOPPETT

Mickey Mantle's 500th home run finally arrived yesterday, in style. He hit it off Stu Miller of the Baltimore Orioles with two out in the seventh inning at Yankee Stadium, and it proved to be the winning run in the New York Yankees' 6–5 victory.

The crowd of 18,872 gave Mantle a standing ovation, which continued through Elston Howard's turn at bat and on into the interval between innings. Mantle's blow, with no one on base, made the score 6–4 and seemed important only ceremonially at that time, because a two-run, pinch-hit homer by Joe Pepitone had given the Yankees the lead in the sixth.

But the crowd's response, and the feat itself—only five other men have hit that many major league home runs—made Mantle so nervous that he almost threw the game away in the next half inning.

"It got to me," he said with a smile afterward. He was more grateful that the game had ended in a victory than that the milestone had been passed. "If we'd lost—and I'd have had to face all those reporters—I don't know if I could have done it."

### Womack Stops Orioles

Only one ruin resulted from Mantle's error, however, and Dooley Womack, who had relieved in the sixth, went on to retire the last four Orioles in order. Womack and Pepitone, therefore, made it possible for Mantle to enjoy the home run he had been anticipating since last year.

It was the first home run he had ever hit off Miller, an experienced pitcher who specializes in slow-speed delivery. It came on a 3-2 pitch and landed deep in the lower right-field stands, where it was caught by Louis DeFillippo, and 18-year-old high-school student from Mount Vernon, N.Y.

DeFillippo presented the ball to Mantle outside the door of the Yankee clubhouse, and received a season pass and some Mantle souvenirs in return. He identified himself as a Yankee fan "all the way" and an amateur center fielder who switched to first base "after Mantle did."

Only Babe Ruth (who hit 714), Willie Mays, Jimmie Foxx, Ted Williams, Mel Ott and Mantle are in the 500 Club, although Eddie Mathews and Hank Aaron will probably join before long.

Even before Mickey's home run, it was an exciting game. Steve Barber, the Baltimore starter, didn't survive the first inning. A walk, single and error filled the bases. Tom Tresh was hit by a pitch, forcing in a run, and Steve Whitaker singled for two more. That gave the Yankees a 3–0 lead, for the second straight game, and again it didn't last. Mel Stottlemyre pitched one-hit ball for five innings, but never got straightened out after Mark Belanger clipped the left-field foul pole for a home run with one out in the sixth.

### Blefary Draws Walk

With two out, Stottlemyre walked Curt Blefary, and Frank Robinson got an infield hit. A 450-foot ground-rule double to dead center by Boog Powell made it 3–2, and after an intentional pass to Brooks Robinson, Charlie Lau poked a ground-rule double to left to put Baltimore ahead, 4–3.

Womack took over from there, and an error by Powell gave the Yankees a base-runner with two out in the sixth. Pepitone, resting a sprained thumb, batted for Bill Robinson and hit his first home run of the season.

In the eighth, the Orioles had men on first and second with one out when Brooks Robinson bounced to short for what would have been a double play—but Mantle dropped the throw at first, losing the third out, and then threw the ball beyond home plate, letting a run score. But Paul Blair flied to right and the festivities were safe.

### MANTLE'S HOMER RECORD

| Year | Home Runs | Year | Home Runs |
|------|-----------|------|-----------|
| 1951 | 13 | 1960 | 40 |
| 1952 | 23 | 1961 | 54 |
| 1953 | 21 | 1962 | 30 |
| 1954 | 27 | 1963 | 15 |
| 1955 | 37 | 1964 | 35 |
| 1956 | 52 | 1965 | 19 |
| 1957 | 34 | 1966 | 23 |
| 1958 | 42 | 1967 | 4 |
| 1959 | 31 | 17 years | 500 home runs |

|  | ab. | r. | h. | rbi. |  | ab. | r. | h. | rbi. |
|---|---|---|---|---|---|---|---|---|---|
| Belanger, ss | 5 | 1 | 1 | 1 | Clarke, 2b | 3 | 1 | 0 | 0 |
| Snyder, cf, | 4 | 0 | 0 | 0 | Howser, 3b | 4 | 1 | 1 | 0 |
| Blefary, 1f | 3 | 1 | 0 | 0 | Mantle, 1b | 4 | 2 | 2 | 1 |
| F. Robinson, rf | 4 | 2 | 2 | 0 | Howard, c | 4 | 0 | 0 | 0 |
| Powell, 1b | 4 | 1 | 2 | 1 | Tresh, 1f | 3 | 1 | 0 | 1 |
| B. Robinson, 3b | 2 | 0 | 0 | 0 | Whitaker, rf | 3 | 0 | 1 | 2 |
| Held, 2b | 2 | 0 | 0 | 0 | W. Robinson, cf | 2 | 0 | 0 | 0 |
| Lau, ph | 1 | 0 | 1 | 2 | Pepitone, cf | 2 | 1 | 2 | 2 |
| Miller, p | 0 | 0 | 0 | 0 | Amaro, ss | 4 | 0 | 2 | 0 |
| Blair, ph | 1 | 0 | 0 | 0 | Stottlemyre, p | 2 | 0 | 0 | 0 |
| Elchebarren, c | 4 | 0 | 0 | 0 | Womack, p | 2 | 0 | 0 | 0 |
| Barber, p | 0 | 0 | 0 | 0 |  |  |  |  |  |
| Bunker, p | 1 | 0 | 0 | 0 |  |  |  |  |  |
| Bowens, ph | 1 | 0 | 0 | 0 |  |  |  |  |  |
| Johnson, 2b | 2 | 0 | 0 | 0 |  |  |  |  |  |
| Total | 34 | 5 | 6 | 4 | Total | 33 | 6 | 8 | 6 |

```
Baltimore       000  004  010—5
New York        300  002  10x—6
```

E—B. Robinson, Belanger, Powell, Amaro, Mantle. DB—Baltimore 2. LOB—Baltimore 5, New York 6. 2B—Powell, Lau. HR—Belanger (1), Pepitone (1), Mantle (4).

|  | IP. | H. | R. | ER. | BB. | SO. |
|---|---|---|---|---|---|---|
| Barber | $\frac{1}{3}$ | 2 | 3 | 2 | 1 | 1 |
| Bunker | $4\frac{2}{3}$ | 2 | 0 | 0 | 0 | 2 |
| Miller (L, 0-4) |  | 4 | 3 | 1 | 1 | 2 |
| Stottlemyre | $5\frac{1}{3}$ | 5 | 4 | 4 | 3 | 6 |
| Womack (W, 3-2) | $3\frac{1}{3}$ | 1 | 1 | 0 | 0 | 2 |

HBP—By Barber (Tresh).

T—2:38. A—18,872.

## No. 500 'Felt Like When You Win a World Series'

"It felt," said Mickey Mantle, "like when you win a World Series—a big load off your back. I wasn't really tense about hitting it, but about everybody writing about it. We weren't doing well and everywhere you'd see 'when is Mantle going to hit 500' instead of about the team winning or losing. Now maybe we can get back to getting straightened out."

That was Mantle explaining his feelings, on television, to Phil Rizutto, once a teammate, now a broadcaster. Phil was making a point of the eagerness everyone felt when Mantle's 500th home run became possible on the next swing, and tried to say that Mantle's quest was making the rest of the team "tight."

Manager Ralph Houk, for one, disagreed with this interpretation of his team's trouble. "Shucks, it's not like it was last week of the season or something," Houk said. "I mean, you knew he was going to hit it, sooner or later. I don't think anybody worried about it too much."

• • •

But there was no denying that the 500th homer had been monopolizing conversation around the Yankees, and now that was over. Mantle spent three-quarters of an hour answering questions after the game, and the other players talked with proper awe of what such a total implies about a career. But then everyone seemed willing to let the subject rest.

Whitey Ford, Mantle's buddy through the years, was asked if he had any other close friends with 500 homers.

"Willie Mays ought to be a good friend of mine, the way he always hit me," Whitey laughed, "or maybe he'd call me a cousin. I had some drinks with Jimmie Foxx in Toots Shor's a few times, and I worked out for Mel Ott when he was managing the Giants and I was in high school, and I knew Ted Williams to pitch to. But I never met Babe Ruth."

• • •

Elston Howard, who batted right after Mantle's seventh-inning homer, did so during a continuing ovation for Mickey.

"I couldn't understand why those people kept cheering me," Howard told Houk, with a grin.

"I thought they were still cheering you for breaking up that no-hitter last month," replied Houk, equally straight-faced.

"I kept hoping Mickey would come out of the dugout and take a bow," Howard explained, "but he just wouldn't."

• • •

Everybody had some Mantle home run to remember. It was repeated over and over that No. 1 had come off Randy Gumpert in Chicago in May, 1951. Houk, who was a bull-pen catcher at the time, singled out the celebrated 565-foot blast out of Washington's Griffith Stadium in 1953, the blow that brought the phrase "tape-measure job" into baseball.

Mickey is partial to a ninth-inning homer that won the game, 2–1, and broke Ruth's record of 15 World Series homers. (Mickey now has 18 Series homers.)

For final commemoration of the occasion, the Yankee management has named tomorrow's game with Cleveland here "500 Night." Some special gift and ceremony for Mantle is being planned, and every 500th customer coming through the each turnstile will be given an autographed baseball.

## 61,157 Hearts Here Throb for Mantle as No. 7 Joins 3, 4 and 5 in Retirement

### By GEORGE VECSEY

Mickey Mantle said, "I wish this could happen to every man in America." But that would not be possible. Only a Mickey Mantle could ever know the feeling of standing in the middle of Yankee Stadium and hearing 61,157 persons cheer him for eight minutes.

It happened yesterday, when a ball park full of people throbbed with love for one man, when Mantle's uniform No. 7 was officially retired by the New York Yankees, when former team-mates and bosses came to honor the man who retired last March 1 after 18 seasons.

They stood and cheered when Mel Allen—a voice from the past—called Mantle out of the Yankee dugout. They cheered so long that Michael Burke, the new-look president of the Yankees, tried to get them to stop. And they cheered even louder when Mantle raised his hands to quiet them. They had bought their tickets to pour out their love and they did not want to stop.

### Speech Stirs Yankee Memories

But finally the crowd gave in, politely, and Joe DiMaggio presented a plaque to Mantle and Whitey Ford presented a uniform to Mantle. Then it was time for Mantle to speak, after another long cheer.

"When I walked into the Stadium 18 years ago," Mantle began, "I guess I felt the same way I feel now. I can't describe it. I just want to say that playing 18 years in Yankee Stadium for you folks is the best thing that could ever happen to a ballplayer. Now, having my number join 3, 4 and 5 kind of tops everything.

"I never knew how a man who was going to die [Lou Gehrig] could say he was the luckiest man in the world. But now I can understand.

Mantle at microphone, thanking the crowd. Behind him are, from the left, Joe DiMaggio, Michael Burke, the Yankees' president, and Lee McPhail, the general manager of the club. (ERNEST SISTO/THE NEW YORK TIMES)

"This is a great day for my wife, my four boys and my family. I just wish my father could have been here. I'll never forget this. Thank you all. God bless you and thank you very much."

The fans understood Mantle's reference to the earlier retirements of the numbers of Babe Ruth, Lou Gehrig and Joe DiMaggio. They remembered that Gehrig had once stood in the center of Yankee Stadium— dying of paralysis—and had said he was the luckiest man in the world. And the fans remembered that Mutt Mantle had died soon after Mickey's rookie season in 1951.

But the mood of the day was not gloomy. Mantle—often withdrawn in the face of adulation—was equal to this moment. As he toured the ball park in a gold cart, he waved to fans in every section and every deck. A few men and one pretty girl even jumped on the field.

Then it ended and the contemporary Yankees took over. But down in the press room Mantle shucked his jacket and tie, commandeered a cool can of beer and described his feelings.

"That last ride around the park," he said. "That gave me goose pimples. But I didn't cry. I felt like it. Maybe tonight, when I go to bed, I'll think about it.

"I wish that could happen to every man in America. I think the fans know how much I think about them— all over the country. I was the most nervous I've ever been—but the biggest thrill.

"The thing I miss the most is being around the clubhouse," he said. "Not the way I played the last four years—that wasn't fun. I've got some guys on this team that are almost like brothers to me—Pepi, Tresh, Stottlemyre. I'm probably their biggest fan. First thing I do every morning is pick up the paper and see how they did.

"But I'm busy. For a retired man, I get around. I travel to openings of my restaurants and my clothing stores. I play golf and—say, did they tell you I'll be working with the Yankees every spring?"

They had. Mantle will help out every spring at training camp, wearing No. 7. But in Yankee Stadium, that number will be seen only in the display case and once a year at Old-Timers Day.


## Guests From Mantle Era

Mel Allen was joined by other men from Yankee history. George Weiss, the former general manager . . . Harry Craft and George Selkirk, Mickey's minor-league managers . . . Yogi Berra (who flew in from San Diego) and Ralph Houk, two of Mantle's managers . . . Tom Greenwade, who signed Mantle . . . plus 12 team-mates from the pennant years: Ed Lopat (1951), Gene Woodling ('52), Joe Collins ('53), Phil Rizutto ('55), Jerry Coleman ('56), Gil McDougald ('57), Whitey Ford ('58), Bobby Richardson ('60), Elston Howard ('61), Tom Tresh ('62), Joe Pepitone ('63) and Mel Stottlemyre ('64) . . . Mantle also presented DiMaggio with a plaque, to hang alongside Mantle's in center field. "Maybe a little higher than mine," Mantle suggested.

Mickey Mantle and Joe DiMaggio at Yankee Stadium on Mickey Mantle Day, 1969, applauding the introductions. (THE NEW YORK TIMES)

August 14, 1995

## Mickey Mantle, Great Yankee Slugger, Dies at 63

### Hall of Famer Loses Two-Month Battle Against Cancer

#### By Joseph Durso

Mickey Mantle, the most powerful switch-hitter in baseball history and the successor to Babe Ruth and Joe DiMaggio as the symbol of the long reign of the New York Yankees, died of cancer yesterday in Dallas. He was 63.

Mantle died at 2:10 A.M. Eastern time at Baylor University Medical Center, succumbing to the disease that had spread from his liver to most of his other vital organs. His wife, Merlyn, and son David were at his bedside.

On June 8, Mantle underwent a transplant operation to replace a liver ravaged by cancer, hepatitis and cirrhosis. At the time, doctors said he would die within two to three weeks if he did not receive a new organ. On July 28, he re-entered Baylor Medical Center for treatment of cancerous spots in his right lung. Recently, he had been suffering from anemia, a side effect of aggressive chemotherapy treatment, and had been receiving blood transfusions. On Aug. 9, the hospital said the cancer had spread to his abdomen.

"This is the most aggressive cancer that anyone on the medical team has ever seen," said Dr. Goran Klintmalm, medical director of transplant services at Baylor. "But the hope in this is that Mickey left behind a legacy. Mickey and his team have already made enormous impact by increasing the awareness of organ donation. This may become Mickey's ultimate home run."

Mantle, who said he was "bred to play baseball," traveled from the dirt-poor fields of Oklahoma to reach

Yankee Stadium in the 1950's and, after his retirement in March 1969, the Baseball Hall of Fame as one of the superstars of the second half of the 20th century.

He commanded the biggest stage in sports as the center fielder for the most successful team in baseball, and he did it at a time when New York was blessed with three great centerfielders renowned as "Willie, Mickey and the Duke," home run hitters who captivated the public in the 1950's as the leaders of memorable teams: Willie Mays of the Giants, Mantle of the Yankees and Duke Snider of the Brooklyn Dodgers.

He outlived the family curse of Hodgkin's disease, which had contributed to the death by heart attack of his 36-year-old son Billy, and the early deaths of his father, at 39, his grandfather and two uncles. He was separated from Merlyn, his wife of 48 years, although they remained friendly. He was an alcoholic, which doctors said was at least partly responsible for causing his liver cancer.

Through all the adversity, he exhibited a quiet but shrewd wit that he often unfurled in a down-home Oklahoma drawl. Of his fear of dying early, he once said: "I'll never get a pension. I won't live long enough." And after years of drinking and carousing with Whitey Ford and Billy Martin as his chief running mates, he joked, "If I knew I was going to live this long, I'd have taken better care of myself."

In the end, though, he had a more poignant message. In a news conference on July 11, a remorseful Mantle told the nation, especially its children: "Don't be like me. God gave me a body and the ability to play baseball. I had everything and I just . . ."

But that's not how he was remembered by teammates. "He was not a phony role model, and I think people really identified with that," former teammate Tony Kubek said. "Mick was never a contrived person, he was a genuine person. He brought a lot of Oklahoma with him to New York and never really changed. He showed a certain amount of humility and never let stardom go to his head."

Said Gene Woodling, who played in the outfield beside Mantle for four seasons: "What can you say about Mickey after you say he was one of the greatest?"

## The Powerful Symbol Of a Yankee Dynasty

He was the storybook star with the storybook name, Mickey, or simply Mick, or Slick to Martin and Ford, who were also known as Slick to one another. He was the blond, muscled switch-hitter who joined the Yankees at 19 in 1951 as DiMaggio was winding down his Hall of Fame career. Wearing No. 7, he led the team through 14 years of the greatest success any baseball team has known before he endured four more years of decline.

He not only hit the ball, he hammered it. He hit often, he hit deep and he did it from both sides of the plate better than anyone else. He could drag a bunt, too, with run-away speed, and he played his role with a kind of all-American sense of destiny. He signed his first contract for $7,500 and his last for $100,000, which seemed princely enough at the time.

But he became wildly famous for his strength, his dash, his laconic manner and, somewhat like Joe Namath in football, for his heroic performance on damaged knees. Long after the cheers faded, so did Mantle, although he revived his image as a kind of fallen hero who carried his afflictions with grace and humor. He acknowledged that some of them were self-inflicted, especially drinking, a habit that had seemed harmless enough when crowds were cheering and he was playing and hitting home runs despite an occasional hangover.

In 1994, while presiding over Mickey Mantle's restaurant in Manhattan as a greeter, he entered the Betty Ford Center in Palm Springs, Calif., to undergo treatment for alcoholism. He came out of the clinic a chastened figure, and his frailty was reinforced by the public decline in his health since June. His transplant revived a debate over whether an alcoholic, even a recovering one, deserves a new liver, and whether his celebrity status had increased his chances of getting one.

Frail, and humbled by the sad events of his later life, Mantle received thousands of letters of support after his transplant operation and discovered that the public could forgive and forget. People chose instead to remember his baseball feats, unforgettably part of the heroic character he portrayed.

He was the anchor of the team for 18 seasons, first in center field and later, when his knees couldn't take the stress anymore, at first base. He played in 2,401 games and went to bat 8,103 times—more than any other Yankee—and delivered 2,415 hits for a .298 batting average. He hit 344 doubles, 72 triples and 536 home runs (373 left-handed, 163 right-handed), and he knocked in 1,509 runs.

He led the American League in home runs four times (in 1955, 1956, 1958 and 1960) and led the league in almost everything in 1956, when he won the triple crown with these totals: a .353 batting average, 130 runs batted in and 52 home runs. He was named the league's most valuable player in 1956, 1957 and 1962. He also hit a record total of 18 home runs in 12 World Series, and 2 more in 16 All-Star Games.

He took such an all-out swing at the ball that he struck out regularly and broke the record set two generations earlier by Ruth. It was a record that Mantle put into perspective when he was inducted into the Hall of Fame on Aug. 12, 1974.

"I also broke Babe Ruth's record for strikeouts," Mantle said. "He struck out only 1,500 times. I did it 1,719 times."

During their empire years, the Yankees built on the mountains of success they had fashioned in the days since Ruth joined them in 1920. In the 1920's, they won six American League pennants and three World Series. In the 1930's, they won five pennants and five World Series. In the 1940's, they won five pennants and four Series. And then came the ear of Mantle.

In 1950, the year before he arrived, the Yankees won the Series again. With Mantle established in the lineup, they won the pennant seven times and the Series five times in the next eight years. And from 1960–64, with the addition of Roger Maris, they won five pennants and two World Series.

Not only that, but in their championship year of 1961, Mantle and Maris provided a seasonlong drama in their chase of Ruth's home run record; Mantle, sidelined by an abscessed hip, dropped out in mid-September with 54, while Maris finished with a record 61.

### Early Baseball Lessons From Both Sides of Plate

Mickey Charles Mantle was born in Spavinaw, Okla., on Oct. 20, 1931. His father, Elvin, nicknamed Mutt, worked in the zinc mines. But he was also a part-time baseball player who had such a passion for the game that he named his son in honor of Mickey Cochrane, the great catcher for the Philadelphia Athletics and a player-manager for the Detroit Tigers. When Mantle was 4 years old, his father would come home from work and teach him how to swing the bat from both sides of the plate while his mother held dinner for them until there was no more daylight.

"When I was a kid," Mantle remembered a few years after he retired, "I used to work in the mines with my dad for $35 a week. Then my dad got me a job cleaning out the area around telephone poles. You see, when you have a prairie fire, if you don't clean out a 10-yard spot around a telephone pole, it will burn the telephone out, and it will cost you a lot of money.

"I was still in high school and we were living out near Commerce in 1948, and we didn't have a hell of a lot. My mother made every baseball uniform I ever wore till I signed with the Yankees. I mean, she sewed them right on me. I was 16 years old then, and my brothers and me would play baseball out in the yard or out back in one of the fields.

"I was also playing semipro ball for a team they called the Baxter Springs Whiz Kids, and one night a scout from the Yankees named Tom Greenwade came through Baxter Springs. The ball park was right beside the road, and he was on his way to watch some guy play in another town. But he pulled his car over and stopped and watched us play. And I hit three home runs in that game, two right-handed and one left-handed, and one of them even landed in the river out beyond the outfield.

"When I graduated from high school in 1949, Greenwade showed up again. He even got me out of the commencement exercises so I could play ball because he was thinking of signing me for the Yankees. I think I hit two more home runs that night. When Greenwade came back a week later, he said he'd give me a $1,500 bonus and $140 a month for the rest of the summer. That's how I signed with the Yankees."

The Yankees started Mantle at Independence, Kan., where they had a Class D minor league club. He hit .313, played shortstop and made 47 errors in 89 games. The next summer, at 18, he played Class C ball in Joplin, Mo., where he hit .383 but made 55 errors in 137 games at shortstop, mostly on wild throws to first base. The team won the pennant by 25 games, and the following spring, he was in Phoenix as a rookie with the Yankees.

Ford, his ally on and off the field for years, remembered how shy and inarticulate the young Mantle seemed when he reported.

"Everything he owned was in a straw suitcase," he said. "No money, none of those $400 suits he got around to buying a couple of years later. Just those two pairs of pastel slacks and that blue sports coat that he wore every place.

"Years later, we were sitting around the dining room at the Yankees' ball park in Fort Lauderdale, and they had this oilcloth on the table, and Mickey said: "This is what we used to have in our kitchen at home. We didn't even have chairs then; we had boxes instead of chairs, and linoleum on the floor. And when it got cold, the draft would raise the linoleum up at the ends."

Mantle was so insecure that he remembered later how he had ducked DiMaggio even though he was playing his final season in center field and Mantle, who had been converted from shortstop to the outfield, was playing alongside him in right.

"Joe DiMaggio was my hero," Mantle said, "but he couldn't talk to me because I wouldn't even look at him, although he was always nice and polite."

### Trip Back to Minors in First Year in Majors

Two months into the 1951 season, Manager Casey Stengel sent Mantle down to the Yankees' top farm team in Kansas City because he was striking out too much. Against Walt Masterson of the Boston Red Sox he struck out five times in one game. He stayed in the minors for 40 games, returned to New York and closed his rookie season hitting .267 with 13 home runs in 96 games.

"Then in the World Series in 1951," Mantle said, "I tripped over the water-main sprinkler in the outfield while I was holding back so DiMaggio could catch a ball that Willie Mays hit, and I twisted my knee and got torn ligaments. That was the start of my knee operations. I had four.

"Once they operated on my shoulder and tied the tendons together. I had a cyst cut out of my right knee another time. And down in Baltimore in 1963, Slick was pitching one night and Brooks Robinson hit a home run over the center-field fence. I jumped up and tried to catch it, and got my foot caught in the wire mesh on the fence, and that time I broke my foot about halfway up."

He became one of the most damaged demigods of sport, but he played with such natural power that he remained the key figure on a team achieving towering success for the fifth straight decade.

His strength as a hitter became legendary. In 1953, batting right-handed, he hit a ball thrown by Chuck Stobbs of the Washington Senators over the 55-hoot-high left-field fence in Griffith Stadium, a drive that was measured at 565 feet from home plate. Three years later, and again in 1963, batting left-handed each time, he smashed a ball into the third deck, within a few feet of the peak of the facade in right field in Yankee Stadium, and no one has come closer to driving a fair ball out of the park.

In 1956, he hit 16 home runs in May. In 1964, he hit two home runs in his final two times at bat on July 4, and two more in his first two times up in the next game the following day. In 1956, he hit three home runs in the World Series, three more in the 1960 Series and three more in the 1964 Series, running his total to 18 and breaking Ruth's record.

"Casey Stengel was like a father to me," Mantle said. "Maybe because I was only 19 years old when I started playing for him, and a couple of years later my own dad was gone. The Old Man really helped me a lot. I guess he even protected me. But I still didn't have it in my head that I was a good major league ballplayer.

"Then Ralph Houk came along and changed my whole idea of thinking about myself. I still didn't have a lot of confidence. Not till Houk came along and told me, "You are going to be my leader. You're the best we've got."

## After Leaving Baseball, Day and Night Drinking

The Yankees stopped winning pennants after the 1964 season, and Mantle stopped playing after the 1968 season. He remembered later what it was like: "When I first retired," he wrote in an article in Sports Illustrated in 1994, "it was like Mickey Mantle died. I was nothing. Nobody gave a damn about Mickey Mantle for about five years." By then, he reported, he was living in a steady haze induced by all-day and all-night drinking.

"When I was drinking," he said, "I thought it was funny—the life of the party. But as it turned out, nobody could stand to be around me. I was the best man at Martin's wedding in 1988, and I can hardly remember being there." Martin died in a one-vehicle accident on Christmas night in 1989. He was legally drunk at the time.

Mantle admitted that drinking had become a way of life even while he was playing. But it finally became a nightmare that undermined his life. And at the request of his son Danny and Pat Summerall, the former football player and current television broadcaster, he checked into the Berry Ford Center in 1994.

He remembered what his doctor told him then: "Your liver is still working, but it has healed itself so many times that before long you're just going to have one big scab for a liver. Eventually, you'll need a new liver. I'm not going to lie to you: The next drink you take may be your last."

There was no next drink, Mantle said. And after leaving the Betty Ford Center, he seemed to be a revived person.

"Everywhere I go," he said, "guys come up and shake hands and say, 'Good job, Mick.' It makes you feel good. It's unbelievable. They give a damn now."

In addition to his wife and son David, he is survived by two other sons, Danny and Mickey Jr.

Funeral services are scheduled for 2 P.M. Tuesday at Lovers Lane United Methodist Church in Dallas.

|        | AB    | HR  | RBI   | AVG. |
|--------|-------|-----|-------|------|
| **1951** | 341   | 13  | 65    | .267 |
| **1952** | 549   | 23  | 87    | .311 |
| **1953** | 461   | 21  | 92    | .295 |
| **1954** | 543   | 27  | 102   | .300 |
| **1955** | 517   | 37  | 99    | .306 |
| **1956** | 533   | 52  | 130   | .353 |
| **1957** | 474   | 34  | 94    | .365 |
| **1958** | 519   | 42  | 97    | .304 |
| **1959** | 541   | 21  | 75    | .285 |
| **1960** | 527   | 40  | 94    | .275 |
| **1961** | 514   | 54  | 128   | .317 |
| **1962** | 377   | 30  | 89    | .321 |
| **1963** | 172   | 15  | 35    | .314 |
| **1964** | 465   | 35  | 111   | .303 |
| **1965** | 361   | 19  | 46    | .255 |
| **1966** | 333   | 23  | 56    | .288 |
| **1967** | 440   | 22  | 55    | .245 |
| **1968** | 435   | 18  | 54    | .237 |
| **TOTALS** | 8,102 | 536 | 1,509 | .298 |

## WORLD SERIES

|        | AB  | HR | RBI | AVG. |
|--------|-----|----|-----|------|
| **TOTALS** | 230 | 18 | 40  | .257 |

August 14, 1995

*Sports of the Times*

## An Imperfect Baseball Deity

### By George Vecsey

People will mourn the tortured man with the hollow eyes and the prematurely wrinkled face, whose liver went fast, just as his knees had done. But the real reason they're mourning Mickey Mantle today is that first he was a young lion who prowled green urban pastures, sleekly, powerfully, unpredictably.

## MILESTONES AND HIGHLIGHTS

**Yankee debut** April 17, 1951
**Triple Crown** 1956
**A.L.M.V.P.** 1956, 1957, 1962
**A.L. home run leader** 1955–56, 1958, 1960
**Home runs** 536 (8th place)
**Home runs from both sides of plate in same game** 10 times, an A.L. record.
**Grand slams** 9
**Most games played for the Yankees** 2,401
**Most at-bats for the Yankees** 8,102
**Three home runs in one game** May 13, 1955
**All-Star Game** 1952–1965
**Gold Glove** 1962
**Uniform retired** June 8, 1969 (No. 7)
**Elected to Baseball Hall of Fame** 1974

Before he was Mickey Mantle the flawed Southwestern folk hero even to cynical Northeasterners, he was Mickey Mantle the athlete who awed people with a swing and a sprint.

He was not merely some case history straight out of the modern soap operas and made-for-television movies, with his recognition of his alcoholism late in his life. Not at all.

People of a certain age are going around with sad expressions today because of the young Mickey Mantle, the one who first captivated them, the one who gave them the intense pleasure of watching an imperfect athletic deity perform extraordinary acts, without the backup of discipline.

There was nobody quite like Mickey Mantle in a baseball uniform. He was not just speed and he was not just power; he was unabashed animal vitality. Even before the fans grew to like him, and then adore him, they were awed by him. They had to watch carefully as he bounded toward first base after hitting a simple ground ball to shortstop. Williams and Musical and Killebrew did not beat out grounders to shortstop. Mantle did. The hitters who could leg out an infield single were "whippets" or "jack rabbits." Mickey Mantle was leonine.

That was the part that turned the fans on. A lot of people watched Mantle slug baseballs to the far corners of the American League. These forty-somethings and fifty-somethings became the emotional base of Mickey Mantle's status as a legend. Little Bobby Costas from Long Island grew up to be an astute broadcaster who knows it is absolutely permissible to openly idolize the Mick.

Mickey Mantle was hot. Male baseball fans talked about him the way they might talk about Marilyn Monroe in another context. Long before there was Mick Jagger, there was Mickey Mantle with more than a trace of menace. He would limp in from the outfield and just before he would duck into the dugout he would spot the prettiest woman in the box seats and he would wink or grin or leer at her. He could get away with it. He was the Mick.

The greatest black players in the first wave had to keep their psychic lids on. Jackie Robinson nearly had a nervous breakdown containing his anger at the racial slurs. Frank Robinson and Henry Aaron and Roberto Clemente had to worry about offending white America with their achievements and their competitive personalities. But Mickey Mantle, the blond Oklahoman who moved to Dallas, could act like a bruiser, like a hothead, like a stud, like a jerk, like a dude, like a jock.

• • •

It is important to remember that the crowd did not always adore Mantle. He was the heir to that most aloof and elegant Yankee, Joseph Paul DiMaggio, who would leave behind one of the great statistics in all of sport: 361 home runs and only 369 strikeouts in his career, a sensational combination of power and self-control.

Mantle would hit 536 home runs and strike out 1,710 times, and when he struck out, he hurled his helmet to the ground, exposing his light hair and his crimson complexion. The crows picked up in his fury, his self-hatred, and it booed, loud and long.

Casey Stengel was awed by Mantle's potential, frustrated by his rawness. In Mantle's sporting fantasies, he was a running back for the University of Oklahoma. Baseball was something city people played. The first time Mantle came north with the Yankees in 1951, they played a preseason game in Ebbets Field, the home of the Brooklyn Dodgers. Stengel marched Mantle out to right field to give him a cram course in how to field the idiosyncratic caroms off the scoreboard. The 19-year-old seemed dumbfounded as the 60-year-old Stengel delivered his lesson.

"He thinks I was born old," muttered Stengel, who had played 14 seasons in the National League. The Old Man was often baffled by his rustic star, but Casey did not turn back the 320 homers Mantle clubbed in a decade on Stengel's watch. He also learned to play the game a bit, and he became a legend for his courage in playing on ruined knees.

So many games come to mind. The rising shot off Bill Fischer and the façade of Yankee Stadium (Mantle pronounced it "fa-KARD"). The feint and dive back to first base, past a stunned Rocky Nelson, in the 1960 World Series. Playing with blood on his uniform from an abscess in the 1961 Series. And the home run off Barney Schultz that broke up a game in the Stadium during the 1964 Series. Everybody has got a favorite.

• • •

Then there was the down side of the legend. Some of the young sportswriters in the 1960's broke the omerta, the unspoken code, by suggesting that Mantle drank too much, caroused too much and was destroying his body. Most fans did not want to know. I called it the "Aw-no, not-the-Mick" syndrome. And a reporter, who dwelled on Mantle's self-destructive, boorish side had to remind himself that Mantle's teammates thought he was not only a great player but also a great teammate, a great guy.

"Mickey was a man," I can hear one specific teammate saying. As I recall, the adulation was for post-night activities rather than pre-midnight. In the pre-addiction-treatment age, in the pre-AIDS age, Mantle's style was considered good, clean fun.

After retirement, Mantle made a living off being the celebrity drunk golfer, America's guest. Few people worried about his dangerous excesses, his broken family, until Mantle got scared and got sober. And then he was forgiven immediately with a great rush of public sympathy. It's too bad Mantle did not have more time, sober and healthy and mature, to enjoy the affection.

August 14, 1995

## Even in the End, Mantle's Circle Remained Unbroken

### Teammates Lifted Spirits In Final Days

#### By Allen R. Myerson

Dallas, Aug. 13—In the end, the muscles that had made Mickey Mantle an emblem of athletic might were gone. His physique was withered not by age but by a liver transplant, cancer and desperate rounds of chemotherapy. He knew, but never told the public, that he had perhaps the most aggressive tumors his doctors had seen.

But he also had his Yankee team mates, his lifelong friends, whose arrival by his hospital bed beginning last Wednesday night rallied his spirits one final time, even when his doctors thought he had only hours, not days.

And at about half past midnight Central time this morning, in his last waking moments, he had his family, however torn. Merlyn, his estranged wife, and David, one of his three sons, each held one of his hands as his awareness faded. He slept about 40 minutes more until they saw his final breath.

If Mantle's redemption came in time for him to start on a new course, it came too late for that course to save him. In his last public appearance, a month ago, he admitted that hard drinking had ruined his health and broken his family, even though he had given up drinking a year and a half ago. He pledged to make amends by helping others as a spokesman for a national organ donor program. In his farewell to the public, a short tape was made two weeks ago and replayed at the hospital today, he urged his fans to request donor cards. Since then, thousands have.

It was a sudden end for a baseball hero whose second career, running fantasy baseball camps and signing autographs, had become more lucrative than his first. He was a vigorous, strapping 63-year-old when he complained to doctors less than three months ago about a nagging stomach ache.

Since then, the drama of his surgery, his recovery and his final defeat has drawn more national attention than the health of almost anyone but a president.

His doctors at Baylor University Medical Center revealed today that they had known even during Mantle's June 8 liver transplant that his outlook was at best uncertain. After removing his liver, they discovered that the cancer had already spread around his bile ducts, and from there probably elsewhere.

By then, they said, the vessels to his new liver had already been attached, so they had no choice but to proceed. They sliced away as much of his bile ducts, crucial to digestion, as they could. But within two days, under a pathologist's microscope, the cancer cells proved to be the most dangerous his doctors had seen.

When Mantle heard the news, he vowed to keep fighting and told his doctors to avoid disclosing just how long his odds were. "I think I'm going to make it," he said a month ago when he was strong enough to begin working out on a treadmill and a stationary bicycle.

Only when Mantle learned on Monday that his cancer had spread throughout his organs, even seizing his heart and his new liver, did he give that fight up. Told that further treatments—radiation, more chemotherapy—were available but probably futile, he asked only that his doctors relieve his pain. His gastroenterologist, Daniel DeMarco, knew that Mantle only had 2 to 10 days left and offered to share his outlook with his patient. Mantle said, "I'll tell you what," according to Roy J. True, a lawyer and friend who was there, "don't even tell me how long I have."

He also didn't want to learn the worst from television and so asked his doctors to remain silent.

As Mantle weakened day by day, his three sons asked his teammates to bid him goodbye. On Wednesday, Danny, his youngest son, told DeMarco that Whitey Ford, the team's star pitcher, was flying in that night and would stop by the next morning.

"You ought to get Whitey here as soon as you can," DeMarco responded. "You bring Whitey here tonight."

Mantle was so cheered by the prospect of seeing his friend that, when Ford visited, he sat up in a chair and traded jokes as if they were on a road trip decades ago. Ford handed Mantle a baseball with autographs from today's Yankee players and an inscription that said, "Get Well Mickey." Mantle kept it by his bedside until the end.

Merlyn Mantle was astounded to see her husband looking better than he has in a week or two. "I thought you said he was sick," DeMarco said she told him.

"I really thought he was going to pass away," the doctor said. "Mickey made a liar out of me, and Whitey Ford helped."

He continued to rally, showing off the autographed ball and watching golf on television, as Bill (Moose) Skowron, Hank Bauer and Johnny Blanchard came in the next day. He had called Skowron every day three months ago when Skowron had double-bypass heart surgery. On Thursday, Mantle wanted to talk about Skowron's health, not his own.

But most of all, Mantle wanted to talk baseball. He reminisced about angrily smashing his favorite bat in two after he hit a shot to distant, dead center field at Yankee Stadium, certain that it would drop for an out.

"Anything hit out there was Death Valley," Blanchard said, recalling Mantle's account.

"Well, this cotton picker kept traveling" for a home run. "And that was a good bat," Mantle said.

Blanchard said that he and others had a difficult time coping with the contrast between the Mantle of the clubhouse and the Mantle before their eyes. "My heart just sank," Blanchard said. "I remember this guy carved out of granite. And to see his face withered and shrunk."

Blanchard, nearly choking—"my Adam's apple was as hard as a rock,"—often had to look away, out the window, anywhere but at his wasted friend.

Mantle was surprised, almost shocked—"Really? Is that right?—to hear Bauer recount how other retired Yankees had tears in their eyes watching a video of him on Old-Timer's Day. On the way out, Skowron and the others told Mantle they wanted to see him again soon. "I'll let you know when," Mantle said.

But Mantle grew ever more feeble, taking morphine instead of milder pain relievers. Sometimes he was too groggy to recognize guests. But he spent much of his final days with Bobby Richardson, a teammate he and his hard-drinking buddies had once ridiculed as "the milk drinker."

When Richardson came in on Thursday, Mantle noticed his bare ankles. "Hey, boys, go buy him a pair of socks," he teased.

Richardson, now a lay minister, helped Mantle pray and, at his request, will preside over his memorial service Tuesday. With Richardson's counsel, Mantle accepted his death with grace and his wide, well-known grin.

"Somebody is lying on their deathbed, and you disturb or awaken them, and the first thing they do is smile at you," DeMarco said. "I've never really seen anyone do that. And then he would lift his hand up and shake your hand."

Mantle's doctors followed his order to avoid heroic measures, but they stayed in close touch. Last night, a Baylor clergyman stood by in his room.

Shortly after 12:30 this morning Merlyn Mantle called DeMarco at home to come immediately. She called on his car phone just after 1 A.M. to say that Mantle has stopped breathing.

DeMarco arrived minutes later to pronounce him dead. "I'm sorry," he said, turning to Merlyn and David. He paused, then added, "He's resting now."

*"My family lost a great friend and a truly wonderful person. Now that both Mickey and Billy are gone, I'll never have friends like them again in my life."*

**WHITEY FORD,**
on former teammates Mantle and
Billy Martin

*"He transcends any game and any team. Just as Jesse Owens was to track and field and Michael Jordan is to basketball, Mickey Mantle is to baseball."*

**GEORGE STEINBRENNER,**
Yankee owner

*"I'll never forget how hard he played all the time, especially the catch he made in my perfect game."*

**DON LARSEN,**
who pitched a perfect game in the 1956
World Series.

*"He could run, throw and hit. There's no telling how good he'd have been with two good legs."*

**YOGI BERRA**

*"He was magnificent. His power, once in batting practice in spring training, I saw him hit the first nine pitches he got over the fence. It was effortless."*

**PHIL LINZ,**
whose locker was next to Mantle's

*"I'd rather go than suffer. He suffered enough in his career."*

**BILL SKOWRON**
Former Yankee first baseman

*"We lost a legend today, and I lost a real friend."*

**MEL STOTTLEMYRE,**
Former Yankee pitcher

*The Death of a Hero: Tears and a Victory at Yankee Stadium*

## Victory by '95 Yankees Becomes Afterthought

### By JASON DIAMOS

The Yankees, black armbands on their sleeves, had tears in their eyes yesterday. So did many of the 45,866 fans in attendance, the third-largest crowd of the season at Yankee Stadium, where the flags flew at half-staff.

There was a moment of silence, as there was at every major league ball park today, followed by a video remembrance of the late Mickey Mantle; the crowd gave a long standing ovation.

"Mickey Mantle, a Yankee Forever," proclaimed the Stadium marquee. One scoreboard message simply read, "7 With Us Forever."

In effect, yesterday was a Mantle farewell along the lines of those for Lou Gehrig, Babe Ruth and Thurman Munson before him. People came to mourn a larger-than-life figure, one of the last great superstars in the Yankee pantheon. They also came to watch a game, an important one played in the heat of a pennant race against the backdrop of a legend's passing.

The Boston Red Sox, whom the Yankees are chasing, were already ahead by 3–0 when David Cone took the mound against the Cleveland Indians. Cone admitted afterward that he was aware of that score.

Inspired by Mantle, and inspired that the Yankees could not afford to fall yet another game behind the streaking Red Sox, Cone (13-6, 4-0 as a Yankee) was sensational. The right-hander delivered the Yankees' second complete game in as many days, striking out nine and yielding just a solo home run, a double and four singles against a ferocious Cleveland lineup.

Paul O'Neill backed Cone with a two-run homer in the first inning, his second homer in as many games. Randy Velarde had three singles and drove in two runs. Don Mattingly had two doubles. Darryl Strawberry added three hits. And the Yankees took their second straight decision over the Indians, 4–1, to close out this five-game set and head to Boston on a strong note—after they had dropped the first three games of this series in heartbreaking fashion.

Boston held on yesterday for its 11th straight victory, a 3–2 decision over Baltimore at Fenway Park. By winning, the Yankees remained nine games behind in the American League East.

"It was pretty emotional," Mattingly, the Yankee captain, said afterward. "I'm sure a lot of the guys don't know Mick, they know of him. Watching the video before the game was tough. I wanted to do something on a day like today. I wanted to go deep, to tell you the truth."

Mattingly nearly did, doubling off the right-field fence before scoring the Yankees' final run in the sixth. But the game was almost an afterthought.

The day started with the news of Mantle's death spreading through the Yankee clubhouse. Players reminisced about their experiences with the outfielder. The Yankees staged an impromptu news conference at which Mattingly, the longtime broadcaster Mel Allen, Manager Buck Showalter, General Manager Gene Michael and Bobby Murcer, Mantle's longtime friend and one-time heir apparent, all spoke.

Murcer, who was once billed—unfairly—as the next coming of the Mantle, was overcome by emotion at the death of his boyhood idol and fellow Oklahoman. "Mickey, the reason people loved him so much is that he portrayed the innocence of what we all want to be," Murcer said. "I don't think to this day Mickey ever realized how people felt about him and how he touched their lives. We've truly lost not only an American hero but a person that portrayed the innocence and honesty that we would all like to have."

Mantle was Showalter's hero, too. He spoke of how, when he was growing up, Mantle was a part of every

# A TALE OF TAPE & TAPE MEASURES

Despite a career full of injuries, Mickey Mantle had a rare ability to power a baseball a long way. Even rarer, he could do it from both sides of the plate. He finished his career with 563 home runs; 373 as a left-handed batter and 163 batting right-handed. He also homered 18 times in the World Series, and no one hit more. Here are some of the more significant home runs Mantle muscled during his career as well as some of the more serious injuries that kept him taped up so often.

### The Power and the Glory

**May 1, 1951** Mantle, 19 years old and batting left-handed, gets his first major league home run, off Randy Gumpert of the Chicago White Sox.

**May 16, 1951** Batting right-handed against Dick Rozek of the Cleveland Indians, Mantle hits the first of this 266 homers at Yankee Stadium. No player has hit more.

**April 17, 1953** The tape measure becomes a figurative fixture after Mantle, Batting right-handed, clubs a pitch from Chuck Stobbs of the Washington Senators out of Griffith Stadium. Best estimate: 565 feet.

**Oct. 4, 1953** In Brooklyn, a bases-filled homer off the right-hander Russ Meyer in Game 5 makes Mantle only the fourth player, to that time, to hit a grand slam in the World Series.

**May 13, 1955** Two homers from the left side off Steve Gromek and one from the right side off Bob Miller give Mantle a three-homer game against the Detroit Tigers at Yankee Stadium.

**May 30, 1956** Another Washington Senator pitcher is tattooed as Mantle's high drive off the right-hander Pedro Ramos hits the upper-deck façade in right field, a foot and a half short of going out of Yankee Stadium for a homer, something no major leaguer has ever done.

**Oct. 8, 1956** Don Larsen grabs the spotlight with a 2–0 perfect game against the Brooklyn Dodgers in Game 5 of the World Series, but Mantle's homer off the right-hander Sal Maglie and a running backhanded catch in deep left-center at the Stadium accent the feat.

**May 22, 1963** Like Ramos seven years earlier, the right-hander Bill Fischer of the Kansas City Athletics watches a pitch nearly leave the Stadium in

child's dreams and how every Little Leaguer used to want to wear No. 7 for the Yankees.

"Part of the whole baseball world passed away this morning," Showalter said. "Old-Timer's Day will never be the same."

Allen, who called many of Mantle's great moments, related a story about how Manager Casey Stengel pleaded with General Manager George Weiss in the spring of 1951 to let him keep the raw 19-year-old. Said Allen: " 'That boy hits balls over buildings,' Casey said.

"Mickey would always say that his grandfather and father had passed away at a young age from Hodgkin's disease. He said, 'It's going to hit me, so I'm going to enjoy life as best I can.' Mickey had this real feeling, he didn't think he was going to live much past that. As he later said, he lived a lot longer than he ever expected."

After the news conference, the Yankees held the on-field ceremony in memory of Mantle, who was 63.

"Today is a sad day for the Yankee family and Yankee fans everywhere," said the public-address announcer, Bob Sheppard, "because today we have lost one of our own, and one of the greatest players in the history of baseball. Please join now for a few moments of silent prayer as we all remember Mickey Mantle."

The Yankee players—many of them had marked a No. 7 on their caps yesterday—were joined by the Indians and fans in bowing their heads. Robert Merrill sang the national anthem. The video tribute was played over the DiamondVision. The fans gave Mantle a standing ovation as a picture of a draped No. 7 pinstriped jersey hung on the scoreboard screen.

Showalter said that for once it was easy to get all his players out of the clubhouse and onto the field.

"I've always liked that, our players realizing our heritage and how much it meant to our fans," the manager said of the tribute. "It was uplifting but it was still a very sad day for the organization."

Velarde said, "It wasn't surprising to me to look down the dugout and see tears in some of the guys' eyes.

The Yankees came out and dominated the Indians behind Cone.

"I walked out and looked at the monuments and the Mickey Mantle plaque before the game," said Cone, who found out about Mantle's passing only when he saw the Stadium marquee yesterday morning. "You can't help but get caught up in all the tradition. It was a privilege to be here. I feel pretty lucky."

Showalter said afterward that, for the second straight game, he had planned not to use his overworked closer, John Wetteland. He did not need to. Cone threw 130 pitches and was in serious trouble only once—in the eighth when Cleveland put runners on first and second with two out.

Cone quickly fell behind, 2-0, to Eddie Murray. The pitching coach, Nardi Contreras, went to the mound.

"Pitching sort of backwards," as Cone called it, the pitcher then threw a split-finer fastball past Murray, who was looking straight fastball. Cone then delivered a fastball away and Murray grounded out to second. Threat over. Game all but over.

"It was almost a copy of what Jack did," Showalter said of Jack McDowell's complete-game victory over the Indians on Saturday night. "I can't tell you how tough it is to go through that lineup."

Victory or no, yesterday was a very long day for Showalter.

"It's just a sad day," he said. "Mickey meant so much to this organization and the game of baseball. Many a kid played this game because he wanted to be like Mickey Mantle.

right. This one misses by three feet, but the ball is still rising when it hits the façade.

**Oct. 10, 1964** With the score tied, 1–1, in Game 3 at the Stadium, Mantle leads off the Yankee ninth and laces the first pitch from the knuckleballer Barney Schultz of the St. Louis Cardinals into the upper deck in right field. It is his 16th World Series homer, surpassing Babe Ruth's mark that stood for 32 years.

**Aug. 9, 1965** On the second pitch ever thrown in an indoor stadium, Mantle, batting leadoff, homers off Dick Farrell of Houston in an exhibition game that officially opens the Astrodome.

**Sept. 20, 1968** Jim Lonborg of the Boston Red Sox is touched for a home run in the third inning at the Stadium. It is number 536, the last of Mantle's career.

### The Big Hurts

**High School** After being kicked in the left shin during football practice, Mantle develops osteomyelitis, an infection of the bone marrow that endangers his knee for years.

**World Series, 1951** Catches his spikes on an outfield sprinkler cover in Game 2 and needs five months for the knee's torn ligaments to mend.

**World Series, 1957** Milwaukee's Red Schoendienst falls on Mantle's right shoulder in a play at second. The injury hampers his throwing and lefty hitting.

**September 1961** Falls out of the home run race with Roger Maris with a virus and a hip abscess.

**June 1963** Runs into an outfield fence, breaking his left foot and doing ligament damage to his left knee. Out of everyday lineup for three months.

August 14, 1995

## 'The Mick. The Mick.' Sad Fans Remember Athletic Excellence

### By BRUCE WEBER

For baseball fans, the spirit of Mickey Mantle has probably never been entirely absent from Yankee Stadium during the past four decades. But its hovering presence yesterday, hours after Mantle died of cancer in a Dallas hospital at the age of 63, infused the Yankees' victory over the Cleveland Indians with a palpable melancholy.

It's really a sad day," said Fred Blickman, a 47-year-old insurance executive from Eastchester who grew up a Yankee fan in the Bronx and was waiting to enter the ball park yesterday with his 9-year-old son, Matthew. "I didn't think it would hit me, but this morning, it really did. I have a large photo of him, taken in 1956. We had it autographed and it's sitting in the den. He was an icon, a man like any other, but still larger than life. He meant a lot to this city."

All over the city yesterday, in fact, people expressed their dismay, both that Mantle had died and that in his final days he had to reclaim his life from alcoholism.

In Prospect Park in Brooklyn, a group of teen-aged ballplayers observed a moment of silence before their game, and another group circled around together and cheered "one, two, three, Mick!"—throwing their bats and gloves in the air.

"I'd like to hit like him," said James Aliperti, 14, a left fielder for the South Shore Dodgers. "I feel bad that he died, but he shouldn't have been drinking."

His manager, Ray Down, added: "He was the Yankees. My brother still thinks he's Mickey Mantle. I wouldn't want my kids to be like him, because he drank too much. Just to play like him."

At Yankee Stadium, there was mourning. The flags around the rim of the stadium—not just the American flags, but the pennants of all the American League teams—were at half-staff, and before the game a seven-minute show of highlights from Mantle's career was shown on the DiamondVision scoreboard; it was followed by a sustained ovation.

Mantle, who played center field and first base for the Yankees between 1951 and 1968, was the central figure on the great Yankee teams of the 1950's and early 1960's, a glamorous player with both speed and power who inherited the role of Yankee hero, the symbol of athletic excellence, from Joe DiMaggio.

DiMaggio, of course, is still alive—he turned 80 last November—and it was part of yesterday's sadness that the line of Yankee descent had been prematurely disturbed once again. Mantle, many fans noted yesterday, outlived one of the heroes who followed him, Thurman Munson, who died in a plane crash in 1979.

"Today is a sad day for the Yankee family and Yankee fans. Today we have lost one of one own, and one of the greatest players in the history of baseball," the longtime stadium announcer, Bob Sheppard, intoned over the loudspeakers.

Indeed, the feelings many fans expressed yesterday showed that Mantle existed for them as not just a ballplayer but an icon who touched them personally.

People found different ways of showing their feelings. There was a run on Mantle memorabilia at the stores across from the stadium along River Avenue. At Ball Park Souvenirs, a salesman said he sold 200 Mantle shirts. "The biggest sales of a single item since the Righetti no-hitter," said the salesman, who gave his name only as Lee, referring to the game pitched by former Yankee Dave Righetti on the Fourth of July in 1983.

And in the seventh inning of the game, a man with no shirt—but with Mantle's No. 7 drawn in marker on his back—jumped from the right-field stands, ran across the field and slid into second base. The man, identified as Craig Kempf, 24, of Queens, was hustled off the field by security personnel, but he was accepting congratulations for his feat on River Avenue after the game.

"I got a court appearance," Kempf said. "I'll pay the fine. I'll do 30 days standing on my head for the Mick."

Others were less demonstrative but more eloquent.

"When I heard about it this morning, I was devastated," said Steve Gentile, a 43-year-old landscaper from Stamford, Conn., who stood for the pre-game tribute at his upper-deck seat near the left-field foul pole, applauding long and hard. Gentile, who came to the United States from Italy in 1966, recalled the overwhelming esteem his American cousins held for a mysterious hero.

"I wondered, 'Who the heck is this Mickey Mantle, God?' " said Gentile, who became a staunch Yankee fan within weeks of his arrival.

It was a year before he attended his first game at Yankee Stadium, but he remembered it well. "We were sitting by the right-field foul pole," he said, pointing across the stadium. "And I caught a foul ball hit by Mickey

Mantle. And he signed it for me after the game. It was maybe 12:30 at night. But then I fell asleep on the train going home. And I lost the ball."

Dick Beyers, 59, a former New Yorker, who, coincidentally, flew in from Los Angeles yesterday just for a trip to Yankee Stadium, wept openly in his seat in the upper deck.

"The Mick. The Mick," he kept repeating. "The Mick."

Beyers said his first wife died of Hodgkin's disease, the same affliction that killed Mantle's father, and that Mantle had sent him flowers.

"My brother called the club and told them about my wife," he said. "Maybe the club sent the flowers, but they were signed by Mickey."

There are, of course, the arguments over who was the best center fielder in New York in the 1950's: Mantle, Willie Mays of the Giants, or the Dodgers' Duke Snider?

"The debates were always good," said Bob Rapp, 58, a lawyer from Miller Place, L.I., who grew up in the Bronx—so he was always in the Mantle camp. "I don't know whether he was a hero, but he was a great ballplayer. He had power, speed. He makes some of these guys today look sick."